INSIDERS' GUIDE® SERIES

INSIDERS' GUIDE® TO

PHOENIX

FOURTH EDITION

SEAN MCLACHLAN AND MARY PAGANELLI

INSIDERS' GUIDE®

GUILFORD, CONNECTICUT
AN IMPRINT OF THE GLOBE PEQUOT PRESS

The prices and rates in this guidebook were confirmed at press time. We recommend, however, that you call establishments before traveling to obtain current information.

INSIDERS' GUIDE®

Copyright © 2002, 2005 by The Globe Pequot Press

A previous edition of this book was published by Falcon Publishing, Inc. in 2001.

Text design by LeAnna Weller Smith
Maps by XNR Productions, Inc. © The Globe Pequot Press

ISSN 1534-2700
ISBN: 0-7627-3457-4

Manufactured in the United States of America
Fourth Edition/First Printing

Arizona Center. GREATER PHOENIX CONVENTION AND VISITORS BUREAU/BABE SARVER

[Top] *Rossib House.* GREATER PHOENIX CONVENTION AND VISITORS BUREAU
[Bottom] *Chinese Cultural Center.* GREATER PHOENIX CONVENTION AND VISITORS BUREAU

Traditional dancers. GREATER PHOENIX CONVENTION AND VISITORS BUREAU/BABE SARVER

Superstition Mountain's hiking area. GREATER PHOENIX CONVENTION AND VISITORS BUREAU

Flowering saguaro. GREATER PHOENIX CONVENTION AND VISITORS BUREAU/RON BOHR

[Top] *Bank One Ballpark.* GREATER PHOENIX CONVENTION AND VISITORS BUREAU
[Bottom] *Downtown Copper Square.* GREATER PHOENIX CONVENTION AND VISITORS BUREAU

[Top] *Kierland Commons.* GREATER PHOENIX CONVENTION AND VISITORS BUREAU/KIERLAND COMMONS
[Bottom] *Orpheum Theatre.* GREATER PHOENIX CONVENTION AND VISITORS BUREAU/ORPHEUM THEATRE

The Phoenician. GREATER PHOENIX CONVENTION AND VISITORS BUREAU/THE PHOENICIAN

Pointe Hilton Peak Resort. GREATER PHOENIX CONVENTION AND VISITORS BUREAU/POINTE HILTON PEAK RESORT

Herberger Theater Center. GREATER PHOENIX CONVENTION AND VISITORS BUREAU/HERBERGER CENTER

Arizona Science Center. GREATER PHOENIX CONVENTION AND VISITORS BUREAU

Horseback riding. GREATER PHOENIX CONVENTION AND VISITORS BUREAU/PETER JORDAN PHOTO.COM

Troon North Pinnacle Course. GREATER PHOENIX CONVENTION AND VISITORS BUREAU/TROON NORTH GOLF CLUB

Hot-air ballooning. GREATER PHOENIX CONVENTION AND VISITORS BUREAU/PETER JORDAN PHOTO.COM

CONTENTS

Directory of Maps

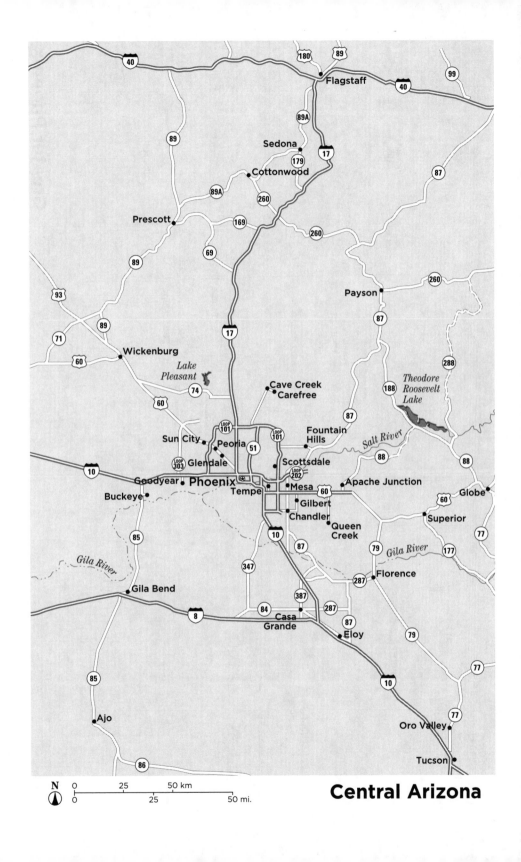

Central Arizona

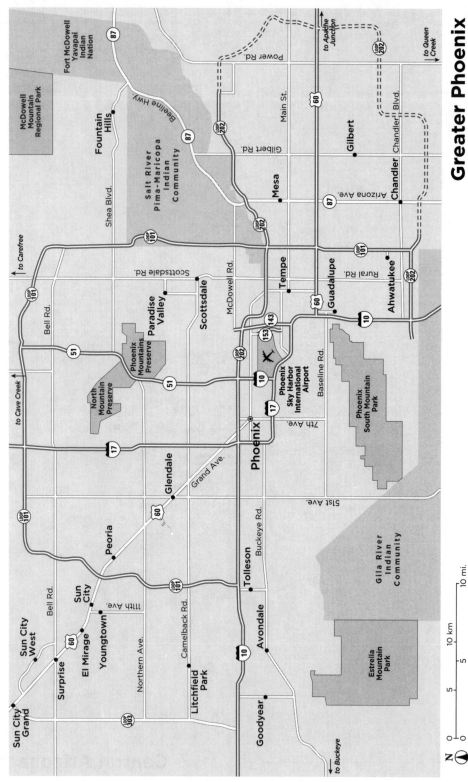

Greater Phoenix

Downtown Phoenix

Phoenix Sky Harbor International Airport

Arizona State Fairgrounds

Arizona Veterans Memorial Coliseum

Heard Museum

Phoenix Art Museum

Civic Plaza

Bank One Ballpark

America West Arena

Union Station

State Capitol

ENCANTO BLVD.

MONTE VISTA RD.

OAK ST.

McDOWELL RD.

CORONADO RD.

PALM LN.

3RD AVE.

CENTRAL AVE.

3RD ST.

7TH ST.

10TH ST.

12TH ST.

16TH ST.

17TH ST.

18TH ST.

19TH ST.

22ND ST.

24TH ST.

ROOSEVELT ST.

McKINLEY ST.

FILLMORE ST.

VAN BUREN ST.

JEFFERSON ST.

JACKSON ST.

MORELAND ST.

2ND ST.

3RD ST.

MONROE ST.

WASHINGTON ST.

LINCOLN ST.

9TH ST.

11TH ST.

16TH ST.

7TH ST.

CENTRAL AVE.

BUCKEYE RD.

PIMA ST.

21ST ST.

RED MTN. FRWY.

PIESTEWA FRWY.

PAPAGO FRWY.

LATHAM ST.

GRAND AVE.

ROOSEVELT ST.

McKINLEY ST.

FILLMORE ST.

3RD AVE.

5TH AVE.

7TH AVE.

CENTRAL AVE.

2ND AVE.

3RD AVE.

7TH AVE.

9TH AVE.

12TH AVE.

15TH AVE.

17TH AVE.

FILLMORE ST.

POLK ST.

VAN BUREN ST.

ADAMS ST.

JEFFERSON ST.

JACKSON ST.

19TH AVE.

20TH AVE.

21ST AVE.

23RD AVE.

24TH AVE.

25TH AVE.

27TH AVE.

GRANT ST.

HADLEY ST.

16TH AVE.

BUCKEYE RD.

PIMA ST.

BLACK CANYON FRWY.

PAPAGO FRWY.

McDOWELL RD.

5TH AVE.

7TH AVE.

202

51

10

10

10

17

60

17

60

17

60

N

0   0.5   1 km

0   0.5   1 mi.

Chandler

Pima Park

E. THATCHER BLVD.

N. McQUEEN RD.

C 200N

C 100E

E. CARLA VISTA DR.

E. FLINT ST.

E. COMMONWEALTH AVE.

E. FRYE RD.

S. McQUEEN RD.

Foley Memorial Park

N. HAMILTON ST.

E. GALVESTON ST.

Gazelle Meadows Park

Armstrong Park

E. CHANDLER BLVD.

E. COMMONWEALTH AVE.
C 0 North/South

N. DELAWARE ST.

N. COLORADO ST.

E. ERIE ST.

E. DETROIT ST.

E. DELAWARE ST.

S. DELAWARE ST.

N. WASHINGTON ST.

ARIZONA AVE.
C 0 West/East

A.J. Chandler Park

S. OREGON ST.

Chandler-Gilbert
Community College
(2626 E. Pecos Rd.)

87

N. CALIFORNIA ST.

S. DAKOTA ST.

W. ELGIN ST.

Navarrete Park

N. IOWA ST.

W. GALVESTON ST.

N. OAKLAND ST.

W. ERIE ST.

W. DETROIT ST.

W. CHANDLER BLVD.

Sheraton San Marcos Country Club

W. FRYE RD.

W. FAIRVIEW ST.

San Marcos Park

N. HARTFORD ST.

N. JAY ST.

N. PLEASANT DR.

N. ALMA SCHOOL RD.

C 1000W

S. ALMA SCHOOL RD.

Arrowhead Meadows Park

N. CENTRAL DR.

Maggio Ranch Park

W. MAGGIO WAY

W. FAIRVIEW ST.

N

0   0.25   0.5 km
0   0.25   0.5 mi.

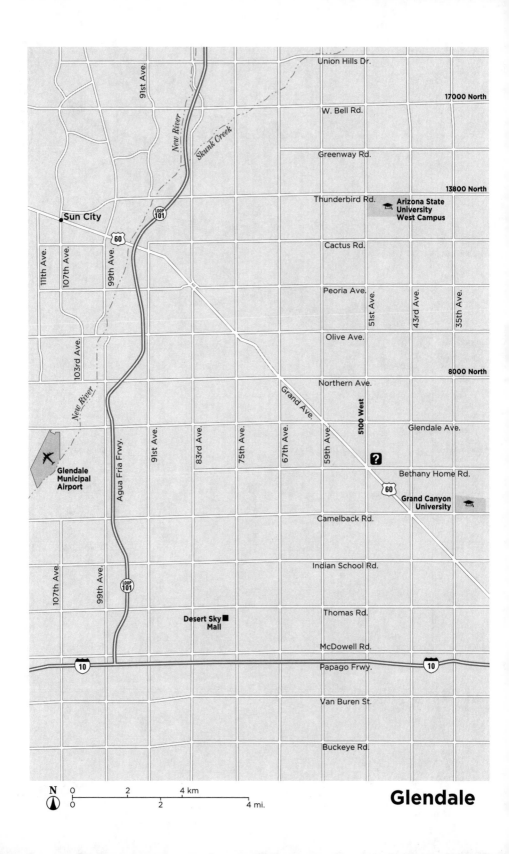

Glendale

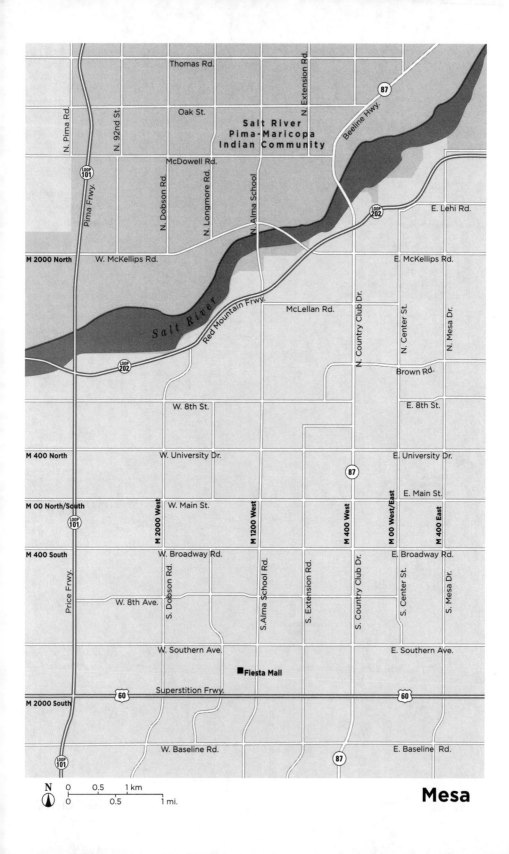

Mesa

Scottsdale

E. GLENROSA ST.

N. 79TH ST.

N. 78TH ST.

4100 North

N. PARKWAY AVE.

E. 3RD ST.

E. 4TH ST.

N. 78TH ST.

Osborn
Park

E. AVALON DR.

N. MILLER RD.

N. MILLER RD.

N. 75TH ST.

Scottsdale
Civic Center

E. STETSON DR.

E. 6TH AVE.

N. DRINKWATER BLVD.

E. DRINKWATER BLVD.

Scottsdale
Mall

Scottsdale
Memorial
Hospital

N. OSBORN RD.

E. EARLL ST.

N. 75TH ST.

N. CIVIC CENTER PLZ.

N. DRINKWATER BLVD.

N. SCOTTSDALE RD.

E. INDIAN SCHOOL RD.

N. BROWN AVE.

E. 1ST AVE.

E. MAIN ST.

E. 1ST ST.

E. 2ND ST.

N. MARSHALL WAY

N. GOLDWATER BLVD.

E. 6TH ST.

N. SCOTTSDALE RD.

N. 71ST ST.

Arizona Canal

N. GOLDWATER BLVD.

N. 70TH ST.

N. 69TH ST.

N. EL DORADO LN.

E. CHERRY LYNN RD.

E. EARLL ST.

N. 68TH ST.

E. 1ST AVE.

E. 2ND ST.

E. 3RD ST.

N. PINTO LN.

N. 66TH ST.

E. CALLE REDONDO

N. INDIAN SCHOOL RD.

N. KACHINA LN.

Paiute
Park

N. 64TH ST.

N. 66TH ST.

N. 64TH ST.

E. EXETER BLVD.

E. CALLE DEL MEDIA

E. CALLE ROSA

E. LAFAYETTE BLVD.

E. CALLE DEL PAISANO

E. CALLE CAMELIA

E. 62ND ST.

N. 63RD PL.

E. ROSE CIRCLE DR.

E. OSBORN RD.

E. EARLL ST.

E. AVALON DR.

N

0   0.25   0.5 km

0   0.25   0.5 mi.

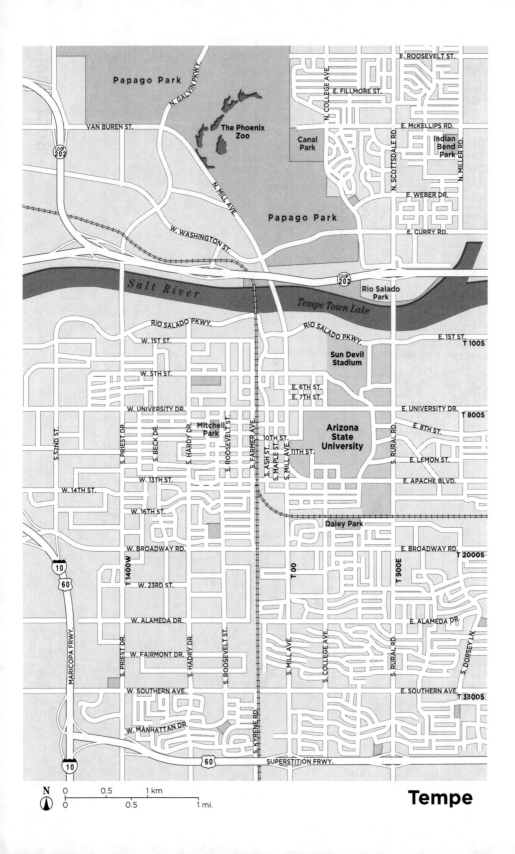

Tempe

ACKNOWLEDGMENTS

For their input, expertise, and assistance in many forms, we thank all who helped with the production of this book at Globe Pequot.

Mary would like to thank Vicki Rider for her invaluable contributions and sends a special thank-you to her husband, Ernest Votto, and son, Eric Votto, for their enthusiasm and patience!

Sean would like to thank all the folks who took time out of their busy schedules to answer his many questions, especially Stacy Reading of the Greater Phoenix Convention and Visitors Bureau. He would also like to thank Mary Paganelli for being such a hardworking and talented collaborator. Another thank-you is owed to Rob, Kat, eXavier, and Kináed for their hospitality, home cooking, and cosmopolitans.

Sean sends a very special thanks to Almudena Alonso-Herrero, whose support, companionship, and patience make his career possible.

We would both like to thank Elizabeth Taylor of The Globe Pequot Press for her keen editorial eye and good suggestions. We salute the efforts of the authors of the first two editions of this book: Salvatore Caputo and Deborah Ross for their first edition and Lori Rohlk Pfeiffer and Paul Morris for the second.

—Sean McLachlan and Mary Paganelli

HOW TO USE THIS BOOK

This guide consists of data-packed chapters that provide useful information for both the weekend visitor and long-time resident alike. You will find a great deal of information in these pages that you will not find in other guidebooks. Not only do we tell you the sights to see, but we fill you in on which neighborhoods are nice places to raise kids and what hospitals have particular facilities. From getting a phone hookup to finding a place of worship, the *Insiders' Guide to Phoenix* is here to help.

We have arranged the information so it is easily accessible. If you are flying into Phoenix for the first time, turn to the Getting Here, Getting Around chapter for information on how to navigate the Valley of the Sun once you have landed. Check out the accommodations chapters for choices on lodging (Hotels and Motels, Resorts, Bed-and-Breakfast Inns, and RV Parks and Campgrounds), browse through the Restaurant chapter to locate the best and closest dining options, and flip through the chapters to discover what to see and do while you are here (Nightlife, Shopping, Attractions, Kidstuff, Annual Events, The Arts, Parks and Recreation, Golf, and Spectator Sports). Price codes are supplied in the restaurant and accommodation chapters to further assist you in those selections. The Kidstuff chapter is especially useful for parents looking to give their child a memorable Arizona experience.

You will notice that throughout the guide we refer to five main areas—downtown Phoenix, the Southeast Valley (which includes Chandler, Mesa, and Tempe), the Northeast Valley (which includes Carefree, Cave Creek, and Scottsdale), the Northwest Valley (which includes Glendale, Sun City, and Surprise), and the Southwest Valley (which includes Goodyear and Litchfield Park). Most chapters are organized by geographical subcategories for your convenience, since the Phoenix metro area is actually several cities. Check out the Area Overview section to find out more.

If you are thinking of moving to this area, you will find the Relocation, Education, and Retirement chapters especially helpful. Filled with tips on how to make the transition to life in the Valley as smooth as possible, these chapters tell how to register your motor vehicle, fill you in on the area school systems, and help you locate the best neighborhood for your needs.

If you are a long-time resident of the Phoenix area, you will find the up-to-date restaurant, nightlife, and annual events listings immensely helpful. Check out the Day Trips chapter for adventures outside of the Valley. Whether you are a visitor or native, don't forget to read the sections on History and Our Natural World. Many city residents aren't fully aware of the rich history and diverse ecozone of the Valley of the Sun.

Generally the title of the chapter will tell you what can be found in it, but some things are a little hard to place. Cafes, for example, are listed in the Nightlife chapter, since they are a popular destination for an after-dinner conversation on our (relatively) cool nights. You will also find some businesses and attractions listed both in the Kidstuff chapter and other chapters. In this case, we tailor the information in the Kidstuff section specifically for those taking care of children.

Scattered throughout the various chapters are special Insiders' tips (indicated by   ) for quick insights. Our guide is written by longtime Arizona residents, and the tips are our way of sharing our insider information. You will also find more lengthy Close-ups with information that is particularly interesting, unusual, or distinctly Phoenix. There is also a table of contents and an index to help you quickly find what you are looking for.

As with any guidebook, use it to get a general idea of the area. Things change, prices go up, restaurants close or move, so once you're in Phoenix ask around for local recommendations. The metro area has several free magazines that list the countless things to do and places to go in the desert city we call home. Get out and get active; you'll find we have a lot to

offer. If you discover something in this book has changed or if you have a recommendation you'd like to share, by all means drop us a line at the following address:

The Globe Pequot Press
Reader Response/Editorial
Department
P.O. Box 480
Guilford, CT 06437

Or you may e-mail us at:
editorial@ GlobePequot.com

AREA OVERVIEW

Welcome to the desert and the Valley of the Sun. You're going to have a good time here and we hope this book will help you find your way around and introduce you to the best the area has to offer. The Valley is big and covers a lot of territory and we thought we'd begin by telling you a bit about the history of the area and then touch on the various cities and geographic regions. You'll be surprised by the diversity of people, cultures, and experiences that you'll discover.

People have visited the Phoenix area for thousands of years and decided to stay, but living here has always been dependent upon access to water. Through the past millennia, civilization in the Valley of the Sun has risen and fallen with irrigation. Centuries before Christ, the Hohokam people began to develop an agrarian culture in the arid Valley, where desert soil hardens within a few inches of the surface. A scant 6 inches of rain falls in the Sonoran Desert each year, just enough to wet the top, percolate through, and still leave a shovel-busting crust. The Hohokam dug through the hardpan to build the hundreds of miles of canals that now form the basis of the Valley's modern canal system. In fact, most of the Valley's irrigation systems follow the paths of these original canals. The Hohokam eventually left the area, leaving behind their waterways to fill with dirt until the next group of people arrived.

The continued growth of the Valley of the Sun still depends on vast waterworks that would make Rome's aqueduct builders envious. And in the last decade, the Central Arizona Project canal diverted water from the 200-miles-distant Colorado River over the Valley's desert acres. In addition, vast reserves of runoff from rain and snow in Arizona's northern mountains are stored behind Roosevelt Dam northeast of the Valley.

Made livable with water and air-conditioning, the Valley draws people like a magnet year after year. Some come for the 300 or so days of sunshine the Valley enjoys each year. Others seek the economic opportunity that this booming desert capital offers. Some come to reinvent themselves in the same way that the pioneers threw off their old lives to find something new in the West. They come to get away from bad weather, bad memories, and bad jobs. Even though about a third of Maricopa County residents leave each year, the influx of newcomers is so great that the Valley keeps growing.

The migration out of the county happens for many of the same reasons that people are coming in. Since so many people move here for work, they have no roots in the Valley and, therefore, when a better job comes up elsewhere, they move there. Job transfers in interstate corporations also play a part. Many of Arizona's major employment fields—such as tourism and the high-tech industry—traditionally attract very mobile employees.

Maricopa County is the 4th-largest county in the country, with a population of more than 3 million, and it ranks 14th in size among counties nationwide. Where do you put all these people? Unlike the already high-density population centers of the East and West Coasts, most cities in the Valley of the Sun are relatively young with no natural growth boundaries. With few exceptions, the cities have nearly free rein to expand and gulp up unincorporated land as they wish in order to accommodate and promote growth. However, growth cannot be allowed to continue unchecked, and boosterism and conserving open spaces are not mutually exclusive concepts. Within recent years the debate over growth boundaries has been fierce, with such groups as the Sierra Club attempting to initiate growth manage-

Phoenix Vital Statistics

Governor: Janet Napolitano

Phoenix city mayor: Phil Gordon

State capital: Phoenix

Area cities: Phoenix, Scottsdale, Paradise Valley, Tempe, Mesa, Gilbert, Chandler, Glendale, Cave Creek, and Sun City

Population: 3 million in the greater Phoenix area

Area: 2,000 square miles

Nickname: Valley of the Sun

Average temperatures: January: high 65° F, low 39° F
July: high 105° F, low 79.5° F

Average rainfall: 7.66 inches

Days of sunshine: 300 days

City founded: October 26, 1870

State founded: Arizona entered the Union on February 14, 1912, as the 48th state. The state flower is the saguaro cactus blossom, the state tree is the palo verde, and the state bird is the cactus wren.

Major universities: Arizona State University, Grand Canyon University, University of Phoenix, Ottawa University, and 10 colleges within the Maricopa Community College District: Phoenix College, Mesa Community College, Gateway Community College, Scottsdale Community College, Glendale Community College, Rio Salado Community College, South Mountain Community College, Chandler-Gilbert Community College, Estrella Mountain Community College, and Paradise Valley Community College

Important dates in history:

1885—Arizona State University, the oldest institution of higher learning in Arizona, founded

1889—Phoenix named as Arizona's capital

1911—Roosevelt Dam, a reservoir that helps supply the Valley's water, completed

1959—Phoenix experiences a boom in new construction and enters a period of steady growth

Community honors:

1993—Best Run City in the World award from the Carl Bertelsmann Foundation

2000—Best Managed City, *Governing Magazine*

2001—Phoenix recognized as the nation's most efficiently run city by the Reason Public Policy Institute (RPPI)

Time zone: Arizona is on mountain standard time and does not change its clocks for daylight saving time. So Arizona is on mountain time half the year and on Pacific time during daylight saving time.

Dress codes: The focus is on comfortable [...] rants require a tie and jacket for gentle[...] for cool evenings from December throug[...]

Major area industries: High-tech manufactu[...]

Sports: Home to the world-champion Arizona [...] World Series

Sales tax: 7.05%

Room tax: The ta[...] Scottsdale.

Visitor centers [...]

Famous sons, daughters, and residents:

Frank Luke, WWI Ace Pilot

Ira Hayes, U.S. Marine who raised the flag on Iwo [...]

Barry Goldwater, politician

Frank Lloyd Wright, architect

Steve Allen, entertainer

Marty Robbins, country singer

Paul Harvey, radio personality

Glen Campbell, entertainer

Erma Bombeck, humorist

Bil Keene, cartoonist

Alice Cooper, rock musician

Francine Reed, blues singer

Steven Spielberg, filmmaker

David Spade, comedian

State/city holidays: Labor Day, Veterans Day, Thanksgiving, Christmas, New Year's Day, Martin Luther King Jr. Day, Memorial Day, Independence Day

Chamber of commerce:

Greater Phoenix Chamber of Commerce
201 North Central Avenue, #2700
Phoenix, AZ 85073-8001
(602) 254-5521, www.phoenixchamber.com

Major airports: Phoenix Sky Harbor International Airport, served by 21 airlines, www.phxskyharbor.com

Public transportation: Phoenix offers bus service throughout the majority of the metro area. Valley Metro: (602) 253-5000, www.valleymetro.org

Military bases: Luke Air Force Base

Driving laws: Seat belts must be worn. Children must be in car seats until they weigh 40 pounds or more. High occupancy lanes are for cars with two or more people.

Alcohol law: You must be 21 years old to purchase alcoholic beverages. Bars are open until 1:00 A.M. You can purchase alcohol on Sunday after 10:00 A.M.

Daily newspapers: The *Arizona Republic* is the largest daily newspaper with a circulation of nearly 400,000. Call (602) 444-8000 or (800) 331-9303 or visit www.azcentral.com.

x rates range from 12.07 percent in Phoenix to 11.67 percent in

town Phoenix
or Information Center
North Second Street (Second & Adams Streets)
oenix, AZ 85004
ours: Monday through Friday, 8:00 A.M. to 5:00 P.M.

Biltmore Visitor Information Center
2404 East Camelback Road
(24th Street & Camelback Road)
Phoenix, AZ 85016
Hours: Monday through Wednesday 10:00 A.M. to 7:00 P.M., Thursday and Friday 10:00 A.M. to 8:00 P.M., Saturday and Sunday noon to 6:00 P.M. Visitor Hotline: (602) 252–5588

Time and temperature: National Weather Service forecast office offers information about weather around the state. Call (602) 275–0073 or visit www.wrh.noaa.gov/Phoenix. Phoenix weather information is also available at www.weather.com.

ment boundaries and policies that actually have some judicial teeth.

As recently as 1950 the city of Phoenix encompassed just 17 square miles and had a population of about 100,000. Since then, the city has pursued an aggressive policy of annexation, which has expanded its area by nearly 400 square miles. The population of Phoenix is nearly 1.3 million, making it the sixth-largest city in the United States.

The Valley's other cities have been just as aggressive in their growth and land annexation. Mesa, the second-largest city in the Valley, had a population of 16,670 in 1950. From the early city center around Main and Center Streets, it has expanded to the edge of Maricopa County on the east. Traveling from Mesa's west end to its east end takes nearly a half hour of driving at the posted 55 mph speed limit on the Superstition Freeway (U.S. Highway 60). The Phoenix-Mesa metropolitan area increased in population by 45.3 percent since 1990. It is the 14th-largest metropoli-

tan area, out of 280 metro areas defined by the U.S. Census. Of all the metro areas, Phoenix-Mesa had the fifth-highest increase in population since 1990 and the eighth-highest percentage increase.

Out of 243 cities nationwide, 8 incorporated cities in the Phoenix metro area (Phoenix, Mesa, Glendale, Scottsdale, Chandler, Tempe, Gilbert, and Peoria) have a population of 100,000 or more. Their national ranking and growth over the last 10 years is as follows:

Phoenix, 6th, 34.3 percent growth
Mesa, 43rd, 37.6 percent growth
Glendale, 81st, 47.7 percent growth
Scottsdale, 88th, 55.8 percent growth
Chandler, 116th, 95 percent growth
Tempe, 129th, 11.8 percent growth
Gilbert, 208th, 275.8 percent growth
Peoria, 214th, 114.1 percent growth

The Valley's economic focus has shifted away from agriculture—though Maricopa County remains one of the

largest cotton-producing counties in the nation—to the service industry, tourism, and high-tech manufacturing. Agriculture began to give way to a defense economy during World War II. After the war the defense industries, such as aerospace, shifted to peacetime production. Electronics companies came to the Valley in profusion in the 1950s, and the high-tech and computer industries followed in the 1980s and 1990s.

Statistics compiled in 2001 by Arizona's Department of Economic Security show that in Maricopa County there is a total civilian workforce of more than 1.5 million with service industries representing the largest employers, with more than 1.2 million employees. U.S. Census Bureau employment statistics for 2001 in Maricopa County were: management, professional, and related occupations, 33 percent; sales and office occupations, 30 percent; service occupations, 15 percent; production, transportation, and material-moving occupations, 12 percent; and construction, extraction, and maintenance occupations, 11 percent. Eighty-two percent of the people employed were private wage and salary workers; 12 percent were federal, state, or local government workers; and 5 percent were self-employed. The median income of households in Maricopa County was $43,096.

Phoenix has a highly diversified economic base, and it serves as headquarters for many large national corporations, including Phelps Dodge, Viad, Aztar, U-Haul, Swift, MicroAge, Petsmart, and Cavco. Leading industries include manufacturing, electronics, high technology, retail trade, services, construction, and tourism.

According to the *Business Journal of Phoenix,* the top five employers in Maricopa County are the State of Arizona, Wal-Mart Stores Inc., Banner Health System, Maricopa County, and the City of Phoenix.

The Valley has also become a sports mecca. This is one of a handful of metropolitan areas to have franchises for all four major-league sports—baseball, football, basketball, and hockey—a claim that even the monstrous Los Angeles metroplex has been unable to make since both the Rams and Raiders deserted la-la land. (See the Spectator Sports chapter.)

As much as the mayors and loyal residents of other Valley cities may bristle, Phoenix has always been the Valley of the Sun's 900-pound gorilla, the hub around which its commerce revolves—so much so that many people refer to the entire Valley of the Sun as Phoenix. Even people who live as far afield as Apache Junction and Avondale have been heard to tell outsiders, "I live in Phoenix."

So just what is the Valley of the Sun? To most, the Valley represents the urbanized portions of Maricopa County. The Valley covers 2,000 square miles, and Phoenix represents about 470 of those. Maricopa County includes 24 incorporated cities and towns, not to mention 32 unincorporated communities. Cities and towns within the county are Avondale, Buckeye, Carefree, Cave Creek, Chandler, El Mirage, Fountain Hills, Gila Bend, Gilbert, Glendale, Goodyear, Guadalupe, Litchfield Park, Mesa, Paradise Valley, Peoria, Phoenix, Queen Creek, Scottsdale, Surprise, Tempe, Tolleson, Wickenburg, and Youngtown. Unincorporated cities include Chandler Heights, Sun City, Sun City West, and Sunflower. From east to west, it stretches 45 miles from Apache Junction to Goodyear. From north to south, it stretches about 40 miles from the northern boundary of Phoenix to Chandler. The outer orbit of the Valley's growth has touched Carefree and Cave Creek in the foothills north of Phoenix, Fountain Hills in the foothills northeast of Scottsdale, and Buckeye to the southwest. Although Wickenburg is about 40 miles northwest of the Sun Cities, it is sometimes considered part of the Valley.

The continuing growth of the urbanized Valley has almost surrounded the Salt River Pima-Maricopa Indian Community, which is located east of Scottsdale and south of north Scottsdale. The reservation's southeastern boundary follows the

Salt River's path north of Mesa. The reservation also touches on Tempe at Hayden Road, south of Scottsdale. The Fort McDowell Indian Community touches the north end of Fountain Hills, while the Gila River Indian Community marks the southern end of much of the Valley.

In many ways Sky Harbor International Airport, operated by the city of Phoenix, is the heart of the Valley. Its eastbound flight paths have sparked noise complaints and a seemingly never-ending battle with the city of Tempe. Yet the sight of the virtually constant air traffic seems symbolic of the Valley's economic vitality. The Valley is a place where, more often than not, shiny new buildings win out over preserving the past. It's a place where people and governments are not afraid to use the latest technology.

Still, it's important to remember that the Valley of the Sun is not just Phoenix, and that although the housing developments that are consuming the desert landscape at the rate of an acre an hour sometimes seem stultifyingly similar, each city does have its own character, history, and attractions.

PHOENIX

As of 1985 Phoenix adopted an "urban village plan" as part of the city's general plan. The idea was that the city had nine distinct areas in which city services and business cores were situated or needed to be situated. The city in its annexations had gobbled up many distinctive neighborhoods such as Maryvale, which began as an affordable bedroom community for young married couples and families when it was developed by John F. Long in the late 1950s and early 1960s, and South Phoenix, where the Valley's African-American and Hispanic populations concentrated.

As was the case with many cities, the central business district of Phoenix became less important as suburbs like Maryvale and Deer Valley arose. Unlike older and more densely packed metropolitan areas such as New York City, Phoenix swallowed its suburbs and neglected its epicenter. The malls in its far-flung neighborhoods helped keep people from heading downtown to do business. Aside from the office workers who went there, Phoenix's downtown was a ghost town after dark through most of the 1980s.

The urban village concept seemed like hokum to some critics, and it's certainly too soon to tell what effect it will have on eight of the nine villages. However, the plan's adoption coincided with major efforts to revitalize downtown, which was one of the nine villages included in the concept. Ever since Phoenix Suns owner Jerry Colangelo decided to build America West Arena in downtown Phoenix, the center of the city has become more vibrant and lively. Now referred to as Copper Square, the 90 square blocks from Third Avenue to Seventh Street, and from Fillmore to south of Jackson, include 95 restaurants and bars, more than 31,000 parking spaces, a free shuttle, and 19 arts, cultural, and entertainment venues, including the state-of-the-art Bank One Ballpark (home of the Diamondbacks), the Herberger Theater Center, the $515-million Arizona Center, the historic Orpheum Theater, and City Hall. With guides on foot or bike seven days a week, and a free shuttle, Copper Square has given people some genuine reasons to head (or stay) there after dark.

A few other clubs and restaurants also have benefited from the rise in foot traffic, which is but a trickle compared with that in other major cities, yet far greater than it was in the 1980s. Bank One Ballpark opened in March 1998 and boosted downtown's fortunes. Further downtown revitalization efforts include the planned expansion of Civic Plaza, which was approved by voters in 2001 and will allow up to $300 million to be earmarked for the expansion of the convention center.

As a city, though, Phoenix remains a huge suburb with interesting pockets of old-time housing such as Encanto Village. There are some very good parks, such as

Papago Park and Margaret T. Hance Deck Park, a 29-acre park above the Interstate 10 tunnel. The park has a paved urban plaza with wooded area, volleyball court, playground, and picnic ramada, along with a Japanese teahouse and garden. Patriot's Square in downtown Phoenix sits atop an underground parking garage and offers an outdoor performing-arts stage, food kiosks, trees, grass, and benches. Since it covers only a city block, it seems packed, especially at lunchtime. There's more brick than grass in it, but it remains a down-town oasis.

The freeway system has improved mobility around the Valley, but people tend to play and shop close to home, and a number of malls serve that purpose—Desert Sky and Maryvale Malls on the west side; Metrocenter in the north-central section; Christown Mall in the central section; the Colonnade and Town & Country shopping center and the Biltmore Fashion Park, all off Camelback Road and the Squaw Peak Parkway (State Route 51); Paradise Valley Mall in the northeastern section; and Arcadia Crossing in the eastern section—and much more shopping has grown up around them. (We provide an overview of shopping hot spots in the Shopping chapter.)

Although Phoenix's neighborhoods are built primarily on a grid and many housing developments are built cookie-cutter style, geographic and economic diversity provide character. In the northeastern part of the city, middle-class to upper-middle-class neighborhoods are punctuated by mountains—Camelback, Squaw Peak, North Mountain, and others. South Phoenix also features some prime housing in the foothills of South Mountain, but as you head north toward the Salt River, the increasing tension of crime-ridden neighborhoods can be felt in the flatlands. Nevertheless, along stretches of Baseline Road in South Phoenix, you'll experience an almost pastoral feeling with small remaining farms and orchards. There's a cozy claustrophobia to Phoenix's Paradise Valley neighborhood, which cannot be

If you are moving to Arizona permanently, you'll want to establish residency soon. Start by getting an Arizona driver's license. (If you're staying less than seven months, you will not need to do this.) If you have a valid license from another state, you can simply apply and have your picture taken. The written and driving tests are not required. For information about car titles, registration, and personalized license plates, call (602) 255-0072.

confused with the upscale town of the same name that sits to the neighborhood's southeast.

The high-rises of the Central Avenue corridor stand in stark contrast to the many old single-story houses just blocks away. A little farther north on Central Avenue, some housing sits on big lots near large apartment complexes—rarely more than two stories tall—and the number of trees increases radically. These are relatively old, established neighborhoods. Far to the west, where housing is relatively new, one can feel an unsettled quietude. The neighborhoods sit flat in the slope toward the Agua Fria River, and the houses are far enough apart that they still seem unsheltered, like pioneer dwellings on the desert floor.

Other far-reaching revitalization projects include the Rio Salado project, a plan to restore the Salt River to its natural state. Once restored, the area will support native wildlife and plant life and create a revitalized river corridor through central Phoenix and, when completed, will offer 10 miles of recreational and interpretive trails; wells and a water delivery system to bring water to the trees and other vegetation; wetlands, canals, ponds and streams, water, shelter, space, and food for wildlife; and an environmental education center. The first stage of the project was realized in June 2001 with the opening of the Gateway, a cyclist and pedestrian plaza on the bank of the Salt River at Central

Avenue that features terraced seating, interpretative gardens, and a 40-foot-by-80-foot shade structure.

One of the six growth areas adopted by the Phoenix City Council in Phoenix's Strategic View of Growth, North Black Canyon, located along the Interstate 17 corridor north of Happy Valley Road, is another area currently under development. There is also a variety of short-term and long-term planning and development activities under way to bring housing and retail developments to the area. In other words, this gorilla city doesn't have a single face. Whatever the fate of the urban-village concept, the planners who created it were certainly right about the diversity of the styles and needs of the city's neighborhoods.

SOUTHEAST VALLEY

Mesa

The Southeast Valley consists of sprawling Mesa, landlocked Tempe, Chandler, Gilbert, and Guadalupe. Some even consider far-flung Apache Junction, a city in Pinal County, to be part of the Valley.

The Southeast Valley is one of the key centers of housing growth, with goods and services following on the heels of new housing builds. Since so much of this area was agricultural mere decades ago, there are few old commerce centers to serve as anchors. Instead, strip malls sprout along the major thoroughfares, spaced on a grid of 1-mile squares. Mesa, Tempe, and Chandler all have core downtown areas that are pedestrian-friendly, but in some neighborhoods in the Southeast Valley it's a daunting task to walk almost anywhere, and local mom-and-pop stores or newsstands are nowhere to be seen.

Mesa is the giant of the Southeast Valley and Arizona's third-largest city. The city was founded by Mormons from Utah and Idaho. They settled on this broad plateau, or mesa, in May 1878 and sought to name the settlement in its honor. However, the post office wouldn't recognize the name "Mesa" because a town named Mesaville existed in Pinal County. The settlers decided to name their community Hayden, after Charles Trumbull Hayden, who at the time ran a ferryboat across the Salt River. This caused confusion in the mails because of an old post office called Hayden's Ferry, so the settlers renamed their town Zenos, after a prophet in the Book of Mormon, in 1886. When Mesaville went out of existence in 1888, the settlers promptly changed the name of the community back to Mesa.

Mormon culture remains dominant in Mesa, giving it a different ambiance from Phoenix and the rest of the Valley. It's not uncommon to see Mormon missionaries, dressed neatly in white shirts and dark ties, riding bicycles and spreading the word.

Given the city's size, the downtown is small and quiet at night. This is not to say that the city is a Mormon city; it's far from it. The influx of population in recent years makes it nearly as heterogeneous as other parts of the Valley. However, the Mormon influence has given rise to the perception that it's a good place for young families to settle. The city also has a larger share of winter visitors and older residents living in trailer parks.

Tempe

Tempe began when Charles Trumbull Hayden built a flour mill and established a ferry service across the Salt River in 1871. Soon, a small community grew up around these enterprises, and the post office recognized it as Hayden's Ferry and Hayden's Mill. The growing settlement took the name Tempe after the suggestion of "Lord" Darrell Duppa. Duppa had a penchant for Greek names, having named Phoenix, and he suggested that Hayden's Ferry be renamed Tempe because to him it resembled the Vale of Tempe in Greece. Hayden became one of the trustees of the Territorial Normal

School, which became Tempe's major asset. The Normal School evolved over the next six decades to become Arizona State University (see the Education and Child Care chapter). Today, the university is central to Tempe's active downtown scene along Mill Avenue, which has been revived and is full of cafes, restaurants, and shopping spots. The presence of students makes Tempe one of the best towns in Arizona for aspiring musicians. Tempe is now Arizona's fifth-largest city.

The university's Sun Devil Stadium is the site of ASU Sun Devil football and the NFL's Arizona Cardinals games. It annually hosts the Fiesta Bowl and was the site of Super Bowl XXX. The stadium also is one of the few venues to have hosted both a papal Mass and Rolling Stones concerts. Large concert scenes from Barbara Streisand's *A Star Is Born* were filmed there, as were scenes in U2's movie *Rattle and Hum.* Other university facilities, such as Gammage Auditorium, also provide easily accessible cultural activities, ranging from touring Broadway plays to classical and pop concerts. The university is also the home of KAET (Channel 8), the Valley's PBS station.

Tempe is unique among the Valley's major cities in that it cannot annex any neighboring land. It is landlocked by Phoenix on the west, Scottsdale on the north, Mesa on the east, and Chandler on the south. However, the city has been making the most of undeveloped land within its limits. The Arizona Mills Mall opened in late 1997 at the junction of the Superstition Freeway (US 60) and I-10. It is the largest mall in Arizona and boasts a range of outlet stores, high-tech play areas, and restaurants.

The newest Tempe attraction is the Tempe Town Lake, where the once-dry Salt River was dammed to create a 2-mile-long recreation area perfect for biking, jogging, skating, canoeing, sailing, and paddleboating.

Aside from Phoenix, Tempe is the only Valley city to be host to two major-league sports teams. The NFL's Arizona Cardinals play at ASU's Sun Devil Stadium (as do the school's Sun Devils), and Major League Baseball's Anaheim Angels play spring-training games at Tempe Diablo Stadium.

Chandler

Chandler is named after Alexander John Chandler, a Canadian who settled in Arizona in 1887. He was the territory's first veterinary surgeon, a post he held until 1892. In the interim, he became one of the Valley's largest landholders. His Chandler Ranch covered about 18,000 acres, and in 1911 he sold his land in plots of 10 to 160 acres. The city of Chandler was established a year later.

The community retained its agricultural character until about 1980, when a building boom propelled it into its status as one of the fastest-growing communities in the state. Chandler has become home to several high-tech manufacturers, including Intel. The city continues to revitalize its downtown on Arizona Avenue with such projects as the Chandler Center for the Arts, which was completed in the early 1990s, and the 1.3-million-square-foot, upscale Chandler Fashion Center, the centerpiece of a 320-acre "urban village" that includes Chandler Festival, Chandler Gateway, and The Boulevard Shops. The San Marcos Hotel, with some updating, was reestablished as the major draw of Chandler's downtown. The hotel, isolated as it was from the rest of the Valley in Chandler's early days, was one of the first to promote itself as a resort for winter visitors. Dr. Chandler lived out his final days at the San Marcos.

For links to Web sites and information for all Valley cities, go to www.maricopa. gov or call (602) 506-3011 or (800) 540-5570. On the Web site, use "Other Sites" to find the official Web sites of cities and towns in Maricopa County.

Gilbert

Gilbert was established in 1912 on land donated by Robert Gilbert. It, too, was an agricultural community. In fact, it was known as the Hay Capital of the World until 1920. In 1980 Gilbert had 5,717 residents, which grew to more than 110,000 in 2001. The fastest-growing community in Arizona, Gilbert has suffered some growing pains. The city is taking in new students faster than it can fund new classrooms and hopes to attract more businesses to balance the residential growth. A hospital and mall are in the planning stages.

Guadalupe

Also part of the Southeast Valley is Guadalupe. A tiny landlocked community, Guadalupe has one of the smallest populations in the Valley. It boasts one of the more colorful municipal histories. Guadalupe was established by members of the Yaqui tribe who fled Mexico in the late 1800s to escape dictator Porfirio Diaz's attempts to relocate them to the Yucatan, which was far from their ancestral home in northwestern Mexico. The name comes from the Virgin of Guadalupe, the patron saint of Mexico. The town's chief landmarks are the mission-style Our Lady of Guadalupe Church and the Yaqui Temple. Today, Yaqui descendants and Mexican-Americans comprise the majority of the town's residents.

It's legal to make a right turn on a red light in the Valley if you make sure to come to a complete stop first. Check the oncoming traffic and then proceed to turn if safe. Many Valley communities have left-turn signals, but those in Scottsdale are slightly different. The left-turn arrows are timed to follow (rather than precede) the green light for the traffic traveling through the intersection.

Public school students go to school in Tempe, which nearly encircles Guadalupe. With a relatively high unemployment rate, Guadalupe officials are seeking more businesses to employ their residents.

Queen Creek

Beyond what is commonly considered the Valley, the farming community of Queen Creek maintains a bucolic lifestyle southeast of Gilbert. The biggest event of the year in the community is Country Thunder, a three-day festival of country music that's heavily attended by RV campers (see the Annual Events chapter). With Gilbert rapidly growing and Williams Gateway Airport growing to its north, Queen Creek may soon be enveloped to become part of the Valley's mainstream instead of remaining on the fringe.

Apache Junction

East of Mesa, all the way in Pinal County, Apache Junction sits at the foot of the Superstition Mountains like an appendix to the Valley. Formerly a fairly relaxed community, Apache Junction has the Valley's growth gene as well. With growth came new zoning restrictions that rankled some longtime residents. Primarily known for the many senior citizens who winter here in trailer and RV parks, Apache Junction may be changing its character as more families settle in the town. Although it is 45 minutes from downtown Phoenix, Apache Junction is likely to be considered part of the Valley's mainstream in the coming years.

Sun Lakes

The unincorporated retirement community of Sun Lakes is wedged between the southern end of Chandler and the northeastern boundary of the Gila River Indian Community. When the community was established in 1972 by developer Robson Communities, it was well separated from Chandler development and not thought of as part of the Valley. Today, the approximately 15,000 residents enjoy golf courses, swimming pools, tennis courts, health clubs, fishing lakes, craft studios, social clubs, and dining facilities. Although separated from downtown Phoenix by a 35-minute drive up I–10, local seniors have little or no need to leave the area to sustain their lifestyle.

Gila River Indian Community

The Gila River Indian Community marks the Valley's southern end. The reservation covers 650 square miles—more than half the size of the Valley—and it houses about 12,000 mostly agrarian residents from the Pima and Maricopa tribes. Although technically outside the Valley, the northern end of the reservation houses attractions that bring in hundreds of thousands of visitors annually. Firebird International Raceway and three casinos have allowed the tribe to improve many community services and add a hospital and fire department.

NORTHEAST VALLEY

The Northeast Valley is considered the Valley's most upscale region. It includes large estates in Paradise Valley and newly developed high-end communities located on land recently annexed by the city of Scottsdale. This area is miles from the Salt River bottom, and, in its gradual slope upward to the Mogollon Rim, foothills become an important geographical feature.

Scottsdale

Scottsdale is top dog in the Northeast Valley. On its eastern side, the city mostly borders the Salt River Pima-Maricopa Indian Community, and to the south it is

If you're a celebrity watcher, Scottsdale is one place where you're likely to run into some. Whether you're out shopping, browsing in art galleries, or taking in the nightlife, keep your eyes wide open and you just might spot a star.

hemmed in by Tempe. Early in its development it squabbled with Phoenix over annexation rights to various tracts on its west side. In the past decade Scottsdale annexed a huge amount of land to the north, which brought communities of ranchers and desert dwellers into its chic fold.

In 1881 Major Winfield Scott homesteaded on the site of the city that would one day carry his name. When Scott retired from the military, he promoted his ranch and the surrounding area as a rest cure and agricultural center. Scottsdale became the official name in 1896, when local settlers sought to establish a school district.

Scottsdale was relatively slow to develop but has boomed in the years since World War II. It was one of the first cities to revitalize its downtown, billing itself as "the West's most Western town." Art galleries abound in downtown Scottsdale, catering to both cowboy-art and modern-art lovers. The downtown is eminently friendly to foot traffic, and Scottsdale Fashion Square and the Borgata of Scottsdale offer upscale shopping not too far from the town center.

The greenbelt that runs for a dozen miles down the Indian Bend Wash made a virtue out of a flooding problem. Since the wash floods during any significant rain, filling it in for development would have been unwise. Instead, the city devised an alternative plan that turned it into a strip of parkland with jogging and bicycle paths and other recreational facilities that would not be unduly affected by the occasional flooding. Floodwaters would irrigate the grass and would be contained by the wide channel.

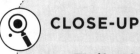

Taliesin West: Architect Frank Lloyd Wright's Personal Favorite

Eleven of Frank Lloyd Wright's buildings are listed by the *Architectural Record* as among the top 100 in the world, but the architect's personal favorite was his architectural school in Scottsdale, Arizona—Taliesin West.

From 1927, when he first visited the Phoenix area to consult on the Arizona Biltmore Resort, to his death in 1959 at the age of 91, the charm of the Sonoran Desert lured Wright to Arizona every winter. He built Taliesin West in the late 1930s and during his tenure there he completed one-third of his designs and his controversial style achieved the recognition he had long pursued.

Taliesin West, now a National Historic Landmark, nestles on 600 acres of desert land. A stroll around the grounds, led by informed tour guides—some of them former Wright apprentices—offers insight into Wright's genius. The school trains about 35 students each year and has an on-site architectural firm. The on-site archives of Wright's drawings and writings draw researchers from around the world. Filmmaker Ken Burns spent two years there researching Wright for a PBS documentary that aired in 1999.

The handful of buildings that comprise Taliesin West recline below the mountains, their profile harmonizing with the desert's rocks and plants. Wright's philosophy of organic design found its spiritual home in Arizona, and he believed the cactus epitomized good design. In a 1940 article for Arizona Highways, he wrote: "The Arizona desert is no place for the hard box-walls of the houses of the Middle West and East. Here all is sculptured by wind and water, patterned in color and texture."

The desert also supplied building materials. Wright worked side by side with his apprentices in the backbreaking work of gathering rocks and sand to create his unique "desert masonry." Hard, flat-sided rocks found in the area, called Taliesin quartzite, were unsuitable for cutting, but he used them to create a textured surface on the thick, concrete walls throughout the campus.

Hands-on work was an integral part of Wright's education philosophy, and his students still learn by doing. Many continue the tradition of constructing their own desert digs in which they live while studying at the school. In Wright's time students worked hard but they also played hard, because the teacher felt that learning how to socialize formally provided good training for the architecture business.

One center of social activity was the living room, dubbed "The Garden Room," whose 56-foot-long space is made even

Taliesin West combines open space, natural materials, and organic shapes to create a building in harmony with its surroundings. ALMUDENA ALONSO-HERRERO

more dramatic by its sloping, translucent roof and spine of windows. Other points of interest on the Taliesin West grounds include the Cabaret Cinema, the Music Pavilion, the Seminar Theater, and Wright's private office. One of Wright's works, the historic Sun Cottage, consists of three large circular rooms framed by glass walls and clustered around a breezeway.

Throughout Taliesin West, redwood timbers crown the buildings and canvas roofs allow sunlight to diffuse through the rooms. His rooms are filled with furniture that he designed. The entrances to his buildings are hidden and mysterious; entryways to rooms are low, opening suddenly into spaciousness and light.

Taliesin West was a work in progress while Wright lived, because the master was forever improving on his designs. Today, his desert camp provides a glimpse into the creative life of a man whose vision is still ahead of its time.

Taliesin West is located at 1261 Frank Lloyd Wright Boulevard in Scottsdale. Tours cost $15 and up. For more information, call (480) 860-2700 ext. 494, or visit www.franklloydwright.org.

Central to the city's image as a cultural leader is the Scottsdale Center for the Arts, which features two art galleries and an 800-seat auditorium (see the Arts chapter). The arts facility is part of the Scottsdale Civic Center complex, also known as the Scottsdale Mall, which includes City Hall, the Scottsdale Library, and other municipal facilities. It is adjacent to Scottsdale Stadium, which hosts the San Francisco Giants during spring training and two teams in the Arizona Fall Baseball League. Another Scottsdale landmark is Taliesin West, a winter residence built by Frank Lloyd Wright in 1937, making Wright's presence a powerful force in the city's cultural fabric. He's claimed almost as a native son. Scottsdale is also home to the Scottsdale Air Park, a busy industrial park that surrounds Scottsdale Municipal Airport around Frank Lloyd Wright Boulevard.

The town of Paradise Valley, nestled among the hills between north Phoenix and north Scottsdale, may be the Valley's most exclusive community. Residents can see the back of Camelback Mountain and look up at a formation called the Praying Monk. The large estates of the community, incorporated in 1961, house many of the Valley's celebrities—Alice Cooper, Geordie Hormel (the heir to the Spam fortune), former major leaguer Joe Garagiola, and Family Circus cartoonist Bil Keane, just to name a few.

As Billie Holiday sang, "Them that's got shall get!" The 13,664 well-heeled residents of Paradise Valley, where most recent figures show that the median home value was $650,000 and the median household income was $150,228, pay no property tax. The town earned some infamy among local drivers when it became the first municipality in the Valley to install photo radar to help its small police force crack down on speeders along Lincoln Boulevard. The mountainside street offers wonderful views of the Valley's lights at night, and it is the main thoroughfare through Paradise Valley from Phoenix to Scottsdale.

Carefree

As Scottsdale and Phoenix aggressively annex toward the north, the Valley almost includes the foothill towns Carefree and Cave Creek, which are almost always mentioned in the same breath. Gordon Lightfoot's song "Carefree Highway" refers to the highway that connects Carefree to I–17, miles to the west. Carefree, established in 1959, is a planned community of luxury homes that rests in the northwestern shoulder of Scottsdale, just northeast of the very northeastern tip of Phoenix. The home of The Boulders Resort (see the Resorts chapter), the town has huge boulders as topographical features. Carefree's population numbers just above 2,000.

Cave Creek

Cave Creek, on the other hand, was founded in 1874, when prospectors found gold to the northeast. Unlike other communities that became ghost towns after a gold rush, Cave Creek was a good area for ranching. The Cave Creek Wash, which flows year-round, and lush springs nearby helped provide water and grazing areas for cattle. The town, just west of Carefree and just north of Phoenix, offers Valley residents a quick, admission-free getaway to the Old West in its Frontier Town, a group of Western-style shops, and its old-timer saloons. Cave Creek's population is around 3,500.

Fountain Hills

Similarly, Scottsdale's growth has nearly brought Fountain Hills into the Valley. From northeast Scottsdale, Shea Boulevard travels through a pass in the McDowell Mountains to enter Fountain Hills. The McDowells form a natural boundary between the mountain community and the Valley. Fountain Hills prides itself on being far from the hubbub and crime of

Area Codes

Once upon a time, the Phoenix area was covered by one area code, 602. Unfortunately, with the breakup of the phone companies and the rapid growth of urban areas all over the country, that's no longer the case. Phoenix and its surrounding areas are now serviced by three different area codes, which makes calling a challenge. The following should help!

602 covers most of the city of Phoenix.

480 covers most of the East and Northeast Valley areas, including Scottsdale, Tempe, Paradise Valley, and Chandler.

623 covers the West Valley communities, including Glendale, Peoria, Tolleson, and the Sun Cities.

And, just so you know, Arizona has two additional area codes: 520 covers most of the Tucson area (Pima County), Pinal, Santa Cruz, and Cochise County and 928 covers the rest of the state, including Flagstaff, Prescott, Payson, Sedona, Yuma, Williams, and the Grand Canyon.

---

the urban center. It was one of "Ten Great Places to Raise a Family" in the May 1997 issue of *Parenting* magazine. When building began in 1970, unincorporated Fountain Hills was seen as being attractive to retirees. The plan called for the then-unincorporated community to expand to 70,000 residents by the time it was built out. Times changed, though, and the market for that type of community evaporated. Now, the town, which was incorporated in 1989, offers upscale, low-density neighborhoods. Its population is a mix of retirees, winter visitors, and families, with a peak-season population of about 20,000. Fountain Hills cannot annex any land because it is surrounded by the McDowell Mountains, McDowell Mountain Park, the Fort McDowell Indian Community, and the Salt River Pima-Maricopa Indian Community. The town takes its name from its fountain, which can spew a plume of water more than 560 feet into the air. Boosters claim that it is the world's tallest fountain, rising 10 feet higher than the Washington Monument. It was designed both as a landmark and a means to disperse the town's effluent.

Because of Fountain Hills' growth, the Fort McDowell Indian Community to the northeast of town is slowly being brought into the Valley's sphere as well. The small community has about 800 registered members. Revenues from tribal enterprises such as the Fort McDowell Casino, a tribal farm, a gas station on the busy Beeline Highway (State Route 87), Fort McDowell Adventures (a tourist destination that offers horseback riding and other activities in the desert), and Fort McDowell Sand and Gravel have helped the community improve its infrastructure and the income of its members.

Salt River Pima-Maricopa Indian Community

Where does the mostly agricultural Salt River Pima-Maricopa Indian Community fit in? It's either the very southern part of the Northeast Valley or the very northern part of the Southeast Valley. Although it has fingers that shoot down south of Tempe's northern boundary, most of the commu-

Quick Reference Guide to the Valley Communities

Phoenix: Ahwatukee, Arcadia, Christown, downtown, Encanto, Maryvale, Metrocenter, and North Central

Southeast Valley: Chandler, Gilbert, Mesa, and Tempe

Northwest Valley: Glendale, Peoria, Sun Cities, Surprise, and Youngtown

Southwest Valley: Avondale, Buckeye, Goodyear, Litchfield Park, and Tolleson

nity is east of Scottsdale, which also bounds the reservation on the north. For the most part, the Salt River marks its southern boundary just north of Mesa and Tempe. Although it is considered the most urbanized of Arizona's reservations, when you pass through the sparsely populated agricultural landscape you feel as though you have left the Valley.

The community's chief crops are cotton, melons, potatoes, onions, and carrots. Along its boundaries with Mesa, Tempe, and Scottsdale, little shops do heavy business selling cigarettes free of state sales tax. The community also benefits from a 140-acre shopping center known as the Pavilions, the largest on Native American land in the nation. The shopping center sits right across from north Scottsdale at Indian Bend and Pima Roads, so it draws a good business from the city. There are also two golf courses and two casinos.

To some extent, Northeast Phoenix is also seen as part of the Northeast Valley.

Be sure to take along plenty of water on all excursions during the summer in Arizona—even if you're just planning to drive or walk a short distance. It's amazing how fast you can dehydrate in the desert heat. If you're waiting for a tow truck in the case of a breakdown, water can feel heaven sent.

With deluxe areas such as the Arizona Biltmore within it, Northeast Phoenix shares the Northeast Valley's reputation for glitzy affluence.

NORTHWEST VALLEY

After the Southeast Valley, the Northwest Valley is enjoying the area's greatest growth spurt. Houses are being built farther and farther out. For our purposes, the Northwest Valley includes Glendale, Peoria, Sun City, Sun City West, Sun City Grand, Youngtown, El Mirage, and Surprise. The housing boom, mostly appealing to young families and retirees, has spawned a major upsurge in amenities in the area in the past decade.

The key to the Northwest Valley's development has always been roads. For most of its existence, Grand Avenue, which also doubles as several highways including US 60, was the main drag that opened commercial development. Acres of industrial buildings line the highway as it progresses northwestward as the only major road in the Valley that proceeds on an angle to the squared-off grid system. Grand Avenue touches on downtown Glendale and downtown Peoria, then offers easy access to Sun City, Sun City West, Surprise, and Youngtown before heading for Wickenburg and Nevada.

The Loop 101 freeway, which begins at Camelback Road and 99th Avenue, heads north to approximately Bell Road and 83rd Avenue before jogging east to connect with I-17. The corridor served by this relatively new freeway has been the center for the Northwest Valley's growth. The Arrowhead Towne Center in Glendale is convenient to residents of Peoria and the Sun Cities, as well as Glendale, and has been the focal point of commercial growth in the area.

Glendale

With a population of more than 225,000, Glendale is the third-largest city in the Valley, fourth largest in the state, and obviously the big dog in the Northwest Valley. It was established in 1892 by members of the Church of the Brethren, but the reason church members had for naming the area Glendale has been lost. For the longest time, the city had a reputation as a blue-collar community and the housing was on a par with that offered in Maryvale. The image of downtown was of a railroad crossing tying up traffic at the triple intersection of Grand, Glendale, and 59th Avenues. The city hired a full-time marketing director in 1987, and its downtown has undergone revitalization, building a reputation as a premiere antiquing destination. The city's library offers notable public arts programming. Glendale is the home of the American Graduate School of International Management (also known as Thunderbird), and since the 1980s it has also housed Arizona State University's West Valley campus, a gem that offers easily accessible cultural activities to the community. The city also recently built a state-of-the-art sports arena at the Loop 101 Freeway and Glendale Avenue for the NHL Coyotes.

To accommodate its rapid growth, Glendale annexed many square miles of unincorporated land to the southwest, including Luke Air Force Base. When Luke Air Force Base was built in 1941, it was expected to be a major economic plum. Unexpectedly, World War II boosted its value. Unlike Williams Air Force Base, which was downsized out of the Southeast Valley due to post–Cold War defense cutbacks, Luke continues to pump money into the economy of the Northwest Valley. However, with Glendale's commercial and residential growth, it has become a target of noise complaints and safety concerns because of flight-training missions based there.

Peoria

Peoria was first settled by Chauncey Clark, who arrived there from Peoria, Illinois, in the late 1800s. A primarily agricultural settlement, the city began to boom in the 1980s, attracting about 400 newcomers a month as housing developments marched over acres previously planted in cotton and other crops. Owing to its young-family orientation, the Peoria schools number among the best in the Valley. The city also opened the Peoria Sports Complex, a spring-training facility along the popular retro-style ballpark lines of Camden Yards, whose proximity to Arrowhead Towne Center has further fueled economic growth along Loop 101. As Peoria's population has grown, Grand Avenue has also developed as a popular business corridor. The city has reached northward in its growth and swallowed up Lake Pleasant and Lake Pleasant Regional Park, one of the most popular weekend destinations among boating and fishing enthusiasts (see the Parks and Recreation chapter).

Sun City, Sun City West, and Sun City Grand

Sun City and Sun City West are developed as far as they can be. They are unincorporated retirement communities established in the past four decades by builder Del Webb. The primary way to reach these communities is via Bell Road, which runs east to west across the Valley, connecting Sun City West to north Scottsdale far away to the east. The streets are designed in twisting, sometimes circular mazes that are nearly surrounded by golf courses. The speed limits are low, and golf carts have the right of way. Besides the golf courses, recreation centers form the center of social activity in the Sun Cities, and the communities' recreation center boards act as a sort of low-level governmental body (see the Retirement chapter).

Shopping and restaurants are available, but the primary attraction of these retirement communities is the low-key lifestyle they offer, which is augmented by easy access to the attractions of Phoenix. Owned and operated by ASU, the 7,000-seat Sundome Center for the Arts offers frequent cultural and entertainment programs, mostly to residents of the Sun Cities since they are so isolated (although popular acts such as the Judds have drawn people from across the Valley). The Sundial Auditorium offers classical music performances.

Youngtown

With an ironic name, Youngtown was the Valley's first master-planned retirement community, begun on 320 acres in 1954. Youngtown was incorporated six years later, when Sun City opened. The community, which is virtually fully developed, encompasses a wedge-shaped area, surrounded by Sun City to the east, El Mirage to the north and west, and Peoria to the south. Since 1995 its annual population growth rate has been 0.8 percent, among

---

the lowest in the Valley. Fortunately, most residents treasure Youngtown's small-town ambiance, so being landlocked is a blessing here.

El Mirage

El Mirage, on the west bank of the Agua Fria River, was settled by migrant farm workers in the early 1930s. A working-class community, many residents have roots that reach back to the city's founding. It's estimated that 75 percent of the town's approximately 6,000 residents are Hispanic, and El Mirage retains a Mexican-American flavor. The city's population growth rate has been even lower than Youngtown's, averaging 0.3 percent annually since 1995. However, city fathers are looking to attract more businesses, particularly distributors and manufacturers. The Santa Fe Railroad and Grand Avenue (US 60) run parallel to one another through the center of El Mirage.

Surprise

Surprise, on the other hand, has become one of the fastest-growing cities in Maricopa County, with an average annual population increase of 18.5 percent since 1995 and a 2001 population of 30,848, a 333 percent growth. It had been 10,737 in 1995. The story goes that one of the city's first settlers back in 1929 said that it would be a surprise if the settlement became a city. Development has been spurred by both family-style and retirement communities. However, Sun City Grand, the latest development by Sun City founder Del Webb Corp., could tilt the community's demographic profile toward the older end of the spectrum. The 3,700-acre Sun City Grand sits on a triangle bounded by Bell Road to the south, Grand Avenue to the northeast, and the proposed Estrella Freeway (Loop 303) to the west. Plans call for Sun City Grand to house 17,500 residents

---

Local chambers of commerce are great sources of information on their areas. They'll be happy to answer questions on neighborhoods, schools, attractions, shopping, and anything else you might want to know. Many have free information packets they can send you before you even get here.

Helpful Web Sites

www.phoenixcvb.com
This is a terrific Web site for visitors and residents alike, developed by the Greater Phoenix Convention and Visitors Bureau. You'll find Phoenix facts, helpful tips, things to do, useful links, and more. Make this your first stop!

www.phoenix.gov
The city government's Web site has lots of useful information on municipal departments and services. There's also a good calendar of events, maps, and pages of local facts.

www.azguide.com
Maintained by the Arizona Guides Association, this site has extensive listings of attractions throughout the state. There are no reviews or descriptions here, but the information is very complete. It's a bit like a phonebook—only the most useful facts.

www.arizonaguide.com
This Arizona Office of Tourism's Web site will give you tons of information on Phoenix and the rest of Arizona too! You can search for information by city, area, or activity; check out online maps; and request free visitor guides.

in 9,500 homes when it is fully developed. Thanks to annexations in the past 15 years, Surprise cradles Sun City West to its northeast and touches Sun City to its east. El Mirage sits to the southeast. Surprise has plenty of room to grow because unincorporated county land stretches from its northwest and southwest boundaries.

SOUTHWEST VALLEY

Phoenix's headlong growth has pushed its fingers into the Southwest Valley, touching such previously outlying cities as Litchfield Park, Goodyear, Avondale, and Tolleson. The pace of development in these communities has almost made Buckeye, which is about 35 miles west of downtown Phoenix, part of the Valley's mainstream.

Litchfield Park

Litchfield Park's main claim to fame is the Goodyear Tire and Rubber Company and its aircraft subsidiary. The company pur-

chased the land that became Litchfield Park and Goodyear during World War I to grow cotton for use in its wartime products. In 1941, as Luke Air Force Base was being established to the north, the government set up a defense plant run by Goodyear Aircraft Corporation in Litchfield Park.

In the late 1960s the city developed a master plan that changed its character from agricultural and defense-oriented to suburban residential. It has since become home to many retired military personnel. The Wigwam Resort, which features three championship golf courses, is Litchfield Park's major employer (with 700 employees) and offers a five-star getaway for locals and visitors alike. Life is easygoing out here, even though I-10 puts downtown Phoenix just 25 minutes away.

Goodyear

The completion of I-10 in the early 1990s sparked a building boom in the town of Goodyear. Although the Goodyear company stopped growing cotton there at the end of World War II, the town remains primarily an agricultural community south of Litchfield Park. But that already is rapidly changing. The Arizona Republic says that Goodyear is expected to be the fastest-growing community in the Valley over the next 40 years. Indeed, its average annual population growth rate of 17.9 percent since 1995 is surpassed only by Surprise (18.5 percent) in the Northwest Valley and Gilbert (18.8 percent) in the Southeast Valley. Family-oriented residential growth is expected to further deplete the area's farmland, and service industries geared to those residents are already booming. Goodyear's population is roughly 19,500.

Avondale

Avondale was first settled by an outlaw named Billy Moore back during frontier settlement, but it wasn't incorporated as a city until 1946. It remains mainly an agricultural community, but like Goodyear to its west, it is undergoing a transformation. City planners want light industry and commercial enterprises to balance residential growth. The plan appears to be working. Its annual average growth rate of 8.3 percent since 1995 is relatively modest compared with Goodyear's. Avondale's growth has encompassed Phoenix International Raceway, which used to sit on unincorporated county land. The raceway, a major draw on the NASCAR circuit, generates a good deal of revenue and traffic for all of the Southwest Valley. Avondale's population is about 40,000 for 2001, with a projected population for 2025 of 104,527.

Tolleson

At a scant 6 square miles, Tolleson sits just a few miles south and west of Desert Sky Mall in the Maryvale section of Phoenix. It, too, has a history as a farming community that has been changed by I-10. Today, a Federal Express service center for all of Arizona and a major grocery-store distribution center are among the large employers taking advantage of the access the freeway provides. The community of approximately 5,000 residents is mostly Hispanic.

Buckeye

At the far west limit of the Valley's expanse, almost to the Palo Verde Nuclear Generating Station, Buckeye is a giant, 100-square-mile agricultural community with a population of around 5,000. Annexation plans call for the town to expand to 500 square miles by 2005. Plans also call for a mix of residential and commercial building to augment the town's agricultural base. The average annual population growth rate has been 1.3 percent since 1995.

GETTING HERE, GETTING AROUND

As a frontier settlement, Phoenix served more as a milepost than a destination point for settlers heading to California. Traveling on the region's first roads was a dusty, bumpy affair and those going by wagon between Phoenix and Tempe had to allow at least a half day to make the trip.

With the area's current cachet as a tourist hot spot and high-tech center, those cow-town days are gone. However, during peak rush hours—from 6:00 to 9:00 A.M. in the morning and 3:00 to 6:00 P.M. in the afternoon—unsuspecting travelers can still be snarled in wagon-pace traffic on one of the Valley's beleaguered interstates. A world-class airport, rationally laid out streets, and clear vistas make the Valley of the Sun welcoming for travelers, but newcomers will quickly realize that the freeway system is racing to keep up with the population explosion. In the 1970s, when an interstate system that would connect Phoenix with Los Angeles was proposed, opponents successfully campaigned against it. Our Valley was left in the dust in terms of freeway construction.

The Arizona Department of Transportation has worked in conjunction with other public and private entities to speed up highway construction and introduce alternative methods of transportation. Loops 202 and 101 are about 10 years ahead of schedule and they will eventually loop around the entire metropolitan area. HOV (High Occupancy Vehicle) lanes encourage carpooling and many companies allow their employees to telecommute.

The Valley leads the pack in building Intelligent Transportation Systems or "smart highways," which—in the not-so-distant-future—will triple the amount of traffic that can travel on a road. In the meantime, visitors may not realize they are driving on smart corridors that tie together disparate traffic signals and computer systems, but they already benefit from faster commutes, fewer accidents, reduced fuel consumption, and lower levels of pollution.

If caught in a traffic jam, drivers are advised to keep their cool and avoid tailgating or other confrontational (and accident-causing) behavior. The mantle of the wild and woolly West has not disappeared altogether; many desert denizens do pack guns. To keep from becoming an accident statistic, the Arizona Department of Public Safety posts safety tips on its Web site.

Travelers should note that most of the Valley's streets are laid out on a grid system, which makes navigation simpler. Major streets are spaced about a mile apart both on an east-west and a north-south axis, creating a grid of square-mile blocks across most of the Valley. (The major exception to the rule is Grand Avenue, which cuts diagonally across the west Valley.) When you know the Valley well, a simple mention of the nearest major cross streets will make it easy for you to plot your route in your head. You'll also know the travel time almost immediately.

Some travelers get away from it all by flying above the crowd. In addition to Phoenix Sky Harbor International Airport, if you can pilot your own plane or are being flown in on a company jet, you can land at one of eight airports around the Valley, which often feature their own on-site amenities, like restaurants.

A trip by air reveals how much the Valley sprawls: Development already covers 3,000 square miles and new buildings gobble up additional desert acreage daily. Although downtown Phoenix remains a major center, the Valley, by and large, is decentralized. This legacy of the automobile presents a challenge for those who eschew a vehicle, though mass transit services are constantly improving. Until light-rail comes to town, consider taking a bus, carpooling, biking, or even walking. Using alternative modes of transportation will help us all in improving Phoenix's air quality and maintaining the quality of life that draws visitors here.

TRAVELING BY CAR

Interstates and Highways

Visitors will find that there are many interesting sites within the Valley that pique their interest, or they may want to venture out on day trips to explore the rest of Arizona. Whatever the case, the Valley's collection of interstates and highways provide the quickest way to go. Here's some information that will help you familiarize yourself with major roads.

INTERSTATE 10

Also called: Papago Freeway, west of the I-17 interchange in Phoenix; Maricopa Freeway, east of the I-17 interchange.

Serves: The cities of Phoenix, Tempe, and Chandler.

Connects: Los Angeles, to the west of Phoenix; Tucson, to the southeast.

Orientation: Mostly east-west, except in Chandler, where it travels north-south before angling southeastward to Tucson. Note that even if you are traveling south for a few miles, the sign still reads east.

Special notes: I-10 twice crosses paths with I-17 to form a loop around downtown Phoenix, once at the southern end of I-17 near Phoenix Sky Harbor International Airport, and again at a major interchange known as "the stack," about a half-mile south of McDowell Road, near 23rd Avenue.

INTERSTATE 17

Also called: Black Canyon Freeway, north of the junction with I-10; Maricopa Freeway, where it converges with I-10.

Serves: Phoenix, Glendale, and Peoria.

Orientation: North-south, except where it becomes an east-west corridor through south Phoenix after rounding the Durango Curve, in the vicinity of 23rd Avenue and Durango Street.

Special notes: Inside the Valley, use this route to get to Arizona State University West. Outside the Valley, it offers the most direct route to Sedona, Flagstaff, and other northern points.

U.S. HIGHWAY 60

Also called: Superstition Freeway.

Serves: Tempe, Mesa, Gilbert, and Apache Junction.

Connects: The East Valley with Miami, Globe, and Native American communities on the east side of the state. Continues to New Mexico.

Orientation: East-west.

Special notes: Good way to reach Fiesta Mall and the Superstition Springs Mall, both in Mesa. The western portion of the Superstition converges with Grand Avenue.

STATE ROUTE 87

Also called: Beeline Highway.

Serves: Chandler, Gilbert, Mesa, Fountain Hills, and Sun Lakes.

Connects: The East Valley with Payson to the north, and it picks up I-10 southeast of the Valley near Picacho.

Orientation: Mostly north-south.

Special notes: This route is a good way to reach Fountain Hills and some of Arizona's cooler northern escapes. North of town, the Beeline Highway becomes a four-lane, sometimes-divided highway, beginning at the intersection of McDowell Road and Country Club on the Salt River Pima-Maricopa Native American Community. In town, the Beeline Highway is a regular city street—Country Club in Mesa and Arizona Avenue in Chandler.

STATE ROUTE 51

Also called: Piestewa or Squaw Peak Freeway.

Intersects: Phoenix and Paradise Valley.

Connects: I-10 and Loop 202 near downtown Phoenix with north Phoenix.

Orientation: North-south.

Special notes: This newly constructed, three- and four-lane route is a good alternative when I-17 is jammed. Previously called Squaw Peak Freeway, elevated portions of this highway offer nice views of the Phoenix skyline and Squaw Peak. Some of the side walls feature public art, such as decorative pots. As of the summer of 2004, construction was still common on this route, and it was often closed on weekends.

LOOP 202

Also called: Red Mountain Freeway.

Intersects: Phoenix, Tempe, and Mesa.

Connects: Downtown Phoenix with northern Mesa.

Orientation: East-west.

Special Notes: Offers good access to Phoenix Sky Harbor International Airport, downtown Tempe, and Arizona State University. It connects with Loop 101, which in turn links with US 60. Offers a nice view of the new Tempe Town Lake and ASU's Sun Devil Stadium.

STATE ROUTE 143

Also called: Hohokam Expressway.

Intersects: Phoenix and Tempe.

Connects: Loop 202 with I-10.

Orientation: North-south.

Special notes: This short stretch of road offers access to the eastern entrance of the Phoenix Sky Harbor International Airport.

STATE ROUTE 153

Also called: Sky Harbor Expressway.

Intersects: Phoenix and Tempe.

Connects: Washington and University Streets on the east end of the airport.

Orientation: North-south.

Special Notes: This fairly new, short stretch of road offers access to the Phoenix Sky Harbor International Airport.

LOOP 101

Also called: Agua Fria Freeway, between I-10 and I-17 on its western end in Glendale; the Pima Freeway, between I-17 and Loop 202 on the northern end in Scottsdale; the Price Freeway, south of Loop 202 on the eastern part of the loop in Mesa. Known generally as the Outer Loop.

Intersects: Glendale and Peoria on its western end; Phoenix and Scottsdale on its northern end; Mesa, Tempe, and Chandler on its eastern end.

Connects: On its western end, I-10 with I-17; on its northern end, I-17 with 56th Street; on its eastern end, US 60 in Mesa with Shea Road in Scottsdale.

Orientation: North-south and east-west.

Special notes: The Arizona State Department of Transportation projects that by 2007 the south end of 101 (which is Loop 202) will form another horseshoe around the east end of the Valley.

HOV Lanes

Take note of the lanes marked by diamonds on I-10, I-17, and Loop 202—they function as High Occupancy Vehicle lanes during rush-hour traffic, Monday through Friday, 6:00 to 9:00 A.M. and 3:00 to 7:00 P.M. Unless you have a passenger, are traveling by motorcycle, or have an automobile that uses alternative fuel, you will be ticketed for driving in HOV lanes during those specified hours. These lanes are mighty convenient during rush-hour times. For example, you can zip by creeping traffic on I-10 from Chandler Boulevard on the south through 91st Avenue on the west. One caution: Keep an eye out for cars in the regular lane that are tempted to zip into the HOV lane. If a collision

If you get caught in a dust storm, pull off the road, turn off your lights, and take your foot off the brake. When visibility is low, you don't want other motorists to mistakenly plow into you because they see your lights and think you are still driving. During Arizona's monsoon season, flooding can render roads impassable and deadly. Never enter a flooded wash. For more driving safety tips, visit www.azdps.com.

occurs, the difference in the speed of the two vehicles can be deadly.

Driving Tips

Even though you will see speeders all around you, posted limits on freeways vary from 65 to 55 miles per hour within the entire metropolitan area, so watch the signs very carefully. We all like to get there as quickly as we can, but speeding does not save considerable time. In addition, the Valley's jam-packed freeways can fluster newcomers, especially since seasoned residents don't yield the right of way as often as they do in the Midwest. Be aware of your exits and the possibility that you may have to cut across several lanes of traffic to reach them. If you don't get over early enough and find yourself cut off, stay on the freeway until the next exit, then double back. Keep a wary eye out for others who might indulge in high-speed lane changes.

Surface Streets

Grand Avenue—Most of the Valley is on a grid system, with major thoroughfares marking each square mile. The major exception is Grand Avenue, which is also called U.S. Highway 60, linking Phoenix to Wickenburg and points north. Grand Avenue's southern end is at Seventh Avenue and Van Buren Street, and it proceeds at a diagonal northwestwardly across the West Valley, traveling from downtown Phoenix to downtown Glendale and Peoria and just southwest of the Sun Cities as it heads out of the Valley.

Central Avenue—Although it is not the geographical center of Phoenix, Central Avenue is central to the street-numbering system. The numbered avenues (First Avenue, Second Avenue, etc.) are north-south thoroughfares west of Central. The numbered streets (First Street, Second Street, and so on) are north-south thoroughfares on the east side of Central. Central Avenue is also the major corridor linking downtown Phoenix with uptown Phoenix, two major areas of high-rise business development.

Van Buren Street—An east-west thoroughfare that runs through downtown Phoenix, Van Buren Street is like Central Avenue in that it's the center point for the north-south streets. For example, north of Van Buren, Central Avenue becomes North Central Avenue. South of Van Buren, it becomes South Central Avenue.

PUBLIC TRANSPORTATION

Valley Metro

Regional Public Transportation Authority, 302 North First Avenue, Phoenix (602) 253–5000
www.valleymetro.org
Valley Metro is the regional identity of the public transit system. This umbrella name was adopted by each city's Regional Public Transportation Authority (RPTA), so the public could experience and interact with a seamless, coherent system.

Buses are equipped with bike racks. Smoking is not allowed. All buses are wheelchair accessible, although not all buses can accommodate all types of wheelchairs. For detailed information on wheelchair accessibility, call the Community Forum at (602) 223–4100.

Routes

Valley Metro buses link 12 Valley communities. Bus frequency varies from every 15 minutes to every hour, depending on the route and the time of day. Sixty-three local routes run from early morning until early evening. Actual hours of operation differ according to the routes. Connections are usually easy because most routes are generally north-south or east-west and intersect with one another.

Twenty-one express routes connect outlying areas with downtown Phoenix. Designed for business commuters, they head inbound to downtown during the morning rush hour, and outbound during the afternoon rush. All of them stop at free park-and-ride lots.

All routes run Monday through Friday, and 57 local routes run on Saturday. Tempe and Phoenix buses run on Sundays and on holidays, thanks to funding initiatives passed by voters. The Bus Book, which contains route and fare information and route maps, can be picked up on any Valley Metro bus, at Central Station at Central Avenue and Van Buren Street in downtown Phoenix, or at the libraries and municipal buildings of the participating cities. It is updated twice a year. The Online Bus Book is available at www.bus .maricopa.gov.

Fares and Transfers

Fares are $1.25 for a local route and $1.75 for an express route. Bring exact change. Transfers are free and are good for an hour after the route reaches the end of the line, a nice deal when trying to cross the Valley by bus. Reduced fares of 60 cents per ride are available for youths ages 6 to 18, seniors 65 and older, and persons with disabilities. Children younger than 6 ride free. For information on reduced fares, bus routes, ticket books, and passes, call (602) 253-5000 from

Because of the heat, it's a good idea to keep a couple of liters of water in your car. An old soda bottle is what a lot of people use. You never know when you might need it to cool your engine or keep yourself hydrated if your car breaks down.

4:00 A.M. to 10:00 P.M. on weekdays and Saturdays, and from 6:00 A.M. to 8:00 P.M. on Sundays and holidays.

Shuttles

DASH, THE DOWNTOWN AREA SHUTTLE

This shuttle service runs every 6 to 12 minutes in downtown Phoenix, from 6:30 A.M. to 5:30 P.M. weekdays. From 6:30 A.M. to 5:30 P.M., it connects the State Capitol with downtown as well. The shuttle is free. Call Valley Metro for more information, (602) 253-5000.

FLASH, THE FREE LOCAL AREA SHUTTLE

FLASH runs through downtown Tempe and around the Arizona State University campus. As the name says, the fare is free. Buses run every 10 minutes or so from 7:00 A.M. to 8:00 P.M. Monday through Thursday and from 7:00 A.M. to 6:00 P.M. on Friday. During the summer, from mid-May through late August, hours are 7:00 A.M. to 6:00 P.M. Monday through Friday. FLASH routes running in a clockwise direction are called FLASH Forward, while those running in a counterclockwise direction are called FLASH Back. For more information, call Valley Metro, (602) 253-5000. Neighborhood FLASH connects the Escalante and University Heights neighborhoods with Riverside/Sunset and Lindon Park neighborhoods via downtown Tempe and Arizona State University. It's a great free way for students and shoppers to get to the area and operates approximately every 15 minutes Monday through Saturday, 7:00 A.M. to 8:00 P.M.

FLASH LITE ON MILL

FLASH is an additional service on Mill Avenue, serving Tempe Town Lake, downtown Tempe, ASU/Gammage Auditorium, and the Papago area. For just Mill Avenue service, it runs approximately every 10 to 15 minutes, five days a week, from 11:00 A.M. to midnight, and Saturday and Sunday from 8:00 A.M. to noon. It serves the Phoenix Zoo and the Desert Botanical Garden on Saturday and Sunday, from 8:00 A.M. to 8:00 P.M. It serves the Papago Center business park Monday through Friday, from 11:00 A.M. to 6:00 P.M. For more information, call Valley Metro, (602) 253-5000.

GUS, THE GLENDALE URBAN SHUTTLE

GUS serves Glendale's central corridor. GUS costs a quarter to ride—10 cents for seniors—and runs Monday through Saturday, 7:00 A.M. to 6:00 P.M. and Sunday 8:00 A.M. to 6:00 P.M. For more information, call (623) 930-3500. (Please note that, because this GUS operates from a cellular phone, the area code differs from Glendale's area code.) For more information, call Valley Metro, (602) 253-5000.

Phoenix is a busy town, so rush hour is a little longer here. Generally locals say the rush hour lasts from about 7:00 to 9:00 A.M. in the morning and 3:30 to 6:30 at night. At this time the highways will be very busy, and the main roads through town, such as Camelback, will be packed. You can find out more about current traffic conditions by calling (888) 411-ROAD or going to www .az511.com. Quick safety tip: Many local drivers don't use or pay attention to turn signals.

SCOTTSDALE TROLLEY

The Scottsdale Trolley—actually just a bus that looks like a trolley—is a free service connecting the Scottsdale Fashion Square with Loloma Transit Center. Its many stops along the way include the Scottsdale Road/Main Street arts district and the Galleria Corporate Center. It operates mid-November through the end of May, Monday through Saturday, 11:00 A.M. to 6:00 P.M. (until 9:00 P.M. on Thursday). For more information, call (480) 421-1004.

Rideshare

The Valley Metro Rideshare program was developed to fight vehicle-emitted air pollution. It can help Valley residents set up carpools, vanpools, telecommuting, and compressed work schedules. Call (602) 262-7433 for information.

Dial-a-Ride

The dial-a-ride service is available in many communities in the Phoenix metropolitan area. For general information and referrals, call (520) 253-4000 or (800) 775-7295. Although it is geared to meet the needs of seniors 65 and older and persons with disabilities, some dial-a-ride systems are available for use by the general public. The Dial-a-Ride Guide is available upon request at (602) 253-5000. Alternative formats are available and callers with text telephone machines can call (602) 261-8208.

People who have a disability that prevents them from using or accessing the regular bus service may qualify for special service under the Americans with Disabilities Act (ADA). They must apply in advance to Valley Metro for certification and must call the respective dial-a-ride at least one day in advance to schedule their service. The certification process may take up to 21 days to complete and may require verification of disabilities from a doctor or other medical professional. Information about ADA eligibility may be obtained by calling (602) 495-5777.

Here are the dial-a-ride numbers for the communities they serve:

El Mirage Dial-a-Ride, (623) 937-0500, serves the general public from 8:30 A.M. to 4:00 P.M. Monday through Friday with no holiday service.

Glendale Dial-a-Ride, (623) 930-3500, serves the general public from 7:45 A.M. to 5:00 P.M. Monday through Friday with no holiday service. Extended service hours for those qualifying under the Americans with Disabilities Act (ADA) run from 6:00 A.M. to 10:00 P.M. Monday through Friday and from 6:00 A.M. to 9:00 P.M. on Saturday. Those seeking ADA service should call Glendale Dial-a-Ride at (623) 930-3515.

Guadalupe Special Services, (480) 730-3092, serves senior citizens and persons with disabilities from 8:00 A.M. to 4:00 P.M. Monday through Friday, with no holiday service.

East Valley Dial-a-Ride, (480) 633-0101, serves senior citizens and persons with disabilities. Days and hours of operation vary from city to city. Call for details.

Maricopa County Special Services, (866) 550-2211, (623) 934-4256, provides services as needed to senior citizens, low-income residents, TANF recipients, and persons with disabilities. No holiday service is provided.

Paradise Valley ADA Service, handled by Phoenix Dial-a-Ride, (602) 253-4000, serves only persons with disabilities and runs from 5:00 A.M. to 8:00 P.M. Monday through Saturday, with no holiday service, unless a fixed route service is provided.

Peoria Dial-a-Ride, (623) 773-7435, serves the general public from 6:00 A.M. to 6:00 P.M. Monday through Friday, with no holiday service. Extended ADA service hours are from 5:00 A.M. to 8:00 P.M. Monday through Friday.

Phoenix Dial-a-Ride, (602) 253-4000, serves seniors and persons with disabilities seven days a week. Weekday service is provided from 5:00 A.M. to midnight, with service requests taken as late as 10:00 P.M.

Weekend service is provided until 10:00 P.M., with service requests taken until 10:00 P.M. Reservations for ADA service must be made at least one day in advance and can be made between 8:00 A.M. and 6:00 P.M. Weekday service for the general public is provided from 5:00 A.M. to midnight, with service requests taken until 10:00 P.M. Weekend and holiday service is provided until 10:00 P.M., with service requests taken between 5:00 A.M. and 9:00 P.M.

Sun Cities Area Transit System (SCAT), (623) 977-8363, serves the general public from 7:15 A.M. to 6:45 P.M. Monday through Friday and from 7:15 A.M. to 4:45 P.M. Saturday, Sunday, and holidays. Extended ADA service hours are from 5:00 A.M. to 8:00 P.M. Monday through Friday.

Surprise Dial-a-Ride, (623) 583-1688, serves the general public from 7:30 A.M. to 4:15 P.M. Monday through Friday, with no holiday service.

AIR TRAVEL

Phoenix Sky Harbor International Airport
3400 Sky Harbor Boulevard, Phoenix
(602) 273-3300
www.phxskyharbor.com

As anyone who looks up at the Valley skies can tell you, Sky Harbor is busy. It's the fifth-busiest airport in the United States and the 15th busiest in the world. It accommodates 1,400 commercial flights a day, serving an average of 36 million people annually. Sky Harbor also serves general aviation, corporate, cargo, and military planes.

The airport began operating in 1929, and in 1935 the city of Phoenix purchased the airport, which then stood on 285 acres. Terminal 1 opened October 13, 1952, and began Sky Harbor's ascent to its current status. The airport handled 296,066 passengers in the first year Terminal 1 was open. In 1961 it served 920,096 passengers. Terminal 2 was built in 1962 for $2.7 million, just as Sky Harbor broke the one-million-passenger-per-year mark. The city strove to make the terminal a lovely gateway to Phoenix and commissioned the late Paul Coze to create a three-panel mosaic mural, known as *The Phoenix*. It still greets passengers in Terminal 2 today. The passenger rate grew to three million in 1971, so planning began for the construction of Terminal 3, which opened in 1979. Growth continued, and the Phoenix City Council authorized construction of Terminal 4 in 1986. The $248 million terminal and four-level parking garage opened in 1990, and Terminal 1 was closed. In 1991 Terminal 4 alone handled 15.4 million passengers, 70 percent of the airport's traffic.

There are 99 gates and 22,000 parking spaces at the airport. Currently, Sky Harbor has three runways, its newest one, which opened in 2000, carries a price tag of $128 million. Rapid growth in the area has put a greater demand on the airport's facilities, and there are numerous construction projects planned. The number of parking spaces at Terminal 4 recently increased by 6,700 spaces. With passenger traffic at about 36 million annually and strict security measures, it's a good idea to arrive at the airport about two hours before your flight is scheduled to leave. A free shuttle travels from economy parking to the terminals every six minutes.

The airport is only five minutes from downtown Phoenix. It's almost centrally located in the Valley and has good access to freeways. Sky Harbor is open 24 hours a day, and car rentals, food service, and catering are available.

Here are the airlines that serve Phoenix Sky Harbor International Airport and their terminals:

Aeromexico—Terminal 4
Air Canada—Terminal 2
Alaska Airlines—Terminal 2
Aloha Airlines—Terminal 3
America West and America West
    Express—Terminal 4
American—Terminal 3
American Trans Air—Terminal 3
Arizona Express—Terminal 2

British Airways—Terminal 4
Continental—Terminal 2
Delta and Delta Connection—Terminal 3
Frontier—Terminal 3
Great Lakes—Terminal 2
Hawaiian Airlines—Terminal 4
Midwest Airlines—Terminal 3
Northwest—Terminal 3
Southwest—Terminal 4
Sun Country—Terminal 3
United—Terminal 2
US Airways—Terminal 2

Ground Transportation

All rates listed below are the maximum allowed under contract with Sky Harbor. Passengers are encouraged to negotiate for better rates.

TAXIS

AAA Cab, Allstate, and Discount have contracts to provide service to Sky Harbor passengers at the following rates: First mile $5.00; each additional mile $1.50; with an airport surcharge of $1.00. There should be no extra charges for more than one passenger in a party or for baggage. You may choose any taxi you wish from the waiting line.

SUPERSHUTTLE

SuperShuttle operates 24 hours a day and offers airport-to-door service. Vans depart every 15 minutes to all areas of the Valley from 9:00 A.M. to 9:00 P.M. and with less frequency from 9:00 P.M. to 9:00 A.M. Flat rates are charged to each geographical area being served and range from $6.00 to $35.00 for a single passenger, with a $7.00 charge for additional passengers within a group. Call (602) 244-9000 or (800) 258-3826 (outside Arizona) for information or visit the Web at www.supershuttle.com. To get to the airport via SuperShuttle, call at the same time you make your airline reservations.

LIMOUSINES

AAA, AM, Affordable, Aries, Arizona Chauffer, Carmel, Empire, Esquire, Luxe, Manhattan, Monarch, Prince, and TLC offer limousine service from Sky Harbor. Their rates are set by mileage and range from $15 to $50. These rates include transport of one or two in a party to the same address. Each additional passenger is $7.00 a head. Feel free to negotiate with the drivers for a lower rate, especially if you wait for other passengers to load and share the fare. Limousines are also available for $30 an hour, with a minimum charge of two hours.

VIP OR PRIVATE SERVICES

A number of companies operate as private carriers from Sky Harbor. Before you make arrangements with a particular company, check to see if they are permitted to operate from the airport, and verify all facets of your arrangement with them.

VALLEY METRO

The Red Line and bus routes 13 and 40 stop at the airport and provide connections to the entire Valley. Call (602) 253–5000 for information.

COURTESY RIDES

Many hotels and resorts provide free pickup and drop-off service for their patrons. To check with your place of accommodation, a courtesy phone center for many hotels and resorts is adjacent to the baggage claim areas in the passenger terminals.

WHEELCHAIR ACCESSIBILITY

Taxis and limousines will transport passengers using wheelchairs as long as the wheelchairs or other appliances can be folded to fit in the trunk with the luggage. Lift-equipped service for passengers in wheelchairs is available from the Super-Shuttle, and passengers should call (602) 244–9000 or, from outside Arizona, (800) 331–3565 for this service. The Valley Metro bus routes that stop at Sky Harbor are also lift-equipped, as are interterminal buses at the airport. Rental cars with hand controls are available from Avis and Hertz. Avis recommends advance notice, and Hertz needs 48 hours' notice. For private carriers, contact the particular companies to find out their wheelchair accessibility.

PARKING

Each terminal has its own parking area and all are wheelchair accessible.

Terminal 2—The short-term parking area sits north of the terminal and features 360 spaces for hourly parking and 2,053 spaces for daily parking. Hourly rates are $1.00 per half hour, with a $16.00 maximum, and a $16.00 lost-ticket fee. Daily rates are $7.00 per day.

Terminal 3—The parking garage adjoins the terminal to the east. It features 2,274 spaces on six levels. Rates are $1.00 per half hour, $16.00 for a daily maximum, and $16.00 for a lost-ticket fee. The garage cannot accommodate vehicles more than 7 feet in height.

Terminal 4—The parking garage sits above the terminal. It has 3,090 regular spaces on four levels and features a 228-space lot for high-profile vehicles that are 7 feet or taller. Rates are $1.00 per half hour, with a $16.00 daily maximum, and a $16.00 lost-ticket fee.

In addition, the airport offers two economy lots for long-term parking. The lot west of Terminal 2 can hold 1,567 vehicles outdoors and can accommodate vehicles more than 7 feet high. The lot east of Terminal 4 has 5,700 spaces, including 2,376 spaces in an eight-level garage, and can accommodate high-profile vehicles as well as vehicles up to 32 feet in length. Both lots have shuttle service to the terminals. Rates are $1.00 per half hour, with a daily maximum of $5.00, and a minimum lost-ticket fee of $5.00.

RENTAL CARS

A number of rental-car companies have counters in the terminals at Sky Harbor, while a number of other companies rent

Important Airport Phone Numbers

Airport Paging
(602) 273-3455

Ground Transportation
(602) 273-3383

Customs/Immigration
(602) 941-1400

Lost and Found
(602) 273-3307

General Information
(602) 273-3300

Parking
(602) 273-0954

cars at the airport but do not have counters inside the terminals. Whether they have counters on-site or not, all of them will shuttle you from the airport to their lots outside Sky Harbor when you arrive (and vice versa when you depart). The following are some of the companies that serve the airport. Use the courtesy phones at the airport to call the companies that don't have on-site counters.

Advantage Rent-A-Car, locations at all terminals, (602) 244-0450
Alamo Rent-A-Car, (602) 244-0897
Avis Rent-A-Car, (602) 273-3222
Budget Rent-A-Car, (800) 527-0700
Discount Car and Truck Rentals, Radisson Hotel, I-10 and University Drive, Phoenix, (602) 437-3477
Dollar Rent-A-Car, (800) 800-4000
Enterprise Rent-A-Car, 2738 East Washington Street, Phoenix, (602) 225-0588
Hertz Rent-A-Car, (602) 267-8822
National Car Rental, (602) 275-4771
Thrifty Car Rental, 4114 East Washington Street, Phoenix, (602) 244-0311

Other Valley Airports

In addition to Phoenix Sky Harbor International Airport, numerous smaller airports in the Valley serve general aviation traffic,

such as corporate and private planes. These airports, known as "relievers," draw a good measure of the general-aviation traffic that would otherwise be served by Sky Harbor.

Chandler Municipal Airport
2380 Stinson Way, Chandler
(480) 782-3540
A general-aviation airport, Chandler handles about 221,000 takeoffs and landings a year. Its control tower is open from 6:00 A.M. to 9:00 P.M. There are hangars, shaded tiedowns, and open tiedowns. About 360 planes are based there, as well as one medical helicopter. Airport-based businesses include an avionics shop, full-service fuel pumps, a repair shop, and three flight schools. Sightseeing tours are available.

Glendale Municipal Airport
6801 North Glen Harbor Boulevard,
Glendale
(623) 930-2188
www.ci.glendale.az.us/airport
The Glendale airport is home base for about 260 planes, both corporate and private, and handles about 140,000 takeoffs and landings per year. Though primarily a general-aviation airport, it is home to about 20 businesses, ranging from airplane hangar sales to an aviation insur-

ance adjuster, and serves two medical evacuation helicopters. A restaurant and gift shop is on-site. The airport also features two flight schools, a terminal, maintenance services, and a Hertz rental-car service. The control tower operates Monday through Friday, 6:00 A.M. to 8:30 P.M. and 7:00 A.M. to 7:00 P.M. on Saturday and Sunday. For charter flights, call Global Aviation at (623) 877–4762.

Mesa Falcon Field
**4800 East Falcon Drive, Mesa
(480) 644-2444
www.ci.mesa.az.us/airport**
Falcon Field handles approximately 274,000 general-aviation takeoffs and landings a year. Falcon Field, which opened in 1941, was used originally by the U.S. War Department to train combat pilots for the British Royal Air Force. When World War II ended, the City of Mesa took over the airport. Today, 900 planes are based there, along with 30 aviation-related businesses, and 50 general commercial enterprises. The control tower operates from 6:00 A.M. to 9:00 P.M., and the airport features a gift shop, a pilot shop, maintenance, fuel, and rental-car services. It's also home to the Champlin Fighter Aircraft Museum and the Confederate (also called the Commemorative) Air Force Museum. In addition, Falcon Field operates a helipad, used mostly by business people heading to meetings in downtown Mesa, which is a few miles away.

Phoenix Deer Valley Airport
**702 West Deer Valley Road, Phoenix
(623) 869-0975
www.phoenix.gov/AVIATION/deervalley/
index.html**
The city of Phoenix Aviation Department, which runs Sky Harbor, has also run this general-aviation airport in the north-central part of the Valley since 1971. The state's second-busiest airport, it had over 370,000 takeoffs and landings in 2000. The control tower operates from 6:00 A.M.

to 9:00 P.M. The airport offers fuel sales, overnight parking, an aircraft maintenance bay, a pilot shop, a restaurant, and a conference room.

Phoenix Goodyear Airport
**1658 South Litchfield Road, Goodyear
(623) 932-1200
www.phoenix.gov/AVIATION/goodyear/
index.html**
The city of Phoenix Aviation Department has managed this airport since 1968. The airport was built in 1943 and originally operated by the U.S. Navy. It served as a support facility for the nearby aircraft division of the Goodyear Tire and Rubber Company. In 1951 the Navy expanded the airport as a base for military aircraft storage, which was its mission until 1965, when the U.S. General Services Administration took over with plans to phase it out. The major tenant is Lufthansa Airlines' Airline Training Center of Arizona. The airport serves the general-aviation needs of western Maricopa County, and air traffic peaked at 142,458 takeoffs and landings in 2000. The control tower operates from 6:00 A.M. to 9:00 P.M. The airport offers fuel sales, overnight parking, a flight-planning and lounge area, an aircraft wash rack, and a conference room.

Scottsdale Municipal Airport
**15000 North Airport Drive, Scottsdale
(480) 312-2321
www.ci.scottsdale.az.us/airport**
Scottsdale Municipal Airport handles approximately 180,000 takeoffs and landings a year. It is surrounded by the Scottsdale Airpark, an industrial park that is home to 25 national/regional corporations and nearly 1,200 small- and medium-size businesses. Commercial charters take off on sightseeing tours from the airport, handling about 8,000 passengers annually. The control tower operates from 6:00 A.M. to 10:00 P.M. The airport features an array of specialty shops, a restaurant, maintenance support and repairs, a rental-car company, limousine services, conference

rooms, a pilot lounge, and aircraft cleaning and storage. A number of flight schools are based there as well.

Williams Gateway Airport
5835 South Sossaman Road, Mesa
(480) 988–7600
www.flywga.org

Williams Gateway Airport is on the site of former Williams Air Force Base, which was closed down in Post–Cold War Department of Defense budget cuts. It handles approximately 240,000 takeoffs and landings per year—including corporate, cargo, general-aviation, and military aircraft. A major economic hub for the area, the airport has about 25 business tenants, including aircraft maintenance, modification, and testing services. It also offers pilot training. Passenger services are planned for the near future. The control tower is operated daily from 6:00 A.M. to 9:00 P.M. Facilities include fuel sales, a pilot lounge, VIP lounge, pilot shop, and a cafe. Arizona State University's east campus is also here.

PRIVATE TRANSPORTATION

Arizona Shuttle Service
5350 East Speedway Boulevard, Tucson
(520) 795–6771, (800) 888–2749
www.arizonashuttle.com

Arizona Shuttle Service runs 13 passenger vans—some with television and VCRs—between Phoenix Sky Harbor International Airport and Tucson. At the airport, it has offices in Terminals 2, 3, and 4. The company offers 18 runs a day, on the half hour from Phoenix from 6:30 A.M. to 11:30 P.M. Fares are $27 one-way and $52 round-trip.

El Paso–Los Angeles Limousine Express
1015 North Seventh Street at Roosevelt
and Seventh Streets, Phoenix
(602) 254–4101

El Paso–Los Angeles Limousine Express has four buses leaving nightly for El Paso, Los Angeles, and Las Vegas. Tickets for El Paso, Las Vegas, and Los Angeles are $35 one-way and $65 round-trip, with special children's rates available. You're advised to purchase tickets in advance, especially for weekend departures, as the buses fill rapidly.

Greyhound Bus Lines
2115 East Buckeye Road, Phoenix
(602) 389–4200
www.greyhound.com

Greyhound can get you here from anywhere in the United States. You'll arrive at its main terminal in Phoenix or around the Valley in Glendale, Chandler, or Mesa. For route and fare information, call (602) 389–4200 or (800) 231–2222. For information in Spanish, call (800) 531–5332.

Sedona Phoenix Shuttle Service, Inc.
P.O. Box 3342, Sedona 86340
(928) 282–2066, (800) 448–7988
www.sedona-phoenix-shuttle.com

Providing service between Phoenix and the Verde Valley area, this company has representatives at each terminal in Phoenix Sky Harbor International Airport. It offers eight trips daily from the airport to Sedona, costing $40 one-way and $65 for a round-trip. Children under 11 ride for half price. Fares are only $30 one-way, $55 round-trip if you only go as far as Camp Verde. The Service prefers that you make reservations at least one week in advance.

TAXIS AND LIMOUSINES

Because of the distances involved in getting around the Valley, taxis, whose fares are based on miles traveled, are not the most popular option. Most Valley dwellers use them as a last resort—usually when cars have given up the ghost in the middle of the night and batteries have so little juice left that even a tow-truck driver can't get them jump-started.

Few cabs cruise for fares here since there are so few locations where enough people congregate to make the endeavor worthwhile. Besides that, hailing a cab is pretty much a lost art among Valley dwellers. If you want a cab, you'll find them lined up at the airport or in front of your downtown hotel. Otherwise, you'll have to give the cab company a call. Rates vary from company to company, although fares hover around $3.00 for the first mile and $1.50 for each additional mile. (A number of taxi companies offer a variety of services, including limousine rentals, package deliveries, and courier services.)

The following taxi companies serve the entire Valley 24 hours a day:

- AAA Cab, (602) 437-4000
- Alpha Cab, (602) 232-2000
- Checker Cab, (602) 257-1818
- Discount Cab, (602) 200-2000
- Tender Loving Care Taxi, (877) 852-8294
- Yellow Cab, (602) 252-5252

On the other end of the spectrum, limousines are as popular here as anywhere because they make a nice splurge for a special occasion—at least, for most of us. Limos are generally rented by the hour, with at least a two-hour minimum rental. Some companies require a higher minimum at busy times, such as weekends and the holiday season. Fares also vary by the type of limo being rented. A 10-passenger limo is going to cost more than

Use logic when finding Valley addresses. By and large, an even number indicates that an address is on the west or north side of a street. An odd number indicates that an address is on the east or south side of a street. Of course, there are exceptions to the rule, but mostly the exceptions are on cul-de-sacs.

a 6-passenger one. You can get a decent limo in Arizona for $45 to $65 an hour, with the two-hour minimum, not including gratuity and tax. Of course, you can always splurge even more than that—ask for a TV or a bar or food service or all of the above. In addition, most limousine companies also offer van and sedan rentals on similar terms.

Here are some of the limousine companies that serve the Valley:

- Arizona Limousines, (602) 267-7097
- Desert Rose Limousine Service, (623) 780-0159
- Driver Provider, (602) 453-0001
- Scottsdale Limousine, (480) 946-8446
- Sky Mountain Limousines, (480) 830-3944
- Starlight Limousines, (480) 905-1234
- Valley Limousine, (602) 254-1955

HISTORY 🏛

Although the Valley's runaway growth within the last few decades makes it seem like a young city, the Phoenix metro area is heir to a rich and varied cultural history. Certainly, very few historical buildings have survived our insatiable development, but the observant visitor or newcomer will be able to look beyond the facade and catch a glimpse of the past. The desert still preserves the foundations of prehistoric towns and the abandoned mine shafts of prospects gone bust. Closer to home there are a number of museums that give an interesting insight into the Valley's past.

Prehistoric Native Americans were the first people attracted to the Salt River Valley. They were hunters and gatherers, living off the land, and their arrowheads can occasionally be found in the more remote areas of the Valley. The first came 20,000 to 40,000 years ago.

The Hohokam (pronounced "hoe-hoe-com") were the first long-term settlers in the Valley. They farmed the Valley and dug nearly 250 miles of irrigation canals to water their fields. This early engineering feat formed the basis of the modern canal system that helped modern Phoenix rise from the desert. After 1,700 years of tilling the Valley, the Hohokam disappeared less than a century before Columbus sailed to America. Archaeologists cannot agree on why their civilization disappeared, but some suggestions include war or economic stresses brought on by bad drought and flooding. Modern Pima in central and southern Arizona trace their ancestry to these ancient peoples. Archaeologists believe that their more decentralized lifestyle proved better suited to the harsh conditions of the desert. After the Hohokam way of life was gone, the Valley remained depopulated. Some ancient hunters camped in the Valley from time to time, but few stayed for long.

THE REFOUNDING OF PHOENIX

The Spanish arrived in the area in 1539. They named it "Arizona," meaning "arid zone" in Spanish. The Tohono O'odham had a similar, and more optimistic, word for their land—"Ali-Shonak," or "place of small springs." Conquistadors and Catholic priests explored the area and sent missionaries far to the north into the Hopi and Navajo lands. They claimed the region for Spain, but the Crown's hold on it was tenuous at best. In 1680 Native Americans rose up against the missionaries and soldiers in what is now called the Pueblo Revolt. The Spanish were kicked out for more than 10 years, but eventually returned in greater numbers. They founded presidios, fortified towns, in Tucson and Tubac. Both are still thriving communities. There were several conflicts between the two peoples for the next hundred years, but Spanish influence gradually increased.

Throughout this time the Salt River Valley was virtually ignored. Occasionally Pima and Maricopa Indians would travel from their traditional lands around the Gila River and farm the area, but there was no permanent settlement.

In 1821 Mexico gained independence from Spain. Soon it and the United States clashed as the Americans tried to expand westward. The Americans thought it was their "Manifest Destiny" to build a country stretching from coast to coast. Anglo settlers in a northeastern Mexican territory instigated and fought a successful rebellion to found the independent Republic of Texas in 1836. It joined the United States nine years later. The United States fought Mexico in 1846 and, after a short but bloody conflict, the Americans won what is now called New Mexico, California, and Arizona. The Treaty of Guadalupe Hidalgo was signed on February 2, 1848, recognizing the region as American and establishing peace between the two nations. The U.S. government established the New Mexico Territory as an administrative state for the eastern part of these new lands. In 1854 the United States expanded this territory with the Gadsden Purchase, which bought a strip of land that is now southern Arizona and New Mexico.

The territorial capital was at Santa Fe, a long way from Arizona, so there was little official help in times of drought or Apache raids. Locals felt they should become a separate territory so their concerns could be voiced more directly in Washington. In 1861, while the country was descending into the bloodbath of the Civil War, a group of local boosters gathered in Tucson, then the largest settlement in Arizona, and voted to form a territory in the Confederacy. The government in Richmond agreed and established a garrison in Tucson. In June 1862 a column of federal troops, including famed mountain man Kit Carson, marched from California and, after a brief skirmish at Picacho Peak, took the entire territory for the Union. It was the westernmost conflict of the Civil War and led to Arizona becoming its own territory on February 24, 1863.

In 1865 the United States Army established Fort McDowell on the Verde River, 18 miles north of the Salt River, to ward off Apache attacks on the small mining encampments in the area. The supplier for the fort was a man by the name of John Y. T. Smith. He built the first European house in the Valley and supplied the fort with hay he found growing in the old Hohokam canals. His home, which is gone now, stood near the eastern end of Sky Harbor International Airport.

Although Smith noticed that the damp earth of the old canals was good for growing hay, it took Civil War veteran Jack Swilling to realize their full potential. Swilling was a bit of a shifty character—he fought for both sides in the war and was known for his short temper. Perhaps a life of fighting made Swilling want something

Remnants of the ancient Hohokam culture survive at The Pueblo Grande Museum and Archeological Park, 4619 East Washington Street, Phoenix, (602) 495-0901 or (877) 706-4408, http://phoenix.gov/PARKS/pueblo.html. Visitors can tour the ruins and ponder why the Hohokam suddenly disappeared around A.D. 1400.

more peaceful. He decided to set up a farm in the Valley and, in 1867, started cleaning up the old canals and putting them back into use. He got financial backing from some investors in Wickenburg and established the Swilling Irrigation and Canal Company. Within a year the first European farm in the Valley, owned by Frency Sawyer, began operations. Swilling started a farm as well, first near Tempe and then near Fort McDowell.

After that the town grew quickly. People found that the old canals were so well designed that the Salt River Valley was one of the best agricultural areas in the territory. As more and more people settled there, citizens formed a committee to name their new home. Swilling wanted to name it Stonewall, after the Confederate General Stonewall Jackson. Apparently, Swilling had fonder memories of fighting for the Confederacy than for the Union. Someone else suggested Salina, in honor of the river that gave the new town life. The name that stuck, however, was suggested by an odd newcomer named Lord Darrell Duppa. Duppa was an educated Englishman and was able to pass himself off as nobility to the provincial Americans of the frontier. He said the site should be named Phoenix, after the mythical bird that rises to new life out of its own ashes. It was apt, and on June 15, 1869, the Phoenix Post Office was established, making the matter final.

Arizona was a true frontier, and Phoenix was still a small and out-of-the-way town. Every necessity or luxury of civilization had to be built, imported, or

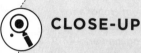

The Hohokam: The Valley of the Sun's First Settlers

For thousands of years prehistoric peoples had roamed southern Arizona, hunting animals and gathering plants for food. Some experimented with farming, but they never developed elaborate civilizations. That all changed when a people known today as the Hohokam (from a Pima word for "those who came before") arrived in the area a little more than 2,000 years ago and began to build large villages, an extensive irrigation system, and a complex society. Archaeologists divide the Hohokam culture into four distinct phases:

The Pioneer Phase (about 300 B.C. to A.D. 550). The origins of the Hohokam are shrouded in mystery. While it is generally thought they arrived in Arizona around 300 B.C. many archaeologists argue for a later date. It is also not known where they came from, but most researchers point to Mexico because of the large Mesoamerican influence on their culture. Settling in what is now Phoenix and Tucson, they developed irrigation canals by about A.D. 300 and lived in small, temporary villages.

The Colonial Phase (A.D. 550 to 900). During this period the Hohokam spread into central Arizona, eventually stopping on the borders of Anasazi, Sinagua, Salado, and Mogollon cultures. The Hohokam culture area eventually encompassed 45,000 square miles. This was also a time of great artistic flowering, during which the Hohokam developed high-quality pottery with detailed geometric or pictorial designs.

The Sedentary Phase (A.D. 900 to 1100). Having reached its farthest geographical extent, the Hohokam culture began to develop larger villages and more extensive irrigation canals. They also began to use ball courts inspired by the ritual games in Mexico. Structures, probably for ritual uses but perhaps for houses for the wealthy as well, were built atop mounds of earth. The quality of the pottery decreased at this time, however, because pots were mass produced and the Hohokam's efforts were focused elsewhere. Trade flourished as the Hohokam set up routes across the Southwest and into Mexico.

The Classic Phase (A.D. 1100 to 1450). Although this period saw the Hohokam at their highest level of population and organization, it was also the period of their decline. Droughts lasting decades hurt the farmers and were followed by floods of the Salt River that destroyed many canals. The towns became impossible to maintain, and the people scattered into bands of hunter-gatherers or small-scale farmers. They eventually developed into the Pima and Tohono O'odham tribes that still live in Arizona today.

Villages and Farming

The Hohokam built dozens of villages along the Salt River and its tributaries. Archaeologists have traced hundreds of miles of canals, some more than 50 feet wide, irrigating thousands of acres in what was otherwise dry desert.

Prehistoric settlers built large towns and complex irrigation systems that can still be seen today. PUEBLO GRANDE MUSEUM

Their main crops were maize, beans, squash, tobacco, and cotton. They also gathered plants from the surrounding desert, such as saguaro cactus fruit, prickly pear pads, mesquite beans, and agave. Hunters tracked deer and rabbits. The Hohokam were experts at gleaning a life from the desert.

The Hohokam, like many other Southwestern cultures, lived in pit houses. These were usually square or rectangular in shape, arranged in groups around a common plaza belonging to an extended family. Pit houses get their name from their floors, which were scooped out of the earth. The walls and roof were made of *jacal,* a latticework of branches pasted over with dried mud. This construction technique made the interior cool in summer and warm in winter. It also had the advantage of being quick to make. When the houses became infested with insects or rodents, the Hohokam simply burned them down and rebuilt on the same spot. Archaeologists have found some villages where the houses have successive layers of floors and estimate that the Hohokam burned and rebuilt their houses about once every 25 years.

For an interesting look at a partially reconstructed Hohokam village, check out the Pueblo Grande Museum and Archeological Park. See the Attractions chapter for more details.

Trade

The Hohokam had a vast trade network stretching from Utah to Mexico, north to the Great Plains, and west to the Pacific. They made ornaments out of shells from the Pacific coast, which they then exported to other cultures. Other materials not found in southern Arizona, such as turquoise and obsidian, were also highly prized. From Mexico the Hohokam imported tropical birds, obsidian, and copper bells.

Religion and Ritual

Little is known about Hohokam beliefs, but we can tell some things from the ruins they left behind. Many sites include ball courts similar to those found in Central America. Those cultures left written records and we know that for them the ball games were a religious ritual, where the creation of the world was symbolically replayed, allowing the community to communicate with the hidden world. It is not known, however, if the Hohokam used the ball games for the same purpose.

Large ritual buildings or houses for the elite were built atop platform mounds. It's not certain what went on in these structures, but they are usually found near the start of the larger canals, so probably had to do with their economic or spiritual upkeep.

The Hohokam left a wide variety of petroglyphs (symbols carved onto rocks) that may reflect their religious beliefs.

Petroglyphs dot the Arizona landscape and make for fun and interesting trips. The closest site is the Deer Valley Rock Art Center. See the Attractions chapter for more details.

Further Reading

The Hohokam: Ancient People of the Desert, edited by David Grant Noble (School of American Research Press, 1999). A short (90-page) introduction to the Hohokam, with chapters written by several experts.

The Archaeology of Ancient Arizona, by Jefferson Reid and Stephanie Whittlesey (University of Arizona Press, 1997). A detailed coverage, more than 300 pages, of the peoples and cultures of the entire state. It includes an extensive discussion of the Hohokam.

Archaeology in the City: A Hohokam Village in Phoenix, Arizona, by David Gregory, Michael Bartlett, and Thomas Kolaz (University of Arizona, 1986). Although it's only 72 pages long, this is a good look at the Hohokam of the Salt River Valley.

invented. While this was a major inconvenience for early pioneers, it also provided endless opportunity for the clever and creative. One such person was Samuel Lount. In the days before refrigeration, the only ice available in summer was what had been stored in specially insulated icehouses from the previous winter. When the summer was hot, demand and inadequate insulation meant short supplies. Lount solved the problem in 1851 by inventing a mechanical ice maker. At first it would seem his fortune was made, but there were two drawbacks to the machine: The process was expensive, and Lount lived in Canada, not exactly a place where people

would pay top dollar for his product. Realizing the old method of icehouses could still compete over the short summer months in the north, Lount moved his family to the more promising climes of Phoenix in the 1870s. It wasn't long before he was one of the richest men in town.

Lount spent his money on real estate in central Phoenix. His business interests expanded and at his death he was able to leave an immense inheritance to his son and daughter. The daughter, Hattie Mosher, was one of Phoenix's biggest developers and advocates for women's' rights. She died in 1945, and there are still a few locals who remember her.

THE YOUNG CITY

Once Swilling, Duppa, and friends got the ball rolling, Phoenix quickly grew in importance. In 1871 it was named the seat of Maricopa County. The city was incorporated in 1878. The canal system continued to be expanded and improved. The Arizona canal, completed by the Arizona Canal Company in 1885, was the largest yet and the first to depart from the old Hohokam routes. New canals fueled new settlements and vice versa. From the 50 or so residents in the Valley when Swilling's company was formed, Phoenix's population climbed into the thousands.

Arizona got a regular lifeline to the outside world in the late 1870s when the transcontinental railroad came through the territory. It missed Phoenix, passing through a small depot named Maricopa, 30 miles to the south. City leaders realized what a railroad connection could do for the local economy and built a stagecoach and freight wagon route to the station. By 1886 they needed more than a road and started building a railway track on the route. The Maricopa-Phoenix line saw its first train on July 4, 1887.

After the transcontinental railroad came through Arizona, the region developed at a rapid pace. Established settlements expanded and mining towns popped up like desert wildflowers after a spring rain. Many died just as quickly. But the population was growing and getting richer, and that meant more tax revenue, more development, and, of course, more wrangling over which town got what piece of the budget pie.

Tucson fought in the legislature to become the capital, but Prescott was able to keep the title for many years. Instead, Tucson got money for the University of Arizona, which opened in 1891 despite the fact that there were no high schools in the territory. Tempe got a school that eventually would turn into Arizona State University. The railway link from Phoenix to Maricopa helped the settlements in the Salt River Valley to grow

and thrive. Soon it was obvious that the center of power was shifting, and in 1889 Tucson's hopes for the capital were forever dashed when it was moved to its present home in Phoenix.

Soon the Valley was home to offices of the federal, territorial, and county governments, good for business. The jobs they brought and the service industry they attracted started a building boom. In the year after Phoenix became the capital, there was nearly $450,000 invested in building projects.

But the boom was not for everybody. There were numerous restrictions on the rights of Native Americans, Mexicans, and immigrants. A city ordinance made it illegal for a Native American to be in town after dark unless he was in the employ of a white resident. In an effort to indoctrinate tribal members, the federal government opened the Phoenix Indian School in 1891. Students were forbidden to speak their native language and required to dress and act "American." Likewise, Hispanics who settled in the city found themselves barred from the Anglo community and power structure, so their lives revolved around their own social and religious institutions. The Chinese, trying to escape prejudice in California, started to move to Phoenix in considerable numbers in the 1880s. While they found a more tolerable atmosphere here, they were still largely relegated to a small Chinatown. Nowadays, Phoenix is home to a wide range of ethnic groups, who celebrate their heritage with special events throughout the year. See the Annual Events chapter for more information.

THE 20TH CENTURY DAWNS

As the new century approached, entrepreneurs opened up railway tracks connecting the capital to various parts of the territory. In 1895 Phoenix became the hub of a line that ran from Ash Fork through Prescott to the Santa Fe transcontinental line.

The new city was doing well, but the harsh conditions of the desert still made life hard for Valley dwellers. The summer heat was almost intolerable. In the 1890s floods raged through the southern half of the city, causing thousands of dollars of damage. In the latter part of the decade, a long drought ruined many farmers.

By the turn of the 20th century, Phoenix had a railroad, many large municipal and private buildings, and all the trappings of civilized society. But the frontier days weren't over yet. In 1910 two teenage brothers named Oscar and Ernie Woodson, perhaps inspired by reading too many dime novels, decided to make their fortune by robbing a train. There hadn't been a train robbery in the territory for years. The days when a desperado could board a train, blow open the safe, and then disappear into the hinterland with the loot were long past. But the Woodson boys weren't exactly the sharpest knives in the drawer, and they decided to give it a try. One fine May evening they boarded the shuttle train running from Phoenix to Maricopa. They had left their getaway horses by the track a few miles out of town. When the train approached the spot, the two desperadoes drew their revolvers and ordered the conductor to stop the train. Then they turned on the passengers and ordered them to empty their pockets. The brothers got a good haul, about $300. Unfortunately, the passengers included many members of the territorial legislature and the sheriff of Gila County. The brothers were now marked men.

The train robbers jumped on their horses and galloped away, heading for the border. It wasn't long before the sheriff of Maricopa County, Carl Hayden, rounded up a posse and set off after them. While his men rode on horseback, Hayden and a friend followed in an automobile. The new invention soon left the rest of the posse in the dust. It wasn't long before they caught up with the Woodsons as they were resting their horses from a hard ride through the May heat. Sheriff Hayden leapt out of the car and whipped out his revolver. The Woodson brothers used their heads for once and surrendered. One of the last train robberies in the history of the West, and the first to be foiled by the use of an automobile, was at an end. The Woodsons did some time and disappeared from history. Hayden eventually became a congressman and then a senator.

FROM TOWN TO CITY

The city's unpredictable supply of water—usually not enough, sometimes too much—led to dam projects sponsored by the federal government. The biggest example near Phoenix is the Roosevelt Dam, about 65 miles northeast of the city at the confluence of the Salt River and Tonto Creek. Construction took seven years and was completed in 1911. Roosevelt Dam gave the city its first reliable flood-control system, hydroelectric power, and a 16,000-acre reservoir.

Soon Phoenix was wired for electricity, a trolley line served the city's burgeoning population, and by 1910 there were more than 11,000 people living in the Valley. Phoenix was the commercial center for several small but growing towns such as

Tempe, Mesa, Scottsdale, Glendale, and Peoria. Arizona was admitted as the 48th state of the Union on February 14, 1912.

By the beginning of the 20th century, Phoenix was developing a reputation as a health resort. Sanitariums offered "rest cures" for those suffering from lung problems, touting the benefits of the Valley's low humidity, mild winter weather, and clean air. While Phoenix was certainly cleaner than the coal-smogged cities of the early modern East, the city has now unfortunately caught up with its older sisters. Rapid development has increased humidity and pollution, making air quality a persistent issue. The northern-style grass lawns favored by some newcomers add pollen to the air and an extra burden on our precarious water supply.

World War I changed agriculture in the area. The war effort led to a huge demand for cotton, used in everything from uniforms to tires to airplane fabric. Many farms that once grew food crops switched to cotton. It is still an important part of the Arizona economy today. There was also a big demand for rubber, and large rubber factories supplied jobs for hundreds of Phoenix residents. These two new industries attracted more workers and by 1920 the city had grown to 29,000 people, the largest in the state.

The influx of people and industry meant that transportation had to be improved. The Southern Pacific Railroad put in a main line to Phoenix in 1926. A year later, commercial airlines took off to Tucson and Los Angeles. Phoenix Sky Harbor Airport opened in 1929. The old dirt roads began to be paved over, and the famous magazine *Arizona Highways* was launched in 1925 to encourage motor tourism.

They weren't the only ones to see Arizona's tourist potential. As early as 1919, the Phoenix-Arizona Club was promoting their city as a tourist destination. "The city where winter never comes" was their motto. The San Carlos and the Westward Ho were two of the luxury hotels that opened in that period. The Westward Ho

is now a retirement home, but the San Carlos is still in business.

The Depression didn't hit Phoenix as hard as some other cities, mostly because of Roosevelt's New Deal projects. Large numbers of Arizonans worked on dam projects or on massive archaeological excavations of the surviving Hohokam ruins. The basis of much of what we know about the ancient society comes from this period. One industry that did grow during the Depression was tourism. A local ad agency touted the metro area as the "Valley of the Sun," a far more appealing moniker than the more accurate "Salt River Valley." Another bit of relief came in the early 1930s with the invention of evaporative cooling. Although this mundane invention rarely makes the history books, it had a profound effect on life in the desert Southwest. Often called "swamp coolers" by locals, they blow air through moist pads, creating a cool flow of air. They are still common today since they are cheaper than modern air-conditioning, but their owners have to sweat a bit during the humid monsoon months when the evaporative coolers aren't as efficient. Cooler homes and offices made life in the desert more bearable, encouraging people and business to move into the area.

World War II saw GIs training for desert combat to the west of Phoenix and several prisoner of war camps throughout the Southwest. Those in Arizona housed German and Italian soldiers. One day, three German POWs from the camp in Papago Park made a break for the border. They had it all planned out. They had

---

The Arizona Historical Society's headquarters at 1300 North College Avenue, Tempe, (480) 929-0292, www.arizona historicalsociety.org, doubles as a museum that focuses on the history of the Valley of the Sun and the central Arizona region. The society also maintains museums in Tucson and Flagstaff.

The westernmost battle of the Civil War—and the only one to take place in Arizona—was the Battle of Picacho Pass, fought near the peculiar split peak of Picacho. Picacho Peak looms over Interstate 10, approximately halfway between Phoenix and Tucson, and is the site of a state park. The wildflowers are plentiful, and it's a great place to hike. Every March reenactors fight the battle once again. Call (520) 466-3183 or go to www.pr.state.az.us/Parks/parkhtml/Picacho.html.

managed to steal a map of Arizona and had found that their camp was very close to the Gila River. Tracing its meandering course, they discovered that it met up with the Colorado River, which flowed south into neutral Mexico. They scrounged enough materials to make a raft, then slipped past their American guards and out into the desert. After evading capture for the first day, they made it to the Gila River—only to find a dry wash. It wasn't long before all three were back in custody.

METROPOLIS IN THE DESERT

The war also attracted defense contractors, a major part of the Valley economy to this day. This trend continued after the war and by the 1950s Phoenix had a booming economy. Modern air-conditioning was now affordable and provided year-round sanctuary from the heat. New communities sprouted up everywhere, such as Maryvale for young families and Sun City for retirees. Office buildings and shopping centers vied for space downtown and in the suburbs. It

was at this time that Phoenix started its aggressive annexation scheme. By 1960 it had expanded to 187 square miles. The city is still growing today, and as you drive in from any direction, you see PHOENIX CITY LIMITS signs long before you see any buildings.

From the 1960s through the 1980s, Valley leaders took the peculiar stance of being pro-growth without developing a mass-transit system or a freeway, and driving became a nightmare. In the 1980s the city government finally decided to build some freeways, including a link to I-10 in 1990. Highway construction and expansion is planned well into the 21st century.

Like many modern city centers, downtown Phoenix experienced a decline, with most people preferring the suburbs. The deterioration seems to have stopped. Shops and bars are now coming back to the area, although parts can still be a bit intimidating after dark. Several big municipal projects such as the Civic Plaza, the America West Arena, the Arizona Center, and the Herberger Theater have lured Phoenix residents back downtown.

Phoenix may be the center of the Valley of the Sun, but its growth fueled the development of other cities—Mesa, Tempe, Scottsdale, Glendale, Peoria, Gilbert, and Chandler. The population of Maricopa County is nearly three million. The desert between the towns is rapidly disappearing, and the Valley looks as if it will turn into one big city within a few years. Many locals worry that the water supply won't be enough for so many people, so the population boom may be over soon. This would be good news for Arizonans who know the value of unsullied desert space and for the few traces of the past that have survived the onset of the 21st century.

HOTELS AND MOTELS

As a prime destination for sun worshipers and tourists, Phoenix and the Valley have been working hard at creating places for all those guests to stay. Seems like there is a new hotel going up every few miles and occupancy rates still remain high. The Phoenix area has been enjoying a boom in hotel construction since the mid-1990s, and several of the places listed in this chapter have opened in the last few years. This tremendous growth in hotels is generally good news for the tired traveler. Lots of hotels and motels means ferocious competition in rates so there are plenty of good values to be found.

This chapter includes older hotels that have retained their special character while keeping their amenities and services up to date. You'll also find many familiar national and regional hotel and motel chains that appeal to budget-conscious vacationers as well as business travelers. However, these listings cannot cover the Valley's many motels and hotels. If you see a favorite chain listed here but aren't sure whether it's the location you want, be sure to inquire with toll-free operators about the chain's other properties in the Phoenix area.

The best places to stay tend to be areas around the Valley where there are clusters of newer hotels and motels. Examples include: the area off State Route 143 near Phoenix Sky Harbor International Airport; the Interstate 17 corridor near Metrocenter in Phoenix; the Superstition Freeway corridor through Mesa; Apache Boulevard in Tempe; the Interstate 10 corridor about 5 miles west of downtown Phoenix; the Camelback Road corridor in east-central Phoenix; the I-10 corridor near Arizona Mills shopping center in Tempe; the area near Arrowhead Towne Center and the Peoria Sports Complex in Glendale and neighboring Peoria; downtown Scottsdale; and north Scottsdale from Shea to Frank Lloyd Wright Boulevards.

Downtown Phoenix also boasts a handful of great hotels near Central Avenue. This puts you right in the center of the action for big events at the civic center and the art museum. Unfortunately, the neighborhood is a bit run down. The city government is working hard to improve the area, and an ambitious development plan is breathing new life into the old city center.

So think about what part of the vast Valley you would like to make your home base during your stay. Then study the listings under the various geographic areas. Each of the four corners of the Valley has certain commendable features.

All the hotels and motels in this chapter offer smoking and nonsmoking rooms. Most have set aside wheelchair-accessible rooms as well. Expect to find cable or satellite TV, with many accommodations offering in-room movies for a small fee. In many cases children stay free as long as they're in the same room as their parents. Small pets are allowed at some hotels and motels; we'll tell you which locations accept them, and you can assume the others do not. If there are certain amenities that are particularly important to you, be sure to ask for details when you call for reservations.

All the accommodations in this chapter accept major credit cards. Many offer senior, group, or corporate discounts. Be sure to ask about these when you call. Because golf is such a popular activity in the Valley of the Sun, we have mentioned a few properties that offer golf packages with your stay.

Prices are based on high-season, double-occupancy rates. Take note, though, that prices go down considerably as summer approaches and stay low at least through Labor Day. So if you're considering a trip to Phoenix in the summer, you'll be pleased with the price of a room. Yes, it's hot then, but almost every accommodation in town has a swimming pool—or pools—and there's always the comfort of air-conditioning. If you will be here in our balmier, non-triple-digit weather, remember to make reservations for lodging as soon as possible. Rooms fill up especially fast in February and March.

Of course, the Valley has options other than hotels and motels. Several upscale hotels are listed here, but if you desire a resort vacation, check the luxurious offerings in the Resorts chapter. Fans of the bed-and-breakfast experience should see the Bed-and-Breakfast Inns chapter. Those traveling in recreational vehicles or vacationers who don't mind roughing it should turn to the RV Parks and Campgrounds chapter.

PRICE CODE

With each location listed in this chapter you will find a pricing guide ranging from one to four dollar signs. The code is based on the price for a one-night, double-occupancy stay in high season, which is January through April. Rates do not include tax. Room tax ranges from 12.07 percent in Phoenix to 11.67 percent in Scottsdale.

$	Less than $100
$$	$100 to $150
$$$	$151 to $250
$$$$	$251 and higher

PHOENIX

Budget Inn Motel   **$**
424 West Van Buren Street, Phoenix
(602) 257-8331
This motel is a good bargain near the city center, but it suffers from being on the edge of a rather dodgy neighborhood. The rooms include a fridge and microwave as well as cable TV and free local calls.

Courtyard by Marriott   **$$–$$$**
2101 East Camelback Road, Phoenix
(602) 955-5200, (800) 321-2211
www.marriott.com
The area near 24th Street and Camelback Road is a great place for accommodations because of all the nearby shopping and fine dining. Courtyard by Marriott is one of the more economical options in that area and within walking distance of Biltmore Fashion Park and the Esplanade retail/restaurant areas. It adjoins the Town & Country Shopping Center. The four-story hotel, built in 1990, has 155 rooms and 12 suites. Amenities include a swimming pool in the courtyard, a hot tub, and an exercise room. In your guest room you'll find a dataport, desk, and complimentary newspaper on weekdays. The hotel serves a reasonably priced breakfast buffet.

DoubleTree Guest Suites   **$$–$$$$**
320 North 44th Street, Phoenix
(602) 225-0500, (800) 222-TREE
www.doubletree.com
Proximity to Phoenix Sky Harbor International Airport makes this a good bet for those traveling by air. The hotel also is near several office towers known as the Gateway Center, the Pueblo Grande Museum, and the new Chinese Cultural Center. Plus, 44th Street provides easy access to the freeways into downtown Phoenix and to Scottsdale. The six-story DoubleTree has 242 newly redesigned and renovated two-room suites furnished with microwaves, wet bars, refrigerators, and voice messaging. A complimentary breakfast buffet adds to the amenities, as do the fitness center, the on-site restaurant, and a large swimming pool surrounded by palm trees.

Embassy Suites
Phoenix—Biltmore   **$$–$$$$**
2630 East Camelback Road, Phoenix
(602) 955-3992, (800) EMBASSY
www.embassysuites.com
The pinkish exterior of this hotel draws your attention if you're near the Biltmore

Fashion Park shopping center. But you'll be even more dazzled by the interior: A giant atrium called the Sonoran Oasis features waterfalls, pools of koi fish, and four-story desert-theme murals. Palms and many other trees are in abundance, plus the atrium offers pleasant, brightly colored sitting areas. Rooms of this five-story hotel look out on the atrium, and the hotel's complimentary breakfasts are served there as well. The Omaha Steakhouse on the premises has been a popular addition to the Biltmore area's many dining options. Lodging consists of 232 two-room suites, each outfitted with a wet bar, microwave, refrigerator, well-lit work/dining area, and sleeper sofa in the living room. Each room also has two telephones with dataports and voice mail, two TVs, a coffeemaker, a hair dryer, an iron, and ironing board. A fitness room and outdoor swimming pool also are at your disposal. Ask about special rates at the nearby Biltmore Country Club golf course.

Four Points Sheraton $$-$$$
10220 North Metro Parkway E., Phoenix
(602) 997-5900
www.sheraton.com
Like the Sheraton Crescent, the Four Points Sheraton serves the accommodation needs of business travelers in the I-17 high-tech corridor. But leisure travelers will love the fact that it's right next door to Metrocenter, with its shops, restaurants, and movie theaters, and down the street from Castles 'N Coasters amusement park. The hotel itself is quite luxurious, with a large, lush central courtyard leading out to an Olympic-size swimming pool. The 284 rooms are spread over 5 floors and include 18 suites. You can ask for a poolside Cabana Suite if you want to live it up. All rooms have coffeemakers, hair dryers, radios and TVs, irons and ironing boards, and telephones with dataport and voice mail. Guest services include a car-rental desk, a gift shop, and an on-call massage therapist. The Coppercreek Bar and Grill is open for breakfast, lunch, and dinner, and an area called the Library offers cocktails

With so many hotels, motels, and resorts in the Phoenix area, there's a lot of competition. Shop around for specials. If you are at all flexible with your travel dates, ask if there are lower rates on other days.

and hors d'oeuvres. Another nice touch: The health club is open 24 hours.

Hilton Garden Inn $-$$
4000 North Central Avenue, Phoenix
(602) 279-9811
www.hiltongardeninn.com
This is the day and age when a hotel's exercise and fitness facilities might be the amenities that draw you to it. Hilton's (formerly Lexington Hotel) Sports Club, at 45,000 square feet, encompasses all kinds of fitness machines, an indoor basketball court, 11 racquetball courts, an aerobics studio, and an outdoor pool. The Courtside Cafe serves a breakfast buffet daily. Another attractive aspect of the Hilton Garden Inn is its location, in Phoenix's uptown financial district. You're midway between downtown and busy Camelback Road. As for the rooms, there are 180 of them divided between a seven-story building and an adjacent three-story building. All have free high-speed Internet. It's possible to ask for a room with a poolside patio in the cabana wing. Other amenities include a beauty salon and an underground garage. Microwaves, refrigerators, and coffeemakers are available for rent upon request.

Hilton Phoenix Airport $$-$$$
2435 South 47th Street, Phoenix
(480) 894-1600, (800) 445-8667
www.hilton.com
Located just 1.5 miles from Sky Harbor International Airport, the Hilton Phoenix Airport offers rooms or suites featuring a Southwestern decor. For the business traveler, this full-service hotel offers dual phone lines and modem hookups in the rooms, as well as meeting or banquet

space for up to 500 people. Other amenities include private balconies, premier cable, heated outdoor pool and spa, on-site rental car desk, and fitness center. There's also Rennick's Restaurant, which serves Southwestern cuisine, and Rimrock Bar and Grille, offering happy-hour specials from 11:00 A.M. to midnight. If you can stay awhile, the luxurious Concierge Level features king-size beds, whirlpool baths in some rooms, and an exclusive lounge serving complimentary cocktails, hors d'oeuvres, and breakfast. The Hilton is located 10 minutes or less from a wide variety of sports, shopping, and dining opportunities.

Holiday Inn—Phoenix West $$
1500 North 51st Avenue, Phoenix
(602) 484–9009, (800) HOLIDAY
www.holidayinnarizona.com
This attractive Holiday Inn is done in pueblo-style architecture with long balconies on the three upper floors and archways on the ground floor. Inside, it offers more Southwestern touches with native plants, ceramic tiles, pastel colors, and various artworks. The 144 newly renovated rooms and 3 suites are decorated in Southwestern shades of turquoise and rose. In-room amenities include coffeemaker, hair dryer, makeup mirror, iron, and ironing board. There are several suites with their own Jacuzzis or private balconies. Also, you can ask for a room with a desk/work area and dataport. A heated pool, whirlpool, sauna, and exercise room are on the premises. The Coyote Grill atrium restaurant serves Mexican food and other fare. The hotel's location gives you easy access to I-10, and you are only about 5 miles west of downtown.

Homewood Suites $$-$$$
2001 East Highland Avenue, Phoenix
(602) 508–0937, (800) 225–5466
www.homewoodsuites.com
This hotel specializes in extended stays, but you can book a room for just one night. Rates decrease for those staying longer than 6 days, and there is also a

special 30-day rate. All 124 rooms are suites in this four-story hotel, which opened in 1997. It's in a prime location near the Camelback Corridor of businesses, retail stores, and restaurants. Three shopping malls—Town & Country, Camelback Colonnade, and Biltmore Fashion Park—are within walking distance. It's 8 miles to downtown Phoenix via the Squaw Peak Parkway. Lodging is a choice between a Homewood Suite, with one king-size or two double beds in the bedroom and fold-out sofa in the living room plus a fully equipped kitchen and dining area, or the Master Suite, where the main difference is the larger living room with fireplace. You can also get a Master Suite with two bedrooms. The hotel rate includes complimentary breakfast buffet, evening social hour, and use of an exercise room, gas grills, and a laundry room. A swimming pool, basketball court, and business center with computers are available for guests to use. Another useful feature is the complimentary transportation to anywhere within a 5-mile radius. Pets are allowed.

Hotel San Carlos $$-$$$
202 North Central Avenue, Phoenix
(602) 253–4121, (866) 253–4121
www.hotelsancarlos.com
George Washington didn't sleep here, but Clark Gable, Marilyn Monroe, Mae West, Spencer Tracy, and Carole Lombard all did. The San Carlos is full of interesting stories, especially from its heyday in the 1930s and 1940s. It was built in 1928 in an Italian Renaissance Revival design, and it was the city's first high-rise, fully air-conditioned hotel with an elevator. Its commitment to preservation has put the hotel on the registry of Historic Hotels of America. The 1930s-era lobby features dark wood paneling, crystal chandeliers, and old photos of downtown Phoenix. A recent $1-million renovation has helped spruce up this old hotel, and there are now two restaurants, a gift shop, a barber shop, and a shoeshine shop on-site. There's also a nice rooftop pool. The hotel is a Phoenix landmark and

is in the heart of downtown. If a proposed downtown development plan gets under way, they should do well. There's a good coffeehouse and an Irish pub on the premises. The hotel has 121 rooms and 12 suites, all with coffeemakers and dataport telephones, but they are not as spacious as modern hotel rooms. Refrigerators and microwaves are available upon request. There's a complimentary continental breakfast.

Hyatt Regency Phoenix $$$-$$$$
122 North Second Street, Phoenix
(602) 252-1234, (800) 233-1234
www.hyatt.com

Long a top player in the downtown Phoenix hotel scene, the Hyatt Regency is a dominant structure of the skyline—a 24-floor building of dark sandstone and glass topped by a popular rotating restaurant called The Compass (see our Restaurants chapter). The hotel itself has 712 rooms, including 45 VIP and business suites. A ride on the glass elevators that slice through the middle of the building affords spectacular views of downtown Phoenix and the Valley beyond. The lobby's huge seven-story atrium is a stunning showcase for hanging abstract sculptures and other artworks. The rooms are tastefully appointed and include coffeemakers. In addition to the Compass Room, the Hyatt has a more casual restaurant, a bagel shop, and a lounge. You'll also find an outdoor swimming pool, a whirlpool, exercise rooms, a concierge desk, and a car-rental desk. Early reservations are important, as the Hyatt is right across from Phoenix Civic Plaza and fills quickly when major conventions are in town.

InnSuites Hotel—Phoenix $$-$$$
1615 East Northern Avenue, Phoenix
(602) 997-6285, (888) 7PHOENIX,
(800) 752-2204
www.innsuites.com

The InnSuites chain of hotels in Arizona and California touts its good service and full slate of amenities. This location is near Squaw Peak and the mountain preserve of north-central Phoenix. As such, it's quite scenic while being close to the Camelback Corridor of shops, restaurants, and offices. Amenities at this 124-suite hotel include complimentary breakfast buffet and refreshments, free local paper, nearby walking and jogging trails, a swimming pool, spa, and exercise room. There are several types of rooms of various sizes, with options on having a king- or queen-size bed and a sleeper sofa and/or a love seat. The Jacuzzi Suite includes a whirlpool tub. You'll find in-room coffee and tea, juice in your refrigerator, and popcorn for your microwave. Pets are allowed. Other InnSuites locations are at 1651 West Baseline Road in Tempe, near I-10, (800) 841-4242; and at 7707 East McDowell Road in Scottsdale, near Eldorado Park, (888) 522-5885.

Phoenix Inn $$-$$$
2310 East Highland Avenue, Phoenix
(602) 956-5221, (800) 956-5221

With a great location just 2 blocks from 24th Street and Camelback Road, the Phoenix Inn specializes in mini-suites—spacious rooms with a king-size bed and sitting area. There are 82 such rooms in the four-story, sand-colored hotel. In addition, there are 24 rooms with 2 queen-size beds and a sitting area; 8 king-size suites with a corner Jacuzzi; 3 family suites with 2 queen-size beds, a sitting area, and a separate king-size bedroom; and 3 presidential suites, which are full 2-room suites. All rooms include microwave, refrigerator, coffeemaker, hair dryer, iron/ironing board, dataport, and voice mail. A swimming pool, Jacuzzi, and workout room are available for use by all guests. The hotel's sunny break-

Here's a bit of movie trivia concerning old Phoenix hotels: The tall hotel with the antennas that you see in the opening scenes of Alfred Hitchcock's Psycho *is the Westward Ho at 618 North Central Avenue, which dates from 1928. It is no longer a hotel, but a retirement home.*

fast room is the place for a complimentary buffet of pastries, cereal, and fruit every morning. A complimentary airport shuttle is available upon request. There's also a complimentary shuttle to corporate offices within 3 miles of the hotel.

i *Many hotels, especially chains, offer discounts to guests who reserve online. When looking up hotels on the Internet, check to see if they have special "Web rates."*

Radisson Hotel—
Phoenix Airport $-$$$
3333 East University Drive, Phoenix
(602) 437-8400, (800) 333-3333
www.radisson.com
The Radisson is one of a cluster of hotels that has opened near I-10 south of Phoenix Sky Harbor International Airport in the last decade or so. With its mirrored glass and concrete incorporated into a modern Southwestern design, the six-floor hotel makes an impressive-looking destination. Inside, the rooms surround an expansive lobby, made inviting by an atrium effect, many plants, and comfortable furniture. The 163 newly renovated rooms include 13 suites; all have coffeemakers, hair dryers, dataports, and pleasing Southwestern artworks. There's a large pool, whirlpool, sauna, and fitness center. Conveniences also include a free airport shuttle and a car-rental desk on the property. The Radisson's restaurant and lounge are called Cafe de Tryst and W. E. Tryst.

Residence Inn by Marriott $-$$$
8242 North Black Canyon Highway,
Phoenix
(602) 864-1900
www.marriott.com
Many vacationers planning extended stays in Phoenix like the homelike atmosphere of rooms in the Residence Inn chain. This location gives you easy access to I-17

through northwest Phoenix. Metrocenter and its village of stores, restaurants, and entertainment are about a mile away via the freeway. Marriott says that Residence Inn's suite floor plans are 50 percent larger than the typical hotel room. Each of the 168 suites has a fully equipped kitchen with full-size appliances, separate living area, full bath, and sleeper sofa. Floor plan options include studio style, a one-bedroom suite, a two-bedroom suite with a fireplace, and a penthouse with a loft-style upper floor. Continental breakfast is complimentary. Plus, there is a weekly social hour. Other amenities include a swimming pool and the Sport Court for tennis, volleyball, and basketball.

Ritz-Carlton $$$-$$$$
2401 East Camelback Road, Phoenix
(602) 468-0700, (800) 241-3333
www.ritzcarlton.com
The 11-story, rose-colored Ritz-Carlton is one of the main buildings to anchor 24th Street and Camelback Road, probably the ritziest intersection in the city. Hotel brochures point out that a rental car is unnecessary for guests because of all the first-class shopping, entertainment, and dining that is within walking distance. Examples include Biltmore Fashion Park, the gourmet restaurant Christopher's, Roy's, Morton's, Hard Rock Cafe, and the AMC Esplanade movie theaters. Golf is also quite accessible, as concierges can arrange for tee times at the Biltmore Country Club a few blocks away. The hotel has 281 beautifully appointed guest rooms, including 14 suites and a private Club Level with extra services. Dark woods and colors of rose and mauve predominate in the hotel's decor, which is quite ornate, down to the wall moldings, gilded frames on artwork, and the many immense chandeliers. The lobby is a wonderful place for intimate conversations, with the space divided into drawing rooms with overstuffed chairs and museum-quality Old World paintings. Each guest room features a marble bath, a refreshment bar, three telephones, an in-

room safe, plush terry bathrobes, and full maid service twice a day. The hotel has two restaurants, one quite formal and the other with a bistro feel. The swimming pool area has a grill-style cafe for alfresco dining, and the Lobby Lounge serves afternoon tea and cocktails. Other amenities include a fitness center, lighted tennis court, and pro shop.

Royal Palms $$$$
5200 East Camelback Road, Phoenix
(602) 840–3610, (800) 672–6011
www.royalpalmshotel.com

In the late 1920s, when New York financier and world traveler Delos Cooke and his wife, Florence, decided to make Phoenix home, they commissioned the building of a mansion in grand Spanish colonial style. Years later, the mansion and its additional casitas were transformed into a hotel that attracted the rich and famous seeking Phoenix sun and solace at the base of Camelback Mountain. But the years took their toll, and the Royal Palms Inn, as it was known until recently, lost clientele to the Valley's newer resorts and hotels. Now it is back in the spotlight, grander than ever thanks to a multimillion-dollar restoration project completed in 1997. Buildings on the nine-acre property were given an exterior face-lift—Italian-stained terra-cotta walls and tiled roofs to recapture the feeling of a Mediterranean-style estate. In addition, some of the best landscape designers in town went to work on the property's orange and palm tree groves, flower gardens, outdoor fireplaces, and fountains. Interior designers carefully revamped the furnishings of the main building and casitas. Touches such as textured walls, tapestry fabrics, deep jewel colors, and handcrafted artifacts help recall the Royal Palms' heyday in the 1940s and 1950s. The nine-hole golf course gave way to residential development, but guests can enjoy the swimming pool, tennis court, and fitness center. The Mediterranean restaurant T. Cook's is arguably one of the best dining rooms in town (see the Restaurants chapter).

Lodging consists of 34 standard rooms on the plaza, 34 plaza suites, 28 standard casitas, 15 deluxe casitas, and 4 villas, all built around the original Cooke mansion. The deluxe casitas in the West Courtyard are the most sumptuous, with a master bedroom suite, luxurious bath, and patio. Other rooms feature king-size beds, mini-refrigerators, and bathrooms with a tub and pedestal sink. There's also the Villa and the Presidential Suite, which are luxurious and quite expensive.

Sheraton Crescent Hotel $$$–$$$$
2620 West Dunlap Avenue, Phoenix
(602) 943–8200, (800) 423–4126
www.sheraton.com

The Sheraton Crescent has the rich ambiance of a grand downtown hotel, even though it's in the I-17 technology/commerce corridor of northwest Phoenix. The interstate makes it fairly convenient to central Phoenix attractions (15 to 20 minutes in nonrush hours), and you'll find the large Metrocenter shopping mall just a few blocks from the hotel. The seven-story building sits on nicely landscaped 13 acres, but the interior is downright opulent with its use of marble, stone, glass, and inviting furniture under twinkling chandeliers. There are 342 guest rooms, 12 of which are suites and 2 of which are top-floor penthouse suites. All have been recently renovated. The two top floors have controlled elevator access, and guests on those floors have exclusive concierge service, complimentary continental breakfast, and evening cocktails. In the other rooms, you'll find high-quality furnishings; a balcony or terrace; a bathroom with Italian marble; two telephones with computer-link and voice-mail capability; a coffeemaker; a safe; a hair dryer; and an iron and ironing board. The bistro Indigo serves breakfast, lunch, and dinner and specializes in fusion cuisine. There's also a bar and a lounge on the premises. On-site recreation includes two lighted tennis courts, sand volleyball, basketball and racquetball/squash courts, and a health and fitness center with steam rooms and a sauna. Golfers enjoy preferred

Arizona does not change its clocks for daylight saving time. So if you are here on the first Sunday in April or the last Sunday in October, realize that national reminders about the time change do not apply to you—at least while you're here.

tee times at nearby courses. At the swimming pool, the family will enjoy Monsoon Mountain, said to be one of the longest hotel water slides in the Phoenix area.

Wyndham Phoenix $$$-$$$$
50 East Adams Street, Phoenix
(602) 333-0000
www.wyndham.com

Formerly the Crowne Plaza, this 19-story hotel in the heart of downtown has been recently bought and renovated by the Wyndham chain. Although the city's downtown renovation plans are far from complete, the location is gradually improving and is within walking distance of the Phoenix Civic Plaza, the Herberger Theater Center, America West Arena, and the shops and restaurants of the Arizona Center. The 532 rooms are spacious and offer the usual amenities as well as business-class additions such as computer rental, dry cleaning, cordless phone, and voice mail. The hotel offers several event and meeting rooms as well as a fitness center with pool and dry sauna, beauty salon, and gift shop. Evenings can be spent dining at Adam's Bar and Grill. Breakfasts are served at Marston's Cafe. There's even a comedy club on-site, called Rascal's, which has shows Thursday through Sunday.

SOUTHEAST VALLEY

Best Western Dobson Ranch Inn $$
1666 South Dobson Road, Mesa
(480) 831-7000, (800) 528-1234
www.bestwestern.com

A pleasant destination in Mesa for almost 20 years, the Spanish-style Dobson Ranch Inn boasts lovely courtyards with fountains and flower gardens, and its 10 acres are crisscrossed with jogging and walking paths. Fronting the inn is the popular restaurant Monti's at the Ranch, serving steaks and continental cuisine. The inn is convenient to the Superstition Freeway and Fiesta Mall. Right down the road is the Dobson Ranch Golf Course. The inn has 213 rooms, with a standard room offering a sitting area and large dressing area. Executive king rooms include a king-size bed, refrigerator, and coffeemaker. The two-room suites include a refrigerator, coffeemaker, microwave, and an additional TV and phone. Other amenities at the inn include a swimming pool, two spas, an exercise room, complimentary buffet breakfast, complimentary welcome cocktail, and free daily newspaper delivered to your door. It's also the spring-training home of the Chicago Cubs, so keep your autograph book handy.

Best Western Grace Inn $-$$
10831 South 51st Street, Ahwatukee
(480) 890-3000, (800) 528-1234
www.bestwestern.com

The six-story Grace Inn is in the ever-growing Ahwatukee area of southern Phoenix. It is close to I-10 and nearby neighborhood shops, restaurants, and malls. Swimming, shuffleboard, and tennis are on the property; golf courses are quite accessible via the freeway. The hotel's spacious rooms have a Southwestern flavor, and guests can choose a king-size bed or two double beds. Larger one-bedroom suites offer separate sleeping quarters and living areas, and the kitchens have a microwave. For more money, there's a Plaza Level of suites with complete concierge amenities. All rooms have coffeemakers and refrigerators. A restaurant on the property offers Southwestern specialties for breakfast, lunch, and dinner. You'll also find a lounge for happy hour and beverage service at the pool.

Best Western Inn of Tempe $$
670 North Scottsdale Road, Tempe
(480) 784-2233, (800) 528-1234
www.bestwestern.com

Opened in 1997, this four-floor hotel is popular with business and leisure travelers who want easy access to the Valley's freeways. It's busy whenever major events at Arizona State University bring people to town. The 103 rooms are accessed from interior corridors, and guests have the option of queen- or king-size beds. There are in-room coffeemakers, dataports, and voice-mail systems. The indoor lap pool has resistance waves for those who like a workout, and the hotel also features an exercise room with five spas. A Denny's restaurant shares the property. Small pets are allowed.

Comfort Inn $-$$
255 North Kyrene Road, Chandler
(480) 705-8882
www.comfortinn.com

A no-frills, budget accommodation with interior access to guest rooms. The Chandler location—convenient to I-10—opened in 1998, offering 72 rooms and giving guests a choice of one or two queen-size beds. The gray-and-white three-story motel has a New England cottage look. The grounds include a heated pool and an extensive vending-machine area. The rooms are small but have desks, modem hookups, ironing boards, and coffeemakers. There's also a free breakfast.

Country Inn and Suites By Carlson, Tempe $
1660 West Elliot Road, Tempe
(480) 345-8585, (800) 456-4000

This location is a good bet if you like suite-style accommodations and want to be close to I-10. The 139 rooms range from studios to one- or two-bedroom suites, all with kitchen facilities. The decor is modern country, with lots of floral fabrics, silk plants, and light woods. The continental breakfast is free. You'll also find a generously sized swimming pool and spa. Pets are allowed, although the hotel asks for a deposit when you check in.

Days Inn—East Mesa $-$$
5531 East Main Street, Mesa
(480) 981-8111, (800) 329-7466
www.daysinn.com

Families will like the casualness and comfort of this attractive Days Inn, located in a growing area of the East Valley 8 blocks from the Mesa airport. It has 61 guest rooms and suites, with your choice of one or two extra-long queen-size beds. A family suite includes a sleeper sofa and breakfast nook with microwave, refrigerator, and wet bar. The outdoor pool is heated and has a nearby Jacuzzi. The continental breakfast is complimentary.

Econo Lodge $
2101 East Apache Boulevard, Tempe
(480) 966-5832, (877) 424-6423
www.econolodge.com

This motel is reasonably priced and has 40 clean, no-frills rooms with a choice of one or two double beds. There's an outdoor pool and a complimentary continental breakfast. It's about 2½ miles to Arizona State University and downtown Tempe with its many shops, restaurants, and nightlife.

Fiesta Inn $$$
2100 South Priest Drive, Tempe
(480) 967-1441, (800) 528-6481
www.fiestainnresort.com

This 33-acre resort-style hotel is a bit off the beaten path yet full of amenities and close to the freeways and Arizona State University. Golfers like the inn's practice facility with a lighted driving range, a practice bunker, and chipping and putting greens. Lessons are available. For other recreation, there are three lighted tennis courts, a swimming pool and Jacuzzi, an exercise room, and a full-service health club within walking distance of the inn. On the premises is a longtime Valley restaurant called Dale Anderson's The Other Place, serving breakfast, lunch, and dinner. Happy hour in the Kachina Lounge includes complimentary hors d'oeuvres. The 270 Southwestern-style guest rooms are divided into 156 standard rooms, 110 mini-suites, and 4 full suites. All rooms have hair dryers, small refrigerators, coffeemakers, irons, and ironing boards. Complimentary limousine service to Phoenix Sky Harbor International Airport is available. Golf packages are available too.

To hear about sporting and entertainment events going on while you are here, try calling the Visitor Hotline at (602) 252–5588. Operated by the Greater Phoenix Convention and Visitors Bureau, the events line is updated weekly.

Hawthorn Suites $–$$
**5858 West Chandler Boulevard, Chandler
(480) 705–8881, (800) 527–1133**

Travelers planning an extended stay in the Valley probably will like the rates of Hawthorn Suites. Rates are discounted for stays of five nights or longer. The Chandler location opened in summer 1998, and the suites feature king-size beds in your choice of one or two bedrooms. Other pluses in each suite: a living room, a fully equipped kitchen with full-size appliances, dual phone lines, full-size ironing board and iron, coffeemaker, and toaster. All rooms are reached by an interior corridor. The hot/cold breakfast buffet is complimentary, plus there's an evening social hour every Wednesday. Recreation amenities include an outdoor heated pool, fitness center, and barbecue area. The well-landscaped grounds also have a small convenience store and laundry room. A hotel shuttle will take you to some of the sights within a 5-mile radius, including the Gila River Casino and Arizona Mills shopping mall.

Hilton Phoenix East/Mesa $$–$$$
**1011 West Holmes Avenue, Mesa
(480) 833–5555, (800) HILTONS
www.hilton.com**

It calls itself a business hotel with resort flair, but Mesa's Hilton is an attractive place with appeal for leisure travelers too. Rooms look out on an eight-story atrium with a curved glass ceiling and lots of palm trees and upscale furnishings. The Hilton is close to Fiesta Mall, a major retail crossroads in the East Valley. For recreation, enjoy the outdoor pool and whirlpool, a nine-hole executive golf course, and a fitness center. There are 263 rooms, 63 of which are suites. All are decorated in soft pastels and have a refrigerator, hair dryer, coffeemaker, iron and ironing board, oversize desk, voice mail, and two phones with modem capability. Those staying in the more expensive suites enjoy a concierge lounge, complimentary continental breakfast, and evening cocktails. The Zuni Bar and Grill Restaurant serves breakfast, lunch, dinner, and Sunday brunch, and the Atrium Lounge is a piano bar with live jazz music. In the lobby is a gift shop and airline reservations desk.

Holiday Inn Express—Tempe $–$$
**5300 South Priest Drive, Tempe
(480) 820–7500, (800) HOLIDAY
www.6c.com**

There's a nicer-than-average lobby at this Holiday Inn Express, with its terra-cotta tile floors, atrium, plants, and pottery giving a feel of casual Southwestern style. The four-story motel has 160 rooms, recently redecorated, with king- or queen-size beds. The outdoor pool area includes a spa. Those traveling in RVs or trucks will find ample parking. Another plus is the proximity of Arizona Mills shopping mall, at Priest Drive and the Superstition Freeway. Pets are allowed.

La Quinta Inn $–$$
**911 South 48th Street, Tempe
(480) 967–4465, (800) 531–5900
www.laquinta.com**

A convenient location 2 miles south of Phoenix Sky Harbor International Airport makes this La Quinta a popular choice for business and leisure travelers. The 128 rooms have a bright look with an earth-tone decor. Rooms come with either two full-size or one king-size bed and, in some cases, also with a recliner and workstation.

You can upgrade to one of the three suites, each of which has a small microwave and a refrigerator. All rooms have a coffeemaker, and Nintendo is available if you ask. In addition to the requisite swimming pool, there's a small putting green in the courtyard. The inn's continental breakfast is free, or you can head to the Denny's restaurant next door. Transportation to and from the airport is complimentary as well.

Mezona Inn $-$$
250 West Main Street, Mesa
(480) 834-9233, (800) 528-8299
www.mezonainn.com

For a medium-priced motel, Mezona Inn has an above-average swimming pool area. Many of the inn's 136 rooms look out on this courtyard. Rooms come with one king-size or two queen-size beds plus a refrigerator, coffeemaker, hair dryer, and makeup mirror. Some rooms have irons and ironing boards. The Mezona is in downtown Mesa—easy to reach from the freeway if you are traveling by car. Fiesta Mall is about a 10-minute drive away.

Sheraton Phoenix East Hotel
and Convention Center $$-$$$
200 North Centennial Way, Mesa
(480) 898-8300, (800) 325-3535
www.sheraton.com

This 12-story in downtown Mesa has sometimes been criticized for being lackluster. Visitors and locals patronize its restaurants: Tuscany's Cucina Rustica, set next to an artificial lagoon and waterfall, serves breakfast, lunch, and dinner, and Grappa's Taverna serves club and bar food. The Sheraton has 273 newly renovated guest rooms and suites, all with coffeemakers, minibars, ironing boards, and a simple but cheery floral decor. The two executive floors offer upgraded amenities, continental breakfast, and evening cocktails. You will probably want a car to venture out to the East Valley shopping malls, tourist attractions, and entertainment. A few small museums and Town Center boutiques are within walking distance.

Tempe Mission Palms $$-$$$$
60 East Fifth Street, Tempe
(480) 894-1400, (800) 547-8705
www.missionpalms.com

Here's a little bit of California in the heart of Old Town Tempe. The Mission Palms hotel is done in mission-style architecture with a lovely courtyard where dozens of palm trees tower above you. Interior appointments are very Southwestern, with the lobby's Native American–inspired pictographs and earth-tone colors. The four-story hotel has 303 guest rooms decorated in shades of teal and plum. Several restaurants, coffeehouses, nightclubs, and boutiques are within walking distance on the popular and trendy Mill Avenue. Or take advantage of the on-site restaurant, Mission Grille, and Harry's Place cocktail lounge with free jazz from Wednesday to Saturday. Other amenities include a rooftop swimming pool, a fitness center, and two lighted tennis courts. Tee times and transportation to the nearby Arizona State University Karsten Golf Course can be arranged. Guests also receive complimentary transportation to and from Phoenix Sky Harbor International Airport.

Travelodge Suites $-$$
4244 East Main Street, Mesa
(480) 832-5961, (888) 515-6375
www.travelodge.com

This motel underwent extensive renovations after being taken over by the Travelodge chain in 1997. Coffeemakers and refrigerators are standard in the 76 rooms, where you have a choice of one or two queen-size beds. The one-bed version has a full kitchen, and the rooms with two beds have space for a microwave. Or you can ask for a full-fledged suite with separate living and sleeping areas. Recreational amenities include an outdoor pool, a Jacuzzi, and shuffleboard. A laundry area is available for guests to use. Pets are allowed for an additional fee if they weigh less than 50 pounds.

At many of the better hotels and resorts, the toll-free reservation numbers are available only during regular business hours. Otherwise, it is best to call the local number.

Twin Palms $
225 East Apache Boulevard, Tempe
(480) 967-9431, (800) 367-0835
www.twinpalmshotel.com
You can find several chain motels and hotels on the stretch of Apache Boulevard between Arizona State University and the Mesa city limits, but the Twin Palms stands out as something refreshingly different. It's a pinkish, seven-story tower, independently owned, sitting directly across from the ASU campus. The hotel says it offers "European hospitality," meaning that it aims to cater to guests' needs with a more personalized approach. Rooms offer higher-quality furniture with contemporary styling. There are 139 rooms and 1 king suite. Rooms have coffeemakers and dataport phones. Other amenities include complimentary use of ASU's massive Recreation Complex, a complimentary newspaper, an outdoor pool, and free 24-hour van transportation to Phoenix Sky Harbor International Airport. Fronting the hotel is a 24-hour International House of Pancakes. Inside the hotel is a bar and lounge.

University Motel $
902 South Mill Avenue, Tempe
(480) 966-7221
A cheap place to stay near the university if you don't want to shell out for the more expensive places up the street. The rooms are basic, but they are clean and offer cable TV and free local calls. The owner is friendly and knowledgeable about the area.

NORTHEAST VALLEY

Comfort Inn $$
7350 East Gold Dust Avenue, Scottsdale
(480) 596-6559, (800) 228-5150
www.comfortinn.com
Near the bustling north Scottsdale intersection of Shea Boulevard and Scottsdale Road, this three-story Comfort Inn puts you fairly close to two major shopping malls and many good restaurants, as well as several premier golf courses. In fact, golf packages are available. Just a few years old, the location has 124 rooms, with the options of a king-size bed, two queen-size beds, a king-size bed combined with a study area, or a suite with its own whirlpool. All rooms have refrigerators, and you can ask for Nintendo. The large outdoor pool has an adjacent whirlpool. The motel serves a complimentary continental breakfast.

Comfort Suites $-$$
3275 Civic Center Boulevard, Scottsdale
(480) 946-1111, (800) 517-4000
www.comfortinn.com
Thanks to a robust tourism industry in Scottsdale, many reasonably priced accommodations have been built, including this one just south of downtown. The three-story, all-suite inn has a pleasing pueblo-style exterior, and the lobby is a small but lovely homage to Southwestern decor, with a beehive fireplace, Santa Fe–style light-wood furniture, and Native American objets d'art. The 60 rooms are junior suites, meaning that a half-wall separates the living and sleeping areas. Rooms include a refrigerator and microwave. A continental breakfast is complimentary. For leisure hours, there's an indoor pool and spa, plus an outdoor spa and sundeck. Restaurant options abound along nearby Scottsdale Road. The hotel is within walking distance of Old Town Scottsdale and the San Francisco Giants' spring-training ballpark.

Hampton Inn—Old Town Scottsdale $$
4415 North Civic Center Plaza, Scottsdale
(480) 941-9400, (800) 426-7866
www.hamptoninn.com

This five-story Hampton Inn is in a quiet corner of downtown Scottsdale near professional and business offices. Yet it's within walking distance of Old Town Scottsdale, which has boutiques and art galleries, and Scottsdale Fashion Square, filled with department stores, smaller shops, and restaurants. The lobby is on the second floor, allowing for parking spaces underneath it. Don't underestimate the pleasure of shaded parking if you're here in the summer. The outdoor pool is small but pleasant enough. Guests receive a complimentary continental breakfast. The 126 rooms and 9 king-size deluxe suites are decorated in deep reds and blues.

Hilton Scottsdale Resort
and Villas $$$-$$$$
6333 North Scottsdale Road, Scottsdale
(480) 948-7750, (800) 445-8667
www.hilton.com

Although it is a compact 20 acres and 185 rooms, the Scottsdale Hilton is a resort-like hotel with beautiful grounds, a relaxing pool area, and impeccably decorated rooms. Adjacent to the hotel is a complex of boutiques and restaurants called Hilton Village, and the exclusive Borgata shopping area is across the street (see the Shopping chapter). The hotel itself has Griff's restaurant, serving up American fare. It's named after hotel owner Merv Griffin of television fame. On the grounds is the Fleming's Steakhouse, a wonderful restaurant for beef and wine lovers. The steakhouse offers 100 specialty wines by the glass. Other amenities include four lighted tennis courts, a fitness center, a gift shop, a beauty salon, and a car-rental desk. Concierges can arrange tee times at one of Scottsdale's many golf courses. The guest rooms range upward from the standard room to rooms with a pool view, poolside rooms with a patio, and luxury suites. Also on the grounds are 45 two-bedroom, two-bath villas that feature full-size living rooms, dining rooms, and kitchens. For an additional cost, you can ask for a private spa.

Holiday Inn Express $$$
3131 North Scottsdale Road, Scottsdale
(480) 675-7665, (800) 228-5151
www.hiexpress.com

This all-suite, three-floor hotel has 171 two-room suites where you have your choice of a king-size or two queen-size beds. Suites come in several floor plans and include kitchenettes. You can upgrade to a Tycoon Business Suite featuring executive desks, well-lit work areas, and computer connections. Each suite comes with a wet bar, an iron and ironing board, two TVs, a microwave, a coffeemaker, and two telephones. The complimentary breakfast buffet offers toast, waffles, cereal, pastries, yogurt, and fruit. For recreation enjoy an exercise room, whirlpool, and swimming pool. Or you can stroll into Old Town Scottsdale, about a 1-mile walk. This hotel was formerly Quality Suites.

Inn at the Citadel $$-$$$$
8700 East Pinnacle Peak Road, Scottsdale
(480) 585-6133, (800) 927-8367

If you're not set on staying close to major tourist attractions, you might want to consider this intimate inn, 30 miles from downtown Phoenix in what's known as the Pinnacle Peak area of north Scottsdale. There is quite a bit of new neighborhood development around the pueblo-style inn, but it doesn't spoil the spectacular view of the McDowell Mountains. The 11 suites are appointed with antique-style furnishings and original artwork. Some suites have fireplaces, others have balconies, and some have both. One suite offers a private hot tub on a terrace with a good view. Guests

---

Virtually all hotels, motels, and resorts in the greater metro area offer non-smoking rooms. When you are making reservations, be sure to specify your smoking preference.

are served complimentary continental breakfasts. In the same complex are an upscale restaurant and a market cafe. Nearby are boutiques and art galleries.

Motel 6 Scottsdale   **$**
6848 East Camelback Road, Scottsdale
(480) 946–2280, (800) 4MOTEL6
www.motel6.com
This is not your usual Motel 6 beckoning you from the freeway. This 122-room location is nestled along Camelback Road as the thoroughfare heads into the heart of Scottsdale. Just steps away is the posh Scottsdale Fashion Square, with its mix of major department stores, boutiques, and trendy restaurants (see our Shopping chapter). And fronting the motel is a remarkably good (and popular) pancake house. The rooms are decorated in light woods and Southwestern colors. You have the option of two full beds or a queen-size bed. The swimming pool offers a pleasant respite under the palms. Pets are allowed.

Ramada Limited Scottsdale   **$**
6935 Fifth Avenue, Scottsdale
(480) 994–9461
www.ramada.com
This three-story, Spanish colonial-style building has changed hands a couple of times in recent years. Formerly Scottsdale's Fifth Avenue Inn, it was bought and remodeled by Econolodge. Now it is a Ramada. Whoever may be running it by the time you read this, the location is good for leisurely window-shopping along Fifth Avenue. Amenities include a quiet, sunny pool area; free continental breakfast; self-serve guest laundry; and refrigerators, hair dryers, iron, and ironing board in every room.

Rodeway Inn   **$**
7110 East Indian School Road, Scottsdale
(480) 946–3456
www.rodeway.com
This location places you near a major crossroads of downtown Scottsdale—Indian School and Scottsdale Roads—

close to shopping, restaurants, and art galleries. That makes it quite a good deal. The motel has undergone both exterior and interior renovations in the last few years. The L-shaped building has two floors, with rooms looking out on a swimming pool. Management is friendly and offers amenities such as free continental breakfast, free coffee 24 hours a day, and a refrigerator and microwave in all rooms. The 65 rooms come with your choice of double, king-, or queen-size beds; a few rooms have been set aside as suites. Ask about golf packages.

Sunburst Resort   **$$$–$$$$**
4925 North Scottsdale Road, Scottsdale
(480) 945–7666, (800) 528–7867
www.sunburstresort.com
The Sunburst, a resortlike hotel, offers some of the same ambiance of major Scottsdale resorts on a smaller scale. It consists of five, two-story structures in a nicely landscaped setting along busy Scottsdale Road, just a few blocks north of Camelback Road. The location puts you in walking distance of plenty of shopping, restaurants, and nightlife. The lobby has a striking sunlit appearance with lots of wood furniture and bright colors. The 210 rooms and suites have a contemporary Southwestern decor. Rooms include refrigerators and private balconies. There's a lot of activity around the Sunburst's sand-beach pool. A restaurant and bar on the premises also keep things lively. There's also a spa, gym, and the chance to go boating or fly fishing on a nearby lake.

NORTHWEST VALLEY

Best Western Inn of Sun City   **$$**
11201 Grand Avenue, Sun City
(623) 933–8211, (800) 253–2168
www.bestwestern.com
There are plenty of shopping, dining, and recreational opportunities in the Sun City area for tourists of all ages. Plus, the recent expansion of the Valley freeway system makes it easier to get from Sun

City to other points. Downtown Phoenix, for instance, is between a half hour and 45 minutes away. This Best Western has 96 rooms furnished with either a king-size bed or two double beds. The majority of rooms include a microwave, refrigerator, and coffeemaker. The inn also has a one-room kitchenette with one queen-size bed as well as a larger three-room apartment with twin beds in the bedroom and a queen-size sofa bed in the living room, plus a full kitchen. All rooms are eligible for discounted rates for those staying seven consecutive nights or longer. The two-story motel has a swimming pool. There's also a complimentary breakfast.

Hampton Inn $$–$$$
8408 West Paradise Lane, Peoria
(623) 486–9918, (800) 426–7866
www.hamptoninn.com
Arrowhead Towne Center, one of the Valley's newer shopping malls, has fostered a boom in retail, office, and residential development in the surrounding area. One new building is this five-story Hampton Inn, which opened in early 1998. The mall is close by and so is Peoria Sports Complex, site of spring-training baseball games and other events (see the Spectator Sports chapter). The 112 rooms here come with either two queen-size or one king-size bed. Standard features include coffeemaker, microwave, and refrigerator. The inn has an outdoor pool and whirlpool plus a laundry room for guests' use. Continental breakfast is complimentary. Pets are allowed.

Windmill Inn at Sun City West $$
12545 West Bell Road, Surprise
(623) 583–0133, (800) 547–4747
www.windmillinns.com
This all-suite hotel has a few intriguing amenities you don't always find, including the free use of bicycles, free use of a lending library of best-selling books, and free coffee and muffin plus a newspaper delivered to your door every morning. The 127 two-room suites are 500 square feet and come with either a king-size bed or two double beds, along with double sinks in the bathroom, a wet bar, a microwave, a refrigerator, two TVs, three telephones, a desk area, and a sleeper sofa. Guests also have the use of laundry facilities. Adding to the amenities are the swimming pool and whirlpool. Pets are accepted. This is a nonsmoking hotel.

RESORTS

A hundred years ago, when winter vacationers first spread out their lawn chairs at Phoenix hotels to soak up the desert sun, they probably had no inkling of what lay ahead for the Phoenix hotel industry. From those simpler times have evolved sumptuous, top-rated resorts in Phoenix, Scottsdale, and other areas of the Valley that attract millions of people and pump billions of dollars into the local economy. In Scottsdale the long row of resorts and high-end hotels along Scottsdale Road helps make tourism the largest economic activity in that city.

Modern resorts don't just have a pool—they have several pools, many of which resemble small lakes. They pay great attention to details in furnishings and architecture, always striving to raise the lodging experience. They always offer golf, if not by building one or two championship courses on their own properties, then by arranging access and trips to nearby courses. You'll always find tennis, notable restaurants, and a full array of guest services, including around-the-clock room service. It's no wonder that Valley resorts have been showered with awards and accolades in surveys, travel guides, and national magazines.

Happily for those of us who appreciate the desert and Arizona's heritage, the fancy resorts respect Southwestern style. We're not Hawaii, after all. Attention is given to desert landscaping, for the most part. Tribute is paid to the state's Native American and Spanish roots through architecture, all kinds of art, and often through the food served in restaurants.

Staying at a Valley resort can be a wonderful experience. The resorts offer great choices for a honeymoon or romantic getaway through special, all-inclusive packages. Some visitors are lucky enough to come to a resort as part of a business meeting or convention. Even if a resort is not in your vacation budget, you might think about splurging on a fine dinner or Sunday brunch in one of the restaurants or sipping cocktails at sunset in one of the lounges. If you're just in for a brief visit, be sure to take some time to walk the main grounds to enjoy the flower gardens and water features.

All the top-rated resorts recognize the importance of offering the spa experience. Steam rooms, massages, facials, whirlpools, lap swimming pools, fitness machines, and free weights are the kinds of indulgences that well-heeled vacationers seek. The Boulders, for instance, offers a special massage with hot rocks. At the Biltmore, you can get a purification treatment loosely based on Native American healing rituals and amenities such as juice bars, aerobics classes, shiatsu, reflexology, aromatherapy, wraps, manicures, and pedicures. You can pick your pleasure in hourlong sessions or daylong packages. Also realize that more and more, a resort's dining options contribute to how highly it's rated. This chapter touches on several award-winning restaurants, but look in the Restaurants chapter for more detailed information.

In recent years, hotels and resorts have begun setting aside smoke-free rooms and wheelchair-accessible accommodations. Be sure to ask about these features when making reservations. All

i

What is a resort casita? Think of it as a mini-house and a home away from home. Often the casitas are individual, stand-alone structures or large guest rooms joined in small groupings with other casitas, town house–style, to create a greater sense of privacy. Often they have their own patios, fireplaces, living rooms, and kitchens.

resorts listed here accept major credit cards. There are no restrictions on bringing children to the resorts, although, as you'll see from our descriptions, some are more kid-friendly than others.

This chapter describes a variety of resorts, starting with what we consider to be the most exclusive, "The Spectacular Six."

PRICE CODE

Resorts were asked for their double-occupancy, daily rates in high-season (generally considered to be January to April, but in some cases including fall months and May). Because resorts tend to offer a variety of accommodations, we have given you dollar codes that represent the range from a standard room to suites, casitas, and luxury villas. Prices indicated here do not include tax, room service, incidental fees or fees for golf, spas, and other amenities. Remember that off-season rates can be dramatically lower than what you see here.

$	$151 to $200
$$	$201 to $300
$$$	$301 to $500
$$$$	$501 and higher

THE SPECTACULAR SIX

Fine weather, friendly people, and beautiful scenery have drawn visitors to the Valley of the Sun for nearly a century. For those with money to spare, Phoenix offers some of the very best resorts in the United States. Golfers come from around the world to try out the incredible variety of professional courses. There's also tennis, Olympic-size swimming pools, and world-class fitness centers to keep guests in shape. For those who want to just sit back and relax, there are shaded groves, luxurious spas, and breathtaking sunsets. It's easy to never leave the grounds, but if you do decide to venture out, the staff are always ready to help with good recommendations and expert service.

Prices for these resorts vary greatly. Assume that the simplest room during high season will cost at least $300 a night, and that prices per night for double occupancy are more typically around $500. For a two-bedroom villa, say, at the Arizona Biltmore, you could pay $1,700. But remember that these are high-season prices, usually lasting from January to April. If vacation plans (and tolerance of the weather) permit you to travel here in the hotter months, the price tag can be much lower. For instance, at the Phoenician, a premium room that goes for more than $500 from January to June can go for $350 in the dead of summer. The Scottsdale Princess has lower rates from April to June and from September to January and even lower rates from mid-June to the end of August. In the slowest part of the year, you could nab a standard room for about $150, less than half the high-season rate, or grab the Presidential Suite for $1,350 ($2,750 in high season). It's also possible to catch some deals around the winter holidays. Many of the resorts offer special bargains on stays between Thanksgiving and New Year's Eve. When choosing a resort, inquire whether the rate varies with how good the view is from your room. The best views command the highest rates. Just remember, you might spend more time by the pool than in your room, so you might be happier without the expensive view. If you're a serious tennis or golf player, or serious about indulging in a resort's spa, ask about programs that include the cost of those activities with your rate. All resorts offer creative packages that will combine sports or spa pleasures with the cost of your room.

Arizona Biltmore $$$–$$$$
24th Street and Missouri Avenue, Phoenix
(602) 955-6600, (800) 950-0086
www.arizonabiltmore.com
Open since 1929, the Arizona Biltmore—crowned "The Jewel of the Desert" at its grand-opening gala—is a cherished part of Phoenix history. Even visitors to town who

are not guests of the hotel should see it to understand how it helped lay the foundation for the Valley of the Sun's resort industry and to appreciate it as an architectural gem. Vestiges of Frank Lloyd Wright can be seen all through the interior and exterior since the Biltmore was designed by one of Wright's apprentices, Albert Chase McArthur. (The extent of Wright's own involvement as "consulting architect" is not known, but that just adds to the hotel's mystique.) The ambiance is one of functional elegance. The geometrically stylized image of a palm tree trunk that's sculpted into many of the exterior concrete blocks sets a theme that's used repeatedly in the decor and landscaping. The lobby has remarkable stained-glass windows, balconies, and Wright-inspired furniture and lighting.

Other interesting facts about the Biltmore: Every U.S. president since 1930 has stayed at the Biltmore; chewing-gum magnate William Wrigley and his heirs owned the resort for four decades; and in 1996, the resort completed a five-year, $50-million renovation and expansion project. The Biltmore continues to be an award-winning resort because its amenities and services keep up with modern times, but face-lifts over the years have not marred its architectural integrity. Although at its debut the Biltmore was on the outskirts of town, Phoenix's phenomenal growth has now placed it at the center of the action. It's only 15 minutes by freeway from downtown and is just a skip away from the Camelback Corridor, a prime retail, restaurant, and office district.

The Biltmore's 730 rooms and villas are furnished in a style reminiscent of Wright's. The one- and two-bedroom villas have full kitchens, indoor and outdoor dining areas, and fireplaces. The Biltmore's 39 acres make it a relatively compact resort. Still, there's space for the Biltmore Athletic Club, along with two championship golf courses at the adjacent Arizona Biltmore Country Club. There's also an 18-hole putting course; three restaurants, including Wright's, featuring impeccable New American cuisine; two bars; eight tennis courts; and an elegant spa offering therapeutic treatments, fitness equipment, steam rooms, and a full-service beauty salon. The resort has become more kid friendly over the years. The Paradise Pool features a 92-foot water slide enclosed in twin towers. The Kids Korral offers a range of supervised activities, as well as special programs such as tennis and yoga on weekends. Lawn games include croquet, volleyball, chess, and shuffleboard, and there are pleasant trails for jogging, strolling, and biking. You will also find poolside private cabanas and swim-up beverage service as well as a salad and sandwich bar.

The Boulders Resort and Golden Door Spa $$$–$$$$
34631 North Tom Darlington Drive, Carefree
(480) 488-9009, (877) 999-3223
www.wyndham.com/hotels/PHXTB/main.wnt

When celebrities want to be seen, they stay at the Arizona Biltmore. When they want privacy, they sneak away to The Boulders. Or so goes the scuttlebutt in Phoenix resort circles. The Boulders, set in the foothills of the far Northeast Valley, is logistically the best place to get away from it all without leaving civilization. It's the kind of place Microsoft founder Bill Gates chose for a retreat. And *Andrew Harper's Hideaway Report,* a travel newsletter that goes out to business executives, has ranked The Boulders the best American resort, in addition to the many other honors it has received over the years.

Carefree, as its name suggests, is a small, laid-back town with beautiful hillside homes about 30 miles north of central Phoenix. The Boulders is on the main route into town and has a 24-hour security gate. Its name pays tribute to the 12-million-year-old geological curiosity at its center: a 90-foot-high mound of boulders. Other rock outcroppings dot the grounds. When the resort was designed and built in the early 1980s, painstaking care was taken to make it as unobtrusive as possible within its desert surroundings. The adobe-style buildings are low-slung and painted to closely match the color of the boulders. Almost all the landscaping is indigenous to the area.

A network of trails on resort grounds lets guests enjoy the mountain scenery, including the reported 350 species of birds and other wildlife in the area. The list of amenities is pages long, topped by The Boulders' two 18-hole championship golf courses. Designed by Jay Morrish, they've won kudos from *Golf* magazine and *Golf Digest*. In harmony with the surroundings, the fairways are covered in local grasses. Staff at the Boulders say service is just as important as amenities. With an eye toward anticipating their guests' every need, they keep detailed preference histories—for instance, who likes feather pillows and who likes synthetic. Concierges welcome questions and relish opportunities to help guests arrange off-resort excursions, such as day trips to the Grand Canyon or hot-air ballooning.

The 160 guest casitas are nestled into the terrain, and each has a fireplace and private patio. Families and golf groups can take advantage of the 35 one-, two-, or three-bedroom villas, complete with laundry facilities and kitchens. All units are furnished in earth tones, and all have wet bars, large dressing and bathroom areas, and wood-beam ceilings.

Dining is exceptional, with five restaurants to choose from, including the casually elegant Palo Verde and The Latilla, offering a more formal menu and views of a waterfall. There are eight tennis courts, with tennis pros offering private lessons and weekly clinics. You'll also find three swimming pools and rock-climbing sessions that guide you up the boulders formation. The Sonoran Spa offers facials, massages, and fitness machines. The resort opened the luxurious Golden Door Spa in 1999. It's a short stroll away from the boutiques and galleries of el Pedregal Festival Marketplace or a short drive to the touristy town of Carefree. Complimentary shuttles get you around the 1,300-acre resort.

Native American art is showcased in the main lodge and dining areas, and the staff even conduct art tours. The world-famous Heard Museum has a satellite museum featuring their renowned collection of Native American art. Transportation to Sky Harbor and Scottsdale airports is available, or you can fly your private plane right into Carefree Airport.

Fairmont Scottsdale Princess $$$$
**7575 East Princess Drive, Scottsdale
(602) 585–4848, (800) 441–1414
www.fairmont.com**

The Scottsdale Princess is probably best known for its association with the Phoenix Open, a key tournament on the PGA tour that annually draws tens of thousands of spectators. It's played on the adjacent TPC Stadium Course. The resort is part of the exclusive chain of Princess Hotels, with branches in Bermuda and Acapulco. The Arizona location blends opulence with Southwestern sensibilities. It's built to resemble a Mexican colonial estate, with lots of arched openings, balconies, railings, and red-tiled roofs. Its terra-cotta color complements the beautiful view of the McDowell Mountains. The Princess is on 450 acres in ever expanding north Scottsdale and has about 650 guest rooms, suites, casitas, and villas. It has the largest hotel ballroom in Arizona, making it a popular place for business conferences. Another prime feature is the Marquesa, the resort's much-heralded restaurant serving Catalan cuisine.

Golf is the big draw here. In addition to the course used for the PGA tour, there's another 18-hole championship course; the Tournament Players Club of Scottsdale operates both. Tennis gets attention here, too, with seven courts, including a stadium court that annually hosts a couple of important tournaments. Other opportunities for recreation include three swimming pools, indoor basketball, sand/water volleyball, a fitness trail, and fishing. Besides the Marquesa, the resort has six other restaurants, including La Hacienda, popular for its Mexican food and strolling mariachis;

a grill at the golf clubhouse; a poolside cafe; and a country-western nightclub. Shopping is well covered, too, with boutiques carrying sports clothing and other fashions, Southwestern gifts, and Indian jewelry. You can indulge yourself in the Spa & Fitness Center with a Turkish steam bath, herbal wraps, or a loofah buff. And how about a Massage in Symphony, where two massage therapists work on one guest, using long, flowing strokes in unison? On the grounds of the Princess are several distinct gardens. Enjoy two cactus gardens, a plaza with 300 decorated pots and a fragrance garden with jasmine, orchid trees, and citrus trees. All rooms have terraces, wet bars, refrigerators, and oversize bathrooms. The 125 casitas are grouped near the tennis courts, while the 75 villas are on the opposite end. Families can take advantage of the Kids Club, which offers supervised activities for kids ages 5 to 12 on weekends.

Resorts aren't just for high-powered business meetings and romantic getaways; they can be great for families too. Many area resorts offer special facilities and activities for kids, such as the Fairmont's Kids Club and water slides and the Wigwam's Camp Pow Wow. Shop around to find the resort that offers what your child would be interested in.

Four Seasons Resort at Troon North $$$$
10600 East Crescent Moon Drive, Scottsdale
(480) 515-5700
www.fourseasons.com

Despite the fame of the above resorts, the Four Seasons can give any resort in the Valley a run for its money. The location is spectacular—surrounded by acres and acres of pristine desert scenery. With 210 guest rooms and suites, arranged in Southwestern casitas, the luxurious accommodations offer views of desert, mountain, and cityscapes. The good news for golf fanatics is that the resort offers preferred tee times on the two renowned golf courses at Troon North. Three restaurants and a lounge provide a wide range of culinary options. The 9,500-square-foot health club and spa offers sauna, steam, and massage therapy.

The Phoenician $$$$
6000 East Camelback Road, Scottsdale
(480) 941-8200, (800) 888-8234
www.thephoenician.com

"Opulence" is the word to best describe the Phoenician. Looking around, you get the sense that no expense was spared in its design and furnishing, from the $8-million collection of paintings, tapestries, antiques, and bronze sculptures to the oval pool tiled in mother-of-pearl and surrounded by lush landscaping with waterfalls, lagoons, and fountains. Then there are the extra touches such as crystal chandeliers, marble floors and walls, and Italian linens. It's unexpectedly palatial for a metropolitan area with such humble beginnings. Yet guests can easily find serenity and relaxation, along with top-notch services, beautiful nighttime views, great golf, and one of the best restaurants in town, all with majestic Camelback Mountain as backdrop.

The Phoenician is better understood through a quick look at its beginnings. It opened in 1988, the "house" that Charles Keating built, as he envisioned building a resort like no other. But when Keating's savings-and-loan empire crumbled and landed him in federal prison, the resort became the property of the Resolution Trust Corp. Recently it's come under the wing of ITT Sheraton Corp. as part of its "Luxury Collection."

The Phoenician is huge, laid out on 250 acres with 654 rooms and suites. Most of the accommodations are in the main building, supplemented by more secluded areas with casitas, suites, and villas. Rooms are furnished with expensive rattan furniture, Berber carpets, oversize bathrooms with

Italian marble, safes, telephones with voice mail and modem capabilities, and limited-edition prints. The resort boasts nine pools and a 165-foot water slide. Guests can stroll through a two-acre cactus garden. A 27-hole golf course, putting green, and clubhouse are also on-site, as is the Tennis Garden with 12 courts, an automated practice court, and a grass court. Staff can arrange for hikes up Camelback Mountain. Croquet, lawn bowling, lawn chess, and billiards provide other amusements.

As for restaurants, the modern French cuisine at Mary Elaine's (named for Keating's wife) is perhaps one of the most expensive and outstanding restaurants in town. The Terrace Dining Room's Italian fare and Windows on the Green's South-western food are popular options. Many Phoenix residents know about the charming afternoon teas in the Tea Court. In addition, you can enjoy a poolside cafe, ice-cream parlor, the 19th Hole Snack Bar, and the Thirsty Camel Lounge. The Centre for Well-Being is a large spa, offering 13 kinds of massages, scrubs and mud packs, facial care, and exercise equipment. For children ages 5 to 12, the resort runs the Funicians Kids Club, where daily themes get them swimming, hiking, making crafts, and playing games under staff supervision. You'll also find a beauty salon, a few boutiques, 24-hour room service, concierge service, and airport transportation.

The Wigwam $$$
300 Indian School Road, Litchfield Park
(602) 935-3811, (800) 327-0396
www.wigwamresort.com
Of the top-five resorts, some say the Wigwam comes closest to capturing the essence of Arizona and the lure of the West. It couldn't exist anyplace but here. This once-private club was built in 1918 to lodge visiting executives of the Goodyear Tire and Rubber Co. and was way out in the country back then. By 1929, it opened to the public, with room for 24 guests. Now expanded to 75 acres, it still carries reminders of a more rugged, cowboy era. Much of the original building from 1918 has

When the relatives visit from out of town, take them out one afternoon to high tea at the Phoenician resort. Served off the lobby, with a spectacular view of the Valley, the tea features exquisite finger-size sandwiches, your own personal pot of tea, wonderful pastries with Devonshire cream, and decadent sweets—all served on fine china. You can munch and chat while listening to soothing piano music. It's guaranteed to impress. Call (480) 941-8200 for reservations and information.

been incorporated into the Main Lodge, including a sitting room with a large stone fireplace that is both cozy and rustic.

This is the only one of the resorts described in this chapter that is in the West Valley. Litchfield Park is a growing area, and thanks to freeways, the Wigwam is now only 20 minutes from downtown Phoenix. Also distinguishing it from other resorts is the fact that it's the only one in Arizona with three golf courses on its property. The Gold and Blue courses were designed by Robert Trent Jones, and Arizona's "Red" Lawrence designed the Red course. All the courses, especially the Gold one, have been praised by those in the know. Also, the Wigwam is home to the nationally known Jacobs' Golf Schools, which run four- and five-day golf sessions. (See the Golf chapter.)

Accommodations are arranged in clusters of casitas—331 in all, plus about 70 suites, decorated with distressed-wood furnishings, stone fireplaces, leather chairs, Mexican ceramic tiles, and Native American-style pottery and baskets. The casitas themselves are made of adobe. Get a taste of Arizona in the Wigwam's best restaurant, the award-winning Arizona Kitchen, where the chef uses ingredients common to the desert and to Native American cooking. Also on the premises are the Terrace Dining Room, plus a casual restaurant with a view of the golf course, and a poolside cafe. The resort has two

How We Live: The Southwestern Lifestyle

Some winter day you'll be relaxing in a Mexican-tiled room bursting with sunlight, enjoying a glass of sun tea, watching the hummingbirds visit a feeder, and you'll say to yourself, "I could never do this in Cleveland!" The truth is, you've hit upon some of the many pleasures of living in a Sunbelt city like Phoenix. Such days are possible—in fact, likely—in the middle of winter. The sun defines our way of life. Longtime residents know it, and newcomers quickly learn it. The things we do in harmony with the climate all contribute to the definition of a Southwestern lifestyle.

The good life here begins by knowing that many outdoor activities and household projects are better left for the cooler months. June through September are for traveling to the nearby mountains, or staying home and splashing in the pool, or relaxing inside air-conditioned comfort, the flip side of hunkering down for the winter in the Snowbelt. Southwestern lifestyle means taking advantage of our glorious nonsummer months by getting outside and enjoying the gorgeous outdoors, whether it's a round of golf or an in-line skating date, hiking or rock climbing, or taking the time to plant your vegetable garden. Locals keep tabs on winter rainfall so that they'll know how colorfully the desert will bloom in the spring. (With all the wildflowers, desert trees, and cacti, it's usually a spectacular display.) You'll begin to acquaint yourself with the native flora and appreciate how shrubs, trees, and grasses are planted with water conservation in mind. It's about seeing the beauty of desert landscaping for homes, roadways, and buildings. Learning the

names of indigenous animals is also important. Yes, we have coyotes, roadrunners, quail, jackrabbits, cactus wrens, lizards, snakes, scorpions, and javelinas. The animals around here can be both wondrous and mysterious.

To enjoy all that nature has to offer here, there are several essentials. One is good outdoor furniture—chairs, chaise longues, umbrellas, and tables that you know will get good use. A good outdoor grill is a must-have too. Many homeowners have grills built into brick or stone walls complementing their backyard design or make do with simpler portable charcoal or propane grills. During the summer months, many people refuse to turn on their ovens for fear of heating up an already hot house. What's a cook to do? Just fire up the grill and cook under the blue skies.

Backyards bring us to swimming pools. Despite their proliferation in residential areas—from an airplane they look like thousands of turquoise dots—pools are not essential, but certainly a great pleasure and actually quite common. There are two schools of thought. Some residents couldn't live without them and find their time in the water rejuvenating and refreshing. Others find their upkeep daunting and worry about pool safety, especially with small children at home. The waste of scarce water and the increased humidity all these pools bring to the Valley are other causes for concern. Some homeowners compromise by buying town houses with common pool areas or by building small water features on their properties, such as fountains,

The outdoor Crescent Moon Terrace at the Four Seasons Resort in Scottsdale blends native plants and scenery with Southwestern architecture. GREATER PHOENIX VISITOR AND CONVENTION BUREAU

ponds, or hot tubs. People without private pools cool off in the summer at public pools, water parks, country clubs, or become very good friends with the neighbors who have pools.

During the Valley's many pleasant evenings, the Southwestern lifestyle is brought out onto patios with ceramic luminarias, or candleholders, and Guadalajara firepots (large cone-shaped ceramic pots for burning wood). Lots of brightly colored Mexican pots and terra-cotta containers filled with cacti and flowers add to the scene. It's not unusual to see twinkly strings of white lights adorning backyards year-round. Another Southwestern twist is to decorate indoors and out with strings of mini-lights that look like red chile peppers.

While you're enjoying the outdoors, don't forget the sunscreen. You can find it at stores year-round, in a variety of strengths and aromas. The aroma is your choice, but if you are smart you will pick a high SPF. The midday sun can be intense, even in temperatures of 60 or 70 degrees. Of course, in summer, people don't even step outside without sunscreen, a hat, sunglasses, or a combination of those.

In addition, locals display their Southwestern lifestyle inside their houses. Homes and hotels gravitate toward the casual elegance of Southwestern design. Also known as Santa Fe style, it incorporates the color palette of the desert, such as terra-cotta and turquoise, and lots of ceramic tile flooring and wood furniture.

Interior designers say contemporary, mission, country, and Spanish colonial styles all fit well in Southwestern homes. Peruse some of the unique furniture and accessories shops in the Valley of the Sun, and you'll see how the style encompasses wrought-iron tables and lamps; large urns filled with cacti or brightly colored paper flowers; chairs and tables with cowhide stretched over them; polished pewter vases, photo frames, and dinnerware; place mats and tablecloths in bright Mexican-inspired stripes; colorful handblown Mexican glasswear; rugs that pay homage to Native American weaving on the floor and on walls; knickknack shelves holding Mexican folk art; large rustic wooden antiques; and hand-forged copper pots.

Once you've found a place dressed in Southwestern style, it's time to dress like the natives yourself. Casual is the word, but not too casual. Worn-in but not worn-out jeans are good, as are khaki pants, shorts, and polo shirts. Contrary to popular belief, all Arizonans do not wear cowboy hats. But if they're for you, you'll be pleased by the selection available. Arizona is also a good place to buy cowboy boots—the kind that John Wayne would be proud to wear. Scan advertisements for stores specializing in

Western wear and don't miss the shops that sell beautiful (and expensive) custom-made boots and belts. Also consider how stylish you would look in Arizona's official neckwear, the bola tie. The classic bola tie is a black leather string that holds a clasp of turquoise set in silver. But stores here sell many wonderful variations that range from small and tasteful to immense and gaudy. You might even find one with a scorpion preserved in a globe of clear plastic.

Speaking of turquoise, you probably won't be in Arizona too long before you break down and buy an authentic piece of turquoise jewelry. It could be a showy squash blossom necklace, a belt buckle, a silver-and-turquoise watchband, or a simple silver ring inlaid with turquoise and other stones native to the Southwest. They can be pricey, but are worth having, for both their beauty and Native American craftsmanship.

The Southwestern lifestyle means learning to talk the talk. Since Arizona's Native American and Hispanic populations have influenced everything from architecture to apparel to food, you'll discover a whole new vocabulary being used. While you're absorbing all these new words with non-English origins—for

pools, the main one more suited for group activities and for having fun on the water slide. The second pool is quieter, nestled among palm trees and flower gardens. Other recreational amenities include nine tennis courts, horseback riding, volleyball, croquet, and trap and skeet shooting. For families on vacation, there's Camp Pow Wow, a supervised recreation program for children ages 5 and older. It's available major holidays, during spring break, and Memorial Day through Labor Day.

EVEN MORE RESORTS

Maybe you haven't won the lottery yet. Don't despair—there are plenty of other great resorts in the Valley that are a notch down in pricing yet provide many of the same amenities and services. Some travelers might rate a few of these resorts even higher than the aforementioned Spectacular Six. Golfers should note that resorts without courses on-site can help you get preferred tee times at nearby public and private courses.

instance, saguaro (sah-WAH-ro) and gila (HEE-la)—take a few moments to learn how to pronounce them. This is especially true at the many fine Valley restaurants, where you'll be confronted with words like pollo (POY-oh) and mole (MOH-lay). Many of the menus will have a glossary that explains the language. Your server will also be happy to translate. The words are easy to pick up once you start.

Local food is a natural offspring of the Southwestern lifestyle. We're talking Mexican food, Native American fare (don't miss out sampling Navajo frybread— puffed, fried dough served with honey or beans), and nouvelle Southwestern cuisine that takes advantage of the many products harvested here. A perfect example is this item from the menu at Arizona Kitchen, the Wigwam Resort's four-star restaurant: filet mignon of beef dusted with guajillo chile powder in a prickly pear Merlot sauce. Of course, it doesn't get that fancy in Southwestern homes, but every good kitchen probably has a Mexican cookbook, a constant supply of tortillas (handmade or store-bought), and several varieties of salsa. And party hosts always bring out a circular platter of chips and salsa. Many people take pride in making their own recipes for salsa, heating them up with chiles or cooling them down with tomatoes.

By the way, if you like to drink beer at parties or restaurants, you might like to try Mexican beer. Many restaurants stock imported brands like Negro Modelo, Bohemia, and Pacifica, in addition to the more commonly known Corona. Or you may choose to drink margaritas, a frozen lime drink made with tequila and triple sec, then served in a salt-rimmed glass. For nonalcoholic drinks, try sun tea, which is brewed by simply placing tea bags in a pitcher of cold water, putting it in the sun for a few hours, and letting the summer heat do the preparation. People here drink it in all kinds of fruit flavors.

Relaxation and socialization in the Southwest is, by and large, not suits and ties, cocktail dresses, and overstuffed chairs in fancy parlors. You can find that at certain resorts, restaurants, or private clubs, but more typically, it's friends gathered in a backyard, casually dressed in jeans, shorts, T-shirts, sandals, and sundresses. Enjoy the laid-back atmosphere. Just don't forget the sunscreen. Come live the Southwestern life.

The choices of Valley resorts are abundant, and this is only a sampling of resorts listed by geographic area, with price ranges included. Again, they are concentrated in Scottsdale, with some in north Phoenix and the East Valley. You may also want to refer to the Hotels and Motels chapter for a look at accommodations with a resort ambiance.

Phoenix

Pointe Hilton Squaw Peak Resort　　　　　　$$-$$$
7677 North 16th Street, Phoenix
(602) 997-2626, (800) 947-9784
www.pointehilton.com
The resort's proximity to the Phoenix Mountain Preserve and the second-highest point in the city, Squaw Peak, gives a scenic setting to this relatively centralized

location. Opened in 1976, it is the older of the two Pointe Hilton resorts in the Valley. It reportedly was the first all-suite resort in the country. Architects gave it a Spanish-Mediterranean look, and the many court-yards and gardens are great for a stroll. The 564 units include mostly two-room suites and some casitas. There are also some boardroom suites, which combine a bedroom with a meeting room for small, executive functions. New to the resort is the Hole-in-the-Wall River Ranch, where families can enjoy tubing amid rocks, foun-tains, and waterfalls. You'll also find a 136-foot slide, a children's camp, a retail area whimsically called Rodeo Drive, and a put-ting course. Golf is available a few miles away, and four tennis courts are on the premises. The spa and fitness center are good places to unwind from all this fun.

Restaurants include Lantana Grille, offering American favorites; the Hole-in-the-Wall, serving Western grub from a 1940s-era ranch house; and Slim Picken's, an informal poolside restaurant.

The Pointe Hilton Tapatio
Cliffs Resort $$-$$$
11111 North Seventh Street, Phoenix
(602) 866-7500, (800) 947-9784
www.pointehilton.com
"Tapatio" means "a place of peace and contentment." This resort is nestled into North Mountain Park, offering tranquil views of desert mountains, desert flora, and cliffs. The 584 suites of the Spanish-Mediterranean-style resort take advantage of the views. So does its best restaurant, Different Pointe of View, where tables are on terraced rows, all facing a floor-to-ceiling window for a beautiful panorama of the Valley. The restaurant is known for its wine cellar as well as its fine American/continental food. The Falls is a three-acre water feature of waterfalls, free-form swimming pools, an enclosed water slide, and an open-air restaurant pavilion. The centerpiece is a 40-foot waterfall that cas-cades into 12 meandering pools, a design inspired by Havasupai Falls in the Grand Canyon. There are 8 recreational pools in

all, plus 11 tennis courts, a fitness room, a full-service spa and salon, an 18-hole golf course, and horseback riding. There's also The Pinnacle, a challenging 10-hole course with a 300-foot drop from the elevated tee. As for the two-room suites, each fea-tures a private balcony. A special Con-cierge Level with upgraded services and amenities is available upon request. There are also some boardroom suites, which combine a bedroom with a meeting room for small, executive functions.

Southeast Valley

Arizona Golf Resort and
Conference Center $-$$
425 South Power Road, Mesa
(480) 832-3202, (800) 528-8282
www.azgolfresort.com
As the name implies, this 187-room resort is for golf lovers. Resort staff can direct you to several nearby courses, but you'll probably be just as happy with the cham-pionship course on the property. It's nicely landscaped with three lakes and mature trees and is a par 71 course. The best accommodation deals are packages that include two to six rounds of golf. Guest rooms include one- or two-bedroom suites, many with private patios or bal-conies that overlook the fairways. Non-golfers receive reduced rates. Amenities include a fitness center, tennis, a pool, and volleyball. The resort's two restaurants are Annabelle's, featuring prime rib and seafood, and Anna's Grill, with lighter, Southwestern fare. The East Valley loca-tion is distant from Phoenix and Scotts-dale, but it's only a mile from the large Superstition Springs Shopping Center.

The Buttes $- $$
2000 Westcourt Way, Tempe
(602) 225-9000, (800) 843-1986
www.wyndham.com
Advertised as a "mountaintop resort," The Buttes is actually nestled in the saddle of the Tempe Buttes. That means the resort is nicely elevated above the city and the

nearby crossroads of two major freeways. We're talking hills, not mountains. Even so, the four-story resort has a well-designed, curvilinear look, and the sunset views from its premier restaurant, Top of the Rock, are almost unparalleled. The huge pool area uses the rocks as a design element, and for kids, there's an aquatic playground and 115-foot water slide. This is a popular resort because it's close to Sky Harbor International Airport. On a mere 25 acres it manages to fit 353 rooms, 4 tennis courts, a fitness center, indoor and out-door pools, and a gift shop. The decor in the rooms is Southwestern style. You'll pay a bit more for a good view. Note to baseball fans: The resort is adjacent to the Tempe Diablo Stadium, the spring-training home of the Anaheim Angels.

Sheraton San Marcos Resort $–$$$
1 San Marcos Place, Chandler
(480) 812-0900, (800) 325-3535
www.sheraton.com
Known as Arizona's original golf resort, the stately San Marcos has been around since 1912, long enough to land the hotel on the National Register of Historic Places. It was designed in the Mission Revival style of architecture popular after the turn of the 20th century. The architect was Arthur Benton of California, an associate of Frank Lloyd Wright's. In fact, it's said Wright spent considerable time at the San Marcos construction site. Today the San Marcos commands an attractive corner of downtown Chandler, which once was a farming community but is now one of the Valley's fastest-growing suburbs.

The 295 rooms and suites have been recently renovated. On the resort's 123 acres is an 18-hole championship golf course, where mature landscaping makes for a pleasant oasis in the desert. Also on the grounds are a putting green, a driving range, lighted tennis courts, golf and tennis pro shops, gift shops, an exercise room, and two pools. Dining options range from an upscale restaurant to a cafe to a clubhouse grill. If you have a chance to wander around the conference facilities

of the resort, you'll notice that meeting rooms are named after illustrious former guests of the San Marcos, including Clark Gable, Errol Flynn, and Gloria Swanson.

Northeast Valley

Carefree Inn $–$$$$
37220 North Mule Trail Road, Carefree
(480) 488-5300, (800) 637-7200
If you like the idea of being close to the mountains near the town of Carefree, this small, nicely hidden-away resort is a good choice. You'll enjoy learning the names and whereabouts of such landmarks as Black Mountain, Elephant Butte, and Skull Mesa. This newly remodeled and expanded resort has 576 rooms, including standard ones with good views, casitas, and luxury villas. Close at hand are several championship golf courses. The inn also caters to bicyclists with tours of the Carefree/Cave Creek area. Spa services, two pools, five tennis courts, a retail shop, a small desert botanical garden, and a fitness center are on-site. The restaurant, Minerva's, is elegantly decorated, distinctively Western, and has been recognized by travel guides. Through concierge services, you can strike out on desert jeep tours, hot-air balloon rides, or horseback riding trips.

Doubletree La Posada Resort $–$$$$
4949 East Lincoln Drive, Scottsdale
(602) 952-0420, (800) 222-8733
www.doubletree.com
As resort swimming pools go, this place has one of the largest around. The half-acre Lagoon Pool features four waterfalls

Live music at the resorts attracts Valley residents and visitors alike. Musicians bring jazz, blues, and light rock to clubs such as Remington's at the Scottsdale Plaza Resort, Different Pointe of View at the Pointe Hilton at Tapatio Cliffs, and the Lobby Bar of the Hyatt Regency at Gainey Ranch.

You don't have to be a guest to enjoy many of the great facilities local resorts have to offer. Many sell day passes to their fine spas, golf courses, and fitness centers. Local businessmen often rent banquet halls and conference facilities for important functions. Dinner at one of the fine restaurants can make for a romantic evening. Call ahead to see what's available.

cascading over big red boulders. Under one waterfall is the weight room and sauna; nearby is the Grotto Bar, if you're seeking a picturesque place for a repast. At a million gallons and the size of a football field, the Lagoon Pool is the largest swimming pool in Arizona and one of the largest in North America, hotel officials say. The resort has many other recreational amenities: a smaller pool, six tennis courts, racquetball, volleyball, and two putting greens. In addition, the resort helps guests get their fill of golf by arranging preferred tee times at off-property championship courses.

At 32 acres, La Posada is relatively small, but it has enough room for 252 casita-like rooms and 10 suites, all with semiprivate patios. The architecture aims for a Southwestern feel by incorporating Spanish and Native American design elements. You'll find lots of archways, columns, red-tiled roofs, and terra-cotta color. Buildings are almost entirely single story, with casitas grouped in quadrants to give the place a residential feel. Restaurant options include the poolside Waterfall Cafe, which serves breakfast, lunch, and light dinner, and the Garden Terrace, serving Mediterranean continental cuisine. La Posada's location at the northern base of Camelback Mountain near Tatum Boulevard makes it convenient not only to Scottsdale, but also to Phoenix and Paradise Valley.

Doubletree Paradise Valley Resort $$
5401 North Scottsdale Road, Scottsdale
(480) 947-5400, (800) 222-TREE
www.paradisevalley.doubletree.com
This is one of the most architecturally attractive resorts on Scottsdale Road. The design incorporates sculpted concrete blocks in a purplish gray for a look that is reminiscent of a Frank Lloyd Wright structure. The central courtyards and pool area of the 22-acre resort are artfully done, with lots of palm trees, fountains, gardens, and waterfalls. The colorful and airy restaurant, EnFuego, offers fusion cuisine with Caribbean and Pacific Rim influences. The 378 rooms all have either patios or balconies. Other amenities include two more restaurants, a lounge with live entertainment, a health club, saunas, a massage service, two indoor racquetball courts, two tennis courts, and a gift shop. The city's main mall, Scottsdale Fashion Square, is within walking distance. Golfing at the McCormick Ranch course is a few minutes' drive away.

Hermosa Inn $$-$$$$
5532 North Palo Cristi Road,
Paradise Valley
(602) 955-8614, (800) 241-1210
www.hermosainn.com
Quietly hidden among the cactus-studded, multimillion-dollar estates of Paradise Valley is the small Hermosa Inn, with 35 casitas and Lon's, an award-winning restaurant, brimming with hacienda charm. The dream project of cowboy artist Lon Megargee, the place was hand-built in the 1930s with adobe bricks, the color of which blends charmingly with the surrounding rock.

Megargee turned it into his home, studio, and guest ranch, and called it Casa Hermosa, or handsome house. Megargee's paintings hang throughout the lobby and restaurant. The inn was extensively renovated in the mid-1990s, and today it's popular not only as an inn, but also as the home of Lon's, a secluded restaurant serving rustic American cuisine (see the Restaurants chapter). Guests of the inn enjoy a pool, outdoor spas, and tennis; golf at nearby courses can be arranged. The four types of casitas, from least expensive to most expensive, are: Rancho, offering one bedroom, a sitting area, and patio; Casita, a king bedroom with a fireplace and patio or a junior queen suite; Hacienda, a one-bedroom suite with a fireplace, wet bar, mini-kitchen, and patio; and Villa, a two-bedroom, two-bathroom suite with a fireplace, wet bar, kitchen, and private patios. All lodging includes continental breakfast at Lon's. The Hermosa Inn is convenient to both central Phoenix and Scottsdale.

Hyatt Regency Scottsdale at Gainey Ranch $$$–$$$$
7500 East Doubletree Ranch Road, Scottsdale
(480) 991–3388, (800) 55–HYATT
http://scottsdale.hyatt.com

Strikingly beautiful inside and out, this Hyatt resort will take you slightly away from the hubbub on Scottsdale Road and into the upscale, lushly landscaped Gainey Ranch—a cluster of office parks, residential development, and retail centers. The main building of the 27-acre resort is a four-story double-H shape, and it houses most of the 493 rooms and suites. All the rooms were fully renovated in 2001. The construction is elegantly modern concrete block and glass with copper and wood accents. A huge, movable wall of glass off the lobby takes advantage of the view— gardens and fountains in the foreground and the McDowell Mountains in the background. The Hyatt's collection of art includes Native American works, bronzes, paintings, pre-Columbian artifacts, and a giant sand painting on the roof of the ballroom. As for restaurants, the Golden Swan overlooks a lagoon, and the Ristorante Sandolo features singing waiters and complimentary rides on a sandolo boat. Golf is available at the three nine-hole courses of the adjacent Gainey Ranch Golf Club. But guests are likely to get sidetracked by the Hyatt's 2.5-acre water playground with its white-sand beach, three-story slide, 10 swimming pools, aqueduct, spa, cold-plunge pools, waterfalls, and other features. The intent is to give guests the feeling of luxuriating in an ancient Roman bath. Also on the grounds are eight tennis courts and the Sonwai Spa, specializing in body treatments inspired by Hopi practices. Jogging and cycling trails are also available. Children can enjoy Camp Hyatt Kachina, where the emphasis is on learning about the culture and geography of Arizona. Deluxe accommodations include casitas and the Regency Club, an area of the third floor where guests receive VIP service.

Marriott's Camelback Inn $$$
5402 East Lincoln Drive, Scottsdale
(480) 948–1700, (800) 228–9290
www.camelbackinn.com

This resort has a lovely, laid-back feel to it, even though it's packed with sophistication and top-notch amenities. A tower above the lobby bears the words "Where Time Stands Still." Guests can relax amid 125 acres in the scenic crook between Camelback Mountain and the Mummy Mountain of Paradise Valley. The hacienda-like resort has earned many awards since opening in 1936. It has needed upkeep over the years, though, with the most recent renovation project totaling $35 million and taking four years. Room interiors were redecorated, and a large pool with fun water features was added, among other things. The property has 427 adobe-style casitas with private patios or balconies, plus 26 suites. Amenities include 6 tennis courts, a golf pro shop, 36 holes of championship golf, and 6 restaurants. The two golf courses are a short distance by car. Also worth noting is the full-service spa, with all kinds of body-pampering therapies. Open since 1989, it was the first spa of its kind in the Valley.

Marriott's Mountain Shadows Resort & Golf Club $$
5641 East Lincoln Drive, Scottsdale
(480) 948-7111, (800) 835-6205
www.marriott.com

Although not an ostentatious resort, Mountain Shadows is a fine choice for golfers. The on-site, 18-hole executive course has nice views of Camelback Mountain and Paradise Valley. Or you can go off-property a short distance to try out two championship courses where Mountain Shadows guests are welcome. Other recreational amenities include three pools, a putting green, sand volleyball, and a fitness center. The resort appeals to tennis players, too, with eight championship Plexiplave tennis courts, which are lighted and open for evening play. The tennis pro can arrange round-robin tennis or match you with a partner. The pro also gives free clinics to resort guests or private instruction for a fee. A sports shop on the premises is stocked with tennis sportswear and souvenirs.

Accommodations at this 40-year-old resort stretch out over several acres to encompass 337 guest rooms and suites, all with recently updated decor. Restaurants on the premises offer a choice of casual meals or fine dining.

Radisson Resort Scottsdale $$-$$$
7171 North Scottsdale Road, Scottsdale
(480) 991-3800, (800) 333-3333
www.radisson.com

Proximity to downtown Scottsdale makes this 76-acre resort an attractive option.

Resorts are all about personal attention, so don't hesitate to sit down with a resort representative to plan what to do during your stay. Most area resorts offer so much you'll probably need their help to sort through it all anyway. Tell the representative what you want: lots of golf? pure relaxations? a chance to see the sights? Resort staff are experts at making you happy. After all, it's their job.

On the premises are 318 guest rooms, villas, and bi-level suites. There are three swimming pools, the fanciest of which is a double-size Olympic pool shaped in an almost perfect circle. The pool is surrounded by deck chairs and palm trees, evoking an idyllic setting. Adding to the generous mix of recreational amenities are 21 tennis courts and 2 18-hole golf courses. Also try the unique 20,000-square-foot Mist Spa for various treatments based on Eastern traditions. Restaurants at the resort are noteworthy: a semiformal dining room called Andre's, serving breakfast, lunch, dinner, and Sunday brunch either inside or on the patio; a French-style patisserie with coffee and pastries in the lobby; and Taps, a pub featuring a dozen microbrews on tap.

An area of the resort called the Arroyo is a small replica of an Old West town, with storefronts and hitching posts made to look like a scene from a John Wayne movie. The Arroyo is used for group functions of up to 900 people, and it's there that the resort caters Western-theme dinners of mesquite-grilled steaks. A full-service spa rivals those at larger resorts and includes Swedish massages, aromatherapy, and body wraps.

Regal McCormick Ranch Resort & Villas $-$$$$
7401 North Scottsdale Road, Scottsdale
(480) 948-5050, (800) 243-1332

A large lake gives this resort a beautiful and almost surreal setting in the desert. Called Camelback Lake, it's open to resort guests who want to rent canoes, paddleboats, and sailboats, or even try fishing. Across the lake is the McCormick Ranch Golf Club, which offers guests two championship courses and one of the Southwest's largest driving ranges. In addition to golf, enjoy a pool and whirlpool, four tennis courts, sand volleyball, and a fitness center. There are 125 rooms and 51 lakeside villas. All rooms have private patios or balconies and feature a Southwestern decor. There are two main restaurants, one of which, the Piñon Grill, serves American/continental cuisine with a Southwestern flair and has won raves from local reviewers.

Renaissance Scottsdale Resort $$–$$$
**6160 North Scottsdale Road, Scottsdale
(480) 991-1414
www.renaissancehotels.com**
This 25-acre resort is tucked into a nice little niche next to the Borgata, an enclave of exclusive shops designed to look like a centuries-old Italian village. That means fun window-shopping and a great restaurant—Mancuso's—are a quick walk away. The Renaissance Scottsdale Resort has a low-slung, adobe look and offers 171 casitas as well as suites. Each of the more expensive suites has a private spa on its patio. All have Southwestern decor with wood-beamed ceilings. For recreation, there are two pools, four tennis courts, and a jogging trail. For those seeking golf, the resort can arrange tee times at one of the well-known championship courses in the area. Choices include the Camelback Golf Club, the Arizona Biltmore Country Club, Stonecreek Golf Club, and Eagle Mountain, all with varying greens fees. The Renaissance Scottsdale Resort staff prides itself on the services to guests, such as delivering a newspaper and complimentary continental breakfast with your morning wake-up call.

Scottsdale Plaza Resort $$–$$$$
**7200 North Scottsdale Road, Scottsdale
(480) 948-5000, (800) 832-2025
www.scottsdaleplaza.com**
This resort, in the style of a Mediterranean villa, prides itself on the way its 404 rooms and suites are arranged to give a residential feel. Lots of arched walkways, stone fountains, and courtyards add to the ambiance. The 40 landscaped acres are in the shadow of Camelback Mountain

When the temperatures climb in the Valley, the prices begin to fall at the various resorts. Summer is when the locals take their vacations at the resorts, enjoying the terrific warm-season values out by the pools. You can wear your sunglasses and pretend that you're a celebrity for a weekend because you'll get the same first-class service that the resort offers in the more expensive seasons.

and afford wonderful views. Its main restaurant, Remington's, is a popular nightspot, while J. D.'s Lounge is an English-style sports pub. For recreation, the resort has five swimming pools, lighted tennis courts, a putting green, ahd indoor racquetball. It has an outdoor whirlpool that is said to be the largest hotel spa in Arizona. The health club has a sauna, exercise equipment, and massage services. For golf lovers, the resort can arrange for preferred tee times at about two dozen courses in the Valley, including Eagle Mountain, Arizona State University's Karsten course, and Scottsdale Country Club.

As for accommodation choices, the range starts with 224 guest rooms, then moves up to 27 patio suites, which offer a private patio overlooking a courtyard. Similar in pricing are the 85 villa suites, which also have private patios. The 58 bi-level suites offer two bathrooms, skylights, and balconies along with the private patio. At the high end of the spectrum are the exclusive Executive Lodge suites, 10 suites offered in four different floor plans. Each is designed as a private residence with extra attention to details, such as four to five telephones, a whirlpool bath, original artwork on the walls, and other fancier furnishings.

BED-AND-BREAKFAST INNS

W ith all the first-class resorts, luxury hotels, and budget motels available in the Valley of the Sun, you might not be aware of the genteel alternative of staying at a bed-and-breakfast. Many seasoned travelers, accustomed to bed-and-breakfast experiences in Europe, New England, and other places, prefer the homier feel they provide. They'll not be disappointed in Arizona. Scenic spots such as the Grand Canyon, Sedona, Prescott, and the mountains near Tucson are filled with bed-and-breakfasts offering ranch-house settings, hacienda digs, and even Victorian mansions.

The Valley of the Sun, however, is another story. You won't find too many bed-and-breakfasts in this metropolis of office parks, shopping centers, and sprawling neighborhoods. Those that do exist operate almost in anonymity, often not known even to their neighbors. Stringent zoning regulations have limited the number and size of these often owner-operated, neighborhood establishments. Ruth Young, who has operated the Mi Casa Su Casa Reservation Service for two decades, says there are a few bed-and-breakfast inns in the rest of Arizona that, like the inns of New England, have 15 to 20 guest rooms and a full slate of amenities. And there are many inns with 10 or so rooms in the rest of the state, but not here. The three commercial bed-and-breakfast inns in Phoenix have five or six rooms, and although they may seem modest by European standards, they offer well-appointed rooms, lovely settings, privacy, and personal attention.

Another accommodation category in the Phoenix area is referred to as host homes or guesthouses, and these are usually operated by couples who have enjoyed traveling to bed-and-breakfasts themselves and now want to reciprocate. They want to show Arizona hospitality to U.S. and international visitors, much like people elsewhere once opened their doors to them. Guests and hosts alike enjoy the opportunity to get to know each other. The hosts lodge guests either in rooms within the main house or in small guesthouses on their property. Private entrances and kitchenettes are frequently available. Guests can take care of breakfast themselves if they want and can come and go as they please. If they do want their hosts to fix breakfasts, they're often treated to feasts of waffles topped with fresh fruit, made-to-order omelets, and luscious pastries.

You'll find that many of the bed-and-breakfast inns are great deals, in addition to being a fun way to see how Arizonans live. Some of the properties have extensive grounds and offer scenic views of the Valley; some have convenient, in-town locations; and some let you see the varied Phoenix residential architecture.

To find out about host homes, contact one of the bed-and-breakfast reservation services listed in this chapter. These homes tend not to advertise and prefer that all their bookings come through a reservation service. That way, the service can ask and answer questions as needed to ensure the guests receive the bed-and-breakfast amenities they're looking for.

In giving the price ranges, we assume your trip will be in high season, from September to May. But if you are coming during the summer, you can find good discounts. Arizona Trails says the low-season rates for the properties it represents can range from $60 to $195 a night. The bed-and-breakfast inns listed here accept credit cards. When choosing a guesthouse, ask the reservation service whether credit cards are accepted.

PRICE CODE

Our pricing indicates the average cost of accommodations during the high season (Labor Day through Memorial Day) minus tax and fees for added services.

$	Less than $125
$$	$126 to $150
$$$	$151 to $200
$$$$	$201 and higher

RESERVATION SERVICES

The reservation services listed here are free to callers. All promise that they have inspected and approved the bed-and-breakfast properties they represent and know them inside and out. In cases where the bed-and-breakfast withholds its address and/or phone number to maintain privacy, we have listed the appropriate reservation service. Roxanne Boryczki, owner of Arizona Trails Bed & Breakfast Reservation Service, says that anyone needing the home's phone number in an emergency can contact the service, which will quickly relay a message. Guests receive the site's phone number and directions upon confirming their reservations.

Advance Reservations Inn Arizona/Mi Casa Su Casa Bed & Breakfast Reservation Service, Tempe
(480) 990-0682, (800) 456-0682
www.azres.com
Ruth Young has owned Mi Casa Su Casa since 1981, so she knows the industry. Mi Casa Su Casa lists more than 250 bed-and-breakfasts in four states but specializes in Arizona. They range from modest homes in quiet neighborhoods to million-dollar homes on large properties. The geographic range includes Phoenix as well as Tempe, Scottsdale, Mesa, Fountain Hills, and Carefree/Cave Creek. Host homes have only one or two guest rooms or a separate guest cottage. Some have magnificent views of the city from the mountain preserves, and some are near mostly undeveloped desert lands. Callers may inquire about heated swimming pools, spas, fireplaces, king- or queen-size beds, and the type of breakfasts served. One guest room affiliated with this service has won an Arizona Society of Interior Designers award. Double occupancy rates range from $75 to $350 a night. There is a one-time service fee of $5.00.

Arizona Trails Bed & Breakfast Reservation Service, Fountain Hills
(480) 837-4284, (888) 799-4284
www.arizonatrails.com
Arizona Trails, established in 1996, handles more than 250 properties around the state. In the Valley that list includes dozens of bed-and-breakfasts inns, guesthouses and hotels in Phoenix, Scottsdale, Tempe, Fountain Hills, and Cave Creek. Owner Roxanne Boryczki says she offers callers a good mix of properties in regard to amenities, location, and price. Many of the bed-and-breakfasts are in scenic locations, even though they might be a long drive from the center of Phoenix. The service keeps track of such things as the age of the house, its decor, availability of kitchen appliances, recreational amenities, convenience to shopping, and tourist attractions, and whether the guesthouse has a private entrance. In addition, hosts are rated on their friendliness, the cleanliness of their accommodations, the safety of the surrounding area, and their breakfasts. You can check out the properties

---

One advantage of staying at a bed-and-breakfast is that many are in old houses, providing a glimpse of how Phoenix residents lived in the days before sprawl. Bed-and-breakfast owners are very proud of their buildings and can provide interesting insights into the architecture and history of the Southwest.

yourself on the Web site. The price range of these bed-and-breakfasts is $75 to $450 a night, double occupancy, and the reservation service is free. Arizona Trails is a member of the Arizona Association of Bed and Breakfast Inns and the Professional Association of Innkeepers International. The service also offers custom itinerary planning.

INNS AND GUESTHOUSES

Phoenix

Camelback Mountain Bed & Breakfast Guesthouse, Phoenix $$$-$$$$
Contact: Arizona Trails
(480) 837-4284, (888) 799-4284

This luxury home perched on the south side of Camelback Mountain was built in the style of famed architect Frank Lloyd Wright. Windows afford great views of the city at night, and interior decoration is contemporary and elegant. The one guest room has a queen-size bed; a cozy sitting area with TV, VCR, and stereo; a kitchenette; a private bath; and a spa on the patio. Also available for use are a swimming pool and game room with a large-screen TV, pool table, pinball, and more. The owners serve a continental breakfast and keep complimentary juices and water bottles on hand. Tee times can be arranged for golfers. No pets are allowed. Smoking is allowed outside the house. Inquire about bringing children.

Harmony House
Bed & Breakfast Inn $-$$
7202 North Seventh Avenue, Phoenix
(602) 331-9554, (877) 331-9554

The Tudor-style Harmony House was built in 1934 as a doctor's residence among acres of citrus trees. Back then it was on the outskirts of Phoenix. Today it offers easy access to central Phoenix. Guests have their choice of five rooms. The Rose Room features Victorian-style decor in forest green and deep rose, a rose-carved king-size bed, a crystal chandelier, and a private bath with a shower and pedestal sink. The Madison Library offers a similar Victorian feel. The Country Garden is upstairs and has charming dormer windows, a king-size brass bed, and a private bath with a pedestal sink, bath, and shower. The Lindsay Room is more secluded, with lots of sunlight, a hunter green decor, a queen-size bed, and an extensive private bath. The Banta Suite has a private bathroom and a knotty-pine bedroom with an adjoining living room to sleep an additional two people. Full breakfasts are served in a family-style dining room or kitchen nook. The Harmony House is a nonsmoking inn. Pets are not allowed. Children older than 12 are welcome.

Maricopa Manor $-$$$
15 West Pasadena Avenue, Phoenix
(602) 274-6302, (800) 292-6403
www.maricopamanor.com

This is an unexpected oasis near the busy intersection of Central Avenue and Camelback Road, and it has been a highly popular bed-and-breakfast inn for several years. The Spanish-style manor house was built in 1928, and the grounds are filled with palm trees and flower gardens. Guests can relax outdoors on the deck, at the pool, or in one of the gathering rooms. The Library Suite has a king-size bed, shelves of leather-bound books, a private deck entrance, and a living-room area with table, sofa, and chairs. The Victorian Suite is done in satins, lace, and antiques and has a sitting room with a breakfast table. The Palo Verde Suite has a large bedroom with a king-size canopied bed plus a guest room with a canopied spool bed. Reflections Past is a large suite with a fireplace in the living room and a bedroom done in periwinkle fabrics. Siesta Suite, with a queen-size bed, offers a large living room, sunroom, kitchen, breakfast area, and private entrance. The Manor Suite is a luxury suite with a three-sided fireplace between the bedroom and living room plus a dining table, chairs, and a desk. The bathroom has a shower and double whirlpool tub. Other suites are offered. All suites have a private bath, cable TV, and telephone. The continental breakfasts feature fresh-baked breads and fresh fruit. Children 12 and over are welcome. Smoking is allowed outside in designated areas. Pets are not allowed.

Southeast Valley

Desert Dreams Bed & Breakfast, Tempe $
Contact: Arizona Trails
(480) 837-4284, (888) 799-4284
This modest Tempe property, about 10 minutes from Arizona State University, offers a two-room suite with a queen-size brass bed and country/antique decor. The sitting room is done in Southwestern style, and the private bath has both a tub and shower. The suite also comes with a mini-refrigerator, microwave, coffeemaker, and TV/VCR. Guests are welcome to swim in the pool. No pets are allowed, and smoking is permitted outside only. Children are welcome. The menu for breakfast varies each day.

Northeast Valley

Hideout at RedBuck Ranch $$$$
30212 North 154th Street, Scottsdale
(480) 471-0011
www.redbuckranch.com
Opened in 1997, the Hideout is hidden in the northernmost reaches of Scottsdale, near the Tonto National Forest and touts itself as a luxurious Western guest ranch. The view stretches uninterrupted for miles and can be enjoyed from the private veranda of the ranch's one guesthouse. Yes, there's only one guesthouse, so you'll get plenty of individual attention. Inside that four-room guesthouse you'll find a bedroom with a custom-made, king-size "mountain man" bed of hand-hewn logs; a

full bathroom with a red, claw-foot slipper tub and a shower surrounded by a rock wall; a living room with a pullout sofa bed, TV/VCR, and gas fireplace; and a kitchen with a wagon-wheel breakfast bar and flagstone countertop. Oh, and don't forget the washer and dryer. The ranch's swimming pool has two waterfalls and a spa. The hosts serve continental breakfasts on weekdays and full breakfasts on weekends, the latter known as a Ranch Hand's breakfast, complete with eggs, biscuits and gravy, sausage, and coffee. Horse lovers will be glad to know that the ranch will stable your horse overnight. For golfers, the hosts can arrange tee times at one of Scottsdale's championship courses. Smoking is allowed outdoors only.

If you're traveling outside the Phoenix area and would like to stay at bed-and-breakfast inns around the state, you'll want to request a free directory from the Arizona Association of Bed and Breakfast Inns. Call (800) 284-2589 or visit www.arizona-bed-breakfast.com. More than 50 locations are listed.

Sleepy Hollow Bed & Breakfast $
5522 East Tapekim Road, Cave Creek
(480) 488-9402
This reasonably priced bed-and-breakfast is in a neighborhood of large properties with desert landscaping. The Sleepy Hollow is at the end of a gravel road, but access to Interstate 17 is only 10 minutes away. It features three guest rooms—two upstairs and one downstairs—in a home filled with antiques and Southwestern wares. The owners also display their antique-doll collection. A porch at the back of the house is a comfortable place for stargazing. Also on the premises is an indoor hot tub. The common living room has a TV/VCR, fireplace, and bar stocked with bottled water and juice. The rooms, called the Owl's Nest, the American, and the Dream Catcher, all have queen-size

Staying at a bed-and-breakfast can be a lovely experience. Often more welcoming and personal than a hotel, the owners are usually longtime residents who love to share insider information about the best places to visit, dine, and shop.

beds and private baths. The Dream Catcher has a sliding door leading to a patio. Breakfast consists of a continental buffet on weekdays and helpings of eggs, pancakes, or waffles on weekends. Smoking is allowed only outside. Pets are not allowed. Children are welcome.

Northwest Valley

Glendale Gaslight Inn $
5747 West Glendale Avenue, Glendale
Contact: Arizona Trails
(480) 837-4284, (888) 799-4284

Antiques lovers will adore this nine-room inn located in historic downtown Glendale and within walking distance of 80 antiques shops. A large lobby features a delightful tearoom and ice-cream parlor, great for relaxing after a day of antiques hunting! The inn is decorated with antiques and all nine rooms feature TV, VCR, refrigerators, coffeemakers, microwaves, telephones, and private baths. Although there are no meals included, the tearoom does offer a lovely buffet breakfast of cereal, juice, coffee, and pastries. Golf packages are also available.

RV PARKS AND CAMPGROUNDS

For those who like to explore the country from a home on wheels, the Phoenix area provides a great place for a break from the highway, especially during the winter months when the desert sun's power has diminished. There are recreational vehicle parks aplenty in the Valley—the Yellow Pages list more than 100. Many nestle in locations with mountain views and come equipped with perks like grocery stores, recreational activities, and spacious shower facilities. Some RV parks are downright luxurious, protected by security gates and enhanced with championship golf courses and resortlike landscaping. The largest of these parks boast between 1,500 and 2,000 spaces. The range of quality and rates offers something for everyone's taste and pocketbook.

Most of the RV parks are in the outlying communities of the northwest and southeast Valley, like east Mesa and the Sun Cities. That's also where most snowbirds, or winter-only residents, like to flock. Apache Junction, a few miles east of Mesa, is composed primarily of retirees who call their RVs and mobile homes home at least part of the year. Consequently, the Valley's RV parks tend to fill with older or retired folks who stay for two to three months, sometimes longer. They hail from snowy climes such as North Dakota, Minnesota, Iowa, and Canada. Repeat visitors often live in park models, which are sized like large RVs and have similar interior appointments, but are not designated for open-road use. Often, these models can be distinguished from RVs by their peaked roofs.

If you're planning to winter in Phoenix at one of these parks, you'll want to make your reservations early—even as much as a year ahead of time. The months of April and October are less crowded than winter. Because space is more available during the hot summer months, you can often find good summer rates if you ask around. If you enjoy your visit to the Valley enough to consider making the transition from resort to RV park, find an RV community you like and reserve a space for the following year.

Some RV parks—especially the large ones with golf courses and other classy amenities—cater to the 55-plus crowd. In accordance with the Fair Housing Act, these parks stipulate that at least one resident of the recreational vehicle must be 55 or older. Although your living quarters won't be multigenerational, these parks compensate by providing a full slate of activities—ranging from softball leagues to computer clubs—to keep their community members busy. In this respect, the scene resembles the lifestyles of the mobile-home communities listed in our Retirement chapter. Folks make a park their home-away-from-home and return to it year after year, developing a sense of community within the neighborhood. Of course, RV parks are pleased to have year-round residents as well. Mobile-home communities

---

You don't need to own your own RV to enjoy the state's wonderful RV parks. Two Valley companies that offer RV rentals are: Cruise America, Inc., 11 West Hampton Avenue, Mesa 85210, (480) 464-7300; and Arizona Travel Center, 5230 East Washington Street, Phoenix 85034, (602) 244-2300. You can also find parts and supplies for your RV in any number of stores on Mesa's Main Street.

A recent survey out of Arizona State University found that 50 percent of the state's winter visitors, or snowbirds, live in mobile-home, RV, or travel-trailer parks while here. Apache Junction alone has approximately 100 mobile-home and RV parks.

that dedicate a certain percentage of their spaces to RVs are another option for visitors, whatever their age. Consult the listings in the Retirement chapter.

The following list of RV parks provides a sampling of amenities and prices and is intended to give a short overview by region. When scouting out accommodations, be sure to ask whether the park accepts only certain types of RVs and if it accepts overnighters as well as long-term guests. Also, many parks offer discounts, such as to members of the Good Samaritan Club, that are worth asking about. For a directory of RV parks not only in the Valley but also near other popular Arizona destinations, write for a copy of the publication *Welcome RV'ers Discover Arizona! 2000*, at 3030 North Third Street, Suite 200, Phoenix 85012, or call the association at (602) 241-8525.

At the end of this chapter, we list options for those campers who prefer car camping or rough camping.

RV PARKS

Phoenix

North Phoenix RV Park
2550 West Louise Drive, Phoenix
(623) 581-3969
This park, in the northwestern stretches of the city limits, is convenient to Interstate 17 and the Deer Valley Road exit. The park boasts 200 spaces to accommodate RVs, with a few cabins available for rent as well. Amenities include showers, a laundry

room, a lounge, a swimming pool, and a store selling propane and other supplies. Pets and children are welcome, and those who desire more seclusion can ask for the no-kids section. Rates are $25 daily, $115 weekly, and $295 monthly, with electricity extra in all cases. Ask about special summer rates.

Southeast Valley

Apache Palms RV Park
1836 East Apache Boulevard, Tempe
(480) 966-7399
www.apachepalmsrvpark.com
This small, modest park with 80 spaces is modern and friendly and will put you close to the action in downtown Tempe. Amenities include a swimming pool, spa, showers, and a laundry room. Rates are $31 nightly and $175 weekly for an elite site with full hookups including free cable TV; rates go down in the summer. Pets are welcome.

Gold Canyon RV Ranch and Golf Resort
7151 East U.S. Highway 60, Gold Canyon
(480) 982-5800, (877) 465-3226
This RV park features 754 spaces right at the base of the Superstition Mountains. It's a bit far from town, but if you like mountain views, this might be the one for you. The 73-acre park is open to those age 45 and older, although most spaces are taken by winter and year-round residents. There's an activity center with swimming and crafts areas, a nine-hole golf course, pro shop, steam room, sauna, and tennis courts. Pets are allowed but limited to one area of the park. Rates are $29 for one night, $190 for a week, $525 for one month, $1,450 for three months, and $3,334 for a year.

Mesa Regal RV Resort
4700 East Main Street, Mesa
(480) 830-2821, (800) 845-4752
A huge, 55-plus RV resort, Mesa Regal offers loads of activities, clubs, and recre-

ational amenities for seniors. Perks include four swimming pools, a library, a computer room, a restaurant, saunas, and putting and driving ranges. The Mesa Regal occasionally has room for short-term visitors among its 2,004 spaces. Rates are $33 per night, $190 weekly, and $498 monthly (electricity extra). A pet section is available.

Orangewood Shadows RV Resort
3165 East University Drive, Mesa
(480) 832–9080, (800) 826–0909
www.orangewoodshadows.com
This 55-plus resort prides itself on its recreational amenities and activities for seniors, including group excursions, shuffleboard, two pools and a hot tub, library, exercise room, and post office. The grounds have more than 800 citrus trees that you can pick from (in season, of course). The majority of its residents are winter visitors who return from year to year. Thus, you should call early to reserve one of its 474 spaces. Daily and weekly rates, including electricity, are $33 and $180, respectively. The monthly rate is $490, and the annual rate is $2,915, with electricity extra. No pets are allowed.

Schnepf Farms RV Park
24810 South Rittenhouse Road,
Queen Creek
(480) 987-3100
www.schnepffarms.com
Here's an unusual find off the beaten path—RV spaces set amid a peach orchard. The Schnepf family leases out spaces for 25 full RV hookups and a large area for dry camping on their 250-acre farm. Guests can partake of the many attractions that bring out locals and others, including pick-your-own produce, a country store, petting zoo, and picnic area. The farm holds several festivals throughout the year and leases its land for the annual Country Thunder country music extravaganza in April, which means some dates are unavailable for campers. Rates are $20 nightly for a full hookup and $12 nightly for dry camping. Weekly

and monthly rates are available; maximum length of stay, though, is 45 days. Children and pets are welcome. Schnepf Farms is open October through March and is closed in the summer.

Tempe Travel Trailer Villa
1831 East Apache Boulevard, Tempe
(480) 968-1411
This 167-unit park caters mostly to permanent residents, who must be 18 or older, except for short-term visits. It's reasonably priced, clean, and in a convenient location near Arizona State University and downtown Tempe. You'll find a laundry area, swimming pool, and showers. Full hookup rates are $25 daily, $140 weekly, $376 monthly, and $2,352 yearly; electricity is extra. Special summer rates are available. Small pets are allowed.

Valle del Oro RV Resort
1452 South Ellsworth Road, Mesa
(800) 626-6686
www.valledeloro.com
This 55-plus park boasts 200 activities each week during high season, making it a popular choice for older winter visitors. A golf coordinator leads trips to nearby courses. Also available are pools, a spa, tennis, a library, theater, and an arts-and-crafts building. The 1,802 spaces have full hookups, and the rates are $35 daily, $195 weekly, $550 monthly, and $3,600 annually; electricity is not included in the monthly or annual rates. Guests are allowed one pet, not to exceed 40 pounds.

Northeast Valley

WestWorld of Scottsdale
16601 North Pima Road, Scottsdale
(480) 312-6802
www.scottsdaleaz.gov/westworld
Horse lovers, take note. This city-owned 120-acre park near The Princess resort is the site of some of the nation's largest horse shows. About 400 RV sites are open to the public on a space-available

Not all RV Parks have space for larger vehicles, and others only have limited space. If you're driving a larger RV, call ahead to check that there's space. Also, some area attractions do not having parking facilities for larger vehicles, so call before you go.

basis. Those traveling with horses can take advantage of overnight stabling too. Those who didn't bring a horse can rent one for a trail ride at Trail Horse Adventures, (800) 723-3538, www.trailhorse adventures.com. If golf is your thing, ask about the 18-hole course, at Sanctuary Golf Course, (480) 502-8200, www .sanctuarygolfaz.com. Pets and children are welcome at WestWorld. Shower facilities are available. Full-hookup nightly rates are $20. There are no weekly or monthly rates since this park is intended for short stays, with a 21-day maximum.

Northwest Valley

Pleasant Harbor RV Resort
8708 West Harbor Boulevard, Peoria
(800) 475-3272, (928) 501-LAKE
www.pleasantharbor.com
Yes, there are lakes in the Phoenix area. This resort is at Lake Pleasant, an intriguing desert setting popular with local boating and fishing enthusiasts. On cool fall and spring weekends, sailors with the Arizona Yacht Club turn out in full regatta and their colorful sails, unfurled against a backdrop of the Bradshaw Mountains, add drama to the setting. The RV park puts you 300 yards from the lake on the east side behind the marina, which is available for those pulling boats. In addition, the 200-space park boasts a clubhouse, an activities slate in high season, pools, spas, putting green, shuffleboard, laundry facilities, a general store, and organized tours. It's adult ori-

ented, but there are no age restrictions. Many people stay three months or longer. All spaces have full hookups, with rates from $28 nightly, $168 weekly, $450 monthly, $1,100 for three months, and $2,700 annually. Discounts are available to those staying longer than three months. Newer sites for larger RVs cost more. One or two pets are allowed per site.

Pueblo El Mirage
RV Resort & Country Club
11201 North El Mirage Road, El Mirage
(623) 583-0464, (800) 445-4115
www.pueblomiragervresort.com
An 18-hole golf course designed by Fuzzy Zoeller is the centerpiece of this 1,200-space resort, which is geared to winter visitors and year-round residents age 55 and older. In addition to golf, guests can take advantage of the two tennis courts, on-site restaurant, pools and Jacuzzis, exercise rooms, billiards, lawn bowling, arts and crafts, dances, and a computer club. With a full-time activity director on board, there's no time for boredom. Full-hookup rates are $30 daily, $525 monthly, and $2,817 yearly. Special spots on the golf course are available at higher rates. Small pets are allowed.

Sunflower RV Resort
16501 North El Mirage Road, Surprise
(623) 583-0100, (800) 627-8637
This gated resort near the Sun Cities is mostly for 55-plus seniors living in park models, who tend to return every winter. About 250 of the park's 1,155 spaces are available for short-term leases to those seniors with any kind of RV. Amenities are ample: an Olympic-size lap pool, spas, a Jacuzzi, a eucalyptus steam bath, organized activities, shuffleboard, tennis, horseshoes, exercise rooms, a wood shop, a ballroom, a library, and modem connections. Pets are welcome. Rates are $39 per day, $243 per week, $561 per month, and $2,856 for a year.

Southwest Valley

Destiny Phoenix RV Park
416 North Citrus Road, Goodyear
(623) 853-0537, (888) 667-2454
www.destinyrv.com
This campground has easy access to Interstate 10, about 5 miles west of Goodyear. This family campground welcomes all ages. Its 282 spaces are open all year and amenities include a pool and spa, shuffleboard, exercise room, classes, and social get-togethers in high season. The rate for one night with a full hookup starts at $35; weekly rates change according to the size of the RV and the season. Two pets are allowed as long as they're medium-size or smaller.

CAMPGROUNDS

The best place for tent camping or rough camping from a truck or RV is in the mountain parks managed by Maricopa County. Not only are they scenic, but they also put you at a distance—though not a great one—from the city's hustle and bustle. The mountains that surround Phoenix aren't terribly tall or verdant with trees, yet they showcase the beautiful Sonoran Desert, with its multitude of cactus species, hardy trees, and wildlife like hawks and coyotes. The parks attract out-of-state visitors and locals for their campsites, hiking trails, horseback riding trails, and picnic sites. All county park campgrounds limit stays to 14 days and generally charge a $5.00 vehicle entry fee. Usually, they ask that RVs be no longer than 35 feet. Note that the heat often forces county campgrounds to close in June, July, and August. Also, Maricopa County does not accept reservations for its campgrounds if you are a small group or individual RV. For large groups, reservations are required. There are no dump fees for those staying in the parks. For information beyond what is listed here, write to Maricopa County Parks and Recreation,

3475 West Durango Street, Phoenix 85009, call (602) 506-2930, or go to www.maricopa.gov/parks.

Southeast Valley

Usery Mountain Recreation Area
3939 North Usery Pass Road,
12 miles northeast of Mesa
(480) 984-0032
In addition to an extensive hiking and horseback-riding trail system, this 3,648-acre recreation area also has an excellent archery range and 50 picnic sites. The area's Buckhorn Family Campground offers 73 sites, several comfort stations, and two campground hosts. A few of the spaces are wheelchair accessible. Individual campsites have electrical and water hookups, a grill, and picnic table. Cost is $18 nightly, including hookup.

Northeast Valley

Cave Creek Recreation Area
32nd Street, 1.5 miles north of
Carefree Highway
(623) 465-0431
A small but scenic recreation area, the Cave Creek park has picnic areas, a horse staging area, and more than 11 miles of trails. Several old mine shafts lie within the park, but they are off-limits. The park has 38 camping sites, all with water and electrical hookups. The comfort stations have showers, and a park host is on the premises. Cost is $18.

During the winter high season, RV parks can be booked up months in advance. Call early to ensure getting a spot. If you can't get into the park you really want, try calling back at a later time; there are often last-minute cancellations.

McDowell Mountain Regional Park
McDowell Mountain Road,
4 miles north of Fountain Hills
(480) 471-0173
This county park, 15 miles northeast of Scottsdale in the lower Verde Basin, rates as one of the most scenic, with an abundance of vegetation and majestic mountain views. Elevation within the park ranges from 1,550 to 3,100 feet. Camping areas are divided into a family campground, group campground, and youth group area, with 76 sites altogether. The nightly rate is $18, including water and electricity. Showers are available.

Northwest Valley

Lake Pleasant Regional Park
99th Avenue, 15 miles north of Sun City
(928) 501-1710
A variety of camping options are available in this 23,662-acre park northwest of the Valley. Popular with boaters, this park contains 25 sites for RVs, and each site has a picnic table, grill, and ramada (an open shelter). The rate of $18 nightly includes water and electricity. There are no dump stations in this county park, but nearby Pleasant Harbor will accommodate that need for a $5.00 fee. For primitive camping, there's space along the lake's shoreline for $5.00 a night. Also, there are about three dozen other sites for tent and RV camping, some with limited access to water and electricity and some with full hookups. Nightly rates range from $8.00 to $15.00 at these sites.

White Tank Mountain Regional Park
Olive Avenue, 15 miles west of Peoria
(623) 935-2505
Comprising more than 29,000 acres of Sonoran Desert mountains, this is the largest park in the Maricopa County park system. Elevations range from 1,400 feet at the park entrance to 4,000 feet at the highest peak. You'll find plenty of picnic areas, ramadas for use by large groups, a

mountain bike trail system, a horse staging area, and two wheelchair-accessible trails. The family campground has 40 sites, each with a picnic table and grill. There are no electrical hookups and no dump stations. Comfort stations have showers. Cost is $10 nightly.

Southwest Valley

Estrella Mountain Regional Park
Estrella Parkway, 5 miles south of I-10
(623) 932-3811
RVers take note—this 19,840-acre park, about 18 miles southwest of Phoenix, not only offers a few areas for rough camping from a tent but has a group campsite with full hookups for seven RVs. The camp is located near tracks for competitive mountain biking, running, and equestrian use. There is a $5.00 vehicle entry fee. Amenities in the park include 65 acres of lawns with picnic tables, a golf course, restrooms, playground equipment, two lighted ball fields, and a rodeo arena. An amphitheater overlooks the picnic area at this park, which is heavily used for group functions. The many trails are for hikers, bicyclists, and horseback riders. The picnic areas, but not the campgrounds, have comfort stations. Full-hookup sites are $18 per night.

ANOTHER OPTION

Lost Dutchman State Park
6109 North Apache Trail, Apache Junction
Near Goldfield Ghost Town,
5 miles north of Apache Junction
(480) 982-4485
www.pr.state.az.us/Parks/parkhtml/
dutchman.html
You will be in the midst of legends and lore about down-on-their-luck gold miners at this 35-site park for tents and RVs, at the base of the Superstition Mountains. Campers will find shower facilities but no hookups. The cost is $10 per night.

RESTAURANTS

Trying to pick a good restaurant out of the Yellow Pages could be quite a daunting task if you're unfamiliar with the Phoenix area. After all, there are thousands of listings. But we're here to help. Within this limited space we describe dozens of restaurants that cover a broad spectrum of choices from upscale, continental dining to neighborhood take-out eateries. Naturally, we had to keep the list to our personal favorites and to places heartily recommended by friends. As a visitor or new resident in the Valley, don't be shy about asking folks for their restaurant recommendations. They are bound to know of wonderful places off the beaten track, and they very well might steer you away from restaurants that are hyped as being great but actually aren't. Why bother with a so-so restaurant when there are so many great places to eat out here?

Restaurateurs are constantly opening places in the Valley, capitalizing on new trends in dining. Breweries serving food have taken off here, as have Pacific Rim restaurants (serving a medley of Asian and American foods with a seafood emphasis). Ever growing Phoenix is an attractive place to set up business, but it also sees its share of restaurant failures. It's a volatile dining scene, which we thought could best be described to you by limiting our list to restaurants that have been open at least a year at the time of this writing. Just keep your eyes open as you drive around the Valley, or read reviews in local newspapers and magazines to stay current on what's hot and what's not.

Be aware that many restaurants cut back on their hours from June to August, when tourist traffic dies down. Realize, too, that restaurants sometimes close suddenly for reasons beyond the quality of their food. Or they change hours. Or change menus. Or change names. It doesn't hurt to call a restaurant before heading to it.

Do call for reservations on weekends in high season, from January to April. Even weeknight reservations might be in order, especially for places with well-known chefs or for those in high-traffic areas such as 24th Street and Camelback Road in Phoenix or downtown Scottsdale.

We've arranged this chapter by geographical regions and types of cuisine. In the mood for a certain kind of food? First find the appropriate geographic area—Phoenix proper, Southeast Valley, Northeast Valley, Northwest Valley, or Southwest Valley, then look for the various cuisine categories under those areas. Try to browse the whole chapter, though, because a restaurant that intrigues you might be listed in one geographic area yet have a second location better suited to your needs.

We created a category called American Fusion to incorporate the many restaurants that succeed on culturally diverse menus—the places that offer pizza next to tamales and sirloin steak next to grilled eggplant. The menus reflect the melting pot that is American food. Mexican food is a regional specialty, so we have included many options in that category. Many restaurants say their cuisine is Southwestern. The term can be a bit vague, but generally it means food that blends Mexican, Spanish, Anglo, and Native American ingredients and cooking styles, usually presented with special touches like brightly colored pepper slices or fruit salsas. To simplify matters, we have grouped Southwestern-style eateries under American Fusion. Folks from other parts of the country and world who want a taste of the Old West—in terms of both atmosphere and culinary offerings—can find those restaurants under the Western category. Casual steakhouses are in this category too. We've also squeezed in a couple of Cajun and Spanish restaurants.

cost of dinner entrees for two, not including beverages, appetizers, desserts, tax, and tip. Obviously, your own bill at a given restaurant may be higher or lower, depending on what you order and on fluctuating prices. These symbols provide a general guide.

$	Less than $12
$$	$12 to $25
$$$	$26 to $50
$$$$	$51 and more

Other categories are Continental and Fine Dining (which includes several luxury hotel and resort restaurants), Seafood, Italian and Pizza, Breakfast, Bakeries, Sandwich Shops, and, last but not least, Asian—in which you'll be surprisingly pleased at the number of Japanese, Chinese, and Thai restaurants. If we have left out a category you're interested in, by all means, check the current Yellow Pages. The Valley is growing increasingly sophisticated in ethnic offerings, and new restaurants open practically every week.

Valley residents often complain that we have too many chain restaurants. Actually, we found in compiling this list that there are plenty of good nonchain restaurants if you take the time to search them out. This chapter does include a few regional chains, names that might not be familiar to you if you hail from the Midwest or East. They are in the list because their quality of food warrants their inclusion. We do not, however, list national chains because you already know what to expect from those places.

Unless we note otherwise, assume that the establishments in this chapter accept major credit cards. Most restaurants have smoking and nonsmoking sections. Wheelchair accessibility is usually not a problem.

PRICE CODE

The price code symbol in each restaurant listing gives you a broad idea about the

PHOENIX

American Fusion

A&J $–$$
**6102 North 16th Street, Phoenix
(602) 241–7519**
An excellent Chicago-style barbecue joint, with ribs, chicken, ham, pork, and all that other wonderful stuff that is supposed to be bad for you. The homemade hot links are especially good. Diners can either eat in at the simple, spare booths (the emphasis is on the food here) or take out. You can order a single plate or a complete meal, but you'd better have a hearty appetite if you go for the second option; A&J's portions are generous. Closed Sunday.

Coopers' Town $$
**101 East Jackson Street, Phoenix
(602) 253–7337**
Alice Cooper, Phoenix's hometown hero of rock 'n' roll fame, opened a casual American eatery near Bank One Ballpark and America West Arena. Billed as "eatertainment," the restaurant/bar features not only rock memorabilia, but also sports memorabilia. Cooper is one of many savvy businesspeople capitalizing on the increased downtown foot traffic associated with the Arizona Diamondbacks and other sports teams. He and his partners have renovated an old warehouse for this restaurant venture. Joining ribs, chicken, and burgers on the menu are two-foot-

long hot dogs, steak grilled on a shingle, and—for the discerning diner—a barbecue feast served in a trash can lid. Look for items served in hubcaps too. (Clean ones, of course.) You can also hear live music here and sometimes famous musicians will sit in with the band. Lunch and dinner are served daily.

Coronado Cafe $$
2201 North Seventh Street, Phoenix
(602) 258-5149
Nestled in a little house, the Coronado Cafe (really more of a restaurant) has become justifiably popular as a lunch destination. The interior is attractively decorated and gives an upscale, homey feel, but the big attraction here is the food, all of which seems excellent. At first look there's the usual assortment of salads, soups, and sandwiches, but the key is in the preparation. Coronado Cafe uses only high-quality ingredients, making a noticeable difference. The portions are generous too. Open for lunch Monday through Saturday and dinner Thursday through Saturday.

Eddie Matney's Epicurean Trio $$$
2398 East Camelback Road, Phoenix
(602) 957-3214
Chef Eddie Matney specializes in bold makeovers of American classics with Mediterranean influences. Examples include a veal chop with sun-dried cherry chipotle au jus; seared tenderloin encased in country mashed potatoes; baked meat loaf; Southwestern-style chicken; and seafood cioppino pot pie. He calls his creations "New American." Lunch and dinner are served daily.

Hard Rock Cafe $$
3 South Second Street, Phoenix
(602) 261-7625
www.hardrock.com
Ogle the memorabilia from the many pop, rock, country, and heavy-metal artists. See the glass-encased costumes from Madonna and Stevie Nicks. Study the

signed guitars from Johnny Cash, Waylon Jennings, Tom Petty, Kurt Cobain, and others. Stare at the Cadillac perched above the restaurant's centerpiece bar. Be amazed by all the signed gold records. Listen to the nostalgic mix of rock music. See for yourself why Hard Rock Cafe is an international phenomenon. And enjoy a decent meal of American and Southwestern fare served by friendly waitstaff. Best bets include the chicken sandwiches and meal-size salads, along with barbecue chicken and fresh fish of the day. Oh yes, the wait for a table is long when it's tourist season. Lunch and dinner are served seven days a week

Omaha SteakHouse $$$–$$$$
2630 East Camelback Road, Phoenix
(602) 553-8970
Familiar with Omaha Steaks International, which sells certified prime Midwestern corn-fed beef through mail order? This is the company's first restaurant venture, and it's a fine way to have someone else cook the T-bone or the rib eye. The restaurant has lovely surroundings in the atrium of the Embassy Suites Biltmore. The menu goes beyond steaks to include shrimp-and-ahi-tuna brochette, rotisserie chicken, rack of lamb, and other items. Side dishes are refreshingly diverse: Lyonnaise potatoes, asparagus with hollandaise, snow peas with red pepper, and more. The steakhouse is open daily for lunch and dinner.

The Original Hamburger Works $
2801 North 15th Avenue, Phoenix
(602) 263-8693
True to name, this casual central Phoenix restaurant dishes out tasty and juicy meat patties, tended to over mesquite charcoal and cooked to your specification. Select what kind of bun and cheese you want, then dress 'em up at the condiment table. Also on the menu are chicken breast and broiled fish sandwiches, and there's a full-service bar. The grill's going daily for lunch and dinner.

Sam's Cafe $$-$$$
455 North Third Street, Phoenix
(602) 252-3545
Reliably good food makes this a bustling
eatery in downtown's Arizona Center. The
restaurant has a Southwestern theme, but
the entrees delve into quite a few different
cuisine categories. Always on the table are
addictive breadsticks served with a spiced
cream cheese spread. Favorite items
include chicken-fried tuna, grilled salmon,
poblano-chile chicken chowder, chicken
Caesar salad, and noodles in a spicy
peanut sauce. The cafe's signature is a
chocolate tamale, your sweet, complimentary ending to the meal—white chocolate
and chopped pecans wrapped in small
cornhusks. Lunch and dinner are served
daily. Other locations are at Biltmore
Fashion Park, 2566 East Camelback Road,
Phoenix, (602) 954-7100; and 10010 North
Scottsdale Road in Scottsdale, (480)
368-2800.

Tom's Restaurant & Tavern $-$$
2 North Central Avenue, Phoenix
(602) 257-1688
Tom's is big on burgers and fries and
blue-plate specials, all of which you can
down while rubbing shoulders with the
mayor of Phoenix and other politicos
known to hang out there. Dark wood,
booths, and a long bar add to the tavern
feel. The restaurant, in an office tower, is
open Monday through Friday for breakfast, lunch, and dinner.

Armenian

Armenia Restaurant $$-$$$
15820 North 35th Street, Phoenix
(602) 863-3300
The Valley has lots of hard-to-find ethnic
restaurants, but Armenian has to be one
of the rarest. Armenia has an ancient culture and has developed its own distinctive
cuisine while taking influences from many
regions. Entrees tend to be hearty and
include kebabs, *julyan* (a soufflé made

with chicken, mushrooms, egg, and
cheese), and *tabaka* (Cornish game hen
with mushrooms and potatoes).

Asian

The Bamboo Club $$-$$$$
2596 East Camelback Road, Phoenix
(602) 955-1288
This restaurant in Biltmore Fashion Park
offers trendy Pacific Rim cuisine in a club-
like atmosphere. The furnishings have a
bamboo theme, and you can opt for
friendly surroundings at the long bar downstairs or more intimate dining upstairs in
the mezzanine. Dishes are served Asian
style—platters come to the table and are
meant to be passed around and shared.
Various kinds of seafood and meats are
steamed, grilled, or cooked in a sizzling
wok. A popular appetizer is the Spicy
Crackling Calamari Salad, which is calamari
cooked in a wok with garlic sauce, peppers,
and mushrooms, then served on a bed of
Napa cabbage. Popular entrees include the
orange scallops, shrimp on crispy spinach,
or Hong Kong steak flambéed with brandy.
Other locations are 699 South Mill Avenue,
Tempe, (480) 967-1286; and 8624 East
Shea Boulevard in Scottsdale, (480)
998-1287. All are open Monday through
Saturday for lunch and dinner and Sunday
for dinner only.

Bamboo Express $
4231 East Thomas Road, Phoenix
(602) 955-1088
"Express" it definitely is, with a kitchen
that whips out Chinese favorites faster
than you can say "General Tsao's Chicken."
Dinner specials include the crispy and
tangy General Tsao's, chicken with broccoli, and sweet and sour pork, all served
with an egg roll, a crab angel (crab and
cream cheese in a deep-fried wonton),
and fried rice. There are two dozen items
to choose from, all reasonably priced.
Lunch specials for $3.50 include teriyaki
chicken and chow mein. Bamboo Express

is suitable for takeout or for dining in. The location is a former bank branch, turned into a pleasant little pastel-toned dining area with green plants and a goldfish tank. Lunch and dinner are served daily. No credit cards.

Big Wong $$
616 West Indian School Road, Phoenix
(602) 277-2870

Authentic foods and a casual atmosphere draw a large Chinese-American clientele. The simple exterior gives way to a pleasant interior that borders on elegant with nicely set tables and lots of Asian adornments on the walls. Many familiar dishes are on the menu, or you can go more exotic with entrees made in a clay pot, such as shrimp with vermicelli. Also recommended are the noodle dishes and steamed chicken in ginger sauce. The restaurant is open for lunch and dinner daily.

China Chili $-$$
3501 North Central Avenue, Phoenix
(602) 266-4463

Don't let the simple exterior fool you, this is a great place for Chinese food. As the name says, many of the dishes are zestier than the average Chinese fare; the spicy garlic eggplant is a local favorite. There's a good selection of soups, meat and seafood dishes, and enough vegetarian offerings to keep the nonmeat-eaters happy. Closed Sunday.

Flavors of India $$
4515 North 16th Street, Phoenix
(602) 277-5546

Flavors of India serves a variety of meals from several regions of the subcontinent. With more than 100 dishes on the menu, including many vegetarian options, you're sure to find something you like. The food generally isn't as fiery as in some Indian restaurants, but, if you want extra spice, the chef will be glad to accommodate you. The chicken makhni, chicken cooked in a clay oven and simmered in a sweet butter sauce with fresh tomatoes and onions, is especially good. Also try some

If you're in one of our many Japanese take-out restaurants, you might notice signs saying that sushi delicacies are not available for carryout in the summer months. This is for your protection, as raw fish can easily spoil in the triple-digit heat.

of the dozen types of fresh-baked breads. Open for lunch and dinner every day. There's a nice lunch buffet where you can fill up for $7.00, and kids 10 and under get it for $4.00.

Gourmet House of Hong Kong $$
1438 East McDowell Road, Phoenix
(602) 253-4859

This is the place for authentic Hong Kong and Cantonese dishes. Be ready for rudimentary decor with Formica tables and tiled floor, but know you're in for the real thing when it comes to the food. Hand-lettered signs on the walls offer lots of specials (all written in Chinese, though). The lunch "Big Plate" is a bargain, with entree plus soup, crab angels, egg roll, and rice for about $5.00. There are lots of noodle dishes for both lunch and dinner. If takeout is your choice, you'll find the service is quite fast. Lunch and dinner are served daily.

Little Shanghai $-$$
4017 East Indian School Road, Phoenix
(602) 957-7666

With all the hoopla that accompanies the opening of trendy Chinese, Japanese, and Pacific Rim restaurants in the Valley, it's easy to overlook the small, neighborhood places that keep on serving regular customers in the same unpretentious style as they have for years. Little Shanghai is such a restaurant—nicely appointed with green plants, primly set tables, and dim lighting, but nothing spectacular. The Szechwan, Shanghai, and Mandarin cuisine is generously portioned and dependably good. Specialties include tangerine beef; Yui-Shan spicy chicken in a cucumber-and-mushroom sauce; shrimp with cream sauce; and moo-shu pork. You can ask for a pot of green tea to be served with your meal. Lunch is served Monday through Friday and dinner every day.

Many area publications publish annual "best of" special issues. Phoenix Magazine, "Get Out," and New Times all run extensive listings of their and their readers' favorite restaurants. Check out their Web pages, listed in the Media chapter, for their online listings.

Persian Garden Cafe $$
1335 West Thomas Road, Phoenix
(602) 263-1915

Persian cooking is one of the great undiscovered delights of world cuisine. It's a bit Mediterranean, a bit Middle Eastern, and a bit . . . something else. The Persian Garden Cafe, which opened in late 2001, has become an important addition to the Valley dining scene. Some of the offerings include chicken kebab, falafel, and steamed veggies. Persians use a broad range of flavorings that are distinct but not too spicy. Saffron is prominent, as is rosewater. The cugurt, a homemade yogurt mixed with cucumber, dried mint, dill weed, and onion, is especially good. There are plenty of options for vegetarians here. Save room for dessert, especially the goopy baklava and the pistachio and saffron ice cream.

Pho Bang $
1702 West Camelback Road, Phoenix
(602) 433-9440

Vietnamese food is the specialty here, so be prepared to sample spring rolls, hearty noodle soups with beef, vermicelli salads, summer rolls, Vietnamese-style grilled shrimp, and other delicacies. Rice bowls are a good lunch option. The ambiance is rather plain, on the order of Formica and vinyl, but tidy enough. Pho Bang, which

you can find in a small shopping center with other Vietnamese-oriented businesses, serves lunch and dinner daily.

Thai Lahna $-$$
3738 East Indian School Road, Phoenix
(602) 955-4658

One of the older Thai restaurants in town, Thai Lahna still packs them in at this small, simply decorated location in an east Phoenix strip shopping center. On the spiciness spectrum, the cooks can prepare your order to the fire-breathing extreme, make it on the mild side, or give you something in between. Recommended dishes include any of the curries, the Pad Thai (thin noodles stir-fried with chicken, shrimp, egg, and bean sprouts), the soups, and the house special of barbecue chicken in a Thai-style chile sauce. Check out the lunch specials Monday through Friday. Dinner is served every day but Sunday.

Tokyo Express $
914 East Camelback Road, Phoenix
(602) 277-4666

Tokyo Express opened around 1980 at a tiny location in east Phoenix and proved to be on the cutting edge of Americans' desire for healthy Japanese-style meals of meat and vegetables over rice. The first location has expanded, and seven other locations have popped up. It has, arguably, the best teriyaki chicken in town—still ringing in at less than $3.00. In addition, many residents had their first experience with sushi thanks to Tokyo Express. We list the Camelback Road location because it's in central Phoenix and because it's next door to an affiliate, the Cherry Blossom Bakery, (602) 248-9090, which always offers interesting tarts, fruit cakes, and carrot cake. Other locations of Tokyo Express are at 3517 East Thomas Road, Phoenix, (602) 955-1051; 5130 North 19th Avenue, Phoenix, (602) 433-1311; 4105 North 51st Avenue, Phoenix, (602) 245-1166; 1120 South Dobson Road, Mesa, (480) 898-3090; 13637 North Tatum Boulevard, Phoenix, (602) 996-0101; 267

East Bell Road, Phoenix, (602) 564–9585; and 9100 East Indian Bend Road, Scottsdale, (480) 948–7500. All locations are open daily for lunch and dinner.

Bakeries

Barb's Bakery $
2929 North 24th Street, Phoenix
(602) 957-4422

While the trendy coffeehouses with big bakery counters spring up in the suburbs, Barb's Bakery tools along just fine at its decades-old location near Thomas Road and 24th Street. It has a small sit-down area for coffee and pastries or spinach-and-cheese croissants, but mostly this is a takeout place for all kinds of muffins, breads, pies, and sweet rolls. The bakery does a brisk business in cakes for special occasions too. It's open Monday through Saturday through the breakfast and lunch hours.

Karsh's Bakery $
5539 North Seventh Street, Phoenix
(602) 264-4874

A busy bakery with an immense whole-sale business along with counter service, Karsh's specializes in Jewish breads—ryes, challahs, and bagels—along with European-style pastries and cookies. Chocoholics will delight in the brownies, tortes, and chocolate coffee rings. Sorry, you'll have to get your cappuccino elsewhere. The bakery is open until 6:00 P.M. every day but Sunday, when it closes at 4:00 P.M.

Old Heidelberg Bakery and
Euro Market $
2210 East Indian School Road, Phoenix
(602) 224-9877

This 30-year-old German bakery recently relocated to new digs closer to downtown and added "Euro Market" to its name to reflect the line of European canned goods, jams, chocolates, and other items that it now carries. The baked goods are scrumptious and reasonably priced. You'll find Danishes, strudels, cookies, and a great selection of hard rolls and breads baked the European way. The store also sells German-language newspapers and magazines. The market is open 9:30 A.M. to 6:00 P.M. Tuesday through Friday and 9:30 A.M. to 5:00 P.M. Saturday.

Barbecue

Honey Bear's $$
5012 East Van Buren Street, Phoenix
(602) 273-9148

"You don't need no teeth to eat our meat," goes their motto. This looks like your typical fast-food joint, but the food is far better. If you choose to dine in the rather basic seating area, you can watch a game and sip a beer. Specialties include pork ribs, chicken, and hot links smothered in tangy Tennessee-style barbecue sauce. The spicy barbecue "Cow-Bro Beans" are recommended as a side order. There's a second location at 2824 North Central Avenue in uptown Phoenix, (602) 279–7911. Both locations are nearly always busy and do a brisk take-away business. They also cater.

Tom's BBQ Chicago Style $
3201 West Indian School Road, Phoenix
(602) 279-8090

Chicago rib tips are the specialty at Tom's BBQ, which has several individually owned locations around the Valley. Meats are slowly cooked over mesquite wood for lots of flavor and are served with coleslaw, potato salad, barbecue-baked beans, and rolls. For those who don't eat red meat, the chicken dinner is a good option. Whatever your choice, you can feed a family of four for less than $25, which makes this an attractive place on weeknights for working couples with starving kids.

Cajun

Baby Kay's Cajun Kitchen   **$$**
2119 East Camelback Road, Phoenix
(602) 955-0011
Surprised to see a Cajun restaurant in the desert? You'll be surprised, too, at the number of desert dwellers who flock to Baby Kay's for jambalaya, catfish, gumbo, etouffee, and other specialties from the red-hot heart of New Orleans. You say it's food with more heat than a 110-degree day? We can take it! Baby Kay's is easy to find in Town & Country Shopping Center. On weekends, just listen for the guitarist playing blues. Outdoor seating on the mall's redbrick plaza is available. Baby Kay's is open for lunch and dinner Monday through Saturday.

Continental and Fine Dining

Christopher's Fermier Brasserie
& Paola's Wine Bar   **$$$$**
2594 East Camelback Road, Phoenix
(602) 522-2344
Christopher's has a sterling reputation for culinary excellence at this prime location at the Biltmore Fashion Square. The cuisine is French based and *c'est magnifique!* Menu items include an excellent truffle-infused sirloin, pasta with house-smoked salmon, seared tuna in red-wine sauce, and wild mushroom and foie gras soup. Of the desserts, we've tried only the chocolate mousse tower, but it was unforgettable in terms of presentation and to-die-for taste. The restaurant serves dinner nightly.

The Compass   **$$$**
122 North Second Street, Phoenix
(602) 440-3166
This revolving restaurant atop the 24-story Hyatt Regency in downtown Phoenix is an excellent choice for those wanting to complement a special night at the symphony, theater, or ballet with a special meal. The Herberger and Orpheum Theaters and Symphony Hall are within walking distance. And the view from the Compass—which makes one clockwise rotation every hour—is incredible. Brass plaques on the windows point out some of the city landmarks you can see from this vantage point. Entrees include roast prime rib of beef, pan-seared salmon, sliced duckling, and pork saltimbocca. Lunch is served Monday through Saturday, when the emphasis is on sandwiches and salads; Sunday brings a fancy brunch. Dinner is served nightly.

Different Pointe of View   **$$$$**
11111 North Seventh Street, Phoenix
(602) 863-0912, (602) 866-6350
www.differentpointeofview.com
The astounding view from the hills of north Phoenix or the regional American cuisine? Which is it that makes Different Pointe of View a great place for a romantic evening out? It's a toss-up, really. This restaurant at the Pointe Hilton Tapatio Cliffs Resort has a terraced design allowing every table to enjoy a good view. (Sunset dining is recommended.) Plus, the menu is certain to please, with entrees such as herb-crusted rack of lamb, tenderloin of Angus beef, roasted Muscovy duck breast, and pecan-smoked venison. The thrill of the evening might be dessert if you choose Bananas Foster prepared in a flaming frying pan. Dinner is served nightly.

Harris'   **$$$$**
3101 East Camelback Road, Phoenix
(602) 508-8888
The eye-catching stucco, red tile, and brick exterior of this large restaurant looks as if it could be someone's lovely Southwestern estate. Inside are high wood-beam ceilings, chandeliers, draperies, and comfortable chairs. Large slabs of meat being hung for dry-aging are displayed behind glass at the front of the restaurant, a reminder that this is a great place for steak and prime rib. The menu also includes lobster, salmon, and chicken. Har-

ris' serves lunch Monday through Friday and dinner Monday through Saturday.

Morton's of Chicago $$$$
**2501 East Camelback Road, Phoenix
(602) 955-9577**
Morton's is an elegant steakhouse with the style and attitude of Chicago transplanted to the desert. You can't go wrong with Morton's prime-grade beef and rib-eye steak. Finish with soufflé for two, available in such flavors as Grand Marnier and raspberry. Dinner is served nightly. Also in Scottsdale at 15233 North Kierland Boulevard, (480) 951-4440.

RoxSand $$$
**2594 East Camelback Road, Phoenix
(602) 381-0444**
One of the big draws in the restaurant-rich Biltmore Fashion Square is RoxSand, a two-level establishment with stylishly modern decor and lots of contemporary art. The name behind the restaurant is RoxSand Scocos, whose culinary creations have put her on the A list of Phoenix-area chefs for several years (see our Close-up in this chapter). The house specialty is air-dried duck with buckwheat crepes, pistachio onion marmalade, and three sauces. Also recommended are the braised veal with polenta and the gourmet pizzas. The vegetarian options are quite extensive too. Desserts such as chocolate tortes and fruit tarts will be hard to pass up. Lunch and dinner are served daily.

T. Cook's $$$-$$$$
**5200 East Camelback Road, Phoenix
(602) 808-0766**
With the recent renovation of Royal Palms, an old-time east Phoenix inn, came a makeover for its restaurant—in regard to both decor and food. The result is a stunner—a beautifully appointed, romantic dining room with top-notch food. The brick walls are painted a soft tangerine color, accented by original tile murals. The focal point of the restaurant is a massive stone fireplace with a rotisserie spit producing many of the signature items on the menu.

The theme is "rustic Mediterranean cuisine," which encompasses items such as rosemary-tied pork loin with baked apples and Tuscan green beans; Cornish game hen coq au vin; and a Mediterranean antipasto platter for two. In addition to lunch and dinner daily, T. Cook's serves breakfasts and Sunday brunch.

Vincent on Camelback $$$$
**3930 East Camelback Road, Phoenix
(602) 224-0225**
Vincent is so well known and respected that it doesn't have to go to great lengths to promote itself. The chef is Vincent Guerithault, a longtime Phoenix resident who some might say put Phoenix on the culinary map. Among his many awards is the James Beard Foundation's "Best Chef Southwest" award (see the Close-up in this chapter). Vincent has worked in different locations over the years but is now settled into a small, modest-looking restaurant next to a convenience store in east Phoenix. The interior, though, is decorated like a lovely country French cottage. The food is known for Southwestern ingredients prepared in a classic French manner. Vincent's signature dishes include duck tamale, grilled lobster with habanera pasta, smoked salmon quesadilla, and roasted corn soup. The menu also features artfully prepared lamb and chicken dishes. Don't miss dessert, with wonderful French pastries and a crème brûlée served in a tacolike shell. Lunch is served Monday through Friday, and dinner is served Monday through Saturday.

Cuban

Havana Cafe $$-$$$
**4225 East Camelback Road, Phoenix
(602) 952-1991**
In the 1980s Chef B. J. Hernandez introduced Valley residents to flavorful Cuban cuisine. Her intimate restaurant has been drawing crowds ever since, and praise goes to such dishes as Ropa Vieja (shredded beef braised with vegetables and red

wine), the moros (Cuban black beans and rice), the paella, Arroz con Pollo (chicken with saffron rice and chorizo sausage), and black bean soup. In the 1990s she opened an offshoot called Havana Patio Cafe at 6245 East Bell Road in Scottsdale, (480) 991–1496. Lunch is served Monday through Saturday and dinner is served nightly.

Irish

Seamus McCaffrey's Irish Pub and Restaurant **$$**
18 West Monroe Street, Phoenix
(602) 253–6081
A friendly little watering hole, McCaffrey's lacks the upbeat feel of Rula Bula in Tempe, but the bar is well stocked and there are British and Irish beers on tap. The food is pretty standard fare with most dishes running about $10. There's live music every Friday and Saturday night. The pub is located next to the Hotel San Carlos.

Italian and Pizza

DeFrancesco's Ristorante **$**
4117 North 16th Street, Phoenix
(602) 279–7409
Look for the red awning to lead you into a warm and cozy home-style dining room. Personal family photographs adorn the walls and the exhibition kitchen is center stage with a wood-burning pizza oven. The family recipes include chicken marsala, tomato basil angel hair, and, of course, pizzas. Open for lunch Tuesday through Friday and dinner Tuesday through Saturday.

Focaccia Phoenix **$**
123 North Central Avenue, Phoenix
(602) 252–0007
Step up to the counter and survey the varieties of plump pasta and simmering sauces behind the glass. Then make your choice. Indecisive types can order a plate with half of one sauce and half of another.

Sandwiches on focaccia bread—using ingredients such as imported air-dried beef, Genoa salami, and fontina cheese— are also top-notch, with a taste rarely duplicated at your local sub shop. Located in cozy, brightly decorated quarters, the eatery fills up at lunchtime with office workers, so be willing to share a table. Open for lunch Monday through Friday.

Lombardi's **$$$–$$$$**
455 North Third Street, Phoenix
(602) 257–8323
If you work downtown and the boss wants to take you out to lunch, immediately suggest Lombardi's, an upscale Italian eatery facing the gardens at Arizona Center. Of course, it's also a fine choice for a nice dinner downtown before or after a cultural or sports event. On the menu are grilled chicken breast, breaded veal scaloppini, scampi with pasta, Italian-style beef tenderloin, and other entrees. Or choose from the assortment of pastas—risotto, fettuccine, cappellini, or rigatoni—prepared with meat or seafood in various sauces. Tiramisu makes a great dessert. Lunch and dinner are offered daily.

Pizzeria Bianco **$$$**
623 East Adams Street, Phoenix
(602) 258–8300
Chef and owner Chris Bianco has won much acclaim for his Neapolitan-style pizza made in wood-fired ovens with toppings such as wood-roasted mushrooms and homemade fennel sausage. Individually sized pizzas, inventive salads, and sandwiches make this a great lunch spot, although you'll have to wait in line with the downtown workers who flock here— but you can always stop in at the wine bar next door. The pizzeria is in a historic building that's part of Heritage Square, next to the Arizona Science Center. It serves lunch Tuesday through Friday and dinner Tuesday through Sunday.

Raffaele Pizza **$$–$$$**
7019 North 19th Avenue, Phoenix
(602) 242–5117

Raffaele's is tucked into the elegant-looking Concord Place office complex at Thomas Road and 44th Street, which offers a pleasant parklike setting. The chef and owner is an Italian named Raffaele Contacessi, who comes up with creative variations on Old World standbys. Menu favorites include a chicken and rigatoni dish in a light cream sauce, seafood in tomato-basil sauce on angel hair pasta, and a dish combining broiled Italian sausage and sautéed chicken in a balsamic vinegar sauce. In addition, Raffaele prepares evening specials. The restaurant is open for lunch and dinner Monday through Friday and for dinner only on Saturday.

Streets of New York $-$$
4757 East Greenway Road, Phoenix
(602) 788-0787
Streets of New York is a 20-year-old Arizona restaurant chain with 17 Valley locations. When you're in the mood for pizza with a bit of panache, this is a good choice. In addition to New York–style pizzas with traditional toppings, Streets of New York offers "Uptown Gourmet" pizzas in varieties such as chicken cacciatore, four-cheese, and garlic shrimp. Calzones, chicken wings, and pasta dinners are tasty too. Most locations have patio seating as well as informal dining rooms where the TV is often tuned into a sports channel. Takeout and delivery are available. The above location is near an Albertsons store at Tatum Boulevard and Greenway Road. Consult the Yellow Pages for other locations.

Mexican

Aunt Chilada's $$
7777 South Pointe Parkway, Phoenix
(602) 431-6470
www.auntchiladas.com
You can tell from the name that this is a fun restaurant. It's gaily decorated and long known for good Sonoran-style Mexican food. Chef Jesse Gonzales puts his heart into the food and uses his family's recipes for solid results. Enchiladas come in cheese,

red meat, chicken, and seafood versions. Of course, standbys like tacos, burros, and fajitas are also on the menu. Whet your appetite with the warm tortilla chips and award-winning salsa. The margaritas—served in a giant cone-shaped, salt-rimmed glass—are awfully wicked too. You can find Aunt Chilada's off Baseline, just west of Interstate 10. Lunch and dinner are served daily. Another location is at 7330 North Dreamy Draw Drive, (602) 944-1286.

Blue Burrito Grille $
4622 East Cactus Road, Phoenix
(602) 787-2775
"Mexican food redefined" is Blue Burrito's motto because it's successfully shown that burritos and enchiladas don't have to be laden with cheese and sour cream to be delicious. The emphasis here is on charbroiled meats, black beans without lard, and vegetarian variations on standard Mexican fare. Many "Heart Smart" meals are available, meaning they're a good option for those watching saturated fats and cholesterol. A family favorite is the Big Blue Burrito, filled with steak or chicken, beans, rice, guacamole, and more, and big enough to serve two. The establishment serves lunch and dinner daily. You can find other locations at 7318 East Shea Boulevard, Scottsdale, (480) 951-3151 and 3815 North Central Avenue, Phoenix, (602) 234-3293.

Los Dos Molinos $$
8646 South Central Avenue, Phoenix
(602) 243-9113
This is a good choice for experiencing fiery hot Mexican food (when in Arizona, do as Arizonans do) and for getting a look at an old hacienda once occupied by old-time cowboy movie star Tom Mix. Enjoy the scenic drive near South Mountain Park while you're at it. As for the tasty menu selections in this family-run restaurant, house specialties include New Mexican-style ribs and green chile enchiladas. Lunch and dinner are served Tuesday through Saturday. Also at 260 South Alma School Road, Mesa, (480) 969-7475.

Scattered around the Valley are small, freestanding taco shops that serve reasonably priced, reliably tasty Mexican food. An added convenience is quick service and, often, drive-through windows. Filiberto's has several locations, but also look for names such as Rolberto's, Aliberto's, and Los Betos.

Manuel's $
2820 East Indian School Road, Phoenix
(602) 957-7540

To those of us who view comfort food as a combination plate of tacos, enchiladas, rice, and beans (with guacamole on the side), the Manuel's chain hits the spot. The restaurant has been in the Valley for almost 35 years and at last count had eight locations. There's festive and colorful decor and friendly, efficient service. If you are watching calories and cholesterol, Manuel's has options such as fajitas and Mexican-style salads. Lunch and dinner are served daily. Additional locations: In Phoenix, 3162 East Indian School Road, (602) 956-1120; 1111 West Bell Road, (602) 993-8778; 5509 North Seventh Street, (602) 274-6426; and 12801 North Cave Creek Road, (602) 971-3680. In Tempe, 1123 West Broadway Road, (480) 968-4437; and 2350 East Southern Avenue, (480) 897-0025. In Glendale, 5670 West Peoria Avenue, (623) 979-3500. In Scottsdale, 8809 East Mountain View Road, (480) 661-1587.

Pico Pica Tacos $
3945 East Camelback Road, Phoenix
(602) 912-0048

Pico Pica is as fun as its name sounds. Although it's a small place tucked into an Arcadia neighborhood shopping center, it's always enlivened by the sound of Mexican pop music and bright interior colors. It's decorated to the max with folk art, Day of the Dead trinkets, Mexican rugs, and paper cutouts, posters, and primitive-looking masks. A Frida Kahlo fan? So are the owners of this establishment, as you can see from the many works of this revered Hispanic artist on the walls. As for food, you'll feel exotic trying the California-style tacos—not just meat varieties, but also potato and fish tacos—or zesty specialties of the house such as mole (meat in a spicy, chocolate-based sauce), carnitas (pork spiked with chiles), and calabacitas (stuffed zucchini). Even the more well-known enchiladas and flautas have a special flair, and the restaurant advertises its use of healthful ingredients. On the beverage end, there are margaritas made from scratch, Mexican beers, and aguas frescas, or homemade fruit drinks. The restaurant is open daily for lunch and dinner; takeout is available. No credit cards.

Richardson's Cuisine of New Mexico $$
1582 East Bethany Home Road, Phoenix
(602) 265-5886

Mexican food of the Southwest has an offshoot called New Mexican cooking, which takes advantage of the range of flavors and heat in various kinds of chiles. Richardson's—through its imaginative enchiladas, quesadillas, and burritos—shows why it has some of the best New Mexican cooking in town. Beyond that, though, it also offers distinctive specialties of the house such as pan-fried top sirloin in a whiskey-lime sauce, swordfish in jalapeño hollandaise, and cilantro paella. The restaurant's seating surrounds a bar, which makes for a lively ambiance. Lunch and dinner are served daily.

Tee Pee Mexican Food $
4144 East Indian School Road, Phoenix
(602) 956-0178

This bustling eatery and bar isn't too exciting on ambiance, but it has been a successful east Phoenix neighborhood hangout since the 1960s. The burritos, tacos, tamales, and chimichangas are reliably good, and this might be the place to try your first Mexican beer. There is another location at 602 East Lincoln Street, Phoenix, (602) 340-8787. Open daily for lunch and dinner.

Sandwich Shops

Kohnie's $$
4225 East Camelback Road, Phoenix
(602) 952-9948

This family-run Arcadia neighborhood lunch spot is tiny, with a few tables inside and a few more next to the parking lot along busy Camelback Road. It's a good place to grab a flavored coffee and pastry on the way to work. The lunch menu offers imaginatively prepared soups, salads, and sandwiches, plus fresh pasta. To accompany your coffee, tea, or soda, try one of Kohnie's scones. At last count, the cafe was churning out 23 varieties, from lemon to raisin to jalapeño-cheese (although not all 23 kinds are available every day). The cafe is open 7:00 A.M. to 2:00 P.M. Tuesday through Friday, 7:00 A.M. to noon Saturday, and 8:00 A.M. to 1:00 P.M. Sunday.

MacAlpine's Soda Fountain and Espresso Bar $
2303 North Seventh Street, Phoenix
(602) 252-3039

In existence since 1928, MacAlpine's boasts an old-time drugstore soda fountain and antique jukebox for good measure. Enjoy the ambiance in this small eatery while trying the hamburgers, tuna sandwiches, cherry phosphates, vanilla cola, and homemade pie. The restaurant is open for lunch only Monday through Friday 11:00 A.M. to 2:00 P.M. and Saturday from 11:00 A.M. to 3:00 P.M.

Pane Bianco $$
4404 North Central Avenue, Phoenix
(602) 234-2100

The first thing that hits you when you come into Pane Bianco is the smell of the focaccia baking in the wood-fired oven in the back. All the sandwiches here are served on this bread, and the restaurant offers salads too. The menu is rather limited, but everything here is made fresh with top ingredients, so it has become a favorite for the lunchtime crowd. Try the sandwich with the housemade mozzarella, local tomato, and basil. You can even order a Bubble Up to wash it down. There are no seats inside, but there are a few on the patio and you can take your sandwich into Cafe Lux next door as long as you get something there too. Open for lunch Tuesday through Saturday.

The Teeter House $$
622 East Adams Street, Phoenix
(602) 252-4682

Unique among Phoenix's many lunch spots, the Teeter House offers sandwiches, salads, and afternoon tea in one of the Victorian houses of Heritage Square, a downtown block of historic homes. The interior is carefully appointed to be a throwback to Victorian times. Long black dresses and top hats are not required, however. Downtown office workers frequently stop by for things like the roast-beef-and-cheese salad or turkey and Havarti on a croissant. Reservations are advised for afternoon tea, in which servers bring on the scones, pastries, fruit, and finger sandwiches to accompany your favorite brew. The Teeter House is open for lunch and tea Tuesday through Sunday.

That's a Wrap! $
2022 North Seventh Street, Phoenix
(602) 252-5051

When the trend of wrapped sandwiches hit America in the early 1990s, this little spot near downtown showed how to create wraps with pizzazz. The selection has grown to 22 kinds of wraps, combining meats, seafood, sauces, and vegetables in several kinds of thin wraps and incorporating flavors from around the globe. The Scottsdale Wrap, for instance, is composed of mahi mahi, shrimp, mushrooms, snow peas, onions, and jasmine rice, topped with garlic sauce and Brie. Accompaniments to the wraps include coffee drinks and smoothies. The restaurant has another location at 2765 North Scottsdale Road in Scottsdale, (480) 941-0484. Lunch and dinner are offered.

Seafood

Steamers $$$
2576 East Camelback Road, Phoenix
(602) 956-3631
The Biltmore Fashion Park location makes Steamers an upscale seafood restaurant, but it's a wise choice if you're hankering for quality fresh seafood, whether it's dinner for two or a family gathering. Recommended dishes include the tuna crusted with mustard seed; prawns stuffed with feta, artichokes, and pine nuts; and the day's fresh catch, grilled to your liking. Meals are accompanied by wonderful cheese scones. Lunch and dinner are served daily.

Soul

Lo-Lo's Chicken and Waffles $-$$
10 West Yuma Street, Phoenix
(602) 340-1304
It's hard to find a chicken and waffles restaurant in the Southwest, but Phoenix is so blessed. Lo-Lo's serves all sorts of combinations of this soul food favorite. You can get your chicken southern style, southern fried, or smothered in gravy and onions. The chicken and waffles can come alone or with grits, eggs, beans over rice, or corn bread. There are breakfast dishes, too, like chicken omelets and breakfast sandwiches. Breakfast is served all day and night, as is the regular menu.

Mrs. White's Golden Rule Cafe $$
808 East Jefferson Street, Phoenix
(602) 262-9256
If you like soul food, this is the place. Since 1964 Mrs. White's has been cooking filling meals of fried chicken, chicken fried steak, fried catfish, and oxtail. Meals come with your choice of sides, such as corn on the cob, mixed greens, and yams. The staff is friendly and welcoming and will show up at random times with free corn bread. The setting is basic, but is livened up with signatures of local sports heroes on the walls. Long a Valley favorite, Mrs. White's gets on lots of Valley "best of" lists. The *Phoenix New Times* dubbed it the "best place to eat if you're starting a diet tomorrow."

Western

Bill Johnson's Big Apple $$
16810 North 19th Avenue, Phoenix
(602) 863-7921
www.billjohnsons.com
Bill Johnson's is a fixture on the Valley's restaurant scene, with lots of red-bandana and cowboy-hat ambiance. The servers wear holsters and toy pistols, so tip big. The steak and chicken are expertly cooked and highly popular due to Johnson's way with barbecue sauce. It's so good it's bottled and sold in stores. For dessert, apple pie a la mode is a fitting ending. Other locations are at 3757 East Van Buren Street, Phoenix, (602) 275-2107; 3101 West Indian School Road, Phoenix, (602) 277-6291; 950 East Main Street, Mesa, (480) 969-6504; 3110 North Arizona Avenue, Chandler, (480) 892-2542; 7322 West Bell Road, Glendale, (623) 776-1900; and 1330 North Dysart Road, Goodyear, (623) 882-8288. Breakfast, lunch, and dinner are served daily.

SOUTHEAST VALLEY
American Fusion

Crocodile Cafe $$
525 South Mill Avenue, Tempe
(480) 966-5883
The Crocodile Cafe's location puts you in the middle of the action along Mill Avenue, so expect crowds on weekend evenings. The restaurant prides itself on "California Cooking," a style combining fresh ingredients with creative marinades, vinaigrettes, and salsas. Many dishes are prepared over an oak-wood grill. The diversity says "California" too—everything from pizza and

calzones to massive salads and Mama's Meatloaf Sandwich. Quesadillas made with chicken or duck are good, as are the burgers and pasta dishes. The restaurant is open daily for lunch and dinner.

Romeo's Euro Café $$–$$$
1111 South Longmore Road, Mesa
(480) 962-4224
www.eurocafe.com
This new, upscale cafe is located in the same building as the Undici Undici Fine Art Coffee House. The menu is long and varied, with more than 20 poultry dishes and 17 types of salad. There's even a whole section for eggplant dishes. Everything is done with good, quality ingredients and in a European style. While you wait for your meal, you can look at the art adorning the walls.

The Weather Vane $–$$
7303 East Main Street, Mesa
(480) 830-2721
Food from the heartland is the theme at the Weather Vane, operating since 1990 in east Mesa. The chicken-fried steak is recommended, or for something a bit fancier at a reasonable price, try the prime rib or fish of the day. Customers come in especially for the restaurant's signature dessert, blackberry cobbler. Lunch and dinner are served daily.

Asian

Happy Bowl Samurai $
5136 South Rural Road, Tempe
(480) 838-2211
The Japanese-language newspapers near the counter and the autographed photos of Japanese baseball stars are a good sign that this is the real thing from the Far East. We recommend the shrimp and vegetable tempura, the chicken teriyaki, and the curry-flavored udon, which are thick noodles served in a ceramic soup bowl. You can purchase items a la carte or obento, which means you get side dishes of egg roll, rice, fruit, and noodles. The

cooler is full of imported carbonated beverages and juices that are fun to investigate. The restaurant is fairly small but more gaily decorated than your typical Japanese fast-food establishment. Lunch and dinner are available Monday through Saturday. No credit cards.

Mint Thai Cafe $$
1111 North Gilbert Road, Gilbert
(480) 497-5366
This tidy little Thai restaurant in a small shopping center is a prime example of the growing sophistication of dining options in the Gilbert area. House specialties include Thai-style pork chops, Sizzling Beef, and a number of spicy seafood entrees. The Mussaman curry, a Thai beef stew, is tasty, as are the chicken satay appetizers and curry noodles. Dessert is cool-down time with a dish of homemade coconut ice cream or Thai custard. The restaurant is open for lunch Monday through Saturday and for dinner nightly.

Saki's Pacific Rim Cafe on Mill Avenue $$$
740 South Mill Avenue, Tempe
(480) 968-7300
You can't miss this restaurant on Mill Avenue—just look for the pillar spouting flames. Saki's has a large sushi bar downstairs that faces an oblong aquarium. The sushi and sashimi varieties number in the dozens—which means you will not only have to ponder whether you want salmon, tuna, eel, scallop, shrimp, or sea urchin, but also what you would like it rolled with and whether you want it cooked, raw, presented in a salad, or tempura-style. You could be there a while. Items beside sushi run the gamut from chicken to filet mignon to noodle dishes. Lunch decisions are a little less complicated, with choices such as chicken curry, seafood tempura, and salmon teriyaki. Similar dishes are available at dinner. The patio upstairs has a misting system to cool down summer diners and heaters to keep winter customers toasty. Saki's is popular at happy hour, where trendies try sake bombers—

Japanese beer with shots of hot Japanese wine. Dinner is served Monday through Saturday and lunch, Monday through Friday. Another location, Sushi on Shea, is at 7000 East Shea Boulevard in Scottsdale, (480) 483-7799. A Scottsdale Fashion Square location, Kona Grill, (480) 429-1100, serves up great food too.

Breakfast

Farm House $
228 North Gilbert Road, Gilbert
(480) 926-0676
A small white farmhouse serving a hearty breakfast from old family recipes sounds too good to be true. But this rustic place still exists even as the once-sleepy town of Gilbert explodes in population. The menu includes eggs, sausage, bacon, pancakes, French toast, Belgian waffles, omelets, home-fried potatoes, and homemade granola. The lunch menu includes sandwiches, burgers, salads, and homemade soups. Or you might catch a lunch special such as meat loaf or chicken and biscuits. The Farm House is open for breakfast and lunch Monday through Saturday. No credit cards.

Continental and Fine Dining

Top of the Rock $$$-$$$$
2000 West Westcourt Way, Tempe
(602) 225-9000
Many view Top of the Rock as tops in elegant dining in the Southeast Valley. It's perched up high as part of the Buttes resort, from which you can correctly conclude that the view of the Valley is wonderful and particularly romantic at sunset. Menu items include mesquite-grilled tenderloin and prawns; pesto-crusted swordfish; and veal chop with saffron orzo. Dinner is served nightly. Sunday brunch is a popular option.

Ethiopian

Blue Nile Cafe $$
933 East University Drive, #112, Tempe
(480) 377-1113
Despite the stereotypes, Ethiopia has a unique and excellent cuisine and in good years actually exports food. With an ancient culture that rivals that of Egypt, it is not surprising that the East African nation has developed a fine culinary tradition. It's hard to compare it to any other cuisine; the taste just has to be experienced. Vegetables and legumes are common, as are stews, chicken, beef, and lamb. The portions are served with homemade *injera* bread, a tangy, spongy creation that looks a bit like a giant crumpet. The food is an interesting blend of spices that are flavorful more than hot. Open for lunch and dinner Tuesday through Sunday, closed Monday.

Irish

Rula Bula: Tempe Irish Pub and Restaurant $$
401 South Mill Avenue, Tempe
(480) 929-9500
www.rulabula.com
The closest thing you'll find to a real Irish pub in Arizona. The wooden bar was made in Ireland, shipped to Phoenix, and reassembled in a historic 19th-century building on Mill Avenue. A variety of Old World drinks are on tap and are served in real European pint glasses, not those undersized American "pints." Choose from a great selection of pub dishes from $8.00 to $23.00. The corned beef is excellent and they bake their own soda bread. On Friday and Saturday nights the place is packed for genuine Irish music and dancing. Bands sometimes show up on other days too. Phoenix isn't exactly the Emerald Isle, but it does have some good Irish acts. Open daily from 11:00 A.M. to 1:00 A.M.

Mexican

Guedo's Taco Shop $
71 East Chandler Boulevard, Chandler
(480) 899-7841

Some say Guedo's (pronounced WE-do) has the best soft-shell tacos around. The freshly made corn and flour tortillas are delicious, and the meat is tender and saucy. Cheese crisps are also a good choice and can be filled with beans, chiles, sour cream, avocado, or a combination. For beverages, check out the good selection of Mexican soda pop and beers, or try horchata, a milky, cinnamon-flavored drink. The salsa bar—with three kinds of salsa, lime slices, onions, shredded cabbage, and cilantro for dressing up your tacos—is attractively draped with a serape, and the colors of the Mexican flag are put to good use in the decor. The Chandler location, in an adobe-style building, is a bit cramped, but you have your choice of indoor or patio seating. Lunch and dinner are served Tuesday through Saturday. Guedo's other locations are 603 West University Drive, Tempe, (480) 317-0115; and 747 North Val Vista Drive, Gilbert, (480) 633-7899.

Macayo Depot Cantina $$
300 South Ash Avenue, Tempe
(480) 966-6677

Macayo's Mexican Restaurants is a family-owned chain that has been operating in Arizona for more than 50 years. It has seven locations in the Valley—all with a colorful, south-of-the-border feel—but we like this one because it has the added attraction of having been transformed from the old Tempe railroad station. The tracks are still just a few steps away. Many of the architectural details of the territorial-style depot have been preserved. Also, the outdoor seating creates a great cantina atmosphere on most balmy evenings. The food is hearty, and we recommend the chimichangas and fajitas. Macayo's also sells special margarita mugs. Additional

locations: 11107 North Scottsdale Road, Scottsdale, (480) 596-1181; 4001 North Central Avenue, Phoenix, (602) 264-6141; 1909 West Thunderbird Road, Phoenix, (602) 866-7034; 7829 West Thomas Road, Phoenix, (602) 873-0313; 115 South Roosevelt Avenue, Chandler, (480) 705-4531; 1920 South Dobson Road, Mesa, (480) 820-0237; 6012 West Bell Road, Glendale, (602) 298-8080; and 12637 South 48th Street, Ahwatukee, (480) 598-5101. All are open daily for lunch and dinner.

Serrano's $-$$
1955 West Guadalupe Road, Mesa
(480) 756-2992

If you're feeling a bit out of the loop as to exactly what Sonoran-style Mexican food is, here's a good place to learn all about it and please your palate in the process. Serrano's is an established local chain with concentration in the Southeast Valley. The extensive menu has many dishes featuring shredded and cubed meats served the Sonoran way with lots of cheese and chiles. They come wrapped in corn or flour tortillas, with spicy rice and refried beans on the side. In addition to the requisite enchiladas, tacos, quesadillas, and burritos, find especiales de la casa such as carnitas, thin slices of charbroiled pork loin, and Pollo Rojo, charbroiled chicken breast covered with a spicy sauce. All meals are preceded by tasty tortilla chips served with a nice chunky salsa and a bean-and-cheese dip. Don't go overboard on those, though, because Serrano's portions are huge and Sonoran food is very filling. The restaurant is open daily for lunch and dinner. Additional locations: 141 South Arizona Avenue, Chandler, (480) 899-3318; 6440 South Rural Road, Tempe, (480) 345-0044; 1964 East McKellips Road, Mesa, (480) 649-3503; 1021 South Power Road, Mesa, (480) 854-7455; 959 North Val Vista Drive, Gilbert, (480) 507-5027; and 3941 East Chandler Boulevard, Chandler, (480) 706-8442.

The Valley's Celebrity Chefs

Rarely does a week go by in the columns of the Phoenix area news media that a local chef is not mentioned. Will RoxSand win that national culinary award? Will Eddie redo the interior of his restaurant? Will Christopher change his fall menu?

Gossip columnists and restaurant reviewers write about chefs with such regularity and familiarity because so many have been elevated to the status of celebrity chefs. Several have achieved national fame, winning prestigious culinary awards, writing cookbooks, and even appearing on cable TV food shows.

Thanks to the growing sophistication of the Phoenix area's restaurant scene over the last decade, many of the country's best and brightest chefs have settled here to work or have added locations of their restaurant chains here. And the Valley benefits from their presence.

You're probably curious about which "name" chefs are associated with the Valley. Here's a quick rundown of who's who, who's where, and who's hot.

One of the Phoenix area's best-loved chefs, Eddie Matney, known for his delicious twists on standard American food, is a popular character in his own right. Visit his restaurant, Eddie Matney's Epicurean Trio, and you're almost sure to see him walking around the room, greeting regulars, and making new friends. He's energetic and passionate about his work. Matney's ebullience about food and frequent public appearances helped stir up business for his restaurant.

Christopher Gross has worked in the Valley since the 1970s and has apprenticed with chefs in California, England, and France. His knowledge of classic and international cooking methods helped make Christopher's an enormous success. Gross was the 1995 winner of the Best Chef in the Southwest award from the James Beard Foundation and has been featured in national food magazines.

Things are cooking as well at Vincent on Camelback, opened in 1986 by nationally known chef Vincent Guerithault, at 40th Street and Camelback Road. This is a favorite destination for Valley residents seeking a special night out enjoying Southwest and French cuisine in intimate surroundings. In a 30-year career, Guerithault has received several awards, including the nod from the James Beard Foundation. Longtime Valley residents know of Vincent's work at other restaurants from the early 1980s. Many consider him the grand master of the Valley's community of chefs. It's interesting to note that, as a teenager in France, Guerithault once worked alongside Wolfgang Puck.

Sandwich Shops

Pita Jungle   **$-$$**
1250 East Apache Boulevard, Tempe
(480) 804-0234

If you would just as soon have your sandwich on pita bread, this place is for you. It's popular with vegetarians, but chicken, turkey, and tuna are on the menu as well, in sandwich concoctions that show a Greek and Italian influence. Specialties

One globally known chef who opened a restaurant here in 1998 was Roy Yamaguchi. Roy's Restaurant, part of an international chain serving Pacific Rim food with a Hawaiian influence, opened in Scottsdale and immediately drew crowds. His restaurant and concept proved so popular, he opened another location at the Camelback Esplande.

As for the Valley's own celebrity chefs, at the top of the list is RoxSand Scocos, whose restaurant, RoxSand, at Biltmore Fashion Park, is always packed and always a culinary adventure. Scocos, a James Beard Award nominee, is known for fusion cuisine that explores Southwestern, Asian, and French cooking. She is frequently involved in community events featuring chefs.

Erasmo "Razz" Kamnitzer began working in the Phoenix area in the 1980s and in 1995 opened Razz's Restaurant and Bar, featuring contemporary international cuisine based on French and classic cooking techniques. The Venezuelan-born Kamnitzer is a seventh-generation chef, and Razz's north Scottsdale customers like the effusive personality he injects into his work. He loves talking food with dinner guests. He has appeared on cable TV's Food Network and has been written up in national food magazines. Kamnitzer and his wife, Bobbi Jo Haynes, founded a charity event—a combination gourmet dinner and art auction—that annually raises money to fight sexual abuse.

Other local star-chefs include James Boyce of the four-star contemporary French restaurant Mary Elaine's at the Phoenician; Michael DeMaria of Michael's at the Citadel, offering funky New American fare; Michale Hoobler at the acclaimed (and tiny) Valencia Lane; the brilliant fusion chef James McDevitt of Restaurant Hapa; and Mark Tarbell at the superpopular Tarbell's.

If you're around the Valley long enough, you will frequently hear chefs' names mentioned in conjunction with charity events. Chefs have gathered together to help raise money for the American Heart Association, as well as for an Arizona charity supporting emotionally troubled teens.

A PBS television series called *Savor the Southwest* brought further limelight to some of the chefs mentioned here. The 13-part series featured Southwestern chefs including: Guerithault, Scocos, Wiley, Lenny Rubin of Medizona, and Robert McGrath of the Roaring Fork.

As a visitor or newcomer to the Valley, keep your eyes and ears open for news about these chefs and others. It's a good way to get to know the best restaurants in town. You also can learn about these chefs' culinary creations in more detail by picking up *The Arizona Chefs' Dine In—Dine Out Cookbook,* featuring 140 recipes from 35 chefs from around the state. The cookbook is available from AJ's Fine Foods, a Valley chain of upscale grocery stores.

include falafel, baba ghanoush (broiled eggplant), and stuffed grape leaves. The hummus with garlic is especially good. The restaurant is fairly small and made intimate by lots of paintings and photographs by local artists on the walls. Pita Jungle is in a funky little shopping center near Arizona State University that also houses a tattoo parlor. The restaurant is open daily for breakfast, lunch, and dinner. A second location is at 1949 West Ray Road in Chandler, (480) 855-3232.

NORTHEAST VALLEY

American Fusion

Arcadia Farms $$
7014 and 7007 East First Avenue, Scottsdale
(480) 941-5665

Arcadia Farms occupies two restored homes across the street from each other in downtown Scottsdale and serves American, bistro-style dishes. There is both indoor and outdoor seating, but when the weather is nice it's hard to resist the patio dining amid the lovely trees on the grounds. The menu ranges from grilled shrimp skewers to salmon medallions on soba noodles to grilled beef tenderloin. The homemade breads and desserts are quite enjoyable. Lunch and dinner are served Monday through Saturday.

Arizona Bread Company $$
7000 East Shea Boulevard, Scottsdale
(480) 948-8338
www.azbread.com

Since 1994 Arizona Bread Company has served a wide variety of fresh artisan breads. Lots of customers pop in after work to get a loaf to take home. You can also eat in at the cafe where they serve sandwiches, soups, and salads. Local soup favorites include vegetable beef barley, chicken noodle, and pasta fagioli. There's another location at 23587 North Scottsdale Road. Open for lunch and dinner on weekdays, lunch only on weekend. Summer hours are often shorter, so call ahead.

Bandera $$
3821 North Scottsdale Road, Scottsdale
(480) 994-3524

Generous portions and reasonable prices—not to mention the best rotisserie chicken we've tasted—make this a popular spot in Old Town Scottsdale. Be sure to try the country-style mashed potatoes with chives, the chile corn bread, and the coleslaw with peanut dressing. The wild mushroom meat loaf is another popular entree. The restaurant is open daily for dinner only. If you're in the mood for a take-out dinner, Bandera has a very efficient drive-through service; call ahead to order, and they'll have it ready for you when you drive up.

Drift $$-$$$
75th Street and Stetson Drive, Scottsdale
(480) 949-8454
www.driftlounge.com

The Valley's newest tiki lounge serves exotic drinks and food in a chic but casual atmosphere. The outdoor patio is pleasant in the evenings, with tiki torches dimly lighting your *pu pu* platters. The drinks come in various weird cups, from the Witch Doctor (a rum and juice mixture served in a skull) to the Grotto (a four-person drink made of just about everything and served in a ceramic tropical lagoon). The drinks are a bit pricey, but they're tasty and add to the atmosphere. Unfortunately, you don't get to keep the cups. The food ranges from standard to spicy and includes various sandwiches and salads featuring tropical fruits and island-inspired glazes. Dig in, the tiki gods will smile upon you.

The Palo Verde $$$$
34631 North Tom Darlington Drive, Carefree
(480) 488-9009

Bright interior colors and lovely views of the Valley from the hills of The Boulders resort make the Palo Verde a good choice, especially if you're intrigued by Southwestern cooking at its toniest. Specialties include smoked lamb shank with pumpkin puree; marinated Arizona ostrich with salsa; pan-roasted snapper with cactus tartar sauce; and red-chile marinated quail. Lunch dishes are a little more mainstream, tending toward salads, sandwiches, and pastas served on thick ceramic plates. Breakfast and lunch are served daily.

Piñon Grill $$$
7401 North Scottsdale Road, Scottsdale
(480) 367-2422

Setting and food make for a memorable experience at Piñon Grill, which is in the Regal McCormick Ranch resort. We suggest seating on the patio, with its romantic views of a large artificial lake. The interior of the restaurant is nice, too, with a Southwestern-casual feel. Entree favorites include the Baked Mexican Shrimp, butterfly shrimp stuffed with spinach and goat cheese; ahi tuna steak with cantaloupe salsa; and veal chop marinated in lime and chiles. Side dishes and corn bread are tastefully presented. Rounding out the fare are innovative appetizers—scallops on blue tortilla shells, for example—chile corn bread, prickly pear margaritas, and yummy dessert crepes. Dinner is served nightly.

Roaring Fork $$$$
4800 North Scottsdale Road, Scottsdale
(480) 947-0795

Named after a river in Colorado, this restaurant is under the steady hand of Chef Robert McGrath. The food concept is described as American Western cuisine so you can enjoy a cast-iron skillet of corn bread with each meal, smoked trout on buttermilk corn cakes, and rib-eye steak slathered in blueberry barbecue sauce. If you're hungry, try the Big-Ass hamburger. Lunch and dinner are served daily.

Rock Bottom Restaurant & Brewery $$
8668 East Shea Boulevard, Scottsdale
(480) 998-7777
www.rockbottom.com

This microbewery was formerly Hops!, but has been remodeled and features an expanded menu. The varieties run the gamut from light, fruit-flavored beers (raspberry ale, for instance) to dark ales and stouts. The food is a pleasing blend of pastas and pizzas, and steak, seafood, and chicken specialties, many of them prepared with the house beers. Lunch and dinner are served daily.

Windows on the Green $$$$
6000 East Camelback Road, Scottsdale
(480) 423-2530

The award-winning chefs at the Phoenician demonstrate their expertise with Southwestern fare at this semicasual restaurant overlooking the resort's golf course. The menu emphasizes indigenous ingredients, such as cilantro, jicama, and nopales cactus combined with traditional meats and wild game. Try the free-range chicken with red chile-honey glaze. There's also a good international wine list. Lunch and dinner are served daily.

Asian

Malee's on Main $$
7131 East Main Street, Scottsdale
(480) 947-6042

Some find this restaurant a bit on the snooty side, being as it is in the heart of Scottsdale's gallery district. We don't recommend it for families with young children, but we can say it has dependably good and artfully served Thai dishes, ranging from meats in lemongrass and mint to satays to curries. Thai iced tea with or without cream makes a most soothing accompaniment if you like your dishes spicy. Malee's (pronounced MAH-ly) is open daily for lunch and dinner.

Roy's Pacific Rim Cuisine $$$
7001 North Scottsdale Road, Scottsdale
(480) 905-1155

Born and raised in Japan and now based in Hawaii, chef and author Roy Yamaguchi has achieved international fame for his cuisine combining elements of European cooking, Pacific seafood, and Asian ingredients and seasonings (see the Close-up in this chapter). A few menu examples: lemongrass tempura chicken with Thai sticky rice; blackened ahi tuna; oak-fired filet mignon; and duck pizza. If you're tantalized enough to try it, we suggest making reservations well in advance. Dinner is served nightly and lunch, Monday through

Small, family-owned restaurants have a tough time everywhere, the Valley included. If you find a place you like, do them a favor and tell your friends. You aren't just helping your friends find a good meal, you're helping a local entrepreneur stay afloat.

Friday. Roy's has a second location at the Camelback Esplanade, 2501 East Camelback Road, in Phoenix, (602) 381-1155.

Barbecue

Don & Charlie's $$
7501 East Camelback Road, Scottsdale
(480) 990-0900
Just remember this four-letter word when considering Don & Charlie's—ribs. Many locals say this longtime establishment in downtown Scottsdale serves the best-tasting ribs around. The prime rib, New York sirloin, and lamb chops are also recommended. Sports memorabilia sets the pace for the decor. Don & Charlie's is open for dinner only, but they're open seven days a week.

El Paso Bar-B-Que Company $$-$$$
8220 North Hayden Road, Scottsdale
(480) 998-2626
For "bar-b-que with an attitude" this restaurant has become quite popular among Valley residents. Special seasonings and the low heat of a pecan-wood pit are the secrets to El Paso's success, the menu explains. We've enjoyed the baby back ribs, beef ribs, and smoked chicken, but be forewarned that the portions are humongous. For something a little different, try the barbecue salmon or lamb barbacoa, which is smoked overnight, Mexican-style. There are sandwich, salad, and burger selections, along with a kid's menu and plenty of alcoholic and nonalcoholic beverages. The decor in the huge Scottsdale location is fairly sophisticated

for a barbecue house—with Southwestern fabrics, log columns, ironwork accents, and cowboy paintings. Lunch and dinner are served daily. Other locations: 4921 East Ray Road, Ahwatukee, (480) 705-5050; 1641 South Stapley Drive, Mesa, (480) 507-7400; and 4303 West Peoria Avenue, Glendale, (623) 931-2438.

Breakfast

First Watch $
4422 North 75th Street, Scottsdale
(480) 941-8464
First Watch gets your day going with an extensive selection of egg dishes and pancakes. There are also several heart-healthy options. Oak furniture and contemporary country decor give it a homey feel. And the constantly poured coffee and tea help you kick it into gear too. It's open seven days a week for breakfast and lunch. Other locations: 9645 North Black Canyon Highway, Phoenix, (602) 943-3232; 1 North First Street, downtown Phoenix, (602) 340-9089; and 61 West Thomas Road, Phoenix, (602) 265-2092.

The Good Egg $
6149 North Scottsdale Road, Scottsdale
(480) 991-5416
Breakfast dishes are imaginatively prepared at this regional chain whose restaurants go by either The Good Egg or The Eggery. You can find omelets, pancakes, and waffles, along with frittatas, a lighter version of omelets called "crepeggs," and Mexican specialties such as huevos rancheros. Many menu items meet nutritionists' guidelines for low-cholesterol meals. Breakfast and lunch (primarily sandwiches and salads) are served daily. This Good Egg is conveniently located in the Hilton Village shopping area. Other locations: 2957 West Bell Road, Phoenix, (602) 993-2797; Park Central Mall, Thomas Road and Central Avenue, Phoenix, (602) 248-3897; 906 East Camelback Road, Phoenix, (602) 274-5393; 13802 North Scottsdale

Road, Scottsdale, (480) 483-1090; 1665 South Dobson Road, Mesa, (480) 831-9044; and 34422 North Scottsdale Road, Scottsdale, (480) 595-1044. Find The Eggery at 5109 North 44th Street, Phoenix, (602) 840-5734; 4326 East Cactus Road, Phoenix, (602) 953-2342; and 50 East Camelback Road, Phoenix, (602) 263-8554.

The Original Pancake House $
6840 East Camelback Road, Scottsdale
(480) 946-4902

Oven-baked apple pancakes and Dutch Babies are a specialty at this cheery breakfast place next to a Motel 6. The crepes are also a good bet as are, naturally, the good ol' buttermilk pancakes. Hours are 7:00 A.M. to 2:00 P.M. daily. There's another location at 402 East Greenway Parkway, Phoenix, (602) 896-9805.

Continental and Fine Dining

Golden Swan $$$$
7500 East Doubletree Ranch Road, Scottsdale
(480) 991-3388

Travel magazines have bestowed accolades upon the Golden Swan, the centerpiece restaurant of the Hyatt Regency Scottsdale. Chefs specialize in regional American cuisine while allowing distinctively local ingredients and cooking traditions to shine through. Examples include beef fajitas with Southwestern herb butter; grilled lamb chop glazed with jalapeño honey mustard and rolled in pistachios; and herb-marinated range chicken baked in an Arizona red-clay pot. The restaurant has a Euro-contemporary feel, with marble and stone floors, ceiling-high glass walls, and black and jewel tones as color accents. Outdoor dining is in a charming pavilion alongside a lagoon inhabited by black swans. Brunch and dinner are offered daily. At brunch you can tour the kitchen and meet the master chef.

Lon's at the Hermosa $$$
5532 North Palo Cristi Road, Paradise Valley
(602) 955-7878

You can get away from it all at this intimate Southwestern-style dining room at the Hermosa Inn, which is tucked into a Paradise Valley residential area. The restaurant is named for Lon Megargee, a cowboy artist who developed this property as a hacienda and studio, then turned it into lodging. The contemporary cuisine features pan-seared scallops on broccoli risotto; breast of duck with foie gras sauce; and wood-grilled salmon with polenta. Lunch and dinner are served Sunday through Friday; it's dinner only on Saturday.

The Marquesa $$$$
7575 East Princess Drive, Scottsdale
(480) 585-2723

Imagine yourself in the Catalonia region of Spain, dining on the finest of regional food, immaculately presented. That's what you'll experience at The Marquesa, one of the Valley's best restaurants. The surroundings are Old World elegant, almost museum-like with the many paintings on the walls. Fare includes sweet red peppers stuffed with crabmeat and cheese; monkfish in a tomato tapenade and white bean sauce; and Paella Valenciana, which is lobster, chicken, pork, shellfish, and Spanish sausage in saffron rice. Dinner is served nightly. The Marquesa is also recognized for its wonderful outdoor Sunday brunch, which exudes a Spanish-marketplace air. The restaurant is closed mid-June through mid-September.

Mary Elaine's $$$$
6000 East Camelback Road, Scottsdale
(480) 941-8200, (480) 423-2530

This is one of the Valley's most celebrated restaurants, thanks to the extraordinary food and special ambiance at the Phoenician resort. You'll be bowled over by the modern French cuisine of Mary Elaine's. The menu changes seasonally, but can include dishes such as Dover sole, squab, rack of lamb, and veal tenderloin. The elegant rooms that form Mary Elaine's have splendid views of the city lights, and all around are gold-framed paintings and sparkling chandeliers. This may be the priciest restaurant in the Valley, but everyone agrees it's worth it! Dinner is served Monday through Saturday.

Razz's Restaurant & Bar $$$
10315 North Scottsdale Road, Scottsdale
(480) 905–1308

Razz's is named for its chef, Erasmo "Razz" Kamnitzer, a Venezuelan and seventh-generation restaurateur who believes in healthy cooking with pizzazz (see the Close-up in this chapter). He uses all kinds of meats, seafood, produce, pasta, herbs, and spices to produce meals low in cholesterol and fat yet intense in flavor. Examples include duck cakes, escargot Bourguignone, nut-encrusted roasted pork tenderloin, halibut Veracruz, and ahi tuna with seasoned soba noodles. Kamnitzer is an exuberant man who likes to schmooze with his customers, which makes Razz's a fun place for a great meal. Dinner is served Tuesday through Saturday.

Italian and Pizza

California Pizza Kitchen $$
10100 North Scottsdale Road, Scottsdale
(480) 596–8300

Pizza with zing is how we think of CPK's selection of more than two dozen wood-fired pizzas, in flavors such as Thai chicken, shrimp scampi, grilled eggplant, and even the less adventurous pepperoni. The menu for this western U.S. chain of restaurants also includes unique pasta dishes—would you believe kung pao spaghetti?—and nicely presented salads. Other locations are at 3163 West Chandler Boulevard, Chandler, (480) 855–3301; 21001 North Tatum Boulevard, Phoenix (480) 473–3336; and 2400 East Camelback Road, Phoenix, (602) 553–8382. Lunch and dinner are available daily.

NYPD Pizza $$$
8880 East Via Linda, Scottsdale
(480) 451–6973

Don't puzzle too long over why a restaurant goes by "NYPD" in the middle of Scottsdale. It stands for New York Pizza Dept., and the pies are made from Old World recipes—Old World as in Brooklyn, not Italy. Order the Greenwich Village (spinach, Roma tomatoes, and garlic), the Pizza Blanca (a white pizza featuring ricotta), or Da Works with, you know, the works. Or fahgeddaboutit and order another variety—even a calzone, some pasta, or an Italian sandwich. The dining room—done up in black-and-white checkerboard—and the take-out counter are open daily for lunch and dinner. There's more at 1949 East Camelback Road, Phoenix, (602) 294–6969; 2580 West Chandler Boulevard, Chandler, (480) 722–0898; and 10433 North Scottsdale Road, Scottsdale, (480) 609–8666.

Oregano's Pizza Bistro $$
3622 North Scottsdale Road, Scottsdale
(480) 970–1860

Oregano's is a hot spot on weekend evenings for its casual Italian bistro feel and inventive pizzas. Thin-crust or Chicago stuffed pizzas come with traditional toppings or in varieties such as Cajun chicken pesto or Mexican pizza with chicken and green chiles. Hoagies and pasta dishes are also on the menu. Other locations are at 523 East University Drive, Tempe, (480) 858–0501; 1008 East Camelback Road, Phoenix, (602) 241–0707; and downtown at 130 East Washington Street, Phoenix, (602) 253–9577. Oregano's is open daily for lunch and dinner.

Ristorante Sandolo $$$
7500 East Doubletree Ranch Road, Scottsdale
(480) 483–5574

It's hard to resist the Venetian charm of this Italian bistro inside the Hyatt Regency Scottsdale. An informal indoor/outdoor cafe, it serves fettuccine Alfredo, mostaccioli Bolognese, and other pasta dishes, with a chopped Italian salad on the side. What's more, the waiters sing, and they'll arrange for you to ride in a gondola-style boat on the Hyatt's lake. The boatman sings, too. Dinner is served nightly.

Mexican

Carlsbad Tavern   **$$$**
3313 North Hayden Road, Scottsdale
(480) 970-8164
Scottsdale certainly has its share of pretentious, pricey restaurants—which makes Carlsbad Tavern a refreshing change. The food—New Mexico–style Mexican with steak and pasta thrown in—is tasty and reasonably priced. The servers are friendly, in a neighborhood tavern kind of way. The newsprint menu pokes fun at "owner" Miguel Guacamole. We recommend the blue-plate special of roasted chicken, the blue corn enchiladas, and the braised lamb grilled over wood in the New Mexican way. Entrees come with green-chile mashed potatoes and corn bread topped with prickly pear butter. Lunch and dinner are served Monday through Saturday, with dinner only on Sunday.

La Hacienda   **$$$$**
7575 East Princess Drive, Scottsdale
(480) 585-4848
We place La Hacienda in the Mexican category with the advisory that it is a cut above most Mexican restaurants in fine-dining ambiance. But you would expect that at a restaurant on the grounds of the ritzy Scottsdale Princess resort. Just a short walk from the hotel lobby, the restaurant occupies an early-20th-century, freestanding Mexican ranch house. Expect first-class table settings, comfortable chairs, a beehive fireplace, extraordinary food, and strolling mariachis to set the tone. Consider spit-roasted suckling pig, grilled seafood, chicken, and beef, all prepared in traditional Mexican style. The place is also known for its coffee drinks that are ordered to cap off a meal. La

Hacienda serves dinner nightly, except on Wednesday, when it's closed.

Old Town Tortilla Factory   **$$-$$$**
6910 East Main Street, Scottsdale
(480) 945-4567
In a renovated adobe cottage dating from 1933, Old Town Tortilla Factory is mega-popular with Valley residents because it's a funky place with nice twists on Mexican and American fare. With entree items like Shawnee Sea Bass and Stuffed Beef Filet, you can see it's not strictly the cheese crisp-enchilada-taco type of Mexican food. Even those items, though, are presented with flair. And the Tortilla Factory makes two dozen varieties of flour tortillas, using ingredients like sun-dried tomatoes and serrano chiles. The bar gets a lot of business, too, and it's quite popular with tequila aficionados, since the place serves almost 100 varieties of the Mexican liquor. Some of the high-end tequilas go for $500 a bottle. The restaurant is open Monday through Saturday for lunch and dinner and Sunday for dinner only.

Sandwich Shops

Chompie's   **$-$$**
9301 East Shea Boulevard, Scottsdale
(480) 860-0475
Chompie's is much more than a sandwich shop, but we include it in this category because its sandwiches are so good. The mile-high sandwiches in this kosher-style restaurant are stacked with your choice of tender corned beef, pastrami, turkey, cheeses, or combinations thereof—congratulations go to the diner who can finish one in a single sitting. The restaurant serves breakfast, lunch, and dinner Tuesday through Sunday (breakfast and lunch on Monday), which makes it tempting to stick around all day, working your way through lox on bagels, eggs, and blintzes for breakfast, then a potato knish and salad for lunch, and then for dinner, a beef brisket special or sweet and sour

cabbage rolls. For dessert you can saunter (or waddle) over to the bakery counter, with its myriad cakes and cookies. Chompie's is a popular neighborhood stop for bagels, which come in about 30 varieties. Additional locations are at 1160 East University, Tempe, (480) 557-0700; and 3202 East Greenway Road in Phoenix, (602) 971-8010.

The News Cafe $
6166 North Scottsdale Road, Scottsdale
(480) 609-1223

You don't have to be a news junkie to hang out here, but with all the different papers for sale, you might turn into one. This is a great place for out-of-towners to sip a coffee and catch up on events back home with their local newspaper. If you are hungry, you can always get a Turkey Classic Column, a Register Roast Beef, a Hot Roast Beef Review, or . . . you get the idea. We especially recommend the bialys, a tasty variation on the bagel. There's another location at 4743 North 20th Street, Phoenix, (602) 957-2236. The one in Scottsdale is in the ritzy Borgata shopping area, a cluster of shops modeled after a medieval Italian village. The one in Phoenix is a bit more laid-back, with a bright sunny interior and nice art on the walls.

Wildflower Bread Company $
15640 North Pima Road, Scottsdale
(480) 991-5180

The owners of this bakery and sandwich shop in north Scottsdale say it's "where the aroma of fresh-baked bread alone solves all of the world's problems for a while." We'll buy that, especially when it's bread in such varieties as good ol' multi-grain or the more exotic ciabatta, focaccia, or wild mushroom. Or when the bread embraces sandwiches like chicken pesto and feta or roast beef and bleu cheese. Also on the menu are salads, from Caribbean Cobb to Oriental chicken. There are cookies and biscotti to go with the good selection of coffees and teas. There are other locations at 3111 West Chandler Boulevard, Chandler, (480) 821-8200;

16059 North 82nd Street, Scottsdale, (480) 951-9453; and 6428 South McClintock Drive, Tempe, (480) 838-9773. Counter service is available for breakfast, lunch, and dinner daily.

Seafood

Restaurant Oceana $$$$
8936 East Pinnacle Peak Road, Scottsdale
(480) 515-BASS

A wonderful seafood restaurant in the Pinnacle Peak area, Oceana features grilled ahi tuna with foie gras, Atlantic salmon, wood-fire roasted Maine scallops, and pan-seared cod in a bacon and leek broth. For diners who want to sample Chef Ercolino Crugnale's signature dishes, there are four- and five-course tasting menus with smaller portions of his seafood creations. Dinner is served daily.

Western

Crazy Ed's Satisfied Frog $$$
6245 East Cave Creek Road, Cave Creek
(480) 488-3317

Things are always hoppin' at the Frog during tourist season. The restaurant shoots for a rollicking Western atmosphere, with sawdust on the floor, a saloon area, honky-tonk music, picnic tables covered with checkered tablecloths, a paper menu filled with cartoons and jokes, and shops on the premises selling Western souvenirs. The food ain't bad, either. We recommend the barbecue ribs or spit-roasted chicken. A children's menu is available. You can sample beers from Crazy Ed Chilleen's (he's a real person) microbrewery. And this is the home of Cave Creek Chili Beer, which features an Arizona-grown chile pepper hand-inserted into every bottle. Lunch and dinner are served daily.

Rawhide Steakhouse $$
23023 North Scottsdale Road, Scottsdale
(480) 502-5600

See how the West was fun at the Rawhide theme park, popular with tourists from all over the world. Then reward yourself with a steak from the restaurant in this re-created 1880s Western town. The baby back ribs and barbecue chicken are also good. We hear tell that the appetizers include deep-fried rattlesnake and buffalo kebabs. We might need a beer from the saloon before we give that a try. Lunch is served Friday through Sunday (October through May), and dinner is served nightly year-round.

NORTHWEST VALLEY

American Fusion

Earl's Mexican-American Food $
9440 West Peoria Avenue, Peoria
(623) 979-0979

There's nothing terribly fancy about this longtime establishment, just wholesome American and Mexican food at reasonable prices. The mesquite-smoked meats with barbecue sauce are a favorite, as are the Mexican combination plates and the hearty breakfasts of eggs and chorizo (Mexican sausage). The full bar sells a lot of margaritas and beer. There are two more locations in Scottsdale, at 4821 North Scottsdale Road, (480) 990-7959; and 15784 North Pima Road, (480) 607-1941. The restaurants are open seven days a week for breakfast, lunch, and dinner.

Mimi's Cafe $$
7450 West Bell Road, Glendale
(623) 979-4500

This restaurant chain out of California is rich in New Orleans French Quarter ambiance. It's a charming change of pace among the eateries fronting the large West Valley mall, Arrowhead Towne Center. For dinner you will have to decide between something light from their great selection of sandwiches and salads or something more robust, such as chicken potpie, beer-batter halibut, or roast pork

loin and red cabbage. Especially recommended are the soups du jour, such as clam "chowda" and Caribbean black bean. Breakfast, lunch, and dinner are served daily. Other Valley locations are at 2800 West Chandler Boulevard, Chandler, (480) 899-5612; 2824 East Indian School Road, Phoenix, (602) 955-5937; 21001 North Tatum Boulevard, Phoenix, (480) 419-5006; 4901 East Ray Road, Phoenix, (480) 705-4811; 10214 North Metro Parkway West, Phoenix, (602) 997-1299; 1250 South Alma School Road, Mesa, (480) 833-4646; and 8980 East Shea Boulevard, Scottsdale, (480) 451-6763.

Breakfast

Kiss the Cook Restaurant & Antiques $
4915 West Glendale Avenue, Glendale
(623) 939-4663

Just a mile from downtown Glendale's antiques district, Kiss the Cook has been dishing out homemade breakfast and lunch goodies since 1980. The family-operated restaurant has a country-cluttered feel, with all the antiques, dolls, birdhouses, and assorted knickknacks on display and for sale. Breakfast gets down to business with buttermilk pancakes from an old family recipe and omelets that you fill with your choice of three ingredients. Also on the table are homemade muffins and apple butter. For lunch, salads are a good choice; select from Cobb, salmon Caesar, Monterey chicken, and Cajun chicken salads, all made from scratch. The restaurant is open every day, for breakfast and lunch only.

German

Haus Murphy's $$
5819 West Glendale Avenue, Glendale
(623) 939-2480

Tucked into downtown Glendale's oldest commercial building (ca. 1900) is a little bit of Germany, a colorful place serving schnitzel, sauerbraten, bratwurst, strudel, and other home-style favorites from Rhineland and Bavaria. Polka tunes and yodeling provide the background music, and weekends bring a strolling accordionist. Sure to catch your eye is the restaurant's vintage soda fountain. It was moved here from Florence, Arizona, where it was featured in Murphy's Romance, starring James Garner and Sally Field. The menu also includes American fare such as chicken sandwiches, pasta, and burgers. Ja wohl, there's a good selection of German wines and beers. From the soda fountain, you can order things like cherry-flavored colas. Haus Murphy's is open for lunch daily, for dinner Monday through Saturday, and for lunch and early dinner (until 5:00 P.M.) on Sunday.

Italian and Pizza

Cucina Tagliani $$
17045 North 59th Avenue, Glendale
(623) 547-2782
This Southern Italian–style restaurant is popular with West Valley families because of its great Pick-A-Pasta deal for $8.99. Diners choose from seven types of pasta and seven types of sauce, then customize their plates further with 20 different add-on items, from sausage, meatballs, and meat sauce to eggplant to bacon to scallops. Meals come with a house salad or soup and focaccia bread. Other items such as sausage sandwiches, antipasto platters, and seafood linguine are also available. Lunch and dinner are served every day.

Southwest Valley

The Arizona Kitchen $$$–$$$$
300 East Wigwam Boulevard,
Litchfield Park
(623) 935-3811
Although this restaurant is off in distant Litchfield Park, it is well worth the drive. This centerpiece restaurant of the Wigwam resort features distinctive entrees such as sautéed medallions of turkey with jalapeño-jack cheese glaze and sun-dried cranberry ancho chile sauce; roasted pheasant glazed with coconut, jalapeños, and mint; and filet mignon dusted with chile powder in a prickly pear Merlot sauce. Plus, the restaurant often uses produce grown just a few miles away in the West Valley's agricultural fields. A dessert treat is a chocolate kahlua taco—the taco shell is a dark chocolate and the filling is fruit and Kahlua mousse. Dinner is served Tuesday through Sunday.

NIGHTLIFE 🍸

"Work hard and play hard!" That's the motto of the people who frequent the Valley's nightclubs. Mostly, it's a young crowd out there—people with the energy to trip the light fantastic and dance until the cows come home. These are the folks who work a busy day, run home and change their clothes, and head out to meet up with friends to explore the good times available around the Valley.

Music lovers are fortunate to live here. On any given night, popular music concerts and other types of performances take place at America West Arena, Arizona Veterans Memorial Coliseum, the Celebrity Theatre, Chandler Center for the Arts, Gammage Auditorium, the Red River Music Hall, Scottsdale Center for the Arts, and the Sundome Center for the Performing Arts, among others. In the summer, you can add such outdoor venues as Cricket Pavilion and Mesa Amphitheater to the mix. That's not to mention the very occasional use of the 70,000-seat Sun Devil Stadium for megaconcerts by the likes of the Rolling Stones or U2. See the Spectator Sports or The Arts chapters for information on getting tickets.

Sometimes nightlife turns up in odd venues. In Glendale the public library has a weekly folk-music coffeehouse. Every now and then, a pop concert like Tony Bennett or k.d. lang will show up at Phoenix Symphony Hall. The America West Arena will feature everything from the circus to Faith Hill and Tina Turner.

In addition, the Valley has just about every type of nightclub imaginable—country, rock, blues, comedy, sports. It also seems that every resort has a lounge with performers of varying quality.

Unless you plan to visit downtown Tempe, don't expect to hit a lot of spots on a single club crawl. Things are just too spread out for that. Downtown Tempe, however, is just off the Arizona State University campus and as a result has numerous bars, nightclubs, and coffeehouses within easy walking distance of each other. Sometimes it seems the whole city is pounding out music.

Drinking and driving is never a good idea and, in the Valley of the Sun, it's particularly bad. Valley police frequently set up roadblocks to check for DUI infractions, and they snag quite a few. There have been a number of high-profile drunk-driving deaths that have stirred community resentment against drunk drivers. Call a cab or use a designated driver if you're out drinking.

For the most part, cover charges for the places listed in this chapter will be in the $3.00 to $10.00 range. Those prices go up when clubs are offering name acts.

The following list is purely subjective, a sample of what we consider the best places Phoenix and the Valley of the Sun have to offer, although there are many fine establishments not listed here. These are the places to start. Of course, we have the tourist havens like the Hard Rock Cafe on Camelback Road, just east of 24th Street in Phoenix. But since you know what to expect from the typical tourist destinations, in this chapter we'll stick to nonchain nightlife. When you're looking for current nighttime things to do, the best places to

We've told you throughout this book that the dress code in Phoenix is casual. The nightclubs are the one exception. If you are planning a night on the town, here's your chance to dress up in those designer duds you've been buying at the city shops. Phoenix isn't as fashion conscious as New York or Los Angeles, but we know how to look good when we want to.

look are the calendars in *Phoenix New Times,* "Get Out," and "The Rep." All of them are published weekly on Thursday and are available for free at convenience stores and in their own freestanding boxes.

BLUES NIGHTCLUBS

Phoenix

Char's Has the Blues
4631 North Seventh Avenue, Phoenix
(602) 230-0205
www.charshastheblues.com

Char's Has the Blues is a friendly, crowded, smoky nightspot where the blues make you sweat and the brews cool you off. Char's has been voted "Best Blues R&B bar" for years in the weekly papers. You're not here to see concerts, but to dance on the postage-stamp size dance floor when one of the local bands gets really hot. There's live music seven nights a week. When the bands take a break, the atmosphere is conducive to genuine conversation like a regular corner bar. No cover on Monday and Wednesday. Doors open at 7:00 P.M.

Monroe's Food and Fine Spirits
3 West Monroe Street, Phoenix
(602) 258-1046

Okay, this is a bit of a dive. But don't let the bras hanging behind the bar fool you—this is a dive with class. Monroe's is a murky little cellar (it used to be a boiler room) that hosts live jazz, R&B, or blues every night except Sunday. The atmosphere is cozy and friendly. Most of the regulars seem to know each other and between sets the bands mingle with the crowd. The music's good, there's local microbrew on tap, and the food is reasonably priced at less than $10 a plate. There's even a ghost, but it's not responsible for the bras. The manager says they "just appear" every morning. Yeah, right. Open 11:00 A.M. to 1:00 A.M. daily.

BREW PUBS

Southeast Valley

Copper Canyon Brewing & Ale House
5945 West Ray Road, Chandler
(480) 705-9700

Use Copper Canyon's six varieties of beer to wash down a menu that includes everything from stuffed salmon and veggie pasta to steaks, burgers, and pizzas. Our taste tends toward the Foothills Honey Blonde and the A-1 Amber Ale, which both have a pleasant tang to them. Although it's situated in a strip mall, Copper Canyon seems anything but storelike. The atmosphere is cool and dark, a refuge for enjoying the brews, and it attracts a mixture of young and middle-age professionals.

Four Peaks Brewing Co.
1340 East Eighth Street, Tempe
(480) 303-9967

Four Peaks Brewing Co. is situated in what used to be the Borden's Creamery in Tempe, giving the place a hip, funky industrial warehouse atmosphere. Even the 72-foot-long bar seems lost in all that space. The brew pub caters to college and young urban professional crowds with 10 different varieties of beer. We recommend the Kiltlifter, a Scottish ale, for its rich body and the Four Peaks Pale, a pale ale, for its lighter taste. The brew pub serves food, including gourmet-style pizzas and sandwiches. Best of all, though, is the shrine to Elvis tucked away behind the right side of the bar (as you look in from the entrance). This kitschy attraction takes on special significance after a pint or two.

Gordon Biersch Brewery Restaurant
420 South Mill Avenue, Tempe
(480) 736-0033

A noisy and busy brew pub/restaurant at the hub of Mill Avenue and Fifth Street. The microbrews are good, and the upstairs seating is a nice place to watch the crowds swirling below. The American cuisine with

Asian influences is very enjoyable, but a bit expensive for what you get. This is a common problem among many Mill Avenue eateries. The patio fills up quickly, but the inside rooms have large windows that make for a bright interior during the day. At night when the lights come up, Mill Avenue can be quite attractive.

Mill Avenue Beer Company
605 South Mill Avenue, Tempe
(480) 829-6775

With 100 beers available, the Mill Avenue Beer Company is really a brew-drinker's paradise. In addition, the menu is full of the munchies that go great with beer—from onion rings to bratwurst. Add in a friendly atmosphere, and Nirvana's just around the corner.

COFFEEHOUSES

Phoenix

Fiddler's Dream
1702 East Glendale Avenue, Phoenix
(602) 997-9795
www.fiddlersdream.org

This isn't your Seattle-type coffeehouse; it's a folk-music coffeehouse where the music is front and center. There's no sound system, and performers are asked to leave their amplifiers home too. The kitchen produces a few snacks to go with the java, and the atmosphere is friendly and relaxed. The low-tech presentation makes it the perfect place to listen and then converse after a set. The little building is tucked behind a Quaker church on the corner of Glendale and 17th Streets.

Lux
4404 North Central Avenue, Phoenix
(602) 266-6469

This hard-to-find cafe is tucked into an unassuming building next to a sandwich shop. It's worth the search. While the food and drink selections are what you'd expect, they are all of high quality. The cappuccinos are especially good, the owner having learned how to make them in Italy. What really makes this cafe one of the best in the Valley is the decor and the people. The owners have a good eye for art, so there are always interesting works by local artists on the walls. Since much of the "art" stuck onto cafe walls ranges from mediocre to bad, this is a refreshing change. The crowd is as select as the art. Lux attracts the Valley's writers, artists, and photographers, so this is a good place to get into interesting conversations.

Willow House
149 West McDowell Road, Phoenix
(602) 252-0272

A great little cafe in a quiet residential neighborhood just off Central Avenue, the Willow House is located in a large, rambling house with plenty of quiet corners. The walls are lined with books and art for sale. Besides the usual varieties of coffees and teas, there's a good selection of fresh bagels, salads, sandwiches, and soups. The crowd here is eclectic, laid-back, and friendly. This is one of the best places in Phoenix to hang out and actually meet people, a challenge in this sprawling city.

Southeast Valley

Essenza Coffeehouse
1350 South Longmore Street, Mesa
(480) 461-0445

One of the great attractions of Essenza Coffeehouse (besides the java, of course) is events like the poetry slam, which turns poetry reading into a wrestling-like competition. You have to see it to understand. Essenza also features acoustic music and an open-mike night.

Undici Undici Fine Art Coffee House
1111 South Longmore Road, Mesa
(480) 962-4224
www.eurocafe.com

Undici Undici is a casual, yet upscale coffeehouse sharing a building with Romeo's

Euro Café. The walls feature work by local artists, and there's a small gift shop with unusual arts and crafts. In the evenings there's often live music. The coffeehouse shares Romeo's dessert counter, so you can try creations such as Fantasy Cake and Intoxicated Love.

Northeast Valley

Authors' Cafe
4014 North Goldwater Boulevard, #104, Scottsdale
(480) 481-3998
Home to a coterie of self-published authors, this cafe is a nice quiet place to relax and scribble after browsing the art galleries around the corner. Books by local authors line the walls, and there are regular signings, discussion groups, and other literary events. Besides the usual coffee drinks, there is a wide selection of teas (also sold by the pound) and a varied menu. The Authors' Cafe is owned by a gourmet chef, and it shows. The meals are consistently good, and the desserts are outstanding. If you are into goopy, sugary concoctions, this is the place. It's not cheap, but you are paying for quality. The cafe is open Monday through Thursday 9:00 A.M. to 10:00 P.M., Friday and Saturday 9:00 A.M. to 11:00 P.M., closed Sunday.

COMEDY CLUBS
Southeast Valley

The Improv
930 East University Drive, Tempe
(480) 921-9877
www.tempeimprov.com
In the Cornerstone Mall, within sight of Sun Devil Stadium, the Improv continues to attract crowds, while most of its mid- to late 1980s rivals have disappeared from the Valley scene. Maybe the secret is location, or maybe it's an example of the Improv's

brand-name appeal. Of course, the lineup of comics might have something to do with it. The Improv, with a capacity of 400, books comedians from Thursday through Sunday. Dinner shows are at 8:00 P.M. each night, and Friday and Saturday feature a nondinner show at 10:00 P.M.

COUNTRY NIGHTCLUBS
Phoenix

Mr. Lucky's
3660 Northwest Grand Avenue, Phoenix
(602) 246-0686
Mr. Lucky's owner, J. David Sloan, is a veteran country performer of the Valley scene. He's been around since Waylon Jennings was a local fixture, and one of his many bands backed up Lyle Lovett on his debut album.

The club has been a country mainstay even longer than Sloan. There's live music and dancing. If you're completely loco, Mr. Lucky's offers mechanical bull riding on Wednesday. For the less loco there are free dance lessons on Thursday.

Southeast Valley

Graham Central Station
7850 South Priest Drive, Tempe
(480) 496-0799
If you're young, rowdy, and want to meet jean-wrapped, boot-wearing members of the opposite sex, the mammoth country palace known as Graham Central Station is your best bet. Blaring music played by a DJ sets the scene for the dancers and revelers.

Northeast Valley

Buffalo Chip Saloon
6811 East Cave Creek, Cave Creek
(480) 488-9118
The cowboy boots nailed to the roof are a clue that you're in the right place. Dine on

barbecue, dance to live music, and enjoy the country culture.

Handlebar-J
7116 East Becker Lane, Scottsdale
(480) 948-0110
The Handlebar-J is another place with a long history. It's been in the Herndon family for two generations. It does a respectable restaurant trade, but its hallmark has been the Herndon family's music. Ray Herndon, who has played with J. David Sloan, Lyle Lovett, and McBride and the Ride, may be the best known of the Herndon Brothers Band members. Although the whole clan rarely gets together on stage, the Herndon Brothers Band remains among the Valley's country royalty. They play Wednesday through Sunday, while the other nights are filled with other bands and dance lessons.

DANCE CLUBS
Phoenix

Bobby McGee's Conglomeration
8501 North 27th Avenue, Phoenix
(602) 995-5982
The dance floor's the thing at Bobby McGee's, although this is also a restaurant and bar with singing waiters. DJs get the crowds pumped up. McGee's also holds events such as bikini contests (Thursday), boxers night (Tuesday), and ladies' night with a men's best-asset contest (Wednesday).

Southeast Valley

Club Rio
430 North Scottsdale Road, Tempe
(480) 894-0533
Club Rio sits on the edge of the Salt River, or Rio Salado, hence its name. The place is of airline-hangar proportions (35,000 square feet), so the dance floor is big. National acts from Todd Rundgren to Ice-T

In Arizona closing time is 1:00 A.M. That doesn't mean you can't have a good long night out, but you've got to hurry up and get out there to do it.

have played here, but most nights it's packed with dancers from ASU looking to groove in all the right places to Top 40, techno, alternative, and modern rock. It's also their favorite meet market. You have been warned (or informed). The outdoor terrace is an especially appealing place on cool evenings, even though it's right under the flight path to Sky Harbor International Airport.

Northeast Valley

Anderson's Fifth Estate
6820 East Fifth Avenue, Scottsdale
(480) 994-4168
Crowded little Anderson's always has a good DJ mix whether it's on classic alternative night, swing night, or trash disco night. The dress on trash disco night is particularly outrageous, almost a game of "how high can you make a platform shoe before a person falls off?" In addition to the DJs, Anderson's features Brit Pop and Industrial dance on Thursday, retro on Saturday, and the occasional concert night.

Axis/Radius
7340 East Indian School Road, Scottsdale
(480) 970-1112
www.axis-radius.com
These two clubs, connected by a glass walkway, are longtime favorites for the college crowd. Axis is the more laid-back of the two. Decked out with ultramodern furniture, the spacious bars and lounges make a good place to meet with friends over a few drinks and food. Radius is the high-energy dance spot, where the dance floors tend to be crowded on weekends and can get pretty packed on weeknights too. The clubs offer a VIP lounge and a cigar bar as

> *If you like Irish music, check out the Arizona Irish Music Society. They can tell you about Irish music performances in the Valley and across the state. Call them at (602) 230–4114 or check listings online at www.azirishmusic.com. Another Celtic clearinghouse is the Irish Cultural Center, at 1106 North Central Avenue, Phoenix, which can tell you about any Gaelic events happening in town, from highland games to Welsh language classes. Many classes and events are held on-site. In 2004 the center opened a faithful reproduction of a 1850s Irish farmhouse.*

well. Both clubs are open Wednesday through Saturday, 8:00 P.M. to 1:00 A.M.

Buzz Funbar
10345 North Scottsdale Road, Scottsdale
(480) 991–3866
This upscale club has dancers moving to the groove of today's Top 40. The place also features a comfy upstairs room to hang out in. On Thursday the scene completely changes with an all-ages night, with live hard-core punk bands.

JAZZ NIGHTCLUBS
Phoenix

Different Pointe of View
11111 North Seventh Street, Phoenix
(602) 866–6350
With any luck, Khani Cole and her band are still at Different Pointe of View when you read this. Her albums on a small jazz label have drawn some favorable attention nationwide, and who knows when she'll itch to wander. She'll have to wander far, though, to find a better situation than the lounge at the Different Pointe of View restaurant. The room overlooks the Valley lights for a romantic atmosphere that

would augment any singer's performance. It's part of the Pointe Hilton Tapatio Cliffs Resort, so you'll feel a little better (and more romantic) if you dress up a bit. In the Valley's casual style, anything from business casual attire to dress clothes fills that bill. As of this writing, Cole performs there Wednesday through Saturday.

Southeast Valley

Bistro Isabelle
7131 West Ray Road, Chandler
(480) 705–9270
This upscale cafe offers jazz Thursday through Saturday from 6:30 to 9:30 P.M., but there are special events too. Sometimes the performances are inside, where musicians can use the grand piano, and sometimes they are under the stars on the bistro's pleasant patio. The food is French continental, including a range of seafood dishes such as mussels, calamari, and seafood crepes.

LATIN CLUBS
Phoenix

La Casa del Mariachi
1420 North 24th Street, Phoenix
(602) 275–8565
This spacious club serves inexpensive and tasty Mexican food while customers enjoy mariachi bands from Arizona and Mexico. While a lot of gringo clubs offer Latin nights, this is the real deal. Spanish is what's usually spoken here, but you can get by in English as well. Check out the colorful Mexican paintings decorating the walls. The mariachi bands play Friday through Sunday in two different lounges. If you want to try it yourself, go to karaoke night on Thursday; the $1.00 beer special will improve your courage, if not your singing voice.

Northeast Valley

Los Olivos
7328 East Second Street, Scottsdale
(480) 946-2256
www.azeats.com/LosOlivos
Los Olivos is the oldest Mexican restaurant in Scottsdale and serves a good selection of dishes. It's the decor, however, that really makes this place unique. The stage features a grumpy-looking idol with glowing red eyes. After a couple of tequilas, you'll think it's looking straight at you. There's mariachi every Thursday and Sunday and Latin music on Friday and Saturday, with a $5.00 cover Friday and $7.00 cover Saturday.

LOUNGES

Phoenix

Chez Nous
675 West Indian School Road, Phoenix
(602) 266-7372
Do you want to travel back to the early '60s? To the days of Kennedy's Camelot, when Frank Sinatra and the Rat Pack were the models of the high life? Then clink a martini glass at Chez Nous. No, this isn't an incredible simulation '60s style; the club hasn't been touched by time since it opened more than three decades ago. You just know the banquettes and flocked wallpaper have been privy to thousands of illicit liaisons and one-for-the-road kiss-offs. Performers, usually duos or solos, play martini music every night.

The Merc Bar
2501 East Camelback Road, Phoenix
(602) 508-9449
No advertising. No sign on the door. This lounge is hidden at the Camelback Esplanade beside the Houston's restaurant. Inside you'll find plush leather sofas, a dark soothing ambiance, and perfectly mixed cocktails. It's very chic.

Northeast Valley

Jet Lag Lounge
7980 East Chaparral Road, Scottsdale
(480) 941-9144
A popular place for the over-50 crowd to gather for ballroom dancing. So popular, in fact, that there's not much room on the moderate-size dance floor. But the music is good, the folks are friendly, and the dress is as casual or as formal as you want it to be. There are a surprising number of singles here, so if you are looking to fall in love under electric starlight, this may be your chance. There's lots of good acoustic jazz too.

POP CONCERT VENUES

Phoenix

America West Arena
201 East Jefferson Street, Phoenix
(602) 379-7800
www.americawestarena.com
Built as the home of the popular Phoenix Suns basketball team, America West Arena can hold about 19,000 people in the basketball configuration and a few thousand fewer for concerts, depending on the size of the performers' stage. For the best views and sound, you'll want to avoid the floor and the upper bowl. Head for seats about midway back in the lower bowl. Still, it's an arena, so sound quality generally is tolerable at best, but you're there for the spectacle, right?

Arizona Veterans Memorial Coliseum
1826 West McDowell Road, Phoenix
(602) 258-6711
The old home of the Phoenix Suns also serves as an occasional concert venue and does nightly duty during the two weeks of the Arizona State Fair in October and November. The fair brings in all sorts of music and the prices are quite reasonable. This hall has seen better days, and the

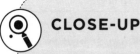

Reservations Bet on Gaming

Valley folks used to satiate their desire for gambling by heading to Laughlin, Nevada, for a weekend getaway with the one-armed bandits. Or they'd drive (or fly) a little deeper into Nevada and hit Las Vegas, the way much of the rest of America does. Otherwise, the alternatives were charity casino games played for prizes, not money, or betting on the races at Turf Paradise and Phoenix Greyhound Park (see the Spectator Sports chapter).

Now, though, casinos are much closer at hand. Four local Indian communities have turned to casinos as a means of generating revenue and employment for their tribal members.

The path to the casinos was an interesting one that started with on-reservation bingo parlors back in the 1970s. The number of tribes with gaming activities grew steadily, until there was a court challenge. As tribes searched for new revenue sources in the wake of Reagan administration cutbacks, gaming became the hot solution. A federal court ruled in 1983 that states had no jurisdiction over regulatory affairs on Indian reservations. That's when Fort McDowell Indian Community, northeast of Fountain Hills, opened its Ba' Ja Bingo Hall. The first Native American bingo parlor serving the Valley was an instant success.

The growth of Indian gaming nationwide prompted Congress to pass the Federal Indian Gaming Regulatory Act of 1988. This created three classes of Indian gaming. Class 1 involved traditional or ceremonial Native American gaming, and it is completely under the jurisdiction of the tribes. Class 2 covers bingo and such numbers games as Lotto and non-bank card games (where the card players play against each other and not the house). This second class is under the jurisdiction of the National Indian Gaming Commission, which was also established by the 1988 law. Class 3 covers high-stakes gaming, including casinos, racing, blackjack and baccarat-style card games, slot machines, and jai alai. To run such games, a tribe must forge a compact with the state in which it is located.

The national law set conflicts in motion between Arizona and tribes that offered gaming. Asserting their sovereignty, tribes such as the Fort McDowell Indian Community began to offer video slots in addition to non-bank card games and bingo even though compacts had not been struck with the state. The state argued that Congress had no power to mandate negotiations between sovereign entities.

On May 12, 1992, federal officials raided reservations around the state and impounded video gaming machines. Fort McDowell was the site of the only major resistance. Tribal members used heavy equipment to blockade the trucks into which federal authorities had loaded the 349 machines seized from Fort McDowell's little casino. The tension was thick. A 10-day cooling off period was ordered. Tribes marched at the State Capitol.

The standoff is generally credited with forcing the state's hand in negotiating gaming compacts. Public sentiment appeared to strongly favor Indian gaming.

Eventually, tribal officials agreed to allow the machines to be shipped off the reservations until a gaming compact was reached. Poker and gaming continued at Fort McDowell even when the machines were impounded. The machines were returned to the tribe on August 27, 1992, in anticipation of a gaming compact. The compact was signed November 25, 1992. The tribe was allowed 475 video gaming machines. Fort McDowell was expected to earn $850 million over the course of the 10-year compact.

In the wake of the Fort McDowell compact, two other tribes near the Valley—the Gila River Indian Community and the Ak-Chin community—also signed compacts. Gila River's casino opened in a tent (or a sprung structure, as the industry calls them) and was so successful that it opened two permanent casinos in 1997.

The future of Indian gaming in Arizona is more secure than it was just a few years ago. The Arizona Gaming Department held in 1997 that poker games must be regulated by the state, not the reservations. This threatened to invalidate existing gaming compacts and the very future of Indian gaming. Luckily for the casinos, moderates in the state legislature convinced the majority that tax revenues generated from the casinos would offset any negative influences of gambling. A compromise was reached and Indian casinos are alive and well.

Here is a partial list of the Valley's nearby casinos:

Casino Arizona at Salt River
Salt River Pima–Maricopa Indian Community, 524 North 92nd Street, at the intersection with McKellips Road
(480) 850-7777, (877) 724-4687
www.casinoaz.com

Opened in a permanent building in 2001, this addition to the Phoenix area features 1,500 slot machines, 50 table games (including poker, seven-card stud, and the popular Texas Hold 'Em), 6 restaurants (serving breakfast, lunch, and dinner), and a stage for live entertainment. There's another location next to Scottsdale's Pavilions Shopping Center and Talking Stick Golf Course. From Phoenix Sky Harbor International Airport, take Loop 202 eastbound to Loop 101 northbound. Exit at McKellips Road, turn right (east), and take a left at 92nd Street. For free shuttle service, call (480) 850-7790.

Fort McDowell Casino
State Route 87 and Fort McDowell Road, Fort McDowell
(480) 837-1424, (800) THE-FORT
www.fortmcdowell.com
The granddaddy of local casinos is popularly known as "the Fort." It started out as the 17,000-square-foot Ba' Ja Bingo Hall in 1983. Today, Fort McDowell Casino features 150,000 square feet of floor space that handles an estimated 10,000 customers each day. The Fort features 475 video gaming machines, poker, keno, high-stakes bingo, and pari-mutuel wagering. It also has seven food outlets offering everything from steak to seafood. To get there from downtown Phoenix, take the Red Mountain Freeway to the Pima Freeway and head north to McDowell Road. Take McDowell Road east to SR 87 (the Beeline Highway), and turn left. Those coming from the Northeast Valley can take Shea Boulevard out to the Beeline Highway and head north. The casino is on the southwest corner of the intersection of Fort McDowell Road and the Beeline Highway.

With live entertainment, dining, and night clubs, casinos such as Harrah's offer more than just gambling. HARRAH'S CASINO

Gila River Casinos Arizona at Wild Horse Pass
Interstate 10 and Maricopa Road, Chandler
(520) 796-7777, (800) 946-4452
This permanent structure near the site of the original Gila River Casino tent boasts 167,000 square feet of floor space. It features a live poker room, high-stakes poker, a $50,000 live keno jackpot, a 1,500-seat bingo hall, and 500 video gaming machines. In addition, a restaurant, deli, and sports bar give patrons a chance to break from the gaming. To get there from central Phoenix, take I-10 to the Maricopa Road exit and head west. The Sheraton Wild Horse Pass Resort is right next door.

Gila River Casinos Arizona at Vee Quiva
51st Avenue, Laveen
(800) 946-4452
With the 66,000-square-foot Vee Quiva casino, the west Valley got into the gaming mode in December 1997. Vee Quiva features live poker, keno, a 500-seat bingo hall, and 500 video gaming machines. There's also a restaurant, deli, and coffee shop. To get there from central Phoenix, take I-10 west to the 51st Avenue exit and head south. The casino, which has no physical address, is 4 miles south of Baseline Road on the east side.

Harrah's Phoenix Ak-Chin Casino Resort
15406 North Maricopa Road, Maricopa
(480) 802-5000
Harrah's Ak-Chin offers 475 video gaming machines, keno, poker, and a 500-seat bingo hall. Food is available at the Range Steakhouse, Harvest Buffet, Agave's Southwest Restaurant, and Munchies Deli. You'll also find a lounge, live entertainment, and a dance floor. To get there from central Phoenix, take I-10 to the Queen Creek Road exit (exit 164). Turn right and follow Queen Creek Road to Maricopa Road and take a left. The casino is about 17 miles from the freeway exit.

sound is very mushy the farther you go from the stage. The best seats are in the lower rows about a quarter-way back from the stage.

Celebrity Theatre
440 North 32nd Street, Phoenix
(602) 267-9373
www.celebritytheatre.com
When it opened as the Star Theatre in the 1960s, this venue was the height of chic, a theater in the round setup with a stage that rotates on a turntable (although some acts opt not to have it turn). For many years it was the premier small hall (about 2,500 seats) in Phoenix, especially for acts that could take advantage of its intimacy. The sound system strains when a heavy act plays there, but when the act is more mellow, the effect is absolute magic. Recently acquired by Toolies Country owner Bill Bachand, the theater has seen a bit of a return to its glory days. The Celebrity is a sentimental favorite of long-time Phoenix residents, although they are wary of the deteriorating neighborhood that surrounds it.

Cricket Pavilion
2121 North 83rd Avenue, Phoenix
(602) 254-7200
www.cricket-pavilion.com
When it opened in November 1990, this amphitheater (formerly called Desert Sky Pavilion) was touted as a year-round venue. After all, the Valley's weather would make outdoor wintertime concerts viable. Maybe so, but what touring act is geared up to do outdoor shows in the winter? Scratch that idea. Still, this is a classy venue, and considering its size (about 22,000 people at capacity), it's easy to get into and out of. The sound is pretty good, especially at dead center in the covered seats.

Orpheum Theatre
203 West Adams Street, Phoenix
(602) 252-9678,
(602) 262-7272 (box office)

The city of Phoenix bought this ancient (in Valley terms) movie theater in 1984 and re-opened it in 1997 after $14 million in cleaning and refurbishing. Originally opened in 1929, the theater's furnishings and decor hearken from the era when movie theaters were meant to be an experience. Check out the drifting clouds on the ceiling, generated by a projector. The 1,400-seat theater is now home to a variety of performing-arts events and is on the National Register of Historic Places. They even show the occasional old-time silent film.

Web Theater
600 East Van Buren Street, Phoenix
(602) 253-7100
Web Theater is another venue with a history. Back in the 1930s through the 1950s, Phoenix had no separate concert venues. The 2,000-seat auditorium at Phoenix Union High School became the city's substitute, bringing in the big names of the era. The property went unused for many years. With a new coat of paint, a lot of cleaning, and a modern sound system, Web Theater has become a good downtown venue for touring contemporary jazz and roots-rock acts. The facility has also been updated for cybercasting concert events.

Southeast Valley

Chandler Center for the Arts
250 North Arizona Avenue, Chandler
(480) 782-2680
www.chandlercenter.org
A pleasant community hall of about 1,500 seats, the Chandler Center hosts nostalgic pop events and the occasional contempo-

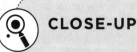

The Glories of Valley Pop

Phoenix isn't known as a regional music center the way that New Orleans, Detroit, San Francisco, Austin, or even (shudder) Tucson are. However, the Valley has produced members of both the Rock and Roll Hall of Fame and the Country Music Hall of Fame.

The hits that made Duane Eddy a rock 'n' roll guitar phenomenon were all recorded in an unobtrusive little studio called Ramsey Audio Recorders, which sat at the corner of Seventh Street and Weldon Avenue in Phoenix until 1964. Eddy racked up 13 Top 40 hits—including "Rebel Rouser," "Ramrod," and "Forty Miles of Bad Road"—while recording at Ramsey's from 1957 to 1962. The studio's unique reverb system played an important part in Eddy's bottom-heavy guitar sound. Producer Lee Hazlewood set up a speaker to feed the sound in the studio into an old water tank out in the building's parking lot. A microphone placed inside the tank recorded the original sound and its reverberations. Sometimes, Hazlewood would have to chase birds off the tank so that their chirping wouldn't get into the recordings.

Eddy was still in his teens when he met Hazlewood, an ambitious radio disc jockey in Coolidge, Arizona. Hazlewood liked Eddy's music and got him some bookings in Phoenix. Hazlewood became a DJ at Phoenix's Top 40 powerhouse KRUX and produced and cowrote Sanford Clark's 1956 hit, "The Fool." Hazlewood struck out to Los Angeles to work for Dot Records for a year, and when he returned it was to work primarily as a record producer in Phoenix. By this point, Eddy was

quite popular in Phoenix's booming country scene, and Hazlewood told him to write an instrumental. On their second shot, Eddy turned out "Rebel Rouser" and became Phoenix's first bona fide rock 'n' roll guitar hero.

Marty Robbins, the country singer best known for the 1959 cowboy ballad "El Paso," was born Martin David Robinson in 1925 in Glendale, or more properly, in an area later annexed by Glendale. Robbins's early life was one of poverty, eased a bit by his grandfather's tales of the Old West. Robbins joined the Navy toward the end of World War II. Returning to civilian life in 1947, he took up the guitar and songwriting. He didn't abandon his day jobs, but did perform casual gigs around Phoenix, eventually landing a spot on KPHO radio and eventually joining *Country Caravan,* a show on KPHO-TV. Robbins's big break came in 1951 when Little Jimmy Dickens did a guest spot on *Country Caravan.* Impressed by the Valley native, Dickens suggested that Columbia Records should sign Robbins. The major label took Dickens's advice, and soon Robbins left for his first recording session in Los Angeles. By 1953, he was a member of the Grand Ole Opry.

Phoenix has always had a thing for country, and both Eddy and Robbins could be on either side of the fence dividing country from rock 'n' roll. The city's cowboy past kept it firmly linked to country music, even though the Western style became an ever decreasing part (except for the hats so many male country singers wear). Waylon Jennings worked in the Valley for six years in the early 1960s between working with Buddy Holly in the late 1950s and signing with Chet Atkins at RCA in 1965. Tanya Tucker only played the Valley for a heartbeat but has been remembered as almost a native daughter ever since. Much later on, Lyle Lovett cut his first country album here, working with a group of musicians who knew Waylon.

But, there were always other kinds of music in town. Dyke and the Blazers may not be as well known as the Hall of Famers, but they nearly immortalized a Phoenix street and nobody knows it! The Blazers were the O'Jays' backup band in the mid-'60s, but on one tour Arlester "Dyke" Christian and the Blazers were stranded in Phoenix when the O'Jays couldn't come up with the money to bring them back to Philadelphia. They made the most of a bad situation and began playing gigs in town. Phoenix became Dyke's home, and by 1967 he and the band had created the song "Funky Broadway" to celebrate the main drag through south Phoenix. It was a rhythm and blues hit for the Blazers, but Wilson Pickett's version of the song was even bigger, crossing over to the pop charts. Dyke and the Blazers had a few other hits, but Dyke was shot to death in Phoenix in 1971.

While Dyke was in the process of set-tling in Phoenix, another band, which would eventually become Alice Cooper, was doing everything it could to get thrown out. Neither the band nor its lead singer was then known as Alice Cooper, but even so, the lead singer says, they were definitely not in step with the Valley of the '60s. Burr-cut Republican Senator and presidential candidate Barry Goldwa-ter was Arizona's political hero, and long-haired fellows who enjoyed the Yardbirds were just a bit too far out. Before they left

town for fame and fortune, the band recorded some demos at Ramsey's Audio Recorders at its then-new studio farther north on Seventh Street. (Alice Cooper wasn't the only rock group from Phoenix to trade in outrage. Members of two pop-ular Phoenix bands who relocated to San Francisco later formed the Tubes.)

A big change happened in the 1980s. Where it had always been wise for acts to leave the Valley if they wanted to attract a national following, the Valley suddenly became big enough to nurture its own bands. The Meat Puppets, a post-punk trio that Nirvana's Kurt Cobain would emulate, grew up here and left the Valley only to tour to a growing legion of under-ground rock fans. They were prophets without too much honor at home, but they were big enough to get London Records to sign them in 1990. A number of their albums earned glowing reviews in magazines like *Rolling Stone*. Cobain had them join in on some numbers on Nir-vana's MTV Unplugged album.

Another group that didn't have to leave the Valley to be signed by a national label was Flotsam and Jetsam, which hooked up with Elektra in 1988 and MCA in 1989. Although this metal quintet never quite broke beyond cult-hero sta-tus, its original bass player Jason New-sted joined metal superstars Metallica.

The most successful of the rock groups that didn't leave home were the tragicomic Gin Blossoms. A group that became synonymous with Tempe's "inde-pendent rock" scene, the quintet played a jangly brand of melodic rock that owed more than a passing nod to REM. Although they were the kingfish of this small pond, they always seemed to be on the verge of breaking up. Band members would stare daggers at one another on stage. Doug Hopkins, the band's most accomplished songwriter, was depressive and an alcoholic. After the group signed with A&M in 1990, his pugnacious attitude in the recording studio prompted the other members to kick him out of the band, even though he'd written most of the songs that were featured on the debut album. Hopkins formed another band and eventually left that one, too, apparently almost incapacitated by his own demons. He shot himself to death on the same December weekend in 1993 that Frank Zappa died. The rest of the Gin Blossoms issued a press release eulogizing Hopkins and continued to tour to keep the album selling. *New Miserable Experience,* the Blossoms' debut, sold more than two million copies. The band's second album, *Congratulations, I'm Sorry,*

didn't do as well, and the road-worn group finally broke up in 1996.

CeCe Peniston, the rhythm and blues diva, also came out of Phoenix. A 1987 graduate of Trevor Browne High School on Phoenix's west side, she became Miss Black Arizona in 1989. When she sang background vocals on an album by Phoenix rapper Overweight Pooch, a talent scout at A&M was so impressed he asked Peniston to record. The result was "Finally," which became the title cut of her debut album in 1992.

This isn't the whole story of the Valley's music scene—which has shown a surprising love for jazz and blues—it's just the story of a few of the acts that made some waves on the pop charts. Not bad for a place that isn't known for its music.

rary touring act. Two seating sections are on turntables and can be turned around to make the hall smaller and more intimate. The acoustics are fairly good.

Gammage Auditorium
1200 South Forest Avenue, near Mill Avenue and Apache Boulevard, Tempe
(480) 965-3434
www.asugammage.com
Frank Lloyd Wright designed this circular building. At roughly 3,000 seats, Gammage Auditorium feels intimate even in the balconies. It's not particularly welcoming to louder acts, but Bruce Springsteen's "acoustic" tour and Laurie Anderson's controlled technological avant-pop proved that this venue is just as good for live pop music as it is for the arts. You can catch touring road companies from Broadway like *The Lion King* and *Phantom of the Opera* as well as performances by opera divas and classical virtuosos.

Mesa Amphitheatre
Center Street and University Drive, Mesa
(480) 644-2560
There are no seats in this 4,000-capacity amphitheater, just a pleasant grassy slope. So stretch out, watch the stars, and enjoy the music. This is the place to catch acts on their way up and acts on their way down. It's very casual, and people bring blankets.

Red River Music Hall
730 North Mill Avenue, Tempe
(480) 829-6779
A 1,000-seat theater, the Music Hall was known as the Red River Opry when it opened, and its main stock-in-trade was a troupe that performed a nightly, Branson-type country-music revue. On summer nights, the Opry established a series of smooth-jazz concerts and country concerts by touring national acts as well as concert dates by pop performers. These

series have continued and the name was changed to better reflect the diversity of entertainment offered. There really isn't a bad seat in the house, and the sound system is among the best.

Northeast Valley

Scottsdale Center for the Arts
7380 East Second Street, Scottsdale
(480) 994-2787
www.scottsdalearts.org
At about 800 seats, the Scottsdale Center for the Arts offers an extremely intimate atmosphere for shows by jazz and folk-music performers, and a contemporary dance series brings in national companies. Touring swing bands also play here. In the summertime, performances in the outdoor amphitheater (within walking distance of the Scottsdale municipal complex) attract acts like the Chieftains and Queen Ida and her Zydeco Band. The sound in the auditorium is stellar, and all the seats provide excellent views of the stage; the sound in the amphitheater is good.

Northwest Valley

Sundome Center for the Performing Arts
19403 R. H. Johnson Boulevard,
Sun City West
(623) 975-1900
Owing to its location in a retirement community, the 7,000-seat Sundome's bill of fare leans generally toward touring pop of another era, but it has seen the likes of Garrison Keillor, The Judds, and Bill Cosby.

ROCK NIGHTCLUBS
Phoenix

The Mason Jar
2303 East Indian School Road, Phoenix
(602) 954-0455
www.masonjarlive.com

The Mason Jar's owner, Franco Gagliano, is a colorful guy. He's been known to pull the plug on acts that peeved him. Fortunately, Gagliano is canny enough to program heavy metal, big-hair rock, and even some alternative music in this venue that looks like an oversize basement rec room. The Mason Jar also has a reputation of being a place to catch national acts on the rise. Jane's Addiction played the Mason Jar on their first trip through Phoenix. You don't have to have any body piercing or tattoos to go to the Jar, but you might see plenty while you're there. Bring your earplugs unless you're unconcerned about hearing loss. Recently the Mason Jar has diversified, so in addition to the punk, metal, and goth, you'll occasionally come across a country band.

Modified Arts
407 East Roosevelt, Phoenix
(602) 462-5516
This is the local venue for the independent labels and alternative groups from the Valley. The walls feature contemporary paintings and the crowd often spills out onto the street. Even without a liquor license, the Modified experience is urban and cool.

Southeast Valley

Hollywood Alley
2610 West Baseline Road, Mesa
(480) 820-7117
www.hollywoodalley.com
The decor comes right out of '70s glam-band heaven, and the music is hard rock and edge of metal. Wear your earplugs. The place gets crowded when popular local bands are playing. In many ways Hollywood Alley reflects the Valley's blue-collar love of all heavy music. On top of that, the club serves good pizza to go with the beer and music.

SHOPPING 🎁

The cultural diversity of the Valley of the Sun, coupled with its cachet as a travel destination, makes for a rich and varied shopping experience. Buying locally made arts and crafts—like Native American jewelry, Mexican pottery, kachinas, cowboy art, bola ties, and cowboy boots—yields one-of-a-kind finds and lasting mementos of your trip. If you are lucky enough to catch an artisan in action, your purchase will be even more meaningful and you'll have a good story to tell the folks at home.

In addition to Southwestern goods, the metropolitan area has nearly every item imaginable, from antique heirlooms to contemporary conversation pieces, teenage trends to evening designer wear, and kitchen classics to outdoor gadgets. Moreover, shopping areas are as plentiful here as jackrabbits in spring. Venues range from historic districts whose quaint shops offer unique and, often, high-end pieces to megamalls that entice with competitive prices and large selections.

Each of the Valley's four corners sports at least one major mall—Phoenix itself has several—with a minimum of three large department stores anchoring a multitude of smaller shops. In addition, you can find even more shopping enclaves on the streets adjacent to the malls. Choose one mall and its outskirts to explore, and you can literally wander the area all day, shopping to your heart's content—or your budget's constraints. Malls are destination points for entertainment seekers, thanks to well-rounded offerings of restaurants, fast-food courts, cinemas, arcades, and, in a few cases, even playgrounds. Plus, malls provide a cool retreat from summer's heat when the sun prevents outdoor pursuits.

The area's open-air shopping districts provide a pleasant diversion for most of the year, whether you have some serious buying in mind or are just in the mood for a stroll and some window-shopping. The Valley holds its own as an antiques hunting destination, with centers in Glendale, Scottsdale, Mesa, and elsewhere. Outlet shopping opportunities have greatly increased in the Valley in the past decade. Even though the outlet malls listed here are on the fringes of the city, they are worth the drive if you're looking for bargains.

To maximize your shopping pleasure, we provide an overview—by geographic area—of the Valley's major shopping destinations. If you are on a mission to find a certain item not mentioned here, be sure to consult the Yellow Pages or ask another Insider. Since great little stores appear in unexpected places, don't be afraid to grab a map and go exploring. As the locals have known for years, you never know what treasures you'll discover.

PHOENIX

Shopping Malls

Biltmore Fashion Park
24th Street and Camelback Road, Phoenix
(602) 955-8400
www.shopbiltmore.com

Biltmore Fashion Park's redbrick sidewalks, shaded walkways, fountains, outdoor cafes, and distinctive storefront architecture all exude elegance and Old World charm. The mall designation may be misleading—yes, it has major department stores mixed with specialty shops, but it also offers a pleasant place to dally and meet friends, even if shopping's not the main event. Don't forget to pick up a guide to the ground's five theme gardens.

Macy's and Saks Fifth Avenue comprise the major department stores, but a big draw for Phoenix residents and international visitors alike is the selection of intimate high-end stores, which include

Gucci, Escada, Ann Taylor, Moda Georgio, Cartier, and Cole-Haan. Even children's apparel goes trendy at OiLily. Dog lovers will go crazy over the homemade treats in the Three Dog Bakery. Williams-Sonoma, Pottery Barn, and Restoration Hardware are fun stops for cooking and home-decorating enthusiasts. Other draws include the Banana Republic, which offers clothing and more, and The Sharper Image, with its fascinating array of high-tech gizmos. Borders Books & Music carries more than 200,000 book, music, and video titles, as well as 2,000 periodicals in 10 languages. It often offers live music. Borders' espresso bar and the children's activity area are great hangouts.

The Biltmore Fashion Park boasts more than 70 fine stores and eating establishments in all, with restaurants clustered on the east end of the mall (see the Restaurants chapter). Fare includes Japanese, Italian, Southwestern, and continental. Stores are open daily. The Greater Phoenix Convention & Visitors Bureau runs an information booth near Saks Fifth Avenue. Valet service and free parking, much of it shaded, is available.

Camelback Colonnade
18th Street and Camelback Road, Phoenix
(602) 274-7642
The Colonnade, one of Phoenix's older shopping centers, has undergone a variety of makeovers through the years to compete with malls in suburban growth areas. Currently, it's a pleasant, not-too-sprawling mixture of large retail stores in an open-air setting, some reached through an indoor mall entrance and some having outdoor entrances. Two of its most popular stores are E & J's Designer Shoe Outlet, with designer shoes and handbags at prices rivaling wholesale, and Last Chance Bargain Shoes & Apparel, with low prices on racks and racks of items for women, men, and children. Returned, reconditioned, and refurbished items from Nordstrom department stores around the country are constantly trickling into Last

Chance. Bargain hunters beware—some of the items have been previously worn or may have flaws.

You'll also find an Old Navy clothing store; Best Buy appliances, music, and computers; Stroud's Linens Outlet; Staples office supplies; Ulta cosmetics store; and two department stores, Mervyn's and Marshall's. If you are hungry, join the locals at the popular Miracle Mile Deli for New York–style bagels and such. The Colonnade is open daily.

COFCO Chinese Cultural Center
668 North 44th Street, Phoenix
(602) 275-8578
This intimate shopping, restaurant, and office complex offers a unique cultural experience where East Asia design meets Western sensibilities. The bold red exterior, green roof tiles, hand-carved pagodas, statues, and an acre of traditional Chinese gardens offer a tranquil refuge. The most interesting store is the Ranch 99 Market, which offers traditional Asian foods and hard-to-find items, from roast ducks to live clams. Oriental Factory Direct has clothing, books, jade, feng shui products, silk clothes, and other gift items direct from Hong Kong. The Art Gallery carries Chinese art, such as rice paper paintings. Imperial Arts and Antiques features hand-painted porcelains and figurines. Yes! I Do, a photography and wedding shop, has a gorgeous selection of handmade wedding gowns, in both Western and traditional Chinese styles.

Desert Ridge Marketplace
Deer Valley Drive and Tatum Boulevard, Phoenix
(480) 513-7586
www.shopdesertridge.com
Just when you thought there couldn't be any more malls to visit, comes Desert Ridge, a $170-million, 1.3-million-square-foot "suburban lifestyle entertainment center" featuring several gated communities, commercial businesses, a Marriott hotel, golf courses, and five unique shopping districts with individual shopping themes. You'll find

more than 100 stores here, with books at Barnes & Noble; groceries at Albertsons; filling feasts at the locally-owned Fatburger; headwear at Hat World; shoes at Famous Footware; and a multiplex theater and eateries, including In-N-Out Burger, Rubio's Baja Grill, and Salute Italian Ristorante. You'll never have to leave!

Many shopping malls make shopping with children fun by providing playgrounds and special events. The Metrocenter has a Castles 'N Coasters that can keep kids occupied while their parents browse the shops. Paradise Valley Mall has a free playground for preschoolers. Call ahead or check the Web site to see what the mall near you offers.

Desert Sky Mall
Thomas Road and 75th Avenue, Phoenix
(623) 245-1400
www.westcor.com
In the early 1990s the old Westridge Mall that serves west Phoenix was revamped into fancier digs—including two new courts and huge skylights—lending it a clean, airy ambiance that fits its mission as a community mall. Nearby is Cricket Pavilion, a popular outdoor concert venue. Now a WestCor property, the mall's department stores include Dillard's, Sears, and Mervyn's. Other shopping venues include a Kitchen & More, Kay Bee Toys, Kit's Camera, and Saba's Western Wear. A Six Shooters Sports Grill features an entertainment facility, and a movie theater is conveniently located on-site. Open daily.

Metrocenter
Interstate 17 between Dunlap and Peoria Avenues, Phoenix
(602) 997-2641
www.shopsimon.com
When it opened in 1973, Metrocenter was not only one of Arizona's first major regional shopping malls, but was America's largest shopping mall. It's still no slouch.

The two-level interior has been remodeled with marble inlay floors, palm trees throughout, and two dancing waterfalls that often stop shoppers in their tracks.

Among its 200 stores you'll find the major department stores of Macy's, Dillard's, JCPenney, Sears, and Robinsons-May. Specialty stores include The Disney Store, B. Dalton Booksellers, Waldenbooks, and Amazing Magic. Clothing stores include Gap, Old Navy, Guess, Structure, Aeropostale, and Express. The mall also offers several Arizona gift stores, including Outwest Gifts.

The food court, dubbed FoodWorks, features many eateries and a Ruby Tuesday restaurant. Harkins Theatres, near the food court, offers stadium seating, 12 screens, and the latest stereo sound system.

Inquire at the customer service center—on the lower level near Dillard's—for more information about merchants, bus schedules, and stroller rentals. The mall is open daily.

Metro Parkway, which circles Metrocenter, is lined with smaller shopping centers, restaurants, movie theaters, and the popular amusement park Castles 'N Coasters. Among the shops facing Metro Parkway is a large Barnes & Noble bookstore, at 10235 Metro Parkway East, (602) 678-0088.

Paradise Valley Mall
Tatum Boulevard and Cactus Road, Phoenix
(602) 953-2959
www.westcor.com
In addition to being one level, Paradise Valley Mall has made its shopping experience more comfortable by adding plush seating areas throughout the mall to give shoppers frequent opportunities to sit and relax. A stream meanders through the food court and the Recipe for a Healthy Me children's playground. Its outdoor patio also features lush landscaping. Anchored by Robinsons-May, Sears, JCPenney, Dillard's, and Macy's, the mall's 160-plus stores also include Ann Taylor, Talbot's, Abercrombie & Fitch, Old Navy,

Brookstone, and Whitehall Jewelers. Mall attractions also include a movie theater and a video game arcade.

Paradise Valley Mall is open daily, and should you need transportation assistance or have questions about the mall, you can find the Customer Service Center near the food court.

The corner of Tatum Boulevard and Cactus Road is also home to three smaller shopping centers, including the Village Fair North shopping center. There, you'll find a large Bookstar at 12863 North Tatum Boulevard, (602) 953–8066.

Phoenix Spectrum Mall
19th Avenue and Bethany Home Road, Phoenix
(602) 249–0670
www.phoenixspectrummall.com
Like the Colonnade, Phoenix Spectrum has shifted its stores and reshaped its philosophy over the years to stay competitive with newer, fancier malls. Its slate of anchors include CostCo and Wal-Mart. It also boasts a Dillard's Clearance Center, which carries unsold new merchandise shipped in from Dillard's department stores in the region. The mall has more than 100 stores, a well-landscaped interior walkway with an abundance of mature trees, and a food court. The complex also has two movie theaters.

Shopping Districts

Arizona Center
Van Buren Street between Third and Fifth Streets, Phoenix
(602) 271–4000
www.arizonacenter.com
By the 1970s most department stores had vanished from downtown Phoenix. A handful of smaller specialty stores remained, but most people shopped in neighborhoods closer to home. The downtown retail scene got a much-needed boost in the 1980s with the construction of the Arizona Center, a two-story, open-air collection of shops, restaurants, and

nightclubs. Incorporated into the design are office towers and numerous gardens, sculptures, and fountains. The main garden, in a sunken area near Van Buren Street, offers a shady oasis for lunch breaks, people watching, or quiet contemplation. The restaurants and bars bustle, but the more sedate atmosphere in the shops provides a pleasant diversion if you're downtown.

The more than 30 shops include New York & Company, Glory-B's, Jayne's Marketplace, Cold Stone Creamery, and Arizona Beach Co. For Arizona books and gifts rustled up by a well-regarded state magazine publisher, check out Cardware. Other specialty shops include Flag World, with an extensive selection of the world's flags; Oak Creek Canyon, with Southwestern home accessories; Sports Fan, featuring sports apparel; the Phoenix International Raceway Gift Shop and Ticket Office, with racing memorabilia; and Smokin Cigar Company, with its fine selection of domestic and international cigars.

Many retail carts are scattered about the Arizona Center selling everything from refrigerator magnets and T-shirts to wind chimes and posters.

The food court packs them in during weekday lunch hours, and it is also open in the evening, making it a convenient place for a quick bite before catching a cultural or sporting event. Another attraction is the AMC 24-screen theater, the only movie house in downtown Phoenix.

The mall is open daily and provides a Guest Services Center in the food court. Find ample parking in the garage on Fillmore Street, which is open to Arizona Center customers, or try to find a spot along Third Street.

Town & Country Shopping Center
20th Street and Camelback Road, Phoenix
(602) 955–6850
www.townandcountryshops.com
In the heart of the Camelback Corridor of retail and business complexes, Town & Country—with its charming blend of red-

tiled roofs, courtyards, and fountains—
makes a nice excursion. About two dozen
shops, mostly on the small and eclectic
side, are connected by walkways lined
with redbrick. Interesting stops include
The Herb Stop, which offers aromatherapy
oils and a cornucopia of herbs; Ye Olde
Pipe & Tobacco Shoppe, for cigar and
pipe aficionados; Table Talk, a kitchen
store; Jutenhoops, an eclectic gift shop
with one of the best selections of greeting
cards in town; and My Sister's Closet,
which offers recycled designer apparel.

The larger stores in the vicinity include
Linens 'N Things, Trader Joe's, and Bookstar. You'll find a coffeehouse, ice-cream
parlor, and a handful of restaurants in the
area, along with a six-screen movie house.
Most of the stores and restaurants are
open daily.

Outlet Shopping

Outlets at Anthem
Interstate 17 at Anthem Way, Phoenix
(623) 465–9500
www.outletsatanthem.com
When heading north on I-17 to the Outlets
at Anthem, you will feel like you're heading out on the open road to Flagstaff. The
shops are 30 to 45 minutes from downtown and, surprisingly, still within Phoenix
city limits. Follow the signs and look for
exit 229.

You'll enjoy bargain hunting in the
pleasant Southwestern-style setting, with
its inviting landscaping and benches. The
more than 90 stores have a wide enough
variety to interest everyone in the family. If
you are shopping for housewares, look for
the Mikasa Factory Store, Kitchen Collection, Le Creuset, Springmaid-Wamsutta,
and other stores. Women's apparel
includes Ann Taylor, Polo Ralph Lauren,
Casual Corner Woman, and Nautica Factory Store. For children, stop by the
Oshkosh B'Gosh Factory Store, Hart-
strings, Carter's, and others. Men can
stock up on clothes and accessories at

Dockers Outlet, Geoffrey Beene, Gap, and
Ashworths. Other stores are Book Ware-
house, Sunglass Outlet, Bose Factory
Store, and Reebok.

You also will find a food court and
playground. Nearby, the Customer Service
Center offers coupon books, stroller
rentals, wheelchairs, and tourist information. The shops are open daily.

Antiques Shopping

Antique Gatherings
3601 East Indian School Road, Phoenix
(602) 956–8203
This large store gathers several antiques
dealers into one location. Each dealer has
a designated space from which he or she
displays and sells wares. You will be
impressed by how tidy this store is, and
it's a delight to browse here even if you're
not in the market for antiques and collectibles. Walking from one dealer's area
to another is like walking among various
tastefully decorated sitting rooms from
different eras. You get a quick sampling of
the Victorian era, the American West, rural
life, and more. Antique Gatherings dealers
sell practically everything except the
kitchen sink (and maybe that, too), including furniture, housewares, books, and
dolls. Prepare to be smitten by fancy pillows, custom-made lamps, artwork, quilts,
tea sets, and doll clothes.

A nice little bonus toward the back of
the store is the Serendipity Tea Room,
which serves sandwiches, high tea, and
salads Tuesday through Saturday. Antique
Gatherings is open daily.

The Brass Armadillo Antique Mall
12419 North 28th Drive, Phoenix
(602) 942–0030
www.brassarmadillo.com
Here's a fun way to browse for antiques
and collectibles all in one building. This
mall—about a mile north of Metrocenter
just off I-17 and Cactus Road—boasts
more than 600 dealers and 39,000 square

feet. Part of a chain of antiques malls headquartered in the Midwest, the Brass Armadillo's easy-to-navigate design includes uncluttered booths and street signs named for states to guide your way.

Be prepared to lose track of time among the vast array of furniture, china, toys, glassware, dolls, vintage jewelry, collectible sports cards, and political memorabilia. If you want to learn more about your finds, you can browse the section of reference books on antiques and collectibles. The mall is open daily.

Specialty Stores

Buffalo Exchange
730 East Missouri Street, Phoenix
(602) 532-0144
www.buffaloexchange.com
Buffalo Exchange, a resale clothing store, has built a reputation among young adults as the place to find stylish clothing on the cheap. But the store has such a good turnover of merchandise and such a wide variety of duds for women and men that we recommend a visit for bargain shoppers of any age. If you're in the recycling mood, Buffalo Exchange will pay you cash or trade for the used clothing that it accepts. The store has another location at 227 West University Drive in Tempe, near Arizona State University (480) 968-2557. There's also a Buffalo Kids at 1720 East Warner Road, Tempe, (480) 545-2868. The stores are open daily.

Candle & Gift Factory Outlet
24th Street and Indian School Road, Phoenix
(602) 522-2704
www.cgfo.com
It's not just the aroma of burning candles that makes a walk through this store a sensory experience. It's also the sounds of soft music and water trickling through indoor fountains, not to mention the eye-catching selection of candles, candleholders, luminarias, sconces, and candle chimneys. Scents include everything from

For a directory of small bookstores in the Phoenix metropolitan area, including stores specializing in used and antiquarian books, check the Valley Independent Booksellers Association Web site at www.bentcover.com. About 60 stores are listed.

florals to rich, chocolate "desserts." Many of the tapers, votives, pillars, and other candles have been made on-site. The candleholders, baskets, and other gift items have been imported from all over the world. There is an especially good selection of folk art. Since this is a factory outlet, prices are reasonable. There are two other locations at 10201 North Scottsdale Road, Scottsdale, (480) 778-1870; and 7229 East Main Street, Scottsdale, (480) 429-3344. The stores are open daily.

Cowtown Boots
2710 West Thunderbird Road, Phoenix
(602) 548-3009
www.cowtownboots.com
After more than 30 years in the business, it's no surprise that almost everything you need to be outfitted in Western style is here at Cowtown, but its specialty is boots. More than 25,000 pairs are on hand, from standard cow leather to more exotic materials like snake, deer, bull, calf, mule, antelope, and ostrich. In addition to the Cowtown label of boots, find Dan Post, Texas, Chisholm, and ACME brands. Factory irregulars are usually on sale, for those looking for a great deal. The store is open daily. Cowtown's other Valley location is at 1001 North Scottsdale Road, Tempe, (480) 968-4748.

Flax Company Inc.
1001 East Jefferson Street, Phoenix
(602) 254-0840
This huge artists' supply store can prove invaluable in finding those perfect creative tools. It is patronized by both casual and serious artists. Flax flaunts one of the state's largest selections of fine writing

instruments, picture frames, artists' paints, canvases, drafting supplies, art studio furniture, and equipment. You can honor your work by ordering a custom frame. It is open every day but Sunday.

Popular Outdoor Outfitters
2814 West Bell Road, Phoenix
(602) 863-2462
www.popularoutdooroutfitters.com
This Arizona-based purveyor of outdoor gear sells such practical items as clothes, tents, and stoves, as well as just-for-fun goods like kayaks and fishing lures. Known for its good selection, Popular often has reasonable prices on hiking boots. Easily accessible from I-17, the store is open daily. Check the Yellow Pages or its Web site for Popular's other Valley locations.

Sportsman's Fine Wine & Spirits
3205 East Camelback Road, Phoenix
(602) 955-7730
This is one of the best liquor stores in the Valley. Not only does Sportsman's offer an impressive range of beer, wine, and spirits, but there's a bar on the premises. Cigars and fine imported cheeses are also for sale. A lot of the products are pricey, but there's plenty for the slimmer budget as well. Complementary wine tastings are held two or three times a week. The crowd here is a little more formal than in most places in Phoenix, but no one will turn you out if you dress casual.

Tracks in Wax
4741 North Central Avenue, Phoenix
(602) 274-2660
If you're looking for vintage vinyl and you don't want to spend a lot of money, this is the place. Unlike a lot of stores of this kind, Tracks in Wax doesn't cater to the collector so much as the listener. You'll find lots of rare albums here, but the scuffed covers keep them from having inflated collectors' prices. One visit uncovered everything from early Blue Oyster Cult to Peter Seger playing frontier tunes on the banjo. We also found the Pogues, the Byrds, the soundtrack to *Barbarella* (no joke), and

even original World War II broadcasts by Tokyo Rose. There are used CDs too.

SOUTHEAST VALLEY
Shopping Malls

Arizona Mills
Superstition Freeway (U.S. Highway 60)
and I-10, Tempe
(480) 491-9700
www.arizonamills.com
Arizona Mills opened to much media hoopla in late 1997, in part because it was Arizona's first shopping center from the Mills Corp., the developer of Ontario Mills near Los Angeles and elsewhere. The company brought "shoppertainment" to the Valley of the Sun, mixing outlet stores from dozens of nationally known retailers with a variety of entertainment venues and innovative restaurants. Arizona Mills strives to outshine the ordinary mall by conveying a lively, almost futuristic atmosphere. The walkway through its oval design wends through six theme neighborhoods that evoke an aspect of Arizona, from desert plants to ancient petroglyphs. Arizona artists designed many of the murals, mosaic tiles, metal sculptures, and pottery. Another fixture in the colorful and decor-intense mall is the profusion of video screens overhead, which blare commercials, mall promotions, and music videos. The shopping is fun, but be prepared for sensory overload.

The retailers, restaurants, and entertainment venues total 175, so there's plenty to see and do. Mall anchors include Last Call from Nieman-Marcus, Ross, Burlington Coat Factory, JCPenney Outlet Store, Linens 'N Things, and Off 5th–Saks Fifth Avenue Outlet. In women's apparel, other stores include Pacific Sunwear of California and Kenneth Cole of New York. You'll also find a Guess? Factory Store, Big Dog Sportswear, and a Van Heusen Factory Outlet. There are a dozen housewares and furniture outlet stores, along with a half-dozen cosmetic stores. It may have more shoe stores than any other venue in the Valley, with options including Nine West Outlet, Skechers Outlet, Bostonian Clarks Shoe Outlet, and an Etienne Aigner Outlet.

Other interesting stops include Vitamin World, which carries all manner of vitamins, supplements, packaged foods, and natural remedies as well as offering a juice bar. The Virgin Megastore is a good stop for compact discs and videos.

There's a food court with an enormous seating area, plus a 24-screen cinema complex, an IMAX theater, and the extremely popular GameWorks, a giant arcade. Arizona Mills is open daily. It has two customer service centers, which also serve as Arizona Tourism Welcome Centers.

Chandler Fashion Center
Chandler Boulevard and Loop 101, Chandler
(480) 812-8488
www.westcor.com

One of the newest additions to the Valley's increasing number of shopping malls, Chandler Fashion Center opened in the fall of 2001. Part of a 320-acre urban village, the mall is home to more than 180 shops and restaurants. You'll find anchor stores Nordstrom, Robinsons-May, and Sears and numerous specialty boutiques. And there are some unique stores, such as Anchor Blue Kids, with cool fashions and great styles in denim for kids ages 7 to 14; The Apple Store, with ongoing demos of the very newest Macs; Eddie Bauer Home; Hollister, with hot West Coast, surfer-styled clothes for teens; Red Rock Trading Post, with Navajo and Hopi crafts; and more. All this and a 20-plex theater and more than 25 eateries and restaurants, including California Pizza Kitchen and Ruby's Diner, an authentic 1940s diner.

Fiesta Mall
Superstition Freeway (US 60)
and Alma School Road, Mesa
(480) 833-4121
www.shopfiesta.com

Fiesta Mall has long been a handy location for Southeast Valley shoppers, with plenty

Traveling with children? Shopping malls are happy to loan out wheelchairs and baby strollers during your visit. Most malls also offer a courtesy escort service to help carry packages or accompany you to your car. Inquire at the mall's Customer Service Center or look for rental kiosks and security stations near the food court.

of variety to meet shopping needs. In addition to the major department stores of Macy's, Dillard's, Robinsons-May, and Sears, the mall houses specialty stores such as Abercrombie & Fitch, Express Men, Frederick's of Hollywood, Waldenbooks, California Daze, Champs Sports, and the Team Shop, with apparel from the Suns, Diamondbacks, and Coyotes. You can also find an Exclusively Arizona, which sells Arizona-made products. There are 135 specialty stores in all, arranged in a two-level mall decorated with Southwestern colors. A food court and children's play area are also featured. The mall is open daily and covered parking is available. For moviegoers, two cinema complexes are within 2 blocks of the mall.

Superstition Springs Center
Superstition Freeway (US 60)
and Power Road, Mesa
(480) 396-2570
www.westcor.com

The Valley's continued growth toward the east has ensured the success of this regional mall, a pleasant destination with 130 stores. The major department stores are Dillard's, Robinsons-May, Mervyn's, JCPenney, and Sears. Several smaller shopping centers sit on the fringes of Superstition Springs Center, making the area a one-stop destination for most shopping needs.

As for the two-level mall, its stores include Carol's Art Gallery, Fast Fix Jewelry Repair, Bath & Body Works, Footlocker, Gapkids, Arizona Images, Waldenbooks, and Paradise Bakery. The interior has a contemporary feel, and in good weather it's quite nice to take a breather from shopping by sitting in the outdoor plaza. Facing the plaza is a playground for children, which features large models of desert animals. There is also a mini botanical garden with a nature trail. Other family-friendly features include the full-size indoor carousel near the food court and a play area with a slide shaped like a dog.

The Customer Service Center is on the lower level near the JCPenney entrance, and the stores are open daily.

Shopping Districts

Mill Avenue
Downtown Tempe
(480) 967-4877

Historic buildings, a mixture of shops, restaurants, offices, and a plethora of people-watching opportunities all combine to make Tempe a desirable place to while away an afternoon. Several dozen shops line Mill Avenue and the surrounding side streets, some tucked away in nooks and crannies. Tempe's central location in the heart of the Valley makes the Mill Avenue area a convenient meeting place; just grab a cup of something to sip at the coffee shops, juice bars, and restaurants with outdoor seating areas. The student population from Arizona State University livens the place up, especially on weekend nights when it bustles like a sophisticated city several times its size.

Clothing, shoe shops, and other stores that cater to college students abound here. Specialty stores include Urban Outfitters, 545 South Mill Avenue, filled with trendy home accessories, books, gifts, and clothing for the young set; Duck Soup, 640 South Mill Avenue, a card and gift shop with a good selection of Arizona and ASU T-shirts, as well as posters, candles, Arizona food products, and jewelry; the Cap Co., 15 East Sixth Street, offering shade for your head in styles ranging from old-fashioned bowlers to sports team

caps; Mazar Bazaar, 514 South Mill Avenue, which offers elegant imported designer clothes and accessories; Those Were the Days; 516 South Mill Avenue, whose unique books and items look like finds from someone's attic; two Campus Corner stores, good places to get ASU apparel before the game. The nearby Gentle Strength Co-op, 234 West University Drive, hits the spot with its selection of health food and cruelty-free products.

You'll also find several stores and restaurants connected to the Centerpoint office and retail development at Seventh Street and Mill Avenue, including a cinema complex. When you are done shopping and want to relax, the Tempe Town Lake is a short stroll to the north.

Antiques Shopping

Antique Plaza
114 West Main Street, Mesa
(480) 833-4844

More than 100 dealers are packed into this two-story antiques mall with 20,000 square feet of exhibit space in downtown Mesa. Find all kinds of furniture from different eras, along with vintage jewelry, table linens, quilts, lamps, Depression glass, trains, toys, and similar small collectibles. Antique Plaza is open daily. There are eight other antiques shops within walking distance. Free public parking is available and a number of restaurants are located nearby.

Specialty Stores

Bookman's
1056 South Country Club Drive, Mesa
(480) 835-0505
www.bookmans.com

This is Arizona's largest seller of used books and music. Bookman's has stores in Tucson, Flagstaff, and Sierra Vista, but this is its only store in the Valley. The selection is as complete as any of the book superstore chains—plus it has so many out-of-print titles that are often hard to find. There's a section devoted to new books, a large magazine section, and an area for used software. You can preview used CDs and cassettes at a listening station. A few chairs and couches are available if you become so engrossed in something that you need to sit down. The personnel are willing to patiently sift through books and magazines you bring in for trade. Bookman's awards cash and/or store credit for materials it's willing to take off your hands. The store is open daily and most evenings.

Changing Hands Bookstore
6428 South McClintock Drive, Tempe
(480) 730-0205
www.changinghands.com
This independent bookstore offers a noteworthy selection of new and used books for dedicated readers. A bin outside the store often offers freebies, and frequent buyers can get discounts when their book card is filled with stamps. Changing Hands offers a number of educational activities for kids and features readings several times a month by local authors. Valley newcomers can keep up to date on activities and new releases through the store's newsletter, which features staff reviews. The adjacent Wildflower Bread Company offers a good meeting point for book clubs, writing groups, and other literature lovers.

Cookies From Home
1605 West University Drive, Suite 106, Tempe
(480) 894-1944
www.cookiesfromhome.com
This cookie bakery got its start in 1981 on Mill Avenue in downtown Tempe, then—thanks to a burgeoning mail-order business—moved to larger quarters in an industrial park. Most agree that these cookies are as good as homemade. They come in eight different varieties and customer favorites include Hunka Chunka, Fudgies, and always Oatmeal Raisin. The retail store is a great place to buy cookies by the pound or as gift packages. There

are a variety of charming tins, baskets, decorated boxes, mugs, and cookie jars in which to present the treats. The store is open Monday through Saturday, but you can prolong the pleasure outside the state by ordering its treats online.

A number of imported imitations of Native American jewelry, arts, and crafts are finding their way into less-reputable stores. Educate yourself before you buy—look for an artist's signature and ask for a certificate of authenticity. When in doubt, buy from the artist directly.

Peppermint Bay
4905 East Ray Road, Ahwatukee
(480) 753-6412
A sweetie of a sweets store, Peppermint Bay sells all kinds of candy either individually wrapped or in bulk. You can peruse the chocolates, candy bars, bubble gums, hard candies, jelly beans, and gummy bears while enjoying the bright decor. You'll wonder whether you've suddenly stepped into a Candyland game. The store has a good variety of sugar-free candies too. Peppermint Bay is open every day and most evenings. If you shop at its other location, at the corner of Baseline and Stapley Roads in Mesa, you can take your candy discreetly into the AMC Theater.

REI-Tempe
1405 West Southern Avenue, Tempe
(480) 967-5494
www.rei.com
Recreational Equipment, Inc.—just REI to those in the know—is the first stop for anyone wanting to explore Arizona's natural wonders. The store carries equipment and related clothing for camping, cycling, climbing, hiking, and more. Staff members often do the sports themselves, so they can help you make an intelligent selection. If you want to try out a sport, you can rent equipment ranging from climbing shoes to kayaks. If you join the Seattle-

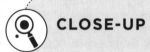

A Taste of Arizona

In your hunt for souvenirs from your visit to this state, some of the best you'll come across will be edible. Arizona is bustling with small companies that turn out innovative food products, many of which have a definite Arizona identity.

One Arizona food success story is Goldwater's Taste of the Southwest, a Scottsdale company started several years ago by the family of former Senator Barry Goldwater. Salsas are its specialty, and they come in a wide range of flavors. Goldwater's was the first in the country to come out with fruit salsa, and now the line includes Paradise Pineapple and Mohave Mango. Goldwater's chunky, medium-spiced Sedona Red Salsa has been rated "excellent" by the *New York Times.* In addition, the company sells Bisbee Barbecue Sauce and The Senator's Chili, a dry mix for beans and beef created by the late senator himself. The products are available in stores around the country. They've even made a dent in the international market. Call (800) 488-4932 for retail locations or order from the Web at www.goldwaters.com.

For something completely different, go home with a box of Fairytale Brownies. The Scottsdale company making these delights has established a lucrative national mail-order business, which you can reach by calling (800) 324-7982 or checking the Web at www.brownies.com. The name comes from a story dreamed up about a fairy with a magic spoon who bakes "in the wee hours of night." The company's old family recipe has won raves from around the country. The 12 gourmet flavors—such as White Chocolate Chunk, Peanut Butter, and Espresso— are available in many Arizona food stores.

More sweet news comes from Glendale and the Cerreta Candy Company. A tour of the company's chocolate-making factory is a popular, mouthwatering diversion in downtown Glendale. The chocolates are available at Smitty's and Fry's supermarkets around the Valley. Call (623) 930-1000 for more information or check the Web at www.cerreta.com.

Since Mexican food is a staple here, it's not surprising that many food companies specialize in salsas, tortillas, and tortilla chips. They can easily be found in Arizona groceries, and you'll have your choice of several variations—reduced-fat, reduced-salt, restaurant-style, black bean-style, lime-cilantro flavor, nacho flavor, and so forth. While in the snack aisle, you might try Poore Brothers Potato Chips. Again, it may be tough to decide which varieties to try—regular, jalapeño, salt and vinegar, or parmesan and garlic. The company is based in Goodyear.

Hot sauces of all sorts are popular too. Southwest Specialty Food Inc. in the West Valley makes a line of "Ass Kickin'" hot sauces and salsas, many of which contain habañero peppers, said to be 10 times as hot as jalapeños. With $10 million in annual sales, this company sells more than 90 different items in retail shops and by catalog in this country and abroad. Call (800) 536-3131 or check www.asskickin.com for a catalog.

Arizona Gunslinger Smokin' Hot Jalapeño Pepper Sauce has also made a name for itself. Its Phoenix-based makers have been distributing it nationally by mail order for almost a decade, and it's often found in airport shops. Gunslinger is made from red-ripened jalapeños, and its thicker consistency means it's suitable on all kinds of food, not just tacos and tostadas. Mail orders are taken at (800) 359–3912 or www.azgunslinger.com.

Other names to look for: Grand Canyon Cookies; Bill Johnson's Big Apple Barbecue Sauce, a 40-year-old recipe from the state's successful Big Apple restaurant chain; and Cave Creek Chili Beer, which boasts a serrano chile pepper hand inserted into every bottle. You can find this unusual beer in a Valley grocery store, or call Chili Beer at (800) 228-9742 for a list of retail shops.

What you take home doesn't necessarily have to be a manufactured food, though. Visit produce stands for home-grown citrus—different varieties of oranges as well as grapefruits, lemons, and tangerines—in the winter and spring. You'll also find dates, pecans, pistachios, piñon nuts, dried fruit, and honey. Arizona is the third-largest producer of citrus and vegetables in the United States.

And would you believe wine is produced in Arizona? The Sonoita-Elgin area of southern Arizona has been successfully making wines since the mid-1980s. Although the wines haven't yet captured more than the local market, they have won awards at various wine festivals. Check labels for these names: Sonoita Vineyards, Terra Rosa Vineyards, and Callaghan Vineyards.

Check out Valley stores for local products, such as Fairytale Brownies. FAIRYTALE BROWNIES

About beverages, here's another thing you ought to know: The ubiquitous AriZona brand of flavored iced teas in the pretty pastel cans and decoratively wrapped bottles comes from eight plants all over the country, none of which are in Arizona.

You can easily find most of the products mentioned while browsing shops in areas popular with tourists, as well as specialty shops in malls. Suggested retailers are Shades of the West on Main Street in Old Town Scottsdale; the Pinnacle Peak General Store in north Scottsdale; Arizona Images, with several mall locations; Cost Plus locations; Exclusively Arizona at Fiesta Mall in Mesa; and the AJ's Fine Foods, with several locations in the Valley.

based cooperative, you also get dividends at the end of the year. The store also has another location in Paradise Valley, at 12634 North Paradise Village Parkway West, (602) 996-5400.

Wide World of Maps
1444 West Southern Avenue, Mesa
(602) 279-2323, (800) 279-7654
www.maps4u.com
This locally grown store carries just about any map your vagabond heart desires and is a vital stop for those who plan on hiking Arizona's rough terrain. If it doesn't carry what you need, Wide World of Maps can map it for you. Its inventory includes travel maps, guidebooks, cookbooks, books on local history, hiking books, topographical maps, atlases, globes, wall maps, CD-ROM maps, and the latest Global Positioning Systems (GPS) and instruction on how to use them. The store also will laminate a map of your choice for maps that will be used a lot. Wide World of Maps is open daily and has another location at 2626 West Indian School Road in Phoenix. The above phone numbers work for both locations.

Zia Record Exchange
105 West University Drive, Tempe
(480) 829-1967
www.ziarecords.com
Founded by Phoenix resident Brad Singer in the early 1980s, Zia has grown from a funky little place selling vinyl to an eight-store, statewide chain. Music lovers appreciate its no-frills approach to providing the widest possible selection of new and used CDs, cassettes, and LPs. Imports are well represented here, and because the inventory is usually alphabetized without regard to genre, it's possible to spy a CD by a country singer snuggled next to one by a heavy metal artist. The local music scene mourned Singer's sudden passing in May 1998, but the stores continue on. Find other Zia's in the Valley at 1940 West Indian School Road in Phoenix, (602) 241-0313; 2510 West Thunderbird Road in Phoenix, (602) 866-7867; and 3851 Thun-

derbird Road in north Phoenix, (602) 482-3119.

NORTHEAST VALLEY
Shopping Malls

The Borgata
Lincoln Drive and Scottsdale Road, Scottsdale
(480) 998-1822
www.westcor.com
You'll do a double take when you spy this replica of a fourteenth-century Italian village, complete with brick towers. The Borgata stands out in more than just the looks department; it guards an elegant array of high-fashion boutiques, jewelry stores, art galleries, and outdoor bistros. The 50 stores include Davinci Collezione, fine Italian men's wear and home accessories; Seven Ring Gallery, fine art from local and national artists; This Little Piggy Wears Cotton, children's clothing; the Dance Centre, selling exercise togs; Impostors Jewelry, selling copies of famous jewelry; The Beach House, selling swim wear to be seen in; and Frankie's Patio Cafe, a shady place to drink and eat. Each Friday, from October through April, the Borgata's cobblestone courtyard is transformed into a farmers' market. The Christmas season brings an incredible display of twinkling white lights and other holiday decorations. The Borgata is open daily.

el Pedregal Festival Marketplace at the Boulders
Scottsdale Road and Carefree Highway, Scottsdale
(480) 488-1072
www.elpedregal.com
With its Moroccan styling, el Pedregal Festival Marketplace harmonizes with its magnificent desert setting—rock-strewn terrain formed millions of years ago. Located where the new housing developments of north Scottsdale give way to the hills and boulders of Carefree, the shopping development is part of The Boulders resort, a

short distance away by foot. One of the main attractions in el Pedregal is the Heard Museum North, which offers exhibitions on a smaller scale than the main Heard Museum in downtown Phoenix and whose gift shop features Native American arts and crafts. More than 36 artisan shops and galleries cluster in this two-level, distinctive building, which overlooks an amphitheater with grassy areas, benches, and cafe tables. The galleries offer everything from local folk art to African sculpture. Other shops include the Conrad Leather Boutique, with custom leather goods and clothing; Rustic Star, with mountain- and desert-themed cards and gifts; and Canyon Lifestyles, which sells Southwestern accessories for the home. Three cafes and a restaurant round out the selection, and special music and art events make a visit even more memorable.

Kierland Commons
7122 East Greenway Parkway, Scottsdale
(480) 348-1577
www.kierlandcommons.com
Designed to look like the Main Street of a small town, with a spacious plaza, shady trellised arcades, natural-colored stone, and an abundance of flowers and trees, Kierland Commons is an upscale retail, restaurant, and office development at Scottsdale Road and Greenway Parkway. The 450,000-square-foot, mixed-use development is the first "urban village" center to be built in the Phoenix area. This addition to the mall scene in Scottsdale features Restoration Hardware, Anthropologie, Sharper Image, Crate & Barrel, and Sur La Table, along with the popular eateries The Cheesecake Factory, and Morton's Steak House.

Scottsdale Fashion Square
Camelback and Scottsdale Roads,
Scottsdale
(480) 921-2140
www.westcor.com
Once a tidy open-air shopping center serving Scottsdale residents, in the past decade Scottsdale Fashion Square has

Shopaholics or those of us with little time to window-shop, should check out eshop arizona, www.eshoparizona.com, an online site that provides a directory of all sorts of shops, galleries, and artisans throughout Arizona, with brief descriptions of their products. You can search more than 21 categories, including accessories, Native American, one-of-a-kind antiques, clothing, crafts, kidstuff, books, leather, Old West, and more. There are helpful descriptions and photos for each listing. The site also covers specials and events and you can search by type of shop or by type of merchandise.

transformed into a ritzy indoor mall that, at 1.8 million square feet, is the largest mall in Arizona. The mall attracts people from all over the Valley, mainly because of its mix of high-powered department stores and classy boutiques.

Scottsdale Fashion Square has Arizona's first Nordstrom and Neiman Marcus. Other anchors include Robinson's- May and Dillard's (the largest in the entire chain). There are 225 stores in all, of which 50 are exclusive stores. In the fall of 1998, Scottsdale Fashion Square not only opened Nordstrom but also finished construction of an enclosed bridge—filled with 50 stores—that connects Nordstrom on the south side of Camelback Road to the main mall on the north side of Camelback.

The ambiance inside the two-level mall makes for a decadent shopping experience. Palm trees tower nearly to the retractable glass ceiling. Fountains throughout the mall make Scottsdale seem more tropical than desertlike, including a two-story "rain curtain" in the center of the food court, which wraps around an open stairway. The food court itself is one of the best in the Valley because of its wide selection—from burgers to international fare that includes French, Mexican,

Chinese, and Japanese fast food. The numerous sit-down restaurants and cafes in the mall draw evening diners.

Stores include Tiffany & Company, the famous New York jeweler; Crate & Barrel; Banana Republic; Z Gallerie, featuring home-decorating accessories; Louis Vuitton; Coach Leather; Guess Kids; The Team Shop, with Phoenix Suns memorabilia; Brentano's Bookstore; J. Crew clothing store; the Build-A-Bear Workshop; and the Everything But Water swimsuit store.

Also find the Scottsdale Kitchen Co., with all kinds of housewares; The Disney Store; Godiva Chocolatier; The Body Shop cosmetics store; and, for souvenir shoppers, Arizona Images. After a hard day of shopping, you can relax at the day spa at Nordstrom or Dillard's or catch a flick at one of the mall's 12 cinemas. Special services provided by the mall include lockers, stroller rental, valet parking, and a roving concierge. The mall is open daily.

Shops at Gainey Village
8787 North Scottsdale Road, Scottsdale and Doubletree Roads, Scottsdale
(480) 488-3381

The Shops at Gainey Village are designed as a series of linked outdoor plazas and buildings reflecting an upscale rustic "village" atmosphere reminiscent of the historic roots of the original Gainey Ranch. The Shops at Gainey Village combine a distinctive blend of upscale shops, boutiques, trendy eateries, and fine-dining establishments. Stores include Pickles & Ice Cream, a maternity boutique; Via Veneto, an upscale, European shoe salon; Xanadu Gallery, with contemporary/representational Impressionistic art; Bella Dimora, featuring bed, bath, and kitchen home accents; and the funky Two Plates Full, with fun, colorful Southwest and contemporary gifts. Hungry? The Coffee Bean & Tea Leaf offers gourmet coffee and much more; there's Thaifoon for Thai food and the Village Tavern, an upscale, casual American restaurant.

Shopping Districts

Carefree
Cave Creek and Tom Darlington Roads, Carefree
(480) 488-3381

Located about 30 minutes north of downtown Scottsdale, the core of Carefree sports several small shops and boutiques that are similar to Scottsdale's Fifth Avenue, but on a smaller scale. They are clustered on Easy Street, Ho and Hum Roads, and Sundial Plaza—all within short walking distance of each other. Peruse stores like the Lemon Tree, 22 Easy Street, (480) 488-3894, which specializes in Hummels, Madame Alexander dolls, and other art collectibles. Stroll through the grounds of the Spanish Village, at the corner of Ho and Hum Roads, (480) 488-0350, and enjoy its specialty shops, clothing boutiques, galleries, and cafes. Most of the shops are open daily.

Fifth Avenue
Downtown Scottsdale
(480) 947-6423
www.downtownscottsdale.com

A number of shopping districts thrive in downtown Scottsdale, each with its own special personality and charm. The merchants of Fifth Avenue cater to tourists and locals alike with a plethora of boutiques and galleries, many with merchandise unique to the Southwest. The Fifth Avenue shops run along 3 blocks of mostly shaded walkways—the fountain with four horses near the center of activity makes a prominent landmark. Shops line both sides of the street and it's worthwhile to explore the establishments on Third Avenue, Stetson Drive, Marshall Way, Craftsman Court, and Main Street. The shops are interspersed with many top-notch art galleries for which Scottsdale is famous. (See the chapter The Arts for more information.)

Here are a few stops along the way to keep in mind as you browse: Kactus Jock, at 7121 East Fifth Avenue, features sportswear made from natural fiber. Arizona

Highways, at 7235 East First Avenue, sells tons of Arizona-related products including hiking books, guidebooks, calendars, address books, posters, cookbooks, local and regional foods, notecards, and more. Cinch a good, custom-fitted swimsuit at Computerized Swimwear Systems, 4020 North Scottsdale Road. Angel Wings and Other Things is an angel-themed gift shop at 7121 East Fifth Avenue. Essentially Books, 6957 East Fifth Avenue, specializes in books on contemporary and Native American spirituality. Some stores are closed on Sunday or limit their hours during the summer.

Main Street
West Main Street, downtown Scottsdale
(480) 947-6423
www.downtownscottsdale.com
The art gallery strip along West Main Street in Scottsdale boasts outstanding collections of arts and antiques. We'll explore the area's reputation more thoroughly in the chapter on The Arts, but note that masterpieces by many of the Old Western masters are represented here, as well as work by folk artists, Native American artists, and contemporary artists. Guidon Books, at 7117 East Main Street, features a serious collection of antique Western and Civil War books, as well as collectible posters and maps.

Marshall Way Arts District
Marshall Way, downtown Scottsdale
(480) 947-6423
www.downtownscottsdale.com
The Marshall Way Arts District—between Craftsman Court and Third Avenue west of Scottsdale Road and north of Indian School Road—is an art lover's heaven. The galleries feature a diversity of media, from limited edition prints to art you can wear, all in a tree-shaded, upscale setting. Many internationally recognized artists have displayed their work here. If you are looking for distinctive jewelry, you might want to check out Jewelry by Gauthier, at 4211 North Marshall Way. Girl of the West, at 7121 East Fifth Avenue, stocks women's

chic western wear, including leather jackets, hats, accessories, and home-decor items. If you get an urge to be creative yourself—or want to pen a perfectly elegant description of your travels to someone you left behind—stop by the Paper Place for fine stationary and writing instruments at 4130 North Marshall Way.

Old Town
Four square blocks around Main Street and Brown Avenue, downtown Scottsdale
(480) 947-6423
www.downtownscottsdale.com
Old Town Scottsdale encompasses many of the city's oldest buildings. The historic shopping district, with more than 150 stores, begins at the corner of Scottsdale Road and Main Street and feathers out a couple of blocks to the east and north. Across Scottsdale Road to the west are the Fifth Avenue shops, another fun shopping district mentioned earlier. Between the two, you are sure to find the perfect memento of your trip to this area or the perfect gift for a friend or relative.

A few Old Town Scottsdale shops to explore include Saba's Western Wear, at 3965 North Brown Avenue, which has been outfitting cowboys and cowgirls since 1927; Cactus Cats, which offers gifts and apparel, at 7233 East First Avenue; the Cactus Hut, specializing in cactus gardens planted in Arizona pottery, located at 7249 East First Avenue; and the Leather Mill, 7225 East First Avenue, which specializes in jackets, belts, hats, boots, and office accessories. Within the Old West Outpost at the corner of First Avenue and Scottsdale Road, shoppers can find several stores that showcase Native American arts and crafts, as well as souvenirs, T-shirts, antiques, and memorabilia.

Scottsdale Pavilions
Pima and Indian Bend Roads, Scottsdale
(480) 991-6007
www.scottsdalepavilions.com
Although its only major department stores are Mervyn's and Target, Scottsdale Pavil-

ions has such a good selection of stores that it has stayed a popular destination since it opened a decade ago. It is on land owned by the Salt River Pima-Maricopa Indian Community and a portion of the revenues go to the tribe.

This open-air mall combines large, freestanding stores flanked by smaller stores, all on both sides of Indian Bend Road. Adjacent to the stores is Fiddlesticks Family Fun Park, an Arizona-grown amusement park with miniature golf, laser tag, and other rides and entertainment. Several chain and nonchain restaurants are interspersed throughout Scottsdale Pavilions. Shoppers can also catch a flick at the movie theater or dine at one of the patio-side restaurants in the food court. Most of the stores and entertainment venues are open daily.

Scottsdale Seville
7001 North Scottsdale Road, Scottsdale
(480) 905-8110
This pastel-colored, Southwestern-style shopping center has several high-end boutiques, including Ap'ropo fashions and accessories; Destiny's Bride, a bridal shop; and Hot Rags fashions. One of the most popular stores is In Celebration of Golf, featuring golf equipment and clothing for all those taking advantage of the golf resorts and championship courses in Scottsdale. There's also a practice tee. Most stores are open daily.

Antiques Shopping

Antiques Super-Mall
1900 North Scottsdale Road, Scottsdale
(602) 874-2900
Just 2 miles south of Old Town Scottsdale is a trio of antiques stores boasting 600 dealers and 120,000 square feet. The largest of the three is the Antiques Super-Mall, housed in a former department store. Just a short walk away are Antique Trove, 2020 North Scottsdale Road, (480) 947-6074; and the Antique Centre, 2012 North

Scottsdale Road, (480) 675-9500. Independent antiques dealers have their own booths within the stores, which encourages a mind-boggling variety of antiques and collectibles at prices ranging from inexpensive to thousands of dollars. On just one quick visit, you can eye hundreds of lamps, clocks, trunks, dressers, all kinds of china, folk art, and interesting collectible toys. The three stores are open daily.

Specialty Stores

Chief Dodge Indian Jewelry & Fine Arts
Papago Plaza, 1332 North Scottsdale
Road, Scottsdale
(480) 970-1133, (800) 553-5604
www.chiefdodge.com
For more than 30 years, this family-run establishment, which offers a wide selection of Native American arts and crafts, allows customers to buy directly from the artisans for a significant savings. Turquoise jewelry is in abundance here, as are crafts such as kachinas, sand paintings, pottery, and baskets. The store also offers art restoration services and on-the-spot jewelry repair. It is open Monday through Saturday.

SMoCA Museum Store
Scottsdale Museum of Contemporary
Art, 7380 East Second Street, Scottsdale
(480) 874-4644
www.scottsdalearts.org
Shopping at the store's two locations within the Scottsdale Center for the Arts makes you feel good because proceeds support the center's programs. Voted "Best Museum Shop" by two Valley publications, its eclectic assortment of eye-popping home accessories, jewelry, art, T-shirts, books, and educational (but fun) toys should delight just about anybody on your shopping list. Many of the works are hand-made by artists, such as studio art glass bowls or hand-painted ice cube tray clocks. Other items, such as neckties sporting Frank Lloyd Wright and Keith

Haring designs, are inspired by famous creative types.

Sphinx Date Ranch
3039 North Scottsdale Road, Scottsdale
(480) 941–2261, (800) 482–3283
www.sphinxdateranch.com
Date farming is quite successful in Arizona, as this little store can attest. Personnel offer samples of several plump date varieties to help you make your choice. Other products, such as cactus jellies and locally made candies, are also available. The store occupies the original home on the date ranch, although the dates come from local farms. The store opens daily.

The Poisoned Pen
4014 North Goldwater Boulevard,
Scottsdale
(480) 947–2974
www.poisonedpen.com
It's no mystery where book lovers go to buy their favorite whodunits. The Poisoned Pen is one of the largest mystery bookstores in the country. In business for more than a decade, the store not only tallies more than 12,000 titles, but it brings in top-rated mystery writers for book signings, hosts book clubs, has its own show on public access television, and even runs its own press. The Poisoned Pen is open daily.

NORTHWEST VALLEY
Shopping Malls

Arrowhead Towne Center
Bell Road and 75th Avenue, Glendale
(480) 979–7777
www.westcor.com
One of the Valley's regional malls, Arrowhead Towne Center serves the needs of residents in Glendale, the Sun Cities, and other new-growth areas stretching to the north and west. Nearby, you'll find the 4,500-acre master-planned community of Arrowhead Ranch, as well as the Peoria

Sports Complex, spring-training headquarters for the Seattle Mariners and the San Diego Padres.

Dillard's, Mervyn's, Robinsons-May, and JCPenney anchor the mall, a high-tech-looking, steel interior featuring a profusion of plants, skylights, and benches. Stores include Casual Corner, Lane Bryant, Victoria's Secret, B. Dalton Bookseller, Animal Kingdom, the Children's Place, GameStop, The Disney Store, General Nutrition Center, Gymboree, Kay-Bee Toys, Kitchen Gourmet, and Nava Hopi Gallery.

In addition to its 150 stores (open daily), shoppers can enjoy an outdoor amphitheater, carousel, two restaurants, a food court, and a movie theater. At press time, the mall was about to undergo a major interior remodeling, which may or may not be completed by the time you read this.

Antiques Shopping

Historic Downtown Glendale
Vicinity of 59th and Glendale Avenues,
Glendale
(623) 435–0556
www.historic-glendale.net
Named by *USA Today* as one of the top antiques destinations in the country, Glendale's charming downtown, with its restored Craftsman bungalows and white picket fences, appears to have sprung from a Norman Rockwell painting. You can find about four dozen antiques stores in the 16-square-block area of downtown. Shops that feature antiques, crafts, tearooms, and even a candy factory are often housed in carefully restored buildings from the early part of the last century. To complete the picture, a trolley transports shoppers through the streets lined with old-fashioned storefronts, streetlights, and park benches in Old Towne and the Historic Catlin Court shopping districts. Old Towne surrounds historic Murphy Park. Catlin Court, which you'll find situated between Myrtle and Palmaire Avenues,

If you are an antiques hunter, pick up The Antique Register, a free bimonthly publication that covers Arizona's many antiques and collectibles shops. It also contains articles and news about collecting. The magazine can be found at most antiques and collectibles shops and markets. There's also a Web site at www.countryregister.com/antique.

and 57th Drive and 59th Avenue, is listed on the National Register of Historic Places.

Many of the stores are open seven days a week, but it's best to call ahead if you're interested in a particular store. Though the stores are too numerous to name, a few of the approximately 100 antiques and specialty shops include The Apple Tree, 5811 West Glendale Avenue, (623) 435-8486, with one of the larger selections of antiques and collectibles; Mad Hatter, 5734 West Glendale Avenue, (623) 931-1991, with vintage toys, dolls, coins, advertising art, and folk art; Coury House, 5802 West Palmaire Avenue, (623) 435-1522, with fine used and out-of-print books; and Bo's Funky Stuff, 5605 West Glendale Avenue, (623) 842-0220, which specializes in 1950s memorabilia and art deco items.

ATTRACTIONS

Are you a museum type? Phoenix has an impressive array of museums spotlighting art and artifacts, from kachina dolls to fighter planes. Are you an outdoorsy type? This area is brimming with attractions that let you enjoy the sunny weather Phoenix is so famous for, while learning something interesting about our city. Do you like to see the world by car? We can recommend a scenic drive up South Mountain or a jaunt into Paradise Valley. Have you come all the way to Arizona to get a taste of the Old West? This chapter rustles up your options in Wild West theme attractions.

We have grouped this chapter's entries by geographic area so that you might consider spending a day in one part of the Valley in order to see one, two, three, or more of that area's attractions. For instance, if you're heading for the Desert Botanical Garden, consider piggybacking it with the Phoenix Zoo, both of which are in Papago Park. If you are touring downtown Scottsdale, that's a good jumping-off point for Frank Lloyd Wright's Taliesin West in north Scottsdale. How about a day seeing the sights of central and downtown Phoenix, such as the Heard Museum and the Arizona Science Center? Want to plan a day of antiques hunting in downtown Glendale? Perhaps you could fit in a stop at the Deer Valley Rock Art Center.

So have a map handy as you read this chapter and think about marking your best route. We have given hours and admission prices for 2004, but you may want to call first to check for any changes.

See the Parks and Recreation chapter for more ideas on how to enjoy our beautiful desert scenery and balmy climate. The Kidstuff chapter will give you a child's-eye view of our best museums and other attractions. Browse The Arts chapter if you'd like to take in some additional culture while you're here.

Whatever your plans for sightseeing, be sure to consider the weather. Some attractions are perfect for those occasional rainy winter days, and others, such as the Desert Botanical Garden, are just glorious on a fall or spring day.

PRICE CODE

With each attraction listed in this chapter you will find a pricing guide ranging from one to four dollar signs. The code is based on single adult admission. Some admissions can vary, for example, if there's a basic admission and a deluxe admission, so there may be a range of price codes. If there is no dollar sign, that means the attraction has no entry fee.

$	$5.00 or less
$$	$5.01 to $10.00
$$$	$10.01 to $15.00
$$$$	$15.01 and up

PHOENIX

Arizona Science Center $$
600 East Washington Street, Phoenix
(602) 716–2000
www.azscience.org
With about 350 interactive exhibits to explore, plus a giant-screen theater and planetarium, you could spend an entire day at the Arizona Science Center. It has proven wildly popular and exceeded attendance expectations since opening in 1997. City boosters rightfully consider it a major factor in the resurgence of downtown. The $47-million four-story structure is eye-catching both inside and out, with its futuristic concrete-and-glass design by noted architect Antoine Predock. Rising into the sky is a nine-story triangular peak, also called a fin, covered with aluminum.

The Science Center is about 10 times the size of the city's old science museum. The planetarium boasts one of the largest domes in the West and offers shows exploring various intergalactic topics. The Irene P. Flinn Theater has a five-story screen using Iwerks technology, which offers a similar viewing experience to the IMAX theaters.

The exhibits are cleverly organized into galleries that explore human physiology, physical forces, transportation, geology, computers, and applied sciences. Almost all the exhibits are hands-on, which is what makes the center so absorbing. There's a physiology station in which you and a partner time yourselves in a wheelchair race, a geology exhibit where you create your own sand dunes, and a station where you simulate piloting an airplane. An area called the Fab Lab is a big draw with kids. They can pull themselves up a rope with a pulley, launch paper airplanes, and roll golf balls along a fast track.

Make time to check out the nifty games, puzzles, posters, books, and other items for sale in Awesome Atom's. The center has a food court with fast-food options, for those who are making a day of it. Also, the cafes of Heritage Square are just next door.

The Science Center exhibits are open 10:00 A.M. to 5:00 P.M. daily except Thanksgiving and Christmas. Admission is $9.00 for adults, $7.00 for seniors and children 3 to 12, and free for children 2 and younger. Higher-priced tickets combining the exhibits and admission to the Iwerks theater and/or planetarium are available.

Arizona State Capitol Museum and Wesley Bolin Memorial Plaza
1700 West Washington Street, Phoenix
(602) 542-4581
As capitols go, Arizona's is a fairly modest granite building with a copper dome. The white, winged figure atop the dome is called Victory Lady. The Capitol Museum is made up of all four floors of the original capitol building, which dates from 1900. In fact, it was built 12 years before Arizona became a state. The Arizona Legislature, having outgrown the building in 1960, meets in newer quarters behind the capitol. Stroll through the capitol to see various murals executed over the decades to depict Arizona's history and scenery and its progress as a state. Also view the old Senate and House chambers, historical photos, and a statue of the state's first governor, George W. P. Hunt. More sights can be found on the capitol grounds and the adjoining Wesley Bolin Plaza, a grassy, 2-block area of sculptures and monuments. It is named after a former Arizona governor. On the eastern end of the plaza rests an anchor from the USS *Arizona*, sunk during the Japanese raid on Pearl Harbor in 1941. The anchor serves as a memorial to those who died aboard the battleship. You'll also find memorials to veterans of the Korean and Vietnam Wars. The plaza is accessible during daytime hours. Capitol Museum hours are 8:00 A.M. to 5:00 P.M. weekdays, 10:00 A.M. to 3:00 P.M. Saturday (January through May only), and admission is free. Call to inquire about guided tours, which are given twice daily.

Burton Barr Central Library
1221 North Central Avenue, Phoenix
(602) 262-4636
www.phoenixpubliclibrary.org
Several major metropolitan libraries with architectural significance have been built since 1990, and Phoenix's central library is one of them. Opened in 1995, the five-story, multimillion-dollar structure was paid for through a city bond election for arts and cultural improvements. Residents looked at its simple exterior of corrugated copper and gray concrete and either loved it or hated it. Then, slowly but surely, the public trickled in, and by viewing it more closely, they began to understand the concept behind local architect Will Bruder's organic design. It is a design inspired by the majesty of Arizona's many copper-colored mesas and rugged gray canyons, and it skillfully uses natural light in opposition to the notion that public

libraries have to be dark and stuffy. The north side of the building has computer-controlled shades, or "sails," outside the windows that rotate and adjust to let in the right amount of light according to the time of day. This makes it one of the most energy-efficient buildings in a state where wasteful construction methods are still the norm. Another remarkable feature is the main entry, where a glass elevator swooshes up and down the five floors while reflecting colored lights into the pool below it. The Great Reading Room on the top floor is considered the largest such room in North America. It's also where you'll notice how the roof is suspended by cables instead of resting on concrete pillars.

The Phoenix library system celebrated its 100th anniversary in 1998 and over the years has grown to 12 branches, in addition to the new Burton Barr library, named after a longtime Arizona legislator. It replaces the old central library at McDowell Road and Central Avenue. The new library includes a good children's area, the Rare Book Room, and the Arizona Room, with resources on the history of the Southwest. Hours are 10:00 A.M. to 9:00 P.M. Monday through Thursday, 10:00 A.M. to 6:00 P.M. Friday and Saturday, and noon to 6:00 P.M. Sunday.

Deer Valley Rock Art Center $
3711 West Deer Valley Road, Phoenix
(623) 582-8007
The Deer Valley Rock Art Center serves as a sanctuary for the 1,500 ancient petroglyphs to be found on this 47-acre desert preserve. Operated by the Arizona State University Department of Anthropology, it provides public access to the Hedgpeth Hills petroglyph site via a quarter-mile nature trail. Signs along the way help interpret what you're seeing. You'll come away with a better understanding of the cultures that made the rock art—the Hohokam and Patayan who inhabited the area from A.D. 300 to 1450. Morning viewing is recommended, and bring your binoculars. The visitor center has various

exhibits, a video room, and gift shop. From October to April the center is open from 9:00 A.M. to 5:00 P.M. Tuesday through Saturday and noon to 5:00 P.M. Sunday. Call about summer hours. Admission is $4.00 adults, $2.00 students and seniors, $1.00 for ages 6 to 12, and free for children younger than 6.

Desert Botanical Garden $$
Papago Park, 1201 North Galvin Parkway, Phoenix
(480) 941-1225
www.dbg.org
Sometimes Valley residents have a hard time convincing outsiders that our Sonoran Desert is a wonderland of trees, shrubs, and flowers. No, not in the magnolia and maple tree sense, but in the sense that we have an amazing variety of plants that can withstand this climate and still bloom brilliantly. The Desert Botanical Garden helps us make our case, immensely. It is one of the nation's few public gardens dedicated to desert plants. Its winding trails pleasantly take you through veritable forests and open your eyes to 4,000 species of cacti, succulents, trees, and flowers.

The garden opened in 1939 as both a showcase and conservation headquarters. Today its collection includes several rare, threatened, and endangered Southwestern species in addition to spotlighting common plants. After a leisurely morning or afternoon in the garden, you will be able to recognize and reel off names of flora such as the ocotillo, the jumping cholla, desert marigolds, the creosote bush, the palo verde tree, the yucca plant, and more. Each trail has signage not only bearing the names, but also explaining the plants' hardiness and desert life in general. Often you will find garden volunteers at information stations displaying specimens you can touch.

The garden is organized around four trails. Plants & People of the Sonoran Desert Trail, which sheds light on desert dwellers' use of plants for food, fibers, and construction, is one-third of a mile. The

Sonoran Desert Nature Trail is a quarter-mile hillside trail focusing on the interactions among plants, birds, reptiles, insects, and mammals sharing the desert. The Desert Discovery Trail encompasses 20 acres and thousands of desert plants from around the world. On the trail are the Cactus House and Succulent House, which showcase plants inside greenhouses. The Center for Desert Living Trail demonstrates the beauty of desert landscaping and explains the water-efficiency of the Desert House, an actual residence within the garden.

At the garden you'll find a visitor center, a gift shop, a cafe, and a plant shop, which has a wonderful selection of plants to buy—instructions included. Also on the grounds is Webster Auditorium, one of the few remaining authentic examples of Pueblo Revival architecture in central Arizona.

Hours are 8:00 A.M. to 8:00 P.M. daily except during the summer, when you can beat the heat by arriving at 7:00 A.M. Admission is $9.00 for adults, $8.00 for seniors, $5.00 for students, $4.00 for children ages 3 to 12, and free for those younger than 3. If you go to the Heard Museum first, keep your ticket—it's good for free admission into the Botanical Gardens. The garden frequently offers guided tours or schedules outdoor concerts; more information is available on the garden hotline, (480) 481-8184.

Hall of Flame Museum of Firefighting $
6101 East Van Buren Street, Phoenix
(602) 275-3473
www.hallofflame.org
A perfect name for the world's largest display of firefighting equipment. The Hall of Flame houses almost 100 restored pieces of hand-to-hand, horse-drawn, and mechanized firefighting equipment dating from 1725 to 1961. The collection includes several well-preserved fire engines, including a fire truck that is safe for children to climb into and pretend to drive. Wannabe firefighters can dress up in coats, helmets, and other gear, or simply browse the four galleries to learn more about this honor-

able profession. The breadth of this museum is quite amazing. There's a gallery devoted to helmets, an area showing more than 2,000 fire department badges, fire safety exhibits, a game area, and an art gallery of firefighting-related scenes. The museum is open 9:00 A.M. to 5:00 P.M. Monday through Saturday and noon to 4:00 P.M. Sunday. Admission is $5.00 for adults, $4.00 for seniors, $3.00 for children 6 to 17, $1.50 for children 3 to 5, and free for children younger than 3.

Heard Museum $$
2301 North Central Avenue, Phoenix
(602) 252-8848
www.heard.org
If you have time to see only one tourist attraction while you're in Phoenix, see the Heard Museum. It has an internationally renowned collection of Native American fine arts and crafts from throughout North America, with emphasis on the peoples of the Southwest. The more than 32,000 works of art and ethnographic objects span several centuries and are handsomely and informatively displayed. All exhibits are presented with a quiet reverence for Native American ways of life.

The Heard Museum was founded in 1929 by Dwight B. and Maie Bartlett Heard, a prominent Phoenix couple who moved to the Valley from Chicago in the mid-1880s. The Heards were avid collectors of Native American artifacts and art, especially those of Southwestern cultures. Their decision to build a museum to share their exemplary collection was visionary. Today, the Heard Museum annually attracts 250,000 visitors from all over the world. It has outgrown its original building—of charming Spanish colonial-style design—and has completed a multimillion-dollar expansion, adding three new galleries, a new auditorium for performances of Native American dance and music, and an Education Pavilion, among other things.

Visitors should spend time at Native Peoples of the Southwest, the Heard's permanent exhibit chronicling the cultures of a number of tribes through art, artifacts, maps, information boards, and videos. Also see the Barry Goldwater collection of 437 historic Hopi kachina dolls, and the C. G. Wallace collection of more than 500 pieces of important Navajo and Zuni jewelry. A couple of galleries concentrate on contemporary paintings, prints, and sculptures by Native Americans, and these are also worth seeing. And here and there you will find art and artifacts from other parts of the world and other cultures, presented for their comparative value. Families ought to.spend time in Old Ways, New Ways, a hands-on exhibit area where youngsters step inside Native American structures, make crafts, and visit with artists.

The Heard Museum Shop & Bookstore is a showcase of Native American jewelry, textiles, pottery, and kachina dolls for sale. If you are a serious collector of Native American art, this is your place. The staff is knowledgeable about the things they sell and can often point you to the finer pieces.

See the Annual Events chapter for special events at the Heard, such as the World Championship Hoop Dance Contest, the Guild Indian Fair & Market, and other events.

The Heard's hours are 9:30 A.M. to 5:00 P.M. daily. Admission is $7.00 for adults, $6.00 for seniors, $3.00 for children 4 to 12, and free for children younger than 4. Save your tickets; they act as free passes into the Desert Botanical Garden.

Heritage Square
Seventh and Monroe Streets, Phoenix
(602) 262-5071

Heritage Square is a cherished niche in downtown Phoenix, a city block that contains the only remaining residential structures from the original townsite of Phoenix. Listed on the National Register of Historic Places, it's a grouping of eight restored Victorian houses in a pedestrian-only enclave. You can find it in the shadow of the new Arizona Science Center and Bank One Ballpark.

Local attractions often host special events and classes related to their theme. The Heard Museum runs many Native American cultural events, and the Arizona Historical Society has lectures on various aspects of the Valley's past. The biggest events are listed in our Annual Events chapter, but there are many more. Call for more information or ask an attendant during your visit. The Phoenix New Times and "Get Out" both have extensive listings of events.

The most eye-catching is the Rosson House, built in 1895, with its expansive veranda and an octagonal gray turret topped by an elaborate finial. The 10 rooms of the Rosson House feature pressed-tin ceilings and parquet floors. It's open for viewing from 10:00 A.M. to 3:30 P.M. Wednesday through Saturday and from noon to 3:30 P.M. Sunday. Tucked next to it is the Burgess Carriage House, which serves as the ticket office and gift shop. The charge for guided tours is $3.00 for adults, $2.00 for seniors, $1.00 for children 6 to 13, and free for children younger than 6.

In the Stevens House is the Arizona Doll and Toy Museum, showcasing antique and modern dolls, dollhouses, and toys. An authentic-looking 1912 schoolroom features antique dolls propped in desks like students. There is a small admission charge of $2.50 for adults and $1.00 for children. Hours are 10:00 A.M. to 4:00 P.M. Tuesday through Saturday and noon to 4:00 P.M. Sunday. The museum is closed in August.

Heritage Square also features the Teeter House Victorian Tea Room, offering lunch, tea and pastries, and a high tea by reservation; Heritage House Café, a self-serve deli in what used to be a mule barn; the Silva House, which has exhibits about early life in Phoenix (admission is free); the Lath House Pavilion, erected in 1980 to facilitate the many outdoor festivals and farmers' markets held at Heritage

Square; the Duplex, a small house that serves as city offices; the Baird Machine Shop, dating from 1929 and now home of Pizzeria Bianco, a popular eatery; and Native Ring, which exhibits and sells fine Native American arts and crafts.

Mystery Castle $
800 East Mineral Road, Phoenix
(602) 268-1581
Built in 1930 in the foothills of South Mountain Park, Mystery Castle has been open for public tours ever since a 1948 *Life* magazine article put it on the map. The 8,000-square-foot castle, built from recycled bottles, old bricks, and granite, was built by an eccentric father as an act of love toward his young daughter. It has 18 rooms and 13 fireplaces. The daughter still lives there and conducts tours from 11:00 A.M. to 4:00 P.M. Thursday through Sunday. The castle is closed from July to September. Admission is $5.00 for adults, $4.00 for seniors, $2.00 for children ages 6 to 15, and free for children younger than 6.

Phoenix Art Museum $$
1625 North Central Avenue, Phoenix
(602) 257-1222, (602) 257-1880
www.phxart.org
Playing an increasingly larger role in the Valley's cultural life is the Phoenix Art Museum, with its permanent collection of 13,000 works spanning several centuries and representing many artistic styles and media as well as many world-renowned artists. The museum officially opened in 1959, although it had thrived as a small community arts center for two decades before that. By the 1980s the museum began to outgrow its space. Thanks to a city bond election, the museum had funds to double its space and make several architectural improvements, which were completed in 1996.

There are several galleries worth seeing at the Phoenix Art Museum, including the Art of Our Time Gallery, with works by Georgia O'Keeffe, Pablo Picasso, Frida Kahlo, Keith Haring, and others; the Western American Galleries, with many Realist

paintings celebrating Western landscape and history; the European Galleries, with paintings and sculptures from the 14th century up to the Impressionists; the Art of Asia Galleries, with works spanning several hundred years; and the Thorne Miniature Rooms, miniature interior replications from America, England, France, and Italy. The museum also hosts traveling exhibitions; recent shows include sculpture by Degas, the Cowboy Artists of America, and silk costumes from Japan.

Children will enjoy the hands-on Art Works Gallery, with games, puzzles, books, and videos that shed light on the museum's collection. You might want to stop by the Art Museum Cafe for light refreshments. The Museum Store is a shopper's delight with unusual gifts, art books, jewelry, and stationery.

The Phoenix Art Museum is open 10:00 A.M. to 5:00 P.M. Tuesday through Sunday, with hours extending until 9:00 P.M. on Thursday. Admission is $9.00 for adults, $7.00 for seniors and students, $3.00 for children ages 6 to 8, and $3.00 for children 6 to 17. There is free admission on Thursday.

Phoenix Museum of History $
105 North Fifth Street, Phoenix
(602) 253-2734
www.pmoh.org
Drop into this museum at Heritage and Science Park if you are visiting the Arizona Science Center or Heritage Square. It will give you a better appreciation of Phoenix's humble beginnings and rise to Sunbelt prominence. The emphases are on territorial and early statehood days in Arizona, along with this area's proud multicultural heritage. Displays include Native American artifacts; the town's first jail; a look at Phoenix as turn-of-the-20th-century haven for the chronically ill; and "aroma barrels" that recreate scents from the past. Sure to catch your eye is the stuffed ostrich, a reminder of the Valley's era as an ostrich-farming center. Cases hold dozens of smaller artifacts to admire, if you don't mind some leisurely browsing.

The museum is open 10:00 A.M. to 5:00 P.M. Tuesday through Saturday. Admission is $5.00 for adults, $3.50 for students and seniors, $2.50 for kids 7 to 12, and free for kids 6 and under. Wednesdays are free from 2:00 to 5:00 P.M.

Phoenix Zoo $$$
Papago Park, 455 North Galvin Parkway, Phoenix
(602) 273-1341
www.phoenixzoo.org

A little-known fact about the Phoenix Zoo: At 125 acres and 7,600 animals, it is the largest privately owned nonprofit zoo in the nation. Open since 1962, it is also internationally known for its efforts on behalf of saving endangered species. For instance, a zoo breeding and redistribution project begun in 1963 has increased the number of the Arabian oryx—a type of antelope—from nine to its present world population of 1,400.

Set among the gently rolling hills, cactus, and craggy red rocks of Papago Park, the Phoenix Zoo draws about 1.2 million visitors a year. It's not unusual to find Valley families who visit the zoo several times a year. Exhibits are continually being updated and added. A recent addition is the Wallaby Walkabout, home to a dozen Australian wallabies. With almost 400 species, the Phoenix Zoo specializes in animals that enjoy warm climates. Exhibit spaces closely resemble the animals' natural habitats. You can see how the spaces change as you move along the zoo's four distinct trails: the Tropics Trail, which is great for bird watching; the Africa Trail, with lions, tigers, and elephants; the Children's Discovery Trail and Harmony Farm, featuring farm animals and farm equipment, a small butterfly garden, and playground; and the Arizona Trail, a must-see for out-of-state visitors. It's here you can view Mexican wolves, coyotes, desert birds, bats, and a spine-tingling array of snakes, scorpions, and other small creatures.

The Safari Train is a popular way to tour the zoo. It offers a 25-minute narrated tour by open-air bus. The zoo hosts

Spend the night at the Phoenix Zoo through a popular program called Night Camp. Chaperoned groups of youngsters 8 and older get to stay up late to walk the zoo trails and find nocturnal animals such as bats. They also participate in animal-related games and see wildlife up close with the help of zoo educators. After a full evening, kids camp out in the Education Building. Call the zoo at (602) 273-1341 for details.

special shows, guided walks, and classes year-round. Ask about the day's events at the gate. If you're visiting in the summer, it's best to get there early in the morning before the animals take an afternoon siesta. There are several snack and beverage bars along the trails. Near the entrance is Trail's End Marketplace, with its fun collection of T-shirts, caps, toys, books, and other mementos.

Zoo hours are 9:00 A.M. to 5:00 P.M. daily, except from June 1 through Labor Day, when they change to 7:00 A.M. to 4:00 P.M. Admission is $12.00 for adults, $9.00 for seniors, $5.00 for ages 3 to 12, and free for those 2 and younger. The Safari Train costs extra. Check our Annual Events chapter for details on two of the zoo's largest events, ZooLights at holiday time and Boo! at the Zoo at Halloween.

Pioneer Arizona Living $$
History Museum
3901 West Pioneer Road, Phoenix
(623) 465-1052
www.pioneer-arizona.com

A mix of authentic buildings and historically accurate reproductions, Pioneer Arizona immerses you in life of the territory at the turn of the 20th century. Its 90 acres feature an 1880s schoolhouse, an 1890s exhibition hall and dress shop, and an 1870s opera house. A stroll down the dusty streets will also lead you to a blacksmith shop, sheriff's office and jail, church, ranch complex, and other buildings. And be sure to saunter through the swinging doors of the Whiskey Road to Ruin Saloon, dating from the mid-1800s. Some of the buildings were moved to the museum from other parts of Arizona, and some were constructed using building plans of the time. Adding to your visit will be the many costumed interpreters, including cowboys, lawmen, and Victorian ladies. The actors demonstrate crafts and stage melodramas. Pioneer Arizona is said to be the largest living-history museum west of the Rockies. It is about 20 minutes north of central Phoenix, just off Interstate 17 at the Pioneer Road Exit. It's open 9:00 A.M. to 5:00 P.M. Wednesday through Sunday, but only from 9:00 A.M. to 2:00 P.M. from June 30 to September 16. Admission is $7.00 for adults, $6.00 for seniors, $5.00 for students, $4.00 for children ages 3 to 5, and free for those younger than 3.

Pueblo Grande Museum and
Archeological Park $
4619 East Washington Street, Phoenix
(602) 495-0901
www.pueblogrande.com
Whenever we modern-day residents need a reminder that we were not the first to civilize this desert valley, we head over to Pueblo Grande. There we can learn to understand and appreciate the world of the Hohokam Indians who flourished in this area for several centuries before mysteriously disappearing in the mid-15th century. The museum, somewhat ironically, is just minutes from that icon of modern civilization, Phoenix Sky Harbor International Airport. Visitors can learn about the Hohokam's many crops, their extensive canal system for irrigation, their use of adobe construction, and their arts and crafts. Most important, once you've seen the indoor exhibits, you'll follow trails around the actual ruins of a Hohokam village that has been unearthed by archaeologists. The Pueblo Grande also has an excellent gift shop with Native American arts and crafts. The museum is open 9:00 A.M. to 4:45 P.M. Monday through Saturday and 1:00 to 4:45 P.M. on Sunday. Admission is $2.00 for adults, $1.50 for seniors, $1.00 for children, and free for kids younger than 6. Free admission for everyone on Sundays.

South Mountain Park Scenic Drive
10919 South Central Avenue, Phoenix
(602) 495-0222
South Mountain and the hills that surround it skirt the southern edge of the city of Phoenix. The city has preserved the area by turning it into a 16,500-acre park, a size that qualifies it as the largest municipal park in the world. It is home to more than 300 species of plant life and critters ranging from rabbits and coyotes to snakes and lizards.

You can drive to the summit of South Mountain, called Dobbins Lookout, by taking Central Avenue south from downtown. Once you pass the entrance gate to the park, simply follow the signs to the summit. The winding, two-lane road climbs for about 5 miles, taking you past picnic sites and trailheads. At the 2,330-foot summit, you will be rewarded by great views of the Valley, including the downtown skyline and the mountains to the east of the Valley. The views were even more spectacular before the Valley started having a smog problem. A springtime drive will introduce you to the desert's colorful wildflowers. The wet spring of 1998 produced one of the most beautiful wildflower displays ever, with lots of lupine, poppies, brittlebush, desert marigolds, and hedgehog cactuses in bloom along the road and on hillsides. The weather has been drier since that time and the wildflowers have not been as prolific but that could change with the next season.

The visitor center at the base of the mountain is open daytime hours and can answer your questions about trails, picnic sites, and how to see the area's petroglyphs. Exhibits in the visitor center and the interpretive center look at area flora and fauna, mining heritage, and the contributions of the Civilian Conservation Corps.

SOUTHEAST VALLEY

Arizona Historical Society Museum $
Papago Park, 1300 North College Avenue, Tempe
(480) 929-0292
www.arizonahistoricalsociety.org
In Papago Park on the Tempe side is a large museum that is quite impressive from the outside, but is only partially completed inside. The Arizona Historical Society is struggling for private and government donations to build exhibits inside the 83,000-square-foot museum. It opened in 1996, with less than half its space in use. There are exhibits spread out through the entire museum now, but it still has an empty feel to it. In the meantime, visitors can spend an hour or so touring what is there. That includes audiovisuals, maps, historic photographs, and a few hands-on exhibits looking at the agriculture, mining, and urban development of central Arizona in the 19th and 20th centuries. One gallery focuses on World War II and its impact on the Valley, including personal letters and photographs from participants in the war effort. On the outdoor terrace is an interesting exhibit explaining the blood, sweat, and tears that went into building the Roosevelt Dam northeast of Phoenix—one of the first federal reclamation projects. Museum hours are 10:00 A.M. to 4:00 P.M. Monday through Saturday and noon to 4:00 P.M. on Sunday. Admission is $5.00 for adults, $4.00 for seniors and students; children under 12 are free. There's free admission for everybody the first Saturday of each month.

Downtown Tempe
Tempe Convention and Visitors Bureau, 51 West Third Street, Tempe
(480) 894-8158, (800) 283-6734
The downtown and campus area blend coffeehouses, nightclubs, trendy restaurants, boutiques, bookstores, offbeat little stores, and office towers, primarily concentrated on Mill Avenue. All this activity makes for a thriving community of students, workers, and tourists who take to the streets all day and into the evening. In fact, downtown Tempe is bustling with nightlife, especially on weekends. But there's also a historic side to Tempe. Several brick buildings built in Victorian or Spanish Colonial Revival styles have been preserved, and new construction does a good job of harmonizing with them. A walking tour should include stops at the Hayden Flour Mill, recognizable by its four silos; Monti's La Casa Vieja Steakhouse, the former home of Charles Hayden, founder of Tempe; Tempe City Hall, a modern, upside-down pyramid of glass and steel; the Andre Building (now housing Paradise Bar & Grill), one of the city's best examples of preservation; and the Laird and Dines Building, a Tempe landmark that now incorporates restaurants, shops, and bars. On the way in or out of town, notice the Old Mill Avenue Bridge, dating from the 1930s.

The Arizona Republic, the Phoenix New Times, and other Valley publications often run coupons for local attractions. Keep an eye out for these. Also, read our listings carefully, because many of these attractions offer free days.

Goldfield Ghost Town & Mine Tours
State Route 88 north of Apache Junction
(480) 983-0333
www.goldfieldghosttown.com
Goldfield was a booming town back in the 1890s, thanks to a gold strike at the base of the Superstition Mountains. For five years, millions of dollars worth of high-grade ore was excavated by eager miners who dreamed of striking it rich. In Goldfield's heyday, it boasted a hotel, boardinghouse, and three saloons. The boom went bust, of course, and the town looks quite battered by time now, but that's what ghost towns are all about. As a tourist attraction, Goldfield offers mine tours, gold panning, a nature trail, and exhibits of antique mining equipment. It is also the

site of Arizona's only operating narrow gauge railroad, which takes you on a short scenic tour of the town. The town's Main Street has a steakhouse/saloon, an ice-cream parlor, and several shops that are fun to browse. If you're there on a week-end, you might catch a gunfight (staged, of course). From Apache Junction in the far East Valley, Goldfield can be reached by driving north on Apache Trail (SR 88). Goldfield is open 10:00 A.M. to 5:00 P.M. daily. Admission is free, with the various attractions priced individually.

NORTHEAST VALLEY

Carefree/Cave Creek
Carefree/Cave Creek Chamber of
Commerce, 748 Easy Street, Carefree
(480) 488–3381
www.carefree-cavecreek.com
These two neighboring communities lie south of the Tonto National Forest and make fun excursions because of their sce-nic surroundings, boutiques, Western shops, and easygoing Southwestern ambiance. The half-hour drive from Scottsdale is pleasant in itself. Head north on Scottsdale Road, and you'll see how acres of new development are inter-spersed with stretches of unspoiled desert. The McDowell Mountains draw your eye to the east, and the northern view spotlights the hills of the national forest. Several miles of Scottsdale Road north of Scottsdale have been designated the Desert Foothills Scenic Drive, and small signs tell you the names of the vari-ous desert plants that flourish in this area.

Using this route you'll reach Carefree first. The planned community was founded in 1956, and today it's dotted with expen-sive hillside homes. The world-class Boul-ders Resort is in Carefree, as is the upscale boutique/art gallery enclave called el Pedregal Marketplace. In the town center are several more boutiques and galleries, along with the K. T. Palmer Sundial, one of the largest sundials in the world. In tune with the town name, Carefree has fun with

street names. Walk along Ho and Hum Roads, for instance, or Easy Street.

While Carefree is on the cosmopolitan side, Cave Creek is the country cousin. Find it by following the signs that point west to Cave Creek Road. You'll know you're there when you start to see store-fronts and restaurants that hearken back to the Old West. Although there is mod-ern residential development springing up all around it, the center of town is able to retain its traditional character. Cave Creek, too, is a fun place for souvenir shopping and antiques hunting. A small museum has Native American artifacts and mining and ranching displays. Take a break at one of the saloons on Cave Creek Road before heading back to the metropolis.

Downtown Scottsdale
Scottsdale Chamber of Commerce,
7343 East Scottsdale Mall
(480) 945–8481
www.scottsdalecvb.com
Downtown Scottsdale is better seen by foot than by car. Scottsdale Road and the east-west roads that cross it are jam-packed with stores, restaurants, and gal-leries. Besides, traffic on Scottsdale Road slows to a crawl in high tourist season, so you might as well leave the car in one of the many public parking lots. Look at the lampposts and elsewhere, and you'll see signage that designates the different areas of downtown, including Old Town Scottsdale, West Main, Marshall Way, and Fifth Avenue. The latter three areas are the domain of shoppers and art connois-seurs and are well worth your time if you are interested in souvenir hunting or in browsing the potpourri of galleries. See the Shopping and The Arts chapters for more information.

A little background on Scottsdale: About 40 acres of virgin desert were turned into town lots in 1894. The little hamlet was named after Army Chaplain Winfield Scott. For many decades Scotts-dale remained a farming and ranching community. Folks rode in by horse on dirt roads from Phoenix and hitched their steeds along what is now Scottsdale Road. This piece of history and others contribute to a slogan that the ultracosmopolitan Scottsdale still hangs onto today (perhaps in vain): "The West's Most Western Town."

You get a sense of the city's Old West heritage on a walking tour suggested by the Scottsdale Historical Society that includes these sites: the intersection of Brown Avenue and Main Street, site of the first general store and post office; the Little Red Schoolhouse on the Civic Center Mall, preserved from 1909 and home of the Historical Society; Cavalliere's Blacksmith Shop at 3805 North Brown Avenue; and the building at 3933 North Brown Avenue, built in 1923 as a pool hall.

Be sure to walk around the Civic Center Mall, a modern complex of government buildings, a public library, a performing-arts center enlivened with gardens, fountains, and sculptures, and the Scottsdale Museum of Contemporary Art. It is a wonderfully conceived oasis and the site of many outdoor festivals and concerts.

Out of Africa Wildlife Park $$$
**9736 North Fort McDowell Road,
Fort McDowell
(480) 837-7779
www.outofafricapark.com**
Think of Out of Africa not as a zoo but as a small version of Sea World that substitutes exotic tigers for the killer whales. The big cats can be seen in natural habitats developed for them at the park as well as in an unrehearsed show called Tiger Splash. Yes, they romp in the water with staff members and perform various tricks. Species include white tigers and Bengals. There are nine animal shows in all, which give the park a chance to show off its other inhabitants, including lions, coatis, foxes, bears, cougars, wolves, pythons, and exotic birds. But Tiger Splash, usually performed once daily, is the most popular. The grounds also include a cafe and gift shop. To get to Out of Africa, take the Beeline (State Route 87) north until you're 2 miles north of

Keep the desert weather in mind when planning an excursion. If you are sensitive to heat, you may want to save the outdoor attractions for the winter months. Many places take this into account and offer longer hours in the cooler seasons. This is also the peak tourist time, so while you will be more comfortable, you may have to contend with longer lines. Try going in the evening, when the crowds thin and the sunsets and starry skies make a beautiful backdrop to your visit. But remember, even at night it's a good idea to use those drinking fountains!

Shea Boulevard, then turn right onto Fort McDowell Road. Winter hours (October 1 to Memorial Day) are 9:30 A.M. to 5:00 P.M. Tuesday through Sunday. Summer hours are 4:00 P.M. to 9:30 P.M. Wednesday through Friday, 9:30 A.M. to 9:30 P.M. Saturday, and 9:30 A.M. to 5:00 P.M. Sunday. In summer (from May to October) you might enjoy the park's dinner shows on the first Saturday of each month. Dinner (included in the admission price) is served from 6:00 to 7:15 P.M., and the first show of the evening starts at 7:30 P.M. Admission, which includes the shows, is $14.95 for adults, $13.95 for seniors, and $6.95 for ages 3 to 12. Children 2 and younger are admitted free.

Paradise Valley Scenic Drive
**Town of Paradise Valley Offices, 6401 East Lincoln Drive, Paradise Valley
(480) 948-7411
www.ci.paradise-valley.az.us**
What's all this fuss about Paradise Valley? What makes it one of the most beautiful examples of mountainous Sonoran Desert? See for yourself why the town of Paradise Valley is the preferred address of the rich and famous. You can't get too close to the luxurious hillside homes because of security gates, but you can see them from a distance by starting at 24th Street and

Camelback Road in Phoenix, then heading north toward Lincoln Drive. Take Lincoln east all the way to Scottsdale Road in Scottsdale, and you'll pass not only fine homes, but also a handful of first-class resorts, including Marriott's Camelback Inn and the DoubleTree La Posada. Turn south on Scottsdale Road, then go west on McDonald Drive for a few miles. The latter street turns into 44th Street, which will bring you back to Camelback Road. This drive affords fine views of Camelback Mountain, including the thumblike rock formation known as the Praying Monk; the Phoenix Mountain Preserve; and the Mummy Mountain range.

Arizona is rich in petroglyphs and pictographs, ancient Native American forms of rock art. What's the difference between the two? Petroglyphs are etched into the rock, and pictographs are painted onto the rock. Explore the various symbols of prehistoric cultures at the Deer Valley Rock Art Center, South Mountain Park, Hayden Butte, and many sites outside the Phoenix area. And please heed this reminder from preservationists and archaeologists: Don't touch.

Rawhide
23023 North Scottsdale Road, Scottsdale
(480) 502-5600, (480) 502-1880
www.rawhide.com
Okay, pardner. Now's the time to dust off that cowboy hat and polish those Tony Lamas. Bring your camera, too, because this 1880s-style Western town is a whole lot of fun if you're in the spirit of reliving the Wild West. With shows by strolling costumed characters and authentic-looking storefronts on Main Street, Rawhide is considered one of Scottsdale's most popular attractions, annually drawing thousands of U.S. and foreign tourists. Featured on its 160 acres are stagecoach, train, and burro rides; gold panning; a

shooting gallery; several shops with Western wear and memorabilia; plus hourly stunt shows complete with explosions, fistfights, gunfights, and falls from buildings. In the Native American Village, watch members of the Apache, Navajo, Tohono O'odham, and Hopi tribes demonstrate traditional crafts and tell stories. Also view Native American structures built at the site using traditional materials. If you time your visit near dinner, you can grab some grub at the popular Rawhide Steakhouse. Hours change with the season, but in winter Rawhide is generally open 3:00 to 10:00 P.M. Monday through Thursday and 11:00 A.M. to 10:00 P.M. Friday through Sunday. Admission is free, and the various activities have tickets ranging from $2.00 to $5.00. Rawhide hosts many holiday-theme and special events throughout the year, often featuring live country music; call the above number for more information.

Taliesin West $$$-$$$$
12621 Frank Lloyd Wright Boulevard, Scottsdale
(480) 860-2700
www.franklloydwright.org
Frank Lloyd Wright's brilliance in creating organic architecture that harmonizes with its surroundings is perfectly exemplified at Taliesin West, Wright's personal winter home, studio, and architectural campus from 1937 until his death in 1959. The 600-acre site is nestled amid cactus and scrub, with wide-ranging views of Phoenix to the south and mountains to the east. The location was once considered quite remote for sightseers, but recent residential development in the far northeast Valley has turned Frank Lloyd Wright Boulevard into a major thoroughfare.

At first glance, you may think Taliesin West looks quite strange. But the eccentricities of its design quickly grow on you as you learn how Wright and his apprentices gathered rocks from the desert floor and sand from the washes to use as building materials. You also will come to appreciate Wright's attention to detail and why he used light and space the way he did.

To see Taliesin West, you have your choice of four guided tours lasting from one to three hours. The one-hour Panorama Tour focuses on Wright's genius in integrating indoor and outdoor spaces. Visitors see the Cabaret Cinema, Music Pavilion, Seminar Theater, and Wright's private office, all linked by dramatic terraces, gardens, and walkways. You'll hear a general overview of Wright's theories of design and learn about the Taliesin Fellowship of architectural students. The tour is offered daily from 10:00 A.M. to 4:00 P.M.; no reservations are needed. Cost is $12.50 for adults, $11.00 for seniors and students, and $3.00 for children ages 4 to 12. Children younger than 4 are admitted free, but tours are not recommended for toddlers unless they are in strollers or in a parent's arms.

The 90-minute Insights Tour includes elements of the Panorama tour plus the dramatic Taliesin West Living Room, with its expansive windows linking it to the garden. Plus, you have an opportunity to sit in Wright-designed furniture. This tour is offered at 9:00 and 9:30 A.M. Monday through Saturday; no reservations are needed. Cost is $20 per person or $16 for seniors, students, and children.

Another option is the Nature of the Site Desert Walk, a 90-minute, in-depth explanation of how Wright's buildings are wedded to their surroundings. You will explore the desert trails that surround Taliesin West buildings and learn how desert vegetation and landforms were translated into design elements by Wright. Cost is $20, or combine it with one of the above-named tours for an additional cost. The walk is held at 11:15 A.M. and 1:15 P.M. Monday through Saturday, and reservations are suggested.

The three-hour Behind the Scenes Tour ($35 per person) allows you to chat with a Wright associate, have midmorning refreshments in the Taliesin Fellowship dining room, and visit all the spots on the Insights tour. Reservations are suggested for this tour, which is held at 9:00 A.M. Tuesday and Thursday.

The above tours are given October through May. Taliesin West is open in the summer, although the heat somewhat limits the number of tours. It's best for summer visitors to call ahead for times.

Be sure to stop in at the Taliesin West Bookstore, which stocks hard-to-find books and prints, along with a nice selection of Wright-inspired clothing and gifts.

NORTHWEST VALLEY

Downtown Glendale
Glendale Chamber of Commerce,
7105 North 59th Avenue, Glendale
(623) 937-4754
www.glendaleazchamber.org
The awnings, the shade of many trees, the brick sidewalks, and the well-preserved buildings all lend a pleasant ambiance to downtown Glendale, the area near 59th and Glendale Avenues. It is an antiques-hunter's paradise, with about four dozen antiques shops within a few blocks of each other. It is said to be the largest concentration of antiques dealers in Arizona. The shops sell everything from Victorian-era furniture to automobile memorabilia to vintage telephones to elegant collectible figurines. Storefronts bear the names Arsenic & Old Lace, Bo's Funky Stuff, and Grandma's House. Also scattered throughout downtown are plenty of specialty shops, such as one selling angel figurines or the shop specializing in handblown glass. Visitors always gravitate toward the 4-block area known as Catlin Court, where century-old bungalows have been preserved and turned into shops and restaurants. Look for trolley stops if you would like a mobile tour of downtown the old-fashioned way. On Saturday from October through May, Glendale stages a farmers' market and crafts fair in Murphy Park.

For refreshments, your options include ice-cream parlors, tearooms, and family-style restaurants. Or you could skip such formalities entirely and head straight to Cerreta Candy Company, 5345 West Glendale Avenue, (623) 930-1000, where you

The white mansion on the hill near 24th Street and Lincoln Drive in Phoenix's ritzy Biltmore Estates neighborhood belonged to chewing gum magnate William Wrigley Jr. He built it in 1931 as a 50th wedding anniversary present for his wife. Currently, the Wrigley Mansion is owned by Geordie Hormel, a Phoenix resident and heir to the Hormel meat-packing fortune.

can watch chocolates and other candies being made in this small, family-owned factory. Stop in anytime during retail hours of 8:00 A.M. to 6:00 P.M. Monday through Saturday. Boxed candies and chocolate by the pound are available for purchase.

Sahuaro Ranch $
9802 North 59th Avenue, Glendale
(623) 939-5782
Listed on the National Register of Historic Places, the 16-acre park known as Sahuaro Ranch is designed to preserve one of the Valley's oldest and finest homesteads. The land was once part of a 640-acre fruit farm developed by a family from Peoria, Illinois, in the late 1800s. In the 1970s the city of Glendale saved several acres from development and turned Sahuaro Ranch into a tourist attraction. You can admire 7 original buildings, a lavish rose garden, and the more than 100 peacocks that roam the grounds. Also on display is a small re-creation of the original fruit orchard as well as a miniature cotton gin, a restored vineyard, various artifacts in the Main House Museum, blacksmithing tools, and various artworks. The park itself is accessible all day every day, but guided tours of the exhibits are given by volunteers and are limited to

Wednesday through Friday 10:00 A.M. to 2:00 P.M., Saturday 10:00 A.M. to 4:00 P.M., and Sunday noon to 4:00 P.M. The tours cost $3.00 for adults and are free to those 11 and younger.

SOUTHWEST VALLEY

Wildlife World Zoo $$$
165th and Northern Avenues,
Litchfield Park
(623) 935-9453
www.wildlifeworld.com
Billed as the place to see exotic animals, Wildlife World Zoo is worth seeing if you like an informal zoo that lets you encounter animals up close. The zoo actually began in 1974 as a breeding farm for rare and endangered species, then opened to the public 10 years later. The collection now runs the gamut from rare species of primates to gazelles, a rhino, a zebra, and a white tiger. A walk through the grounds allows you to see dozens of interesting animals in fenced enclosures—about 200 species in all. Many visitors come to see the impressive collection of birds, such as pheasants, toucans, macaws, cockatoos, stilts, and ostriches. Most of the birds are displayed in a large, walk-in aviary. The zoo houses reptiles, an aquarium, and a petting area for children. At the giraffe feeding station, you can mount a platform that puts you at eye-level with the giraffes, which then eat pellets out of your hand. You can also feed the lories, small parrots that like apple wedges. The zoo has guided tours, a snack bar, and a gift shop. It's open 9:00 A.M. to 5:00 P.M. daily, with admission prices of $13.95 for adults, and $5.95 for children ages 3 to 12. It's free to children younger than 3.

KIDSTUFF 👥

Just as the lure of wealth fueled the imagination of the Old West's early settlers, the region's mystique still packs plenty of imaginative punch for kids. Our legends and lore, unforgettable landscapes, and unique cultural traditions make a rich and memorable experience for the young set . . . and plenty of photo opportunities for doting parents. Whether you hanker to ride a horse, inspect a rattlesnake, float down a river, pan for gold, eat spicy foods, or bed down under the stars, there's plenty of family-friendly events and attractions.

Though the Phoenix metropolitan area is practically a living-history textbook, Western-themed attractions are only part of the equation. The area offers a plethora of entertainment options, including playgrounds, arcades, fun parks, zoos, and toy shops. Phoenix has bragging rights to several world-class museums whose hands-on activities keep kids entertained. The Valley's vibrant arts community means that plenty of outlets exist for keeping those creative juices going—from hands-on art venues to special theater performances just for kids.

Keep in mind that the weather plays a big part in deciding how to have fun. From May through September, the temperature ranges too high to spend long periods of time outdoors—unless you plan to keep your cool in a pool, lake, or water theme park. Therefore, we suggest options for both indoor pursuits and outdoor adventures.

For more ideas see the Spectator Sports chapter for places to watch professional sports year-round. See the Parks and Recreation chapter to scope out ideal sites for desert hikes or for whiling away an afternoon.

PRICE CODE

With each attraction listed in this chapter you will find a pricing guide ranging from one to four dollar signs. The code is based on admission for an adult and one child. Please note that small children often get in cheaper or for free. Some admissions can vary, for example, if there's a basic admission and a deluxe admission, so there may be a range of price codes. If there is no dollar sign, that means the attraction has no entry fee. For restaurants the price is for a meal for two, not including drinks and dessert.

$	$5 or less
$$	$5.01 to $10
$$$	$10.01 to $20
$$$$	$20.01 and up

INDOOR PURSUITS

Museums

Arizona Museum for Youth $$
35 North Robson Street, Mesa
(480) 644-2467
www.arizonamuseumforyouth.com
You can really kid around in this downtown Mesa museum, named one of the country's best children's museums by *USA Today,* where youth enjoy an introduction to the world of fine arts. Visitors can experiment with hands-on activities that stimulate creativity and artistic savvy. Hours vary due to season and special events, so call in advance. Admission is $3.50 per person and free for children younger than 2.

Arizona Science Center $$$
600 East Washington Street, Phoenix
(602) 716-2000
www.azscience.org

The folks at the Arizona Science Center have fun down to a science. The multimillion dollar structure houses four floors' worth of hands-on, engaging exhibits that make learning seem like second nature. Its futuristic concrete-and-glass design by noted architect Antoine Predock is worth a look in and of itself. It gets even better inside. Look for a planetarium with one of the largest domes in the West; a theater with a five-story screen using Iwerks technology; and 350 exhibits cleverly organized into galleries that explore human physiology, physical forces, transportation, geology, computers, and applied sciences. Exhibits change frequently so families can stop by more than once. Experiments your budding Einsteins can try include making giant bubbles, testing paper airplanes, and measuring their skin in square inches. Near the food court, you'll find the center's store, Awesome Atom's, which is a required stop to stock up on gadgets for the thinking set. The Science Center exhibits are open 10:00 A.M. to 5:00 P.M. daily, except Thanksgiving and Christmas. Admission is $9.00 for adults, $7.00 for seniors and children ages 3 to 12, and free for children 2 and younger. Ask about special rates for large groups. Shows at the Iwerks theater and the planetarium cost extra. If you like what you see, the center runs a special summer camp for children 12 and younger, as well as continuing classroom programs for preschoolers during the winter months.

Challenger Space Center $$
21170 North 83rd Avenue, Peoria
(623) 322-2007
www.azchallenger.org

Part of a network of 41 centers worldwide, this location is home to the Knight Space Science Education Center and the Challenger Learning Center of Arizona. Kids of all ages will love the planetarium, but the most intriguing thing here is the Technology Flight Deck, which features nearly $1 million in technology, including a Mission Control room designed after Johnson Space Center. Wanna-be astronauts can participate in a simulated mission on Saturday from 10:30 A.M. to 12:30 P.M. and 1:00 to 3:00 P.M. Reservations are required and tickets cost $17.50 for adults and $15.00 for children. This is not recommended for children under age 6, and kids 7 to 10 must be accompanied by a ticketed adult. There's also a great gift shop, the Galaxy Gift Shop, full of out-of-this-world gifts. The center is open Monday through Friday, 9:00 A.M. to 4:00 P.M. and Saturday, 10:00 A.M. to 4:00 P.M. Admission is $6.00 for adults and $4.00 for children and seniors.

Hall of Flame Museum of Firefighting $$
6101 East Van Buren Street, Phoenix
(602) 275-3473
www.hallofflame.org

Fire trucks intrigue the child in all of us, but the array of firefighting gear at the Hall of Flame Museum will amaze even the most jaded museumgoer. Here's a chance to get a close-up view of almost 100 restored fire engines and firefighting apparatus dating from 1725 to 1961—said to be the world's largest such display. You can board a fire engine, slide down a firehouse pole, and dress up in firefighting gear. There's a gallery devoted to helmets, an exhibit of more than 2,000 fire department badges, fire safety exhibits, and a display of firefighting lithographs and prints by Currier and Ives and others. A kids' area teaches safety through activities geared for ages three and older. Perhaps the most intriguing display in the museum is an original Phoenix Call Center, whose working scanner still does duty. The museum is open 9:00 A.M. to 5:00 P.M. Monday through Saturday and noon to 4:00 P.M. Sunday. Admission is $5.00 for adults, $4.00 for seniors 62 and older, $3.00 for children 6 to 17, $1.50 for ages 3 to 5, and free for children younger than 3.

Heard Museum $$
**2301 North Central Avenue, Phoenix
(602) 252–8848
www.heard.org**

This world-renowned museum provides one of the best ways to learn about the cultures and the arts of Native Americans of the Southwest. It has the largest selection of katsinas (kachina dolls) anywhere. The museum's 32,000 works of art and cultural artifacts will keep the whole family interested, though children will love the exhibits geared especially for them. Best of all, visitors learn not only about the past but find out about modern-day Native American life. Duck inside authentic houses—including a Navajo hogan, an Apache wickiup, and a Hopi corn-grinding room. Work on an oversize bead loom, design Zuni jewelry, visit a Kiowa dance arbor, and walk through a re-creation of a Zuni pueblo. Be on the lookout for demonstrations by Native American artists, as well as performances of Native American music and dance. In the Museum Shop and Bookstore, you'll find books for young readers and toys that will continue to hold their interest at home. See our Annual Events chapter for special events at the Heard, such as the World Championship Hoop Dance Contest and the Guild Indian Fair & Market. The Heard is open 9:30 A.M. to 5:00 P.M. daily. Admission is $7.00 for adults, $6.00 for seniors, $3.00 for children 4 to 12, and free for those younger than 4. Guided tours are available and parking is free.

Mesa Southwest Museum $$
**53 North Macdonald Street, Mesa
(480) 644–2230
www.mesasouthwestmuseum.com**

At the Mesa Southwest Museum, visitors can explore Arizona without ever leaving town. The natural history museum doubled its space and added several galleries in 2000. A 200 million-year-old *Camarasaurus* may be ancient history, but he's one of the stars of the museum's Prehistoric Wing, which focuses on the age of dinosaurs. There, a three-story mountain presents a life-size peek at the Mesozoic Era—just watch out for the animated dinosaurs and the flash floods. Modern Arizona's beauty is revealed in the *Arizona Highways* Magazine Gallery, a permanent exhibit that features 45 top images from past issues of the magazine. Kids whose curiosity is piqued can get their kicks at the Discovery Room, where computers, books, and classes offer answers to questions that might stump the adults in their entourage. The museum is open from 10:00 A.M. to 5:00 P.M. Tuesday through Saturday, and from 1:00 to 5:00 P.M. Sunday. Admission is $6.00 for adults, $5.00 for seniors and students with an ID, $3.00 for children 3 to 12, and free for children younger than 3.

Phoenix Art Museum $$$
**1625 North Central Avenue, Phoenix
(602) 257–1222, (602) 257–1880
www.phxart.org**

Family Sunday Programs at the museum are held on the third Sunday of each month, when the museum hosts a participatory art experience for kids ages 5 to 12 and their parents. Each Sunday includes art-making activities, self-guided explorations of the museum, and, on selected Sundays, related performances. Activities are available on a first-come, first-served basis and portions of most Family Sundays are bilingual (Spanish and English). There is a similar program on the second Saturday of every month. There is no additional fee, and the programs are free with museum admission, but preregistration is requested. The museum is open 10:00 A.M. to 5:00 P.M. Tuesday through Sunday with hours extended to 9:00 P.M. on Thursday. Admission is $9.00 for adults, $7.00 for seniors and students, $3.00 for kids 6 to 17, and free for children under 6. Admission is free on Thursday.

Pueblo Grande Museum and Archeological Park $
**4619 East Washington Street, Phoenix
(602) 495–0901
www.pueblogrande.com**

Learn more about the Hohokam people whose villages once dotted the Valley more than six centuries ago. At the ruins of one of these villages, you can see the preservation work being done by archaeologists and wander among the interpretive exhibits both on the grounds and inside the museum. Kids can attend a workshop to become a junior archaeologist or can be immersed in ancient studies at one of the park's archaeology summer day camps held June through August. Petroglyph hikes outside the park, led by experts, also appeal to wanna-be archaeologists. Pueblo Grande is open 9:00 A.M. to 4:45 P.M. Monday through Saturday and 1:00 to 4:45 P.M. Sunday. Admission is $2.00 for adults, $1.50 for seniors, $1.00 for kids 6 to 12, and free for children 5 and younger. Sundays are free.

Taste of the Old West

Goldfield Ghost Town & Mine Tours
State Route 88 (Apache Trail), 4 miles
north of Apache Junction
(480) 983-0333
www.goldfieldghosttown.com
Flash back to the 1890s and get a feel for the excitement of the gold rush. Once a thriving town of 4,000 when gold fever was at its peak, Goldfield offers underground mine tours, gold panning, a nature trail, exhibits of antique mining equipment, and a narrow-gauge train ride. If you're there on a weekend, you might catch a gunfight (staged, of course). From Apache Junction in the far East Valley,

---

Rawhide plays host to the largest clown gathering in the Southwest in early August. The event includes a parade and lots of entertainment, such as face painting, balloon sculpting for the kids, and fireworks at the end of the night. Best of all, it's free. Call (480) 505-2661 or visit www.rawhide.com.

Goldfield can be reached by driving north on the Apache Trail, also known as SR 88. Goldfield is open 10:00 A.M. to 5:00 P.M. daily. A steakhouse and saloon are open until midnight. Admission is free, with the various attractions priced individually.

Pioneer Arizona $$$
Living History Museum
3901 West Pioneer Road, Phoenix
(623) 465-1052
www.pioneer-arizona.com
Did you know Arizona was the 48th state to join the Union? Here's a chance to experience what Arizona was like as a territory at the turn of the 20th century, from a period of 1880 until it became a state in 1912. Pioneer Arizona is said to be the largest living-history museum west of the Rockies. Its 90 acres feature 29 historic buildings, including a schoolhouse, a sheriff's office and jail, a church, ranch complex, and a teacherage, which is a cabin where a teacher once lived. At the blacksmith shop, you'll see a real working blacksmith who has been plying his trade for nearly 25 years. You might even catch a melodrama playing in the Opera House. In the fall, costumed interpreters—cowboys, lawmen, and Victorian ladies—make the era come alive. The museum is about 20 minutes north of central Phoenix, just off Interstate 17 at exit 225. The museum is ramping up a full schedule of events, including Statehood Days, a Christmas lighting, and a Mountain Man Rendezvous. The grounds have a full-service restaurant, the Pioneer Café, and an antiques shop. The museum is open daily, from 9:00 A.M. to 5:00 P.M., except from June 30 to September 16, when the hours are 9:00 A.M. to 2:00 P.M. Admission is $7.00 for adults, $4.00 for children ages 3 to 5, and free for children younger than 3.

Rawhide
23023 North Scottsdale Road, Scottsdale
(480) 502-5600, (480) 502-1880
www.rawhide.com
One of Scottsdale's most popular attractions, Rawhide draws tourists from the United States and abroad, all of whom

hanker for a glimpse of the Wild West. The 1880s-era town comes complete with passenger stagecoach, train rides, burro and horse rides, a rock-climbing wall, a water corral, gold panning, a shooting gallery and arcade, and mechanical bull dubbed the Widowmaker. Gunfighters roam the streets (character actors, we presume) and might challenge your tyke to a shoot-out. The antics at the Six-Gun Theater are as good as any spaghetti Western, with plenty of cliff-hanging stunts like roof rolls and explosions. Learn more about Native American traditional dances and costumes at the Spirit of the West Theater. If time allows, browse through the Western-style shops, visit the petting ranch, watch a working blacksmith, and grab some grub at the steakhouse. Rawhide is open daily but hours change according to season, so call ahead to check its hours, admission charges, and annual events.

Theater for Young Audiences

The Valley is home to a number of theater troupes whose offerings are geared for kids, many of whom feature child actors. Childsplay, a resident company of the Herberger Theater Center with an international reputation, is perhaps best known in the state. The Valley's children's theater offerings include pared-down adult fare, musicals, fairy tales, and—at the Great Arizona Puppet Theater—there's even puppetry. Note that most companies go on hiatus for the summer, save for small productions by kids in summer camps or workshops. If you are a Valley newcomer, your kids might want to take a shot at the stage themselves; many of these troupes offer theater workshops.

Childsplay $$$$
132 East Sixth Street, Tempe
(480) 350-8101
www.azeats.com/childsplay

Named by *American Theatre* magazine as one of the four leading theaters for young audiences in the nation, Childsplay has been entertaining the young and young-at-heart since 1977. A recent sampling of shows included *Time Again in Oz*, which revisited Frank Baum's classic works; *The Velveteen Rabbit*, a fanciful story about a toy that comes to life; and *The Imaginators*, about three children using their imaginations to turn their garage into an exciting world of adventure. In addition to the classics, Childsplay's themes can provoke essential family conversations, especially with such works as *The Beauty Machine*, about vanity and self-image. Catch performances at the Herberger Theater Center, 222 East Monroe Street, Phoenix, (602) 252-8497; at the Tempe Performing Arts Center, 132 East Sixth Street, Tempe, (480) 350-8119; or at the Scottsdale Center for the Arts, 7380 East Second Street, Scottsdale (480) 425-5340. Ticket prices range from $11 to $18, and performance times vary.

Cookie Company $$$$
100 East McDowell Road, Phoenix
(602) 254-2151
www.phoenixtheatre.net
An affiliate of Phoenix Theatre, the Cookie Company built a stellar reputation for taking old stage favorites and putting a modern spin on them. Recent shows included *Rapunzel*, *Treasure Island*, and *Taking the Wrath out of Math*. The Cookie Company, made up primarily of adult actors, has also tackled fables, fairy tales, and contemporary works. Its Saturday afternoon performances are often presented in both English and Spanish and tickets cost $12 for adults and $10 for kids. And the theater is aptly named—audiences chomp on cookies and milk after each performance during a meet-the-actors reception.

Greasepaint Scottsdale
Youtheatre $$$$
7020 East Second Street, Scottsdale
(480) 990-7405
www.greasepaint.org

Founded in 1984 by Wendy Leonard, a director with many years of experience in children's theater, Greasepaint is known for its reliably fun productions and its ability to nurture young talent. Performances usually take place on weekends on its home stage at the Stagebrush Theatre, with tickets costing $15 for adults and $12 for children and students. Aspiring thespians should check out the company's summer workshops.

> A valuable resource for getting to know what Phoenix has to offer families is a monthly magazine called Raising Arizona Kids. It carries a comprehensive calendar of events and thoughtfully written articles about issues of concern to parents. The magazine is available at most Valley grocery stores and bookstores and via subscription on the Web at www.raisingarizonakids.com.

Great Arizona Puppet Theater $$$
302 West Latham Street, Phoenix
(602) 262-2050
www.azpuppets.org

These puppeteers have been delighting audiences since 1983. They create and manipulate all kinds of puppets, including rod puppets, hand puppets, and marionettes. The shows often celebrate Arizona culture. Productions have included *Hotel Saguaro, The Elves and the Shoemaker, Trouble at Haunted Mountain,* and *The Christmas Mouse.* The theater also occasionally hosts guest puppeteers from around the country, such as Chinese Puppet Master Yang Hui. Performances vary with season and show, so call ahead. Tickets cost $6.00 per child, $8.00 per adult.

Jester'Z Star Theater $$$
7117 East McDowell Road, Scottsdale
(480) 423-0120, (480) 423-5111
www.theater168.com

Jester'Z improvisational theater is funny enough for adults but clean enough for kids. Its shows steer clear of raw language and crude situations, and alcohol and smoking are prohibited on the premises. Performances are fast paced and interactive, and members of the audience yell out suggestions for scenes, games, and exercises. Catch the show playing every Thursday, Friday, and Saturday night at 8:00 P.M. Tickets cost $8.00 for the Thursday shows, $10 for Friday and Saturday. There's also a 10:00 P.M. show on Saturday. Reservations required. If your kids get an itch for show business after the show, sign them up for classes and workshops.

Mesa Youtheatre $$$
155 North Center Street, Mesa
(480) 644-2681

Award-winning Mesa Youtheatre, under the direction of Jennifer Akridge, strives to present plays that speak to kids at their level, yet still challenge their minds. Costumes, set designs, and staging further demonstrate the theater's professionalism. Their repertoire—with classics like *Really Rosie, Alice in Wonderland,* and *Summer of the Swans*—encompasses both comedy and drama suitable for ages 5 and older. Performances usually take place Friday through Sunday, and tickets are $9.00 for adults and $7.00 for students. Acting and drama classes are also available for toddlers to adults.

Shopping

In this section we list a few of our favorite toy stores and specialty shops for kids. These stores may not be as well-known or as huge as places like Toys 'R' Us, the Disney Store, KAY-BEE, and Warner Bros, which are also in the Valley, but you're bound to find something that's both fun and educational. Two of the especially family-friendly malls are listed along with a few specialized bookstores. If you don't see your favorite store here, see the Shopping chapter for a more extensive listing of Valley malls.

Arizona Mills
Superstition Freeway (US 60)
and Interstate 10, Tempe
(480) 491–9700
www.arizonamills.com
The Valley's newest mall is full of manu-facturers' outlets that appeal to adult shoppers, but it also has a kid-friendly side, notably because it contains Game-Works arcade, an IMAX theater, which shows interesting shows on faraway places, and a 24-screen movie house. The Rainforest Cafe delights with the sights and sounds of an actual Amazon rain for-est. Stores your kids will like include Funzy's, which carries cool toys; Way to Glow!, which lights up with glow-in-the-dark paraphernalia; and Awesome Atom's, a branch of the store at the Arizona Sci-ence Center. Arizona Mills can be reached from I–10 near the junction with US 60.

Atomic Comics
1120 South Country Club Drive, Mesa
(480) 649–0807
www.atomiccomics.com
The Valley has several good comic-book stores, but this is one of the best, offering a stock of more than one million comics. It also features comic-related video games, collectible cards, and action figures. It sponsors Pokemon seminars and tourna-ments on Saturdays. Atomic Comics has three other Valley locations: 10215 North 28th Drive, Suite A1, Phoenix, (602) 395–1066; 5965 West Ray Road, Suite 19, Chandler, (480) 940–6061; and 4537 East Cactus Road, Phoenix, (602) 923–0733.

Brainstorms
Paradise Valley Mall, 4550 East Cactus
Road, Phoenix
(602) 996–8088
This store has both a serious and a fun side. You'll find books and kits on astron-omy, anatomy, zoology, and other science areas that are educational and fun. It also includes kid-pleasing, absurd, wacky, and gross items, such as fake eyeballs, pillows made of shredded money, or rubber hands you toss around like balls. Arts-and-crafts

items, nursery toys, puppets, games, and puzzles also fill this compact store.

Gardner's Book Service
16461 North 25th Avenue, Phoenix
(602) 863–6000
www.gbsbooks.com
This store may be hard to find because it doesn't advertise and is literally a ware-house of educational resources, but once you peek inside the 12,000-square-foot treasure trove you'll agree it's worth the effort. The store is actually geared toward book distributors, teachers, and librarians—who receive discounts on purchases—but family shoppers are welcome. The selec-tion includes juvenile fiction for all levels of readers, picture books, young-adult novels, and nonfiction.

Hobby Bench
Paradise Valley Mall, 4550 East Cactus
Road, Phoenix
(602) 996–7200
This is a toy store as much as a hobby store. It carries many brand-name toys, such as BRIO, LEGO, and Playmobil, but it also has an immense variety of arts-and-crafts items for all skill levels. Here's the best place to add to your model train set and find model-building kits for your bud-ding rocket scientist or aviator. Hobby Bench has other Valley locations at 8058 North 19th Avenue, Phoenix, (602) 995–1755; 4240 West Bell Road, (602) 547–1828; and 1781 East Highway 69, Prescott, (928) 776–1535.

Superstition Springs Center
Power Road and US 60, Mesa
(480) 396–2570
www.westcor.com
This mall makes a nice destination for a family outing not only because it houses several major department stores and dozens of specialty stores, but also because it has a couple of nice features for those moments when you're shopped-out and need a respite. Young children can take a break by riding the carousel near the food court or by exploring the

indoor play area. Another play area outside, below the food court, features rocks to climb on and tunnels to skinny through, plus a slide that looks like a Gila monster. A pleasant sitting area, a botanical garden, and a short nature trail with marked sites that explain desert plants complete the picture.

Kid-Friendly Restaurants

Chuck E. Cheese $$–$$$
8039 North 35th Avenue, Phoenix
(602) 973–1945

856 South Alma School Road, Mesa
(480) 834–9322

8890 East Indian Bend Road, Scottsdale
(480) 951–1991
www.chuckecheese.com
This is a chain restaurant, but the kiddie rides, arcade games, and a ball pit make this a popular choice when the little ones get to choose the restaurant. Chuck E. Cheese and his mechanical puppet band pop out onto a stage every now and then to perform a few numbers and crack jokes. Pizza is the specialty, but sub sandwiches and a salad bar are also on the menu. The restaurants are open daily for lunch and dinner. There are several more locations in the Valley; we've just shown the three most central here. Check the phone book or Web site for more.

Ed Debevic's $$$
2102 East Highland Avenue, Phoenix
(602) 956–2760
You want atmosphere? You got atmosphere, plus plenty of fast-talking, insult-hurling, and bubble gum-chewing waiters and waitresses. The fabulous 1950s set the theme at this chain restaurant, as you can guess from the retro attire, jukebox, linoleum, and signs on the walls. Expect burgers, fries, chicken, and spaghetti, diner-style, with enough variety for kids' fussy tastes. Be sure to order a genuine milkshake, served in a

tall metal cup. The restaurant is open daily for lunch and dinner.

**Pinnacle Peak Patio
Steakhouse** $$$–$$$$
10426 East Jomax Road, Scottsdale
(480) 585–1599
www.pppatio.com
Your youngsters will experience a blast from the past when they are deputized by the Old Timer at this Western-themed restaurant. In addition to receiving their own badge, there's a coloring book and a kids menu to amuse them—or you can challenge them to count the ties that have been cut from the necks of naive tenderfoots and hung from the ceiling. Hint: There's close to a million. A Valley institution since 1957, the Pinnacle Peak Patio serves steak, chicken, and ribs.

Rustler's Rooste $$$–$$$$
Pointe Hilton South Mountain Resort,
7777 South Pointe Parkway, Phoenix
(602) 431–6474
www.rustlersrooste.com
Your gang will enjoy hanging out at this taste of the Old West atop South Mountain, which offers great food and wide-open views of the city. If you can wrest your kids away from the popular slide, you can pick out Valley landmarks. Authentic touches include a barn-wood exterior, sawdust on the floor, and ranch and farm implements on the walls. Entertainment includes a live country band and colorful characters who wander from table to table, telling tall tales, and performing magic tricks.

Other Indoor Retreats

Alltel Ice Den $$$
9375 East Bell Road, Scottsdale
(480) 585–7465
www.coyotesice.com
Attention, fans of NHL hockey. The Phoenix Coyotes' practice ice rink is open for public skating several times a week. The ice is almost exactly like the America

West Arena rink in downtown Phoenix, where the Coyotes play their home games. The facility offers figure skating and hockey programs for children and adults, plus a pro shop, concessions area, and restaurant. Public sessions vary by the season, but usually last two hours every weekday, with the addition of two-hour evening sessions Thursday through Sunday. Admission is $7.00 for adults and $5.00 for those 6 to 15, with skate rental being an additional $4.00 for hockey skates or $3.00 for figure skates. Kids under 5 skate for $5.00, skate rental included. There's teen night on Friday and family night on Saturday. A family of four can skate on Wednesday and Sunday for $28.00, skate rental included.

Arcadia Ice $$
3853 East Thomas Road, Phoenix
(602) 957-9966
www.arcadiaice.com
Ice-skating might not be as popular in Phoenix as it is in colder climes, but it sure feels good on a hot day. Arcadia Ice is inside the Desert Palms Power Center and has public skating sessions during both days and evenings, with skating lessons on weekend afternoons. Day skating sessions are 1:00 to 3:30 P.M. Monday through Friday; 7:00 to 9:00 P.M. Friday night; noon to 2:00 P.M. Saturday; and 7:30 to 9:30 P.M. Saturday night. Admission is $4.50 for adults, $3.50 for kids 3 to 12, and $2.50 for skate rental.

Burton Barr Central Library
1221 North Central Avenue, Phoenix
(602) 262-4636
www.phoenixpubliclibrary.org
We recommend a stop at Phoenix's main library because of its fine selection of children's books and its fanciful design. The five-story library is copper and concrete on the outside, with lots of natural light flowing into the inside. If you're interested in architecture, we recommend checking out the Great Reading Room on the fifth floor, where you can inspect the cable-suspended roof more closely. And believe it or not, on

the way to the library's restrooms, you can see a body heat-sensitive fiber-optic display along translucent walls. In addition, the glass elevators reflect colored lights as they swoosh up and down. The children's area has lots of cozy, creative sitting places, thanks to a City of Phoenix public art program that enlisted artists to design the furniture and book kiosks.

Cerreta Candy Company
5345 West Glendale Avenue, Glendale
(623) 930-1000
www.cerreta.com
This redbrick building is a landmark in downtown Glendale, but we're much more interested in what goes on inside—the making of delicious Cerreta chocolates and candies. You can stop in anytime during retail hours of 8:00 A.M. to 6:00 P.M. Monday through Saturday to watch candy being made at this family-owned factory. TV screens near the candy-making machines show a video that helps explain the process. Boxed candies and chocolate by the pound are available for purchase.

Jeepers $$$
4961 West Bell Road, Phoenix
(602) 439-9200

2726 South Alma School Road, Mesa
(602) 820-8300
www.jeepers.com
Jeepers has the feel of a mini state fair with all its amusement park rides, video games, noise, and colored lights. Luckily for all those families looking for something to do on a hot day in the Valley, it's all indoors. The playlands are geared to children 12 and younger, offering small but fast roller coasters, carousels, and other kiddie rides. Preschoolers like the three-level soft playground with tunnels, chutes, and ladders. Hours are 10:00 A.M. to 9:00 P.M. Monday through Thursday; 10:00 A.M. to 10:00 P.M. Friday and Saturday; and Sunday, 11:00 A.M. to 8:00 P.M. You can buy individual ride tickets or passes. Passes for unlimited rides are $7.99, with toddlers under 36 inches getting a $2.00 discount.

Kiwanis Park Wave Pool $$
6111 South All-America Way, Tempe
(480) 350-5201

This indoor pool at Kiwanis Community Park is not a full-fledged water park, but it has continuous waves and a giant water slide. It's popular when it's too hot to be outside, yet you can take away a bit of the chill from swimming with a few moments of sunning on the pool's outdoor deck. Hours vary by the season; sometimes the wave pool is only open on weekends. Admission is $6.00 for adults and $3.00 for children ages 3 to 17. The pool is not recommended for toddlers. Tube rentals, snacks, and beverages are available.

Laser Quest $$$
3335 West Peoria Avenue, Phoenix
(602) 548-0005

2035 South Alma School Road, Mesa
(480) 752-0005
www.laserquest.com

Laser Quest is part of a national chain capitalizing on the game of laser tag, in which participants chase each other around a maze in the dark, shooting laser guns at each other for almost a half hour. Totally cool, say kids and adults who have tried it. Hours vary, depending on the season, but are typically 5:00 to 10:00 P.M. Monday through Thursday; 5:00 P.M. to midnight Friday; 10:00 A.M. to midnight Saturday; and noon to 10:00 P.M. Sunday. It opens a few hours earlier in the summer. The cost is $6.50 per person, and you get to keep your personalized scorecard.

Mystery Castle $$
800 East Mineral Road, Phoenix
(602) 268-1581

Once upon a time in the 1930s, a daddy decided to build a dream castle for his little princess. He built it in the desert, of native stone. It took 15 years to complete and has 18 rooms, 13 fireplaces, parapets, and many nooks and crannies. Inside and out, it looks like a castle and, at 8,000 square feet, is large enough to host royalty. Today, Mary Lou Gulley still lives in the castle her father built for her and conducts tours. Her fairy-tale abode is now on the Historical Registry and has been spotlighted by various media. Tour hours are 11:00 A.M. to 4:00 P.M. Thursday through Sunday. Cost is $5.00 for adults, $4.00 for seniors, $2.00 for children ages 6 to 15, and free for children younger than 6. It is open October through June.

Oceanside Ice Arena $$
1520 North McClintock Drive, Tempe
(480) 941-0944
iskateaz.com

At a cool 50 degrees Fahrenheit, Oceanside provides a nice escape for East Valley residents. Public skating sessions vary week to week, though. You can usually get in during the afternoons or evenings, but call ahead for hours. Admission is $4.50 for adults and $3.50 for children 12 and younger. Figure skate rentals are $3.50 and hockey skate rentals are $4.50. Inquire about lessons for beginning skaters or children's hockey.

Scottsdale Civic Center Library
3839 North Drinkwater Boulevard,
Scottsdale
(480) 312-2474
www.library.ci.scottsdale.az.us

This large library is a focal point of Scottsdale's Civic Center Mall, and its children's area is one of the most eye-appealing Valley libraries. It's designed to resemble a giant pop-up book, complete with cutout trees, clouds hanging from the ceiling, a castle facade, a reading tower with a drawbridge, carpeting in the color of a forest floor, and a "stream" running through shelving areas. Cozy seating can be found in the picture book area. In the young-adult fiction area, find an oversize chess set available for anyone's use, and just around the corner is a dollhouse on display. The library is open 9:00 A.M. to 9:00 P.M. Monday through Thursday; 10:00 A.M. to 6:00 P.M. Friday and Saturday; and 1:00 to 5:00 P.M. Sunday.

FUN IN THE SUN

Appreciating Nature

Deer Valley Rock Art Center   **$**
3711 West Deer Valley Road, Phoenix
(623) 582-8007
Better your understanding of the symbolism and beauty of rock art, or petroglyphs, and the earliest inhabitants of this region at the Deer Valley Rock Art Center, where you can view more than 1,500 petroglyphs along a quarter-mile path through a desert preserve. From October through April the center is open from 9:00 A.M. to 5:00 P.M. Monday through Saturday; and noon to 5:00 P.M. Sunday. Guided tours are available at 10:00 A.M. on Saturday. From May through September, the center is open from 8:00 A.M. to 2:00 P.M. Tuesday through Friday; 9:00 A.M. to 5:00 P.M. Saturday; and noon to 5:00 P.M. Sunday. Admission is $4.00 for adults, $2.00 for students and seniors, $1.00 for ages 6 to 12, and free for those younger than 6. Kids can also explore the past more deeply at the Deer Valley Rock Art Center's summer day camp.

Desert Botanical Garden   **$$$**
Papago Park, 1201 North Galvin Parkway, Phoenix
(480) 941-1225
www.dbg.org
We would put the Desert Botanical Garden high on your to-do list. You might have seen botanical gardens before, but you probably haven't encountered one that celebrates the glory and variety of desert flora. You'll learn about dozens of varieties of cacti and succulents by winding through the garden's many nature trails. Often you'll find garden volunteers who have set up learning stations, perhaps even with hands-on activities. If you head to the garden in the spring, you will be amazed by the variety of cactus blooms, desert trees, shrubs, and flowers—which seems to include every color in the rainbow. Hours are 8:00 A.M.

to 8:00 P.M. daily, except during the summer, when you can beat the heat by arriving at 7:00 A.M. The center is closed on holidays. Admission is $9.00 for adults, $8.00 for seniors, $5.00 for students, $4.00 for kids ages 3 to 12, and free for kids 2 and under. Learn more about the garden in the Attractions chapter.

Hayden Butte
First Street and Mill Avenue, Tempe
(480) 350-5200
Not too grueling and not too easy, this hike up a craggy hill is just right for families with young children. Also known as A Mountain, the butte is popular with Arizona State University students, who get a kick out of constantly repainting the concrete A near the top. The hike up is quite steep in parts, but it only takes a half hour. Watch for rocks with petroglyphs on the way. Be rewarded with great views of the Salt River and East Valley.

Katydid Insect Museum   **$$**
5060 West Bethany Home Number 4, Glendale
(623) 931-8718
www.insectmuseum.com
If your kids are into creepy crawlers, then this is the place for them! This fascinating museum features 8,000 insects, all displayed in specimen cases (thankfully!). Kids with nerves of steel can hold live Madagascar hissing roaches, bearded dragon lizards, millipedes, fence lizards,

---

Looking for an evening out with the family? Check out the Movies in the Park series at Kiwanis Park Lake in Tempe. Held every Friday evening at dusk from March through May at the Kiwanis Park Lake Fire Circle at Mill Avenue and All America Way, the kid-friendly movies (think Finding Nemo, Daddy Day Care) are free. Take a picnic and a few chairs and enjoy the evening out on the lawn. Call (480) 350-5200 for a schedule.

---

and a variety of beetles. There are several kinds of live specimens, including nine types of scorpions under black lights and a tarantula with a 12-inch leg span. A small gift shop, lots of video tapes, and craft items round out the museum offerings along with monthly workshops. Admission is $4.00 for adults, $3.00 for students and seniors, $2.00 for kids ages 7 to 11, $1.00 for kids 3 to 6, and free for kids under 3. Open Monday through Friday, 11:00 A.M. to 4:00 P.M.

MacDonald's Ranch $$$$
26540 North Scottsdale Road, Scottsdale
(480) 585-0239
www.macdonaldsranch.com
Take a horseback ride among desert scrub and tall saguaros, with the McDowell Mountains as your backdrop. For decades, MacDonald's Ranch—a real ranch that raises horses—has been teaching young people about these magnificent animals, through lessons and day rides. The ranch also specializes in cowboy cookouts on the trail to complete your Western adventure (groups of 10 or more). Reservations are recommended for the cookout, and the ranch suggests this activity for children ages 7 and older. There are pony rides at the ranch for those younger than 7. Sample prices: A one-hour guided trail ride is $30 per person; a one-hour ride with a cowboy luncheon is $55 per person.

Out of Africa Wildlife Park $$$$
9736 North Fort McDowell Road,
Fountain Hills
(480) 837-7779
wwww.outofafricapark.com
Tigers in Arizona? This wildlife park has developed a natural habitat for white tigers and other species of predators, who star in the park's unrehearsed shows. The most popular show is Tiger Splash, where visitors can see tigers practicing hunting techniques as they splash in and out of the water with staff members. The park presents nine animal shows in all, featuring not just tigers but lions, coatis, foxes, bears, cougars, wolves, pythons, and

exotic birds. Other features include a cafe and gift shop. To get to Out of Africa, take the Beeline Highway (State Route 87) north until you're 2 miles north of Shea Boulevard, then turn right onto Fort McDowell Road. Winter hours (October 1 through Memorial Day) are 9:30 A.M. to 5:00 P.M. Tuesday through Sunday. Summer hours are 4:00 to 9:30 P.M. Wednesday through Friday; Saturday, 9:30 A.M. to 9:30 P.M.; and Sunday, 9:30 A.M. to 5:00 P.M. Admission, which includes the shows, is $14.95 for adults, $13.75 for seniors, and $6.95 for children ages 3 to 12. Children 2 and younger get in free.

The Phoenix Zoo $$$
Papago Park, 455 North Galvin Parkway,
Phoenix
(602) 273-1341
www.phoenixzoo.org
The Phoenix Zoo is such a lively place that regular visitors have found they can head there several times a year and still find exhibits to explore. The 125-acre zoo is well organized and easy to traverse if you just have a few hours to spare, but we recommend making a day of it if the weather is pleasant. Each of the trails has a theme, such as the tropics, Africa, or the Arizona desert, and that's how you'll find any animals you're particularly interested in, from baboons to coyotes to zebras. Be on the lookout for the unfamiliar, too: Kori bustards, Mexican wolves, warthogs, and Chacoan peccaries. One of the zoo's most popular attractions is the Forest of Uco, featuring spectacled bears. If you're new to Arizona, don't miss the zoo's Arizona Trail, with its unique exhibit of rattlesnakes, scorpions, and other creepy-crawlies—some of them viewed in a dark tunnel under special lights. The Discovery Trail features a small butterfly garden and a farm area with hands-on activities. The Safari Train takes visitors on guided tours for a small fee. Hours are 9:00 A.M. to 5:00 P.M. daily from Labor Day to Memorial Day. In the summer, hours change to 7:00 A.M. to 4:00 P.M. (In the summer, the earlier you go, the better.) Admission is $12.00 for

adults, $9.00 for seniors, $5.00 for ages 3 to 12, and free for those 2 and younger. Check our Annual Events chapter for details on two of the zoo's largest events, the pageantry of the holiday ZooLights and the Halloween festivities of Boo! at the Zoo.

South Mountain Park Bike Trails
10919 South Central Avenue, Phoenix
(602) 495-0222
If you've never had the experience of mountain biking in the desert, this is a great place to try it. The ridges and crests of South Mountain Park are higher than you think, so be ready for a workout. The average trail is 20 miles long, but along the way you will enjoy vistas of the city, the desert brush, wildflowers, and interesting rocks. You'll see trail markings when you enter the park from Central Avenue. Be sure to pack plenty of water to avoid dehydration.

Wildlife World Zoo $$$
1605 West Northern Avenue,
Litchfield Park
(623) 935-9453
www.wildlifeworld.com
This zoo is a trek to reach, but it's worth seeing because of its unusual and rare animals—more than 200 species in all. For example, the new indoor-outdoor penguin exhibit features black-footed penguins from Africa. Wildlife World's denizens are also easier to see than in some zoos, so visitors get a close-up look at rhinoceroses, llamas, tigers, lions, and antelopes. A new feature is the Australian Boat Ride, where you can ride a pontoon through the Outback and see emus, kangaroos, and cockatoos. Kids will get a kick out of the giraffe feeding station, where a platform puts them at eye-level with the giraffes, where they can literally have these graceful creatures eating out of their hands. You can also feed small parrots called lories, which are partial to apple wedges. On-site amenities include a gift shop, food service, and free parking. The zoo is open 9:00 A.M. to 5:00 P.M. daily, with admission

prices of $13.95 for adults and $5.95 for children ages 3 to 12. Admission is free for children younger than 3.

Amusement Parks

Castles n' Coasters $$$$
9445 Metro Parkway East, Metrocenter,
I-17 and Dunlap Avenue, Phoenix
(602) 997-7575
www.castlesncoasters.com
This amusement park catches your eye from I-17 and the best way to get there is to take the Peoria exit. The park's name comes from its castle replica, which anchors the center of the amusement park, and the two roller coasters, one of which is Arizona's largest. If the thrills and chills of that double-loop coaster, Desert Storm, are too much, try the slightly tamer log ride, bumper boats, or NASCAR racers. The park also features a smaller coaster and carousel, along with four miniature-golf courses. Inside the castle are video games and snack areas. Teens favor this amusement park as a hangout place on weekend nights, while younger kids enjoy having birthday parties there on weekend days. Castles 'N Coasters opens at 10:00 A.M. year-round, but hours for the rides are seasonal. Usually the rides run on Friday evenings, all day and until 11:00 P.M. on Saturday, and all day until 10:00 P.M. on Sunday. Call for hours on weekday evenings. Rides are priced individually (Desert Storm costs $4.00), or you can buy an unlimited ride pass for $18.00 or an unlimited ride and golf pass for $23.00.

CrackerJax $$$$
16001 North Scottsdale Road, Scottsdale
(480) 998-2800
www.crackerjax.com
Miniature-golf aficionados like this place for its three courses of varying difficulties. You can also try your hand at real golf on the two-level driving range, which has enough space for 60 duffers. This amusement park also keeps kids young and old

happy with bumper boats, go-karts, sand volleyball, batting cages, video games, and an arcade. You can load up on eats at the park grill and eatery. Park hours vary by season, but generally it opens at 10:00 A.M. daily for golf and batting cages, with most rides operating by 4:00 P.M. Rides start at 10:00 A.M. on Saturday and Sunday. The park stays open until 10:00 P.M. Sunday through Thursday and until midnight on Friday and Saturday. All-day passes are available and are sold according to your height: The smallest children pay $12.50, and from there it goes up to the adult price of $16.50.

Enchanted Island at Encanto Park $$$
1202 West Encanto Boulevard, Phoenix
(602) 254-1200
www.enchantedisland.com
Encanto Park, a public area, stretches for several blocks between Thomas Road and Encanto Boulevard. Should you happen to meet any adults who are natives of Phoenix, they will tell you this was the place to go in their childhood, particularly because of its resident amusement park, Enchanted Island. The park continues to be a favorite gathering place for families, especially those living in central Phoenix. Enchanted Island's most nostalgic attraction is a carousel that has graced the park since 1948. Another longtime favorite is the C. P. Huntington train that winds around the park. For more amusement, there's a pirate ship, kiddie roller coaster, rope climbing, bumper boats, action play stations, and more. There are also plenty of picnic areas adjacent to Enchanted Island. At Encanto's lake, try a little paddleboating, canoeing, or fishing. You can rent boats from Encanto Park Boat Rentals at (602) 254-1520. Enchanted Island hours vary, so call ahead. An unlimited ride pass costs $10.00 for guests less than 54 inches tall and $6.00 for those above. Individual rides costs $1.00.

Fiddlesticks Family Fun Park $$$$
1155 West Elliot Road, Tempe
(480) 961-0800

8800 East Indian Bend Road, Scottsdale
(480) 951-6060
www.fiddlesticksaz.com
The family that plays together will have oodles of fun at Fiddlesticks, where the amusements include miniature golf, bumper boats, go-karts, batting cages, and video games. The Scottsdale location has all the above features, plus a kiddie land, a roller coaster, an elephant ride, and the favorite among amusement parks aficionados—laser tag. The Tempe location has a lighted driving range popular with golfers of all ages. Families can buy value packages that allow entrance to a combination of attractions; the packages are $16 for adults and $12 for children under 59 inches tall. Hours vary so please call ahead.

Water Parks

To fight off the summer doldrums and beat the heat, many Valley families head to water parks. This area is fortunate to have three big ones—all packed with fun features and millions of gallons of cool, refreshing water. Parents and kids cool down with lots of soaking, splashing, sliding, and tubing. All three water parks are run by Golfland Entertainment Centers and are convenient to reach from anywhere in the Valley. The parks usually open Memorial Day weekend and remain so through Labor Day weekend. The less crowded days tend to be Monday through Wednesday.

We give admission prices for all three parks, but be ready for add-on costs, such as inner tube, inflatable raft, or boogie board rentals; locker rentals; and the food and beverage tab, since rules prohibit bringing your own.

A couple of other tips: Consider wearing slip-on aqua shoes—the concrete surrounding the pools is hotter than you think. Also, be mindful of the ratings given

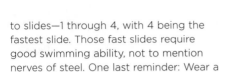

to slides—1 through 4, with 4 being the fastest slide. Those fast slides require good swimming ability, not to mention nerves of steel. One last reminder: Wear a good sunscreen lotion and apply it hourly.

Admission prices change from year to year, but most recently they were $17.00 for those 12 and older and $14.00 for children ages 4 to 11. Children 3 and younger get in free. The water parks offer discounts for late admission, which is after 3:00 or 4:00 P.M., depending on the park.

Big Surf $$$$
1500 North McClintock Drive, Tempe
(480) 947-7873
www.golfland-sunsplash.com
This almost 30-year-old park brings back fond memories for any adult who grew up in Phoenix. It's legendary as the place to hang out; it was one of the world's first artificial-wave pools and is still probably the largest in the world. The massive pool—as big as four football fields—lets you ride the waves every 90 seconds. Its surrounding landscaping and decor lend the park a Polynesian theme. Big Surf has 11 giant slides and assorted other slides. Little ones will enjoy a wading pool with sprinklers and easy slides. Hours are 10:00 A.M. to 6:00 P.M. Monday through Saturday and 11:00 A.M. to 7:00 P.M. Sunday.

Golfland/Sunsplash $$$$
155 West Hampton Avenue, Mesa
(480) 834-8319
www.golfland-sunsplash.com
The gigantic wave pool here differs from Big Surf's—you get 10 minutes of calm and 10 minutes of wave action. Another feature that appeals to relaxation seekers is a circuitous "river" that you can lazily float upon in your inner tube. The kiddie area is quite big, with easy concrete slides, a waterfall, sprinklers, and hoses for lots of safe water play. This Caribbean-theme park has 10 tube and giant slides. For indoor diversion, there's a huge arcade area with games for any skill level, which is a favorite date place for Valley teenagers. The park also has a new laser

A steamboat ride, in Arizona? Believe it or not, you and the family can take a scenic cruise on the Dolly, a 100-foot-long replica of an early-American riverboat sternwheeler. The boat cruises the original path of the Salt River on Canyon Lake, 16 miles northeast of Apache Junction. The drive is worth it for the spectacular 90-minute narrated nature cruise of this beautiful lake. The boat leaves the dock daily at noon and 2:00 P.M. After the ride, the kids can swim or just wade in the river. There's a picnic area nearby, a snack bar on deck, and a restaurant. Call (480) 827-9144 or get more details at www.dollysteamboat .com. Adult fare is $15.00; children ages 6 to 12, $8.50. Reservations are strongly suggested. It's a real kid pleaser.

tag area. Also popular are the miniature-golf courses adjacent to the arcade. The water park is open 10:00 A.M. to 8:00 P.M. Monday through Thursday; 10:00 A.M. to 9:00 P.M. Friday and Saturday; and 11:00 A.M. to 7:00 P.M. Sunday. Golfland is open 10:00 A.M. to 10:00 P.M., Sunday through Thursday; and 10:00 A.M. to midnight Friday and Saturday.

Waterworld Safari $$$$
4243 West Pinnacle Peak Road, Phoenix
(623) 581-1947
www.golfland-sunsplash.com
This water park with an African safari theme is popular with folks in the West Valley. Its newest attraction is the Zambezi River, a 1,100-foot-long lazy waterway that's perfect for relaxing. The wave pool is designed to give 10 minutes of calm and 10 minutes of wave action. Little ones have a great time on the easy slides and the rapids. The Jungle-Jim's children's play pool has a self-latching, fenced area. Lifeguards are on duty. For adventure-some older kids and adults, there are eight larger slides of the super-speedy, scream-eliciting variety. Hours are 10:00

A.M. to 8:00 P.M. Monday through Thursday; 10:00 A.M. to 9:00 P.M. Friday and Saturday; and 11:00 A.M. to 7:00 P.M. Sunday.

Other Parks

Crow's Dairy $$
10505 West Broadway Road, Tolleson
(623) 936-4435
www.crowsdairy.com
This is a fourth-generation, working dairy farm where families can pet and feed barnyard animals and watch milking demonstrations. Never taken a hayride? Here's your chance. Tours are offered by appointment only, from September through May, for $5.00 per person with a minimum of 20 participants.

Desert Breeze Railroad $
Desert Breeze Park, Ray Road and McClintock Drive, Chandler
(480) 940-1685
Ride on a reproduction of an 1880s train in this small but pleasant park in a suburban neighborhood. When—or if—the tots should tire of that, there's plenty of playground equipment in the park and a carousel. The train runs 10:00 A.M. to sunset Thursday through Saturday, 11:00 A.M. to 5:00 P.M. on Sunday, and closes in July and August because of the heat. Amenities include a snack bar and a covered patio. A train ride costs $1.50, kids under 18 months ride free. The carousel costs $1.50. A 10-ride pass is available for $12. Special seasonal rides are offered on Halloween and Christmas.

Desert West Skateboard Plaza
Desert West Park, 6602 West Encanto Boulevard, Phoenix
(602) 495-3700
When this skateboard park opened in 1997, Phoenix was the first city in Arizona to have such a park. It has been packed ever since with teens wanting to perfect their jumps and turns. The massive park features several bowls, a central four-sided pyramid, and various ledges for the

daredevil in you. It makes good sense to wear helmets and other protective gear, by the way. Hours are 7:00 A.M. to 10:00 P.M. daily. Admission is free.

Indian Bend Wash Bike Path
Along Hayden Road, Scottsdale
(480) 312-7901
This is an easy, meandering bike path along a greenbelt, but the route stretches for 11 miles. So decide beforehand how much of it you want to tackle. There are several good starting points, such as north of downtown Scottsdale at Chaparral Park at Hayden and Jackrabbit Roads or the Bike Stop Rest Area on Thomas Road between Miller and Hayden Roads. You can head north toward Shea Boulevard or south toward McKellips Road in Tempe. Along the way you'll meet many other bicyclists—this is a popular route because the greenbelt and its small lakes and golf courses make pleasant surroundings. In-line skaters, strollers, joggers, and dog walkers share the route. It makes dips here and there under major traffic arteries. The greenbelt is slightly below street level because it's the place that catches the flow of rainwater after big storms and thus prevents flooding of nearby homes.

McCormick-Stillman Railroad Park $
7301 East Indian Bend Road, (Indian Bend and Scottsdale Roads), Scottsdale
(480) 312-2312
www.therailroadpark.com
Scottsdale residents love their railroad park—it's often overflowing with people enjoying birthday parties and picnics on weekends. The park has added an antique carousel and clock tower. The resident train is a 5/12-scale model of the Rio Grande Western Railway, and it chugs a little over a mile through 30 acres of parkland. You board at Stillman Station, a replica of a historic train depot at Clifton, Arizona. Railroad buffs should head to the corner of the park housing displays of railroad memorabilia. There you'll find a Pullman car that was used by several United States presidents, a 1906 Baldwin locomo-

tive, a 1914 Santa Fe baggage car, and a machine shop dating from 1903. For most of the year, rides on the train and carousel are offered daily, starting at 10:00 A.M. and running until 6:30 P.M. On summer weekends the hours are the same, but on summer weekdays, the train runs only from 4:00 to 8:30 P.M. Tickets cost $1.00, with children younger than 3 riding free. Next to the carousel is a sandy playground with lots of climbing equipment and slides. A Southern Pacific caboose houses a snack bar. In October the park hosts its annual Railfair celebration, with displays, games, and other fun events for the entire family.

Play cowboy for a day by taking a trail ride at any Valley outfitter, such as All Western Stables in Phoenix, (602) 276–5862; Fort McDowell Adventures, in Mesa, (480) 816–1513; or Saguaro Lake Ranch in Mesa, (480) 984–0335. You can also pack them off to a dude ranch for a stay—John F. Kennedy spent time on an Arizona ranch long before his stint as president. Call the Dude Ranchers' Association in Colorado for more information, (307) 587–2339, or check out www.duderanch.org

ANNUAL EVENTS

Thanks to El Sol, the Valley of the Sun bustles with outdoor festivals. The season of festivals and major outdoor events—including a number of arts and sports related events—usually begins in late October and runs through April. Throughout the year, the Valley plays host to many festivals celebrating diverse cultures—Mexican American, Native American, Japanese, Scottish, Greek, you name it. These festivals not only reflect our unique heritage, but also show our desire to share it with all those around us.

The Valley's pleasant winters allow all kinds of holiday-related outdoor festivals, including the popular ZooLights at the Phoenix Zoo and Las Noches de las Luminarias at the Desert Botanical Garden.

The event calendar drops off in the summer, when the triple-digit temperatures have driven out the tourists, as well as many residents. Hardy souls turn up the heat even higher by plunging into our great Cinco de Mayo festivals and celebrating our country's independence at the Valley's Fourth of July shows.

The Arizona Office of Tourism estimates that there are at least 4,000 events around the state annually. In the Phoenix area that translates to several hundred large public gatherings a year. This chapter will bring you up to speed on several not-to-be-missed events, as well as a few smaller festivals that may pique your interest.

We have supplied approximate dates for these various events, but be aware that they are subject to change, as are admission prices.

JANUARY

Celebration of Fine Art
Chauncey Equestrian Center, 18500
North Scottsdale Road, Scottsdale
(480) 443-7695
www.celebrateart.com

This open-air exhibition and festival hoists its big white tents every year for about 11 weeks, starting in January. Touted as an outstanding art event, it provides a chance to see the on-site studios of more than 100 artists, including painters, jewelers, photographers, weavers, ceramists, and a sculpture garden. One of the attractions of the event is the chance to see artists in action. It is no wonder that *Art & Antiques* magazine called this "one of the West's premier art events." It is usually open during daytime hours, and admission is $7.00 for adults, $6.00 for seniors and military; children under age 12 are free.

Barrett-Jackson Classic Auto Auction
WestWorld, 16601 North Pima Road,
Scottsdale
(480) 421-6694
www.barrettjackson.com
Rightly dubbed "the Oscars of the collector-car world," this is an auction and show of hundreds of classic cars, almost all in excellent original or restored condition. Along with the Phoenix Open and the Arabian Horse Show, the Barrett-Jackson Classic is one of Scottsdale's top three events, attracting high-rolling auto enthusiasts from around the world. In 2003 total sales exceeded $27 million. The year's big ticket item was a 1957 Jaguar XK-SS Roadster that went for $1.1 million. Other cars included a 1967 Ford GT 40 Mark 1 ($347,760) and a 1932 Auburn Cabriolet Coupe ($180,360).

Even if you aren't one of the lucky few who can afford to shell out more money for a car than most people spend on their homes, you can at least enjoy the wide selection of good food and browse the auto memorabilia on sale. Just looking at the cars will spark a lifetime of daydreaming. The event runs five days in mid-January, with daily general admission tickets costing $15.00 each, $10.00 for students and seniors (62 and over), $6.00

for youths ages 6 to 12, and free for children under 6. A four-day pass costs $50.

The Phoenix Open
Tournament Players Club of Scottsdale, 17020 North Hayden Road, Scottsdale
(602) 870-4431
www.phoenixopen.com
The Phoenix Open is considered the world's most-attended golf tournament. And who wouldn't want to catch a glimpse of famous golfers in the beautiful setting of a Phoenix winter? In addition to being the place to be for serious and casual golfers, the Open is a highly successful fund-raiser. The sponsoring organization, the Thunderbirds, raises money for various Arizona charities, especially those bringing sports to disadvantaged youths. The tournament lasts four days, generally around the last weekend in January. But the event stretches to fill out the week with such things as celebrity tournaments, a Skills Extravaganza, a "Dream Day" of golf for inner-city youth, and a Special Olympics putting clinic. Tickets at the gate cost $25 per person; children 17 and younger are admitted free when accompanied by an adult. The TPC course is adjacent to the lovely Scottsdale Princess Resort (see the Resorts chapter).

American Express Invitational Native American Arts Festival
West Valley Fine Arts Center, 387 Wigwam Boulevard, Litchfield Park
(623) 935-6384
www.wvfac.org
This outdoor festival showcases more than 200 Native American artists and craftspeople from the Southwest. You'll find a wonderful array of jewelry, sculpture, weavings, and paintings plus hands-on crafts activities for children. Native American music and dance performances are also featured. The event is organized by the West Valley Fine Arts Council. Admission is $8.00 for adults, $5.00 for children 11 to 16; children under 11 are admitted free. Look for this two-day event the second or third weekend in January.

Sunday A'Fair
Scottsdale Civic Center Mall, 7380 East Second Street, Scottsdale
(480) 994-ARTS
www.scottsdalearts.org
Mini arts festivals, the Sunday A'Fairs make an appealing way to while away a Sunday afternoon on the grassy mall of Scottsdale Civic Center Mall. They feature outdoor concerts by well-known and emerging Valley musicians. Expect a variety of musical styles, including Cajun-zydeco, reggae, Delta blues, and mainstream pop. Also find Arizona-made arts and crafts and plenty of food and beverage booths. Admission is free, and the A'Fairs generally are held each Sunday afternoon from January through mid-April, unless a larger festival or special event is using the mall. Hours are noon to 4:30 P.M.

FEBRUARY

Scottsdale Indian Artists of America Show
Civic Center Mall, 7380 East Second Street, Scottsdale
(866) 398-2226
www.indianartistsofamerica.com
Since 1995 the Indian Artists of America juried exhibition has drawn more than 100 of the nation's finest potters, weavers, jewelers, sculptors, and painters, representing a number of tribes. Usually held on a Saturday and Sunday in mid-February, the show also spotlights Native American dancing and music, fashion shows, and bird of prey demonstrations. Admission is $8.00 for adults; free for children 12 and younger.

Scottsdale Jaycees Parada del Sol
WestWorld, 16601 North Pima Road, Scottsdale
(480) 990-3179
www.scottsdalejaycees.com
Parada del Sol—or a walk in the sun—offers a chance for the increasingly cosmopolitan Scottsdale to live up to a slogan it coined several decades ago: "The West's Most Western Town." Yes, there

was a time when cowboys traveled the dirt roads into Scottsdale to hitch their horses on Main Street while they grabbed a beer at the saloon. This event, founded in 1959, celebrates this tradition. During Parada del Sol Week, cowboys, pioneer women, and mountain men reclaim their place in Scottsdale history. Events include the Hashknife Pony Express, in which riders deliver mail via horseback on a 225-mile ride from Holbrook to Scottsdale; the Parada del Sol Parade, a Saturday morning spectacular that's believed to be the world's largest and longest horse-drawn parade; the Parada del Sol Rodeo, four days of bronc riding, steer roping, rodeo clowns, and more, sanctioned by the Professional Rodeo Cowboys Association; a Rodeo Dance; and a Trail's End Celebration, featuring food, drinks, kids activities, and gunfight performances. Parada del Sol events usually take place in late January or early February. The parade is free.

World Championship Hoop Dance Contest
Heard Museum, 2301 North Central Avenue, Phoenix
(602) 251-0255
www.heard.org
You won't see this too often: More than 40 Native American hoop dancers from the United States and Canada gathering annually for one of the few hoop dance competitions in the country. Originally, the hoop dance was part of a healing ceremony meant to restore balance and harmony. In Native American tradition the hoop symbolizes the cycles of life. At this early February event, you'll see members of various tribes in their colorful buckskin costumes bearing jingling metal trinkets. Dancers use as many as 50 hoops to form shapes and suggest images, while showing off their fluid grace and precision. It's quite hypnotic! Admission is $7.00 for adults, $6.00 for seniors, $3.00 for kids 4 to 12, and free for children 3 and under. Tickets include admission to the museum.

Arizona Renaissance Festival and Artisan Marketplace
East of Apache Junction on U.S. Highway 60, Apache Junction
(520) 463-2700
www.royalfaires.com
A Phoenix tradition for more than 10 years, the Arizona Renaissance Festival is a great way to escape from modern drudgery and go back to a simpler time of lords and ladies. It's amazing how the 600 costumed performers who descend on us every year are able to turn a bare 30-acre lot near the highway into a colorful 16th-century village. Actors, jugglers, fools, and acrobats all vie for attention. Knights joust three times a day in the tournament area. Children can try pursuits such as archery, ax throwing, or pony and camel rides. Arts and crafts are for sale and there is enough food at the feasting booths to satisfy Henry VIII. Bring your gold, though; it gets a bit pricey. Admission is $16.00 for adults, $6.00 for children ages 5 to 12. Children under 5 are free. Check advertisements for retailers selling discounted tickets. Signs will point you to the festival grounds from US 60. The drive from central Phoenix is less than an hour.

Scottsdale Arabian Horse Show
WestWorld, 16601 North Pima Road, Scottsdale
(480) 515-1500
www.scottsdaleshow.com
Founded in 1955, the Scottsdale Arabian Horse Show is a huge event for Scottsdale and attracts more than 200,000 spectators. This is, in fact, one of the world's

Bookaholics, beware. If you're in town in late February, you're likely to hear the buzz about Phoenix's favorite used-book sale: the Visiting Nurses Service Association Sale, which is held at the Arizona State Fairgrounds Exhibit Building. The Saturday and Sunday event features a half-million used (and new) books plus maps, magazines, videos, CDs, and books on tape. Admission is free, but, more important, books are cheap.

largest Arabian horse shows, with 2,000 of the world's finest steeds competing for more than $200,000 in prize and scholarship money. A main arena and two secondary arenas run simultaneous classes in halter, English pleasure, trail horse, hunter, jumper, dressage, Western pleasure, and other categories. But if you're thinking this show is just for horse lovers, you're wrong. Two huge tents become display space for more than 250 exhibitors from around the world selling clothing, jewelry, fine art, food, and horse accessories. The pomp and pageantry are enough for anyone's eyes to drink in. And there's always a chance of spotting celebrities. Seen at the show in previous years have been Wayne Newton, Beach Boy Al Jardine, and actor Patrick Swayze, to name a few. Daily admission to the 10-day extravaganza is $10.00. Look for it in mid-February.

Fountain Hills Great Fair
Avenue of the Fountains, Fountain Hills
(480) 837-1654
www.fountainhillschamber.com
The town of Fountain Hills looks forward each February to welcoming thousands to this three-day outdoor fair featuring the creations of almost 500 professional artists and craftspeople. Also on the bill are food courts, live entertainment, carnival rides, games, and an early morning hot-air balloon race—all taking place on the expansive park in the center of Fountain Hills. You can't miss it—this is where you'll see one of the tallest fountains in the world, shooting 500 feet into the air at set intervals. From the intersection of Scottsdale Road and Shea Boulevard in north Scottsdale, head 12 miles east to Fountain Hills. Admission is free.

Matsuri: A Festival of Japan
Heritage and Science Park, Seventh and Washington Streets, Phoenix
(602) 262-5071
You will have many ethnic and cultural festivals to choose from during a Phoenix winter, but this is probably the loveliest. Since 1984 Matsuri organizers have

brought together the sights and sounds of Japanese classical dancing, taiko drummers, natives dressed in beautiful kimonos, and artists displaying unusual crafts. Martial arts play a big part in the festival, too, with demonstrations in judo, Shotokan karate, swordsmanship, and tae kwon do. Exhibits include bonsai demonstrations, origami folding, kite construction, fabric art, and cooking demonstrations. You can also participate in a traditional tea ceremony. Booths serving Japanese food are in abundance. Matsuri usually takes place the fourth weekend in February and admission is free.

Arizona Scottish Gathering and Highland Games
Mesa Community College, 1833 West Southern Avenue, Mesa
(602) 431-0095
www.arizonascots.com
Have a Gaelic old time at this celebration of all things Scottish. The two-day event in mid-February offers athletic events you've probably never heard of, such as the hammer throw and caber toss. On top of that are historical reenactment groups, bagpipe and drum competitions, dances, and children's activities. One-day general admission passes are $12.00 for adults, $10.00 for seniors, $5.00 for children ages 5 to 15, and children younger than 5 are admitted free.

Greek Festival
Chandler Community Center, 125 East Commonwealth Avenue, Chandler
(480) 899-3330
www.st-katherine.org
Immerse yourself in Greek folkways and food at the annual Greek Festival, held each year since 1985 in mid- to late February. You'll find live Greek music, dancing, wine, imported products, and carnival rides throughout this weekend-long festival. You can also try out a free lesson in Greek folk dancing. Specialty food items include baklava, calamari, and fresh lamb roasted on a spit. Proceeds benefit the St. Katherine Greek Orthodox Church. Admis-

sion is $2.00 for adults, with children younger than age 12 admitted free.

For the latest news about special events, the City of Phoenix has a recorded information line at (602) 534-FEST. You can also call the city's Parks and Recreation Department at (602) 262-4627.

Lost Dutchman Days
Apache Junction Rodeo/Event Center, Lost Dutchman Boulevard at Tomahawk Road, Apache Junction
(480) 982-3141
www.apachejunctioncoc.com
The legend of Jacob Waltz—the Lost Dutchman—and his futile quest for gold in the Superstition Mountains has been celebrated since 1964 in Apache Junction. Lost Dutchman Days features a parade, a senior pro rodeo, various vendors, a carnival, gold panning, and food booths. The event lasts for three days and is generally held around the end of February. Admission is free to most events, except the rodeo and carnival rides.

MARCH

Heard Museum Guild Indian Fair & Market
Heard Museum, 2301 North Central Avenue, Phoenix
(602) 251-0255
www.heard.org
If you are in town the first weekend of March, heed this advice: You must go to the Guild Indian Fair & Market. Of the many events put on by the world-renowned Heard Museum, this is the best. As always over the past 40 years, the fair nurtures respect and admiration for the visual and performing arts of various tribes. More than 600 of the nation's finest Native American artists show their work. Plus you will see various tribal dances, with performers in full regalia, and hear a vari-

ety of Native American music. Children will have fun with craft activities, and the food booths are numerous, letting you choose among Native American, Mexican, and other fare. The event runs daytime hours on a Saturday and Sunday. Tickets are $10.00 for adults, and $3.00 for children ages 4 to 12. It's free for children younger than 4. Admission to the fair includes admission to the Heard's seven galleries.

Chandler Ostrich Festival
Downtown Chandler
(480) 963-4571
www.ostrichfestival.com
This wacky, three-day family festival hearkens back to the days of ostrich farms in the Valley and was featured as a backdrop to the 1995 film version of Terry McMillan's book, *Waiting to Exhale*. From the streets of historic downtown Chandler, you'll be amused by ostrich-themed events, including jockeys riding ostriches as if they were thoroughbreds. Numerous food booths give you a chance to sample ostrich burgers—or something more familiar. There is a carnival midway and live entertainment. Three stages of entertainment feature a slate of national and local talent, playing anything from classic rock to Hispanic music. The Ostrich Festival usually takes place the second weekend in March, and admission is free. Seeing the ostrich races costs $3.00 for adults, $2.00 for seniors, $1.00 for kids 5 to 12, and those under 5 are free. There are separate admission charges for the carnival rides—$1.00 tickets or $15.00 for unlimited rides for one person. Prices can be more at the gate, so book in advance.

Scottsdale Arts Festival
Civic Center Mall, 7380 East Second Street, Scottsdale
(480) 994-ARTS
www.scottsdalearts.org
The work of more than 185 artists and artisans is featured in this juried outdoor show that is ranked among the top art festivals in the country. Adding to the ambiance are musical performances on

two stages, food and beverage booths, and an area for children. The event takes place on a Friday, Saturday, and Sunday in mid-March. Admission is free.

The National Festival of the West
WestWorld, 16601 North Pima Road, Scottsdale
(602) 996-4387
www.festivalofthewest.com
From old-time fur traders to modern-day ranching, this festival commemorates the romance, lore, and legend of the American cowboy and the settling of the American West. Over four days, the festival presents Western music and movies, cowboy poetry, and costume contests. Western heroes and peddlers dressed in period costumes stroll the festival grounds. Features include an exhibit of Western art and cowboy col-lectibles, the National Cowboy Mounted Shooting Championships, and ranch rodeo-style arena events. One of the highlights of the show is the Chuck Wagon Cook Off, in which chuck wagons from across the coun-try come to compete for prizes. Visitors can sample their old-fashioned cooking. Each year in mid-March, the festival hon-ors individuals who have helped preserve the Western lifestyle. Past honorees have included Gene Autry, Ben Johnson, and Denver Pyle. Admission is $12.00 for adults, $11.00 for seniors, and $4.00 for children.

Tempe Festival of the Arts
Downtown Tempe
(480) 967-4877
www.millavenue.org
You will marvel at the ingenuity of crafts-people as you wander through this three-day outdoor festival of juried works. Vendors show everything from jewelry and pottery to photography and blown glass. The streets of downtown Tempe, including several blocks of Mill Avenue, are blocked off to traffic for this pedestrian-friendly event. Adding to the festive atmosphere are street musicians and jug-glers, booths offering a wide range of eth-nic cuisine, and activities for kids. This

event in the last weekend of March and a similar festival the first weekend of December are organized by the Mill Avenue Merchants Association. Both are well attended, but crowds only add to the fun. Admission is free.

APRIL

Phoenix Film Festival
Various locations
(602) 955-6444
www.phxfilm.com
The Phoenix Film Festival is held every spring and brings together independent, minority, and experimental filmmakers from the local area and around the world. It runs for several days and showcases an amazing variety of work. It also hosts the largest competition of low-budget films in the world, allowing people from all walks of life to screen their work. While there are some art films here with high produc-tion values and good funding, the empha-sis is on the more cutting edge, marginalized filmmakers. This leads to a freshness of the work and allows some interesting, otherwise unheard views to make it to the screen. One nice aspect is that attendees have a chance to mingle with the directors, actors, and writers and share ideas on their favorite medium. Fea-tured filmmakers also present seminars on the art of film and give tips on making your own films. Individual screenings are as low as $10, but a festival pass is a bet-ter value. Passes run from $30 for one day to $100 for the whole festival.

Arizona Book Festival
Carnegie Center, 11th Avenue and Washington Street, Phoenix
(602) 257-0335
www.azbookfestival.org
This free book fair draws thousands of readers every year. Local authors rub shoulders with national best-sellers and conduct signings, talks, and panel discus-sions on their work. Past guests have included J. A. Jance, Ursula LeGuin, and

Sherman Alexie. There's a great dealers' room with used and new books for sale and plenty of activities for kids.

Tostitos Southwest Salsa Challenge
Scottsdale Stadium,
Osborn Road and Civic Center Boulevard, Scottsdale
(602) 955-3947
www.salsachallenge.com

Bring your taste buds to this event, where a saucy selection of some 50 salsas vie for the People's Choice Award in this annual benefit for the Hemophilia Association. The flavors span the salsa spectrum from sweet, fruit-flavored to four-alarm-fire varieties. Celebrity judges award top honors in business, restaurant, and individual categories. The event also includes live musical entertainment. The last two years it has taken place on a Saturday in early April, but the date varies. It's usually a springtime event, though. Admission is $8.00 for adults, $3.00 for kids, and free for children 3 and younger.

This chapter contains only a sampling of the biggest and most popular annual events. Check out your local chamber of commerce, church, and parks and recreation department for other special events. Most happen in the cooler months, but summer nighttime events often lure Phoenix residents out when the worst of the heat is over.

Sunday on Central
Central Avenue, downtown Phoenix
(602) 534-FEST

You might think the good people of Phoenix have gone crazy—whizzing down the middle of busy Central Avenue on bicycles, skateboards, in-line skates, and even on foot. Actually, they're celebrating Sunday on Central, during which all of Central Avenue, from Virginia Avenue to Osborn Road, is closed to traffic so that

families can play on the street. The event includes musical entertainment, street performers, food vendors, crafts displays, and a pet parade. Of course, it's okay just to walk around if you're not on wheels. The daytime event is free. This event used to be in April but in 2004 was held in March. As of press time, there was no date set for future Sundays on Central.

Scottsdale Culinary Festival
Scottsdale Civic Center Mall, 7380 East Second Street, Scottsdale
(480) 945-7193
www.scottsdaleleague-arts.org

This long-running annual event is a week-long salute to the culinary arts, held the middle of each April. Events include: Tour Culinaire, in which participants hop around town by trolley to progressively sample courses of a meal, which costs $175 per person; an authors luncheon; Cooks and Corks, offering food demonstrations and wine tastings; and the event that fills the grassy mall to overflowing—the Great Arizona Picnic, offering food booths from dozens of Valley restaurateurs and caterers. The picnic takes place the second weekend of the festival. Live music on two outdoor stages goes on throughout the day and evening of that Saturday and Sunday, so there's plenty to excite the senses. Tasting coupons at the picnic are available individually, and there's usually a beer garden in one corner of the mall. For more information on this annual fund-raising event, call the Scottsdale Center for the Arts box office at the above number or call the sponsoring organization, the Scottsdale League for the Arts, at (480) 945-7193.

Country Thunder USA
Queen Creek, near Schnepf Farms
(480) 966-9920
www.countrythunder.com

Country music fans from around the Southwest—as many as 30,000 per day—flock to this four-day festival. Country Thunder takes place in mid- to late April at a large campground site in Queen Creek, enabling those traveling in RVs to stay close to the festivities. There are activities for kids, shows of glowing hot-air balloons, and food booths to go along with the concerts. Admission at the gate in 2004 was $59 per person for one day, with camping and VIP tickets costing considerably more. Discounted tickets are available in advance of the show.

MAY

Cinco de Mayo
Mesa Southwest Museum, 53 North Macdonald Street, Mesa
(480) 644-2230
Cinco de Mayo (Fifth of May) celebrates the victory of Mexican forces over the French in 1862. Mexican restaurants around the Valley go all out with fiestas and special meals. At Mesa Southwest Museum, the fun includes ethnic cuisine along with live entertainment, lectures on Mexican history, and authentic Mexican crafts. The event starts the Friday evening closest to May 5 and runs through the next day. Admission is free.

Cinco de Mayo Festival
Patriot's Park, Central Avenue and Washington Street, Phoenix
(602) 279-4669
The weekend near the fifth of May brings a huge Mexican-themed street celebration to downtown Phoenix. The live entertainment includes mariachi bands, folklorico dancers, and headliner acts from the United States and Mexico. Performers have included Laura Flores, Los Lobos, and Freddy Fender. The celebration, which includes numerous food booths, children's activities, local bands, and various contests, usually begins about noon each day and continues into the late evening. Admission is $3.00 for adults, and free for children 12 and younger.

JULY

Fabulous Phoenix Fourth
State Capitol, 17th Avenue and Washington Street, Phoenix
(602) 534-FEST
Patriotic hearts swell with pride at the sight of fireworks above Arizona's Capitol building. This is how the city of Phoenix celebrates the Fourth of July—with a 25-minute fireworks spectacular and numerous events scattered on 120 acres. Hear the oohs and aahs of the 250,000 people around you. The event begins at 4:00 P.M. and features various stages of entertainment, food vendors, and crafts displays. In the past few years, Fabulous Phoenix Fourth has managed to book top-name country entertainment, including The Dixie Chicks, Alabama, Toby Keith, and The Mavericks. Fireworks start at 9:30 P.M. Admission is free.

Summer Spectacular Art Walk
Art district of downtown Scottsdale
(480) 990-3939
www.scottsdalegalleries.com
For more than 10 years, shortly following the Fourth of July, the dozens of galleries of downtown Scottsdale collaborate on a Thursday evening Art Walk filled with artists' receptions, refreshments, musical entertainment, and other special events. An after-dark stroll through the galleries of Marshall Way, Main Street, and other avenues offers a good way to beat the heat, especially because the galleries roll out the red carpet by presenting works from nationally known artists. The Art Walk is free.

OCTOBER

Arizona State Fair
State Fairgrounds, 19th Avenue and McDowell Road, Phoenix
(602) 252-6771
www.azstatefair.com

So much to do, so little time. Even though the Arizona State Fair runs for 18 days beginning in mid-October, it's easy to walk away feeling you haven't seen or done nearly enough. Just giving attention to the hundreds of agricultural, livestock, fine arts, crafts, and collectibles displays can take a day. But if you want just a daylong outing, then of course you need to leave time for enjoying the midway rides and games. Family favorites include the Ferris wheels and a roller coaster. But there are plenty of other rides—tame and not so tame—to choose from. You also want time to indulge in barbecue, hot dogs, meat on a stick, Navajo frybread, cotton candy, and the many other treats sold at booths throughout the fair. Don't forget to peruse the fair's various merchant booths, especially those selling Native American jewelry and imported Mexican goods. We haven't even mentioned the live entertainment nightly in Veterans Memorial Coliseum at the fairgrounds. The lineup includes national headliners in country, rock, and pop. Expect to pay around $8.50 for adults, $4.00 for seniors 55 and older and kids ages 5 to 15; it's free for kids younger than 5. Ride tickets and games cost extra. The concerts are free with admission; reserved seats for the concerts are available for an extra fee and can be purchased in advance. Check advertisements in local newspapers to see which Valley retail outlets are selling discount tickets or admission/ride package deals. Parking costs $7.00 per vehicle.

Boo! at the Zoo
Phoenix Zoo, 455 North Galvin Parkway, Phoenix
(602) 273-1341
www.phoenixzoo.org
This is one of the Phoenix Zoo's most popular annual events—not surprising since it gives children a chance to come to the zoo in their Halloween costumes. And that provides a chance to scare a lion instead of vice versa. In addition to seeing regular zoo exhibits, kids can participate in hands-on activities and hear educa-

tional talks about animals from zoo staff. Zoo admission is $12.00 for adults, $9.00 for seniors, $5.00 for children ages 3 to 12, and free for children younger than 3.

NOVEMBER

Metris Thunderbird Balloon Classic
WestWorld of Scottsdale, 16601 North Pima Road, Scottsdale
(602) 978-7797
www.t-birdballoonclassic.com
Aficionados of hot-air ballooning know that this is one of the premier events on the national circuit. Launched in 1974, the classic features races with more than 130 balloons and, despite the huge crowds, it is definitely worth seeing. The corporate balloons are a show in themselves: Flying high in past years have been a Burger King Whopper, Tony the Tiger, Planters Mr. Peanut, and Air Shamu, to name a few. Proceeds benefit scholarships at Thunderbird, the American Graduate School of International Management. The competitions usually take place early mornings on the first Saturday and Sunday of November. Related events—which include activities for kids, skydiving exhibitions, nighttime shows of glowing hot-air balloons, and crafts booths—start the Friday evening before. Daily admission per event is $10 at the gate, with an all-events pass costing $25.

Glendale Glitters Holiday Light Extravaganza
Downtown Glendale
(623) 930-2299
Glendale does indeed glitter around the holidays. All the buildings in a 10-block area are decked out in lights—more than one million of them. The light display extends into Murphy Park. In Catlin Court, an antiques shopping district, the buildings sparkle with icicle lights. On Friday and Saturday evenings, the antiques shops and restaurants stay open late. There's also music, arts and crafts, and carriage and trolley rides. On other nights, you can stroll

and enjoy the quiet beauty of one of the Valley's nicest neighborhoods. The lights are switched on with much fanfare and fireworks on the night following Thanksgiving and stay on until mid-January. The event is capped off in style with Glendale Glitter and Glow, another nighttime street festival. Bands and street performers gather for a giant block party during which dozens of hot-air balloons light up the night. All events are free.

Sun City Arts & Crafts Festival
Sundial Auditorium, 14801 North 103rd Street, Sun City
(623) 876-3000

For more than 30 years, the seniors of Sun City have organized an annual show of their multifaceted talents in arts and crafts. Through clubs at the recreation centers of Sun City, seniors produce photography, calligraphy, ceramics, knitting, metalwork, lapidary, leatherwork, needlework, quilts, stained glass, woodworking, paintings, and more. Billed as the largest senior craft show in Arizona, the show always runs on Thanksgiving weekend in November. Admission is free.

DECEMBER

Celebration of Basketry and Native Foods Festival
Heard Museum, 2301 North Central Avenue, Phoenix
(602) 251-0255
www.heard.org

Held the first weekend in December, the Celebration of Basketry and Native Foods Festival at the Heard Museum is the largest event of its kind in the United States, bringing together Native American basket makers and native food producers from all over the world. Throughout each day you'll see basket weaving exhibits, traditional dancing, and food demonstrations and tastings by famous chefs and traditional native cooks. Watch Hopi piki bread and parched corn being made over open flames and buy food products to take

home too, like Tohono O'odham tepary beans and cholla buds, hand-harvested Diné pine nuts, homemade chokecherry jam, smoked salmon jerky, and more. The festival is open from 10:00 A.M. to 4:00 P.M. Admission is free.

Tempe Festival of the Arts
Streets of downtown Tempe
(480) 967-4877

This arts-and-crafts extravaganza, founded in 1998, usually attracts a crowd as diverse as the artworks being shown. Cast your people-watching eye upon babies in strollers, senior citizens, young urban professionals, Arizona State University students, alternative hipsters, and others. Oh, the art is pretty eclectic too. This is a juried exhibition, so expect high-quality ceramics, photographs, glass art, sculpture, handmade toys, weavings, and jewelry galore. The Holiday Zone features seasonal crafts, including ornaments. Add to this carnival mood a variety of street performers, from jugglers to cellists to unicyclists. The main stages of entertainment feature locally known bands. The Mill Avenue Merchants Association–sponsored festival takes place annually on the first weekend of December. Admission is free.

APS Fiesta of Light Electric Parade
Central Avenue, downtown Phoenix
(602) 261-8604

Phoenix has dozens of holiday events put on by both public and private sponsors. This one, run by the Parks, Recreation, and Library Department, is the biggest. Up to 300,000 people crowd 3 miles of sidewalk along Central Avenue on the first Saturday of December to watch more than 100 brightly lit floats. Some of them are truly spectacular, with tens of thousands of lights in spectacular designs. There is also a variety of light-covered cars and trucks, marching bands, clubs, and school groups, all glowing brightly in the Arizona evening. Even the marchers carry strings of lights. It's quite a sight and many locals have grown up seeing it every year. This has been going on since 1987, and it just seems to keep getting bigger. Admission is free.

Las Noches de las Luminarias
Desert Botanical Garden, 1201 North Galvin Parkway, Phoenix
(480) 941-1225
www.dbg.org
For more than 20 years, volunteers at the beautiful Desert Botanical Garden have marked the holiday season with Las Noches de las Luminarias. Southwestern-style luminarias are paper bags weighted down with sand, with each bag containing a lighted candle. It's a holiday tradition to place luminarias along a path to brighten the way in the dark nights of winter. At this three-night event, usually held the first weekend in December, the garden paths glow with 7,000 luminarias, which makes for quite a sight. Musical entertainment adds to the scene. This is a popular event, so buy tickets as soon as possible. Cost is $12.50 for adults and $4.00 for children 5 to 12, with members getting a discount. Ticket are not sold at the door, and it's best to buy yours far in advance.

Good sources of information on what's happening in town are as close as the nearest news rack. Pick up a free copy of "The Rep," The Arizona Republic's *entertainment section. Or get ideas from "Get Out," the entertainment section of the* Tribune *newspapers. There's also the freebie,* New Times. *All three are published on Thursday.*

ZooLights
Phoenix Zoo, 455 North Galvin Parkway, Phoenix
(602) 273-1341
www.phoenixzoo.org
This is a delightful holiday-time outing for families and out-of-town visitors. The Phoenix Zoo strings more than 600,000 lights along the pathways and up in the trees. Look carefully, and you'll see light displays of butterflies, birds, spiders, snakes, and larger creatures. Some displays are "animated," such as frogs that jump across a lake, and some displays move in time to holiday music. Also captivating are the many costumed characters, the dancing trees, and Grandmother Oak, a talking tree. ZooLights hours are from 6:00 to 10:00 P.M. nightly from the first weekend in December to the second weekend in January (closed on Christmas Eve). Admission is $6.00 in advance and $7.00 at the gate.

Pueblo Grande Museum Auxiliary Indian Market
South Mountain Park Activity Complex, 10919 South Central Avenue, Phoenix
(602) 495-0901, (877) 706-4408
www.pgmarket.org
For almost 30 years, the Pueblo Grande Museum in Phoenix, site of an ancient Hohokam village, has organized a wide-ranging outdoor exhibition of Native American arts and crafts. The show has become so popular—representing 450 artists from more than 60 tribes—it has moved to South Mountain Park. Most artwork is reasonably priced, and you have the satisfaction of knowing they are authentic. Those in the holiday mood will surely want to look for Native American–themed Christmas ornaments. The two-day event in mid-December also features native music and dance. Admission is $7.00 for adults; children younger than 12 are admitted free.

Victorian Holiday Celebration
Heritage Square, Monroe and Seventh Streets, Phoenix
(602) 262-5071
The feeling of an old-fashioned Christmas is in store when you check out the displays and entertainment at Heritage Square for this weekend event in mid-December. The square, where some of Phoenix's earliest homes have been preserved, is a perfect setting. Enjoy arts and crafts, hands-on activities, carriage rides,

train rides, puppet shows, and musical entertainment—all evoking days long ago. Admission is free.

Peoria's Oldtown Holiday Festival
Osuna Park, Oldtown Peoria
(623) 773-7198
www.peoriaaz.com

Since 1986 Peoria has been celebrating the season with an old-fashioned Christmas celebration. Events and attractions include a Valley-wide high school choral contest, a snow area, a merchant scavenger hunt, cookie decorating, make-and-take crafts, and hay wagon rides. Santa wouldn't miss this for the world. The event runs one evening in early December, from 5:00 to 9:00 P.M. Admission is free.

Tempe Tostitos Fiesta Bowl Block Party
Downtown Tempe
(480) 350-0900
www.tostitosfiestabowl.com

This is no neighborhood block party. Named one of the top eight places to spend New Year's Eve by *USA Today,* more than 150,000 people ring in the New Year in the Southwest's version of Times Square. Sponsored by Tostitos, the event officially welcomes the Fiesta Bowl football teams and their fans to Tempe. The city blocks off downtown streets and clears the way for live entertainment from nationally known performers like Billy Idol, Sugar Ray, The B-52s, The Goo Goo Dolls, REO Speedwagon, and LeAnn Rimes. Food and beverage booths, kiddie rides, and fireworks displays round out the

event, as well as a pep rally with each visiting team's marching band and drill squad. The action begins about 4:00 P.M., with the pep rallies starting after dark. Two rounds of firework displays top the event, at 9:00 P.M. and again at midnight. Admission is $15, with additional charges to attend other Fiesta Bowl events.

Fiesta Bowl Parade
Central Avenue in downtown Phoenix
(480) 350-0900
www.tostitosfiestabowl.com

The Fiesta Bowl college football game at Sun Devil Stadium in Tempe is the center of attention this time of year in the Valley. The bowl game brings the Fiesta Bowl Parade, a lively spectacle of floats plus dancers, equestrians, pompom groups, and walking groups from schools and clubs, all colorfully presented. Also in the spotlight are national award-winning high school marching bands. Past grand marshals include baseball great Ryne Sandberg, skater Kristi Yamaguchi, football player Danny White, and basketball player Charles Barkley. The parade, which heads down Central Avenue, usually takes place two to three days before the big game. The date varies from late December to early January. The free event is a big draw for residents and tourists alike, many of whom support one team or the other in the Fiesta Bowl by wearing the appropriate team colors. Expect a crowd of about 400,000, but there's plenty of room along the parade route, which runs for several blocks.

THE ARTS

If you look at the expressive petroglyphs carved in stone by the Valley's first dwellers, you might come to the conclusion that Arizona has always inspired artists.

You'd be right. In addition to those early peoples, artists were among those who spearheaded Western expansion by painting the beauty of the region for all to see. In the 1850s Henry Cheever Pratt, Seth Eastman, and John Russell Bartlett, landscape artists, were part of a border commission to survey the area. Other visual artists who worked in Arizona included well-known black-and-white photographer Ansel Adams; surrealistic German painter Max Ernst; and Maynard Dixon, a turn-of-the-20th-century post-Impressionist who used the mountains of Arizona as backdrops for his fanciful Greek scenes. The abstract artist Jackson Pollock spent some of his teenage years on his family's dairy farm in Phoenix, and he was one of the Works Projects Administration artists who worked in Arizona during the 1930s. Depression photographer Dorothea Lange, known for her heart-wrenching images of migrant farm workers, also found plenty of material in Arizona.

The city of Phoenix began building a foundation for arts and culture early in the 20th century. The Heard Museum opened in 1929, the Phoenix Art Museum traces its beginnings to the 1930s, and the Phoenix Symphony recently celebrated its 50th anniversary. Since the mid-1980s the Valley of the Sun's arts community has matured. The Valley's economic boom has influenced the arts in much the same way a desert rain helps bring life to the desert. Nevertheless, the lure of the outdoors diverts much attention and funds away from the arts, so even top-ranked companies like Ballet Arizona have trouble maintaining financial stability.

Despite the financial challenge, the arts—visual, music, drama, dance, and literature—play an important part in the Valley's quality of life. Artists in all media draw on the combination of ethnic, regional, and classical influences that stem from our unique heritage. If you take a gander in any gallery district, you'll find Native American pottery, katsinas (kachinas), jewelry, weaving, and more. Hispanic culture is well represented by dance and music, and its varied pottery styles—from Mata Ortiz to Oaxacan—can be found in many museums and shops.

Cowboy art is an important tradition in the Valley. The Cowboy Artists of America was founded in 1965 in Sedona, and its annual auction is a premier Valley art event. Modern art has found a haven here as well, but perhaps the best combination of the two styles is the work of Ed Mell. This Arizona native draws on Western themes for his cubist renditions in oil and bronze.

Another form of art that has allowed people around the world to enjoy Arizona's natural wonders is photography. The photographers of the magazine *Arizona Highways*—with more than 75 years of publishing—have established the benchmark for this type of landscape work. Its first color cover featured a photograph taken by one of Arizona's famous politicians, Barry Goldwater, who documented Native American life.

One of the top contemporary artists in the world hangs his hat near Flagstaff. James Turrell uses light as a medium to produce optical illusions. One-part science and one-part creativity, his interactive sculptures warp viewers' perceptions of light, space, and matter. In addition to maintaining a constant flurry of exhibitions and installments around the world—such as a Skyspace proposed for the Scottsdale Center for the Arts—his passion has been funneled into his large-scale environmental project near Flagstaff. There, he has worked 28 years to bring the Roden Crater project to fruition. The celestial gallery provides a complex array of viewing spaces from which visitors can experience the cosmos. His grand plan is expected to become another Arizona landmark.

As for theater, rarely does a week go by when there isn't something hot going on in regional and local drama or national touring productions. Many musicians and theater professionals from the East and West Coasts have made the area home, and the Valley scene has blossomed to include an estimated 60 professional and community theater companies, ranging from the mainstream to experimental. There are also active theater departments on the main and west campuses of Arizona State University. In Tempe you can catch a variety of productions—small works, staged readings, video productions, and experimental works—at the Lyceum Theatre, the Prism Theatre, the Intelligent Stage, and Drama City. At ASU West, theater students stage their works in the University Center Building. The Valley has several children's theater companies and even a puppet theater. These are listed in the Kidstuff chapter.

Community-level arts are alive and well too. The Sun Cities, for instance, have modern dance groups, choruses, all manner of arts classes, and a continuing slate of events at the Sundome and the Sun Cities Museum of Art.

Community arts centers are a focal point of cultural activity in several other cities in the Valley, including Scottsdale, Tempe, and Mesa. They not only host art exhibitions and live performances, but also have a community outreach goal to bring in families for classes and other events.

Observers say a healthy national economy and better marketing have helped boost attendance and revenues for symphonies and other classical music groups. After many rough years, the Phoenix Symphony is in a period of relative financial stability. The symphonies of smaller Valley cities, notably Mesa, Tempe, Sun City, and Scottsdale, continue to draw audiences. Arizona State University has a symphony,

as well as chamber ensembles and a concert band. Around the Valley you'll find string quartets, Baroque music ensembles, and piano trios regularly playing at small venues. Arizona Opera has gone beyond traditional performances to attract a new generation of fans. For those who like rock, pop, alternative, and New Age music, Phoenix will not disappoint. It attracts most of the major tours, from the Rolling Stones to Yanni. The jazz scene also sizzles, thanks to local music promoters who bring in regional and national artists known for classic jazz, easy-listening jazz, Dixieland, and other styles. (See the Nightlife chapter for jazz and pop music venues.)

Outside the Valley, art also flourishes. To the north, Sedona is home to approximately 200 working artists, many of whom have fled urban areas to draw inspiration from the town's red-rock vistas. A $9-million performing arts center, the Sedona Cultural Park, opened in 2000. Jerome, near Sedona, and Bisbee, to the south, are both former mining towns that have also retooled themselves as art communities. Tourists find plenty to see and do in these areas, as the chapter on Day Trips illustrates in more detail.

In this chapter we give an introduction to arts in the Valley—though a comprehensive listing would be longer than this book. You'll find contact information for many of the performing art organizations, as well as the venues where they usually can be seen.

THEATER

Actors Theatre of Phoenix
P.O. Box 1924, Phoenix 85001
(602) 253-6701,
(602) 252-8497 (box office)
Formed in 1984, this professional theater company goes by the slogan "theater that's just slightly off-center, off-Broadway, just downtown." After stints at different venues, ATOP has settled into the downtown Herberger Theater Center, 222 East Monroe Street, Phoenix, as a resident

company, performing on Stage West. It aims for five productions per season, and past hits include a "slightly off-center" version of *A Christmas Carol, The Complete History of America (abridged),* and *Nixon's Nixon.* Ticket prices range from $25 to $32.

Arizona Jewish Theatre Company
444 West Camelback Road, Suite 208, Phoenix
(602) 264-0402
www.azjewishtheatre.org

As the only Jewish theater company in the state, the AJTC produces plays that reflect the Jewish experience and introduce Jewish culture to the community. The nonprofit theater came into being in 1988 and performs at The Playhouse on the Park, 1850 North Central Avenue, inside the Viad Corporate Center in Phoenix. The company does both drama and comedy, and recent productions have included *Door to Door* and *King Levine.* It prides itself on its multicultural perspective, with cast and crew from all walks of life. Curtain Call, the company's educational division, provides a variety of theater workshops for children from all backgrounds, both during summer and after school. AJTC season subscriptions or individual tickets ($29 to $32) are available. Performances are usually Thursday through Sunday evenings, with afternoon performances on Sunday.

Arizona Theatre Company
502 West Roosevelt Street, Phoenix
(602) 256-6899,
(602) 256-6995 (box office)
www.arizonatheatre.org

"The equal of anything on Broadway." That's been said about productions of Arizona Theatre Company, the state's nonprofit resident theater, whose work has won national recognition and a presidential citation. ATC annually puts on six main-stage productions in both Phoenix and Tucson. In Phoenix, the ATC performs at the Herberger Theater Center, 222 East Monroe Street in downtown Phoenix. The company formed in Tucson in 1966 as the

Arizona Civic Theatre, then in 1978 added performances in Phoenix and changed its name. David Ira Goldstein has served as artistic director since 1992. In choosing plays, ATC says its mission is to offer a broad range of theatrical styles, confront a spectrum of issues, and deepen ATC's commitment to cultural diversity. Recent productions included *Othello* and *A Streetcar Named Desire.* Expect first-class costumes, lighting, and sound and stage design from ATC. Performances usually run Tuesday through Sunday, with a few matinees. Single-ticket prices range between $27 and $45; season subscriptions are available.

Black Theatre Troupe
333 East Portland Street, Phoenix
(602) 258-8128,
(602) 258-8129 (box office)

The Black Theatre Troupe performs four to five productions a year at the Helen K. Mason Center for the Performing Arts, a modest stage in downtown Phoenix at Third and Portland Streets. Concentrating on productions that illuminate the African-American experience, this troupe's previous works include *Strivers Row* and *Sweet Thunder.* Tickets range from $22 to $30.

Childsplay
132 East Sixth Street, Tempe
(480) 350-8101
www.azeats.com/childsplay

Of all the theater companies for children that have blossomed in the Valley, this one stands out. Named by *American Theatre* magazine as one of the leading theaters in the nation for young audiences, its out-of-the-ordinary productions have been providing unforgettable experiences for children and adults alike since 1977. The award-winning troupe of adult professional actors is led by artistic director David Saar, who's not afraid to tackle serious subjects and bring them to a child's level of understanding. Comedies, musicals, and mainstream works, such as *Anne of Green Gables,* are all part of the Childsplay repertoire. Its production of *The Vel-*

veteen Rabbit has become so popular that it's been presented every holiday season since the mid-1980s.

Childsplay's mission is "to create theater so strikingly original in form, content, or both, that it instills in young people an enduring awe, love, and respect for the medium, thus preserving imagination and wonder, the hallmarks of childhood." To that end, Childsplay tours to schools statewide and brings school groups to the theaters where it performs, including the Herberger Theater, 222 East Monroe Street in Phoenix, (602) 252-8497; the Tempe Performing Arts Center, 132 East Sixth Street in Tempe, (480) 350-8119; and the Scottsdale Center for the Arts, 7380 East Second Street in Scottsdale, (480) 425-5340. Most public performances are on Friday evenings and Saturday and Sunday afternoons. Season subscriptions or individual tickets are available. Single-ticket prices range from $11 to $18.

Desert Foothills Theater
33606 North 60th Street, Cactus Shadows Fine Arts Center, Carefree
(480) 488-1981
www.desertfoothillstheatre.com
The award-winning Desert Foothills Theater, which plays at the Cactus Shadows Fine Arts Center in Cave Creek, celebrates more than 25 years of community theater. It is sponsored by the Foothills Community Foundation. It puts on four performances a year, with shows like *The Pirates of Penzance, You Can't Take it With You, Tomfoolery,* and *Guys and Dolls.* Tickets vary in price, and you can get special theater and dining packages. Call for information on specific performances.

Ethington Theatre
3300 West Camelback Road, Phoenix
(602) 589-2871 (box office)
The resident theater of Grand Canyon University has added to the cultural life of the West Valley since 1950. Its student-faculty productions are known for being innovative and energetic. One season's ambitious productions for this small venue

included *Tartuffe, The Mousetrap, Accidental Death of an Anarchist, Hansel and Gretel,* and *The Gondoliers.* Performances are usually Friday and Saturday evenings at 8:00 P.M., with Sunday matinees at 2:00 P.M. Admission is $10.00 for adults, $8.50 for seniors and children.

Phoenix Theatre
100 East McDowell Road, Phoenix
(602) 258-1974,
(602) 254-2151 (box office)
www.phoenixtheatre.net
Organized in 1920, Phoenix Theatre claims to be the state's oldest theater company. Its season runs September through May, and it presents productions that exhibit a commitment to little-known gems along with big-name works. Recent productions include *Morning's at Seven* and *Chicago.* A popular sidelight is the Cookie Company, a troupe that performs theater for children—and serves cookies too. Both troupes offer season subscriptions and individual tickets; call for prices.

Scottsdale Community Players
7020 East Second Street, Scottsdale
(480) 990-7405
www.stagebrush.bizhosting.com
One of the Valley's oldest community theaters, Scottsdale Community Players has been bringing down the house since 1952. Its stage is the Stagebrush Theater, a barn-like building in Old Town Scottsdale. It performs six regular-season shows and two shows during the summer season. Recent performances have included *A Man for All Seasons, The Miracle Worker,* and *Closer than Ever.* Individual tickets cost $18 for adults and $17 for seniors and students. The Stagebrush is also home to Greasepaint, a children's theater company.

Southwest Shakespeare Company
Mesa Amphitheater
251 North Center Street, Mesa
(480) 641-7039
www.swshakespeare.org
This is a modest company with only a few productions per season, but it can be a

good way to spend an evening with the Bard. The company performs at the Mesa Amphitheatre, 251 North Center Street in Mesa, (480) 644-2560. Recent productions have included *Julius Caesar* and *Richard III*. Each production usually runs two weekends in a row. Season tickets cost $45, individual tickets are $20 for adults, $16 for seniors and students; and group discounts are available.

Theater Works
9850 West Peoria Avenue, Peoria
(623) 815-1791,
(623) 815-7930 (box office)
www.theaterworks.org
Theater Works came into being in 1986 to fill a void in the Northwest Valley. It bills itself as Arizona's largest community theater, offering comedies, dramas, and children's programs like *Sweet Charity, Love Letters,* and *Songs for a New World*. Ticket prices are kept low ($15 to $21), in keeping with the theater's mission of making high-caliber entertainment accessible to everyone. The season consists of seven shows presented September through May, plus four summer stock shows. Workshops and classes are popular with children in the community.

DINNER THEATER

Copper State Dinner Theatre
3801 East Washington Avenue, Phoenix
(623) 937-1671,
(602) 279-3129 (box office)
This is an institution on the dinner theater scene, having been around for two decades. The Copper State Players perform comedies both Friday and Saturday evenings. The dinner menu offers American fare. The cost is $32.95 per person.

Mystery Mansion
3950 East Campbell Avenue, Phoenix
(480) 994-1520
www.mysterymansion.com
Treat yourself to food, laughs, and shivers at Mystery Mansion's production, *Murder*

at Greystone Manor. This audience-participation murder mystery is complemented by a three-course Italian dinner, served by the adjoining Pronto Ristorante. The show and meal cost $33 and are offered every Friday and Saturday at 7:30 P.M.

MUSIC

Arizona Opera
4600 North 12th Street, Phoenix
(602) 266-7464
www.azopera.com
This is not your parents' opera—even the initially dubious cannot help but be impressed by the grand themes, costumes, and scenery they'll see and hear on the Arizona Opera stage. Its innovative productions rock the traditional opera world. It uses the latest in theatrical and technical advances, such as subtitles (for those who need to brush up on Italian) and rear projectors. The organization won international acclaim under longtime Director Glynn Ross. David Speers has taken over as general director and has attracted a number of rising stars to his stage. Recent productions have included *The Mikado, Sweeney Todd,* and *La Bohème*. The opera plays October through April at Phoenix Symphony Hall, 225 East Adams Street, Phoenix, and sometimes offers a Great Singer Series at the Orpheum Theatre, 203 West Adams Street, Phoenix. If you can't catch them in Phoenix, you can also grab a show in Tucson—Arizona Opera duplicates its entire season there. Call the opera for tickets or Ticketmaster at (480) 784-4444. Season tickets are available, and individual tickets range from $25 to $115.

Phoenix Boys Choir
Helen C. Lincoln Center for the Phoenix
Boys Choir, 1131 East Missouri Avenue,
Phoenix
(602) 264-5328
www.boyschoir.org
This isn't just any boys choir, but one with an international audience, several record-

ings, awards, and alumni that have made their way as professional musicians. Its 170 members play in five choirs. They are mostly boys ages 7 to 14, but an ensemble of 30 Boys Choir graduates sing as the Men of the Phoenix Boys Choir. Successful choir alumni include pop musician Richard Page, former lead singer of '80s pop stars, Mr. Mister; Carl Gayles, international pianist; Brian Kunnari, who arranges scores for Disney Studios; and Martin Davitch, who composed the theme music for *ER*. Founded in 1948, the choir owes much to artistic director Harvey K. Smith, who was at the helm from 1960 until his retirement. Artistic director Georg Stangelberger is now at the choir's helm.

The touring members of the choir have traveled to Austria, Paris, France, London, Taipei, Beijing, and Sydney. Their repertoire includes English choral classics, sacred music, folk music, jazz, show tunes, and holiday programs. The choir's recording of Penderecki's "Credo" won an AFIM "Indie" award for "Best Recording of 1999" as well as a 2000 Grammy for "Best Choral Performance." Performances are held at Phoenix Symphony Hall, 225 East Adams Street in Phoenix; the Chandler Center for the Arts, 250 North Arizona Avenue in Chandler; the Orpheum Theatre, 203 West Adams Street in Phoenix; and Arizona State University West "La Sala", 4701 West Thunderbird Road in Phoenix; Scottsdale Center for the Arts, 7830 East Second Street, in Scottsdale; as well as several area churches. Individual tickets ($15 to $25) and season subscriptions are available.

Phoenix Chamber Music Society
(602) 252-0095
www.phoenixchambermusicsociety.org
Founded in 1961, the Phoenix Chamber Music Society had modest beginnings by bringing together a quartet of Phoenix Symphony Orchestra members for a small concert series. It has grown to host performances by chamber musicians from all over the world. The 2004–05 season includes the Ying Quartet, Chicago Chamber Musicians, the Paris Piano Trio, and more. Performances are at the Scottsdale Center for the Arts, 7380 East Second Street, and individual tickets are $25.

One way that Valley residents while away the long, hot summers is to attend outdoor concerts—after the sun's gone down, of course. Concert series that are free or charge a small admission take place at several spots, including the Desert Botanical Garden, (480) 941–1217; Kiwanis Community Park in Tempe, (480) 350–5201; Murphy Park in downtown Glendale, (623) 930–2820; el Pedregal Festival Marketplace in Carefree, (480) 488–1072; and Encanto Park in Phoenix, (602) 262–6412.

The Phoenix Symphony
455 North Third Street, Suite 390, Phoenix
(602) 495-1117 (office),
(800) 776-9080 (box office)
www.phoenixsymphony.org
The Phoenix Symphony has battled financial problems and indifference in the Valley, but it has been commended by the National Endowment for the Arts for its high level of musicianship and successfully selling itself to tough Southwest audiences. Founded in 1947, it became a full-time symphony in the 1980s and has won two recording awards from the American music industry, plus continental Europe's equivalent of the Grammy. In 1997–98 spirits were high as the Phoenix Symphony celebrated its 50th anniversary season. Hermann Michael came aboard as conductor and music director. A native of Germany, he has guest-conducted a number of U.S. orchestras over the years. His predecessors have included James Sedares in the early 1990s and Theo Alcantara through most of the 1980s. The 75 musicians of the Phoenix Symphony Orchestra play classics, chamber, and family concerts at Symphony Hall, 225 East Adams Street, and provide music for Bal-

The House of Native American Music

Canyon Records sits atop the Native American music mountain. It's not a very big mountain, mind you, but the Phoenix-based record company's position in this special genre makes Canyon a noteworthy presence in the national music scene.

Canyon Records' story is that of Ray Boley, an Anglo, and the two Native American musicians—Ed Lee Natay and R. Carlos Nakai—who changed his life.

In 1951 Boley opened Canyon Films, a company that made commercials and industrial films, after running his own recording studio in Phoenix for three years. That's when Phoenix Little Theatre, a local stage company, asked Boley to record some songs for a production.

Chances are that if you're not from a Native American reservation, you've never heard of Navajo singer Ed Lee Natay. Boley hadn't either. So when he first heard Natay sing traditional vocal chants, accompanying himself with a drum, Boley was awestruck. The theater job involved recording Natay performing four songs, but when the project was over, the music lingered in Boley's mind. He vowed to record an album of Natay's chanting. Using a single microphone, Boley captured Natay and his drum for posterity. That album, *Natay—Navajo Singer,* was the first Canyon Records release.

Boley soon found out that almost nobody was recording Native American music, and the few companies that did—such as Folkways—did so for ethnographic purposes rather than for the love of music. That is, they weren't Native American records made for Native American people, but were marketed to those

interested in learning how Native American music sounded. That's not what Canyon Records was about. For the next 20 years, Boley and his wife, Mary, made seeking out and recording Native American music their hobby, while Boley's main stock-in-trade remained the film company. They went to different tribes seeking different sounds, and Native Americans came to Canyon Records to hear their music. During that time Canyon's catalog of albums was small, but included quite a few singles.

Although these were popular records, the Native American market itself was tiny. A record that sold 20,000 copies was considered a runaway hit. However, Boley's devotion to the music grew, and in 1971 he sold off the film company to concentrate on Canyon Records. In the next year he and his wife nearly doubled the label's catalog of albums to 50 titles. They recorded songs from many nations, including the Arapaho, Chippewa, Cree, Kiowa, Papago, and Pima. They recorded war dances, round dances, lullabies, and peyote chants. Boley was not a purist, and thus he went beyond tribal and traditional music to record modern entertainment such as "chicken scratch" music, which takes the European polka and gives it a tribal twist.

The Boleys opened their own retail store, Canyon Records and Arts, on December 2, 1972. The site, at 4143 North 16th Street, perches across from the Phoenix Indian Hospital. Boley hired Numkena Associates, headed by Hopi architect Dennis Numkena, to design the building in the adobe brick and earth

R. Carlos Nakai is a premier Native American flutist. CANYON RECORDS

tone Southwestern pueblo style. The opening was a gala affair, and 800 people from Arizona tribes attended. The building was blessed by a Catholic priest and an Apache medicine man. Although Canyon Records' products predominated, the Boleys also sold other Native American recordings, books, crafts, and artwork. Boley, preferring to work on the recording end, sold the retail part of the business to Bob Nuss in 1983. Nuss kept the Canyon Records and Arts name until July 1987, when the store became known as Drumbeat Indian Arts. Still, the store serves the same social function it has for many years, complete with a bulletin board that lists local Native American event and pow-wow information.

Enter R. Carlos Nakai. Boley met Nakai in the mid-1980s, when Canyon Records was already well established. As Natay had done 35 years earlier, Nakai changed everything for Boley. Nakai, of Navajo-Ute heritage, was trained as a classical trumpeter. However, he wanted to improvise, and although the ghosts of Louis Armstrong, Miles Davis, and Dizzy Gillespie might argue with him, Nakai felt he couldn't improvise on the trumpet. Nakai adapted the wooden flute—common among tribes of the Great Plains—to his musical needs. He played traditional Plains melodies and wrote and improvised his own haunting tunes. He even paired his wooden flute with synthesizers, creating a sound that fit comfortably into the then-mushrooming New Age category.

Once again, Boley was fascinated. He took a chance on Nakai, whose ideas deviated from traditional notions of

Native American music, and the payoff was surprising. The market for Canyon Records' products immediately expanded as Anglos began buying Nakai's music, which received exposure off the reservations. Today, Nakai can rightfully be called "the superstar of Native American music," having sold more than 2.5 million albums since he started recording in 1985. Nakai has more than 20 titles in his Canyon Records catalog and perhaps a dozen more on other labels. One album, *Canyon Trilogy*, has sold more than 500,000 copies worldwide. A prolific performer and composer, Nakai's efforts include those with a band called Jackalope and team-ups with other performers and composers. He opened the door for many more Native American performers to find their place in this new crossover market.

Boley retired from Canyon Records in 1992, selling the label to Robert Doyle. By the time he retired, the label had more than 400 titles in its catalog. The Phoenix Indian Center honored Boley with a benefit dinner on April 15, 1995. His willingness to record Native music helped preserve and promote traditional culture among Native Americans and, ultimately, to the world at large.

Under Doyle's management Canyon Records continues to thrive and has expanded its offerings. In addition to Native American flute music, recent recordings have included nouveau flamenco, jazz, New Age, and even rap. You can find its recordings in the Valley under "World Beat" or "Native American" categories at Tower Records, 1110 West Southern Avenue, Mesa; Drumbeat Indian Arts, 4143 North 16th Street, Suite 1, Phoenix; or at any Borders Books & Music stores. For more information about the label's catalog sales and tour details, or for general information about Native American music, call (800) 268–1141, or visit their Web site at www.canyonrecords.com

let Arizona, the Arizona State University Choral Union, and the Phoenix Boys Choir, along with other performance groups.

In the last decade the symphony has produced three recordings, all of which spent time on *Billboard*'s classical music charts. Among its guest artists over the years are Pablo Casals, Van Cliburn, Yo-Yo Ma, Itzhak Perlman, and Wynton Marsalis. Doc Severinsen has served as principal pops conductor since 1982. The Phoenix Symphony's season runs September through May. Tickets are sold individually and by subscription and range in price from $20 to $53. Seats at special Family Concerts are available for $10 and $15, but make reservations early. Some concerts are preceded by lectures discussing the music to be performed.

Sun Cities Symphony of the West Valley (623) 972–4484 (business), (623) 975–1900 (Sundome Box Office)
This organization recently celebrated its 30th anniversary. Performances are at the Sundome, 19403 R. H. Johnson Boulevard in Sun City West. James Yestadt, longtime music director and conductor, leads classical music programs that often feature well-known soloists, such as flutist Eugenia Zuckerman or violinist Eugene Fodor. The symphony also offers an annual pops concert. Classical concerts are preceded by one-hour talks that delve deeply into the music to be featured. Tickets range in price from $20 to $45.

DANCE

Ballet Arizona
3645 East Indian School Road, Phoenix
(602) 381-0184, (602) 381-1096,
888-3BALLET (box office)
www.balletarizona.org

Ballet Arizona was founded in 1986 and is already one of Arizona's largest performing-arts companies. Its repertoire has included demanding classical ballet works, major 20th-century works, world premieres of new works, and cutting-edge choreography. Its annual performance of *The Nutcracker*—performed at Symphony Hall, 225 East Adams Street, Phoenix—draws thousands of families who might otherwise not be interested in ballet. In recent years Ballet Arizona has made strides in community and educational out-reach and in introducing cultural diversity to its performances. The Ballet Arizona School has more than 250 students. The company's major performance venues include the Orpheum Theatre, 203 West Adams Street, Phoenix; and the Herberger Theater, 222 East Monroe Street, Phoenix. Season subscribers receive discounted rates on tickets; single tickets range all the way from $7.00 to $100.00, with discounts for seniors and students.

Ballet Etudes
(480) 844-2788

The dancers of Ballet Etudes are between ages 9 and 18. They're selected annually by open auditions and are expected to meet rigid standards of study, rehearsals, and performances, with the goal of emulating a professional ballet company. The young dancers receive training from professionals and vast stage experience. Members have gone on to study or perform with the Jof-frey Ballet, Ballet West, and other presti-gious organizations. The highlight of each season is *The Nutcracker,* presented on Thanksgiving weekend at the Chandler Center for the Arts, 250 North Arizona Avenue in Chandler. Also attracting family audiences is the annual springtime produc-tion, *Dancing with Fairytale Favorites,* also

at the Chandler Center. The company occasionally performs with the Phoenix Symphony and the Mesa Symphony Orchestra. Tickets are available from the Chandler Center box office, (480) 782-2680, for $9.00 to $12.00.

Center Dance Ensemble
231 West Frier Drive, Phoenix
(602) 997-9027,
(602) 252-8497 (box office)
www.centerdance.com

The Herberger Theater Center created the Center Dance Ensemble as its resident modern dance company in 1988. The small company of nine dancers has become highly respected under the leadership of Frances Smith Cohen, artistic director and choreographer. Cohen helped found the dance program at the University of Ari-zona in the early 1970s and has been an influential local dance teacher for many years. She received the Governor's Out-standing Artist Award in 1994. One of her greatest works with the ensemble has been *Snow Queen,* based on a Hans Chris-tian Andersen fairy tale. Other works by Cohen have tackled issues such as the Holocaust and bigotry and have shown a willingness to experiment with many forms of music. The ensemble performs four times a year at the Herberger, 222 East Monroe Street in Phoenix, and tickets are available from the center's box office. Admission is generally $19.50 for adults, $16.50 for seniors, and $8.50 for students.

Southwest Arts and Entertainment
2248 East Christy Drive, Phoenix
(602) 482-6410

As a nonprofit presenting organization, Southwest Dance still brings top-quality dance ensembles from around the world, but it has recently changed its name and expanded its focus. It attracts world-class companies, from ballet to contemporary, such as Ukrainian National Dance and Bal-let Folklorico de Mexico. It also brings in world music, jazz, and other attractions to Arizona, such as the Preservation Hall Jazz Band. Venues include Phoenix Symphony

Hall, 225 East Adams Street in Phoenix; the Orpheum Theatre, 203 West Adams Street in Phoenix; the Chandler Center for the Arts, 250 North Arizona Avenue in Chandler; and the Cactus Shadows Fine Arts Center, 3606 North 60th Street, Cave Creek. Single tickets, ranging from $20 to $40, are available from the Civic Plaza box offices for Phoenix performances, and from the Chandler Center box office or Ticketmaster for Chandler performances. You also can order tickets at www.tickets.com or by calling (800) 905-3315.

VENUES

Chandler Center for the Arts
250 North Arizona Avenue, Chandler
(480) 782-2680 (box office),
(480) 782-2683 (administration)
www.chandlercenter.org

The high-tech Center for the Arts, completed in 1984, has contributed to the coming of age of downtown Chandler. Its concerts, road shows, and theatrical productions draw people into what not too long ago was a sleepy city center. The center is known for the "turntable" design of its auditorium—two seating sections in the rear rotate 180 degrees to face two more intimate stages. Walls move, too, meaning the center can run three events simultaneously. The Main Stage seats 1,000; the Little Theater, 365; and the Recital Hall, 255. For big shows all the seating is combined for the single performance. State-of-the-art acoustics, expansive dressing rooms, a dance studio, a television studio, a scene shop, and tunnel access connecting stage areas are among its amenities. Past performers include Jay Leno, Crystal Gayle, the Stars of the Bolshoi, and Le Ballet National du Senegal. More than two dozen regional arts organizations regularly use the center. In addition to the more than 1,000 activities held each year in the three theaters, the center continuously runs visual arts exhibitions and educational programs. An adjunct of the center, the Vision Gallery, is at 80 South San Marcos Place in Chandler. The nonprofit Chandler Cultural Foundation manages the center for the City of Chandler.

Grady Gammage Memorial Auditorium
Arizona State University, Gammage Parkway and Mill Avenue, Tempe
(480) 965-3434
www.asugammage.com

One of the Valley's architectural jewels, Gammage was designed by Frank Lloyd Wright and completed in 1964. A redesigned adaptation of Wright's never-built Baghdad Opera House, 50 concrete columns support the round roof, which has a pattern of interlocking circles. A few years ago the 3,000-seat auditorium underwent an extensive renovation and continues to be known for its acoustic excellence as well as its beauty. This is the place to see touring Broadway shows, and in the past Gammage has hosted *Cats*, *The Phantom of the Opera*, *Rent*, and *Riverdance*. It also books smaller theatrical performances and pop and classical music concerts. The stage accommodates a full symphony orchestra and a massive pipe organ. You can catch a guided tour of Gammage daily; call ahead at (480) 965-4050 for an appointment.

Herberger Theater Center
222 East Monroe Street, Phoenix
(602) 254-7399,
(602) 252-8497 (box office)
www.herbergertheater.org

A block north of Phoenix Symphony Hall, the Herberger has two stages designed to provide an intimate theater experience. The Center Stage seats 802 on three levels, and Stage West seats 320 in a proscenium, or horseshoe, configuration on four levels. When the orchestra pit is not being used, it can be raised or lowered to accommodate set designs. Acoustics are designed to facilitate the spoken word, making the Herberger a popular venue for theater. With five resident companies and several rentals to community groups, the Herberger bursts with about 600 performances a year. The companies are Arizona Theatre Company, Ballet Arizona, Actors Theatre of Phoenix, Center Dance Ensemble, and Childsplay. The Herberger is ADA compliant and it now has an infrared system for audio-described and listening-impaired systems. Concessions are available. An orientation for volunteers is held the first Saturday of every month.

Kerr Cultural Center
6110 North Scottsdale Road, Scottsdale
(480) 596-2660
www.asukerr.com
Tucked in amidst the glitzy resorts and shopping centers of Scottsdale Road, Kerr (pronounced *care*) Cultural Center is a 300-seat adobe studio built in 1959 by composer/violist/arts patron Louise Lincoln Kerr. The studio was designed for chamber music, and such notables as Pablo Casals and Isaac Stern have played here. Today, Kerr's programming includes jazz, folk, world music, theater, lectures, cameo theatrical events, and family concerts. It is run by Arizona State University. The entrance to Kerr is a little tricky. Follow the signs at the stoplight at Rose Lane near the Borgata Shopping Village.

Orpheum Theatre
203 West Adams Street, Phoenix
(602) 252-9678,
(602) 262-7272 (box office)
Renovate it, and they will come. The Orpheum was built in 1929 as an ornate art-deco theater to showcase vaudeville acts and movies. Later it attracted Broadway shows and all kinds of stars. In the 1970s it moved into Hispanic-theme concerts. But time was not kind to the Orpheum; it fell into disrepair and closed in the 1980s. Thanks to city bond funds and private donations, the theater reopened in early 1997, after $14.2 million in renovations. Visitors today can enjoy the architectural wonders of the Spanish Colonial Revival-style building. The winding staircases, embellished doors, gilded proscenium, murals, and starlight-painted ceiling are worth seeing. Technical amenities have been brought up to date as well. The the-ater has hosted Carol Channing in a production of *Hello Dolly,* international ballet stars, and regional theatrical productions. It has no resident company, but is used primarily by Southwest Arts and Entertainment, Theatre League, Ballet Arizona, JAM Theatricals, and Peoples Pops. The 1,400-seat Orpheum is another triumph in the revitalization of downtown Phoenix.

School of Music Building
Arizona State University, Gammage Parkway and Mill Avenue, Tempe
(480) 965-8863 (events hotline)
Frank Lloyd Wright's Taliesin Architects designed the Music Building to complement Gammage Auditorium. A Southwestern-style addition, completed in 1991, blends well with surrounding architecture. The building is home to Katzin Concert Hall, the Music Theatre, Recital Hall, and Organ Hall, which boasts a 1,800-pipe organ. The halls are used for a variety of performances, particularly concerts by students of ASU's up-and-coming music school.

Scottsdale Center for the Arts/Scottsdale Museum of Contemporary Art
7380 East Second Street, Scottsdale
(480) 994-ARTS
www.scottsdalearts.org
The vibrant offerings by the Scottsdale Center for the Arts and its new Scottsdale Museum of Contemporary Art (SMoCA) contribute to the city's reputation as a fine-art destination. A cultural hub for the region, the SCA offers a first-rate venue for nationally-known performers. It hosts more than 60 music, dance, and theater performances, as well as several screenings of independent films throughout the season. Tony Award–winning star of Broadway Betty Buckley, Downbeat Lifetime Achievement jazz pianist Marian McPartland, virtuoso violinist Joshua Bell, the illusionist dance company Pilobolus, and Ireland's ever popular Chieftains are just a few of the high-energy talents that have graced the stage of the center. Presentations by the Phoenix Chamber Music Society, the Phoenix Symphony Chamber

Orchestra, and the Scottsdale Symphony Orchestra can be heard on a regular basis.

Some concerts are held under the stars in the center's outdoor amphitheater, and on Sunday afternoons from January through mid-April, the SCA presents Sunday A'Fair from noon to 4:30 P.M. when concerts and artist booths are offered free to the public outside on beautiful Scottsdale Civic Center.

Scottsdale Civic Center, an oasis of grassy lawns, beautiful flower gardens, fountains, and sculptures, is also the setting for the Scottsdale Arts Festival.

The stunning architecture of SMoCA's Gerard L. Cafesjian Pavilion, designed by Arizona's renowned Will Bruder and opened in 1999, mirrors the top-quality art and design on exhibit within its walls. The large dichroic glass wall by New York artist James Carpenter incorporated into the exterior of the building, serves as a beacon to museumgoers. Visitors to SMoCA can experience exhibits like Almost Warm and Fuzzy: Childhood and Contemporary Art, a delightful mix of innocence and nostalgia; an exhibition of works by internationally acclaimed Flagstaff-based artist James Turrell, including an overview of the artist's monumental Roden Crater project and a new Turrell Skyspace; Donald Sultan's Pop-influenced, still-life images; and a retrospective of works by German sculptor Wolfgang Laib, among other shows. In April 1999 SMoCA was awarded the highest honor a museum can receive: accreditation by the American Association of Museums (AAM). Among more than 8,000 museums nationwide, only 750 have been accredited by the AAM Accreditation Commission.

The joy of shopping has not been overlooked at SCA and SMoCA. Each has an award-winning museum store that offers a selection of unusual and artsy objects. For the visitor's dining pleasure, Scottsdale Civic Center is ringed by a number of fine restaurants that include a gourmet coffee shop, Indian food, Spanish fare, and top-quality American cuisine.

The SCA and SMoCA are managed by the Scottsdale Cultural Council. Tickets can be purchased online through www.tickets.com or by phone by calling (480) 994-ARTS. Museum hours are 10:00 A.M. to 5:00 P.M. Tuesday, Wednesday, Friday, and Saturday; 10:00 A.M. to 8:00 P.M. Thursday; noon to 5:00 P.M. Sunday. The museum is closed on Monday. Admission is $7.00, $5.00 for students, and free for members and children 15 and younger. Admission is free on Thursday, sponsored by New Times.

Second Stage West
Arizona State University West, 4701 West Thunderbird Road, Phoenix
(602) 543-ARTS
Downstairs in the University Center Building at ASU West, this stage principally serves the Department of Interdisciplinary Arts and Performance. Though primarily a development space for works in progress by both students and well-known performers, you also can catch experimental and live performances.

Sundome Center for the Performing Arts
19403 R. H. Johnson Boulevard, Sun City West
(623) 975-1900
www.asusundome.com
The largest single-level theater in the nation, the Sundome seats 7,033. It was completed in 1980 and over the years it has hosted such acts as Bob Hope, Tom Jones, and George Burns. In recent years it has added country music and mainstream pop acts to lure younger audiences. Still, it's a source of pride for the seniors of the Sun Cities. The Sundome operates under the aegis of Arizona State University.

Symphony Hall
Phoenix Civic Plaza, 225 East Adams Street, Phoenix
(602) 262-6225,
(602) 262-7272 (box office)
The home of the Phoenix Symphony Orchestra and the Arizona Opera often

hosts touring performers and Broadway shows as well. The hall, which has the largest proscenium stage downtown, is known for its good acoustics, plush interior, and stunning chandeliers. It seats 2,600 on the main floor and balcony. Symphony Hall faces a large terrace that's frequently the setting for city-sponsored festivals and outdoor concerts.

VISUAL ARTS

In the 1980s the people of Phoenix got serious about raising the city's stature as a cultural center and approved a vast amount of bond money to help improve museums and libraries. One of the funding recipients was the Phoenix Art Museum, whose space had become severely cramped. A gleaming, $25-million remodeling of the museum was completed in 1996. Building design improvements by a well-known New York architectural firm have helped put the museum in the national art spotlight. Equally important are the exhibitions the museum has been able to mount in the past few years; these, too, have garnered national attention.

Any survey of the Valley visual arts scene has to include Scottsdale. With its dozens of galleries in the downtown arts district and elsewhere, Scottsdale is considered one of the top-five art destinations in the nation. It competes with Santa Fe for top honors in promoting Southwestern art. Many well-known painters and sculptors live and work here, and the roster includes Native American artists who excel not only in painting and sculpture, but also jewelry, weaving, woodcarving, and pottery.

Museums and galleries are one way to immerse yourself in the Valley's fine-arts scene. The area's many arts-and-crafts fairs are another. Always drawing crowds are the Heard Museum Guild Indian Fair & Market; the Scottsdale Arts Festival; the Old Town Tempe Festival of the Arts in the spring and fall; the Fountain Hills Great Fair; and the Indian Artists of America show in Scottsdale. Check our Annual Events chapter for details on these shows and others.

Art Centers

Cactus Shadows Fine Arts Center
33606 North 60th Street,
south of Carefree Highway, Cave Creek
(480) 488-1105, (480) 488-1981 (theater)
This arts center on the campus of Cactus Shadows High School serves the small but ever growing communities of Cave Creek, Carefree, and far-north Scottsdale. The Foothills Community Foundation oversees programming, which includes exhibits by the area's professional artists and by public school students; four productions per season by the award-winning Desert Foothills Theater, (480) 488-1981; and plays by the high school drama club. Many dance performances are held here, such as work by the regional troupe Ballet Etudes. Every fall, the Missoula Children's Theater stops by on its world tour to produce a show with local kids. The center also hosts several of the concerts in Musicfest, (480) 488-0806, an annual classical music series for Foothills residents. You can check them out at www.azmusicfest.org. Foothills Film Society, (480) 488-1090, offers an eclectic variety of independent films such as *Smoke Signals, Carnal Knowledge,* and *Women in Love.* The center's hours and fees vary according to performances and exhibits, so call ahead.

Mesa Arts Center
155 North Center Street, Mesa
(480) 644-2056
www.mesaarts.com
This arts center wears many hats in serving Arizona's third-largest city. It supports the visual-arts exhibitions of Mesa Contemporary Arts; the children's plays of Mesa Youtheatre; a series of outdoor concerts; more than 600 visual- and performing-arts classes for all ages; a film

series; and special events. Many events, such as the Thanksgiving gospel-music festival and Cinco de Mayo, reach out to Mesa's diverse cultural communities. Examples of the concerts the center sponsors are the Out to Lunch series at Community Center Plaza; Concerts at the Amp at Mesa Amphitheatre; and Concerts in the Park at Dobson Ranch Park, all with free admission. Mesa Contemporary Arts is perhaps best known for its annual "Vahki" exhibition, which for 20 years has featured the best of contemporary American crafts through a national, juried show. The gallery is open noon to 8:00 P.M. Tuesday through Friday and noon to 5:00 P.M. on Saturday. The art exhibits rotate for several weeks at a time, and admission is free. Design plans for Mesa's new Arts and Entertainment Center are now under way. The new facility, which opened in 2004, includes four theaters, new art galleries, and performing- and visual-arts classrooms. The new facility replaces the existing Mesa Arts Center and is located on the southeast corner of Center and Main Streets downtown.

Nelson Fine Arts Center
Arizona State University, Mill Avenue
and 10th Street, Tempe
(480) 965-2787
http://asuartmuseum.asu.edu
This is one of the newest and most impressive additions to the ASU campus—a highly modern building of textured purple-gray stucco designed by Antoine Predock, an internationally known architect who also designed Phoenix's Arizona Science Center (see the Attractions chapter). The Nelson Center has outdoor performance spaces, water features, and a 12-foot wall that serves as an outdoor projection screen. The center is home to the ASU Art Museum. The museum is spacious for a university collection and hosts both national and internationally recognized artists. There is usually a good collection of local work too. They are especially known for their collection of 19th- and 20th-century American paint-

ings, Latin American art, and contemporary crafts. Photography and installation pieces are often featured as well. Admission is free. Hours are 10:00 A.M. to 9:00 P.M. Tuesday, 10:00 A.M. to 5:00 P.M. Wednesday through Saturday, and 1:00 to 5:00 P.M. Sunday. The center is also home to the intimate Paul V. Galvin Playhouse and the University Dance Laboratory.

Art Museums

Heard Museum
2301 North Central Avenue, Phoenix
(480) 252-8848
www.heard.org
The world-famous Heard Museum is a must-see on your visit to the Valley. The museum's 10 spacious exhibit galleries offer valuable insight into Native American cultures and arts, both historical and modern. Its outdoor bricked courtyards, graced with traditional and contemporary Native American art, are a joy to see. The Heard Museum's 50,000-square-foot expansion nearly doubled its public spaces. New features include three galleries, a 400-seat auditorium, an education center, an expanded museum shop and bookstore, and an indoor/outdoor cafe. For simple enjoyment of Southwestern Native American baskets, pottery, rugs, sculpture, paintings, and artistic jewelry, plan to spend time in the Heard's many galleries and its shop. Also have a look at the Barry Goldwater collection of more than 400 Hopi katsinas (or kachinas). Contemporary paintings and other works by well-known artists are often on view in temporary exhibits. An especially good time to visit the Heard is during one of its special events, which are discussed in more detail in the Annual Events chapters. For more about the Heard, read the Attractions chapter. The Heard is now open daily, from 9:30 A.M. to 5:00 P.M. Admission is $7.00 for adults, $6.00 for seniors, and $3.00 for children ages 4 to 12. Children younger than 4, museum members, and Native Americans get in free.

Heard Museum North
Scottsdale Road and Carefree Highway, Scottsdale
(480) 252-8840
www.heard.org
Heard Museum North is an 8,500-square-foot branch of the Heard Museum. Opened in 1996 at el Pedregal Festival Marketplace near Carefree, it shows changing exhibitions of Native American art, hosts guest artists, and showcases special events. The small shop on the premises offers the highest-quality arts and crafts, purchased directly from Native American artists. Hours are 10:00 A.M. to 5:30 P.M. Monday through Saturday and noon to 5:00 P.M. Sunday. Admission is a suggested donation of $3.00. Entrance to the shop is free.

Phoenix Art Museum
1625 North Central Avenue, Phoenix
(602) 257-1222
www.phxart.org
Back in the 1930s, when Phoenix was a much smaller town, surrealist painter Philip C. Curtis and others developed the Phoenix Art Center. With the postwar population boom, the city gradually became more serious about its cultural life, and the Phoenix Art Museum opened in 1959. Now the largest art museum in the Southwest, it mounts more than 20 exhibitions a year, including most of the blockbusters that tour the country. Recently, it has exhibited a major collection of western art and artifacts from the Forbidden City in China. In 1996 the museum entered a new era with the completion of a $25-million expansion and renovation project that more than doubled its space to 160,000 square feet. The project also gave the museum some first-class improvements in lighting, wall space for massive works of art, an architecturally intriguing Great Hall, a state-of-the-art lecture hall, and better storage space.

The museum boasts more than 14,000 works in its permanent collection, including works on paper, paintings, textiles, and sculpture. Make time to visit the galleries with contemporary art; the Thorne Miniature Rooms showing historic interiors; an excellent Art of Asia Gallery; the European Galleries; and the Western American Art Gallery. You'll be delighted by the prestigious, international array of artists, with works that date from 1600 to the present.

Children will enjoy the hands-on Art Works Gallery. Inquire with the museum about the schedule for art workshops for children and adults, docent talks, lectures, and special concerts. For refreshment, there's Eddie's Art Museum Cafe. For gifts, art books, jewelry, and many other items, stop in the Museum Store. During cooler months you can relax in an attractive entryway filled with sculptures and fountains. The Phoenix Art Museum is open 10:00 A.M. to 5:00 P.M. Tuesday through Sunday, and it stays open until 9:00 P.M. on Thursday. Admission is $9.00 for adults, $7.00 for seniors and students, $3.00 for youths aged 6 to 17, and free for children younger than 6. Admission is free on Thursday.

Shemer Art Center and Museum
5005 East Camelback Road, Phoenix
(602) 262-4727
This small museum makes an interesting side trip, as much for the building itself as for the artwork within it. The first house built in Arcadia (a stately neighborhood at the base of Camelback Mountain), it houses galleries and art classrooms. The Santa Fe mission–style adobe structure was built in the 1920s and purchased in 1984 by Martha Shemer for donation to the city of Phoenix. It's been expanded and renovated over the years but maintains an "old Phoenix" character. Inside you'll find contemporary works by local artists and an intriguing 1890s miniature mansion for dolls. Bold steel sculptures and a citrus orchard enliven the center's grounds. The annual Sunday at Shemer family art festival in November is a popular event. In addition to a variety of art classes for all ages, the museum sponsors an Artists' Cafe series where local artists can keep abreast of trends and issues.

There's a lot of money in the Valley art scene, and that draws top talent from across the country and around the world. While the big institutions like the **Phoenix Art Museum** *and the* **Herberger Theater Center** *will grab your attention with excellent traveling exhibitions and shows, be sure not to miss equally good events at smaller venues. Check out the listings in the* **Phoenix New Times,** *the "Rep," "Get Out," and* **Phoenix Downtown.** *All are available for free in shops, restaurants, and streetside boxes. Another free magazine,* **Art-Talk,** *features in-depth articles as well as listings. It's harder to find, being a monthly publication instead of a weekly, but look for it in the Scottsdale arts district.*

Gallery hours are 10:00 A.M. to 5:00 P.M. Monday through Friday; 9:00 A.M. to 1:00 P.M. Saturday; and extended hours on Tuesday from 10:00 A.M. to 9:00 P.M. Admission is free.

West Valley Art Museum
17420 North Avenue of the Arts, Surprise
(623) 972-0635
www.wvam.org
The stately look of this midsize museum and its collections tells you the seniors of the Northwest Valley are pretty serious about their art. Exhibits change often; a gallery might have realistic landscapes one month and contemporary art another month. The stature of some of the shows is well worth the visit, as the museum often exhibits heavyweights like Leonard Baskin, the world famous sculptor and printmaker, and Philip C. Curtis, Arizona's surrealistic master. The museum's collection of ethnic costumes from more than 60 countries, acquired from all over the world, is worth seeing, as is the sculpture garden. The museum has an extensive permanent collection of the works of American realists George Resler and

Henry Varnum Poor. The museum offers art classes, and it hosts a weekly series of concerts and art lectures called Artful Afternoons on Tuesdays. You'll find books, cards, and gifts in the small museum store. The Classic Café offers daily lunches and Sunday brunch. Hours are 10:00 A.M. to 4:00 P.M. Tuesday through Sunday. Admission is $7.00 for adults and $2.00 for students; children 5 and under are free.

Galleries

So abundant are the art galleries in Scottsdale, Phoenix, and other parts of the Valley that we can't list them all here. Instead, we've given a small sampling of galleries to illustrate the area's diversity. You'll find spaces specializing in Native American art, modern art, Western art, objets d'art, eclectic art, and high-quality crafts. Many of the downtown Scottsdale galleries are open Thursday evenings for Art Walk. Many are closed Sundays.

Bentley Gallery
4161 North Marshall Way, Scottsdale
(480) 946-6060
The Bentley specializes in abstract and minimalistic contemporary painting and sculpture, with a roster of artists that includes Pat Steir, Helen Frankenthaler, Martin Mull, and Vernon Fisher. This is where interior designers find marvelous steel sculptures. The gallery is open only during the day and is closed Sunday.

Chiaroscuro
7160 Main Street, Scottsdale
(480) 429-0711
www.chiaroscurogallery.com
This gallery displays consistently good work from a variety of contemporary artists and is viewed by locals in the art scene as one of the best contemporary galleries, along with Vanier just up the street. The focus here is on sculpture of various materials, but there is an interesting array of paintings too. Work includes

the evocative wood sculptures of Munson Hunt and the elaborate floral paintings of Barbara Rogers.

Eleven East Ashland Gallery
11 East Ashland Avenue, Phoenix
(602) 257-8543
Far from the glitz of downtown Scotts-dale's arts district lies a small, independent art space that has been here for more than a decade. Eleven East Ashland is in an old house in central Phoenix and has a reputation for showing talented local artists who prefer not to make the Scotts-dale scene. Here you'll find unusual, thought-provoking paintings, photogra-phy, and mixed media works, as well as performance art. Gallery hours are limited to 3:00 to 9:00 P.M. on Wednesday, noon to 5:00 P.M. on Saturday, and other times by appointment.

Gilbert Ortega Museum Gallery
3925 North Scottsdale Road, Scottsdale
(480) 990-1808
You'll see the Gilbert Ortega name on sev-eral storefronts in Scottsdale. Ortega, a fourth-generation trader in Native Ameri-can arts and crafts, boasts a dozen loca-tions around the Valley. If you're in the market for authentic Native American jew-elry, baskets, rugs, and pottery, it's a good idea to get a sense of the variety by stop-ping in at one of his stores. His newest location, listed here, is one-part retail store and one-part display area for several museum-quality pieces from Ortega's pri-vate collection.

Joan Cawley Gallery
7135 East Main Street, Scottsdale
(480) 947-3548
www.jcgltd.com
Another veteran of the Scottsdale gallery scene, Joan Cawley showcases American contemporary and Southwestern art. Among the artists represented are Dick Phillips, R. C. Gorman, and Jean Ekman Adams. Their corporate offices are located at 1410 West 14th Street in Tempe, (480) 858-0929.

Lisa Sette Gallery
4142 North Marshall Way, Scottsdale
(480) 990-7342
A gallery loved by serious contemporary collectors represents national and even international artists. Even those who don't know much about art will appreciate works such as those by William Wegman, whose clever dog photos have picked up commer-cial appeal. Other artists represented include Francis Whitehead, Fred Stone-house, Marie Navarre, and Luis Gonzales.

As you peruse local galleries, you might notice they stock a large amount of con-temporary and older Russian art. This is no accident. Gallery owners have been eagerly carrying works from Russian artists for the past 10 or 15 years. Russ-ian Impressionism, Soviet Realism, and Russian contemporary art have become big sellers. Gallery owners say that the artists' attention to detail, hard-work ethic, and centuries of tradition have helped make them some of the big names in the art scene.

Lovena Ohl Gallery
7144 East Main Street, Scottsdale
(480) 946-6764
The late Lovena Ohl is considered one of the pioneers in generating interest in Native American art. Her name has been revered among Southwestern art dealers and buyers for more than two decades. This gallery continues her efforts by repre-senting such well-known artists as painter Michael Kabotie, Santa Clara potter Grace Medicine Flower, sculptor Larry Yazzie, and jeweler Harvey Begay.

Materia/The Hand and the Spirit
4222 North Marshall Way, Scottsdale
(480) 949-1262
A gallery like this helps you appreciate the artistry and variety in the realm of crafts by showcasing the best work available. You'll find high-quality contemporary

Care for an art stroll through a large college campus? With walking shoes and a map in hand, head for Arizona State University in Tempe. There you'll find the Nelson Fine Arts Center, Gammage Auditorium, the Gallery of Design, the Computing Commons Gallery (computer-generated art), Northlight Gallery (photography), and the College of Law Art Collection. Or seek out student art at the Memorial Union Gallery, the Harry Wood Art Gallery, or Step Gallery 369. For a map to all these campus galleries, stop by the ASU Visitor Center at Rural Road and Apache Boulevard.

crafts in wood, ceramics, and glass, plus wearable art in jewelry and clothing. Open 10:00 A.M. to 5:00 P.M. Tuesday through Saturday.

May Gallery
The Borgata, 6166 North Scottsdale Road, Scottsdale
(480) 998-2424
Located in the ritzy Borgata shopping village, the May Gallery features Realism, Impressionism, and Western works by leading artists. Its studio glass art is especially fine, and museum-quality Southwestern jewelry is available.

Overland Gallery
7155 East Main Street, Scottsdale
(480) 947-1934
www.overlandgallery.com
Overland is known for its collection of early-20th-century Russian paintings of everyday people, painted in the style of the Impressionists. This is the place to pick up Western and American representational art for your formal living spaces.

Rima Fine Art & Custom Framing
7077 East Main Street, Suite 1, Scottsdale
(480) 994-8899
www.rimafineart.com

This gallery specializes in contemporary Russian painters, but also has a nice collection of French Impressionists. Among the more interesting pieces are rare sculptures by Pierre-Auguste Renoir. While they may seem a bit out of place next to the dreamlike paintings of Evgeni Gordiets or the Byzantine-inspired images of Yuri Gorbachev (cousin of the former Soviet leader), the consistent quality of the artists really sets this place apart from the bronze cowboys and Indians offered by the more mundane galleries along the street.

Riva Yares Gallery
3625 North Bishop Lane, Scottsdale
(480) 947-3251
The Yares Gallery is set a bit apart from the crowd, both geographically and philosophically. Two blocks south of most of the galleries, its high-tech exterior looks freshly transplanted from New York City. That metropolitan attitude carries over to the gallery's collection, which emphasizes abstract and contemporary art.

Vanier Galleries
7106 East Main Street, Scottsdale
(480) 946-7507
www.vanierart.com
Another mainstay of Scottsdale galleries, this space represents several nationally known contemporary artists. The gallery is one of the largest in Scottsdale and has numerous exhibitions throughout the year. Pieces run the gamut of media from massive paintings to delicate metalwork. Along with Chiaroscuro, it is well known and respected among local art lovers as showing some of the best contemporary art in town.

Art Walks and Festivals

Evenings during the Valley's cooler months are a lovely time to be out walking, and evenings are a lovely time to stroll among the galleries in our art districts. Scottsdale galleries have a long-standing tradition of opening their doors to browsers on Thursday evenings. Central Phoenix art studios currently offer open houses and self-guided tours one Friday evening a month. Smaller-scale art walks have sprung up as well. You don't have to be a serious art buyer to go on an art walk. Artists and galleries appreciate the chance to introduce their works to a wider audience. Often the artists will be on hand, and many galleries serve light refreshments and feature great, live entertainment.

This section also includes information about a few of the big outdoor art exhibits held during tourist season. They, too, welcome browsers and art collectors alike.

Celebration of Fine Art
18500 North Scottsdale Road, Scottsdale
(480) 443-7695
www.celebrateart.com
The open-air exhibition area called Celebration of Fine Art hoists its big white tents every year for about 11 weeks starting in January. It offers a chance to see the on-site studios of more than 100 artists, including painters, sculptors, jewelers, photographers, weavers, and ceramists. In 1998 the show moved north to the grounds of the Chauncey Equestrian Center. It's usually open 10:00 A.M. to 6:00 P.M. daily during those 11 weeks, and admission is $7.00 for adults, $6.00 for seniors, children under 12 free.

Hidden in the Hills Studio Tour
Cave Creek
(480) 488-3381
Once a year, the artists who live and work in the hills around Cave Creek open their studios for a public tour. The tour is presented by the Sonoran Arts League and represents more than 100 artists. The event offers a chance to see interesting sculptures, paintings, glasswork, and pottery, some by nationally known artists. The event is usually held two weekends in November. Maps to the studios are available from area retailers or the Cave Creek Chamber of Commerce by calling the number listed.

The art exhibits in the terminals of Sky Harbor International Airport are a welcome diversion when waiting for a flight. In fact, Sky Harbor has one of the largest airport art programs in the United States, with at least 20 display areas and a permanent collection worth $2.1 million. Look for a variety of art media, along with historical and regional memorabilia, celebrating Arizona's heritage. For more information, call (602) 273-2006.

Magic Bird Festivals
Locations vary
(480) 488-2014
The Magic Bird Gallery in Cave Creek organizes outdoor arts and crafts festivals at several locations from October through April. The festivals usually feature dozens of booths, imported wares, food, music, and family entertainment. Locations include McDonald's Ranch, 26540 North Scottsdale Road, Scottsdale; and the Peoria Sports Complex, 16101 North 83rd Avenue, Peoria. Hours typically run from 10:00 A.M. to 5:00 P.M. Friday through Sunday. Admission and parking are free.

Phoenix First Fridays
Downtown Phoenix
(602) 256-7539
www.artlinkphoenix.com
This art walk, held the first Friday of each month from October to June, is an opportunity to see mainstream and avant-garde artists. At Janet deBerge Lange's studio, for instance, see her complex assemblages of found objects. At Studio LoDo, check out work by a dozen professional artists. The Icehouse is an old cold-storage compound now used for large-scale experimental exhibitions. The participating studios are clustered in downtown Phoenix, but you'll need a car. Also along the self-guided tour find the Phoenix Art Museum and the MARS Artspace. First Friday hours are 7:00 to

CLOSE-UP

Art in the Public Eye

You don't need to go to a museum or gallery to see great art in the Valley—just look around. Not only will this keep travel-tired kids busy, but admission is free and the work can be enjoyed even if you are just passing by.

Dozens of artworks grace public spaces in the Valley, adding style in unexpected places. Gargantuan lizards, prickly pear cacti, and Native American motifs jazz up the walls that line the Pima Freeway in a 6-mile-long work called *The Path Most Traveled* by artist Carolyn Braaksma. Windswept metal trees and sculptural saguaros, conceived by artist Joe Tyler, transform six bus stops along Shea Avenue. Whimsical sculptures of trumpet flowers and hummingbird-attracting plants brighten the view of nursing home residents near Civic Center Boulevard and Earll Drive in the Hummingbird Sanctuary Garden, the brainstorm of artist Kevin Berry.

This visual feast illustrates the commitment of Valley residents to support the arts and beautify their cities, a notion that has gained momentum since the mid-1980s when many cities started investing in public art programs. In addition to adding some much-appreciated eye candy, the artwork you'll see is often utilitarian. Artists add their embellish-

ments to the functional infrastructure of civic works, such as sound barriers, bus stops, canals, and libraries. Even the unused areas surrounding interstate interchanges have designs formed from landscaping rock, sort of like sand painting on a giant scale. Let's hope they keep it up; there's still a lot of concrete in the Valley!

The city of Scottsdale—whose residents approved a Percent for Art Ordinance in 1985—boasts perhaps the most thriving public art program in the Valley. Since then, more than 35 public art projects have been created throughout the city, and many more are in the works. Take a stroll through the Scottsdale Civic Center Mall, 7380 East Second Street, and you'll see a number of outstanding works. Nearly seven acres of gardens contains 16 works of art, including the beloved Windows on the West sculpture by artist Louise Nevelson. The mall provides a quiet retreat on weekdays; on weekends it buzzes with special events, like concerts, art fairs, and festivals.

The Scottsdale Center for the Arts also resides on the mall. In addition to its galleries, it will soon be exhibiting a piece by James Turrell. Considered to be one of the top 10 contemporary artists in the world, this Flagstaff, Arizona, resident creates optical illusions with light and

10:00 P.M. Call the sponsoring organization, Artlink, at the above number for a map of studios. Also inquire about Art Detour, an extended version of First Fridays, held each spring.

Scottsdale Art Walk
Various locations
(480) 990-3939
If it's Thursday evening and the weather is pleasant (9 times out of 10 it is), several streets in downtown Scottsdale will be

shadow. His Skyscape, a viewing room for contemplating the sky's changing light, is expected to draw national attention.

A sample of other public art works in the Valley include:

• The 540-foot-long mural overlooking Tempe Town Lake from the wall of Loop 202, was fashioned by Rebecca Ross and Jeff East from thousands of handmade tiles. The playful critters and images that represent the past, present, and future of the Salt River were made with the help of Tempe schoolchildren.

• Michael Maglich's whimsical sculptures on the columns in front of Phoenix Civic Plaza, which pay tribute to Arizona's official neckwear, the bola tie.

• Marilyn Zwak's Native American–inspired wall relief for the Thomas Road bridge of the Squaw Peak Parkway.

• John Waddell's sculpture, *Dance,* which captures attention in front of the Herberger Theater. Waddell is a well-respected Arizona artist who works in bronze.

• Trevor Southey's 9-foot male nude, *Full Life Reach,* at Central Avenue and Washington Street.

• Doug Hyde's massive bronze tribute to Arizona's Navajo Code Talkers at Central Avenue and Thomas Road.

• Memorials to Vietnam and Korean War veterans at Wesley Bolin Plaza, 19th Avenue and Jefferson Street, next to the State Capitol.

• The 180-foot-long, bright green pedestrian bridge, designed to resemble

A stroll around the gallery district in Scottsdale reveals several works of public and private art, such as this bronze statue in the window of the Vanier Galleries. ALMUNDENA ALONSO-HERRERO

a grasshopper, at Cave Creek Wash in Moon Valley Park, north of Coral Gables Drive.

For a map of a self-guided tour and a map to the City of Scottsdale's public art sites, contact the Scottsdale Cultural Council at (480) 994–ARTS.

brimming with pedestrians hopping from gallery to gallery. Head for Marshall Way, Fifth Avenue, First Avenue, Main Street, and Craftsman Court and ogle artworks in many media, some of them worth thousands of dollars. The art walk is presented by the Scottsdale Gallery Association, and the 75-plus members open their doors from 7:00 to 9:00 P.M. every Thursday. Also find free entertainment, refreshments, and artist demonstrations.

Scottsdale is the heart of the Valley arts scene. To help find your way around, check out www.scottsdalegalleries.com, which lists gallery hours and provides handy maps. You'll also find links to some of the galleries featured on the Web site.

Thunderbird Artists
15648 North Eagles Nest Drive,
Fountain Hills
(480) 837-5637
www.thunderbirdartists.com
Those interested in buying paintings or sculptures—especially in the Southwestern genre—should check out the juried fine art and fine crafts festivals organized by Thunderbird Artists. The group, which represents about 150 U.S. artists, often exhibits work in conjunction with themed festivals. The Carefree Fine Art & Wine Festival, held on various weekends from November to March, turns the streets of Carefree into one big art gallery. The Scottsdale Fine Art & Chocolate Festival, held in February, stimulates the senses with art, spectacular sculptures, and 20 chocolate booths. The free shows usually run on weekends from 10:00 A.M. to 5:00 P.M.

 The intersection of Scottsdale Road and Main Street is the heart of the Scottsdale arts district. You can spend a good couple of days exploring the galleries, shops, restaurants, and cafes without seeing everything. But there's one unusual feature about this neighborhood you'll soon notice. To the west of Scottsdale Road lie the finest galleries and better restaurants, priced accordingly. To the east of Scottsdale Road are dozens of touristy trinket shops and cheaper restaurants. It's all a matter of taste, but there does seem to be some unspoken rule about who sets up business where.

ARTS ORGANIZATIONS

Arizona Artists Guild
8912 North Fourth Street, Phoenix
(602) 944-9713
Founded in 1928, the Arizona Artists Guild provides a nurturing environment for artists. It meets the third Tuesday of each month, September through April, at 7:00 P.M. at the guild building. Meetings include talks and demonstrations by nationally known artists, which nonmembers can attend. Members with an interest in a specific medium, such as sculpting, get together regularly. Other activities include juried exhibitions, critique groups, and a fund-raiser.

Arizona Commission on the Arts
417 West Roosevelt Street, Phoenix
(602) 255-5882
www.arizonaarts.com
Among the many good works of this state-funded commission is its roster of state artists—in the visual and performing arts—who travel to schools and community centers. In addition, its grants help keep many small, multicultural art groups running. A monthly bulletin helps keep artists abreast of workshops and job opportunities.

COMPAS (Combined Metropolitan Phoenix Arts & Sciences)
3110 North Central Avenue, Phoenix
(602) 287-9300
Founded in the early 1960s, COMPAS funds more than 40 art organizations and venues, fulfilling its slogan, "Giving a Hand to Our Cultural Community." Recipients have included the Phoenix Art Museum, the Heard Museum, the Phoenix Zoo, and the Desert Botanical Garden. Recently, COMPAS has expanded its grant-giving to include several other arts- and science-related nonprofit organizations, both large and small, particularly new ones. It holds two fund-raising events annually.

Phoenix Arts Commission
200 West Washington Street, 10th Floor, Phoenix
(602) 262-4637
Since its creation in 1985 by the Phoenix City Council, the Arts Commission's mandate has been to enhance the arts in Phoenix and raise the public's awareness and involvement in preserving, expanding, and enjoying the arts. The commission also directs a public art program—outdoor sculptures, murals, and other works—and fosters arts education in the schools. Many of the city's cultural activities are funded by matching grants from the commission. About two dozen citizens serve on the commission; city staff administer programs and services.

Scottsdale Artists' School
3720 North Marshall Way, Scottsdale
(480) 990-1422, (800) 333-5707
www.scottsdaleartschool.org
For more than 20 years, the nonprofit Scottsdale Artists' School has been a small oasis of art instruction, attracting adults of all skill levels from all over the country and abroad. One reason the school is so popular is its roster of working artists who serve on the faculty. Students have a chance to learn portraiture, still-life painting, figure sculpture, and dozens of other techniques from artists well-regarded in their fields. Annual enrollment is more than 2,200, and early registration is recommended. Call the school to receive its annual schedule of classes.

Scottsdale Cultural Council
7380 East Second Street, Scottsdale
(480) 994-2787
www.sccarts.org
The Scottsdale Cultural Council is a nonprofit arts management organization contracted by the City of Scottsdale to oversee its cultural affairs, including management of the Scottsdale Center for the Arts, SMoCA (Scottsdale Museum of Contemporary Art), the Scottsdale Public Art program, and the Scottsdale Arts Festival. The council has been recognized for its contributions to the community with accolades and awards, including an Arizona Humanities Council Distinguished Organization Award.

The Valley's earliest art—petroglyphs—is being preserved. The city of Phoenix built a large retaining wall to preserve more than 160 petroglyphs at 19th Avenue and Greenway Road. In Tempe, find petroglyphs along the hike up "A" Mountain near Arizona State University. For more information on petroglyphs, visit the Deer Valley Rock Art Center in north Phoenix, or call (623) 582-8007.

West Valley Fine Arts Council
387 East Wigwam Boulevard, Litchfield Park
(623) 935-6384
www.wvfac.org
The arts scene in the far West Valley is small but poised to grow as new residents trickle in. Keeping on top of the situation is the West Valley Fine Arts Council, which was founded in 1989. It operated as the Cultural Arts Society West for 20 years before that. The council, which receives funding from COMPAS, the Arizona Commission on the Arts, and elsewhere, is entrusted with developing, enhancing, and promoting quality arts and arts education in an area that encompasses Litchfield Park, Avondale, Goodyear, Buckeye, and parts of west Phoenix, Glendale, and Peoria. The council's annual Native American Festival, a showcase of authentic crafts, music, and hands-on activities for families, generally kicks off with a performance by award-winning Native American flutist R. Carlos Nakai. Other events include a mariachi festival, the Phoenix Symphony pops concert, an annual jazz festival, and an annual youth arts festival.

OUR NATURAL WORLD

Weather forecasters don't have to work too hard in Phoenix. For more than 300 days of the average year, the forecast is sunshine. But visitors and newcomers soon find out that the natural world of Phoenix offers much more than sun.

The desert's plants, birds, animals, and insects make a powerful impression on first-timers. Black widows or scorpions may lurk in a dark recess of an unoccupied park bench. On the fringes of the city, drivers brake for brazen coyotes. Jackrabbits bound out of hiding in suburban neighborhoods. Tall saguaro cacti stand like sentinels in the popular desert landscapes around many homes. Those who opt for grass lawns will pull up a bounty of desert weeds. (People who try to tell you the desert is barren just aren't paying attention to the world around them.)

Sometimes it seems as though the developers who keep chewing up the desert at the rate of an acre an hour, as one local newspaper likes to say, don't see anything but a vast, flat, barren plain in the Valley of the Sun. Yet the selling point, especially for the fringe-area, upscale developments, is the pristine beauty of the unforgiving desert, the natural world that wins over the heart of a true desert dweller.

A ROCKY DESERT

Phoenix and the Valley of the Sun sit at the northern extreme of the Sonoran Desert, an ancient seabed that's now almost devoid of moisture. Mentioning a desert may call to mind movie panoramas of windblown sand dunes, but that's the wrong picture. Before humanity's intrusion, the Sonoran Desert was an endless tract of eroded, brown mountains punctuated by valleys of patchy desert grass, palo verde trees, saguaro cactus, and creosote bushes. The sand is brown, reddish-brown, or a gravelly gray. It doesn't accumulate in dunes or even seem like sand really, but rather a surface grit.

At a distance, the desert's precipitous mountains look like piles of precariously balanced rocks ready to come tumbling down if a crucial stone is pulled out. This is an illusion created by erosion. The topsoil has been stripped away by the eons, and today we view the bedrock, the skeleton of these mountains. The smoothness of their surfaces recalls their origins at the bottom of an ancient sea.

Other mountains, still brown, slope more gently toward the sky. More hospitable than the rock-faced giants, these mountains' sides are dotted with cacti, and the surfaces seem coarse and pebbly. Some of the mountains are relics of ancient volcanic activity, but today those forces of nature sleep soundly. Although Arizona is the next-door neighbor of seismically active California, it's relatively inactive as far as earthquakes are concerned.

THE LAY OF THE LAND

The Valley of the Sun, where Phoenix and its neighboring cities dwell, sits about 1,000 feet above sea level. Essentially, this is the Salt River Valley. The metropolitan area is bisected and bounded by rivers. The Salt River, or Rio Salado, cuts across the Valley, and its ready supply of water was Phoenix's initial reason for being. To the east of the Valley, the Salt meets the Verde River as both wend their way down from mountain ranges. To the west, the Salt flows into the Gila River, which continues westward to the Colorado River on Arizona's border with California. Like a western boundary line for the Valley of the Sun, the Agua Fria River flows from the north into the Gila.

The nearly imperceptible slope of the Salt River Valley gives the Phoenix metroplex the appearance of a plain ringed by gigantic, jagged teeth, something like an impossibly huge bear trap.

Phoenix looks northwest to the Bradshaw Mountains; its topography to the north and east gradually rises to the steep ascent known as the Mogollon Rim (pronounced "muggy-OWN"). To the south, South Mountain creates a wall within the city only recently girdled by new housing developments spreading ever southward. The Sierra Estrella and the White Tank Mountains rise to the southwest and west, respectively. The Superstitions float like heat-borne apparitions to the southeast, while the McDowell Mountains to the northeast could never be mistaken for a mirage.

Humanity has made South Mountain, which sits south of the Salt River, among the Valley's most identifiable summits. Broadcast towers blinking their red warnings to aircraft are clustered atop the mountain. On a clear night, they can be seen from the ground upwards of 50 miles away, like a homing beacon for returning travelers.

Other easily identified prominences include Camelback Mountain and Squaw Peak. As its name implies, Camelback huddles like a sleeping camel of the desert amid the northern Valley's suburban sprawl. Progressively more expensive estates climb not quite halfway up its side, ignored like fleas by the dozing giant. To the west, Squaw Peak provides a vexing sensitivity problem from a politically incorrect time. The name has been decried by many—but not all—Native American groups as derogatory. Its name may change, and the change could come quickly, or the issue could drag on for another century. Whatever the case, its

The Sonoran landscape is dotted with old abandoned mine shafts, especially in the mountains around Phoenix. While it might be tempting to explore these relics of old-time prospectors, don't. Most were dug by inexperienced Easterners who had more ambition than technical skill, so they weren't too safe to begin with. A hundred years later they are extremely prone to cave-ins.

conical shape makes it an easily recognizable spot on the Phoenix landscape.

From a distance, the Papago Buttes, which today overlook the Phoenix Zoo and the Desert Botanical Garden, look like smooth bumps separating Phoenix from Scottsdale and Tempe. Their reddish-brown surfaces make them look like close cousins to Camelback well to the north. Come closer and you'll see that those seemingly smooth surfaces are pockmarked by shallow openings.

WEATHER AND CLIMATE

You won't melt in Phoenix. You can't fry eggs on the blacktop here, even though TV weather people try it for the camera every now and again at summer's high point. If you come here in summer, you will soon learn why people are fond of saying, "It's a dry heat."

Low humidity lets the summer mercury rise high. The hottest days peak at more than 120 degrees Fahrenheit. And summer ignores the calendar here, with 100-degree days sometimes stretching from May to October. On the upside, the lack of humidity means the shade of a leafy tree offers considerable relief. Swimmers emerging from a pool on a hot summer day may suddenly feel chilled because the water evaporates so quickly off their skin, supercooling them. This effect makes it possible to use a relatively inexpensive form of air conditioner, known technically as an evaporative cooler and

Although there are a few untouched areas close to the central part of town, the sprawl that is Phoenix forces serious hikers to hop in their cars and head out of the Valley. Check out the Day Trips and Parks and Recreation chapters for good places to see the wilderness. You may be in the middle of a big city, but an hour or two on the road can get you to the middle of nowhere.

popularly as a "swamp cooler," to cool homes for most of the summer. In these systems, a fan takes in hot outside air and then blows cool air created by the rapid evaporation of water soaked up by special pads. These coolers become ineffective when the dew point hits 55 degrees or higher. (The dew point is the temperature at which water vapor in the air will condense on an object. The lower the dew point, the less moisture there is in the air.) For Arizona, a dew point of 55 means the air is holding a high percentage of moisture. In the Valley, the dew point hits that level during the late-summer rainy season. As long as the air is dry, many say that 105 degrees in Phoenix is more comfortable than 95 degrees in a humid climate.

A desert left to itself undergoes vast temperature fluctuations each day. The scorching midday heat gives way to a chill in the dead of night. The desert doesn't have an insulating coat of humid air (dry heat makes way for dry cold) or a thick blanket of vegetation to hold the day's heat close during the night.

Such is not the case for the Valley of the Sun, except on its very fringes. A "heat sink" effect is a direct result of the Valley's staggering growth. In 1940 Phoenix was a cow town of 65,000 and Scottsdale was a hamlet of 1,000. Today, the Valley is home to almost two million people. The sun beats down on pavement, sidewalks, and buildings all day. These structures store the heat, and at night they radiate it back into the air. Average summer low temperatures have been

climbing for decades, and it is not unusual to experience 100-degree temperatures well after dark. This is a major change from the days when agriculture was the dominant industry here.

Agriculture in the desert? Believe it or not, with irrigation provided by the federal Salt River Project, certain crops grow extremely well in this climate. Desert soil that had never seen the plow proved rich in nutrients. In 1915, soon after the completion of the Roosevelt Dam, which created Roosevelt Lake, Phoenix's primary water source, there were 250,000 acres of alfalfa, cotton, citrus, grain, and other crops under cultivation. The large number of irrigated fields provided significant cooling at night, although not the same degree of cooling that uncultivated desert affords because humidity moderates temperature extremes, and the irrigated fields were humid.

During the winter, temperatures creep down to below freezing in the Valley's colder locations, and people have to protect frost-sensitive citrus and other plants and flowers. These low temperatures usually occur only in the dead of night and any accumulated frost or ice melts away by midmorning. On very rare occasions, some snow may fall, but unless it falls in the area's higher elevations, it usually disappears as it hits the ground or even sooner. Valley dwellers can look out from their homes and see snow atop Four Peaks, the Superstitions, or the Bradshaws. They can smell the snow in the air, feel a little chill, and still work or play outside in shirtsleeves. Winter is also the most likely time to see fog in Phoenix, as cool air close to the ground holds the winter moisture.

Like the heat sink, the problems associated with the winter temperature inversion are directly related to the Valley's growth. During the winter a warm air mass traps the cold air close to the surface like an invisible bowl held over the Valley, creating what the television weatherman will call an "inversion layer." The surface air stagnates, and pollutants accumulate to unhealthy levels, waiting for a weather front to push them out. In an effort to fight this situation, Maricopa County declares no-burn days when wood-burning stoves and fireplaces, long popular accoutrements for Valley homes, may not be used. Also, the use of oxygenated fuels is mandated for Valley vehicles in the winter months. Ordinances banning the installation of wood-burning fireplaces in new construction have also been passed by Valley municipalities.

The Monsoon

During the late summer, humidity builds up into a rainy season, known locally as "the monsoon." The presence of the monsoon is not determined by the presence of storms but by the measure of moisture. When the average dew point hits 55 degrees for three days in a row, the monsoon season is considered to be up and running.

Like its namesake in southern Asia, the Arizona monsoon depends on a shift in the prevailing winds. During the rest of the year, these winds come from the east, but as the monsoon builds, sometime in late June or early July, the prevailing winds begin to come out of the west. Moisture flows up through Mexico from the Pacific Ocean and the Gulf of California, stirring up torrential rains, impenetrable dust, and dazzling lightning.

To desert dwellers, the process can be excruciatingly gradual. One day, a single cloud is visible in the distant sky. The next day, perhaps, it's a few. Then, a few more and so on, until huge billows of storm-bearing cumulonimbus circle the Valley like huge, white anvils.

The surrounding mountains and the Valley's superhot air seem to form a barrier that has to be hammered away by the increasing strength of the monsoon system. Each day, the thunderheads creep closer but then dissipate in rain over the mountains. The Valley almost resists the incursion of these summer storms, even as Valley dwellers wish the tease would end

and the rains begin. After all, the humidity is building, and desert living is at its most uncomfortable. Everyone anticipates the welcome release of the rain, knowing it will refresh the landscape and all that lives within. Finally, heaven's gates open.

These storms cause flash flooding through the normally dry channels of washes and arroyos. In a matter of minutes, gentle trickles become hell-bent torrents that can sweep away the unwary. This is the natural course of storms in the desert where the vegetation is sparse and the underlying hardpan resists rapid percolation of the water. The hard ground refuses to absorb the water so it runs off, accumulating in the washes. The gathered waters flow rapidly to a low point—in this case the Salt River. The Valley's building boom aggravated those natural tendencies, and new developments are required to have flood-retention basins to stave off flash flooding in neighborhoods.

Although the Valley is occasionally surprised by morning blows, the monsoon storms generally occur in the late afternoons and early evenings after the atmosphere has had the whole day to saturate itself with moisture. The National Weather Service's storm warnings usually expire no later than midnight. In the wee hours of the morning, the cycle begins again as the moisture deposited earlier starts to evaporate and form clouds.

Often, the thunderstorms are preceded by pillars of blowing dust whipped up from the desert surface to thousands of feet in the air. An approaching dust storm looks like a tidal wave of airborne dirt and can make the daytime dark. In the worst case, visibility goes down to zero. In some rare instances, the dirt stays in the air even after the rain hits, and the water showers everything with tiny blobs of mud.

There's no official measure of when the monsoon ends. The humidity suddenly stops anywhere from late August to mid-September, and weather observers recognize immediately that it's over for another year.

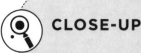

Hummingbirds in the Valley:
A Blur of Feathers

Why not invite some of the prettiest desert dwellers into your own yard? Putting up a hummingbird feeder is an excellent way to make new friends with one or two of these tiny birds.

Once you decide to start looking for hummingbirds, you'll begin to see them just about everywhere. They live throughout the Valley and seem to follow regular routes each day, moving from flower to flower, feeder to feeder, on fairly regular schedules. Be sure to look at any red flowers (they love bright reds and pinks, but they'll visit flowers of all colors). Also look at the tops of pine trees and even along telephone lines. Hummingbirds spend part of their day sitting down (if you had to flap your wings that fast, you'd sit down too).

Two species are commonly seen in the Valley. The Anna's hummingbird (look for a flashy red head and throat) and the black-chinned hummingbird (distinguished by a deep violet crown and extended bib) are regulars here. You'll see them darting between flowers only to pause and look around momentarily and then rocket out of sight. They are fiercely possessive of feeders and will defend them from other hummingbirds in dramatic shows of aerobatics.

Most of the hummingbird's day is spent flying between flowers and feeders to eat, with pauses for sitting, napping,

flirting, preening, and defending territory. They have a heart rate of 1,260 beats a minute. And to feed that metabolism, they require some 155,000 calories per day (compared to 3,500 for a 170-pound man). Scientists estimate that to match the energy requirements of a hummingbird, a human would have to consume 285 pounds of hamburgers a day.

The source for most of these calories is the sugar-packed nectar of flowers, with the occasional insect thrown in for variety and protein. To the dismay of spiders, hummingbirds are notorious for raiding the bugs from spider webs. The birds don't suck nectar from flowers. Instead they lap it up with long trough-shaped tongues at 13 licks per second.

With such a high metabolism, the birds do something odd each evening in order to survive the long night. Many hummingbirds slow their breathing and heart rates until they enter a state of hibernation. They sleep this way until warmed by the sunlight of dawn when their vital signs return to normal.

Hang your feeder where you can see it throughout the day (so you can enjoy the birds' visits). Don't use the premixed feeder solutions sold in stores (the red dye in the solution is not needed and may harm the birds). Instead, make your own by boiling one part sugar to four parts water. Let it cool and fill up your feeder.

Be sure to change the sugar water every two weeks or so, removing any black mold that may develop. A clean feeder is essential for the bird's health. Once a bird has adopted your feeder as its own, it will expect you to keep it filled. People tell stories about empty feeders and impatient birds darting up to house windows and hovering there, expectantly, reminding you that they are hungry.

Once you've hung the feeder, be patient. Keep an eye on it over the next several weeks and eventually a hummingbird will find it and adopt it as a regular watering spot. Hummingbirds have fixed routines, visiting certain flowers, flying to various yards, and it will take some time before the birds will find yours. After a few visits, they will add your sugar water to their daily routine and become regulars. The birds will soon become used to seeing you too. You can get very close to them if you hold still when they visit, as sudden movements will startle the birds. Eventually you and the hummingbirds can enjoy breakfast on the patio together. When that happens, you know that you've been accepted as a true desert dweller.

Once you've seen your first hummingbird, you might turn your attention to looking at some of the other birds that frequent the area. Here are some of the best places to see the local species.

Desert Botanical Garden
1201 North Galvin Parkway
in Papago Park
(480) 941-1225
www.dbg.org

Many desert birds, including hummingbirds, make their homes in the natural setting of this lovely garden. The garden frequently sponsors a docent-led bird walk (call for times), but you don't have to take a tour to see hummingbirds here; you just need a bit of patience.

The Phoenix Zoo
455 North Galvin Parkway
in Papago Park
(602) 273-1341
www.phoenixzoo.org

Although the Phoenix Zoo does not officially have hummingbirds on display, they frequently can be seen buzzing around the grounds. During the warmer summer months, the zoo opens at 7:00 a.m. and offers misted paths to cool visitors, Animal Encounters education shows, and even puppet shows. The birds and animals are much more active in the morning hours and are easier to view. Come later in the day and they tend to be napping, often hidden from sight.

Boyce Thompson Arboretum
U.S. Highway 60,
just 3 miles west of Superior
(520) 689-2811
http://arboretum.ag.arizona.edu

Only an hour from Phoenix, this remarkable series of gardens offers a wide range of habitats that attract birds of all kinds (including hummingbirds). Since the location is higher than the Valley, it is noticeably cooler during the summer and a terrific place to have a picnic, watch birds, and admire spectacular flowers.

Compared with the monsoon storms, most other rains in the Valley are gentle. The unabashedly corny storytellers are fond of joking, "We had a 6-inch rain last night. The raindrops were 6 inches apart."

Some years, the monsoon season is much drier than others. Even less dependable is the winter rainy season, which can fluctuate wildly in intensity. Generally, the winter rains are soft. Yet the worst flooding in the 1980s and 1990s resulted from winter storms fanned by the Pacific Ocean weather condition known as El Niño. Despite all that stormy weather, the average annual rainfall is listed as a mere 7.66 inches.

THE DESERT AS GARDEN

The winter rains make the spiny defensiveness of desert vegetation explode into colorful profusion in a too-short spring. The palo verde tree's bright green bark and leafless, bony branches explode into bright yellow blooms. As the ironwood tree blossoms purple, the yucca wears white, the ocotillo sports red, and the saguaro crowns itself with waxy white flowers high above the desert floor.

Varieties of cacti abound precisely because they are so well-adapted to the undependable rainfall of the desert. Cacti fall under the classification "succulents" because they store up water in preparation for bone-dry years. The girth of a century-old saguaro may be punctuated by a number of thin waists representing the various dry periods. The saguaro's circumference may increase by 20 percent during the monsoon season. The saguaro

is among the largest of cacti, and mature plants can grow to be 50 feet tall and weigh up to 20 tons—98 percent of which is water. Aside from the Grand Canyon, the image of the saguaro with a pair of arms upraised as if startled or facing an armed burglar is the most familiar in Arizona—and the trademark of the Sonoran Desert. Its stunning white bloom is Arizona's state flower. The giant dwells only in the desert lowlands, below 3,600 feet. Sixty miles north of Phoenix, the saguaro disappear as the ground level rises. Unfortunately, the saguaro is a suffering species, withered by the Valley of the Sun's air and noise pollution.

Another familiar sight is the barrel cactus, particularly since it's quite popular as a landscaping plant. The barrel cactus grows to about 5 feet tall. Its spines are not thin and fine like hair, yet they resemble hair in the way they cover the barrel's stubby body. This is the cactus a lost desert traveler could dig into for water.

Most people already know the prickly pear cactus. Although it is native to the Western Hemisphere's deserts, it can grow in less arid and colder climes. The prickly pear comes in 300 varieties that have been cultivated around the world. Unlike most cacti, it is not tubular. Its flat pads look like thorny, oval-shaped oven mitts. Fruit and flowers bud atop the edges of the pads.

The cholla (CHOY-uh), especially the breed known as the teddy-bear cholla (or jumping cactus), has numerous barbed spines, which make the plant look like an unkempt, hairy hermit. The spines dig into flesh and, because of their barbs, are hard to get out. The jumping cactus likes to trick the unsuspecting: People tend to misjudge the spines, walk too close, and brush against them. The teddy-bear joints detach easily upon contact. First-timers will say the cactus jumped out to get them, hence the name. (Of course, it also makes you jump.) Botanists maintain that the cholla cannot jump; the rest of us are not so sure and remain wary.

Saguaros and many other desert plants and trees on public lands are protected by law. Attempting to take them to landscape your yard or to give as gifts is illegal.

Another desert plant that's popular in landscaping is the ocotillo (oh-ca-TEA-oh), which is not a succulent. Its strategy of defense against long dry periods is to remain dormant most of the time, its thorny arms like octopus tendrils praying for water. After a rain its brown arms sprout thousands of tiny green leaves and then shed them to prevent water loss by transpiration.

The agave (ah-GAH-vay), or century plant, lives up to 75 years to bloom just once. Imagine artichoke leaves several feet long but opened up rather than clenched. At the end of its life, the agave sends up a stalk that might grow to be 30 feet high. The stalk holds the precious blooms, and once that work is done, the agave dies. Yuccas, which bear a close resemblance, also show up in desert landscaping.

The palo verde tree, a Spanish name that translates as "green pole," generally grows in desert washes. The state tree of Arizona, it bears leaves for a short time, but sheds them as the ocotillo does, to conserve water. Photosynthesis continues though. The tree's bark is green because of the presence of chlorophyll, the catalyst of photosynthesis, and the surface of the branches sustains the tree the way leaves do in other trees.

Mesquite (mess-KEET) trees are not native to the Sonoran Desert. They were imported from Texas, but they love it here. They can grow up to 30 feet tall, and their root systems will spread out as much as twice that distance to trap as much water as possible during a rain. Grazing cattle, eating the tree's beans and depositing them elsewhere in their droppings, helped the trees multiply rapidly in Arizona's rangeland.

The creosote bush dominates the Sonoran Desert, and its survival strategy seems to be birth control. The plants are widely spaced so that they don't vie with each other for water. Scientists believe this happens partly because the mature plants produce substances that inhibit seedlings.

CRITTERS GREAT AND SMALL

Without air conditioning and irrigation, only hardy creatures can survive the Sonoran Desert's extremes of climate. Before humanity got here, inhabitants developed their own means to cope with the desert's undependable rainfall and extreme heat. In a land where food is scarce for all creatures, they developed vicious defenses against becoming food themselves, whether the spiny barbs of the jumping cactus or the poisonous sting of the scorpion. The desert's bag of surprises for the unwary includes 16 species of rattlesnake and more than 20 species of scorpions, not to mention 4 species of skunk and the Gila monster, the only species of poisonous lizard in the United States. Two poisonous spiders—the Arizona brown spider (cousin to the brown recluse) and the black widow—also make their home in the desert's dark spots, where flies serve as plentiful food.

As much as the mention of these creatures might raise goosebumps, there is tremendous beauty in them. The black shell of the black widow is almost luminescent, and the red hourglass shape on its belly offers aesthetic contrast. The black-and-orange skin of the Gila monster looks like an exquisitely beaded belt.

The Arizona Public Lands Information Center is an excellent resource for anyone interested in exploring Arizona's wilderness areas. They have information on everything from panning for gold to adopting a wild horse (no, you don't get to take it home). Their storefront sells maps, trail guides, and fish and game permits. The staff is very knowledgeable and helpful. Hours are 8:30 A.M. to 4:30 P.M. Monday through Friday. Visit them at 222 North Central Avenue, Suite 101, Phoenix, or call (800) 986-1151. They're on the Web at www.publiclands.org.

Important Information on Desert Safety

The desert is a beautiful and fascinating place. Many Arizonans are avid fans of one or more outdoor sports such as hiking, rock climbing, mountain biking, and bird watching. But it is important to remember that the desert is also a harsh and unforgiving place. Every year people are injured or even killed because they do not follow some basic safety rules and simple common sense. Please remember the following tips:

- Bring plenty of water (not soda, not alcohol, water). A liter per person for every two hours is recommended. If it's especially hot, it is a good idea to bring more. Drink frequently, not just when you get thirsty. If you are thirsty, you are already a bit dehydrated. It's also a good idea to drink before you set out.
- Bring a pair of tweezers. Many desert plants have thorns, so look, but don't touch. If you get stuck by one, don't try to pull the thorns out with your fingers. Trying to pull a thorn out without tweezers may just transfer it to your finger, and that will hurt a lot more!
- Dress appropriately. Cool clothing that covers most of your skin and a broad-brimmed hat are best. Sturdy shoes or hiking boots are important, and long pants will help protect you from thorns.

- Use sunscreen with a high SPF. Arizonans have a very high rate of skin cancer. The desert is not a place to work on your tan. Sunburn can happen before you know it and can lead to dehydration and heat prostration.
- Never hike alone.
- Do not try to touch or handle any wildlife. Many will bite or sting if threatened and some are poisonous.
- Don't stick fingers or toes anywhere you haven't looked in first. Snakes and scorpions often hide in dark crevasses.
- If you are bitten, remain calm. Even rattlesnakes and scorpions are rarely fatal. Have your fellow hikers drive you immediately to the nearest ranger station or hospital. While snakebite kits may provide some help, they are no substitute for proper medical attention.
- Tell someone where you are going and when you expect to be back. Find out about your hike first. Outdoor shops and national parks can provide maps and information for a wide variety of hikes.
- Stay on trail. This will reduce your chances of getting hurt or lost. It will also help preserve the desert's fragile ecosystem.
- "Take only pictures, leave only footprints." It may be a cliché, but it's still good advice.

The relentless sun can heat the desert floor to 150 degrees, so many desert creatures are nocturnal. Foremost among these is the coyote. In Native American lore, the coyote is a wily trickster, but in the dead of night, a coyote's howls sound plaintive rather than self-assured. Perhaps the notion of being a trickster comes from the coyote's speed, which can fool those unfamiliar with it. Another factor in the coyote's trickster image is that coyotes hunt in packs in clever fashion. One will chase the prey while others rest, and then one of the rested will take up the pursuit if necessary. The prey never gets to rest, of course, and eventually tires. Coyotes also are opportunistic, so they don't often work hard to find food. They eat carrion, diseased animals, and even plants. Coyotes are generally gray and weigh in at between 15 and 45 pounds. The Valley's relentless growth has driven back the coyote to the fringes, but outlying homeowners and campers know not to let domestic cats or small dogs out where they will become easy prey for the coyote.

After all those Warner Bros. cartoons, it's only natural to mention the roadrunner here. The birds are rarely seen in the Valley since they've mostly been driven out by settlement, but it doesn't take too much travel to see them.

Like the coyote, predators such as the mountain lion, the bobcat, and the badger don't hang around the Valley much, although it's within their range. Neither do elk and mule deer. Most of the remaining wildlife in the Valley is pretty good at hiding itself. Fleet-footed jackrabbits and cottontails may jump out of suburban hiding places. Rodents and squirrels do a good job of hiding out too. People don't see owls much, but they're up there, waiting to come out at night and catch some of those rodents. Any number of small lizards will dwell in your backyard, and toads will occasionally show up. Life near a small stream will turn up frogs as well.

The Valley's diversity of birds is great, but you're most likely to see pigeons, sparrows, finches, woodpeckers, doves, ducks, and geese. Every yard seems to have a mockingbird. Set out a hummingbird feeder, and the spoon-size birds will show up hungry. (It takes a lot of fuel to power those wings.) The state bird is the cactus wren. It is the largest North American wren, but it prefers the open desert to the confines of civilization—although it frequently turns up in the Valley. It loves to nest in cholla, where its home is pro-

Don't drive off-road in the desert. It's unsafe, illegal, and can upset the desert's delicate balance of life.

tected from predators by the cholla's spines. The Gila woodpecker and the flicker, on the other hand, cut holes into a saguaro cactus and nest inside. Some hawks make their nest in the crook of the saguaro's arm, although they're not likely to do it in your backyard.

Bats also lurk here. Although feared by many, bats are prized by some for their ability to keep the insect population down. Some people even build bat houses—something like birdhouses except they have space inside for the bats to hang upside down—to attract them.

Poisonous snakes such as the diamondback rattlesnake, which can grow to more than 6 feet long, prefer to stay away from humanity. However, Valley residents have occasionally found rattlesnakes on their doorsteps in the spring. Usually, such snakes are halfway dazed as they come out of hibernation and have wandered someplace they don't really want to be in search of a place to sun themselves. If you see one, don't assume it will give you a warning before it strikes. They are very quick and don't necessarily rattle their tails before striking. Call an animal-control officer. They're prepared for this.

Although pest extermination is a big business, the Valley still harbors the poisonous black widow and Arizona brown spider. The spiders don't need much maintenance in order to thrive. Just give them a dark place buzzing with flies. The black widow female is usually about a half-inch long, a glossy black with a red hourglass on her underside. The male is seldom seen and carries red marks along the sides of its abdomen. (Maybe he's seldom seen because the female has a habit of eating him after mating.) Widows will eat other spiders along with other insects and centipedes. They are easily provoked when guarding an egg sac but otherwise don't

---

Don't panic at the bites of venomous bugs or snakes. Stay calm and call the Poison Center-Samaritan Regional Emergency Hotline, (602) 253–3334.

---

agitate too easily. Not strictly a desert dweller, the black widow is found in the warm regions of all 48 contiguous states, but its presence in the hard-bitten desert seems almost symbolic of the desert's cruel beauty. The spider's venom causes muscle spasms and on rare occasions can be fatal.

The Arizona brown spider is about four-tenths of an inch long, with a yellow-orange hue and a violin shape on its back. Like a true desert dweller, it is nocturnal, and it paralyzes small insects with its poison to trap them before feeding. Its bite is rarely fatal, but this is a creature you don't want in your house. They have been known to bite sleepers, leaving ugly round scars where the venom kills the skin.

If you want to get a human Valley dweller upset, talk about a scorpion bite. Scorpions don't bite. They sting. They have pincers that make them look something like tiny lobsters, but the sting is in the tail. Scorpions are found under rocks in the desert, so be careful if you're turn-ing over a stone. Generally, the smaller the scorpion, the more dangerous its sting. *Centruroides sculpturatus* is the deadliest in Arizona and can kill humans, although this rarely happens anymore. This tiny scorpion is distinguished by a thin tail and straw-colored body about 2 inches long.

Relative newcomers to the pantheon of Valley pests are the Africanized honeybees, commonly known as "killer bees." These bees arrived in Arizona from Mexico in the late 1980s and by the early 1990s had extended their range to include the Valley. They are uncommonly aggressive in defense of their hives and will swarm over a perceived intruder and sting relentlessly. Depending on the susceptibility of the victim, even the gentler European honeybee can kill, so the killer bees' threat is greatly exaggerated. Still, caution is advised. The basic preventive measure is to watch for bee activity and call a beekeeper if it appears that there's a hive forming on some part of your property.

Scary, but not dangerous, is a critter commonly known as a "sewer roach." These are big, brown beetles that can be about 2 to 4 inches long and look an awful lot like the common cockroach subjected to some evil nuclear experiment—except they don't glow in the dark.

PARKS AND RECREATION

With more than 300 days of sunshine a year, the Valley of the Sun provides perfect weather for playing outdoors. When it's just too hot or when the occasional rain falls, indoor recreational opportunities abound as well. A number of Phoenix municipal parks are in mountain surroundings, including South Mountain Park, the largest municipal park in the world. The mountain parks provide desert views for picnics, as well as such activities as hiking, mountain biking, and horseback riding. Even rock climbing is available within the city on the sheer walls of Camelback Mountain.

Of course, there are times when you'd rather cool off than sweat your way up a mountainside. As you might imagine, municipal pools are popular in the Valley's hot climate. Such commercial water parks as Big Surf, which has a wave pool to simulate the pounding of the sea, are another wet alternative. Nearby wilderness and lakes afford Valley residents and visitors easy access to boating and fishing as well, not exactly activities you'd expect to find in the desert, but certainly ones that provide hours of entertainment and some relief from the summer heat.

We have participatory sports leagues and tennis courts—and so many great golf courses we decided to dedicate a whole chapter to the subject (see the Golf chapter). In addition to sports and various forms of exercise, municipal parks and recreation departments and YMCAs offer a variety of relatively sedate leisure activities from dance lessons to quilting, too numerous to list here.

To give you an overview, we've divided this chapter into two sections. The first is Parks, in which we list the major parks in and around the Valley of the Sun and the variety of recreational offerings each offers. The second section is Recreation, which focuses on specific recreational activities, like horseback riding and soaring. For information on camping in the Valley, see the RV Parks and Campgrounds chapter.

PARKS

National Forest

Tonto National Forest
Mesa District Ranger Station,
26 North Macdonald Street, Mesa
(602) 225-5200
www.fs.fed.us
Tonto National Forest is adjacent to the Valley, bordering north Scottsdale and Mesa, and Valley points in between. The forest covers nearly three million acres of wilderness, and the Forest Service says it is one of the most heavily visited national forests. It covers rugged territory, rising from the desert into mountains covered with pine trees. (The elevations range from 1,300 to almost 8,000 feet.) There's no admission charge to enter the forest, although there are charges for camping and other activities.

Many Valley dwellers are attracted to the water-based activities in the forest on the Verde and Salt Rivers and at such reservoirs as Saguaro Lake. They are also fond of the cool clime of Payson in summer. (See the write-ups on Saguaro Lake and Payson in the Day Trips chapter and the write-ups under the Boating, Fishing, and Tubing headings in this chapter.) The Forest Service says the white water on the upper stretches of the Salt River is world-class.

When you encounter wildlife in Arizona's back country, appreciate the encounter, but leave the animals alone. They will return the favor.

Tonto National Forest offers 900 miles of hiking and equestrian trails. Those closer to the Valley are better suited to novices. Other trails are deep in remote areas and will challenge the most experienced hiker and rider.

It's always a good idea to check up on conditions and fire restrictions out in the wild before starting on a backcountry trip. The Mesa District Ranger Station offers a convenient place to pick up trail maps and other forest recreational information.

State Park

Lost Dutchman State Park
6109 North Apache Trail, Apache Junction
(480) 982-4485
Jacob Waltz, known as the "Dutchman," traveled through the Superstition Mountains east of the Valley in 1880s searching for gold. The name of the park is a bit of a misnomer because it makes it sound as though the Dutchman was lost. Waltz claimed he had found gold in the Superstitions, and as proof he used gold to buy supplies when he returned to civilization. Waltz always eluded anyone's attempts to follow him to the mine, and when he died, the location of the mine was "lost"—if it wasn't a figment of Waltz's imagination, which seems most likely. Ever since, people have searched for the "Lost Dutchman Mine." For the record, Waltz was German, not Dutch.

The park was established in 1977 after the U.S. Bureau of Land Management sold the Lost Dutchman Recreation Site to the state. The 320-acre park's facilities include a visitor center, picnic areas with tables and grills, a campground with 35 units, a dump station, trails, restrooms, showers, and group-use areas. Saguaros are everywhere in this desert park. At night, the lights of the Valley are visible. A hiking-equestrian trail leads into the rugged Superstition Wilderness area of the Tonto National Forest. Park rangers advise that the grade of the trail makes it tough on horses and recommend the park's lower-level trails, on which hiking, mountain biking, and horseback riding are all permitted. One of the most accessible hikes is a pretty tough 4.5-mile round-trip route that gives stunning views of Weaver's Needle, an imposing outcrop of volcanic rock. The entrance fee is $6.00 per vehicle with up to four people. To get there, take the Superstition Freeway (U.S. Highway 60) east to the Idaho Street (State Route 88) exit. When SR 88 becomes the Apache Trail, follow it about 5 miles northeast to the park entrance.

Maricopa County Parks

The Maricopa County Parks system describes itself as the largest county parks system in the country. It offers ample opportunities for fun—hiking, camping, swimming, and many other activities. Daily hours of operation vary, so call the county for information at (602) 506-2930, or go to www.maricopa.gov/parks.

Adobe Dam Regional Park
43rd Avenue and Pinnacle Peak Road,
Glendale
(623) 465-0431
This 1,526-acre county park includes a number of recreational facilities: the Victory Lane Sports Complex for softball, Waterworld water park, Arizona Kart Racing Association and Phoenix Kart Racing Association tracks, the 500 Club golf course, an airport for ultralight aircraft, 26,000 feet of model railroad operated by the Maricopa Live Steamers, and the Arizona Model Pilots Society complex. To get

there, take Interstate 17 to the Pinnacle Peak Road exit and then head west to 43rd Avenue. There is no daily fee.

Cave Creek Recreation Area
37019 North Lava Lane, Cave Creek
(623) 465-0431

This 2,922-acre county park is within the town of Cave Creek. Its entrance is on 32nd Street, 1.5 miles north of the Care-free Highway (State Route 74). Interesting rock formations and scenic views are the park's hallmarks. There are a number of old mine shafts in the park, and visitors are advised not to enter them because they are hazardous. The park includes 43 individual picnic sites available on a first-come, first-served basis. There are four large ramadas for group picnics, and these can be reserved for a fee. There are 38 individual camp sites plus a group campground that is available by reserva-tion only. There is also a horse-staging area. The park has six well-maintained trails, totaling 11 miles. All are multiuse, unless otherwise marked. The daily fee is $5.00 per vehicle. To get there from downtown Phoenix, take I-17 north to the Carefree Highway exit and head east to 32nd Street. You can also reach the park from north Phoenix by taking Cave Creek Road or from Scottsdale by taking Scotts-dale Road. When you reach the Carefree Highway from either road, proceed west to 32nd Street.

Estrella Mountain Regional Park
15099 West Casey Abbott Drive N.,
Goodyear
(623) 932-3811

The 19,840-acre Estrella Park features 65 acres of turfed area with picnic tables, grills, restrooms, playground equipment, two lighted ballfields, and a rodeo arena. An amphitheater nestles against a hill overlooking the picnic area. Ten ramadas with electricity can be reserved. Group camping is available with reservations. Water is available in picnic areas. The park has 33 miles of trails for hiking, horseback riding, and biking. A new competitive

track with two loops that total 11 miles has been added to the park. This track is intended for high-speed training for mountain bikers, equestrians, and runners. The daily fee is $5.00 per vehicle. To get there take the Estrella Parkway exit south from Interstate 10. About 5 miles south of I-10, head east on West Vineyard Avenue. The park entrance will be on your right.

Lake Pleasant Regional Park
41835 North Castle Hot Springs Road,
Morristown
(928) 501-1710

This is a 22,662-acre park surrounding Lake Pleasant, which was formed when the New Waddell Dam was built to store water brought into Maricopa County by the Central Arizona Project canal. The lake is nearly 10,000 acres and is 225 feet at its deepest point. The park has two boat ramps—a 10-lane one at the south end of the lake and a 4-lane boat ramp accessi-ble through the north entrance. Two campgrounds are open for tent or RV camping. Reservations are not accepted for the 144 sites, which have electrical and water hookups. Nearby restrooms have showers, and all sites have picnic tables and firepits. Shoreline camping is allowed in the summer and fall months. A Desert Outdoor Center is available for rent. There is no electricity or public telephone at the park. The park is open 24 hours a day, and the daily fee is $5.00 per vehicle plus $2.00 per watercraft. Lake Pleasant is located 20 miles northwest of Phoenix in Peoria; take SR 74 to the Castle Hot Springs Road exit. Drive north approxi-mately 2 miles on a paved road, where you'll find the entrance to the main camp-ing areas and the visitor center.

McDowell Mountain Regional Park
15612 East Palisades Drive, Fountain Hills
(480) 471-0173

This 21,099-acre park in the McDowell Mountains features 88 picnic tables, com-fort stations, a youth-group camp area, and family and group campgrounds. The campgrounds offer 80 sites with a dump

station, water, electricity, and shower facilities. Water is available in the picnic areas.
There is a 14-night limit on camping, and
advance registrations are required for the
group and youth-group camp areas. The
park features hiking, mountain-biking, and
horseback-riding trails. A competitive
track offers three loops of varying diffi-
culty for competitive training away from
recreational users. Mountain bikers, equestrians, and runners are invited to use this
track. The daily fee is $5.00 per vehicle. To
get there from downtown Phoenix, take
I-10 east to Loop 202 (Red Mountain
Freeway), continue heading east to Loop
101 (Pima Freeway), and head north to
McDowell Road. Take McDowell Road east
to the Beeline Highway (State Route 87).
Follow the Beeline north to the Shea
Boulevard exit that leads into Fountain
Hills. Take Shea Boulevard to Fountain
Hills Boulevard and turn north. The park
entrance will be on your left a few miles
outside Fountain Hills.

Usery Mountain Recreation Area
3939 North Usery Pass Road, Mesa
(480) 984-0032

Usery Mountain Recreation Area is a
3,648-acre park on the edge of the Tonto
National Forest and Pinal County. Just 12
miles northeast of Mesa via the Apache
Trail, you know you're really in the desert
here. The park features a 73-unit family
campground and a group campground
that requires reservations. Water, electricity, showers, and a dump station are available. The facilities also include a
reservations-only group-picnic area, comfort stations, and 60 individual picnic sites
with grills, tables, ramadas, and water. The
facilities include an archery range, a
horse-staging area, and a network of 11
trails, 7 for hiking or horseback, the other
4 for hiking only. Closing times at the picnic areas, staging area, and archery range
vary. The park is closed to all off-road
travel, and horseback riding is restricted
to existing trails. The daily fee is $5.00 per
vehicle. To get there from the Superstition
Freeway (US 60), take the Ellsworth Road

exit north. Ellsworth Road becomes Usery
Pass Road about 4 miles north of the
highway. The southern boundary is a short
distance north of McDowell Road; the
main entrance will be on the right-hand
side, about a mile farther.

White Tank Mountain Regional Park
13025 North White Tank Mountain Road,
Waddell
(623) 935-2505

This park, among the White Tank Mountains just to the west of the Valley, seems
almost a secret to Valley dwellers. It's
rarely crowded and makes a good place
to enjoy the desert. The 29,217-acre park
includes 260 picnic sites with grills, tables,
ramadas, and restrooms; a 40-site campground; and a group campground that
requires reservations. Three group picnic
areas are available. The park also has a
mountain-bike race course and 29 miles of
trails for hiking. Some trails lead to walls
that are good for rock climbing. The park
has two barrier-free trails, which lead to
ancient Native American petroglyphs.
Numerous petroglyph sites dot the park,
and educators can provide information or
guided hikes. The entry fee is $5.00 per
vehicle. To get there from downtown
Phoenix, take I-10 west to Cotton Lane.
Head north to Olive Avenue and then go 5
miles west to the park.

Municipal Parks

All the Valley's cities have parks. Some are
lush and green, others revel in a rocky
desert landscape. Some are not much
more than a large lot with playground
equipment, while others feature multiple
ball fields and artificial lakes. We note
some of the popular municipal parks in
the following listings. The parks departments of each city can provide a complete list.

The Phoenix Parks, Recreation, and
Library Department, (602) 262-6861,
administers almost 26,000 acres of desert

and mountain parkland within Phoenix's city limits. In addition to the standard picnic areas and recreational facilities, such as basketball courts and playgrounds, these desert parks offer more than 100 miles of trails for hiking, biking, and horseback-riding enthusiasts. Phoenix parks are open from 5:30 A.M. to midnight daily.

Bonsall Park
59th Avenue and Bethany Home Road, Glendale
(623) 930-2820
Known to many Insiders as "Chicken Park," for the ranch that preceded it, Bonsall Park has attracted generations of families for picnics. Activities include feeding the resident ducks or admiring the Air Force jet perched in simulated flight on a concrete stand. Amenities include picnic tables, grills, a pool recreation center, and a new in-line skating rink. Courts for volleyball, tennis, and basketball are available.

Desert Breeze Park
Ray Road and McClintock Drive, Chandler
(480) 940-1685
Desert Breeze Park is home to the Desert Breeze Railroad, described as a one-third-size replica. The train, which features both an 1880-style locomotive and a modern diesel locomotive, takes passengers through a tunnel and around the lake in the park's center. The train runs 10:00 A.M. to sunset, Wednesday through Sunday, and closes in July and August because of the heat. Amenities include a snack bar and a covered patio. A train ride costs $1.50, although infants and toddlers ride free. The carousel costs $1.25. A 10-ride pass is available for $12.00. The depot is decorated like a Western village. A snack bar and a carousel ($1.00 per person) also provide entertainment. The park has playground equipment and picnic areas that are available for rental through the City of Chandler Community Services Department at the number above. Reservations are taken 12 months in advance. Nonresidents are charged more than Chandler residents for reservations. Fishing is also allowed. See the Fishing section in this chapter for more details.

Echo Canyon Recreation Area
East McDonald Drive at Tatum Boulevard, Phoenix
(602) 261-8318
When Phoenix was small, Camelback Mountain's south side was its familiar face and the north side was as mysterious as the dark side of the moon. The north side is where the Echo Canyon Recreation Area sits. The rock here, which rises some 200 feet in places, is redder than in most Phoenix mountain parks, except for Papago Park. This area doesn't have the usual park amenities—the only water available is a water fountain at the trailhead—just hiking trails and the opportunity to go rock climbing. The views of the city are wonderful and lure experienced rock climbers and hikers. The upper portions of Cholla Trail become rugged and may be unsuitable for small children. The park is open May through September, from 6:00 A.M. to 7:30 P.M.; and October through April, from 7:00 A.M. to 5:30 P.M. See the Hiking and Biking section in this chapter.

Encanto Park
15th Avenue and Encanto Boulevard, Phoenix
(602) 261-8994
A lush, grassy enclave in the heart of Phoenix, Encanto Park is the easiest way for people caught up in the swirl of downtown business to take a breather. It's also a spot for family picnics and recreation. There's boating and fishing on the small lake, a children's amusement park, a lighted basketball area, an exercise course, golf, handball and racquetball courts, a playground, a pool, and softball fields.

Fountain Park
El Lago and Saguaro Boulevards, Fountain Hills
(480) 816-5124
A 64-acre park surrounds Fountain Lake, where Fountain Hills' namesake fountain can shoot water up to 560 feet into the air.

> *For trips into the back country, Arizona State Parks officials recommend carrying along at least five gallons of water for drinking. They also recommend not going alone and always telling a responsible person what your backcountry travel plans are and providing a map if at all possible.*

Normally, the fountain's plume, created by two 600-horsepower turbine pumps, is 330 feet. (A third pump is kept idle as a backup, and it's only on the rare occasions when the third pump is turned on that the 560-foot stream is possible.) The fountain has a utilitarian purpose. It is used to help evaporate effluent (or treated wastewater). Through most of the year it operates for 15 minutes at the top of the hour from 10:00 A.M. to 9:00 P.M. The schedule can increase during winter when there's more effluent to evaporate. The fountain's plume can be seen from the Beeline Highway shooting up over mountaintops. The park is a perfect place for picnicking on the grass, jogging, and playing on playground equipment. Fountain Park is also a popular place for weddings and other group events, but reservations are required. For details, call the number above.

Indian Bend Wash
Along Hayden Road, Scottsdale
(480) 312-2304

The greenbelt that is Indian Bend Wash can be looked at as one huge park, although it's not. An 11-mile path used by bicyclists, joggers, walkers, and skaters connects a series of golf courses and city parks in one vast stretch of green, roughly through the center of Scottsdale. Four city parks sit among the golf courses: Chaparral Park, at 5401 North Hayden Road; Indian School Park, at 4289 North Hayden Road; Eldorado Park, at 2311 North Miller Road; and Vista Del Camino Park, at 7700 East Roosevelt Road. The facilities include softball fields, tennis courts, basketball courts, volleyball courts, playgrounds, and picnic areas. For more information on facilities, call the number above. Both Chaparral and Eldorado Parks have municipal pools; see our Aquatics section for more details. Fishing is permitted at Chaparral Park; see the Fishing section.

Kiwanis Community Park
Mill Avenue and All America Way, Tempe
(480) 350-5200

The facilities at green Kiwanis Park, the biggest park in south Tempe, are extensive, including lighted softball/baseball fields, batting cages, lighted sand volleyball courts, a lighted basketball court, picnic tables, playground equipment, a lake, a wave pool, horseshoe courts, soccer fields, and a recreation center that includes 15 lighted tennis courts. For information on recreation center activities, call (480) 350-5201. Boat rentals are available for Kiwanis Lake. Tempe residents may reserve picnic ramadas, ball fields and volleyball courts up to 11 months in advance by calling (480) 350-5200. Fishing is also permitted. See the Softball, Fishing, and Tennis write-ups in this chapter for more details.

McCormick-Stillman Railroad Park
Indian Bend and Scottsdale Roads, Scottsdale
(480) 312-2312
www.therailroadpark.com

The railroad at McCormick-Stillman Railroad Park is a 5/12-scale railroad modeled after the Rio Grande Western Railway. People board at Stillman Station, a replica of a historic Arizona train depot, and the train takes them on a mile-long ride through the 30-acre park. Also at the park are displays of railroad memorabilia, along with a Pullman car used by several United States presidents, a 1906 Baldwin locomotive, and a 1914 Santa Fe baggage car. The park features a playground and carousel. For most of the year, rides on the train and carousel are offered daily, starting at 10:00 A.M. and running until 6:30 P.M. On summer weekends the hours are the same, but on summer weekdays the train runs only from 4:00 to 8:30 P.M. Tickets cost $1.00, with children younger than 3 riding free. Next to the carousel is a sandy playground with lots of climbing equipment and slides. A Southern Pacific caboose houses a snack bar.

North Mountain Recreation Area
10600 North Seventh Street, Phoenix
(602) 262-6696

Situated on and around North Mountain and covering a small section of the North Mountain Preserve, the North Mountain Recreation Area looks down over Sunnyslope and the major part of Phoenix to the south. It offers basketball and volleyball courts, a playground, a ramada and picnic area, restrooms, and hiking and riding trails.

Papago Park
Van Buren Street and Galvin Parkway, Phoenix
(602) 256-3220

Papago Park marks Phoenix's boundary with Scottsdale and Tempe. The reddish hue of its soil makes it seem more colorful than Phoenix's other desert parks. The air somehow seems crisper here too. Within the park boundaries sit the Phoenix Zoo, the Desert Botanical Gardens, a lighted softball complex, a baseball complex, an archery range, fishing, horseshoe pits, an orienteering course, ramadas and picnic areas, restrooms, an exercise course, and hiking and riding trails. The views toward the rest of Phoenix and other parts of the Valley are gorgeous.

Red Mountain Park
7745 East Brown Road, Mesa
(480) 644-5300

At Red Mountain Park you get away into a marshland against the backdrop of the Superstition Mountains. At the center of the park's artificial lake is a marsh environment where ducks and other birds hide out when they're not out on the water. The park offers picnic ramadas that can be reserved, playground equipment, a cement volleyball court, soccer fields, and basketball courts—all lighted. Reservations require a permit that must be obtained at least one business day in advance, and permits for Friday and Saturday use must be obtained by Thursday. For details, call (480) 644-5319. Across Brown Road and to the east of the main developed portion of the park is the park's lighted softball complex. Fishing is also permitted. See the Softball and Fishing write-ups in this chapter for more details.

Sahuaro Ranch Park
59th Avenue and Mountain View Road, Glendale
(623) 930-2820

Walk around Sahuaro Ranch Park for just a minute, and you're bound to run into a peacock or peahen. More than 50 of them roam freely around the grounds. About a century ago, Sahuaro Ranch began to bloom as a citrus orchard out in then-remote desert. Today, it is part of Glendale's mainstream. The park's major draw is the 60-acre recreation area that includes three daytime soccer fields and one lighted one, four lighted softball fields, four lighted sand volleyball courts, picnic areas with grills, nine lighted ramadas, a playground, and restrooms. The remainder of Sahuaro Ranch Park is a historical area that gives visitors a view of the orchard operation. It's buffered from the rest of the park by original citrus groves. A variety of buildings have been preserved or restored, such as the Adobe House and Guest House, which let visitors see the rustic furnishings of pioneer life. In addition, the ranch's fruit packing shed was converted into an art gallery in 1995. The 80-acre park is open April through October from 6:00 A.M. to midnight daily and from November through March from 6:00 A.M. to 10:00 P.M. daily.

South Mountain Park
10919 South Central Avenue, Phoenix
(602) 495-0222

At 16,000 acres, South Mountain Park is billed as the largest municipal park in the world. More important than that to Valley dwellers and visitors, it offers an easy way to get an overview of the Valley. You can

Parks and Recreation Departments

Your municipal parks and recreation departments are the best sources for information on park facilities, sports leagues, fitness programs, and much more. Here is a list of those in the Valley and their phone numbers and Web pages.

Chandler
(480) 782-2727
www.chandleraz.org

Fountain Hills
(480) 816-5152
http://fh.az.gov/parksrec

Gilbert
(480) 503-6201
www.ci.gilbert.az.us/parks

Glendale
(623) 930-2820
www.ci.glendale.az.us/recreation

Maricopa County
(602) 506-2930
www.maricopa.gov/parks

Mesa
(480) 644-2351
www.ci.mesa.az.us/parksrec

Peoria
(623) 773-7137
www.ci.peoria.az.us

Phoenix
(602) 262-6861
www.phoenix.gov/parks

Scottsdale
(480) 312-2722
www.scottsdaleaz.gov/parks

Tempe
(480) 350-5200
www.tempe.gov

see virtually everywhere in the Valley from Dobbins Lookout, and a "compass" points you in the direction of such landmarks as Four Peaks, a mountaintop in Tonto National Forest to the northeast, and the Sierra Estrella, a mountain range to the southwest. This is also the best place in the Valley to see saguaro and other desert flora in their natural habitat. A park road hairpins up and down the mountain to serve both autos and daredevil bicyclists. In addition, the park offers an interpretive center to learn about all the desert flora and fauna; an activity complex; ramadas and picnic areas; restrooms; and a network of hiking and riding trails. See the Horseback Riding and the Hiking and Biking sections in this chapter.

Squaw Peak Recreation Area
2701 East Squaw Peak Drive, Phoenix
(602) 262-7901
On the south end of Phoenix Mountains Preserve, a vast preserve of desert mountain land that sits just about midcity as Phoenix's current boundaries are figured, Squaw Peak Recreation Area is one of the area's most popular desert parks. Although it has ramadas and picnic areas situated in a cul-de-sac below Squaw Peak, the main draw here is the hiking trails, particularly the Summit Trail, which attracts joggers, hikers, and casual walkers in droves each morning. The trail is strenuous and rough in places, so be careful and bring water. See the Hiking and Biking section in this chapter.

Staggs Park
**Litchfield Road and Villa Nueva Drive S.,
Litchfield Park
(623) 935-9040**

The Southwest Valley is still mostly rural and agricultural. Tiny (less than 3 square miles) Litchfield Park, the home of the Wigwam Resort, has been a shady, suburban residential oasis amid the vast tracts of farm and ranch land in the area. (New housing developments in neighboring Avondale and Goodyear are quickly changing things.) Staggs Park is, like the town, a sleepy little place. The park is shaped like a cane, with the upper part of the cane surrounding the west end of the lake and the length of the cane running along the north side of the lake. Residential properties line the south end of the lake. Across Litchfield Road sits a field with a baseball backstop and playground equipment. Fishing in the lake requires both a state license and a permit from the city. (No net fishing is allowed.) Boating also requires a permit.

Thunderbird Park
**59th Avenue and Pinnacle Peak Road,
Glendale
(623) 930-2820**

Thunderbird Park boasts 1,185 acres of conservation park that offer great views of the northwest Valley. Part of Hedgpeth Hills, the natural desert park includes hiking, biking, and equestrian paths; covered picnic areas with grills; wildlife-viewing areas; and a pond.

RECREATION

Ballooning

Adventures Out West
**Scottsdale
(602) 996-6100
www.adventuresoutwest.com**

Adventures Out West has been flying people over the desert since 1973. The company offers what it calls the Five Star Vacation flight, which includes a 60- to 90-minute flight, brunch, and a videotape of the flight. Flights cost from $150 per person. Group rates are also available. The company also offers a basic flight, which includes a one-hour flight and a small brunch. Flights take off from the Northeast Valley over State Trust lands every morning at sunrise and in the late afternoons from November through March. The company also offers flights that take off from the Southeast Valley and fly over housing and farmland south of the Valley. Call for reservations one to three weeks before flying.

Looking to join a team? Visit the city's Team Sports Office at 1802 East Encanto Boulevard, Phoenix, or call (602) 262-6485. Disabled kids and adults can get involved in sports through Adaptive Recreation Services. They are located at 1946 West Morningside Drive, Phoenix. Call (602) 262-4543 or (602) 534-2491 (TTY).

Zephyr Balloon/A Aerozona Adventure
**7418 East Cortez Street, Scottsdale
(480) 991-4260, (888) 991-4260
www.azballoon.com**

The owners of A Aerozona have been taking people aloft over State Trust lands between Cave Creek Road and 99th Avenue since 1974 and have garnered a perfect safety record. They have flights every day of the year, weather permitting. They arrange to meet you at the launch site about 15 minutes before dawn. After a dawn launch you'll be floating anywhere from treetop level to 1,000 feet high over 200 miles of open desert the company leases. You'll touch down from 45 to 90 minutes later and enjoy a champagne brunch in the desert as you and other passengers reflect on the flight. Then, they drive you back to your car. Rates are $125 per person if you go to the launch site and $145 if you want to be picked up. Gift certificates and group rates are available.

Reservations should be made one to three weeks before a flight. The owners recommend making reservations four weeks before a holiday flight. Late-afternoon flights are available from November through March.

Boating

Arizona is among the top states in per-capita boat ownership, another fact to add to your store of desert trivia. The opportunities to go boating in nearby waters include the most popular options of Lake Pleasant in the Northwest Valley and Saguaro Lake in the Tonto National Forest. If you don't own your own boat, boat rentals are available at a number of urban lakes, such as Kiwanis Park and Encanto Park. Check with each city's parks department for information. If you go out in a speed boat or with Jet Skis, show courtesy to swimmers, water skiers, and those in kayaks, sailboats, and canoes.

In Arizona, all aquatic vehicles—from sailboards to Jet bikes to large boats—must be registered with the Arizona Game and Fish Department. The only vehicles exempted are nonmotorized inflatable boats that are less than 12 feet in length. Registration costs $4.00, plus the license tax of 45 cents per foot, up to 18 feet, and 68 cents per foot for over 18 feet. Non-resident fees cost $20.00 for registration, plus a license tax of $2.90 per foot, up to 18 feet and $5.50 per foot for over 18 feet.

Practice Plus-One Boating, meaning what you take out on your boating trip be sure to bring back plus one—one piece of litter or debris, every time. If it floats, net it. If it blows out, go back and get it. Act ethically and responsibly to keep our waterways clean for the enjoyment of all.

A life jacket is required for every person aboard, and those younger than 12 must wear their life jacket while aboard. Further information on boating licenses is available at the Arizona Game and Fish Department, 2222 West Greenway Road, Phoenix, (602) 942–3000; or 7200 East University Drive, Mesa, (480) 981–9400.

Lake Pleasant Regional Park
SR 74, Peoria
(928) 501–1710
From most parts of the Valley access to Lake Pleasant is fairly easy, which, of course, means crowds on weekends. But despite the rush of kamikaze Jet Skiers, the lake also is an abode for the members of the Arizona Yacht Club, who frequently use the lake as a venue for their weekend regattas. The lake, formed by the Waddell Dam, offers gorgeous views of the mountains surrounding it. The park crawls with wildlife, including coyotes, burros, and a shy pair of nesting bald eagles. The lake permits parasailing as well as boating. You pay $5.00 per motor vehicle to get into the park; $7.00 for vehicles pulling watercraft. The park's main entrance (the first as you come up from the Valley) gives access to a 10-lane boat ramp, which is adjacent to parking for 590 vehicles with boat trailers. The second (north) entrance is 3 miles past the first and gives access to a four-lane ramp, which has space for 112 vehicles with boat trailers. Both launching ramps are on the western shore of the lake. Before you come upon the main entrance, you'll pass Pleasant Harbor Road, which gives access to the Pleasant Harbor Marina on the lake's eastern shore. Lake Pleasant Watercraft rental offers boat storage and complete repair facilities. Camping and shower facilities are available.

Saguaro Lake Recreational Area
Off Bush Highway, in Tonto National
Forest about 10 miles northeast of Mesa
(480) 610–3300, (602) 225–5200

Saguaro Lake is the closest of three lakes formed by dams along the Salt River. As such, it gets crowded on summer weekends, but it's still a great place to enjoy watery fun. There are two Forest Service boat-launch ramps on the north end of Saguaro Lake. You can come straight up and launch, park your land vehicle nearby, and take the boat on out. When coming from Mesa, the launch ramps can be reached by taking the turn off Bush Highway for the Sheriff's Aid Station and the Saguaro Lake Marina. The lake is closed to parasailing (it's just as well since the surrounding mountains close off the lake from prevailing winds). Those with boats and Jet Skis should be considerate of water skiers and kayakers. For boat storage, service, and rentals, call the marina at (480) 986-5546. Boating maps are available at the Mesa District Ranger Station, 26 North Macdonald Street, Mesa, (480) 610-3300, and at the Tonto National Forest Office, 2324 East McDowell Road, Phoenix, (602) 225-5200. The entry fee is $4.00 per day, per vehicle, with $2.00 extra charged for watercraft.

Climbing

Camelback Mountain
Echo Canyon Recreation Area,
East McDonald Drive at Tatum Boulevard,
Phoenix
(602) 261-8318
Camelback Mountain offers quick access to great climbs in the Valley, but the crumbly sandstone walls make the situation a bit dicey. The 80-foot tower called the Praying Monk, one of the most popular climbs, offers a sheer angle, a great view of the Valley, and permanent—though aging—bolts fixed along the route. The east face is rated at a 5.4, the southeast corner at a 5.6. Hikers beware—do not climb these rocks without the proper gear, protection, and instruction.

Arizona is a top destination for rock climbing, attracting international climbers. For more information on climbing in the Valley, check out **Rock Climbing Arizona,** *by Stewart M. Green. If you want to get some practice on a good indoor gym, try the Phoenix Rock Gym in Tempe's Aztech Court (1353 East University). Check out their Web site at www.phoenixrockgym.com.*

Fishing

If you're 14 or older and plan to fish in Arizona, you need to be licensed by the state Game and Fish Department. Some local jurisdictions require a special permit as well, so it's good to check on local regulations before you decide to test out an interesting new fishing spot.

Licenses are issued annually to residents for an $18 fee, but several license options are available for nonresidents. A tourist can pick up a one-day license for $12.50, a five-day license for $26.00, and a four-month license for $37.50. These licenses entitle you to catch warm-water fish in any body of water in the state, including the Valley's canals. To catch trout, you pay $10.50 more for an annual trout stamp.

The exception to this rule is the Urban Fishing program, which costs $16 annually for residents and visitors alike. An Urban Fishing License costs the same as the general fishing license, but it entitles you to fish only at certain park lakes in the Phoenix and Tucson areas. To fish anywhere else in the Valley or the state, you need the general license. The advantage of the urban fishing program is that the license fees pay for the stocking of these specific lakes with catfish in the summer and trout in the winter.

The Urban Fishing License covers fishing at these Valley parks: Cortez Park, 35th and Dunlap Avenues, Phoenix; Desert West Park, 6602 West Encanto Boulevard, Phoenix; Encanto Park, 15th Avenue and Encanto Boulevard, Phoenix; Papago Park, Van Buren Street and Galvin Parkway, Phoenix; Chaparral Park, 5401 North Hayden Road, Scottsdale; Canal Park, McKellips Road and College Avenue, Tempe; Kiwanis Community Park, Mill Avenue and All America Way, Tempe; Desert Breeze Park, Desert Breeze Parkway, Chandler; Red Mountain Park, 7745 East Brown Road, Mesa; and Riverview Park, 2100 West Eighth Street, Mesa.

Further details on fishing licenses may be obtained from the Arizona Game and Fish Department, 2222 West Greenway Road, Phoenix, (602) 942-3000; or 7200 East University Drive, Mesa, (480) 981-9400.

Lake Pleasant
Off SR 74, Peoria

Lake Pleasant presents the angler with bass, catfish, and crappie. Because the lake is so popular, the serious, but bleary-eyed, angler is going to be out in the water well before dawn.

Roosevelt Lake
Off the Apache Trail, SR 88, about 30 miles northeast of Apache Junction in Tonto National Forest

Serious anglers recommend Roosevelt Lake because of its good fishing. Although it's a bit of a haul from the Valley, you can easily do an overnight turnaround. From the Valley, Roosevelt Lake is the farthest of the four lakes formed by dams along the Salt River. Despite being the highest of the lakes, it's fairly warm because it's shallow. Thus, the fish grow well. Spring is the best time to catch bass up there. Catfish are best caught in the spring and summer. Crappies are abundant in spring. You can fish the lake year-round, though, and still turn up some good catches.

Saguaro Lake
Off Bush Highway, about 10 miles northeast of Mesa in Tonto National Forest

Saguaro Lake is a challenging place for anglers because the lake is so popular. It's tough to make a good catch here. The best time to fish Saguaro Lake is in the winter, when most of the boating traffic dies down. Anglers who can't wait for winter will get up well before dawn or stay up into the wee hours to partake of Saguaro Lake's bounty of bass and catfish in some secluded cove.

Hiking and Biking

A number of Valley cities have bike paths along urban streets; call the respective city parks and recreation departments for information and maps. More interesting because they are away from the roads are the paths along the canals through the Valley of the Sun. These canal paths are shared by bicyclists, hikers, joggers, horseback riders, and the occasional dog, but they generally offer a tranquil route through the Valley.

We can't emphasize enough, though, that you should take adequate water along with you for your trip. On the urban trails, where you can quickly turn off and hit a convenience store, this may not be much of a concern, but when you get more isolated, you want to keep well-hydrated, even in winter.

Grand Canal
The Grand Canal travels across the Valley from where it emerges from an underground aqueduct southwest of the intersection of Washington Street and Mill Avenue in Tempe. The canal path heads northwestward into Phoenix, north of Indian School Road and past the Phoenix Indian Medical Center before it heads almost due west between Phoenix Central High School and Brophy College Preparatory School and then curves southwest. South of Indian School Road and I-17, the

Bicycle Rental and Repair

If you're visiting and want to use a bicycle to check out some of the trails, a few places rent bikes for that purpose. Most rent on a daily basis. The number of bike-rental places is diminishing due to insurance concerns and theft, so it's best to call and check first. All the places here repair and sell bicycles as well.

Arizona Outback Adventures
16447 North 91st Street, Scottsdale
(480) 945-2881
www.azoutbackadventures.com
Arizona Outback Adventures has been leading hiking and biking tours since 1990. They vary depending on what you want to see and how long you can go. The more independent-minded can rent a bike and strike out on their own. There is a wide variety of cruisers and mountain bikes ranging from $25 to $65 per day and $50 to $210 per week. All rentals include the free use of a helmet.

Tempe Bicycle
330 West University Drive, Tempe
(480) 966-6896
www.tempebicycle.com
Tempe Bicycle is located just a bit off Mill Avenue in downtown Tempe. The shop rents bikes from $15 to $40 a day. Weekly rates range from $45 to $75.

canal begins to travel west. It travels to the northwest a little north of 56th Avenue and Osborn Road. It travels into Glendale at 75th Avenue and Camelback Road, continuing northwest to Bethany Home Road and 83rd Avenue, where it heads due west to about 107th Avenue and ends.

Indian Bend Wash Bike Path
Along Hayden Road, Scottsdale
(480) 312-2722
This bike path meanders for 11 miles along the sunken greenbelt constructed for flood control through the center of Scottsdale. It's not a challenging trail at all, but it offers the chance to quickly get out in some greenery and unwind. There are several good starting points, such as north of downtown Scottsdale at Chaparral Park at Hayden and Jackrabbit Roads or the Bike Stop Rest Area on Thomas Road between Miller and Hayden Roads. The path ends at Shea Boulevard in the north and at McKel-lips Road, on the line with Tempe, in the south. You'll pass a number of public golf courses, small lakes, and municipal parks along the way. You won't have to worry about auto traffic, but pedestrians, skaters, and joggers share the path.

Mormon and National Trails
South Mountain Park,
10919 South Central Avenue, Phoenix
(602) 495-0222
These are fun trails for mountain biking, although they're shared by hikers, so be careful and courteous. From the mountain-bike point of view, Mormon Trail is a technical single track. The trail climbs to a mountain ridge, follows it, and then hooks up to the National Trail. At this point, a rider can choose to return to the trailhead by turning left down the National Trail. By turning right you continue upward on the National Trail. At "the waterfall" bike riders are forced to carry their bikes up a short distance, and then it's 3 to 4 miles back to

the parking lot. The bike ride down is very bumpy.

Summit Trail
Echo Canyon Recreation Area, East McDonald Drive at Tatum Boulevard, Phoenix
(602) 256-3220

At 2,700 feet, Camelback Mountain happens to be the tallest in Phoenix, so its Summit Trail takes hikers to the top of the Valley's world. However, you don't get the reward of a magnificent view without a little work. This is a popular place among overachievers, and the park rangers rate it a difficult hike. The mile-long path is steep with slippery patches of gravel, but it's well worth the effort.

Taking kids for a walk in the desert is a great way for them to learn to appreciate nature and get a sense of place lacking in the big city. Remember, though, that children are especially prone to sunstroke and dehydration. Don't rely on them to tell you if they aren't feeling well, since their enthusiasm may outstrip their endurance. Take it on yourself to give them plenty of water and make sure they're dressed appropriately.

Summit Trail at Squaw Peak
Squaw Peak Recreation Area,
2701 East Squaw Peak Lane, Phoenix
(602) 262-7901

We hesitate to mention the Summit Trail at Squaw Peak because it's already so popular and crowded. This 1.2-mile trail doesn't go as high as Camelback's Summit Trail (it's only 2,600 feet), and it isn't as difficult. However, the view is just as good.

Sun Circle Trail
Maricopa County
(602) 506-2930

The Sun Circle Trail incorporates paths along some major canals as it makes its

110-mile circle through the Valley. The trail—open to pedestrians, bicyclists, and horseback riders—was conceived and mapped by the Arizona State Horsemen's Association Trails Committee and then presented to the county Board of Supervisors back in the early 1960s. In 1965 the county obtained cooperation from the Salt River Project and the U.S. Department of the Interior to have the trail run alongside the canals. Parts of the trail remain unfinished, as flood-control clearance and rights of way are sought, but a good deal of the trail is continuous. Signs mark the trail at intervals. Maps are available from the county Parks and Recreation Department at the number above.

The Arizona Canal, a major part of the completed portion of the Sun Circle Trail, travels west from the Granite Reef Dam on the Salt River east of the Beeline Highway (SR 87) across Scottsdale to roughly Hayden Road, and then it jogs south toward Indian School Road, which it parallels into Phoenix. Then, it heads northwest to Glendale and Thunderbird Paseo Park, where it terminates at approximately 75th Avenue and Thunderbird Road. Along the way, it passes such bike-friendly parks as the Phoenix Mountains Preserve, North Mountain Park, and Squaw Peak Park.

The southern portion of the Sun Circle Trail connects with the Arizona Canal path at the Granite Reef Dam. It travels southwestward along the South Canal, a bit south of the Salt River. The Sun Circle Trail then follows the Consolidated Canal eastward through Mesa and then south into Gilbert. The trail then turns west on the Western Canal, north of Elliot Road, and travels through Chandler and into Tempe. When the Western Canal veers to the north near Tempe's Kiwanis Park, the trail continues westward into South Mountain Park in Phoenix.

Points of interest along the trail include Papago Park, Granite Reef, South Mountain Park, the Agua Fria River, and the Salt River Indian Community.

Hockey Organizations

Desert Youth Hockey Association
1520 North Hayden Road, Scottsdale
(480) 994-9119
This association organizes youth hockey leagues and tournaments and coordinates participation in national tournaments.

Valley of the Sun Hockey Association
Phoenix
(602) 379-0333, (602) 957-9966
www.vosha.org
The association organizes youth ice hockey leagues and tournaments.

Hockey

Although ice hockey in the desert seems a non sequitur, it's been popular in the Valley forever—or at least dating from when the late, minor-league Phoenix Roadrunners came to town. Roller hockey made the game even more popular with kids. After the advent of in-line skates, kids could set up a net in their cul-de-sac and play, instead of having to find an ice rink or a roller rink willing to let them play.

Listed here are rinks dedicated solely to in-line roller hockey. Look under Ice Skating and Roller Skating headings to find facilities that offer hockey leagues, in addition to open skating.

Casey at the Bat
Union Hills Drive and 40th Street, Phoenix
(602) 971-3224
Casey at the Bat is a sports complex that includes a roller rink for hockey league-only use. The nearby batting cages are available for use for $1.00 for 16 balls.

In-Line Hockey Rink
Bonsall Park, 59th Avenue and
Bethany Home Road, Glendale
(623) 930-2820
This City-of-Glendale-owned rink offers free open play by age group, as well as clinics on how to improve their game to both youth and adult hockey leagues. For details on hours, league schedules, and group reservations, call the number above.

Horseback Riding

Phoenix is not far removed from the Wild West, so you can bet that horseback riding remains dear to many folks out here. People who own horse properties out on the fringes of the Valley just get up on their horses and ride out into the rural area or wilderness nearby, which is not exactly advisable for people who don't know the area. It's easy to get lost in the wilderness. If you ride from the stables listed below, you will have a trail guide regardless of your experience with horses. Also, remember to take plenty of water, especially in the wilderness areas.

Arizona Horselovers Park
19224 North Tatum Boulevard, Phoenix
(602) 262-6696
This park has three equestrian arenas open sunrise to sunset seven days a week, except when they are reserved for special events (it's best to call ahead). It's open some evenings from 6:00 to 9:00 P.M.

Hikers, bikers, equestrians, and off-road motor-vehicle enthusiasts share many trails in Arizona's parks. They're urged to leave as little mark of their passing as possible and to show courtesy to one another.

Glendale Parks and Recreation Department
5850 West Glendale Avenue, Glendale
(623) 930-2820

Thunderbird Park and Thunderbird Paseo Park both offer horseback-riding trails. The trail at the Thunderbird Paseo Park links with the Arizona Canal, while the trails at Thunderbird Park are favored by many Valley equestrians. Call for information and maps.

Lost Dutchman State Park
6109 North Apache Trail, Apache Junction
(480) 982-4485

With all those saguaros out there, you'll know you're in the Arizona desert at Lost Dutchman State Park. A hiking-equestrian trail leads into the rugged Superstition Wilderness area of the Tonto National Forest. Park rangers advise that the grade of the trail makes it tough on horses and recommend the park's lower-level trails, on which hiking, mountain biking, and horseback riding are all permitted. The entrance fee is $6.00 per vehicle with up to four people. To get there take the Superstition Freeway (US 60) east to the Idaho Street (SR 88) exit. When SR 88 becomes the Apache Trail, follow it about 5 miles northeast to the park entrance.

MacDonald's Ranch
26540 North Scottsdale Road, Scottsdale
(480) 585-0239
www.macdonaldsranch.com

For decades MacDonald's Ranch—a real ranch that raises horses—has been taking people through the magnificent McDowell Mountains. The ranch also specializes in cowboy cookouts on the trail to complete your Western adventure (groups of 10 or more). Reservations are recommended for the cookout, and the ranch suggests this activity for children ages 7 and older. There are pony rides at the ranch for those younger than 7. Sample prices: A one-hour guided trail ride is $30 per person; a one-hour ride with a cowboy luncheon is $55 per person.

Maricopa County Parks and Recreation Dept.
3475 West Durango Street, Phoenix
(602) 506-2930

The county Parks and Recreation Department can supply maps and information on the horseback trails at Estrella Mountain Regional Park, Usery Mountain Recreation Area, and McDowell Mountain Regional Park. Maps can also be picked up at the parks' ranger stations. The department is also the place to go for maps and information on the Sun Circle Trail, which travels through urban areas and wilderness alongside the Arizona Canal and other major canals in the Valley. The Maricopa County Parks and Recreation Department has horseback-riding concessionaires on or adjacent to the Cave Creek Recreation Area, (623) 465-0431; White Tank Mountain Regional Park, (623) 935-2505; Estrella Mountain Regional Park, (623) 932-3811; and Usery Mountain Recreation Area, (480) 984-0032. These outfits have special use permits that allow them to lead trips into the regional parks and recreational areas managed by Maricopa County.

Papago Riding Stables
400 North Scottsdale Road, Tempe
(480) 966-9793

Papago Riding Stables will take you on trails through the red rocks of Papago Park. Trail rides are $15 per hour, per person. The stables open at 8:00 A.M. each day, but the closing hours vary with the season and weather. In the summer the stables shut down at the hottest hours of the day and reopen in the late afternoon. It's best to call ahead for times.

Phoenix Parks, Recreation, and Library Dept.
200 West Washington Street, Phoenix
(602) 262-6861

North Mountain Recreation Area, Papago Park, and South Mountain Park all offer horseback-riding trails, and they are very popular places to make a quick getaway into desert scenery without leaving the

Valley. The department can provide maps to the trails.

Ponderosa Stables
10215 South Central Avenue, Phoenix
(602) 268-1261
www.arizona-horses.com

Ponderosa Stables offers horseback riding in South Mountain Park. The stables are open daily from 8:00 A.M. until dark. Trail rides are $22 per person per hour. A four-hour ride is $60 per person on weekdays, $65 on weekends. Ponderosa also gives riding lessons at $25 an hour per person. The lessons are one on one. Ponderosa's wranglers will also take groups out on cookout rides, featuring steak and chicken or hamburgers and hot dogs. There's an eight-person minimum on those, and reservations are needed.

Ice Skating

Think about it. It's the middle of summer and you want to get some exercise, but you'd like to stay cool too. Ice skating is just the right prescription, and it's fun year-round, even though you'll never see a frozen Valley pond.

Alltel Ice Den
9375 East Bell Road, Scottsdale
(480) 585-7465

The Phoenix Coyotes' practice rink is open for public skating several times a week. The ice is almost exactly like the America West Arena rink in downtown Phoenix, where the Coyotes play their home games. The facility offers figure skating and hockey programs for children and adults, plus a pro shop, concessions area, and restaurant. Public sessions vary by the season, but usually last two hours every weekday, with the addition of two-hour evening sessions Thursday through Sunday. Admission is $7.00 for adults and $5.00 for those 6 to 15, with skate rental being an additional $4.00 for hockey skates or $3.00 for figure skates. Kids under 5 skate for $5.00, skate rental

included. A family of four can skate on Wednesday and Sunday for $28, skate rental included. Call for league information.

Arcadia Ice
3853 East Thomas Road, Phoenix
(602) 957-9966
www.arcadiaice.com

Arcadia Ice is open for skating and lessons. Located inside the Desert Palms Power Center, it has public skating sessions during both days and evenings, with skating lessons on weekend afternoons. Day skating sessions are 1:00 to 3:30 P.M. Monday through Friday and from noon to 2:00 P.M. Saturday. Night sessions are from 7:00 to 9:00 P.M. Friday and 7:30 to 9:30 P.M. Saturday. Admission $4.50 for adults, $3.50 for kids 3 to 12, and $2.50 for skate rental.

Oceanside Ice Arena
1520 North McClintock Drive, Tempe
(480) 941-0944
www.iskateaz.com

This facility, named for its location next to Big Surf water park, is open for skating and lessons. You can usually skate during the afternoons or evenings, but call ahead for hours. Admission is $4.50 for adults and $3.50 for children 12 and younger. Figure skate rentals are $3.50 and hockey skate rentals are $4.50. Inquire about lessons for beginning skaters or children's hockey. Adult leagues play there too.

Jeep Tours

Desert Storm Hummer Tours
15525 North 83rd Way, Scottsdale
(480) 922-0020, (866) 374-8637
www.dshummer.com

Head out into the Four Peaks Wilderness Area of Tonto National Forest in one of the sturdiest 4 x 4 vehicles around, a Humvee. This vehicle can take you places a jeep couldn't, like 4,000 feet up the side of a 6,000-foot mountain. Humvees replaced the old military jeeps in 1979 and became available commercially in 1992.

Desert Storm Hummer Tours has been in operation since 1997. It has six hummers leaving seven days a week for the Four Peaks Wilderness Area. For a four-hour tour, the price is $95 per person; children 12 and younger ride for $75 apiece. For resort or home pickup, the price is $100 per person. There's also a night desert tour using night-vision equipment. That tour costs $125 for adults and $100 for kids. Call as early as possible for reservations in the busy season from October through June. From July through September, the company says it can usually take people who call the day they want to go.

Rafting

Desert Voyagers
Scottsdale
(480) 998–7238
www.desertvoyagers.com
Desert Voyagers can take you on a variety of raft rides in the desert rivers near the Valley. Funwater Floats take a half-day, with a two-hour float through the Tonto National Forest. The price is $59 per person. Or, for the same price, you can share

Water sports are a great way to cool off in this hot, desert environment, but remember that you still need to drink a lot of water and apply regular doses of sunscreen. The water reflects and magnifies the sun, so if you're in a boat, inner tube, or pool, you can burn even quicker than if you were on a hiking trail. You may have noticed that we keep repeating warnings about the heat. That's because every year visitors get sick or even die of sunstroke here. We are very serious about these warnings. You may be the healthiest person on the block, but you are not stronger than the desert sun. Really.

a "Funyak" with someone and paddle behind one of the guided rafts on a Funwater Float. The company also offers the Best of Arizona, which combines a desert jeep tour with a raft trip for $135 per person, with a minimum of four people. Reservations are recommended.

Roller Skating

When it comes to roller skating, you can choose from rinks that allow in-line skating or those that are strictly the old-fashioned, roller-derby style skates. (The in-line rinks may also have hockey leagues.) The Valley has enough rinks to keep fans of both styles happy.

Great Skate of Arizona
10054 North 43rd Avenue, Glendale
(623) 842–1181
The Great Skate boasts the largest rink in Arizona, and it allows both in-line and roller-derby style skates. The skating schedule changes regularly, so the Great Skate suggests you call ahead for the current schedule. Prices range from $3.00 to $8.00, and skate rental is included. The rink is available for private parties and also offers lessons.

Rollero Family Roller Skating Center
7318 West Indian School Road, Phoenix
(623) 846–1510
www.rollero.com
Rollero has been in business for more than 45 years and maintains a family atmosphere. It's open on all major holidays, with open skating sessions on most nights of the week. Prices can vary daily, ranging from $3.00 to $8.00 per person depending on the day and time. There is no charge for skate rental. The schedule changes depending on the season and to accommodate private parties (Rollero specializes in birthday parties), so it's best to call ahead. Rollero does not allow in-line or street skates.

Surfside Skate
1625 East Weber Road, Tempe
(480) 968-9600
www.surfsideskateland.com

Tempe's Surfside Skate is an indoor roller rink near Big Surf water park, and it offers in-line skating and skating lessons. Open skating sessions take place Friday through Sunday. Hours change to accommodate lessons and private parties, so call ahead. Admission ranges anywhere from $2.00 to $10.00, depending on the day, time, and activity. Skate rental costs $2.00 to $3.50. Surfside Skate also hosts artistic skating, speed skating, and youth hockey leagues, so call for more information.

Soaring

Arizona Soaring, Inc.
Estrella Sailport, State Route 238,
Maricopa County
(520) 568-2318, (800) 861-2318,
(480) 821-2903
www.azsoaring.com

How about soaring silently through desert sky at about 4,000 feet? Although Estrella Sailport is well south of the Valley, you can see the Valley spreading northward from your perch. Weather and geography are kind to Estrella Sailport, offering conditions right for soaring almost every day of the year. Arizona Soaring is open 11:00 A.M. to 5:00 P.M. Monday through Friday and 9:00 A.M. to 5:00 P.M. Saturday and Sunday. Sailplanes are taken up and released at 3,500 feet and, by riding the air currents, generally reach an altitude of about 5,000 to 6,000 feet. The high-performance craft can soar to 10,000 feet on a good day. A ride in a trainer lasts 20 minutes and costs $69.95 per person. A 20-minute ride in a high-performance sailplane costs $89.95 and a 40-minute ride costs $129.95. Daredevils may want to try the 15-minute aerobatic ride for $99.95. Arizona Soaring also offers longer rides and lessons. To get there take I-10 east to exit 164 and head toward Maricopa. Follow the road for 15 miles and then turn west on SR 238. You'll come upon Estrella Sailport 6.5 miles later.

Softball

Softball has been big in the Valley of the Sun ever since fast-pitch softball (the type with the windmill windup as opposed to slow underhand pitching) was a major spectator sport out here in the early 20th century. Slow-pitch softball has been growing nationwide since the 1960s, and its growth in the Valley mirrors the national trend. When we talk softball as an adult recreational activity, it's slow-pitch that rules in the Valley. Fast-pitch is generally played by women's teams. Slow-pitch is generally played by men's and corecreational teams.

If you've got a softball team, and you want to play more than an occasional pickup game, there are many different leagues and tournaments open. Company and industrial leagues, church leagues, and ethnic leagues are mostly closed to people outside those particular groups.

City leagues are open to all participants, sometimes with a residency requirement or restriction (i.e., teams that have no residents from the specific city may be last in line to be registered). Tournaments sponsored by the two major sanctioning bodies—the Amateur Softball Association and the United States Slo-Pitch Softball Association—are open to member teams.

Chandler Community Services Department
125 East Commonwealth Avenue,
Chandler
(480) 782-2727

Chandler offers men's, women's, and corecreational slow-pitch league play in winter, spring-summer, and fall seasons. The league plays by ASA rules. Games are played at the Snedigar Sportsplex, 4500 South Basha Road, and Folley Memorial Park, 601 East Frye Road. Registration

Softball Organizations

The American Softball Association sponsors a number of tournaments at such Valley venues as the Rose Mofford Sports Complex and Victory Lane Sports Complex. You can get information on those and on tournaments held outside the Valley by calling (928) 445–5725. Although the ASA is dedicated foremost to preserving fast-pitch softball, its rules for both fast-pitch and slow-pitch softball are observed by a number of Valley city softball leagues.

information is available at the phone number above.

Gilbert Parks and Recreation Department
119 North Gilbert Road, Gilbert
(480) 503–6201

Gilbert offers men's, women's, and corecreational slow-pitch league play year-round. The league plays by ASA rules. Games are held at Freestone Park, 10190 East Juniper Avenue. Registration information is available at the phone number above.

Glendale Parks and Recreation
5850 West Glendale Avenue, Glendale
(623) 930–2820

Glendale offers men's, women's, senior's, and corecreational slow-pitch league play in spring and fall. In summer Glendale offers corecreational play only. The league plays by ASA rules. Games are played at Sahuaro Ranch Park, 59th Avenue and Mountain View Road; Foothills Park, 57th Avenue and Union Hills Drive; and Paseo Racquet Center, 63rd Avenue and Thunderbird Road. League and reservation information is available at the number above.

Mesa Community Services Department
Parks and Recreation Division
125 North Hobson Street, Mesa
(480) 644–2351

Mesa offers men's, women's, and corecreational slow-pitch league play year-round. The league plays by ASA rules. Games are held at Red Mountain Park's Softball Complex, 7808 East Brown Road; Riverview Park, 2100 West Eighth Street; Ellsworth Park, 107 South Horne Road; and Kleinman Park, 710 South Extension Avenue. Registration information is available at the phone number above.

Peoria Community Services
8401 West Monroe Street, Peoria
(623) 773–7137

Peoria offers men's, women's, and corecreational slow-pitch league play in spring, summer, and fall. The league plays by ASA rules. Games are played at Varney Park, 11820 North 81st Avenue. Reservation information is available at the number above.

Phoenix Parks, Recreation, and Library Dept.
200 West Washington Street, Phoenix
(602) 262–6861

Phoenix offers year-round league play for upper levels of competition at Rose Mofford Sports Complex, 9833 North 25th Avenue, Phoenix, (602) 261–8011; and Papago Softball Complex, 6201 East Oak Street, Phoenix, (602) 261–8841. Leagues vote on using ASA or USSSA rules. For other levels of competition, five geographical districts in the city field their own leagues. Call the department for further information.

Scottsdale Community Services
7447 East Indian School Road, Scottsdale
(480) 312-0227

Scottsdale offers men's, women's, and corecreational slow-pitch league play year-round. The league plays by ASA rules. Games are played at Horizon Park, 15440 North 100th Street; Chaparral Park, 5401 North Hayden Road; and Eldorado Park, 2311 North Miller Road. Registration information is available at the phone number above.

Tempe Community Services
3500 South Rural Road, Tempe
(480) 350-5207

Tempe offers men's, women's, and corecreational slow-pitch league play in the spring, summer, and fall. The league plays by modified ASA rules. Games are held at Kiwanis Community Park softball fields on All America Way; Tempe's Papago Park, Curry Road and College Avenue; Daley Park, College Avenue and Encanto Drive; Tempe Diablo Stadium Complex, 2200 West Alameda Drive; Clark Park, Roosevelt and 19th Streets; and Escalante Park, River Road and Orange Street. Registration information is available at the phone number above.

Swimming

Swimming is big in the desert. What better way to stay cool, after all? The offerings include the following municipal pools:

Chandler

Chandler has five municipal pools open from various dates in the spring and summer. Fees are 50 cents for kids 17 and younger, 75 cents for seniors 55 and older, and $1.50 for adults. Lessons are available. Hours vary, so call ahead. The city runs an aquatics hotline at (480) 782-2733.
- Arrowhead Meadows Pool, 1475 West Erie Street, Chandler, (480) 732-1064
- Desert Oasis Aquatic Center, 1400 West Summit Place, Chandler, (480) 732-1061, (480) 732-1062

- Folley Pool, 600 East Fairview Street, (480) 732-1063
- Hamilton Aquatic Center, 3838 South Arizona Avenue, (480) 782-2630, (480) 782-2631
- West Chandler Aquatic Center, 250 South Kyrene Road, (480) 783-8261, (480) 783-8262

Gilbert

Fast-growing Gilbert has two municipal pools open from mid-May through mid-August. Fees are $1.00 for kids 18 and younger, and $1.75 for adults 19 and older. Swim passes are available through Gilbert Parks and Recreation, (480) 503-6201. Lessons are available. Call for hours.
- Gilbert Municipal Pool, 1016 North Burk Street, Gilbert, (480) 926-1030
- Mesquite Aquatic Center, 100 West Mesquite Street, Gilbert, (480) 503-6292

Glendale

Glendale has a seven-pool system that operates from June through August. Schedules vary for each pool. For the full range of aquatic activities and swimming lessons offered, it's best to call (623) 930-2820 for information or the individual pools at the numbers listed below for schedule details.
- Apollo Pool, 8045 North 47th Avenue, Glendale, (623) 915-2713
- Cactus Pool, 15500 North 63rd Avenue, Glendale, (623) 412-5532
- Cardinal Pool, 6350 West Glendale Avenue, Glendale, (623) 915-1679
- Community Pool, 6000 West Olive Avenue, Glendale, (623) 915-2775
- Ironwood Pool, 12603 North 61st Avenue, Glendale, (623) 412-5868
- O'Neil Pool, 6448 West Missouri Avenue, Glendale, (623) 915-2803
- Rose Lane Pool, 5003 West Marlette Avenue, Glendale, (623) 930-7905

Mesa

Mesa's 13 municipal pools have been voted the "best in the nation." Pool hours vary at different times of the summer, so it's best to call Mesa Parks and Recreation, (480) 644-2351, for more details. Fees are 75 cents for kids 17 years and younger and $1.50 for adults. Swim passes are also available at the Parks and Recreation number. Lessons are available. A $19-million indoor competitive, instructional, and therapeutic aquatics complex, the Mesa Indoor Aquatics Center, in Mesa Town Square, was supposed to have been complete in 2003, but the project is on hold due to budget problems.

- Brimhall Junior High Pool, 4949 East Southern Avenue, (480) 644-5087
- Carson Junior High Pool, 525 North Westwood Street, Mesa, (480) 644-2374
- Falcon Field Pool, 4800 East Falcon Field Drive, Mesa, (480) 644-2375
- Fremont Junior High Pool 1001 North Power Road, Mesa, (480) 644-2369
- Kino Junior High Pool, 848 North Horne Street, Mesa, (480) 644-2376
- Mesa Junior High Pool, 828 East Broadway Road, Mesa, (480) 644-2377
- Parkway Recreation Center Pool, 1753 East Eighth Avenue, Mesa, (480) 644-2864
- Poston Junior High Pool, 2433 East Adobe Street, Mesa, (480) 644-2371
- Powell Junior High Pool, 855 West Eighth Avenue, Mesa, (480) 644-2378
- Rhodes Junior High Pool, 1860 South Longmore Road, Mesa, (480) 644-2550
- Shepherd Junior High Aquatics Complex, 1407 North Alta Mesa Drive, Mesa, (480) 644-3037
- Stapley Junior High Aquatics Complex, 3250 East Hermosa Vista Drive, (480) 644-4977
- Taylor Junior High Pool, 705 South 32nd Street, Mesa, (480) 644-3036

Peoria

Peoria has two pools as well as Sunrise Pool and Family Center, opened in May 2004. Pools are open from Memorial Day weekend through mid-August daily and on weekends through Labor Day weekend. Fees are 50 cents for children and $1.50 for swimmers 17 and older.

- Centennial Pool, 14388 North 79th Avenue, Peoria, (623) 776-9555
- Peoria High School Pool, 11200 North 83rd Avenue, Peoria, (623) 979-3456
- Sunrise Pool and Family Center, 21321 North 86th Drive, Peoria, (623) 773-8495

Phoenix

Almost all the Valley's communities have at least one municipal pool, but Phoenix's system is extensive. Phoenix's Parks, Recreation, and Library Department's Aquatic Section operates 28 pools city-wide. Pools open for weekend swimming in May and are open seven days a week from the first Monday in June through Labor Day.

Admission for each pool is 50 cents for swimmers younger than 18 and older than 50, and $1.50 for everyone in between. Season passes are available for the summer as well.

Learn-to-swim programs, water-safety and specialty classes, and recreational team programs are offered throughout the summer at many of the pools. For more information on the city's aquatic programs, call the city's Swim Line at (602) 534-7946 or TDD (602) 262-6713.

Deer Valley, El Prado, Paradise Valley, and Starlight pools are equipped with water slides. Many of the pools have diving boards. Most of them have separate wading pools for very young children. Paradise Valley pool has a large mushroom in its wading area, which provides a cool shower of water for the children to play in. For persons with disabilities, the city operates Telephone Pioneer pool. Telephone Pioneer is equipped with lifts, dry- and wet-access ramps, and a separate therapy pool. Lessons are available. Pool hours vary; call for hours of operation and directions if you need them.

- Alkire Pool, 1617 West Papago Street, Phoenix, (602) 261-8787
- Cactus Pool, 3801 West Cactus Road, Phoenix, (602) 262-6680
- Cielito Pool, 4551 North 35th Avenue, Phoenix, (602) 262-4752

- Coronado Pool, 1717 North 12th Street, Phoenix, (602) 262-6709
- Cortez Pool, 3434 West Dunlap Avenue, Phoenix, (602) 262-7107
- Deer Valley Pool, 19400 North 19th Avenue, Phoenix, (602) 534-1842
- Eastlake Pool, 1549 East Jefferson Street, Phoenix, (602) 261-8729
- El Prado Pool, 6428 South 19th Avenue, Phoenix, (602) 261-8638
- Encanto Pool, 2125 North 15th Avenue, Phoenix, (602) 261-8732
- Falcon Pool, 3420 West Roosevelt Street, Phoenix, (602) 262-6229
- Grant Pool, 714 South Second Avenue, Phoenix, (602) 261-8728
- Harmon Pool, 1239 South Fifth Avenue, Phoenix, (602) 261-8733
- Hermoso Pool, 5749 South 20th Street, Phoenix, (602) 261-8731
- Holiday Pool, 4530 North 67th Avenue, Phoenix, (602) 261-8031
- Madison Pool, 1440 East Glenrosa Avenue, Phoenix, (602) 262-6494
- Marivue Pool, 5625 West Osborn Road, Phoenix, (602) 261-8929
- Maryvale Pool, 4444 North 51st Avenue, Phoenix, (602) 262-6685
- Mountain View Pool, 1104 East Grovers Avenue, Phoenix, (602) 534-1347
- Paradise Valley Pool, 17648 North 40th Street, Phoenix, (602) 534-5161
- Perry Pool, 3131 East Windsor Avenue, Phoenix, (602) 262-7367
- Pierce Pool, 2150 North 46th Street, Phoenix, (602) 262-6199
- Roadrunner Pool, 3502 East Cactus Road, Phoenix, (602) 262-6789
- Roosevelt Pool, 6246 South Seventh Street, Phoenix, (602) 262-6832
- Starlight Pool, 7810 West Osborn Road, Phoenix, (602) 495-2412
- Sunnyslope Pool, 301 West Dunlap Road, Phoenix, (602) 262-7165
- Telephone Pioneer Pool, 1946 West Morningside Drive, Phoenix, (602) 495-2404

- University Pool, 1102 West Van Buren Street, Phoenix, (602) 261-8730
- Washington Pool, 6655 North 23rd Avenue, Phoenix, (602) 262-7198

Scottsdale

Scottsdale has three municipal pools; the Cactus and Eldorado pools are open year-round. Fees are $1.50 for adults and $1.00 for kids 17 and younger. Lessons are available. Call for hours.

- Cactus Pool, 7202 East Cactus Road, Scottsdale, (480) 312-7665
- Chaparral Pool, 5401 North Hayden Road, Scottsdale, (480) 312-2361
- Eldorado Pool, 2311 North Miller Road, (480) 312-2484

Newcomers seeking recreational opportunities for their children should check with the local school district. Many districts host after-school and summer recreational programs and can direct parents to such opportunities as Little League and other youth sports programs. Another good source is the local recreation department.

Tempe

Tempe has three outdoor municipal pools and the Kiwanis Park Wave Pool inside the Kiwanis Park Recreation Center. The pool season runs from the last week of May through mid-August. Hours vary, so it's best to call the pools at the phone numbers listed below. Fees for the outdoor pools are 75 cents for kids 6 to 17 years old and $1.50 for adults. Lessons are available. Fees for the wave pool are $6.00 for adults and $3.00 for children ages 3 through 17. Tempe residents pay $4.00 for adults and $2.00 for children. In addition, the wave pool is open for "float-in" movies once a month in June, July, and August. For more information, call the city's Parks

CLOSE-UP

Yoga in the Valley of the Sun

Yoga has become increasingly popular as a way to relieve stress, increase flexibility, and get into shape. There is a bewildering array of styles, so talk to the studio to see what kind of yoga is best for your goals. With more than 20 studios in the metro area, Phoenix is an exciting place for practitioners of any tradition. Many of the city's gyms and resorts also offer classes.

One advantage of going to a studio regularly is the people. A good yoga teacher will try to foster a sense of community in the class, and students who attend a particular class on a regular basis will find themselves making friends with other regulars.

Please note! Yoga is not just for people who are in shape. Overweight, muscle pain, or stiffness is no barrier. As a matter of fact, you will find these problems reducing with steady practice. One local yoga instructor told us of a one-armed veteran who ended up becoming quite adept at various yogic postures. The only requirements are a willingness to learn

and some dedication; you can't pick it up in just a few classes.

Another myth is that yoga requires a certain religious doctrine. Yoga did indeed evolve from Hindu tradition, but this is not how it is generally taught in the United States. You will find some classes that do involve a great deal of Eastern philosophy and others that don't mention it at all. Just as you can always find a class tailored to your physical needs and goals, you can find a class suited for your philosophical beliefs as well.

Below, we list a handful of the more popular studios. All of them offer beginning, intermediate, and advanced classes. Look around; it's best to get the feel of a few studios before settling on one.

Arizona Yoga specializes in Anusara yoga. The hallmark of the studio is a consistent training program, providing the beginner with a solid base from which to develop. This makes it easy to switch from one class to another without having to adjust to a new teaching style. Serious

and Recreation office at (480) 350-5200 or TDD (480) 350-5050.
- Clark Park Pool, 1730 South Roosevelt Street, Tempe, (480) 350-5208
- Escalante Pool, 2150 East Orange Street, Tempe, (480) 350-5800
- Kiwanis Park Wave Pool, 6111 South All America Way, Tempe, (480) 350-5701
- McClintock Pool, 1830 East Del Rio Drive, (480) 350-5202

Tennis

Racquet sports have always been popular here, although not quite as popular as golf. Most of the parks and recreation departments offer tennis courts, many lighted after dark, that are available in local parks on a first-come, first-served, no-charge basis. Call the respective city parks department for a complete list of

Anusara students, and teachers in training, come from across the state to attend classes here. Arizona Yoga is located at 2334 North Scottsdale Road, #126, Scottsdale, (480) 941-6855, and at www.azyoga.net.

For a more eclectic offering, try the **Bodyworks Studio.** In addition to Kundalini, Hatha, and Vinyasa, Bodyworks gives classes in drumming, belly dancing, massage, aromatherapy, and dozens of other subjects. Bodyworks Studio emphasizes a family-friendly environment. Kids will find plenty to do, whether it's Mommy and Me Yoga, theater or crafts. In its efforts to nourish all aspects of life, Bodyworks Studio has support groups for men's issues, career building, psychodrama, and more. Bodyworks is located at 1801 South Jen Tilley Lane, Suite B-8, Tempe, (480) 894-2090, and at www.bodyworks-studio.com.

Founded in 1987, **Desert Song Yoga** is one of the oldest studios in Phoenix. It offers small, friendly classes with lots of individual attention. Students are encouraged to linger after their class to talk, meditate, or read in the studio's shady courtyard. Desert Song provides a homey

Yoga is a great way to relax from the bustling city life. It keeps the body young and fit, too. THE PHOENICIAN

feel that makes it the longtime favorite for many locals. The teachers encourage students to realize both their physical and spiritual abilities. Desert Song is located at 4811 North Seventh Street, Phoenix, (602) 265-8222, and at www.adesert song.com.

courts. The following are some of the public, pay facilities in the Valley.

Gene Autry Sports Complex
4125 East McKellips Road, Mesa
(480) 644-2149
This complex features 16 lighted tennis courts, a practice wall, showers, and a small pro shop. Drop in tennis hours are Monday through Saturday at 7:30 A.M. and Sunday at 6:30 P.M. Hours of operation vary, so call

ahead. Court rental is $4.50 during the day and $6.50 in the evening for singles play; doubles play costs $7.00 during the day and $9.00 during the evening.

Kiwanis Park Recreation Center
6111 South All America Way, Tempe
(480) 350-5701
The Kiwanis Park Recreation Center has 15 lighted hard courts. It has been recognized by the U.S. Tennis Association as

one of the outstanding public tennis facilities in the country. Fees are $4.50 per court for 90 minutes before 7:00 P.M. and $6.00 per court after 7:00 P.M. The center also offers lessons and tennis leagues. Its hours are 7:00 A.M. to 10:00 P.M. Monday through Thursday; 7:00 A.M. to 7:00 P.M. Friday; 8:00 A.M. to 6:00 P.M. Saturday; and 8:00 A.M. to 9:00 P.M. Sunday.

Mountain View Community Center
1104 East Grovers, Phoenix
(602) 534–2500

This center has 20 lighted tennis courts. Use of the courts costs $1.50 for 90 minutes during the day and $2.20 for the same period at night.

Paseo Racquet Center
6268 West Thunderbird Road, Glendale
(623) 979–1234

The Paseo Racquet Center features 14 hard courts and one red-clay court, all lighted. The center opens at 7:00 A.M. in July and August and at 8:00 A.M. the rest of the year. It closes at 9:30 P.M. Monday through Friday and at 2:00 P.M. on Saturday and Sunday. Fees are $2.00 per person for 90 minutes. At night add on a $3.00 light fee per court. The Paseo Racquet Center won an Outstanding Public Facility award from the U.S. Tennis Association. Reservations are taken 24 hours in advance and are recommended. The facility has a pro shop, lockers, and showers. Group and private lessons are available. The center also hosts about 20 tournaments per year.

Phoenix Tennis Center
6330 North 21st Avenue, Phoenix
(602) 249–3712

The Phoenix Tennis center features 22 lighted, hard-surface tennis courts. It's best to call the day before you want to play to make reservations. Rates are $2.00 per person for 90 minutes, $3.00 at night. The facilities include lockers and showers.

Tubing

Salt River Recreation Inc.
North Bush Highway and Usery Pass Road, Mesa
(480) 984-3305
www.saltrivertubing.com

Floating down the Salt River on an inner tube is one of the great joys of Valley life. This part of the Salt River, south of the Stewart Mountain Dam that forms Saguaro Lake and north of the confluence with the Verde River, is always running. You get a faster ride on days after a rain and a slower ride when the weather's been dry a while. Park at the south end of the route, rent your tube (or bring your own), then ride a shuttle bus up to your desired starting point. The company has drop-off points for various lengths of ride. Allow yourself about three hours. Then, let the cool current carry you past desert scenery. When you've come to your route's end, you're right where you parked your car. Keep your car keys in something waterproof and attached to you. In some very minor white water, your rear end may skid on some rocks. Some people outfit their tubes with floating coolers and entertainment centers. We haven't seen a barbecue grill on a tube yet, but we're sure someone's working on it. Salt River Recreation is open from May 4 to October 1 each year, though days and hours of operation vary. Tube rental and shuttle bus service costs $12 per person. Children must be older than 8 to rent an inner tube, and life jackets are recommended.

Water Parks

Water parks in the Valley are popular because they offer an active way to cool off. Consider wearing slip-on aqua shoes— the concrete surrounding the pools is hotter than you think. Also, be mindful of the ratings given to slides—1 through 4, with 4 being the fastest slide. Don't forget to apply good sunscreen on the hour.

Admission prices change from year to year, but most recently they were $17 for those 12 and older and $14 for children ages 4 to 11. Children 3 and younger get in free. The water parks offer discounts for late admission, which is after 3:00 or 4:00 P.M., depending on the park.

Big Surf
1500 North McClintock Drive, Tempe
(480) 947-2477
www.golfland-sunsplash.com
Big Surf lays claim to being the original water park in the Valley and is a legendary place to hang out. As big as four football fields, it probably still is the largest wave pool in the world. Its surrounding landscaping and decor lend the park a Polynesian theme. Big Surf has 11 giant slides and assorted other slides. Little ones will enjoy a wading pool with sprinklers and easy slides. Hours are 10:00 A.M. to 6:00 P.M. Monday through Saturday and 11:00 A.M. to 7:00 P.M. Sunday.

Golfland/Sunsplash
155 West Hampton Avenue, Mesa
(480) 834-8319
www.golfland-sunsplash.com
Golfland/Sunsplash offers a miniature-golf course and water-park combination. The park's water slides are big fun. It also features a wave pool and a tunnel known as the Black Hole. Another feature that appeals to relaxation-seekers is a circuitous "river" that you can lazily float upon in your inner tube. The kiddie area has easy concrete slides, a waterfall, sprinklers, and hoses for lots of safe water play. This Caribbean-theme park has 10 tube and giant slides. For indoor diversion, there's a huge arcade area with games for any skill level, which is a favorite date place for Valley teenagers. The park also has a laser tag area. Also popular are the miniature-golf courses adjacent to the arcade. The water park is open 10:00 A.M. to 8:00 P.M. Monday through Thursday; 10:00 A.M. to 9:00 P.M. Friday and Saturday; and 11:00 A.M. to 7:00 P.M. Sunday. Golfland is open 10:00 A.M. to 10:00 P.M. Sunday through Thursday and 10:00 A.M. to midnight Friday and Saturday.

Waterworld Safari Water Park
4243 West Pinnacle Peak Road, Phoenix
(623) 581-1947
www.golfland-sunsplash.com
Waterworld may be the best of the Valley's water parks. It boasts the six-story Avalanche speed slide along with waterfalls, a wave pool, kiddie pools, and other slides for all levels of daring. The Zambezi River, a 1,100-foot-long lazy waterway, is perfect for relaxing. The wave pool is designed to give 10 minutes of calm and 10 minutes of wave action. Little ones have a great time on the easy slides and the rapids, curving waterways that zip you down to a shallow pool. The Jungle-Jim's children's play pool has a self-latching, fenced area. Lifeguards are on duty. For adventuresome older kids and adults, there are eight larger slides. Hours are 10:00 A.M. to 8:00 P.M. Monday through Thursday; 10:00 A.M. to 9:00 P.M. Friday and Saturday; and 11:00 A.M. to 7:00 P.M. Sunday.

YMCA

YMCA Valley of the Sun
YMCA Metropolitan Office,
350 North First Avenue, Phoenix
(602) 257-5138
The YMCA offers a wide variety of athletics, fitness, and sporting activities, from basketball leagues and in-line hockey to swimming pools and aerobics. The YMCA Valley of the Sun has 10 locations across the Valley.

GOLF

In Arizona, golf is life. Golfers build their personal and work schedules around their tee times and build their houses around the golf course. Deal-makers and rock stars are often spotted on our links, and dozens of pro athletes live here in their off-seasons so they can be on the courses every day. Some people joke that the reason football free agents come to talk to the lowly Arizona Cardinals is because the golf is so good and plentiful here. People schedule business trips and conventions in the Valley, knowing that when the work is done, the golf course awaits.

Many communities are built around golf courses, boasting the course as an amenity just the way homeowners once boasted of indoor plumbing. In places such as the retirement haven Sun City, drivers will see diamond-shaped yellow road signs with the silhouette of a golf cart, warning them of golf-cart crossings. Certainly, the number of retirees out here helps boost the numbers, but golf is played avidly by every age group in Arizona.

Dubbed the "Golf Capital of the World" by the National Golf Foundation, Phoenix is considered one of the world's top golf destinations. A few mind-boggling statistics: 11 million rounds of golf are played in Arizona every year. More than 2 million tourists and over 500,000 residents spend nearly $1 billion on golf and related products. Fifteen of the top 100 golf instructors live in the Phoenix area, including Jim Flick at the Tournament Players Club of Scottsdale, Mike and Sandy LaBauve at Kierland Golf Club, and Peter Kostis at Grayhawk, just to name a few. Ranked the sixth most popular golf destination, Phoenix courses also have the highest average greens fees in the United States after Hawaii and Las Vegas. As they say, you get what you pay for!

Golf course construction, like every other kind of construction in the Valley, is booming. Arizona has more than 300 golf courses and 15 commercial driving ranges, and nearly 75 percent of the state's courses are open to the public. Arizona adds courses and makes additions to existing courses at an average of eight a year. Most of that construction is in the Valley. The Arizona Golf Association estimates that Arizona could sport more than 400 courses by 2010!

In real estate terms, building a home along golf-course frontage property increases the value of both multifamily and single-family housing from 15 to 30 percent. Homes with extraordinary views and golf frontage, a combination found on many of the Valley's newer courses, can increase real-estate values anywhere from 50 to 200 percent. Putting the money issues aside, golf courses are just beautiful places to live beside. Sitting in your backyard, you can enjoy the illusion that all that nearby fairway is part of your yard. Of course, you may have to put up with occasional errant golf balls in your yard, but balance that with the chance to enjoy the sweet smell of newly cut grass.

Golf began to take hold in Arizona when Harry Collis and Will Robinson designed a course at the San Marcos Golf Resort in Chandler back in 1912. Soon after, the Phoenix Country Club had a course as well. In those days, traditional Midwestern and Scottish links designs ruled the courses, with lush greens transporting golfers out of the desert and back to the places they left—only without the snow to cramp their games.

Arizona's rapid growth has changed that trend. Growth makes water an increasingly scarce commodity in a desert environment, which affects the types of design and landscaping used by course architects. Even architects who design more traditional styles tend to surround the fairways with desert landscaping. The Arizona Department of Water Resources allows courses in the Phoenix area to have 90 acres of primary turf and 30 more acres of rough turf, which has a lower water-application rate. Course designs in Arizona have to account for circumstances that differ wildly from those in other golf meccas such as Florida and the Carolinas. The hostile desert environment, the rocky soil, and restrictions on water use have forced course architects to become creative with placing turf. Desert target courses tend to be among the most challenging available, and they really test the skills of the average golfer. You should count on spending some time looking for your ball out among the cacti and brush.

With more than 200 golf courses within 50 miles of downtown Phoenix, your golfing choices are plentiful. Many great course architects are represented here—Gary Panks, David Graham, Tom Weiskopf, Jay Morrish, Robert Trent Jones Jr., Tom Fazio, Pete Dye, even Arnold Palmer.

The Valley's near-constant sunshine makes year-round golf a pleasant prospect. Granted, it's a little tough in the summertime, but that's also the time when course traffic eases up considerably, and bargains are the rule. Summer is the perfect time to play all the courses you can't afford to try during the pricey peak season.

The high season for golf in the Valley is from late December through April. The weather for golf is at its best then, with sunshine and mild temperatures. The influx of winter visitors, who vie with full-time residents for time on the links, makes demand even greater. Because the law of supply and demand is in effect, you'll pay the highest fees in winter. The low season runs from May through August, and avid golfers who don't mind the heat can find fees reduced greatly. The cost of the extra sunscreen you'll need will eat up only a small fraction of the greens fees' savings. Some courses have different fees for short-lived shoulder seasons between the high and low seasons. These fees are usually 'tweeners, not as high as the high-season fees but higher than low-season fees. Some courses charge less on weekdays, when demand is lower than on week-

You'll find course and resort reviews, a course and lodging guide, and golf-related features on the megasite www.GolfArizona.com. If you're not on the Web, you can call them at (480) 837–2184 for information on golf packages.

ends. For golf-planning purposes, assume that a weekend is Friday, Saturday, and Sunday and that weekdays are Monday through Thursday. These price breaks are noted in the listings below. All fees listed include a golf cart, unless otherwise noted.

Greens fees vary considerably and are affected by many factors, including the weather, the economy, and the time of year. The best bet is to call the course directly for the exact cost and to find out if there are any special deals. The fees listed here will help you determine the range of prices out there, but shouldn't be taken as gospel.

There is no easy rule to follow when reserving your tee time. The earliest you can reserve a tee time on most crowded municipal courses is three days in advance. At Papago, easily the busiest Phoenix municipal course, no advance reservations are taken, so people camp out in their cars to be first in line when the course opens for the day. On the other hand, Encanto, another busy Phoenix municipal course, proudly boasts they'll get walk-ups on the course within a half hour. Some of the high-end semiprivate courses will allow you to book a tee time a month in advance, but you'll pay a hefty reservation fee because if they're going to hold a time for you that long they want to make sure you'll show up. Demand is high on those courses, and they want to keep things flowing smoothly.

Remember the seasonal nature of demand too. In summer, some courses change their tee-time reservation policies. The best advice is to call a week to two weeks before you plan a golf outing, find out the reservation system of the course at that time, and make your plans accordingly. For information on the Valley's well-known golf tournaments, see the Spectator Sports chapter.

What follows is a list of some of the semiprivate and public courses in the area. Of course, there are many exclusive private and members-only courses in town as well, but these are not open for public play. Listings of these courses can be found in the many area golf publications available free at visitor centers in town or at the airport.

Golf is pervasive here. You can get golf packages almost anywhere—hotels, motels, resorts, even some RV parks. Just ask when you're checking in.

PHOENIX

Arizona Biltmore Country Club
2400 East Missouri Avenue, Phoenix
(602) 955-9655
www.arizonabiltmore.com
The Arizona Biltmore has represented the upper crust of Valley accommodations for decades, and the Biltmore's Adobe course has been part of the amenities since 1932. The Links course, equally top-notch, offers a modern alternative to the Adobe. These are semiprivate courses, with resort guests having priority on tee times.

As you might suspect from its age, the Adobe is a traditional 18-hole course. The par 72, 6,122-yard course features landscaping that's an extension of the hotel grounds' lush greenery. The signature hole is the No. 3, a 423-yard par 4 that features water before the hole, a bunker to the right, and a pine tree to the left.

The par 71, 6,300-yard Links course wraps around the outer edge of the Biltmore grounds and offers good views of Camelback Mountain and downtown Phoenix in the distance. Seven lakes add challenges to your game.

Amenities include a clubhouse, pro shop, driving range, and the resort hotel's restaurant and swimming pool. The greens fees, cart included, are $165 in high season (January through June), $75 in the shoulder season (September through December), and $48 in the low season (July through August). There's also an 18-hole putting course, which is free to guests.

Cave Creek Golf Course
15202 North 19th Avenue, Phoenix
(602) 866-8076
www.ci.phoenix.az.us/SPORTS/golf.html
Averaging about 100,000 rounds a year, Cave Creek Golf Course surpassed Papago Park as the most popular Phoenix municipal golf course in recent years. Like the other Phoenix courses, this is a traditional 18-hole course. Very unlike the other courses, this land was once a landfill reclamation project. Cave Creek runs through the middle of the course, and nearby hills and mountains add color. The 6,290-yard, par 72 course is difficult, with the toughest being the 450-yard, par 4 No. 8 hole.

The greens fee in high season (October through May) is $21 for Phoenix residents and $31 for nonresidents, golf cart included. In low season (June through September), the greens fee is $15 for residents and $25 for nonresidents. There are also discounts for seniors and juniors and a variety of other discounted fees. Amenities at Cave Creek include a clubhouse, a pro shop, a driving range, putting and chipping greens, and a snack bar.

Encanto Golf Course
2755 North 15th Avenue, Phoenix
(602) 253-3963
www.ci.phoenix.az.us/SPORTS/golf.html
Encanto Park offers its surrounding homes a bucolic and green reprieve from desert dwelling, so it's only natural that its golf course, enhanced by mature palm and salt cedar trees, would do the same. The par 70, 6,386-yard municipal course was designed by William P. Bell and is a favorite among local golfers. Completed in

1935, Encanto is billed as the third-oldest golf course in Arizona. Encanto has level, wide fairways and a limited number of hazards. The ambiance is relaxed and amiable, a perfect place for the average golfer to just enjoy being out there knocking the ball around. The course features eight par 4s that are more than 377 yards. Half of those are the last four holes, which are 430, 413, 400, and 403 yards.

The greens fee in high season (October through May) is $30 for Phoenix residents and $44 for nonresidents, golf cart included. In low season (June through September) the greens fee is $21 for residents and $25 for nonresidents. There are also discounts for seniors and juniors and a variety of other discounted fees. In addition to its clubhouse, golf shop, driving range, practice area, and lessons, Encanto has a swimming pool, tennis court, and a reasonably priced restaurant called Mulligan's.

Maryvale Golf Course
5902 West Indian School Road, Phoenix
(623) 846-4022
www.ci.phoenix.az.us/SPORTS/golf.html
When you're driving by Maryvale Golf Course with the windows rolled down late on a summer's night, you'll feel the temperature go down dramatically. Nighttime irrigation of the grass on this 18-hole traditional municipal course produces the natural air conditioning. Of course, it helps that eucalyptus, cottonwood, and palm trees shade the course as well. And let's not forget that there's water on the course. Designed by William F. Bell (who also designed San Diego's Torrey Pines course), Maryvale is not nearly as busy as Phoenix's other municipal courses, which makes it both a bargain and a mellow experience. The toughest hole is No. 3, a par 4 that's 421 yards, but generally speaking this 6,191-yard, par 72 course is good for all skill levels.

Maryvale's amenities include a clubhouse, a pro shop, a driving range, a practice area, lessons, and a snack bar. The city touts the course's junior golf school, where many of the state's golf pros learned the game. The greens fee in high season (October through May) is $34 for Phoenix residents and $39 for nonresidents, golf cart included. In low season (June through September), the greens fees average around $22 for both residents and nonresidents. There are also discounts for seniors and juniors and a variety of other discounted fees.

Papago Golf Course
5595 East Moreland Street, Phoenix
(602) 275-8428
www.ci.phoenix.az.us/SPORTS/golf.html
This 7,000-yard course undoubtedly is Phoenix's most attractive municipal golf course; as a result, it's very busy. Golfers play about 85,000 to 90,000 rounds a year at Papago. And why not? It's one of the best municipal courses anywhere. With the red rocks of the Papago Buttes dominating the views, golfers know full well they're in the desert Southwest even though they're walking through a traditional, tree-lined course. Designed by William F. Bell, the course features wide, flowing fairways and large, rolling greens. It's playable but challenging for the average player, with demanding doglegs and interesting holes. For instance, the finishing hole, a par 4, 443-yarder, doglegs uphill to a wide green. Papago is also the home of the Phoenix Open qualifying round. Amenities include a clubhouse, a

Die-hard golfers should book early-morning tee times in the summer and take advantage of the summer rates, which are quite a bit lower than the high season. You can get a lot of golf in before it grows too hot, and you don't have to compete with crowds of winter visitors for a good tee time. And don't be shy about slaking your thirst from the drinking fountains around the course and when the beverage cart stops—bottled water is always a good choice.

pro shop, a driving range, a practice area, lessons, and the Double Eagle Cafe.

The greens fee in high season (October through May) is $35 for residents, $46 for nonresidents, golf cart included. In low season (June through September), the greens fee is reduced. There are also discounts for seniors and juniors and a variety of other discounted fees.

The Raven Golf Club at South Mountain
3636 East Baseline Road, Phoenix
(602) 243-3636
www.ravengolf.com

The Raven, designed by David Graham and Gary Panks, opened in November 1995 on what used to be farmland at the base of South Mountain. It has quickly earned a favorable reputation for its enjoyable course layout and top-of-the-line service that rivals members-only clubs. A 6,264-yard, par 72 course, The Raven offers well-manicured, wall-to-wall grass in the Midwestern traditional golf style. Thousands of pine trees line the wide, undulating fairways, giving the golfer a sense of solitude. The Raven is very playable, with challenging holes. The par 3 7th hole is very intimidating. It has water and sand all the way down the left-hand side of the fairway. The 18th hole, a par 4, is one of the best finishing holes

around. A lake sits in front of the green and to the right is a three-tiered waterfall. South Mountain rises in the background, making it scenic as well.

The Raven has played host to the Southwest section of the PGA Championship and the LPGA Mitsubishi Invitational and is the host for the Arizona Golf Association's State Stroke Play Championship.

Greens fees in high season (December 25 through May 17) are $169, cart included. In the low season (June 1 through August 31), they're $79. In the two shoulder seasons, greens fees are $115. Amenities include a golf shop, a locker facility, the Raven Grill with an outdoor pavilion and banquet facilities, and a highly regarded practice facility with a golf academy, putting green, and chipping area.

SOUTHEAST VALLEY

ASU Karsten Golf Course
1125 East Rio Salado Parkway, Tempe
(480) 921-8070
www.asukarsten.com

Karsten, opened in 1989, was designed by Pete Dye to accommodate players of all skill levels. Dye molded land near the Salt River into a stunning Scottish-style links course, with rolling hills, plenty of bunkers, and water. The 6,200-yard, par 72 course is adjacent to Tempe's Town Lake, a project that reclaimed part of the river bottom for use as an urban lake. Views of the man-made lake add beauty to the surroundings, which already provide a great view of ASU's Sun Devil Stadium leaning against "A"Mountain. With water lining the left-hand side, bunkers on the right-hand side, and water on the approach, the 18th hole has a lot of character and has become a favorite.

Karsten serves as the practice facility for ASU's men's and women's golf teams and hosts NCAA and other regional championships. The amenities include a clubhouse and golf shop, a driving range and practice area, a private dining room, lessons, and the Trophy Room restaurant. In addition, the staff stresses service, treating players well in the fashion of the best resort courses.

Greens fees, golf cart included, Friday to Sunday, in high season (January through April) are $89. In low season (June through September), they're $35. In the shoulder seasons, they're $60.

Dobson Ranch Golf Course
2155 South Dobson Road, Mesa
(480) 644-2270

Dobson Ranch, sequestered in a suburban Mesa neighborhood, rivals Phoenix's Cave Creek and Papago Park courses as one of the busiest in the state. Built in 1972, this 6,593-yard, par 72 course is a very traditional, very playable, and forgiving course. Dobson Ranch is well-groomed with fast, often undulating greens. The layout is open, but the course features many trees to make it more scenic in a traditional vein. It's also an easy course to walk. The 8th hole, sitting next to a creek that runs down the whole right side of the course, is the signature hole. The sloped green of this par 4 hole sits among bunkers on three sides.

The course features a golf shop, a clubhouse, lessons, putting greens, a chipping area, a lighted driving range, and the Ranchhouse restaurant. The greens fee in high season (November 1 through March 31) is $39, including cart. In the shoulder season (April 1 through May 30), the fee is $34, and in the low season (June through October), it's $18.

Ken McDonald Golf Course
800 East Divot Drive, Tempe
(480) 350-5250

Ken McDonald Golf Course is a traditional municipal golf course in Tempe. As such, it sees quite a bit of use; it can host almost 100,000 rounds a year. This course prides itself on running a tight ship. Despite the volume of players, tee times are the times you will be hitting the ball off the first tee. The 6,743-yard, par 72 course is like a little park tucked away in a suburban develop-

ment. McDonald is so unassuming it shares a parking lot with the Tempe YMCA. The flat layout is easy to walk, and the tree-lined fairways make it desirable to do so. Playing here is not overly demanding either. The landing areas off the tees are relatively generous. One of the more interesting holes is No. 17, a par 3. There is water to the right and bunkers to both left and right, and the green undulates. This is no cheap shot.

Tempe residents have preference in reserving tee times. Greens fees, including golf carts, are $34 for residents and $37 for nonresidents in the high season (November 1 through April 30). They are $19 and $25 in low season (May 1 through October 31).

The amenities include a pro shop, a clubhouse, lessons, club repair, practice areas, two putting greens, a chipping green, dining facilities, and Pete's 19th Hole snack shop.

Ocotillo Golf Resort
3751 South Clubhouse Drive, Chandler
(480) 917-6660, (888) 624-8899
www.ocotillogolf.com

A basic description of Ocotillo Golf Club would mention water, houses, and grass. Ocotillo's 27 holes—three separate nines called Blue, White, and Gold—feature 27 miles of shoreline. The nines are built on a traditional design, with 23 of the 27 holes involving water and houses surrounding the perimeter. Designed by Ted Robinson, Ocotillo opened in 1986 as something of a break from the beat-you-up target courses. Although the water threatens, the fairways are wide. The Blue course is shortest but has the most water, while the Gold has the least, making for the safest and easiest passage. The White is the toughest of the three. The Blue-White combination is a 6,513-yard, par 71; the White-Gold combination is a 6,592-yard, par 71; and the Gold-Blue combination is a 6,729-yard, par 72.

The 4th hole on the Gold course is a par 4 with water down the left side and water on the approach to the green. It's very pretty but not too forgiving. Similarly, the 4th hole (par 4) on the White course carries water off the tee and water off the second shot. With a waterfall to the left of the green and the clubhouse behind the green to the right, this is the prettiest hole on the course. And guess what the 8th hole on the Blue course features? More water. It's a par 4 with water down the right-hand side and more water that you have to cross twice before the green.

The greens fees are $155, golf cart included, in the high season (January through March), $95 in the shoulder seasons (April through May), $115 for October through December, and $65 in the low season (June through September).

Ocotillo has a 28,000-square-foot clubhouse facility that includes a restaurant, outdoor dining area, and special-events pavilion. The amenities also include a golf shop, lessons, a putting green, and a full driving range.

The Greater Phoenix Convention and Visitors Bureau offers a free 48-page book entitled Greater Phoenix Golf *that's filled with useful information. Call (877) 225-5749 to get a copy.*

San Marcos Golf Resort
**100 North Dakota Street, Chandler
(480) 963-3358
www.sanmarcosresort.com**
The San Marcos has a claim to being the oldest golf course in Arizona because its original nine, which is now where the Chandler Public Library sits, was built back in 1912 by Harry Collis and Will Robinson. The current 18-hole golf course is ancient by Arizona standards, too, having been opened by Collis in 1922. The San Marcos was a ritzy getaway when such celebrities as Fred Astaire, Bing Crosby, Errol Flynn, Clark Gable, and Jimmy Stewart played here in their heyday. Even Al Capone played here.

The 6,500-yard, par 72 course is a traditional, Midwestern style, built long before current water restrictions began to limit the amount of turf. Because of its age, it has a mature ambiance and plenty of grass and trees, such as salt cedar, eucalyptus, willow, and palm, that offer shade from the desert sun.

Greens fees, including cart, are $95 in high season (January through March), and they go down to $49 after 2:00 P.M. each day. In low season (June through August), fees are $32. In the spring shoulder season (April through May), the fees are $59, and $39 after 2:00 P.M. each day. Fees vary considerably, so call ahead. Hotel guests have first dibs on tee times. The amenities include a clubhouse, pro shop, driving range, putting and chipping greens, and a restaurant.

Toka Sticks Golf Club
**6910 East Williamsville Road, Mesa
(480) 988-9405
www.tokasticks.com**
Toka Sticks began as an Air Force golf course as part of Williams Air Force Base. The Gila River Indian Community bought the course in 1996 and renamed it after a traditional field-hockey game played by the women of the Pima tribe. The Pimas upgraded the course to the tune of $2 million, adding new cart paths and bunkers and sprucing up the greens. The 6,680-yard, par 72 traditional course was built in two phases. The Air Force built the first nine holes in the early 1950s, and the second nine, designed by civil engineers, were added in the early 1980s. The course is lined with trees such as eucalyptus and salt cedar. The toughest hole on the course—a par 5 of 541 yards—is saved for last. Amenities include a clubhouse, a pro shop, a driving range, putting and chipping greens, and a snack bar.

Greens fees are $50, including cart, in high season (December through March), $28 in the shoulder season (April through May), and $20 in low season (June through September).

NORTHEAST VALLEY

The Golf Club at Eagle Mountain
14915 East Eagle Mountain Parkway, Fountain Hills
(480) 816-1234
www.eaglemtn.com

Eagle Mountain lets you look down on the East Valley as you golf. Perched as it is in the foothills of the McDowell Mountains, many prominent peaks add to the course's picturesque quality. Although Eagle Mountain is not a target course—there's grass from tee to green—its landscaping is nontraditional. When you're off the fairways and greens, you're in the desert where saguaros and desert scrub dot the surroundings. The 6,755-yard, par 71 course, designed by Scott Miller and opened in January 1996, takes advantage of desert ravines to make the course, which wraps around Eagle Mountain, seem set apart rather than an expected part of the Eagle Mountain master-planned community. One of the best examples of the course's scenic charms is the closing hole. The tees are at the highest point on the golf course, with the green at the bottom of a slope. A lake and bunkers sit to the right, and the hole is framed by a dramatic view of Red Mountain.

Greens fees, including cart, range from $135 in high season to $65 in the summer. Weekdays are considerably cheaper, and there are specials for Arizona residents.

The service and ambiance of Eagle Mountain are comparable to those of a private country club. The amenities include a clubhouse, a full practice facility, a golf shop, lessons, locker rooms and showers, and The Grille restaurant.

Grayhawk Golf Club
8620 East Thompson Peak Parkway, Scottsdale
(480) 502-1800
www.grayhawkgolf.com

Grayhawk features two desert-style courses—Talon and Raptor. Set in the foothills in north Scottsdale, it offers views of the McDowell Mountains, Pinnacle Peak, and the Valley. The sheer beauty of the desert almost overwhelms the golf here. Talon, designed by David Graham and Gary Panks, is a 6,391-yard, par 72 course. Despite its wide landing areas, Talon features 14 acres less grass than Raptor and plays more like a target course. Take, for example, the 17th hole, a par 3 with an island green. Raptor, a 6,620-yard, par 72 course designed by Tom Fazio, features its own challenges, such as the 16th hole. A lake and a creek run alongside this par 3 that plays anywhere from 185 yards to 200 yards. It's definitely challenging.

Greens fees, including cart, range from $225 in the high season (late January through March) to $150 in the hot months. There are discounts for weekdays during the warmer months, as well as for twilight golfing.

Grayhawk features a 42,000-square-foot clubhouse, two dining areas, a golf shop, lessons, the Kostis-McCord Learning Center, and Phil's Grill. Phil Mickelson is the tour representative at Grayhawk.

Kierland Golf Club
15636 Clubgate Drive, Scottsdale
(480) 624-1000
www.westin.com/kierlandresort

Kierland, which opened in 1996, features three nine-hole layouts—Ironwood, Acacia, and Mesquite—that golfers can combine for a 27-hole, par 72 round. Scott Miller designed a lush parkland with undulating greens for all three nines. Each layout, named for the predominant trees in its landscape, has its own identity. A wide-open topography allows for views of Pinnacle Peak, Camelback Mountain, and the McDowell Mountains. (In fact, the beginning holes are oriented to each of these landmarks.) Interestingly, Miller's design takes advantage of golden-colored native grasses—instead of rocks and cactus—to give strong definition to the fairways. So it looks like a target course but is less forgiving. With lakes at all three finishing holes and dry washes throughout the course, Kierland offers playability and drama. The

> *A number of courses offer price breaks for twilight rounds. Duffers leave work early, grab their clubs, and play until sunset. Some courses offer special rates in the morning, others in the late afternoon. The mornings are cooler, even a bit cold in the winter. In summer the late afternoon will be very hot, but doable if you're a fanatic (and drink lots of water).*

yardages are: Ironwood-Acacia, 6,247; Acacia-Mesquite, 6,263; and Mesquite-Ironwood, 6,298.

In 2003, the club saw some big changes as the Westin Kierland Resort & Spa was opened, offering the usual amenities for those tired out from long hours on the greens. The course got a new 19,000-square-foot clubhouse, as well as enhanced bunkers and TifEagle greens.

Amenities include a clubhouse, a pro shop, food and beverage service, a practice facility, and the *Golf Digest* Golf School under the direction of pros Mike and Sandy LaBauve.

Greens fees, including cart, range widely from $170 in the high season to $75 in the low season. There are several shoulder seasons, with rates hovering at $140.

The Phoenician Golf Resort
6000 East Camelback Road, Scottsdale
(480) 423-2449
www.thephoenician.com
Since luxury is the calling card of the Phoenician resort, no one should be surprised that its semiprivate, resort-golf experience is equally luxurious, featuring impeccably manicured grass and gorgeous landscaping. The Phoenician has 27 holes, three distinct nines. These wrap around the resort so that they can be played in three 18-hole patterns. Before the Phoenician opened in 1988, a public course sat on this site, but it was completely redone for the resort. The Phoenician's facility opened with 18 holes designed by Homer Flint. Ted Robinson Sr.

designed the other nine holes, which opened in 1996.

The Oasis Course lives up to its name with plenty of water features that please the eye but trouble golfers; the Desert Course is a challenging target course that skirts the base of Camelback Mountain; and the Canyon Course is lushly landscaped and undulates across the southern slope of Camelback. The three 18-hole combinations are each a par 70. The Oasis-Desert combination is 6,300 yards; the Desert-Canyon combination is 6,068 yards; and the Oasis-Canyon combination is 6,258 yards.

The clubhouse and golf shop are as well-appointed as the resort's hotel. The package is completed by a driving range, club rentals, and lessons. Lessons can be augmented with the Swing Solution video-analysis system, which offers a complex analysis of a player's swing.

Although winter is the high season, there's no set date when the winter rates begin because overseeding with winter grass plays havoc with the schedule. Nonetheless, the high rates go into effect sometime after Labor Day. Rates are the same for guests and nonguests and range from $180 in the high season to $90 in the summer. Hotel guests have tee-time priority.

Tournament Players Club of Scottsdale
17020 North Hayden Road, Scottsdale
(480) 585-4334, (888) 400-4001
www.tpc.com
As the home of the FBR Open, the Tournament Players Club of Scottsdale can be thought of as the premier professional challenge in the Valley. There are two courses at TPC—Stadium and Desert. The team of Tom Weiskopf and Jay Morrish designed the courses to take advantage of the desert setting and excellent views of the McDowell Mountains. Both courses feature lush fairways surrounded by desert landscaping and punctuated by lakes and bunkers. The 7,089-yard, par 71 Stadium course is aptly named, using mounds and terracing to provide a stadium-like area for spectators to watch

PGA Tour events such as the FBR Open. The Desert course, a 6,423-yard, par 70, is more level than the Stadium course, and the greens are larger, making it more playable for the average golfer. Amenities include clubhouses, a golf shop, lessons, and the Grill Restaurant.

Stadium course greens fees are $218 for peak season, $139 to $186 for shoulder season, and $88 for the summer. Desert course greens fees are $53 for peak season (January 1 to May 2 and October 1 to December 31) for nonresidents, $49 for residents; and $42 for low season (May 3 to September 30) for nonresidents, $37 for residents.

Troon North Golf Club
10320 East Dynamite Boulevard, Scottsdale
(480) 585-7700
www.troongolf.com
Troon North offers two courses—Monument and Pinnacle. Monument, the older of the courses, was designed by Tom Weiskopf and Jay Morrish before they went their separate ways. Weiskopf designed the Pinnacle course. Both of these courses are tough for the average player. Golf Magazine ranks Troon North among America's Top 100. It's ranked No. 1 in Arizona by *Golfweek* magazine.

Monument's flow through its 6,636 yards is smooth, yet the par 72 course is a desert target style—very tough. Every hole presents a challenge. The 3rd hole is the Monument hole, a par 5 with a 25-foot tall boulder in the middle of the fairway. The ambiance—with views of the McDowell Mountains, Pinnacle Peak, and the Valley—convinces the golfer that the everyday world is far away. Pinnacle's front nine are the most scenic holes at Troon North. For example, the 6th hole of this 7,044-yard, par 72 course runs up the side of a hill where Pinnacle Peak dominates the background.

Troon North is a semiprivate facility, and members have preference for booking tee times. Greens fees, including cart,

vary immensely depending upon the season and how far in advance tee times are booked; weekend peak fees come in at a high of $275 and low season fees at as low as $75.

The amenities include a clubhouse, a pro shop, a driving range for players with tee times, a practice area, lessons, dining facilities, conference rooms, and The Grill at Troon North.

A great way to make friends and new golf buddies is to play in one of the many amateur golf tournaments. The events are festive and frequent. For information on upcoming amateur golf tournaments, contact the Arizona Golf Association, 7726 North 16th Street, Phoenix 85020, call (602) 944-3035 or (800) 458-8484, or check the Web at www.azgolf.org.

NORTHWEST VALLEY

The Legend at Arrowhead
21027 North 67th Avenue, Glendale
(623) 561-1902
www.americangolf.com
Arnold Palmer and Ed Seay designed this traditional, grass-from-tee-to-green course as the centerpiece of the master-planned Arrowhead Ranch community in Glendale. This area is booming because its gray-black hills and generous lots keep suburbia looking like the desert. Although the Legend is a traditional course featuring six lakes, it is built on those dark hills and can't be mistaken for a Midwestern-style course. This 7,005-yard, par 72 course becomes much more difficult when played from the championship tees, but if you choose your tee boxes well, it can be very enjoyable. In fact, golf doesn't get any better than the 5th hole. It's a 426-yard, par 4 that's played from elevated tees to an hourglass-shaped green with water on the right.

Greens fees, cart included, vary seasonally from $55 to $175. Amenities include a clubhouse, restaurant, a pro shop, lessons, a driving range, a practice area, Nike Golf Learning Center, and an all-grass chipping and putting green.

SOUTHWEST VALLEY

The Wigwam Resort
451 North Litchfield Road,
Litchfield Park
(623) 935-9414, (800) 909-4224
www.wigwamresort.com
The Wigwam Resort is another bastion of the old high life of Arizona resorts. Originally built as the private domain of Goodyear executives, the Wigwam is open to those who can pay the price for these elegantly rustic surroundings. And the same goes for its three golf courses. The Wigwam has earned *Golf Magazine*'s Silver Medal Resort honors and *Links Magazine*'s Best of Golf Award. In addition, the Gold course was ranked as the top resort course on *Golf Digest*'s list of Arizona's Best Courses.

The Gold course features a traditional layout designed by Robert Trent Jones Sr. A 7,074-yard, par 72 course, the Gold is a tough one to play with elevated greens, narrow landing areas, bunkers, and water. At 6,085 yards, the par 70 Blue course is the shortest layout at the Wigwam, but that doesn't make it the easiest. It's a fairly unforgiving links-style course. The 6,865-yard, par 70 Red course was designed by Arizona's Robert "Red" Lawrence and V. O. "Red" Allen, and features lakes, creeks, and huge greens. It's a traditional layout that is something like comfort food compared with the others, although it still presents a challenge.

The greens fees for all three courses are $120 for high season, $95 for shoulder season, and from $37 to $65 for low season. All fees include carts. Amenities include a clubhouse, pro shop, driving range, and practice area as well as tennis courts, spa, dining facilities, and lessons.

SPECTATOR SPORTS

Fall, winter, spring, or summer, sports fans won't have any trouble getting their fill of good things to see in Phoenix and the Valley of the Sun. The market is one of the few in the country to boast four big-league franchises—football's Arizona Cardinals, baseball's World Series champions the Arizona Diamondbacks, hockey's Phoenix Coyotes, and basketball's Phoenix Suns.

The Valley also welcomes Major League Baseball's Anaheim Angels, Oakland Athletics, Milwaukee Brewers, Chicago Cubs, San Francisco Giants, Seattle Mariners, and San Diego Padres for spring training in the Cactus League. The other teams in the league—the Diamondbacks, Colorado Rockies, and Chicago White Sox—play their home games in Tucson but are frequently in the Valley for games against their league opponents. In the 2001 World Series at Bank One Ballpark, the Diamondbacks beat the New York Yankees in games six and seven to win the World Series for the first time.

Bubbling just below that level in the Valley's sea of sports is the WNBA franchise, the Phoenix Mercury, and the two-time Arena Football champions, the Arizona Rattlers. Meanwhile, Major League Baseball's Arizona Fall Baseball League lets Valley dwellers and winter visitors get a peek at up-and-coming baseball players.

In addition to the professional sports, Arizona State University's Sun Devils field competitive teams in football (men's), basketball (men's and women's), baseball (men's), and fast-pitch softball (women's). The Valley is also home to such annual events as the Phoenix Open, a natural in a place where golf is the preeminent participation sport, and the Fiesta Bowl, which hosted the first unified national college championship game in 1999.

The Valley loves auto racing, and crowds of 100,000 show up on race day for the NASCAR Winston Cup series in the fall and the Indy Racing League Phoenix 200 in the spring at the relatively remote Phoenix International Raceway on the far west side of the Valley.

ARENA FOOTBALL

Arizona Rattlers
America West Arena, 201 East Jefferson Street, Phoenix
(602) 514-8300
www.azrattlers.com
Ever since America West Arena opened in 1992, the expansion team Arizona Rattlers have been a major participant in the Arena Football League. Football purists may scoff at the indoor arena game, which is played on a 50-yard field with eight players on the field, but tickets are very affordable and you will appreciate sitting in air-conditioned comfort. Players play offense and defense with the exception of the kicker, quarterback, offensive specialist, kick returner, and two defensive specialists. However, the speedy, offense-oriented contests pack about 16,000 fans into the arena on summer weekends. The off-field atmosphere is raucous, with lots of flashing lights, ear-splitting music, and sound effects. There are plenty of give-aways and half-time and pregame festivities that feature the team mascot, Fang, a fierce-looking biker who rides into the arena on a huge Harley to rev up the crowd's response (and his motorcycle).

The Rattlers have played under coach Danny White, the former Dallas Cowboys quarterback, since their inception. In 2003 Rattlers wide receiver Hunkie Cooper became The Arena Football League's all-time leader in kickoff returns, wide receiver Randy Gatewood was names the league's Ironman of the Year, and the Rattlers became the first team in AFL history to score 80-plus points in consecutive games. Rattlers' gear is available at the Team Shop in the arena. The team is involved in many community events and sponsors a flag-football tournament.

The Rattlers' 14-game season begins in April and ends in August. Season-ticket rates range from $40 to $364, which includes a preseason game and the first shot at buying playoff tickets. Single-game tickets range from $5.00 to $48.00.

AUTO RACING

Firebird International Raceway
20000 Maricopa Road, Chandler
(602) 268-0200
www.firebirdraceway.com
Drag racing rules at Firebird. Funny cars and jet dragsters roar around one of three tracks so the events are noisy and festive. The east track is 1.25 miles long and features 10 turns. The west track is 1.2 miles long with 11 turns. The Firebird Course is 1.6 miles with 14 turns. Drag racing is held most Friday nights throughout the year. Major annual events at Firebird include the NHRA National Time Trials, the NHRA Checker Schuck's Kragen Nationals, and the NHRA Division 7 Opener. Adjacent Firebird Lake also is the site of drag-boat racing. Admission varies with events. Firebird Raceway is easily accessible from Interstate 10, just west of the Maricopa Road exit.

Phoenix International Raceway
7602 South 115th Avenue, Phoenix
(602) 252-3833,
(602) 252-2227 (box office)
www.phoenixintlraceway.com
Situated in view of the ruggedly gorgeous Estrella Mountains, Phoenix International Raceway serves as a setting for many TV commercials that highlight cars moving against a pristine desert backdrop. The track is in use 300 or more days a year for auto testing, driving schools, commercials, and, especially, the racing events.

The raceway, described as the fastest 1-mile oval in the world, opened in 1964 in an unincorporated part of Maricopa County about 30 miles west of downtown Phoenix. Back then its location was way, way out in the Valley, and even now, with tendrils of development creeping out that way, it remains an isolated desert experience. The NASCAR Winston Cup, held in November, draws about 100,000 people to the D-shaped track. The Indy Racing League's Phoenix 200 in mid-March draws about 35,000, as does the Copper World Indy 200 in mid-March. Schedules are available at the track's office in Phoenix.

To reach the track from Phoenix, go west on I-10 to 115th Avenue. Head south on 115th about 4 miles until 115th Avenue takes a turn to the west into Baseline Road.

BASEBALL

Arizona Diamondbacks
Bank One Ballpark, 401 East Jefferson
Street, Phoenix
(602) 462-6500
www.azdiamondbacks.com
Just about the biggest event in Arizona sports was the incredible victory of the Diamondbacks over the New York Yankees to win the 2001 World Series Championship. In a memorable World Series, the 1-2 pitching force of co-MVPs Randy Johnson and Curt Schilling brought owner Jerry Colangelo and the state of Arizona its first World Series win.

The Diamondbacks' story began with the Phoenix Suns basketball team. Suns owner Jerry Colangelo announced in 1993, the year his basketball team went to the NBA finals, that he was putting together an ownership group to try to purchase a Major League Baseball franchise for Phoenix. In 1995 Colangelo received the franchise, which would start play in 1998.

Almost immediately, work began on Bank One Ballpark (affectionately dubbed BOB), a retractable-roof stadium with a natural-grass playing surface. It was built in the current MLB fashion to offer the old-time, single-use baseball stadium feel. At the same time, it is air-conditioned to

make a capacity crowd of 49,033 comfortable during the summertime game schedule. BOB even boasts a swimming pool for patrons who want to stay wet during a game. The opening of the roof even has its own dramatic theme music. In 2000 the team revealed its mascot, D. Baxter the Bobcat.

When former New York Yankees coach Buck Showalter signed on in 1995, 18 months before the Diamondbacks would play their first game, the tone was set for good, fundamental baseball. Alas, it was still an expansion team despite having a team of talented veterans—including gold glover Matt Williams at third base and former St. Louis ace Andy Benes pitching—and exciting prospects such as former Olympic first baseman Travis Lee. The Diamondbacks stuck to the bottom of the National League West division in 1998. The next year, the D-Backs, with the help of demon pitcher Randy Johnson, took the National League's Western Division Championship. For a new team, the Diamondbacks have quickly moved to the top ranks of the majors.

Season tickets range from $456.50 for the uppermost level to $6,000 plus for the Clubhouse level. Single-game tickets range from $7.00 to $95.00.

There are approximately 33,600 parking spaces available within a 15-minute walk of BOB, which (using a 1.5 persons per car average) would seem to mean there's enough parking for everyone. However, BOB is downtown and thus take up parking spaces. The Diamondbacks' home schedule also will overlap with home games of the Phoenix Suns, Phoenix Coyotes, Phoenix Mercury, and Arizona Rattlers on many nights, which means an additional 10,000 to 19,000 people downtown on some game nights. Though parking hassles have been minimal, you should allow for extra time to park if you want to arrive in time for the national anthem.

The best way to get there from outlying areas is to take I-10 to the Seventh Street exit and head south to Washington Street. Then head west to Fourth Street, where BOB sits just 1 block south. Canny drivers will avoid parking headaches by getting downtown early and parking blocks away from the stadium. The walk will help burn off some of those hot dogs.

Looking for baseball tickets? The Arizona Diamondbacks release 400 tickets on game days that sell for $1.00 each. The bargain pricing helps reduce scalping outside the ballpark, but the seats are placed way up in the stratosphere, so bring binoculars if you have them. You'll have to pick these tickets up in person, so call first for details, (602) 462-6500.

Cactus League
120 North Center Street, Mesa
(480) 827-4700
www.cactus-league.com

The Cactus League is Arizona's wing of Major League Baseball's spring training. Ten teams begin working out in Arizona in the last week of February, which still counts as winter in all but baseball's peculiar logic. They play exhibition games against one another through March, when the regular season begins.

Compared with Florida, where the other 20 MLB teams take their training, Arizona is a relative newcomer. The Cactus League's roots stretch back to 1947 when the Cleveland Indians moved their spring training to Tucson and convinced the San Francisco Giants to hold theirs in Phoenix. In 1951 Del Webb, the builder who created Sun City, was a co-owner of the New York Yankees and had his team switch places with the Giants for one season of spring training. In 1952 the Chicago Cubs, dissatisfied with spring training on Catalina Island where they could get no other teams to come, settled in the Valley for spring training.

For most of the 1950s and 1960s, the Cactus League was anchored by the

Indians, Giants, and Cubs, with a number of other teams, including the Boston Red Sox, Baltimore Orioles, and Houston Colt .45s, filling in a fourth slot. With the 1969 expansion, the Seattle Pilots and the San Diego Padres settled into the Cactus League as well. (Both are still in the league, although the Pilots are now known as the Milwaukee Brewers.) The league had eight teams for most of the 1970s and 1980s, seven in the Valley and one in Tucson.

In the late 1980s the original Cactus League team, the Cleveland Indians, packed its bags and moved to Florida, and the Arizona league looked in serious danger of collapse as Florida had passed legislation to make it more attractive for teams to hold spring training there. Even the Cubs, whose games were the highest-attended in spring training, were thinking of moving to the East Coast. A group of Valley boosters formed the Cactus League Association, and then-Governor Rose Mofford created the Arizona Baseball Commission in efforts to keep spring training in Arizona.

With the addition of the Arizona Diamondbacks and Chicago White Sox, the Cactus League now stands at a healthy 10 teams in seven stadiums. The current teams have long-term leases, and all the stadiums are either new or have been renovated in the past decade.

The volunteer Cactus League Association says the economic impact of spring training on Arizona, thanks to the teams and fans who spend money here, is about $200 million annually.

Ticket information changes each spring. The Cactus League Association can provide league schedules and stadium locations, but has no hand in ticketing. For tickets, fans can call the individual teams or stadiums (see subsequent list), or Ticketmaster, (480) 784-4444, depending on which ticket agency covers games at a particular ballpark.

The league's current participants, their spring-training ballparks, and the phone numbers for each team's ticket office are:

- Anaheim Angels, Tempe Diablo Stadium, 2200 West Alameda Drive, Tempe, (602) 438-9300
- Arizona Diamondbacks and Chicago White Sox, Tucson Electric Park, 2400 East Ajo Way, Tucson, (866) 672-1343
- Chicago Cubs, Hohokam Park, 1235 North Center Street, Mesa, (480) 964-4467
- Colorado Rockies, Hi Corbett Field, East Broadway Boulevard and Randolph Way, Tucson, (520) 327-9467, (800) 388-7625
- Kansas City Royals, Texas Rangers, Surprise Stadium, 15754 North Bullard, Surprise, (623) 594-5600
- Milwaukee Brewers, Maryvale Baseball Park, 3600 North 51st Avenue, Maryvale, (623) 245-5500
- Oakland Athletics, Phoenix Municipal Stadium, 5999 East Van Buren Street, Phoenix, (602) 392-0217
- San Diego Padres and Seattle Mariners, Peoria Sports Complex, 16101 North 83rd Avenue, Peoria, (623) 878-4337, (800) 409-1511
- San Francisco Giants, Scottsdale Stadium, 7408 East Osborn Road, Scottsdale, (480) 312-2586

MLB's Arizona Fall Baseball League
10201 South 51st Street, Phoenix (480) 496-6700

Compared with spring training and the Diamondbacks, the Fall League is a well-kept secret with a total attendance of about 50,000 people at 138 games. Here's your chance to see the stars of tomorrow play. The league is totally owned by Major League Baseball so that each of the 30 teams has a piece of it.

A developmental league that began in October 1992, the Fall League is essentially an all-star league of double-A and triple-A players. Each MLB team sends six such prospects to the league, and they are assigned to one of the league's six teams. About 400 of the players from 1992 through 1997 graduated to the majors, including such stars as the Los Angeles Dodgers' Mike Piazza and the Boston Red Sox's Nomar Garciaparra. In 1994 the league drew its biggest crowds ever because of double-A player Michael Jordan, who had already made his name in some other sport.

The schedule is set by about the middle of June, and the games are played from the beginning of October through November. Game times are 1:05 and 7:05 P.M. Season passes and schedule details are available through the league office. Plenty of walk-up tickets ($5.00 for adults, $4.00 for seniors and children) are available on game days at the individual stadiums.

The teams and their stadiums are:

- Grand Canyon Rafters and Scottsdale Scorpions, Scottsdale Stadium, 7408 East Osborn Road, Scottsdale, (480) 941-1930
- Maryvale Saguaros, Maryvale Baseball Park, 3600 North 51st Avenue, Phoenix, (623) 247-2727
- Mesa Solar Sox, HoHoKam Park, 1235 North Center, Mesa, (800) 905-3315
- Peoria Javelinas, Peoria Sports Complex, 16101 North 83rd Avenue, Peoria, (623) 486-2800
- Phoenix Desert Dogs, Phoenix Municipal Stadium, 5999 East Van Buren Street, Phoenix, (602) 681-9363

BASKETBALL

Phoenix Mercury
America West Arena,
201 East Jefferson Street, Phoenix
(602)514-8333,
(602) 252-9622 box office
www.wnba.com/mercury
In 1997, the WNBA's inaugural year, the Phoenix Mercury professional women's

basketball team won the Western Conference title. The team drew an average attendance of 13,703, tops in the eight-team league. Team owner Jerry Colangelo, confident that there was an untapped market in women's basketball, hired Cheryl Miller to be head coach and general manager of the Mercury. Miller was known for building winning records as a coach at USC from 1993 to 1995. The Mercury had a 16-12 record the first year.

Since then, the WNBA has seen more expansion with two new teams and a 30-game regular-season schedule. The play-offs also changed from single-game semifinal and final rounds to two best-of-three series.

Fans of the Mercury are noisy and festive, making these games a lot of fun to attend.

Ticket prices range from $10 to $80 per game, while season tickets range from $189 to $1,755 on the floor. Season tickets include a preseason game and first dibs on postseason tickets. For individual tickets, call (480) 784-4444; for group or season tickets, call (602) 252-9622.

Why wait in line at the ticket booth when you can avoid it with a little planning? If you order early enough, you can have tickets mailed to you and walk right through the turnstiles when you arrive for the event. Another approach is to order tickets beforehand and have them waiting at the will-call window, where the lines are always shorter.

Phoenix Suns
America West Arena,
201 East Jefferson Street
(602) 379-7900,
(602) 379-7867 box office
www.nba.com/suns
The Phoenix Suns opened up shop in 1968 as an NBA expansion franchise, the first big-league club in Phoenix. Befitting an expansion franchise, their first few seasons

Phoenix: Sports Town USA

Why are Phoenix and the Valley of the Sun so big on sports? Is it something in the water? Is it the high proportion of Chicago-area transplants longing for their Bears, Bulls, Cubs, White Sox, and Blackhawks?

A cynic might say that the media here hyped sports into a big thing. The cynic would be right, but the media are just playing to the market.

Let's go in for a little pop psychology here and attribute the hold sports has on the Valley to the huge number of people who have relocated and are now seeking some kind of hook to make them feel Arizonan. Sports teams with their geographic names fill the bill easily. Relocating from the frozen north, many people feel like they're just camping out here in their initial years. As vast and spread out as it is, the Valley hardly seems settled if you've relocated from a megalopolis. With earning a living as their major preoccupation, many transplants have a hard time sinking roots in their communities. They buy the house and meet the neighbors, but the very architecture of homes built in the last two decades (cinder-block fences and the lack of front porches) combined with increasingly tight schedules keep casual neighborly contact—something you almost can't avoid back East—to a minimum. Although people often work hard to become part of their communities by forming neighborhood associations and block watches, the common denominators to conversations are often sports.

Meet a stranger, and within three minutes one of you will remark about a sports team with a comment like, "How about those D-Backs last night!" Besides, people working that hard at everything need something to distract them.

When the Phoenix Suns landed Charles Barkley in 1992 and catalyzed the team to only its second run to the NBA finals, for the first time in almost anyone's memory strangers in the Valley had something to talk about besides the weather. The phrase "How about those Suns?" had the power to form instant bonds. When a Suns game was on, particularly once the playoffs started, everyone seemed to be tuned to KTAR listening to play-by-play announcer Al McCoy. In fact, if you were sitting at an intersection with the car radio on, you could expect passing pedestrians to wave and ask for the score.

But not everybody was sold. Many people in the Valley revel in keeping their old allegiances. When the Suns met the Bulls in the finals, it was not uncommon to see Bulls banners on cars and homes, although there were many more "Go Suns" markings out there. This old allegiance thing crosses many lines. Some love life in the Valley, but they hang on to their old team as a link to their old home, even though they don't want to shovel snow anymore. Others see the Valley as just a stopping-off point in their lives, and they'll stick with whatever city they really care about.

The oddest of these are the longtime Valley dwellers, some of them natives, who refuse to switch allegiance from the Dallas Cowboys to the Arizona Cardinals, which, by the way, is the only Arizona big-league franchise that doesn't play in downtown Phoenix. They say that before the Cardinals got here in 1988, the Cowboys were the team they followed and they see Dallas as their home team. When the Cowboys play the Cardinals, the only home game sure to sell out in a Cardinals season, the Cowboys' fans envelop the Cards' red-garbed fans in a sea of blue.

However, even those naysayers are a testament to the sports obsession in the Valley. After the Suns' big run, forests of backboards, portable and permanent, popped up seemingly overnight in the acres of tiled-roof Valley developments.

Of course, the pop psychology goes out the window when you consider that there isn't much home-team identification when it comes to motor sports and golf, which are both big in the Valley sports scene. So there must be another factor (or factors) to the sports craze here.

One of them is the environment. With its almost perpetual sunshine and low humidity, the Valley is a comfortable place to play sports almost year-round. Even in the dog days of the summer monsoon, evening recreation is tolerable. Golfers golf. Kids shoot hoops. Tennis courts jam. Soccer leagues fill playgrounds. Softballers and Little Leaguers play on their respective diamonds. That's not to mention swimming, running, skiing, snowboarding, and mountain biking, all of which have their own adherents. Many, many Valley dwellers are active in their leisure time, and their participation in sports tends to make them more interested in them. Add in couch potato sports watchers, who probably outnumber the active types, and you've got an extremely fertile field for sports obsession.

One of the interesting things about the Valley's sports nuttiness is that it's one of the few things that unites the average citizens with Phoenix's movers and shakers. Valley boosters have been obsessed with getting major sports events, such as the Super Bowl, to town for decades--at least since the formation of the committee that created the Fiesta Bowl in 1969. Although many average Joes resent the deals the movers and shakers cut with sports franchises to build stadiums and arenas, many more follow the games.

In fact, the downtown redevelopment of Phoenix has hinged on the Suns' popularity. When owner Jerry Colangelo moved the team to its downtown America West Arena digs in 1992, smaller entrepreneurs began to see the value in opening such businesses as sports bars and restaurants downtown. The success of the Suns put Colangelo in the position to be the linchpin in turning the Winnipeg Jets NHL franchise into the Phoenix Coyotes and to lure Major League Baseball here, making the Valley one of the few markets with four major-league teams. Colangelo also got Phoenix in on the ground floor of the WNBA, which seems likely to be a league of the future. With both the baseball stadium and arena drawing thousands downtown, redevelopment is in full swing. So much development raised the question of whether the Valley community can support all these teams. Signs seem to point to yes.

So, yeah, Phoenix is a sports town. Most definitely.

were terrible. Their bad luck didn't end with a 16–66 mark in their first season. Thanks to the last-place finish, the Suns had the opportunity to flip a coin with expansion mates the Milwaukee Bucks to decide who would get the No. 1 pick in the 1969 draft. The Bucks won the toss and got Lew Alcindor (soon to be much better known as Kareem Abdul-Jabbar). In 1971 he led the Bucks to the NBA Championship. The Suns are still waiting for their turn.

The team made a run to the finals in the 1975–76 season, parlaying up a 42–40 season record. When they met the Boston Celtics in the finals, the series was tied after four games. The Suns took Game 5 to triple overtime at the Boston Garden before losing to the Celtics. They lost the series in the next game. The NBA finals didn't see another triple overtime game for 17 years, until (guess who?) the Phoenix Suns met the Chicago Bulls in 1993. Although the Suns, led by the irrepressible Charles Barkley, won the triple overtime this time, the Bulls still prevailed in six games thanks to Michael Jordan. The list of impressive Suns players goes on to include Kevin Johnson, Dan Majerle, Stephon Marbury, and Shawn Marion.

The Suns have sold out America West Arena's 19,023 basketball seats ever since the arena was opened in the fall of 1992. Tickets range from $10.00 in the uppermost seats to $5.00 on the floor. Season tickets range from $500 in the uppermost seats to four digits for the club seats. The Suns ticket office can be reached at (602) 379-7867.

COLLEGE SPORTS

Arizona State University Sun Devils Ticket Office, Sun Devil Stadium, Stadium Drive, Tempe
(480) 965-2381, (888) SUN-DVLS
www.sundevils.com
When the Sun Devils football team made its 1996 run to the Rose Bowl, it capti-

vated the Valley, often outdrawing the NFL's Cardinals in the same stadium each fall weekend. Average home-game attendance was 63,884 that year.

The university's athletics programs have been an important part of the Valley's spectator sports spectrum since their inception. As is the case with most sports programs, the men's ball teams—football, basketball, and baseball—have the highest profile. However, there is a strong following for the school's women's basketball and softball teams as well.

ASU has 21 varsity sports and has won 129 national championships, including 11 in women's golf and 5 in baseball. Former Sun Devils include "Mr. October" Reggie Jackson, former Dallas Cowboys quarterback and current Arizona Rattlers coach Danny White, and golfer Heather Farr, who died in 1993.

Football, far and away, is the dominant sport in terms of fan support and can fill Sun Devil Stadium's 73,379 seats. (Somehow they squeezed 74,963 people in to see ASU beat California, 35–7, on November 9, 1996.) The annual game with arch rival University of Arizona is one of the most spirited and competitive events in college football.

Men's and women's basketball teams play at the University Activity Center, a 14,198-seat facility that was built in 1974 at a cost of $8 million. Baseball players try to knock it out of the park at Packard Stadium, a 7,875-capacity ballpark built in 1974. Softball pitchers do their windmill windup at Sun Devil Club Stadium, a 600-seat field. Track and field events take place at the Sun Angel Stadium/Joe Selleh Track, which has a 5,000-seat grandstand and movable bleachers that can accommodate another 4,000 for big events such as the annual Sun Angel Track Classic. There's an aquatic center for the swimming teams, and ASU Karsten Golf Course gives the golf teams dedicated space for practice. The Sun Devil Ticket Office has information on all sports tickets at ASU.

Tostitos Fiesta Bowl
120 South Ash Avenue, Tempe
(480) 350-0900
www.fiesta-bowl.com
The Fiesta Bowl is part of the College Football Bowl Alliance, formed in 1997 to create a system to guarantee a true national championship game each year. The championship game rotates among the four members of the alliance, which, besides the Fiesta Bowl, includes the Sugar, Orange, and Rose Bowls.

The idea that the Valley should have a football bowl game was first floated in a speech by ASU president B. Homer Durham at an athletic awards banquet in 1968. Boosters seized on the idea and formed a group called the Arizona Sports Foundation. They prepared a pitch that emphasized that the Rose Bowl was the only bowl game being played outside the South, that Arizona's climate would be a natural ally in the game's success, and that a number of worthy Western Athletic Conference teams had been overlooked by the existing bowls. They also framed it as a charity event that would aid the fight against drug abuse. They made the pitch to the NCAA in 1970 and were turned down. The next year, though, the NCAA gave its approval.

The first Fiesta Bowl was played December 27, 1971, with ASU beating Florida State before a crowd of 51,098. CBS televised the Fiesta Bowl from 1974-77 and NBC took over in 1978. Over the years the Fiesta Bowl spawned dozens of auxiliary events including the Fiesta Bowl Parade, four tennis events, a three-on-three basketball tournament, and a gigantic New Year's block party in downtown Tempe. In 1987 the Fiesta Bowl pitted top-ranked Miami against second-ranked Penn State in a national championship that sold out the stadium with a crowd of 73,098 and a television audience of 70 million. The Fiesta Bowl played host to the first unified National Championship Game in 1999, at Arizona State University's Sun Devil Stadium. Ticket and event information is available by calling (480) 350-0911 or (800) 635-5748.

DOG RACING

Phoenix Greyhound Park
3801 East Washington Street, Phoenix
(602) 273-7181
www.phoenixgreyhoundpark.com
Even people who never bet on the dogs can enjoy an evening out at Phoenix Greyhound Park. The ambiance at the clubhouse restaurant, with excellent views of the track and tableside TVs for watching the races and offtrack races around the country, is comfortable and, well, club-like. Dinners are buffet-style and reasonably priced, and servers can even explain the betting to novices. If you choose instead to sit out in the grandstands, the trackside cafe is your food option.

The track was established in 1954 and underwent a $20-million renovation in 1990. The quarter-mile track is used for both 550-yard and 680-yard races all year long. Races from other tracks are also piped in, and off-track wagers are taken.

Admission is $3.00 for the air-conditioned clubhouse and free for the grandstand. General and preferred parking is free every day; valet parking is available for $2.00.

FOOTBALL

Arizona Cardinals
8701 South Hardy Drive, Tempe
(602) 379-0102
www.azcardinals.com
The short course in Arizona Cardinals history goes like this: 1899, Morgan Athletic Club (Chicago); 1900, Racine (Chicago) Normals; 1901-1921, Racine (Chicago) Cardinals; 1922-1959, Chicago Cardinals; 1960-1987, St. Louis Cardinals; 1988-1993, Phoenix Cardinals; 1994-present, Arizona Cardinals. The oldest continuously operating professional sports franchise (dating from 1898) represented the NFL's

As almost anywhere, parking is some-thing of a hassle when you're trying to reach a sporting event. Football tail-gaters have the right idea. Get to the event early and make a day of it. Most facilities have concession stands and restaurants to make it easier to pass the time before the event. If you're heading to Cardinals or Sun Devils events, there are numerous restaurants, taverns, and coffee shops within walking distance in downtown Tempe where you can enjoy a meal before or after the game. The same holds true for America West Arena and Bank One Ballpark events in down-town Phoenix.

youngest team in 2001. Coming off a dis-appointing 3–13 season in 2000 that included a head coaching change midway through the campaign, the young Cardi-nals entered the 2001 season with few in the media and public expecting success. The energy and passion of new Head Coach Dave McGinnis combined with the commitment and desire of a hungry young team resulted in more than double the number of wins from the year before and a team widely considered to be one of the most promising in the NFL today. Season highlights included big upsets over Oak-land and Philadelphia on the road and a strong finish, winning five out of the final eight games. The Cardinals' playoff run fell just short as they finished the year 7–9. Both 2002 and 2003 were disappointing to the fans, as the Cardinals finished 5–11 and 4–12 respectively. With new Head Coach Dennis Green at the helm, fans are looking forward to the 2004 season.

Represented by players like all-pro wide receiver David Boston; Rookie of the Year candidate offensive lineman Leonard Davis; hometown hero quarterback Jake Plummer; and fan favorite free safety Kwamie Lassiter, the Arizona Cardinals have a bright future in the Valley of the Sun. The future became even brighter in

2000 with the passing of Proposition 302, clearing the way for the construction of a new multipurpose facility, which will include a new football stadium for the team. The new stadium will offer fans a first-class game-day experience. Air-conditioning, a retractable roof, individual seats with cup holders, exclusive club level seating and lounges, increased restrooms and concessions, and even a retractable field will make it the NFL's premier foot-ball venue, affording the Cardinals unprecedented home-field advantages and fans spectacular views and amenities.

The Cardinals currently play their home games at Sun Devil Stadium on the campus of Arizona State University. In 2002 the Cardinals offered the lowest ticket price in the NFL. Single-game tick-ets ranged from $25 end-zone seats to $220 50-yard-line loge-level seats. Season tickets are offered with an exclusive 10 to 20 percent discount on all locations. Sea-son tickets are available in the lower level beginning at $225 for end-zone seats, $280 for corner end-zone seats, and $360 to $440 for sideline seats. Season ticket holders in 2002 also receive, among many other exclusive amenities, a free Cardinals-fan jersey for every two tickets purchased. Also, season ticket holders will have exclu-sive priority on seat selection in the Cardi-nals new stadium over subsequent ticket sales campaigns to the general public. Anticipating continued success on and off the field, now is definitely the best time to check out the team. To learn more about season tickets or to reserve seats, call the Cardinals at (602) 379–0102 or visit the team Web site, www.azcardinals.com.

Stadium parking is offered for season ticket holders, and there are many lots close to the stadium that provide paid parking. Don't try to park in ASU lots, which require a campus parking decal.

Sun Devil Stadium is easily reached from U.S. Highway 60, where you can take either the Rural Road or Mill Avenue exits north. From Mill Avenue, the stadium is a right turn off Fifth Street straight onto Stadium Drive. From Rural Road, take a

Getting Tickets

- **Box Office:** Most of the sports arenas also have their own box offices that will be happy to sell you tickets if they have them. When events are sold out, many people can locate seats by asking around and networking with coworkers who own tickets that they are unable to use. Etiquette demands that you repay the owner for the face value of the tickets. Be aware that this rule goes away during playoffs and important rivalry games. Then the value of the tickets is what the market will bear.

- **Ticketmaster:** Ticketmaster is the major agency offering off-site sales of tickets to sporting events. Ticketmaster does add fees for credit-card service over the phone and for mailing. You can reach Ticketmaster at (480) 784-4444.

- **Ticket Brokers:** Don't call them scalpers, please. Reselling tickets at a handsome markup, a practice that's known as scalping elsewhere, is perfectly legal in Arizona. You just can't do it right outside the venue itself. So ticket brokers tend to park themselves about a block from any venue, asking passersby if they need to buy or sell tickets. If the brokers are overstocked, their markup tends to go down as the event gets closer.

Are those tickets real or counterfeit, though? There is no way to protect yourself from a ripoff in a situation like that. If you can't get tickets from the venue itself (either because it doesn't have the seats you want or because the show or game is sold out), you'll be better off visiting one of the 20 or so ticket brokers who are listed in the Phoenix Yellow Pages. There'll be someone at their offices who's accountable if your tickets turn out to be counterfeits.

A $3.50 ticket to a sold-out 1998 Arizona Diamondbacks vs. Seattle Mariners game went for $15 at one of these ticket brokers' offices. We didn't feel scalped. We got to see Ken Griffey Jr. hit a home run, after all.

---

left on University Drive and then take a right onto Stadium Drive. However, you can avoid many headaches by parking some distance away in the lots and streets around Mill Avenue or Rural Road.

GOLF TOURNAMENTS

Phoenix Open
7226 North 16th Street, Phoenix
(602) 870-4431
www.phoenixopen.com
The Phoenix Open is the one of the top-drawing sporting events in Arizona, attracting the 500,000 spectators in 2004 for the weeklong event, held the third week of January at the Tournament Players Club of Scottsdale, 17020 North Hayden Road, Scottsdale. Although its now officially named the FBR Open, everyone still calls it the Phoenix Open.

It wasn't always that way. Only about 600 people were in the gallery to see Ralph Guldahl finish five strokes better than John Perelli to win the tournament in 1932. The tournament was abandoned during the depths of the Depression but was revived by the special events

---

Always bring sunscreen and a hat to outdoor events in Arizona. Sunburn can happen with less than 20 minutes' exposure.

committee of the Phoenix Chamber of Commerce in 1939. The committee was expanded to become the Thunderbirds, a service group that has been putting on the Phoenix Open ever since. The Thunderbirds put on the Thunderbird Collegiate Invitational and the Thunderbird Junior and Senior Golf Classics each summer. Most of the Thunderbirds' efforts support the new Thunderbirds Golf Club and First Tee Youth Academy in South Phoenix, which will cost over $11 million and is being funded by a combination of sources, including an ongoing fund-raising campaign and operating revenues. The 27-hole complex includes a nine-hole par-3 Short Course, created by renowned designer Tom Fazio.

The 2004 Phoenix Open raised more than $1 million in donations to support various area charities, including the Boys and Girls Clubs and the Special Olympics.

The Phoenix Open PGA event includes such pretournament activities as a junior golf clinic, four Pro-Am events, a pro-celebrity shootout, and a long-drive contest.

Prices are $25 for general admission each day. Children 17 and younger get in free with an adult. Information is available year-round at the Thunderbirds office number listed above.

---

i *Outdoor arenas tend to charge more for shaded seats. Consider spending the extra money. While the sun may not seem so bad at first, by halftime you may be begging for a time out.*

Ping Banner Health
1441 North 12th Street, Phoenix
(602) 495-4653
For almost 20 years, the LPGA has been coming to the Moon Valley Country Club for this tournament, held the third week of March. At 6,435 yards, Moon Valley's course is the longest on the LPGA tour. With a million-dollar purse, this has

become the fifth-highest-ranked event on the tour. The event, which benefits the cancer programs at Banner Health System medical centers in Arizona, draws tens of thousands of spectators over the course of a week. Tickets are $15 a day and $50 for the full week. Moon Valley Country Club is on Moon Valley Road in Phoenix, north of the intersection of Thunderbird Road and Coral Gables Drive.

TENNIS

Franklin Templeton Tennis Classic
Princess Resort, 7575 East Princess Drive, Scottsdale
(480) 473-4444
http://Arizona.scottsdaletennis.com
The Franklin Templeton Tennis Classic is the ATP Tour event in Arizona and brings top stars from around the world. The tournament, which draws about 50,000 people for the week, includes matches by 32 singles players and 16 doubles teams. Surrounding events include the annual draw party, celebrity auction, and the ATP Tour kids' day. Tickets range from $14 to $72 per match, and event packages are $110 and up. It is held the first week in March.

HOCKEY

Phoenix Coyotes
Glendale Arena, 9400 West Maryland Avenue, Glendale
(623) 772-3200
www.phoenixcoyotes.com
Arizona sports fans were thrilled when hockey legend Wayne Gretzky—the NHL's all-time greatest player—joined developer Steve Ellman in the purchase of the Phoenix Coyotes. When the new ownership team took over the hockey club in February 2001, Gretzky assumed the role of managing partner and wasted no time making changes to the Valley's ice-hockey team. Gretzky hired a front office consisting of proven, experienced hockey men including Cliff Fletcher, Michael Barnett, and Dave Draper. This hockey man-

Best Seats in the House: Valley Sports Bars

The big game you wanted to see sold out? Tickets too expensive? Don't get angry, get smart! There's an inexpensive way to see most of the Valley games, and you're guaranteed a chance to get a good seat.

As a big-time sports town, Phoenix and the Valley have a wide array of big-time sports bars. These are the friendly lounges that specialize in sports as much as they do in pouring beverages and serving food. The atmosphere is always convivial and it's easy to make friends. After all, you all have the same thing in common—you're there for the games.

These cordial venues not only have immense video screens, they also have many of them, allowing the lucky viewers to watch all the college football games at the same time. With the advent of satellite dish technology, sports bars now have access to an unbelievable amount of sports action from around the country and from across the globe. In addition to the expected football, baseball, basketball, and hockey, you can also watch events like motor sports, skydiving, skate boarding, and even sumo wrestling from Japan. And they even rerun old games from years past so you can still watch your sport when it is out of season.

A few bars do charge a cover, but in return, you'll usually find nicer munchies and an upscale atmosphere. During the regular Monday Night football games, many sports bars host trivia contests and games of skill. You might find yourself throwing a nerf football at a basket across the room in hopes of getting a free appetizer or trying to predict the score for the next quarter.

The pleasures of the sports bar are many. The seats are always good. Beers by the bottle far exceed the quantity (and quality) of the offerings at the local stadiums and are far cheaper. Peanuts and assorted munchies are often free at the lounge and you'll have an entire menu at your fingertips for dining during the game. Perhaps you'll order up some hot wings or nachos as an appetizer—the options are extensive. You also can pay with a credit card. (Try asking the peanut vendor at the game to charge it!)

Perhaps the best thing about watching the game with other people at the bar is the feeling of camaraderie. You can cheer together and boo as a group. Like a good joke, the pleasures of the game are heightened when shared.

Go ahead and look closely at those shots of the fans at the game. They look a little bit hot, don't they? Well, you're sitting in air-conditioned comfort in August watching the same game. So tip your glass in their direction and sit back with your buddies and enjoy the game.

Big Screens and Good Times

Ahwatukee

The Sports Bar, Pointe South Mountain Resort
7777 South Pointe Parkway
(602) 431-6476

Shannon's Grill
1334 East Chandler Boulevard
(480) 283-8750

Cave Creek

Harold's Cave Creek Corral
6895 East Cave Creek Road
(480) 488-1906

Chandler

Damon's
7450 West Chandler Boulevard
(480) 961-7427

Draft House Sports Café
393 West Warner Road
(480) 963-5520

Famous Sam's Restaurant and Sports Bar
940 North Alma School Road
(480) 812-1177

First Round Draft
7200 West Chandler Boulevard
(480) 961-3080

Gallagher's Food and Fun
2050 North Alma School Road
(480) 963-0093

Howie's Pub & Eatery
6045 West Chandler Boulevard
(480) 961-4488

The Stadium Club
2060 West Chandler Boulevard
(480) 963-3866

Downtown Phoenix

Alice Cooper's Town
101 East Jackson Street
(602) 253-7337

America's Original Sports Bar
455 North Third Street
(602) 252-2112

Jackson's On Third
245 East Jackson Street
(602) 254-5303

Majerle's Downtown
24 North Second Street
(602) 253-9004

Gilbert

Champions Sports Saloon
211 North Gilbert Road
(480) 545-9669

Famous Sam's Restaurant
and Sports Bar
720 West Ray Road
(480) 899-9804

First Round Draft
1520 West Warner Road
(480) 497-2445

Mesquite Grill and Sports Bar
75 West Baseline Road
(480) 892-0807

Mesa

Benchwarmers Grill
801 South Power Road
(480) 854-8670

agement crew knows how to build a winner and immediately transformed the Coyotes roster into a younger, faster, and stronger team. Forget the failures and short-lived successes of the past; this new team will compete for hockey's ultimate prize, the Stanley Cup, for years and years to come. These new Coyotes

Famous Sam's Restaurant and Sports Bar
2860 East Main Street
(480) 924-1305

430 North Power Road
(480) 924-8778

2730 East Baseline Road
(480) 497-1252

Sluggo's Sports Grill
161 North Centennial Way
(480) 844-8448

Three Cheers
5750 East Main Street
(480) 985-1244

The Vine Tavern & Eatery
6102 East Main Street
(480) 396-2472

Scottsdale

Brennan's Sports Bar
13610 North Scottsdale Road
(480) 951-8837

Famous Sam's Sports Bar
7134 East Thomas Road
(480) 994-4488

Goldie's Neighborhood Sports Cafe
10135 East Via Linda
(480) 451-6269

J. J.'s Sports Cantina
409 North Scottsdale Road
(480) 990-3477

Stooges Sports Pub
7919 East Thomas Road
(480) 990-1114

Tempe

Ball Park Pub
1855 East Guadalupe Road
(480) 838-9585

Doc & Eddy's
909 East Minton Drive
(480) 831-0635

McDuffy's
230 West Fifth Street
(480) 966-5600

Philly's Sports Bar and Grill
1826 North Scottsdale Road
(480) 946-6666

Prankster's Gar & Brill
1024 East Broadway Road
(480) 967-8875

The Vine Tavern and Eatery
801 East Apache Boulevard
(480) 894-2662

975 East Elliot Road
(480) 730-6313

West Valley

Max's Restaurant & Sports Lounge
6727 North 47th Avenue, Glendale
(623) 937-1671

embark on a new era, one of action, one of change, one of transition. With a brand-new arena opened in 2003, the Coyotes are looking great!

Single-game tickets start at $9.00, and season-ticket prices start at $450.00, which includes all 41 regular-season games, four preseason contests, and first

i *While season tickets are generally handled by the arena or organization, individual tickets for many sports are handled by Ticketmaster. They can be reached at (480) 784-4444.*

dibs on playoff tickets for the "White Out." Check the newspaper and you'll see special offers on single tickets from time to time that sometimes include a drink and a hot dog. The ticket-office number is (480) 563-7825.

HORSE RACING

Turf Paradise
1501 West Bell Road, 19th Avenue
and Bell Road, Phoenix
(602) 942-1101
www.turfparadise.com
Riders up! Turf Paradise features live thoroughbred racing and betting on simulcast races from late September to early May. Although the main attraction is horse racing, the track's floral gardens, olive grove, three lakes, orchid trees, palm trees, and

waterfall let the track live up to its name. The exotic avian wildlife includes swans, flamingos, and herons. The tranquil setting contrasts with the high adrenaline in the grandstand.

Walter Cluer announced he would build a horse track on the 1,400-acre site back in 1954, when the spot was many miles from Phoenix. Now, although encircled by growth, it maintains its desert oasis atmosphere.

Among the big days of the year is Super Saturday, held the first Saturday in February, featuring three major races—the Turf Paradise Breeders Cup, with a $150,000 purse; the Turf Paradise Derby, with a $100,000 purse; and the Arizona Oaks, with a $75,000 purse.

Renovated in 2000 to the tune of $5 million, the raceway now features book-style betting carrels and a trackside, resort-style swimming pool, in addition to two restaurants (the elegant Turf Club and the casual Clubhouse). There are also two rooms for banquets and the top-level Director's Suite. All provide good views of the racing action. Admission is $2.00 for the grandstand and $4.00 for the clubhouse levels.

DAY TRIPS 🚗

Although there are enough hot spots within the Phoenix metropolitan area to keep visitors and residents busy, you would be remiss if you did not venture outside the Valley to experience the rest of Arizona. Getting out of town on one of the Valley's crowded arterial roadways might seem like a hassle on a Saturday morning, but you will be amply rewarded. There's enough to do and see in Arizona that our state magazine, *Arizona Highways,* has been going strong for more than 75 years and has yet to run out of fascinating places and landscapes to feature. Moreover, the state's climate varies—from sunny desert to cool pine forests—so that in the winter you can literally golf in the morning in the Valley and ski in the afternoon in the White Mountains or Flagstaff.

The Grand Canyon is, of course, our top destination, but there are plenty of other areas to discover within a three-hour drive. Of course, our foray into the rest of the state is only an introduction—to cover it thoroughly, we'd need to publish another book—so you might want to do further research into some of the areas that pique your interest. Destination points that are worthy of a visit, but require more than a

day to do, include Lake Powell, Canyon de Chelly, Monument Valley, and the Painted Desert in the northeast part of the state. Toward the east, the White Mountains offer ample skiing, hiking, and fishing opportunities. To the southeast, the frontier town of Tombstone and the mining-turned-artist community of Bisbee are worth a visit. In this chapter we'll touch on some destination points closer to the Valley that can be done in a day, organizing our trips into those that can be reached via Interstate 17 and those that can be reached via Interstate 10.

UP INTERSTATE 17

Arcosanti

Visitors may know about our famous architect, Frank Lloyd Wright, but few know about one of his students, Paolo Soleri, who has been gathering international acclaim for his experimental city that is the antithesis of Phoenix's urban sprawl. Arcosanti, about 50 miles north of Phoenix, is east of I-17 at the Cordes Junction exit. This prototype city is compact and meant to leave little impact on the surrounding landscape—a refinement of Italian hill villages, where people live in clustered housing while the fields where they work stretch out for miles around.

The cement structures, although cast in futuristic geometric shapes, look rustic, at least in part because they're unfinished—something like a ghost town from tomorrow. Privately funded—with most of the legwork being done by students and volunteers—Arcosanti may never be completely finished. The environmentally sensitive philosophy behind the project has made it attractive to ecological idealists and artisans and fascinates anyone interested in ways to solve the problems of diminishing

Being a desert area doesn't keep Arizona from having a winter. Valley winters are mild, so we have to remind ourselves when we're traveling to northern Arizona that snows can be heavy and unexpected. Tire chains are recommended for those making winter trips into the Mogollon Rim country or up to Prescott or Flagstaff. Check the travel weather reports on television or call the state Department of Public Safety for reports on highway conditions along your route at (888) 411-7623.

energy resources and a dwindling supply of open land. Soleri has been internationally recognized for his innovative designs.

Some of the funding for the project comes from the sale of distinctive Soleri-designed wind bells, which are sold in the gift shop. Guided tours of Arcosanti take about an hour, but you can walk around the grounds, visit the cafe and bakery, and even stay overnight if you wish. For details, call (928) 632–7135, or visit www.arcosanti.org.

Flagstaff

Flagstaff—140 miles north of Phoenix on I-17—makes an easy day trip from the Valley, but be aware that the two cities are practically polar opposites when it comes to weather. While you may be enjoying a round of golf in February in the Valley, the 52,000 residents of Flagstaff are likely to be hunkered down in their homes, staying warm by the fire. While Phoenix is one of the warmest cities in the nation, Flagstaff is one of the nation's snowiest cities, with 84 inches a year. Not surprisingly, the annual snowfall bodes well for Flagstaff's ski area, the Arizona Snowbowl, nestled in the San Francisco Peaks.

Come summer, Flagstaff is bustling with Valley residents escaping the blistering heat for the pines, the peaks, and temperatures that usually top out in the low 80s. Many Phoenix residents have summer cabins in the Flagstaff area. The highway to the north continually dips and rises as the Sonoran hills become more mountainous and the landscape of saguaro and cholla turns green with cottonwoods and other trees. After a drop down into the Verde Valley, you climb up into the thick forests of pine that form the gateway into Flagstaff, elevation 7,000 feet. The city's backdrop is the San Francisco Peaks, where you will find 12,643-foot Mount Humphreys, the highest point in Arizona.

Over the last decade Flagstaff has made a lot of progress sprucing up its downtown. We recommend a day in downtown Flagstaff if you enjoy browsing arts-and-crafts stores and soaking up the historic ambiance of this major east-to-west railroad stop. Northern Arizona University is also interesting to see, as is the Museum of Northern Arizona. Probably, though, you will want to combine Flagstaff with two or three other sights in the northern and central parts of the state. See this section for descriptions of Sedona, Jerome, and Montezuma Castle, which are all within about a 90-minute driving radius of Flagstaff. We've put Flagstaff, or "Flag" as many call it, in the day trips section, but it really is worth staying for a night or two. Use it as a base for seeing the Grand Canyon and the numerous archaeological sites in the area. (For further information on these destinations, check out the *Insiders' Guide to Grand Canyon and Northern Arizona*.)

Here's the lowdown on a few of Flagstaff's major attractions, places to stay, and restaurants.

The Arizona Snowbowl's ski season usually runs from December to mid-April. There are more than 30 trails and 4 chairlifts. In summer those chairlifts turn into the Scenic Skyride, lifting you to an elevation of 11,500 feet. The ride is open daily mid-June through Labor Day and for a limited time through mid-October. The Snowbowl is 14 miles north of Flagstaff on U.S. Highway 180. For information, call (928) 779–1951, or visit www.arizonasnow bowl.com. For the Snow Report, call (928) 779–4577.

About a mile from downtown is Lowell Observatory, where the planet Pluto was discovered in 1930. Lowell has a visitor center, hands-on exhibits, tours, lectures, and sky shows. It is at 1400 West Mars Hill Road, (928) 774–2096, or visit the observatory at www.lowell.edu. The Northern Arizona University campus also has an observatory, offering weekly public viewing of the night sky. Their phone number is (928) 523–7170, or visit www.nau.edu.

The Museum of Northern Arizona, 3101 North Fort Valley Road, (928) 774–5211, or www.musnaz.org, is a good place to learn about the anthropology, biology, and geology of the Colorado Plateau region. Also, there is often an exhibit focusing on Native American arts and crafts. The museum's short nature trail with its cliff overlooks is worth walking. In 2003 the museum celebrated its 75th birthday.

Fairly close to Flagstaff are two interesting natural attractions: Sunset Crater Volcano National Monument, an extinct volcano surrounded by a surreal landscape of cooled lava flows; and Walnut Canyon National Monument, with a paved nature trail leading to Sinagua cliff dwellings built into steep canyon walls. Sunset Crater is 15 miles north of Flagstaff on U.S. Highway 89, (928) 526-1157. Walnut Canyon is 7 miles east of Flagstaff on Interstate 40, (928) 526-3367.

Lodging is plentiful in Flagstaff because of its ski industry and its reputation as an Arizona summer getaway. The city is also convenient for those traveling cross-country on I-40. Reservations are essential in the height of summer. Radisson Woodlands Plaza Hotel, 1175 West Route 66, (928) 773-8888, is one of the fancier spots in the city. Scenically situated in a ponderosa forest is the Little America Hotel, 2515 East Butler Avenue, (928) 779-7900, (800) 352-4386.

If you want to be more in the center of things, the historic Weatherford Hotel, at 23 North Leroux Street, has been a favorite for more than a century. There are two bars—a relaxing one upstairs that has a great view of the town and mountains and a loud one downstairs that features live music. The rooms are somewhat basic, and noise filters up from the carousing downstairs, but the convenience and great atmosphere outweigh any disadvantages. The hotel can be reached at (928) 779-1919 or www.weatherfordhotel.com.

Chain motels and hotels are well-represented and include Days Inn at 2735 South Woodlands Village Boulevard, (928) 779-1575; Econo Lodge at 2480 East Lucky Lane, (928) 774-2252; and Quality Inn at 2000 South Milton Road, (928) 774-8771, (800) 228-5151. A charming

bed-and-breakfast is the Inn at 410 in a century-old home. It offers nine different rooms, some with saunas and others with beautiful views of the San Francisco Peaks. The location is good too—an easy walk to the center of town. The Inn at 410 is online at www.inn410.com. It's located at 410 North Leroux Street, (928) 774-0088, (800) 774-2008. Another great bed-and-breakfast is the Birch Tree Inn at 824 West Birch Avenue. The owners of this country Victorian bungalow provide excellent good and a relaxed atmosphere. It's an excellent place for a writer and his girlfriend to elope. The Birch Tree Inn can be reached at (888) 774-1042 or www.birchtreeinn.com. Campgrounds include the KOA Campground at 5803 North US 89, (928) 526-9926, and the Fort Tuthill Coconino County Park Campground off I-17 just south of Flagstaff, (928) 774-5139, October through April; or (928) 774-3464, May through September.

Flagstaff's dining choices have become more sophisticated over the years. Country French cuisine is served at Chez Marc, 503 North Humphreys Street, (928) 774-1343, www.chezmarc.com. For American and continental food, try Buster's Restaurant & Bar, 1800 South Milton Road, (928) 774-5155. For Italian food, try Pasto "Fine Italian Dining" at 19 East Aspen Avenue, (928) 779-1937. Another fine restaurant is Racha Thai, which serves great Thai dishes at $6.00 to $10.00 per entree. It's located at 104 North San Francisco Street, (928) 774-3003. Breakfasts are good at Brandy's Restaurant and Bakery, 1500 East Cedar Avenue, (928) 779-2187, www.brandysrestaurant.com. As a college town, Flagstaff attracts coffee-house intellectuals, artists, and outdoors enthusiasts. Their hangouts include Cafe Espress, 16 North San Francisco Street, (928) 774-0541, and Macy's, 14 South Beaver Street, (928) 774-2243—which serve great vegetarian dishes, coffees, and pastries. Cafe Espress has the best breakfasts in town.

One of Flagstaff's major annual events is the Winterfest in February. Highlights include sled-dog races, sleigh and snow-mobile rides, snow sculpture contests, concerts, art shows, winter stargazing, and various winter sports. Every winter Flagstaff also hosts the Arizona Book Festival. For more information, call the Flagstaff Chamber of Commerce at (800) 842-7293. During the summer you'll find various art and music programs like A Celebration of Native American Art held at the Northern Arizona University, (928) 774-5213, www.musnaz.org. The Wool Festival features sheep, goat, and llama shearing; animal shows; and demonstrations of spinning, felting, dyeing, and weaving. For more information, call the Arizona Historical Society Pioneer Museum at (928) 774-6272. In June you won't want to miss the Pine Country Pro Rodeo at the Coconino County Fairgrounds, on U.S. Highway 89A, a few miles south of Flagstaff. For information, call (928) 774-4505, or visit www.pine countryprorodeo.com.

Find antiques stores and art galleries downtown along the famous Route 66, San Francisco Street, and Beaver Street, as well as in other parts of town. For outdoor gear, go to Babbitt's Backcountry Outfitter's at 12 East Aspen Avenue, (928) 774-4775. They rent or sell just about everything you need. A cheaper option with almost as much selection is Peace Surplus at 14 West Route 66, (928) 779-4521 or www.peacesurplus.com. The staff is very friendly and knowledgeable, and the prices are the lowest in town. For an interesting and eclectic collection of old books, including some rare and fascinating antiques, go to Starrlight Books, 15 North Leroux Street, (928) 774-6813. Famous writers do signings there during the annual Northern Arizona Book Festival, held in late April.

For more information, contact the Flagstaff Convention and Visitors Bureau at 211 West Aspen Avenue, (928) 779-7611, www.flagstaffarizona.org, or the Flagstaff Visitor Center, 1 East U.S. Route 66, (800) 842-7293.

Grand Canyon

What's a visit to the Grand Canyon State without a visit to the Grand Canyon? We don't mean to be overbearing here, but if you have come all the way to Phoenix from the eastern half of the United States or abroad, go to the Grand Canyon! It is, after all, one of Mother Nature's most awe-inspiring sights.

If you only have the time to do the canyon as a day trip, do it, but pace yourself accordingly. The South Rim is about a five-hour drive from Phoenix and half the trip is on interstates. To get there, take I-17 north for about two and a half hours to Flagstaff, then get on US 180, heading north, for about another two hours. All told, it's about 220 miles from Phoenix. Private vehicles pay $20 to enter Grand Canyon National Park. Many of the park's scenic overlooks are accessible by car but, because of the large number of visitors at the park, some are closed parts of the year and you should be prepared to catch a shuttle bus to the rim. The East Rim Drive (State Route 64) is open year-round and follows the canyon rim for 26 miles east of Grand Canyon Village to Desert View, the park's east entrance. The West Rim Drive is closed to private automobiles from mid-March through mid-October, during which times the park runs a free shuttle bus. When it is open, you can follow the rim for 8 miles from Grand Canyon Village west to Hermits Rest.

Backcountry hiking through the 1.2-million-acre Grand Canyon National Park requires a permit. The cost is $10.00 per person plus an additional $5.00 per person for each night you camp in the canyon. Write to: Backcountry Office, Grand Canyon National Park, P.O. Box 129, Grand Canyon 86023, or call (928) 638-7875. Please note that the phone is answered only between 1:00 and 5:00 P.M. As part of an effort to promote hiker safety and emphasize the importance of packing enough water and food, the Park Service will send you a free video called

Hiking the Grand Canyon. Be sure to apply for any permits well in advance.

NORTH RIM

Since the North Rim is quite a way from Phoenix and is better reached from Colorado or Utah, we'll give only a quick overview and then focus on the South Rim. To reach the North Rim from Phoenix, take I-17 north to Flagstaff, then take I-40 east to US 89 north. This is a mostly two-lane road of more than 100 miles through some rather desolate stretches of the Navajo and Hopi Reservations. But you're not done yet—at Bitter Springs, take US 89A west, cross the Colorado River at Navajo Bridge and continue on to Jacob Lake. Head south on State Route 67 through beautiful pine forests to the North Rim entrance. This is an all-day drive, but you will be rewarded with a more peaceful Grand Canyon experience. Park Service cabins are available for overnight lodging. For details on the North Rim, we recommend a look at the *Insiders' Guide to Southwestern Utah* and *Insiders' Guide to Grand Canyon and Northern Arizona,* or call Grand Canyon National Park at (928) 638-7888, www.the canyon.com. Since the North Rim is a couple of thousand feet higher than the South Rim, many Park Service facilities there are open only from mid-March through late October.

SOUTH RIM

"I hiked the Grand Canyon!" proclaim T-shirts proudly worn by the hardy souls who make the daylong hike from the rim of the canyon to the Colorado River a mile below. The trails are more winding than a coiled snake; they are steep, rocky, and dusty—and rather dangerous in spots. We don't recommend a hike to the bottom if you're doing the canyon as a day trip. But you can set out on the popular Bright Angel Trail for a spell just to see what it's like. Be sure to wear your best sneakers with treads or, better yet, hiking boots. Also, pack water and sunscreen. There is

no water along the trail, and you will need it no matter what time of year it is. Hiking is advised only when it is not snowing or raining at the canyon. In fact, spring and fall are excellent times to see the South Rim because the crowds lessen a bit (actually, it's gotten to the point where there is no downtime for tourism here) and because the walking is easier in balmier weather. Summer temperatures at the canyon are about 80 degrees on the rim and about 100 degrees at Phantom Ranch along the Colorado River. However far you take the trail, remember that the hike back up will take almost twice as long as the hike down. If you don't feel like hiking, you can arrange to descend the canyon by mule.

Don't feel bad if you decide to skip the hiking altogether. The scenic drives give excellent views, and there are several observation points where you can get out of the car and take in the wonderment of it all. Unfortunately, pollution has made the canyon a little less photogenic than it used to be. To better capture the definition and depth of the red rocks, gray cliffs, and tree-studded mesas, try taking your pictures at sunrise or sunset.

If you want to learn more about the park or simply catch a shuttle bus, visit the Canyon View Information Plaza. Here visitors can catch their first glimpse of the canyon in relative serenity away from the noise of traffic. Here you can also get an overview of the park's recreational options, including information on the shuttle buses, biking, hiking, and ranger-guided activities. In 2004 the park's mass-transit system,

If you type "Grand Canyon" into a search engine on the Internet, you'll come up with a boggling array of Web sites, many run by private firms that show only their own services. The two official sites are the National Park Service's Web site at www.nps.gov/grca and the one run by the Grand Canyon Chamber of Commerce at www.thecanyon.com.

Seniors 62 and older may obtain a Golden Age Passport for a one-time fee of $10, which grants them free admission for life to all National Park Service sites in the country. Annual Grand Canyon passports, valid for the calendar year, are available to everyone for $40. Those who are physically or mentally challenged may apply in person for a Golden Access Passport, which also offers free admission for life to all our national parks. The rest of us can purchase the National Parks Pass for $50, which is good for a year of unlimited entries to all the national parks. For more information, call (888) GO-PARKS or visit www.nationalparks.org.

including alternative fuel buses and light-rail, was completed. Visitors will also have access here to the Grand Canyon Greenway, a trail system that will eventually extend from Canyon View Information Plaza to the future Grand Canyon Transit Center north of Tusayan, which is 7 miles south of the South Rim.

We hope you'll do more research about the Grand Canyon if you plan an extended stay here. Here are a few other things to think about as you plan your trip:

If you take the Bright Angel or South Kaibab Trail all the way down, you might consider arranging for overnight lodging at Phantom Ranch, which has bunkhouses, cabins, and a few other simple amenities to revive you after the hike. But reservations are a must; in fact, you should make them a year in advance. The number is (928) 638-3283.

During the canyon's busiest times, it's likely that portions of the scenic drive along the rim will be closed to private automobiles and you will be asked to take one of the free shuttle buses operated by the Park Service. It's part of an effort to reduce pollution and parking problems at this tourist haven which receives more than five million visitors a year from all

over the world. Eventually, the Park Service hopes to bring visitors in by light-rail mass transit from Tusayan, 7 miles south of the South Rim.

Have you considered taking a train to the Grand Canyon? From a depot in Williams, west of Flagstaff, you can catch the scenic Grand Canyon Railway to the South Rim. For information, call (800) 843-8724.

Still other ways to see the canyon include small airplane and helicopter flights; mule rides; motor-coach tours; white-water rafting trips; mountain biking; and guided walks with a park ranger.

Lodging at Grand Canyon Village ranges from rustic cabins ($64 per night and up) to Western-style lodges ($48 to $126 per night) to the historic El Tovar Hotel ($129 per night and up). The El Tovar, dating from 1905, recently underwent $1 million worth of renovations. Once visited by the likes of former President Theodore Roosevelt and Western writer Zane Grey, many of the rooms offer wonderful views. The hotel decor resembles an elegant hunting lodge, with massive wood-beam ceilings, fireplaces, and chandeliers. All reservations are made by calling (303) 29-PARKS, faxing (303) 297-3175, or visiting www.grandcanyonlodges.com. You can also call (888) 297-2757. The hotel and lodges have various high-end restaurants, steakhouses, cocktail lounges, coffee shops, and cafeterias. You can also find several reasonably priced restaurants and motels in Tusayan. Campers should call the Grand Canyon National Park Campgrounds at (800) 365-2267 for reservations, or check online at http://reservations.nps.gov.

See the Grand Canyon on a seven-story IMAX screen at the Grand Canyon National Geographic Theater in Tusayan, 7 miles south of the South Rim. A film called The Hidden Secrets gives a history of the 277-mile-long canyon, including the story of Major John Wesley Powell and his trip down the Colorado River in 1869. For information, call (928) 638-2203, or go to www.grandcanyonimaxtheater.com.

For a trip planner and other information, write to Grand Canyon National Park at P.O. Box 129, Grand Canyon 86023; call (928) 638-7888; or visit www.the canyon.com.

Jerome

Located 130 miles north of Phoenix in the Central Arizona hills, Jerome has evolved from a mile-high ghost town into an eclectic artist community. Browse art galleries, sip latte at an outdoor cafe, and admire the buildings that survived Jerome's long-gone heyday as a copper mining town. To get there from Phoenix, head north on I-17, then take State Route 260 west until you hit US 89A, which will pass through the small towns of Cottonwood and Clarkdale. Jerome beckons you from high upon its precarious perch on the side of Cleopatra Hill, overlooking the Verde Valley. The short, steep, and winding drive provides plenty of fun.

Miners struck it rich in Jerome in the mid-1800s. The population boomed in the 1920s to about 15,000, but that didn't last. Today, Jerome's population totals about 500 residents.

Don't expect a ghost town in the sense that it's devoid of people. Actually, they come in droves, especially on weekends with good weather. Jerome is a popular day trip for Phoenix residents. And word has gotten out—don't be surprised to see plates from all over the country. Jerome also seems to be on the A-list for motorcyclists.

While in Jerome wander around to the historic buildings, or what's left of them. A "traveling jail" still stands, even though a dynamite explosion in the 1920s moved it 200 feet from its original foundation. The mansion of mining king "Rawhide Jimmy" Douglas has been turned into Jerome State Historic Park. Old photographs and exhibits of the region's copper mining days can be seen at the Jerome Historical Society Mine Museum, Main Street and Jerome Avenue, (928) 634-5477. The Gold

King Mine Museum, Perkinsville Road, (928) 634-0053, has a replica of a mine shaft. Several of Jerome's historic homes open each May for the town's annual home tour. Call the Jerome Chamber of Commerce for more information about the tour or any other aspect of the town. The chamber can be reached at 50 North Main Street, Jerome, (928) 634-2900. The historical society has a useful Web site about the town at www.jeromehistorical society.org.

You might want to combine a trip to Jerome with a look at Tuzigoot National Monument near Clarkdale, where you'll see the ruins of a 100-room pueblo inhabited by the Sinagua from the 12th to 15th centuries. For information, call (928) 634-5564. Also, Clarkdale is the departure point for the Verde Canyon Railroad, which affords a scenic, 40-mile round-trip through cottonwood groves and desert mesas. For more information, contact the Cottonwood/Verde Valley Chamber of Commerce at 1010 South Main Street, Cottonwood, (928) 634-7593, or visit www.ci .cottonwood.az.us. You can also call the railroad directly at (800) 320-0718 or visit www.verdecanyonrr.com.

Both Jerome and the Cottonwood area have plenty of lodging options, many in historic buildings. Choices include the Inn at Jerome, 309 North Main Street, (928) 634-5094, (800) 634-5094, and www.innatjerome.com; the Ghost City Inn, 541 North Main Street, (928) 63-GHOST, and www.ghostcityinn.com; and the Surgeon's House, 100 Hill Street, (928) 639-1452, (800) 639-1452, a bed-and-breakfast converted from the home of a mining-company surgeon. Their Web site is www.surgeonshouse.com. All of these inns are several decades old but have been carefully restored. In Cottonwood try the Best Western Cottonwood Inn, 993 South Main Street, (928) 634-5575.

For dining, your options include chain restaurants in Cottonwood and Clarkdale. In Jerome take your pick of several reasonably priced cafes along Main Street. One interesting restaurant is The English

When you are traveling on Native American land, be respectful. Don't take any pictures without permission, and be sure to inquire about all the necessary permits and licenses if you plan on going hiking, hunting, or fishing. Keep in mind that dances are often part of religious ceremonies and visitors should exercise the same deference they would in church. Alcohol is not permitted on reservations. For more information on enjoying Native American destinations, contact the Arizona Office of Tourism at (602) 230-7733. You can also call the Arizona American Indian Tourism Association at (520) 523-7320.

Kitchen on Jerome Avenue, (928) 634-2132, which claims to be the oldest continually operating restaurant in Arizona. It was originally built in 1899 by Charley Hong, an immigrant from China, and served miners and travelers alike.

Montezuma Castle National Monument

A nice side trip on the way up to Flagstaff or Sedona is Montezuma Castle National Monument. These cliff dwellings, some of the best preserved of Arizona's ancient structures, had nothing to do with Montezuma and the Aztecs. However, early white settlers thought they did and thus misnamed them after the Aztec ruler.

The buildings are relics of the Sinagua, a Native American tribe that vanished without a trace in the 1300s. You can't enter these pueblos, but Montezuma Castle is a startling sight. As you come upon it from the trail, you see a cave high up in the cliffside holding a five-story stone building, defying our modern sense of where a building should be. Obviously, these ancient peoples had more sense than we did because this building and its

mud-plastered walls have been virtually untouched by the elements in the intervening years. The other ancient building at this location, which stands so much more sensibly at the bottom of the cliff, has been weathered by rain and wind.

There is a visitor center with exhibits of artifacts from the pueblos. Admission to Montezuma Castle is $3.00 for adults and free for kids 16 and younger. It is open year-round. To get there, take exit 289 east off I-17 and follow the signs. For details call (928) 567-3322.

Prescott

Arizona's first capital, Prescott (pronounced press-KIT) sprang up amid the nation's largest contiguous forest of ponderosa pines back in 1863, shortly after gold was discovered in the nearby hills. Today, Prescott is the county seat of Yavapai County (named after a local Native American tribe) and an easy two- to two-and-a-half hour trip from Phoenix. Take I-17 north to the Cordes Junction exit and then head west on State Route 69 until the junction with State Route 89, where a quick jog south puts you in the heart of the city.

SR 69 wends through pretty, mountainous country on the way to Prescott. Most of the highway has been widened to four lanes in recent years to accommodate local residential traffic and the increasing number of visitors from the Valley. You'll pass the tall smokestack of a long-abandoned smelter in the one-time mining town of Mayer. A fairly natural stopping point is Young's Farm in Dewey at the junction with State Route 169. This is the place for fresh produce. Its coffee shop and bakery are open daily. For more information, call (928) 632-7272 or visit www.youngsfarminc.com.

Just before the turn onto SR 89, you traverse the Yavapai Reservation, where casino gambling adds another attraction for visitors.

A more challenging "back way" from the West Valley offers a scenic ride through the ponderosas of Prescott National Forest. From Phoenix, take Grand Avenue northwest to Wickenburg. In Wickenburg U.S. Highway 60 splits off to the west. From that point, continue northwest for about 7 miles and take the turnoff for SR 89 and the town of Congress. From Congress, SR 89 climbs northeast up steep Yarnell Hill. The view back toward Wickenburg becomes a bird's-eye view panorama, and the scenery near Yarnell Hill quickly becomes mountainous evergreen forest. SR 89 brings you into Prescott on Montezuma Street, which is better known as Whiskey Row.

If you choose to take this route for a day trip, it's advisable to take it one way, either into or out of Prescott, and to use the I-17 route for the other portion of the trip. The back way adds an hour or more, mostly because you're heading farther west and then cutting back to Prescott. Mountain switchbacks tend to slow the progress of even the most intrepid driver.

Young professionals are likely to motor up to Prescott on the weekend to soak up the local nightlife around Whiskey Row (so named because it is where all the town's saloons and bawdy houses used to be), stay the night, and then head back down to the Valley. Despite the appearance of the smart set, Prescott offers plenty of attractions for families as well. The city boasts 525 buildings listed on the National Register of Historic Places—a pleasant contrast to the Valley's penchant for tearing down any building that's been up for a while.

Courthouse Plaza—bounded by Gurley Street on the north, Montezuma Street on the west, Goodwin Street on the south, and Cortez Street on the east—is the heart of Prescott. Tree-shaded and cool (Prescott averages about 20 degrees cooler than Phoenix), the plaza invites visitors to dawdle while checking out the courthouse, which dates from Prescott's stint as the territorial capital.

Prescott's pace feels slower than the Valley's. The restored brick buildings that house the restaurants, antiques stores, saloons, and other businesses around the plaza are authentic reminders of Arizona's Wild West days. Shopping for antiques certainly fits the setting.

To get a full appreciation of Prescott's past, visit the Sharlot Hall Museum, 2 blocks west of the plaza at 415 West Gurley Street, (928) 445-3122, www.sharlot.org. Sharlot Hall came to the territory at age 12 in 1882. Her fascination with Arizona, its history, and its artifacts led her to become the official territorial historian in 1909. The museum she opened in 1928 encompasses the original Governor's Mansion, a log home built in 1864, two 1870s vintage homes, and utilitarian buildings such as a blacksmith's shop and a schoolhouse, among others. The Sharlot Hall Building, opened in 1934, is itself old enough to be considered historic in this neck of the woods. It houses the museum's exhibits on Prescott and Native American history. The museum also is host to major annual events such as the Folk Arts Festival during the first weekend of June, the Arizona Cowboy Poets Gathering held the third weekend in August, and the Indian Arts Market held the first weekend of October. From April through October, the museum is open 10:00 A.M. to 5:00 P.M. Monday through Saturday and 1:00 to 5:00 P.M. Sunday. From November through March, it closes at 4:00 P.M. Admission is a $5.00 donation.

Another Prescott museum, The Smoki Museum, 147 North Arizona Street, (928) 445-1230, displays artifacts from many Native American tribes, including clothing, ornaments, and ceremonial paraphernalia from the Sioux, Apache, and Woodland tribes. Many items in the collection were donated by Arizona son Barry Goldwater, who was a member of the Smoki People. Hours are 10:00 A.M. to 4:00 P.M. Monday through Saturday and 1:00 to 4:00 P.M. Sunday.

Of the many annual events in Prescott, the Frontier Days/World's Oldest Rodeo celebration around the Fourth of July is the city's biggest draw. Prescott also plays host to an Intertribal Powwow in June, and the Yavapai County Fair in September.

Prescott's setting at the edge of a mountain-studded plain makes it a natural spot for hiking, fishing, boating, and other activities that take in the scenery. Off Thumb Butte Road west of downtown, Thumb Butte—which resembles a giant thumb—offers a picnic area and hiking trails. North of town, on SR 89, the Granite Dells, giant slabs of yellowish-brown granite, rise on both sides of the highway. Sparse vegetation clings to the sides of these smooth, rounded rock towers, which will take much longer to wear away than the soil that once covered them.

As you might expect, the nearby Prescott National Forest is well worth a visit for hiking and camping. In 2001 area trail advocates dedicated the 5.5-mile Prescott Peavine Trail. It will eventually expand to a 12-mile trail along a historic railroad route and will serve as a link to other trail systems in nearby Chino and Prescott Valleys.

Maps and information are available at the Prescott National Forest Main Office, 344 South Cortez Street, (928) 771-4700.

If you want to spend the night in Prescott, the Hassayampa Inn at 122 East Gurley Street, (928) 778-9434, (800) 322-1927, is one of Prescott's many historic buildings and offers accommodations in the $100-a-night range. The Hotel St. Michael, 205 West Gurley Street, (928) 776-1999, (800) 678-3757, offers accommodations from $59 and up. It sits next door to a Whiskey Row cowboy bar, and a ghost supposedly haunts the building—possibly because the cowboys are keeping it awake.

If you want to grab a bite while you're in Prescott, forget all the national fast-food chains and check out Kendall's Famous Burgers and Ice Cream, 113 South Cortez Street, (928) 778-3658. The burgers are big and tasty. For Southwestern-style prime rib, go to Murphy's at 201 North Cortez Street, (928) 445-4044. Sit-

uated in one of Prescott's many historic buildings, Murphy's is very popular with folks in Prescott, and reservations are recommended for lunch and dinner, especially on the weekends. Murphy's offers its own microbrews and private-label wine too. To dine elegantly, the Peacock Room at the Hassayampa Inn, 122 East Gurley Street, (928) 778-9434, ext. 104, is the place for continental cuisine.

These are just a few of the accommodations, activities, and points of interest in Prescott. For more information, contact the Prescott Chamber Tourism Information Center, 117 West Goodwin Street, (928) 445-2000, (800) 266-7534, or visit www.prescott.org.

Sedona

The artists' community of Sedona, named after one of the town's original settlers, Sedona Schnebly, nestles among towering red rocks that form one of the most beautiful spots in Arizona. The rock formations are imbued with deep hues from iron oxides; their names—Cathedral Rock, Bell Rock, the Cockscomb Spires—are inspired by their strange, windblown shapes. A top tourist attraction, Sedona nevertheless offers plenty of places to sequester oneself from the madding crowd. Some locals and many visitors believe that the area's natural electromagnetic fields—dubbed "vortexes"—have rejuvenating properties. Decide for yourself by making the fairly easy, two-hour drive to Sedona from Phoenix. Follow I-17 north to State Route 179, then turn west toward Sedona.

You'll find plenty to do walking through town, especially if you like arts and crafts. Possessing much the same ambiance as the Scottsdale art scene, but with more of a crowd, Sedona's galleries showcase top-notch paintings and sculptures in a variety of media, from Native American arts and crafts to modern studio art glass. One celebrity artist to check out is Robert Shields, once a member of the popular mime duo Shields and Yarnell, whose fanciful creations are showcased in his studio, Robert Shields Design, at 181 SR 179, (928) 204-2123. Just behind Robert Shields Design, at 175 SR 179, is The Book Loft, an excellent source of new, used, and rare books. It has a good section on local history and nature and the best view of any bookstore we've ever seen—a huge window looks out over a verdant valley with red-rock mesas beyond. The Book Loft can be reached at (928) 282-5173.

Altogether, Sedona has more than three dozen galleries, which congregate not only along the main road, US 89A, but also at Tlaquepaque Arts and Crafts Village, at 336 SR 179, (928) 282-4838, a re-creation of an old Mexican village graced with all manner of galleries. Tlaquepaque is located on your left just off SR 179 on your way into town. Another must-see is the Sedona Arts Center, at US 89A and Art Barn Road, (928) 282-3865, in the center of town, which has changing exhibits by regional artists.

Sedona's weather is usually pleasant throughout much of the year, but be warned that it does snow there in the winter, and summer temperatures can go as high as 100 degrees. Because of the nice weather, outdoor festivals are popular. One new venue is the city's $9-million Sedona Cultural Park, 250 Cultural Park Place, (928) 282-0747 or www.sedonaculturalpark.org, which features an outdoor amphitheater and arts education center. Some of the town's biggest annual events involve the performing arts: the Sedona International Film Festival in March; the Sedona Chamber Music Festival in May; and Sedona Jazz on the Rocks in September, (928) 282-1985. In December folks come from all around Arizona to see Sedona Red Rock Christmas Fantasy, whose more than one million lights illuminate several acres at Los Abrigados Resort.

If you feel spiritually uplifted after your visit, that's probably because of the vortexes that draw New Agers from around the country. There are said to be about a dozen such vortexes, including those at Cathedral Rock and Bell Rock. Nonbeliev-

ers can still enjoy earthly delights such as massages and spas offered by Sedona's New Age stores and traditional resorts.

If the city shops make you feel fenced in, there are better things to do out of town. Stop by the Sedona Heritage Museum, at 735 Jordan Road, Sedona Historical Park, (928) 282-7038, for a peek at Sedona's past, including its location as a site for old westerns. Hiking along Oak Creek Canyon is popular, as is the creek's natural water slide at Slide Rock State Park. Northern Light Balloon Expeditions runs hot-air flights above Sedona; call (928) 282-2274 or (800) 230-6222. Jeep tours, four-wheeling, and horseback riding are fun too. There are several companies in town offering excursions, but the oldest one is Pink Jeep Tours at (800) 873-3662 or www.pinkjeeptours.com, or go to their office at 204 North US 89A. If you drive a high-clearance vehicle, try Schnebly Hill Road, which connects Sedona with I-17 and Flagstaff and offers great views of the red rocks and Verde Valley.

You might be tempted to stay overnight in Sedona (maybe it's those vortexes pulling you in), and if so, your choices will run the gamut from luxury golf resorts to intimate inns to chain motels. Known for a long time to Phoenix residents wishing to splurge on a romantic getaway is L'Auberge de Sedona, a re-creation of a French country inn at 301 L'Auberge Lane, (928) 282-1661, (800) 272-6777, and online at www.lauberge.com. We also recommend Junipine Resort on US 89A, (928) 282-3375, (800) 742-7463; Los Abrigados Resort, 160 Portal Lane, (928) 282-1777, (800) 521-3131, www.ilx resorts.com; and Radisson Poco Diablo Resort, 1752 SR 179, (928) 282-7333.

There are several nice bed-and-breakfasts, some along Oak Creek Canyon north of town. Look into the Lodge at Sedona, 125 Kallof Place, (928) 204-1942; the Territorial House, 65 Piki Drive, (928) 204-2737 or (800) 801-2737; Canyon Villa Bed & Breakfast Inn, 125 Canyon Circle Drive, (928) 284-1226, (800) 453-1166; or the Inn on Oak Creek, 556 SR 179, (928)

282-7896, (800) 499-7896. The budget-conscious traveler might consider the Comfort Inn Sedona, 725 SR 179, (928) 282-3132, (800) 228-5150, or the Sedona Super 8 Motel, 2545 SR 89A, (928) 282-1533, (800) 858-7245. The Manzanita Campground in Oak Creek Canyon is small but scenic. It has about 18 sites for non-RV campers—there are no hookups, but you will find tables, grills, toilets, and drinking water. The phone number is (928) 282-4119. There are also several Forest Service campgrounds along Oak Creek, north of Sedona. Pine Flat Campground has 58 camping spots on two sites and can be reached at (877) 444-6777.

At last count, Sedona had more than 60 restaurants covering the spectrum from fast food to Mexican to gourmet. We heartily recommend the Heartline Cafe, 1610 West US 89A, (928) 282-0785, which serves exquisite continental cuisine. Check them out online at www.heartlinecafe.com. Another nice place is the Plaza Cafe, an Italian-owned cafe and sandwich shop. The coffee is excellent and salads, sandwiches, and other dishes are made with top ingredients. They are open for breakfast and lunch every day. Plaza Cafe is located at 1449 West US 89A, (928) 203-9041.

The Sedona-Oak Creek Canyon Chamber of Commerce can be reached at P.O. Box 478, Sedona 86339, (928) 282-7722, (800) 288-7336, www.sedonachamber .com. Their office is at 331 Forest Road.

UP THE BEELINE HIGHWAY (STATE ROUTE 87)

Payson

Located approximately 95 miles away from downtown Phoenix, Payson is the closest summer getaway for people in the East Valley. From downtown, you get on the Red Mountain Freeway (202 east) to its junction with SR 87. It's a simple buzz north up the Beeline Highway, through the Salt River Pima-Maricopa and Fort McDowell Yavapai reservations, through the Mazatzal (pronounced, believe it or not, ma-tah-zall) Mountains, and into the cool pine forests of Payson.

At an elevation of 5,000 feet, the temperature in Payson is typically 20 degrees lower than in the Valley. The Payson area also enjoys about 21 inches of rain a year, about three times the Valley's annual rainfall. Payson sits in the Tonto Basin, about 20 miles south of the Mogollon Rim, the steep lip of a 7,000-foot plateau that stretches eastward to New Mexico. The Rim separates Arizona's northern plateau area from the state's central and southern regions. The huge rock wall stands like a shorter Grand Canyon wall. The Rim dominates the landscape; hence the Payson area is also known as Rim Country.

Founded in 1882 as a mining settlement, Payson has gone through phases as a ranching and lumber town. Today, tourism and retirement industries dominate the local economy. You'll find 15 antiques shops in the area, nine motels, a number of bed-and-breakfasts, cabin facilities, nine RV parks, and six campgrounds.

Payson bills itself as the Festival Capital of Arizona, and the annual events in Payson include the World's Oldest Continuous Rodeo in August. (Say, isn't that what Prescott called its rodeo?) There are a number of other festivals as well, including the Arizona State Old Time Fiddlers' Contest in September.

Set in the middle of the Tonto National Forest, Payson is a place to enjoy outdoor activities year-round. It's a place to view spring wildflowers, to stay relatively cool in summer, to view colorful foliage in the fall, and to do cross-country skiing in winter. The area's mountains, lakes, and streams lure anglers, bird watchers, boaters, campers, hikers, horseback riders, hunters, swimmers, and water skiers.

Western novelist Zane Grey fell in love with the Rim Country and set many of his cowboy novels in this region. He built a hunting lodge near Payson in 1920, writing there often. For many years after his death in 1939, the cabin was preserved as a historic site featuring exhibits on the novelist and the Wild West. Unfortunately, it was one of 61 homes that burned down in the Dude forest fire in 1990, the effects of which still can be seen outside Payson, where the forest is slowly growing back. The Zane Grey cabin site is now owned by a private developer and no longer open to the public, but you can find plenty of Zane Grey history in Payson proper.

In fact, the Rim Country Museum, 700 Green Valley Parkway, (928) 474-3483, has plans to re-create the Zane Grey cabin on its grounds in Payson to complement its exhibits on the author. The museum, which has exhibits on all aspects of the area's history from pre-Columbian times through today, resides in the original Tonto National Forest Ranger Station, built in 1907. Admission is $3.00 for adults, $2.50 for senior citizens, $2.00 for students, and free for kids 12 and younger. It's open from noon to 4:00 P.M. Wednesday through Sunday and closed on holidays.

While you're out that way, you may want to tour the Tonto Creek Fish Hatchery, (928) 478-4200. It's a 17-mile drive from Payson to the turnoff to the hatchery on SR 260. The road is marked with a sign and you'll turn north on Forest Service Road 289. The hatchery has been stocking Rim Country creeks and lakes with trout for 50 years. You can tour their facility free of charge from 8:00 A.M. to 4:00 P.M. seven days a week, excluding holidays. Stop by their visitor center, where you'll learn more about the whole process.

Down the same road as the hatchery is the Tonto Creek campground. The campground's upper section features 9 sites, while the lower has 17. You're in the forest out here—nestled amid ponderosas, junipers, and oaks. Tonto Creek flows nearby, and it's stocked with rainbow trout. This is a rustic site with no toilets or electricity. It's open April 1 through October 30. The fee for camping is $8.00 per day.

Payson is just 10 miles south of Tonto Natural Bridge State Park, on SR 87, (928) 476-4202. The natural rock formation that gives the park its name is the largest travertine, or limestone, bridge in the

When driving the highways and byways of Arizona, keep an eye out for roadside vendors. These folks sell everything from Navajo and Mexican blankets to the ubiquitous strings of dried red chiles. Although the quality of the merchandise varies, you can often find nice souvenirs and get into interesting conversations with the Arizonans most tourists never meet.

world. The bridge is 400 feet wide and 180 feet high and crosses a 150-foot-wide canyon. In fact, it is so big that, when you arrive at the old lodge and park your car you have no idea you are actually on the bridge. Viewpoints are easily accessible, but most exciting is a steep climb down a trail at the side of the canyon wall, which will lead you under the bridge. The site was discovered by prospector David Gowan in 1877 during a skirmish with Apaches. A lodge that Gowan's nephew built in 1927 has been restored on the site. Admission is $6.00 a carload. Hours vary, so call ahead.

On the way to Tonto Natural Bridge, you may want to check out the Shoofly Indian Ruin. It's just north of Payson, off SR 87 on Houston Mesa Road. The only remains of this ancient settlement are primitive rock pit houses, abandoned by their residents about A.D. 1250. No one knows why, or where they went.

About 19 miles north of Payson on SR 87 is the town of Strawberry, home of the oldest schoolhouse in Arizona. Turn left at Strawberry Lodge in the center of town and about 1.5 miles later you'll find the log schoolhouse, built in 1884. The last classes were held there in 1916.

Strawberry is just below the Mogollon Rim. You can climb SR 87 another 10 miles to the top of the Rim. Watch for the signs to Forest Road 300, which turns off to the east. This gravel road, maintained only in summer and passable by passenger car, offers spectacular lookouts from the edge of the Rim as well as picnic areas and campgrounds. It also affords access to a number of lakes that are great for fishing. If you follow the road for its entire 45-mile length, you'll end up on State Route 260, approximately 30 miles east of Payson.

Anglers can pick up information on good fishing locations in Rim Country lakes and streams (as well as other information on Payson-area attractions and activities) by visiting the Rim Country Regional Chamber of Commerce at the corner of SR 87 and Main Street, (928) 474-4515 or (800) 672-9766.

For hikers, a number of trails wander through the area. A popular choice is the Highline National Recreational Trail, which travels for 51 miles beneath the Mogollon Rim. Some trails branch off from the Highline up to the Rim itself. From the Pine Trailhead, 15 miles north of Payson off SR 87, the Highline heads toward the 260 Trailhead, 27 miles east of Payson off SR 260. For more details on trails in the Tonto National Forest, pick up trail guides available at the U.S. Forest Service Ranger's District Office at 1009 East SR 260 in Payson, (928) 474-7900. The office also has information on nearby Forest Service campgrounds.

If you want to wrap up the day gambling with a one-armed bandit, there's the Mazatzal Casino, a half-mile south of Payson on the east side of SR 87 at milepost 251, (928) 474-6044 or (800) 777-7529. The casino is run by the Tonto Apache tribe.

If you want to stay the night, lodgings include Motel 6, for $60, at the corner of SR 87 and Phoenix Street, (928) 474-4526, and the Best Western Paysonglo Lodge, with rooms ranging from $70 and up double occupancy, at 1005 South Beeline Highway (SR 87), (928) 474-2382. Remember, though, if you want to stay in Payson over a summer weekend when things are really hopping, you'll need to make reservations well in advance. For more information, call the Rim Country Regional Chamber of Commerce, (928) 474-4515 or (800) 672-9766, or visit www.rimcountrychamber.com.

At lunchtime, check out the Small Café at the Twin Pine Shopping Center, Beeline Highway and SR 87, (928) 474-4209, which serves sandwiches, soups, and salads. Take the Christopher Creek exit from SR 260 in Payson to get to the Creekside Steakhouse & Tavern, (928) 478-4389, where they serve well-prepared steaks and plenty of suds to wash them down.

Saguaro Lake

Boating, Jet-Skiing, fishing, picnicking, and camping can be enjoyed at a number of different lakes around Phoenix. One of our favorites is Saguaro Lake, about an hour-and-a-half drive out of the central part of the Valley. From Scottsdale take Shea Boulevard east to Fountain Hills, then catch SR 87 going north. About 10 miles past Fort McDowell Casino, you will see the signs directing you to Saguaro Lake. You can also get to SR 87 (nicknamed the Beeline Highway) from Mesa, where Country Club Drive turns into the Beeline as it heads north.

Saguaro Lake is part of a chain of four lakes formed by Salt River dams built in Tonto National Forest over several decades of the 20th century. The most famous of these is Roosevelt Dam. Completed in 1911, it is the world's largest masonry dam, constructed entirely of quarry stone. The dams provide the Valley of the Sun with hydroelectric power, irrigation, and flood control. Roosevelt Lake is the easternmost of the four lakes, and the chain moves to the west with Apache and Canyon Lakes, then Saguaro—the second-smallest at 1,200 acres.

Anglers catch bass and trout in Saguaro. Jet-Skiers and motorboaters ply the elongated stretches of the lake with wild and wet abandon. If none of these appeal to you, consider a one-and-a-half-hour paddleboat cruise on the *Desert Belle*. It allows you to see much of the lake's 22-mile shoreline, and the captain provides occasional commentary to enhance your visit. You have your choice of sitting in an open or covered area. The weather will be a bit cooler than in the Valley, and you'll get a breeze off the lake, so dress appropriately. The scenery is an intriguing juxtaposition of rocky desert outcroppings against the blue water. You will pass dozens of rock formations, narrow canyons, and caves as well as cliffs streaked with black varnish where waterfalls once cascaded. Flora includes many varieties of cacti, desert trees, and, in the spring, a good smattering of desert wildflowers. Wildlife sightings are part of the fun. It's not unusual to see coyotes, javelinas, rabbits, squirrels, mule deer, and bighorn sheep. Birds are quite abundant, and if you're lucky you'll see turkey vultures, hawks, owls, blue herons, and even bald eagles. From October through January, the *Desert Belle* leaves the dock at 12:30 P.M. Wednesday through Sunday. In high season (February through April) the cruise is offered at 12:30 and 2:30 P.M. daily. In summer (May through August), the gears shift to a sunset cruise, at 5:00 P.M. only, on Saturday and Sunday. The cost is $13.00 for adults and $7.00 for children. If you're not picnicking for this day trip, we suggest lunch at the Lakeshore Restaurant, (480) 984–5311, open daily, where you can get a nice view of the lake and marina from the patio. For more information on the Lakeshore Restaurant or the *Desert Belle*, call (480) 984–5311 or visit www.saguarolake.net.

Information on other amenities at Saguaro Lake is also available from the Tonto National Forest Service by writing P.O. Box 5348, Phoenix 85010, or calling (602) 225–5200. Those with boats and Jet Skis should be considerate of water skiers and kayakers. For boat storage, call the marina at (480) 986–5596; for service and rentals, call (480) 986–0969. Boating maps are available at the Mesa District Ranger Station, 26 North Macdonald Street, Mesa, (480) 610–3300, and at the Tonto National Forest Office, 2324 East McDowell Road, Phoenix, (602) 225–5200. The entry fee is $4.00 per day, per vehicle, with $2.00 extra charged for watercraft.

When driving out of the Valley into other parts of the state, travelers can be surprised at how cool it is at their destination. When the elevation is 5,000 feet above the Valley floor, the temperature drops quickly, so dress accordingly. Even if you stay within the Valley, the desert floor does not retain its heat during the night and you can freeze.

Canyon Lake also offers cruises, in this case aboard the *Dolly Steamboat*, a 100-foot replica of an old double-decker riverboat. You have to take a different route to reach Canyon Lake, which lies 16 miles north of Apache Junction off State Route 88, also called the Apache Trail. Cruise times vary by season, but generally the 90-minute Nature Cruise, which costs $14 plus tax, departs at noon and 2:00 P.M. daily. The Twilight Dinner Cruise varies depending on the season and costs $39.95. Call ahead for the latest prices, schedules, and reservations at (480) 827–9144 or visit www.dollysteamboat.com.

DOWN INTERSTATE 10

Tucson

For a look at Arizona's second-largest city, you need only drive about two hours southeast of Phoenix on I-10. The distance is 115 miles, and Arizonans joke that it is the most boring drive in the state. Luckily, the 75-mph speed limit helps you breeze past the desert scrub toward the more interesting sight of Tucson's Santa Catalina Mountains. One stop to consider along the way, though, is Picacho Peak, near Eloy, site of Arizona's only Civil War battle. It is commemorated with a monument and a flagpole.

Like Phoenix, Tucson is a highly livable desert metropolis seeing tremendous growth. It has beautiful residential developments, a respectable cultural scene, and a healthy economy. Plus, it's in a lovely setting surrounded by five mountain ranges, including the blue-tinged Santa Catalinas.

Tucson encompasses about three-quarters of a million people in a metropolitan area of 500 square miles. Its residents by and large love their "Old Pueblo," preferring it over Phoenix, which they see as being way too urbanized and sprawling. You'll often hear residents of the two cities banter over which place is better.

Tucson does seem to have a slight advantage concerning weather. It boasts 350 days of sunshine a year, compared with Phoenix's 300 days. Also, those familiar with both cities say the summer daytime heat is somewhat less oppressive, and the nights are crisper in Tucson, although 105 degrees in June is not uncommon. Tucson is 1,000 feet higher than Phoenix, which partially explains the weather difference. Winters feel a bit more like winter thanks to the sight of snowcaps on the surrounding mountains. As expected, for at least six months of the year, Tucson's weather is wonderful.

Tucson makes a great day trip from Phoenix, but its scenery, major attractions, and resorts make it a fine vacation destination in and of itself. What follows are several suggestions on making the most of your excursion. For further details, see *Insiders' Guide to Tucson.*

On your way to Tucson, consider stopping off at Casa Grande National Monument. This was the site of a large Hohokam town sustained by a network of canals. It gets its name from a four-story adobe structure that is unique in southern Arizona, built around A.D. 1350 Archaeologists aren't sure why the Hohokam built this impressive house, bringing 600 beams of juniper, pine, and fir from distant mountains. It may have been the home of a clan leader or a communal dwelling. Researchers say the windows may have been used to mark the rising and setting of important stars, sort of a high-rise agricultural calendar. It's not the most impressive archaeological site in Arizona, but if you are passing by, it's well worth the time. The monument has a museum and a small bookshop. Entry is $3.00. Casa Grande is a few miles off I-10 Take exit 185 east along State Route 387. Take a right onto SR 87 and follow the signs. For information, call (520) 723-3172 or go to www.nps.gov/cagr.

If we had to name two things you must see while you are in the area, they would be the Arizona-Sonoran Desert Museum and Mission San Xavier del Bac. So plan your day with that tip in mind.

The Arizona-Sonoran Desert Museum is about 10 miles west of Tucson at 2021 North Kinney Road. It offers a terrific look at the plant and animal life of the Sonoran Desert, with more than 300 animal species and 1,200 kinds of plants in a natural landscape. One exhibit features nocturnal desert dwellers such as kit foxes and tarantulas. An underwater viewing area lets you see beavers, river otters, and desert fishes. There's also a hummingbird aviary and a prairie dog colony. A walk-through cave leads you to an exhibit of gems and minerals from this region. All around are blooming desert gardens and displays of cacti. Admission is $12.00 for adults, November to April; $9.00 May to October; $4.00 for children ages 6 to 12; $2.00 May to October; and free for children younger than 6. Hours are 8:30 A.M. to 5:00 P.M. in the fall and winter and 7:30 A.M. to 5:00 P.M. in the spring and summer. From June through September, the museum is open until

10:00 P.M. on Saturday nights. For more information, call (520) 883-2702 or visit www.desertmuseum.org.

The mission at San Xavier del Bac is easy to reach from Interstate 19. Heading south about 10 miles from Tucson, look for the San Xavier Road exit. The gleaming white towers and domes of the mission are unmistakable. Against a clear blue sky, this mission—dating from 1783—is a one-of-a-kind image, so be sure to bring your camera. The interior architecture is wonderful as well, thanks to many years of meticulous restoration work. Called the "Sistine Chapel of North America," the mission features artwork on practically every square inch and in practically every nook and cranny. This includes paintings, frescoes, and statues. Arizonans know the mission as the "White Dove of the Desert." As you wander around, learn about the Jesuit missionary and explorer Father Eusebio Francisco Kino and other men of the cloth who served here. Located on the Tohono O'odham Reservation, the mission is one of the last Spanish churches still serving its Native American parishioners. The mission is open for view daily from 8:00 A.M. to 6:00 P.M., and no admission is charged, although donations are welcome. Masses are held each morning and four times on Sundays. For more information, call (520) 294-2624.

If you're exploring Tucson by car, don't miss a drive through Saguaro National Park, where you will find the largest concentration of saguaro cacti in the state and in the world, for that matter, since saguaros grow only in the Sonoran Desert. For Saguaro Park West, the western district, or the area surrounding the Tucson Mountains, exit at Ina Road from I-10 and drive west, following the signs. For Saguaro Park East, the eastern district, or the area surrounding the Rincon Mountains, continue on I-10 until you reach southern Tucson, then take Houghton Road north and follow the signs for about 8 miles. The western district's number is (520) 733-5100; the eastern district's is (520) 733-5153.

For a taste of the Old West, one of the best bets in Arizona is Old Tucson Studios, originally built as a set for the movie *Arizona* in 1939. It has since been used as the backdrop for more than 200 movies, TV shows, commercials, and documentaries. Old Tucson is tourist friendly, with lots of staged gunfights, stunt shows, trail rides, costumed characters, tours of movie sites, films, old-fashioned shops, stagecoach rides, cowboy-style dinners, and saloons. It's 12 miles west of Tucson, next to Saguaro National Park's western entrance. The address is 201 South Kinney Road. In the winter, hours are generally 10:00 A.M. to 6:00 P.M. daily, closed Thanksgiving and Christmas Day. Admission is $14.95 for adults, $9.45 for children ages 4 to 11, and free for children younger than 4. For more information, call (520) 883-0100 or visit www.oldtucson.com.

Another Tucson-area attraction worth visiting is the Pima Air & Space Museum,

---

In 1974 two Arizona cavers discovered Kartchner Caverns near Benson in southeastern Arizona, a pristine cave that includes 13,000 feet of passages, rare multicolored formations, and two rooms as long as football fields. They explored the cave for two years before revealing their secret to the property owners. The public learned about the cavern in 1988, when Arizona State Parks purchased the property. The cave, a Discovery Center, hiking trails, hummingbird garden, and campgrounds, were opened to the public in 1999. The cavern's features include a thin stalactite "soda straw," which measures 21 feet long, nitrocalcite "cotton," and "birds nests" formed from rare quartz. Fossils from sloths, horses, and bears that roamed the area more than 40,000 years ago were also unearthed. The park is located 160 miles from Phoenix, 9 miles south of I-10 in Benson, Arizona. Reservations are required. For more information, call (520) 586-CAVE.

The much-lauded Arizona Trail, a 790-mile recreation trail cutting through the state from Utah in the north to Mexico in the south, was finished in 2002. The trail is open to hikers, equestrians, mountain bicyclists, cross-country skiers, and other outdoor enthusiasts. The trail links up with the Grand Canyon, the San Francisco Peaks, the Mogollon Rim, Saguaro National Park, and other important sites. For a map and more information, write the Arizona Trail Association at P.O. Box 36736, Phoenix 85067; phone (602) 252-4794; or visit www.aztrail.org.

6000 East Valencia Road, (520) 574-0462, www.pimaair.org. It has more than 250 civilian and military airplanes on display. It's open from 9:00 A.M. to 5:00 P.M. daily, with admission costs of $9.75 for adults, $8.75 for seniors and military, $6.00 for children ages 7 to 12, and free for those younger than 7.

The University of Arizona also makes an interesting stop. Highlights of the campus include the planetarium and observatory at the Flandrau Science Center, (520) 621-4515; the Ansel Adams and Alfred Stieglitz collection at the Center for Creative Photography, (520) 621-7968; and the exhibits on Native American cultures at the Arizona State Museum, (520) 621-6302.

If you don't mind going a little farther afield, the Biosphere 2 Center in Oracle is an unusual sight. About 30 miles north of Tucson on State Route 77, Columbia University's Biosphere 2 is the new incarnation of the original Biosphere 2, which you may remember as the place where several scientists lived under a roof of glass and steel in a small version of Earth and its various climates. The scientists no longer live there; it is now a research center with daily tours and plenty of interesting exhibits, including global warming and rain forest plant life. Admission is $19.95 forages 13 and up, $12.95 for ages 6 to 12; kids under

6 free. For more information, call (520) 838-6200, or visit www.bio2.edu.

Colossal Cave, one of the largest dry caverns in the world, is 20 miles east of Tucson, (520) 647-7275. The Titan Missile Museum, about 30 miles south of Tucson, features a tour of the underground silo housing the world's only Titan II ICBM. The phone number is (520) 625-7736. Tombstone, with its famed OK Corral, is about 70 miles southeast of Tucson. Call (888) 457-3929 for information or visit www.tombstone.org. Even Nogales, Mexico, with its border-town ambiance and tons of colorful shops, is within reach by going 60 miles south of Tucson on I-19.

Tucson is known as the "Astronomy Capital of the World," thanks in large part to clear desert night skies and to Kitt Peak National Observatory, which houses the largest collection of telescopes anywhere, including the largest solar telescope. You can find it about 50 miles southwest of Tucson via a steep and winding mountain road. The visitor center at the observatory is open from 9:00 A.M. to 3:45 P.M. daily, except Thanksgiving, Christmas Eve and Day, and New Year's Day, and offers guided tours. Inquire about evening stargazing programs. For information, call (520) 318-8726, www.noao.edu. The Flandrau Science Center at the University of Arizona also offers programs in its planetarium and public observatory. Call (520) 621-4515 or visit www.flandrau.org.

Hiking enthusiasts can head up to Sabino Canyon in north Tucson. From I-10, exit east on Grant Road, then take the Tanque Verde Road turnoff. Tanque Verde leads to Sabino Canyon Road and the visitor center. The Sabino Canyon Recreation Area can be reached by calling (520) 749-8700.

Although Tucson's event calendar is not quite as lively as Phoenix's, you might be on the watch for several major events. In February Tucson hosts the Tucson Gem & Mineral Show, an international exposition, (520) 322-5773. Also in February is the huge, PRCA-sanctioned rodeo, La Fiesta de los Vaqueros, preceded by the world's largest nonmotorized parade, (520) 741-2233. Throughout March look out for spring-training baseball at Hi Corbett Field and Tucson Electric Park for the Colorado Rockies, the Chicago White Sox, and, last but not least, the Arizona Diamondbacks, (888) 683-3900.

Shopping is a good diversion in Tucson, thanks to a mix of major metropolitan malls and cozy boutique districts. Foothills Mall at Ina Road and La Cholla Boulevard, (520) 742-7191, offers several outlet stores, a movie theater, a brewery, and an indoor games and rides area for children. Park Place is at 5870 East Broadway Boulevard, (520) 748-1222. And the Tucson Mall is at 4500 North Oracle Road, (520) 293-7330. Old Town Tucson, near Main Avenue and Franklin Street, is a quaint place for browsing, and shops have a good selection of Native American and Southwestern arts and crafts. Old Town Artisans, a marketplace dating from the 1850s, can be reached at (520) 623-6024, (800) 782-8072, or by visiting www.old townartisans.com. Also, several great little shops are clustered on Fourth Avenue. For studio art glass check out the work of Arizona master Tom Philabaum at Philabaum Contemporary Art Glass at 711 South Sixth Avenue, (520) 884-7404. Tucson's Antique Mall is at 3130 East Grant Road, (520) 326-3070.

Should you decide to stay overnight in Tucson, the city has a good selection of chain hotels and motels, including Courtyard Marriott at the Tucson Williams Center, 201 South Williams Boulevard, (520) 745-6000. Another possibility is The Hilton Tucson East at 7600 East Broadway Road, (520) 721-5600, with 233 rooms in an atrium-style upscale hotel. Tucson also has several nice bed-and-breakfasts, including Casa Alegre at 316 East Speedway Boulevard, (520) 628-1800 or (800) 628-5654, and the El Presidio Inn, 297 North Main Avenue, (520) 623-6151, (800) 349-6151.

First-class resorts help feed Tucson's tourism industry. Those with a national reputation include the Arizona Inn, a restored hotel dating from 1930. It is at 2200 East Elm Street, (520) 325-1541, (800) 933-1093, or www.arizonainn.com. Spa enthusiasts can't go wrong with Canyon Ranch and its full slate of fitness activities, nutrition counseling, beauty treatments, and gourmet meals. It's tucked away at 8600 East Rockcliff Road, (520) 749-9000, (800) 742-9000, or www.canyonranch.com. Golf resorts, all brimming with amenities, include: Loews Ventana Canyon Resort, 7000 North Resort Drive, (520) 299-2020, (800) 234-5117, or www.loewshotels.com; and Westin La Paloma, 3800 East Sunrise Drive, (520) 742-6000, (800) 937-8461, or www.westin.com. Expect rooms at these resorts to go for at least $200 a night double occupancy in high season.

Restaurant options are plentiful in Tucson. Two of the best-known upscale dining rooms are the Ventana Room, 7000 North Resort Drive, (520) 299-2020, and The Tack Room, 7300 Vactor Ranch Trail, off Sabino Canyon Road (watch for the giant cowboy boot), (520) 722-2800. Quite popular is the Southwestern fare at the Cafe Terra Cotta, 3500 East Sunrise Drive, (520) 577-8100. Mexican restaurants are a good option: Check out El Charro Mexican Cafe, the oldest family-operated Mexican restaurant in the United States, at 311 North Court Avenue, (520) 622-1922; or Cafe Poca Cosa, 88 East Broadway Boulevard, (520) 622-6400, for Mexico city cuisine. Or tap into the University of Arizona scene with a visit to Gentle Ben's Brewing Company, 865 East University Boulevard, (520) 624-4177, or www.gentlebens.com, a bar and restaurant with several of its own brews on tap.

Detailed information on Tucson's many attractions, restaurants, accommodations, and shopping can be obtained by calling or writing the Metropolitan Tucson Convention & Visitors Bureau, 100 South Church Avenue, (800) 638-8350 or by visiting www.visittucson.org.

RELOCATION 🏠

It's a buyer's market in Phoenix and the Valley of the Sun. Developers are busy building new homes on the far edges of the Valley and, with many people moving to the area, real estate is a booming industry.

In fact, the metro Phoenix housing market is one of the most dynamic in the nation, continually competing with Las Vegas for the top spot nationally. Arizona ranks first or second in the United States in new single-family housing starts. According to the *Arizona Republic,* a record number of new and used homes sold across the Valley in 2003, and Phoenix's relatively low cost of living is attracting many people looking to relocate.

In 2003 the median price of a new home in the Valley was $176,500. With a median price of $155,000, resale homes in the Valley are also a bargain.

The state has one of the lowest income-tax structures in America. During the last decade, the state reduced income tax by 31 percent. Couple that with the relatively low property taxes and buying and keeping a home in the Valley becomes a terrific bargain. Maricopa County collects property taxes for itself, the state, cities, school districts, the community college district, the Central Arizona Water Conservation District, and any other taxing districts within which a residence is located. Arizona has a sales tax of 5 percent. Maricopa County adds an additional 7 percent tax on top of that. The various towns and cities in the Valley also add an additional tax, which varies by city or town. Property tax in Maricopa County is 10 percent of the property's current full-cash value as determined by the Assessor's Office.

In this chapter we take a look at the Valley's booming real-estate scene. We introduce you to some of the Valley's well-known neighborhoods and to some of the area's established real-estate agents who can help you find the perfect home, should

you like the Valley so much you decide to move here. The Valley is known for its retirement communities, and we have listed those in greater detail in the Retirement chapter. For information on Valley school districts, see the Education and Child Care chapter.

OVERVIEW

If you're considering relocating to the greater Phoenix area—congratulations! There's nowhere better than the Valley of the Sun for retirement or a new start. And there's a lot to consider—what neighborhood to live in, where to send the kids to school, how much to spend on housing, what style retirement community works for you. Once you make the decision to move here (and we hope you do!), there are all the details that go into a big move—how to get a driver's license, find a real estate agent, and, for some, begin a new career. We'd like to help make things a little easier! Here's a quick resource guide for newcomers. Welcome!

Libraries

All Maricopa County residents are eligible for a free Phoenix public library card with proof of ID. To get one, stop by any Phoenix Public Library branch, or preregister online and then go to any branch to pick up your card. A list of locations and hours is at www.ci.phoenix.az.us/library .html

Education

There are numerous school districts, private schools, and charter schools here, along with several community colleges, universities, and technical schools. In short, there are lots and lots of options. You'll find detailed listings in the Education and Child Care chapter. Here are some additional resources to have at your fingertips:

**Arizona Charter Schools Association
(928) 779-2761
www.azcharters.org**

**Arizona Department of Education
(602) 542-4361
www.ade.state.az.us**

Child Care

The area abounds with child-care options from national child-care centers to nanny services and preschools. The Education/ Child Care chapter provides comprehensive listings and services. A great referral service is the Association for Supportive Child Care at (480) 829-0500 or (800) 308-9000 and on the Web at www.arizonachildcare.org.

Health Care

Home to several top hospitals, including the world-renowned Phoenix Children's Hospital and the Mayo Clinic in Scottsdale, the metro area is well known for top-notch medical services of all kinds. The Health Care chapter provides an exhaustive and detailed list of all the major hospitals and medical services in the greater Phoenix area. For additional information or an overview, you can also contact:

**Arizona Medical Association
(602) 246-8901
www.azmedassn.org**

**Arizona Medical Board
(480) 551-2700
www.bomex.org**

If you're looking for comprehensive information on relocating to the Phoenix area, check out the **Phoenix Relocation Guide** *($11.00); it provides vital statistics, detailed housing information, and listings of relocation professionals. A great all-in-one tool for relocating. Call (480) 515-0620 or (800) 291-8060 to order.*

**Arizona Department of Health Services
(602) 542-1000
www.hs.state.az.us**

Motor Vehicle Information

If your car is already titled or registered in another state, you must get an Arizona title, registration, and license plate when you become an Arizona resident. If you work in Arizona, remain in the state for seven months or longer during any calendar year, or put children in school without paying nonresident tuition rates, you are considered a resident.

**Vehicle registration
Arizona Department of Transportation
(602) 255-0072
www.dot.state.az.us/mvd**

EMISSIONS

For the metro Phoenix area, your vehicle must first be emissions-tested if it is a model year 1968 or newer, including diesels. For more information, contact the Arizona Department of Environmental Quality at (800) 284-7748, or check www.adeq.state.az.us/environ/air/vei.

DRIVER'S LICENSE

If you have a valid license from another state, you have to present it and one other form of ID in order to get an Arizona license. A vision test is required but not a written test. For motor vehicle department locations, call the Arizona Department of Transportation at (602) 255-0072. Their Web site, www.dot.state.az.us/mvd, provides a list of all locations and their hours.

Real Estate

As the sixth-largest metropolitan area in the United States, Phoenix and Maricopa County are rapidly expanding. There are over 20 cities and towns, all with distinct personalities and price ranges, and things are growing and changing fast. Here are some housing resources, but for much more detail, read the Real Estate Agencies and Neighborhoods section of this chapter.

Arizona Association of Realtors
(602) 248-7787
www.aaronline.com

Arizona Department of Real Estate
(602) 468-1414
www.re.state.az.us

Relocation Services

Arizona Insights Relocation Center Inc.
10446 North 74th Street, Suite 100,
Scottsdale
(480) 481-8401, (800) 899-7356
www.cbsuccess.com
Arizona Insights has been in business since 1982 to help corporate transferees, new hires, and candidates. It is now associated with Coldwell Banker Success Realty, and the company's services include an area orientation, home-finding and rental assistance, temporary housing, spouse/partner career assistance, and school counseling. It's a one-stop center for information on relocating to the Valley and can even help with finding doctors, day care, and auto registration locations. It also offers the same services to Valley residents seeking to relocate worldwide.

Retirement

Ready to retire? Maricopa County is a great place to do so! A leader in the development of "active-adult" communities, the Valley of the Sun affords lots of choices for retirees of all types. Looking for an active retirement, you'll find year-round golf, tennis, swimming, and lots of senior-friendly activities to choose from here. Check out the Retirement chapter for details and listings of retirement services and communities. A terrific central resource is the Area Agency on Aging, (602) 256-2277, www.aaaphx.org.

Chambers of Commerce

These are great resources for local information and many provide free relocation packages. Here are some of the larger ones. For a comprehensive list and online links to each one, go to www.phoenix.about.com/cs/businesschamb/index.htm.

Greater Phoenix
(602) 254-5521
www.phoenixchamber.com

Scottsdale
(480) 945-8481
www.scottsdalecvb.com

Southwest Valley Chamber of
Commerce, Goodyear
(623) 932-2260
www.stvalleychamber.org

Carefree/Cave Creek
Chamber of Commerce
(480) 488-3381
www.carefree-cavecreek.com

Chandler
(480) 963-4571, (800) 963-4571
www.chandlerchamber.com

NEIGHBORHOODS

Most Valley housing is relatively new and, consequently, so are most neighborhoods. The neighborhoods that people can pick out by name usually have some history to them. Phoenix, at least partly because of the way it has annexed unincorporated communities, has neighborhoods with names. In Phoenix, neighborhoods such as Encanto, Arcadia, Maryvale, Paradise Valley, and Sunnyslope are among the best known.

To the rest of the Valley, a neighborhood usually is the name of a development. With so many new developments popping up, any listing would quickly become a litany of names and features without any context. It's much more useful to think of the Valley outside of Phoenix in geographic terms. North and South Scottsdale are distinct from one another, so are North and South Tempe and East and West Mesa. The neighborhoods and developments within each geographic area are very similar.

With very few exceptions, the great truth about Valley development is that the farther you get from the Valley's core, the houses being built are bigger and the landscaping is more desertlike.

The oldest Valley neighborhoods were built to help the residents forget they were in the desert. Greenery abounds thanks to lawn irrigation. In these neighborhoods, lawns were often sunk an inch or two below the surrounding sidewalks and bounded by grass-covered mounds. The lawns are flooded at night so that they look a bit like rice paddies. They stay green.

As time went on, the Valley became more water-conscious. The neighborhoods built in the 1950s through the 1970s saw a mixture of green lawns and desert landscaping, with grass lawns still tending to outnumber the desert landscapes. By and large, these neighborhoods are full of ranch-style houses built without basements on concrete pads. Because the elements (except for the sun) were relatively kind to autos, many homes built in that era featured carports rather than garages. Most of these homes were built in cozy proximity for young, blue-collar and lower-middle-class families.

The developments built in the past 15 to 20 years tend to have a more spacious feeling. Two-story houses have become more common. Garages are the norm. The developments themselves have sunken greenbelts for flood protection, which opens up the landscape of a neighborhood. The greenbelts become places to jog, walk the dog, ride your bike, or just meander. Many newer developments are built around artificial lakes or golf courses to add a touch of cool, green relief to the surroundings. On the higher end of the price scale, some communities are gated and have their own security.

Homeowner associations have become more common, both in older neighborhoods and in new developments. In new developments especially, they act as a form of low-level government, enforcing various restrictions in the property deeds in an effort to keep property values up for all association members. Enforcement is usually through fines, after the homeowner has been given some warnings. The associations use their dues to keep up common areas, such as greenbelts and roadside landscaping. Restrictions can be as loose as making sure that all the houses are painted in a similar palette of colors or as tight as not allowing outdoor speakers in a patio area. Outdoor remodeling and building additions often have to be reviewed by the associations in order to ensure that they comply with the deed restrictions. This is in addition to any review procedure that a city might have.

The associations evolved because of the vast differences in neighborhood upkeep, especially in Phoenix proper. You can drive down one half-mile of a street in a development and find nothing but immaculately kept homes and landscapes, and then proceed the next half-mile through blocks of badly kept rentals. The associations help keep this patchwork from developing any further.

Phoenix

Sprawling for more than 400 square miles, the city of Phoenix encompasses many neighborhoods. The following are some of the more identifiable.

ARCADIA

The Arcadia area is one of the more mature neighborhoods. Sitting beside Camelback Mountain and stretching to Scottsdale, this neighborhood developed mostly in the postwar era. Within its confines a mix of wood-frame, brick, and painted cinder-block homes can be found. The landscaping is mature, and the streets are lined with trees, making it an attractive area for middle-class families and young urban professionals. The houses have more character than many of the homes built in later years, although some of the older ranch-style homes are being torn down and replaced with large, Tuscan- and Southwestern-style residences.

DOWNTOWN PHOENIX

Downtown Phoenix, considered the area from McDowell Road south to the Southern Pacific railroad tracks and Seventh Street west to Seventh Avenue, is undergoing a revitalization spearheaded by the location of two major venues in the area: America West Arena and Bank One Ballpark. The new Dodge Theatre is also a main attraction. This growth has brought an explosion of interest in opening businesses—particularly restaurants, coffeehouses, and nightclubs—that take advantage of the sudden influx of nighttime foot traffic in the area.

What little housing there was in the area before downtown's resurgence was older and housed mostly lower-income people. This housing, generally small, single-story houses with mature, water-intensive grass-and-tree landscaping, is being torn down to make way for upscale condominium and town-house sorts of housing. However, it is an area where concerns about crime and personal safety are legitimate. It's now referred to as Copper Square, and the Downtown Phoenix Partnership is working with residential developers, the business community, civic leaders, and current residents to attract housing here that fits the urban character of downtown, including lofts, upscale apartments, and housing priced to meet many budgets. The partnership has greatly increased the number of services available in the downtown area. There are security guides, streetscape improvements, parking and traffic assistance, the DASH (a free downtown area shuttle), and downtown information directories. Downtown residents now have access to concert halls, theaters, cinemas, shopping, offices, groceries, coffee shops, restaurants, galleries, cultural and sports attractions, and more. Considering the pace of change, this is becoming a very desirable neighborhood very quickly.

ENCANTO

The neighborhood around the 222-acre Encanto Park, Encanto Village, which forms a good portion of the square mile defined by Seventh Avenue, Thomas Road, 19th Avenue, and McDowell Road, is very good-looking and home to most of Phoenix's historic district. The homes are older, dating from as far back as the 1920s, and feature mature landscaping. There's a sense of being in an oasis that has a bit of a Midwestern look. Unlike developments built after water restrictions came in, this is a neighborhood that relies on grass for landscaping rather than desert styles. Being in a relatively flat area of central Phoenix that is only a few miles from the Salt River, the neighborhood's trees and grass insulate and isolate the area. You don't notice the surrounding mountains so much here, just the neighborhood. As a desirable little enclave close to downtown Phoenix, Encanto's housing is relatively expensive, filling the neighborhood with professionals and their families. The Encanto neighborhood is of a similar character to a number of neighborhoods within 5 miles of downtown Phoenix, including the Willo, Coronado, and Phoenix Country Club neighborhoods.

CHRISTOWN

By and large, the homes in the area around Christown are affordable and close to the amenities of downtown and the state fairgrounds. The neighborhood streets, developed from the 1950s through the 1970s, are wider than those in older neighborhoods such as Encanto, so it doesn't seem so isolated from the desert.

The postwar housing reflects a suburban imperative. Single-story structures, either of wood-frame or painted cinder-block construction, dominate, with mature landscaping and grass-blanketed yards. If not for the palm trees and desert mountains visible in the distance, this would be a suburban area that would fit comfortably in any part of the country.

In many ways, the Christown area is mirrored east of Central Avenue by similar unnamed neighborhoods (or neighborhoods whose names are obscure) and west of Interstate 17 by the vast Maryvale neighborhood. They present a line of demarcation between the old Phoenix of the 1950s, with its working-class ambiance, and the outlying upper middle-class areas (often defined by desert landscaping) farther out from the city's core.

MARYVALE

Maryvale has become almost synonymous with the west side of Phoenix. In actuality, Maryvale was a 1950s development by builder John F. Long. (He named it after his wife, Mary.) The units were affordable for young families, looking something like desert versions of the house in the Dick Van Dyke Show. The streets were broader than the old cozy developments like Encanto, but the general suburban desert feeling was the same. Occasionally, you see some desert landscaping, but most

Arizona housing is being built at a fantastic rate. Developments are spreading into the desert rapidly. The newer developments offer more of a desert flavor than the older neighborhoods, but established neighborhoods already have their own distinctive cultures and flavors, which can be a good source of support during any transition.

reminders of the desert are the occasional cactus or saguaro that's part of a conventional grass lawn. Maryvale still attracts working-class and lower-middle-class folks.

Many builders followed Long's lead in subsequent decades, and the effect is a similar style of single-story tract housing for many miles around. The only difference is that with newer developments, desert landscaping began to catch up with and rival the predominance of grass lawns.

Some areas of Maryvale have deteriorated and face high crime, although westside business has been growing since the completion of Interstate 10. The housing, which depended on lower-cost materials for its affordability, goes south very quickly when not maintained properly. That desert sun is murder on asphalt shingles and sprayed-paint exteriors.

Cricket Pavilion (formerly called Desert Sky Pavilion), an open-air entertainment amphitheater that opened on Maryvale's west side in 1990, helped fuel a major economic revitalization of the area. The then-moribund Westridge Mall, which is across Encanto Boulevard from the amphitheater, has since been renamed Desert Sky Mall and is thriving. The area is also home to 8,000-seat Maryvale Baseball Park, spring-training home of the Milwaukee Brewers.

METROCENTER

The area around Metrocenter mall, which runs alongside I-17 from the Arizona Canal to Peoria Avenue, is newer than Christown. Looked at as a geological exercise, this neighborhood reflects the next strata in the Valley's growth. The developments around the mall are more likely to feel like suburban enclaves than those in Christown. The Metrocenter neighborhood's streets feature more twists and turns that keep nonresidents from cutting through, a legitimate concern in light of the mall's heavy traffic. Here some desert landscaping starts to creep in among the suburban lawnscape. The landscaping is mature, and houses may be just a tad farther apart. Again, single-story structures dominate, and there is less of the painted cinderblock and more of the wood-frame type of house. By and large, this area is a bedroom community for middle-class families or professionals who work downtown or in nearby office-industrial parks.

NORTH CENTRAL

From the 1920s on, an address along the northern parts of Central Avenue meant the occupants were wealthy. Keep in mind that northern is a relative term. The city has expanded far to the north of Northern Avenue, which once was the northern boundary of the city. This well-heeled section of Central Avenue begins at Camelback Road on the south and extends to just north of Northern Avenue. Houses here were built over a long period. Some reflect an older, more stately style, while others are upscale suburban ranch houses. The streets are narrow and cozy. You'll find a tree-shaded walking path on both sides of Central Avenue, the remains of an old riding trail for horses. The landscaping is mostly a lush green. The neighborhood is upscale and filled with professionals.

SUNNYSLOPE

Sunnyslope began as a place where indigent people came to seek cures for lung ailments. The Valley's dry climate made it the perfect place for such cures, but cure seekers were banned from pitching tents in Phoenix proper. So they went north to around Dunlap and Central Avenues to the foothills where they would sit on the "sunny slopes" and recover their health. Eventually a sanatorium was built there, and a small, thriving lower-middle-class community arose.

The beauty of Sunnyslope is that the neighborhood feels cozy. It's a strange perception because the houses aren't really any closer together than elsewhere. Perhaps the maturity of the landscaping and the way the community nestles at the foot of the North Mountain Preserve makes it feel more enclosed than some other areas. Homes in the area are mainly ranch style, and the character of the neighborhood is generally middle class to lower-middle class.

PARADISE VALLEY

The Paradise Valley neighborhood of Phoenix borders on the town of Paradise Valley, but don't confuse the two. They're very different. The Paradise Valley neighborhood is a visually busy area that creeps up to the north end of North Mountain. It also rises toward the foothills to the north. Houses here are peopled by blue- and white-collar types. The construction is generally single-story tract homes, with many taking advantage of desert landscaping, which tends to become more of the norm in the areas immediately around Phoenix's mountains.

SOUTH PHOENIX

Technically, South Phoenix would include Ahwatukee and an extremely wide variety of houses and neighborhoods. Farms, ranches, nurseries, orchards, and industrial parks, as well as the luxurious area around the Pointe South Mountain Resort—all are part of South Phoenix.

Unfortunately, in popular parlance, South Phoenix is the wrong side of the tracks—actually, the wrong side of the Salt River. Some (and we stress the word *some*) sections of South Phoenix come as close as you'll find to an urban war zone in the Valley.

There's a strong effort among community members to fight blight and crime. South Phoenix, like many other Valley areas, is an area of suburban tract homes, many of them built in the past 20 to 30 years. A few developers are rediscovering the area and building pockets of upscale homes near the base of the South Mountain. These developments offer great values on mountain-view housing. Even when you exclude the more luxurious areas of South Phoenix, the income levels vary widely, from middle class to poor.

Southeast Valley

AHWATUKEE

Sitting south of South Mountain, Ahwatukee began growing in the 1980s and 1990s and is still growing today. Terra-cotta roofs and stucco predominate, and the neighborhood is generally walled off from the main streets, with a few entry points. This is a neighborhood full of young urban professionals, a mix of families, and a small pocket of retirees. Be warned that commuter traffic during rush hour can be slow. The housing, generally single-story or two-story homes and a wide variety of upscale apartments and town homes, ranges from the moderately priced to the expensive.

CHANDLER

Chandler has a small downtown core with some housing that dates from the city's founding. Chandler didn't see an immediate postwar growth boom, and thus remained a largely agricultural community until residential developments began sprouting at a good clip in the late 1970s and early 1980s. In recent years Chandler has continued to grow at a fast pace, with residential subdivisions taking the place of farms and ranches. Again, the newer developments are predominantly of the tile-roof and stucco style, but there are also wood-frame neighborhoods and neighborhoods akin to Maryvale in the older sections. Chandler is attractive to

young families and middle-class professionals, particularly since Intel became a major employer here. Its retail sectors are also a main attraction, with the refurbishment of the downtown business district and the addition of Chandler Fashion Center mall.

GILBERT

Like Chandler, Gilbert had been an agricultural community for most of its existence. Then in the 1980s residential development started to boom. In recent years the city has exploded with new residential and retail developments. So, the vast majority of housing in Gilbert is relatively new, which means tile roofs and stucco. The older places in town—those that are still left—are a mixture of horse properties and small ranches. The city of Gilbert attracts young families and middle-class professionals.

MESA

At 122 square miles, Mesa is not as vast as Phoenix. Still, the east-west drive across Mesa is long and makes the city seem to stretch on forever. Most of the city's growth in the past two to three decades has been in housing developments that spread eastward from the more mature area surrounding downtown.

Downtown Mesa—The center of downtown spreads out from the intersection of Center and Main Streets. The streets are

Look across the Valley and you'll see a sea of red-tile roofs. Developers take their knocks for building so many homes with tile roofs and stucco walls, but there are advantages to such construction. The stucco is applied to wire mesh over insulating foam panels for added protection from the summer heat, which helps reduce utility bills. The tile roofs stand up to intense desert sun better than any other roofing surface. The average owner will never have to reroof a tile-roofed house.

wide and lined with trees. There's plenty of space for parking, and a number of the streets are wide enough so that you can park diagonally head on to the curb. Many of the streets have substantial grassy medians. Much of the housing is from before World War II. Exteriors of redbrick, painted brick, and painted cinder block and stucco are the norm here. The area ranges from middle class to blue-collar.

East Mesa—The eastern portion of Mesa is a progression of new housing developments. The farther east you travel, the stucco and tile-roof style that predominates in the Valley's new developments is just as predominant here. However, you're also more likely to see wood-frame housing reminiscent of the East or Midwest here than you are in other new areas. These new suburban developments are encroaching upon older areas that contain horse properties and little clusters of old trailer parks and rentals. The area also includes huge trailer-park complexes, such as Leisure World.

The spaces between the old development clusters and the new are still fairly wide open as you near Apache Junction and the Superstition Mountains; however, this land, too, is slowly being gobbled up by development. These older areas grew up around the old alignment of U.S. Highway 60, which followed Main Street and the Apache Trail to points east. (Main Street becomes Apache Trail as it heads east of Power Road.) The newer alignment of US 60 along the Superstition Highway and the completion of the highway through Mesa makes it an easy hour's drive to downtown Phoenix, thus fueling the building boom.

With the addition of Williams Gateway Airport, the growth of east Mesa has also expanded southward, again with new developments of tile-roof and stucco housing. The area features a mixture of young families and middle-class professionals.

West Mesa—Much of this area was developed from the 1960s through the 1970s and features suburban housing tracts that are similar to the Maryvale,

Christown, and Metrocenter areas of Phoenix. You'll find a mix of lawns and desert landscaping here and more shingle roofs than tile. The vast majority of homes are single story. The developments are very similar in character to those in neighboring areas of Tempe. The area's residents include young families, blue-collar workers, and middle-class professionals.

TEMPE

Although there are many smaller neighborhoods in Tempe, the city breaks down into essentially three areas—north of the Salt River, the Arizona State University area, and south Tempe.

The area north of the Salt River resembles and is adjacent to south Scottsdale. A quick rise from the river toward the Papago Buttes gives the well-kept, single-story tract housing an attractive background. The neighborhoods up here are pretty well settled with mature landscaping, usually grass and palm trees.

Redevelopment and the addition of Tempe's Town Lake have changed the face of downtown Tempe, which is adjacent to the ASU campus south of the Salt River. The neighborhoods surrounding downtown and ASU are mostly older areas, with mature trees and grass landscaping. The wood-frame and brick houses are small but have individual character. These are pleasant and shady neighborhoods of old-time flavor, almost a stereotype of the college town. The area attracts mostly students and faculty. However, some new high-end loft homes have recently gone up and are attracting urban professionals to downtown.

South of Southern Avenue, Tempe essentially becomes the land of red tile roofs and stucco. Housing here tends to start from the $140,000s, and in some enclaves goes well beyond that. As you move south, the lots grow larger with a few horse properties and even pricier homes. So the area attracts middle-class, upper-middle-class, and, depending on the development, a few wealthy folk.

Northeast Valley

CAREFREE

Carefree was founded in the 1950s and is one of the earliest planned communities in Arizona. Famous for its giant sundial (the largest in the Western Hemisphere) and unique rock outcroppings, Carefree is 36 miles from downtown Phoenix and encompasses about 8.8 square miles. With a population of around 3,000, this upscale community has a reputation for a laid-back lifestyle evidenced by city streets named Ho and Hum Roads and Easy Street. According to census information for the year 2000, median resident age was 55.2 years, median household income $88,702, and the median house value, $411,200.

CAVE CREEK

Cave Creek was settled in the 1870s by miners and ranchers, but did not become incorporated as a municipality until 1986. Just northwest of Scottsdale, it's only 36 miles from downtown Phoenix and has a population of just under 4,000. Census data from 2000 show the median resident age at 44.7 years, a median household income of $59,937, and a median house value of $270,500. This area is booming with new housing developments. People are attracted to Cave Creek's Old West feel and cozy atmosphere.

FOUNTAIN HILLS

Isolated from the rest of the Valley by the ridge of the McDowell Mountains, Fountain Hills revels in its small-town atmosphere. Residents swear by the friendliness of neighbors. In 1997 *Parenting* magazine featured Fountain Hills in an article called "Ten Great Places to Raise a Family." A planned community, Fountain Hills set its sights on retirees when it opened in 1970. The area had previously been a cattle ranch. The houses were intended to be small to fit the needs of the retired couple. Life would center on the golf course that wends its way through town along Saguaro Boulevard and on Fountain Park, where the world's tallest fountain can send a jet of water up to 560 feet into the air. The town's master developer, MCO Properties Inc., says that the market changed and demanded larger houses. Most of what's available in Fountain Hills is of the stucco and tile-roof variety, but there's more variation within that style than you'll see in many recent developments. Fountain Hills is attractive to older families, professionals, and retirees.

PARADISE VALLEY

Now, if you really want to go upscale, check out the town of Paradise Valley, which is adjacent to (but not to be confused with) the Paradise Valley neighborhood of Phoenix. Surrounded by Phoenix and Scottsdale, this community boasts a vast array of well-to-do celebrities, including baseball's Joe Garagiola and rock star Alice Cooper—talk about diversity! With the reddish-brown rock of Camelback and Mummy Mountains dominating the hilly landscape, this is a place where desert landscaping abounds. Exclusively zoned for single-family residents, many of the houses are done in variations of Mexican home architecture, giving them a cool quality in the bright heat of the sun. People with money are buying up perfectly good older homes, tearing them down, and building mansions on the expensive earth. The spaces between houses seem vast and are peppered with desert plants.

SCOTTSDALE

Scottsdale essentially is two cities—north and south. The southern portion of the city is the area developed from the 1950s through the 1970s as a result of booming employment in aerospace and other industries. Palm trees dot the landscape and let the sun shine through. The housing, mostly single-family tract homes, is affordable and has been, for the most part, well maintained. It's an area that attracts faculty and students from nearby ASU as well as middle-class families.

As you move northward, toward Shea Boulevard and beyond, the housing values rise from the low $200,000s up to infinity (or at least close). New developments of the red-tile roof and stucco variety seem to be going up constantly, eating up more of the pristine desert that two decades ago wasn't even part of the city. There are even some communities that offer Tuscan-style architecture. These are all upscale developments, some of them featuring artificial lakes, others dependent on golf courses, and all basking in the splendor of the nearby mountains. You can't forget you're in the desert up here, even though most of the subdivisions have plenty of trees and greenery.

Northwest Valley

GLENDALE

Glendale has three faces. The part of Glendale that bounds the north-central section of Phoenix is much like that part of Phoenix in character. As you go north from the Glendale line at Camelback Road and 43rd Avenue, the developments get newer. The southern end is much like the Christown neighborhood of Phoenix, giving way to developments more like those around Metrocenter. The southern end has more young families, and in the northern end more established professionals predominate.

Downtown Glendale has been through quite a face-lift in recent years. It has a charming, small-town quality that belies the city's status as the third largest in the Valley. This is where you'll find the city's oldest prewar houses (some of them pre–World War I), a number of them being reclaimed by professionals who like their charm. As with most housing from the Valley's early days, redbrick and white stucco are the norm.

Then, there's the rest of Glendale, which has boomed and expanded over the past two to three decades to the southwest and to the north. The growth has been in areas that once were covered with farm fields and orchards. True to the character of most suburban development in the area, there is much tile-roof and stucco. Given that Glendale once had a reputation as a blue-collar town—old industrial parks dot Glendale's south end—the new development is surprising. For it's not only middle- class, but also upper-middle-class in character. Arrowhead Ranch in northwestern Glendale typifies this up-and-coming face of the city. The 4,000-acre development features artificial lakes with 14 miles of shoreline and two championship golf courses.

The biggest thing to hit Glendale in recent years is the new Glendale Gateway, a complex that includes the 17,000-seat Glendale Arena—home to Arizona Coyotes hockey and Arizona Sting lacrosse, along with other sporting events, shows, and concerts—and the new Cardinals football stadium, which is currently under construction and set to open in 2006. Glendale will host the Super Bowl in 2008 at the new stadium, and residential and commercial development is booming in and around Glendale Gateway.

PEORIA

Peoria was founded in 1886 by settlers from Peoria, Illinois, and was a small farming community until recent years. The housing developments that have exploded across Peoria in the past few decades are mostly of the tile-roof and stucco variety with desert landscaping, although you'll also find some wood-frame styles mixed in. The city is attractive to both younger and older families and also to a number of retirees residing in Westbrook Village, which is just east of Sun City. Peoria is also home to the new 11,000-seat Peoria Sports Complex, which hosts both the San Diego Padres and Seattle Mariners spring-training games.

SUN CITY

Sun City is a well-planned retirement community that offers every amenity to its residents. Life here revolves around the golf courses and recreation centers, where senior citizens defy old stereotypes with an active lifestyle. The 1,200 acres of golf links create belts of green relief among houses that were built from 1960 through 1980. Sun City is an unincorporated area of Maricopa County. (See the Retirement chapter for more about Sun City.)

SUN CITY GRAND

Like its sister communities, Sun City Grand, located in Surprise, is a growing retirement community for active adults. The 4,000-acre community will have 9,800 homes and 17,500 residents upon completion (8,500 homes have already been sold). Sun City Grand offers all the amenities Del Webb communities are known for: state-of-the-art recreational facilities, championship golf courses, indoor and outdoor pools, and spas.

SUN CITY WEST

Separated from Sun City by the usually dry Agua Fria River, the Sun City West retirement community opened when Sun City was just about built out in 1980. Sun City West is a bit grander in scale than Sun City. The houses are bigger and essentially for more well-to-do seniors. Sun City West also reflects a general housing trend in the Valley toward bigger, less-crowded development. However, in its basics, Sun City West is much like Sun City, revolving around its golf courses and recreation centers. Sun City West is an unincorporated area of Maricopa County. (See the Retirement chapter.)

SURPRISE

Surprise officials say that a new home is completed in Surprise every three and a half hours, so the old town is quickly disappearing. Surprise has attracted new development as young families look farther from the Valley's core to find lower-cost property. Surprise also includes two large retirement communities: Arizona Traditions and Sun City Grand.

YOUNGTOWN

Youngtown was established as a strictly retirement community in 1954 and was incorporated in 1960. And although the town's age restrictions were lifted in 1998, most of the residents remain age 55 and up. The housing, of 1950s through 1960s vintage, reflects the retirement imperatives of the time—simple, small ranch houses. The retirees here typically have less income than in Sun City and Sun City West. Youngtown also has much more of a small-town atmosphere than either Sun City or Sun City West, which seem more like resorts than towns.

Southwest Valley

With the advent of Loops 101 and 303 on the west side of Phoenix, the Southwest Valley has absolutely exploded with growth, both residential and commercial. As this part of the Valley becomes more accessible, and more affordable than the east side, people from all over are flocking here, where mostly master-planned communities are being built.

AVONDALE

Avondale was founded during World War II to provide housing for workers from the tire and rubber factory in nearby Goodyear. Homes in the older section retain their small-town feel, and this downtown neighborhood reflects Avondale's history as an agricultural community. Three rivers traverse the city—the Gila, Salt, and Agua Fria—and their banks serve as recreation areas. However, with all the new development occurring in Avondale, the town is certainly changing. The new communities, aimed at young families and professionals, are heading in the tile-roof and stucco direction. Years ago, the city annexed the area around Phoenix International Raceway, and although this neighborhood used to be surrounded by an area of large, relatively isolated homes, you can now find new subdivisions here too.

BUCKEYE

Buckeye was once a small farming community, with most of its housing contained in a small town center. Not any more. With the construction of master-planned communities like the 8,800-acre Verrado, with 14,000 homes and its own city hall, this once-sleepy little town is booming. The tile-roof and stucco neighborhoods now under construction in Buckeye offer a plethora of amenities—such as lakes, golf courses, and hiking trails—and are luring single professionals, families, and even retirees. Plans are underway for as many as 160,000 homes around the White Tank Mountains, and Del Webb is slated to build another Sun City here, once Sun City Grand is full. Buckeye's proximity to Phoenix, about 30 to 45 minutes via I-10, makes it desirable to anyone who wants to get away from the hustle and bustle of Phoenix and get more house for their money.

GOODYEAR

In 1917 the Goodyear Tire and Rubber Company purchased 16,000 acres in Arizona to grow cotton to be used in making its rubber tires. The town of Goodyear grew up around these fields, and in the 1940s, when the cotton market declined after the war, the company opened an airplane plant in town. For years Goodyear had a company-town feel to it, since its single-family homes were initially built for plant workers. Over the years, however, Goodyear's cotton fields gave way to other crops, and this land has now been used for residential development. The planned communities moving into Goodyear offer everything from affordable starter homes to a variety of upscale residences, including casitas and mountainside or equestrian estates. Currently, the largest development in Goodyear is the 20,000-acre community of Estrella Mountain Ranch, which is nestled at the base of the Estrella Mountains and offers single-family and custom homesites, along with two lakes, a yacht club, a golf course, and a 40-acre park. Goodyear is attractive to both young families and professionals, many of whom commute to Phoenix.

LITCHFIELD PARK

Litchfield Park was also founded by the Goodyear Tire and Rubber Company and, as Valley sizes go, it is a small town both in area and population. In the older part of town, the streets are shady and the homes are situated on large lots. No walls separate Litchfield Park from the rest of the Valley, but it nonetheless feels like an enclave. The town has developed over the past three and a half decades in the shadow of the Wigwam Resort, which remains the town's top employer. However, even though Litchfield Park has little room for growth in area, a few new tile-roof and stucco housing developments have sprung up in recent years. Litchfield Park has, in a sense, merged with the town of Goodyear, since Litchfield Park is so small and Goodyear is expanding so greatly. Litchfield Park is also just 3 miles from Luke Air Force Base, and many of its residents are retired military personnel.

TOLLESON

Tolleson is a largely Hispanic town with a farming-community past. Like the other Southwest Valley cities, it, too, is evolving. In recent years new tile-roof and stucco subdivisions have been built next to the town's older single-family homes, and its proximity to I-10 has made it attractive for both residential and commercial growth. The town is home to a variety of manufacturing and distribution companies, including the American Italian Pasta Company and Fry's and Albertsons' distribution centers.

APARTMENT LIVING AND OTHER RENTALS

Extensive growth in the Valley has put an upward pressure on the rents charged by apartment complexes. Still, the Valley remains a very affordable place for renters. Broadly speaking, good one-bedroom units with a minimum six-month lease range from the low $550s per month in Phoenix to $900-plus monthly in north Scottsdale.

All Rentals & More
5835 North 16th Street, Suite J, Phoenix
(602) 279-9578

All Rentals & More opened its doors in 1989 and is a full-service real estate company that works with several hundred apartment communities in the Valley. The agency can also assist with house and townhome rentals and has three offices serving the Valley of the Sun. The agents can help find long- and short-term leases and will escort potential renters to the properties. Information includes floor plans, lease terms, and move-in costs, among other details. The service is free to prospective renters.

Apartment Finders
3554 West Northern Avenue, Phoenix
(602) 841-5055
www.aptfind.com

In business since 1981, Apartment Finders has a computer network that offers current information on more than 300,000 units in the Valley of the Sun. The information available includes floor plans, amenities, school information, and other details. The company's licensed agents can help find long-term and short-term leases for winter visitors and corporate relocators. They even escort apartment seekers to the properties and are experts in handling challenging rental issues such as income and credit problems or finding properties that allow large dogs. The company is paid by the property owners, so its services to renters are free. It has four offices (two in Phoenix, one each in Tempe and

There's lots of information available for renters both on the Web and at local stores. Check out Apartments For Rent *(www.forrent.com) and* Apartment Rentals *(www.azcentral.com/class/real estate.html); both are free and cover the greater Phoenix area.*

Mesa) serving the entire Valley. The Valleywide number for the company is (602) 957-7000.

REAL ESTATE AGENCIES

Century 21 A.M. Realty
1730 East Warner Road, Suite 7, Tempe
(480) 831-1114
www.century21.com

Century 21 A.M. Realty opened its doors in 1980 and is the oldest Century 21 franchise in Maricopa County. The agency focuses on the East Valley, although it can find and sell homes across the Valley. Through Century 21 and the VIP Referral System, the agency can accept and refer relocation clients worldwide. Century 21 has dozens of independently owned and operated affiliates in the Valley that offer similar services.

Coldwell Banker Success Realty
10446 North 74th Street, Suite 200, Scottsdale
(480) 481-8400
www.cbsuccess.com

Success Realty has more than 25 sales offices serving every portion of the Valley of the Sun. It is the largest multioffice company within the Coldwell Banker Real Estate Corporation affiliate network in Arizona. Founded in 1950, Success Realty, including its offices in Tucson, employs more than 2,200 real estate professionals. The company has a full-fledged relocation division. Coldwell Banker is a full-service real estate company and also offers relocation services, a developers' marketing service, and concierge services.

Besides the real estate classifieds of the Arizona Republic *and the* Tribune, *a number of publications can aid home shoppers. Look for* Homes & Land, The Real Estate Book, Homes Illustrated, *and* Harmon Homes. *Each offers several editions zoned to specific areas, and all of them include photos of the houses. They're all available free at various grocery and convenience stores, usually in racks by the exits so they're easy to grab on the way out.*

ERA Encore Realty
678 East Thunderbird Road, Phoenix
(602) 938-2000
www.era.com
Encore Realty is one of the top 50 offices in sales in ERA's international franchise network. Based in Phoenix, Encore handles sales in all areas of the Valley with more than 50 agents. Encore is a member of the National Military Broker Network and specializes in meeting the needs of service members from Luke Air Force Base.

John Hall and Associates
11211 North Tatum Boulevard, Suite 200, Phoenix
(602) 953-4043, (800) 477-0105
www.johnhall.com
John Hall and Associates, in business in Arizona since 1974, has 5 offices and more than 800 real estate professionals covering the Valley. It is a full-service agency that offers complete relocation services for individuals, brokerages, and corporations.

Keller Williams Realty
3420 East Shea Boulevard, Suite 200, Phoenix
(602) 787-2000
http://new.kw.com/kw
Keller Williams Realty maintains 10 sales offices in the Valley of the Sun. This is the north Phoenix location. The firm provides local sales and relocation services as part of the Keller Williams network.

MCO Realty Inc.
9617 North Saguaro Boulevard, Fountain Hills
(480) 837-2500, (800) 237-2501
www.mcorealty.com
You can't miss MCO Realty, because its two-story headquarters stand prominently at the busy intersection of Saguaro and Shea Boulevards. Another Fountain Hills office can be found at the Plaza Fountainside, next to Fountain Park. A wholly owned subsidiary of MCO Custom Properties, the master developer of Fountain Hills, MCO Realty focuses on selling both new and resale homes as well as custom homesites in Fountain Hills.

Molly Bridgeman Realty
7145 North 57th Avenue, Glendale
(623) 934-0095
Molly Bridgeman loves Glendale and Peoria, and she puts her money where her mouth is. Most of her properties are in the Northwest Valley. Bridgeman has been in Arizona real estate for 23 years and has had her own agency for the past 18 years. Her office, a remodeled 1913 red-brick house in downtown Glendale, is near the Catlin Court antiques-store district. The six-agent office handles new homes, resales, relocation services, and property management for investors.

Russ Lyon Realty
6710 North Scottsdale Road, Suite 180, Scottsdale
(480) 778-8000
www.russlyon.com
Russ Lyon Realty, a Valley firm that opened for business in 1947, has more than 575 sales associates in 10 sales offices based in Ahwatukee, Carefree-Cave Creek, Mesa, Peoria, Phoenix, Paradise Valley, and north Scottsdale. This is their corporate and relocation office. Russ Lyon is an affiliate of RELO, a nationwide relocation service, and is also an affiliate of Sotheby's International Realty, specializing in luxury properties.

Realty Executives
301 East Bethany Home Road,
Suite 187 C, Phoenix
(602) 264-0605
www.realtyexecutivesphx.com
This is the central Phoenix office of the
Realty Executives franchise operation,
which was born in the city in 1965. Today,
there are more than 1,000 Realty Executives franchises worldwide. Reflecting its
hometown roots, Realty Executives
Phoenix has 17 offices in the Valley of the
Sun, as well as its corporate headquarters.

RE/MAX All Stars
8079 North 85th Way, Scottsdale
(480) 998-6000
www.realestate-arizona.com
RE/MAX All Stars is one of many RE/MAX
offices across the Valley of the Sun. It
offers full-service real estate sales and
service and relocation services through
RE/MAX's international network.

West USA Realty
11022 North 28th Drive, #100 Lake
Biltmore Corporate Center, Phoenix
(602) 942-1410
www.westusa.com
West USA Realty is a Phoenix firm that
opened its doors in April of 1986 and has
since grown to six branch offices and
seven franchise offices, with a network of
more than 1,400 real estate professionals

*If yours is a low-income household, you
can learn about the many services and
programs available to you in Arizona by
obtaining the* People's InfoGuide. *Published by the* Arizona Community Action
Association, *it lists senior services along
with places to go for assistance with
employment and training, health care,
housing, understanding Social Security
benefits, and help in paying utilities. For
the annually updated guide, contact the
association at 2627 North Third Street,
Suite 2, Phoenix, (602) 604-0640, or
visit www.azcaa.org/PIG.htm to down-
load the guide from the Internet.*

in the Valley. This office serves the metro
Phoenix area. West USA's other offices are
scattered Valleywide.

Why USA Penelope Realty
Waddell
(623) 935-3804
www.peneloperealty.com
Penelope C. Myer has been in real estate for
more than a decade and has had her own
agency for the past seven years. Although
she sells homes Valleywide, she concen-
trates on the West Valley and specializes in
residential and retirement properties. The
four-agent office sells horse properties
and offers relocation services as well.

RETIREMENT 🌴

In Phoenix you can talk to retirees who have traveled the world—for leisure, business, or military service—people who know they have a wealth of choices for a retirement nest, and they'll tell you why they chose this city above everywhere else: climate, of course. Tired of shoveling snow and skidding on ice, many retirees opt for the Valley of the Sun. They also like the fact that Phoenix is so welcoming to seniors. The cost of living is relatively low, the people are friendly, there's plenty to do, and the active retirement communities here have gained international fame.

Between 1995 and 2000, according to U.S. Census data, 134,583 seniors moved to Arizona. According to the *Arizona Daily Star,* during that period Arizona attracted 6.5 percent of senior interstate movers, replacing California as the second-highest destination for people older than 60.

We call these part-time winter residents, who are usually at least 50 years old, snowbirds—although the chamber-of-commerce types prefer the term "winter visitors." Snowbirds flock to a variety of Valley roosts—apartments and condos with short leases, relatives' homes, their own part-time homes, and, most notably, mobile homes and RV parks. In many cases they find enclaves of like-minded seniors, easing their way into feeling at home in the big city.

Seniors tend to congregate on the fringes of the metropolitan area. In Apache Junction, in the far Southeast Valley, for instance, there are literally dozens of mobile home and RV parks that attract the older set, those here either year-round or part of the year. Diagonally across the Valley, in the far Northwest, is the world-famous, first-of-its-kind Sun City, along with similar age-restricted communities marketed as havens for seniors.

One enclave for the mature set is Youngtown, about 12 miles northwest of Phoenix. Technically, Youngtown—not Sun City—was the nation's first master-planned retirement community, established in 1954 and welcoming residents in 1960. It shies away from the glitz of Sun City and instead prefers to remain a quiet, incorporated town of about 3,000. Recently, it repealed an ordinance that had been in place for many years requiring at least one member of each household to be 55 or older.

Here in the Valley, part-time and permanent residents alike defy the stereotype of crotchety, stay-at-home "old people." As long as they're blessed with good physical and mental health, seniors remain actively engaged in intellectual, recreational, and community pursuits—and glorious, year-round golf.

Active retirement communities fit many to a T. Developers across the Valley have poured millions of dollars into championship golf courses and recreation centers that complement comfortable—and in many cases, luxury—homes. Ever since Sun City, the golf-resort concept has been copied or elaborated upon by several Valley developers. The concept continues to be even stronger as baby boomers mature.

If you're in your second childhood, you will be amazed by the diversions here. Note that travel becomes a major part of the lives of seniors. Often they join their retirement community on tours to exotic places arranged by organizations. Or they're looking for adventure from the seats of their motor homes and recreational vehicles. Or perhaps it's classic car road rallies and motorcycle clubs that beckon them.

Some seniors are exercise lovers and many embrace active lifestyles. You'll find more than 10,000 participants in the Valley's Senior Olympic State Games. And we're talking medalists in sprinting, swimming, cycling, tennis, fitness walking, powerlifting, and more.

Many in the age-55-plus crowd, though they may have chosen to settle down in neighborhoods with people of their age and interests, do choose to continue working, part-time or full-time. Volunteer work is another option, and communities such as the Sun Cities and Sun Lakes are known for the mighty volunteer corps they send out to social service agencies, hospitals, and schools. Add to that your choice of arts-and-crafts clubs and hobby groups geared to seniors around the Valley.

There are a number of ways for a newcomer to make friends, notably the "state clubs." At many retirement communities, clubs have formed to represent every state in the union, not to mention some foreign countries. Folks with any kind of tie to a club's state or country can join in on picnics and other social events.

Not all the Valley's senior citizens choose a Sun City–like lifestyle, of course. You might decide you don't like the homogenous feel of living only near other seniors, or you might find the pristinely kept streets and houses a little too tidy for your tastes. You might decide you don't want to live in a place quite so active, or perhaps the country-club life is not your scene.

Many seniors live in the older neighborhoods of Phoenix, in homes they bought when their families were younger. Now they live side by side with younger couples starting their families. Many have chosen neighborhoods where they can downsize to garden apartments, patio homes, condominiums, or mobile homes. Even within the age-55-plus communities, there are options besides owning a single-family home. Especially popular for cost-saving reasons are villas, which are virtually maintenance-free and often lie adjacent to golf courses or greenbelts.

In addition, Phoenix is a desirable place for seniors who need a bit of assistance because there are so many options. Several new and established complexes offer "active independent living," where seniors can enjoy one- or two-bedroom suites, with some meals provided, as well as health aides, housekeeping, swimming pools, and planned activities.

For those not living in retirement communities, the Valley's many senior centers can become the avenue to keeping active. The centers are well spread geographically across the Valley, and they are bustling with bingo games, dances, holiday parties, intergenerational get-togethers, and educational programs.

As an age-55-plus volunteer at the Sun City West Visitor Center said after reeling off a long list of the area's amenities, "If you're bored, it's your own fault."

ACTIVE-ADULT COMMUNITIES

Ever wonder how "active adult" became the catch phrase for seniors-only communities? The concept of vibrant retiree neighborhoods—where grannies biding their time on rockers are far from the norm—got its start in the Valley of the Sun. In 1960 pioneer builder Del Webb completed Sun City, a tidy community of homes northwest of Phoenix. Sun City homes were built on circular streets, with major roads bisecting those streets and leading the way to clusters of activity—shops, banks, and recreation centers as well as acres and acres of golf courses. Now, the community is so self-contained that many residents prefer to get around in golf carts instead of cars. Cultural life flourishes thanks to the 7,000-seat Sundome Center for the Performing Arts as well as a well-tended art museum and various musical, dance, and theatrical groups. And, over the years, the place has filled to the brim with social groups catering to a wealth of interests. The requirement to buying into this paradise: At least one member of the family has to be 55 or older, and no one younger than 18 is allowed, except for visits.

The concept has taken off like Arnold Palmer with a 9-iron. Developers' bill-boards all over the Valley display the happy faces of couples that look just barely older than 55—playing golf, swim-ming, reveling in a lifestyle that, suppos-edly, is "like being on vacation every day!" Sun City remains the largest retirement community in the country, and it set the standard for other active-adult communi-ties from Florida to California.

After Sun City, Del Webb Corp. fol-lowed up with two other communities in the Northwest Valley, opening Sun City West in the late 1970s and launching Sun City Grand in 1996. While these original communities are all sold out, and available for resale only, Del Webb continues to build new ones. In the Southeast Valley, Robson Communities got on the band-wagon with Sun Lakes in the 1970s. More than a dozen other active-retirement com-munities—designed by different develop-ers but offering similar amenities—dot the Valley, mainly in the suburbs. Here's a quick rundown of those by Robson and Del Webb, the two leaders in the concept, followed by the names of Valley develop-ers whose projects include age-55-and-older communities.

Corte Bella
22415 North Padaro Drive
Sun City West
(623) 544–5200, (888) 717–9777
www.cortebella.com
Corte Bella is Del Webb's first active-adult country club and the first club of its kind in the Phoenix area. With only 1,850 homes, it is considered small and intimate compared to most communities. Ten mod-els from 625 to 1,850 square feel range from $89,000 to $300,000. Like all Del Webb operations, the amenities are top-notch. The golf club's par-72, 18-hole championship course, by designer Greg Nash, offers four sets of tees, from 5,145

yards to 7,000 yards, with an expansive putting green, short-game practice area, and a generous driving range with target greens. There are separate men's and women's locker rooms and a fully equipped pro shop, as well. A 7,500-square-foot social club is a great spot for casual dining at the cafe, with large patios overlooking the golf course. The fitness club and spa at Corte Bella offers more than 10,000 square feet of basic cardio- and weight-training areas and an aerobics studio. Services include spa treatment rooms, separate men's and women's lounges and locker rooms, indoor whirlpool and steam rooms, and private sun patios. Additional services such as massages and facials can be arranged by request. The minimum age for this Del Webb community is 55.

Sun City
16824 North 99th Avenue, Sun City
(623) 977–5000
www.delwebb.com
In this first active-adult community built by Del Webb, the average home price is $100,000. Although sold out, resale homes are available through real estate brokers and directly from owners, and there may be some development of about 200 addi-tional homes in the future. There are over 40,000 residents and 27,000 homes, with a median age of 73.5 in this amazing miniature city. You can visit anytime; make your first stop the visitor center.

Run by a volunteer group called the Sun City Ambassadors, the Sun City Visitor Center, 9903 West Bell Road (Promenade Center), (623) 977–5000, (800) 437–8146, is chock-full of pamphlets, maps, fliers, and magazines describing the dozens of recre-ational opportunities, housing options, social clubs, and more for would-be resi-dents. It's also the place to arrange for a guided tour. Hours are 9:00 A.M. to 4:00 P.M. Monday through Saturday.

Sun Cities Information and Referral, 9451 North 99th Avenue, Sun City, (623) 974–4713, has volunteers on hand to answer general questions about amenities,

Retirement Guides

Thinking about retiring to sunny, warm Arizona? You're not alone! In addition to the myriad of travel guides and brochures, there are several magazines that focus on retirement in our popular state. Here are a few to check out:

Arizona Living, published by Madden Press, is designed exclusively for active boomers and retirees thinking about or planning to retire in Arizona. This glossy publication is available at newsstands or free from some area visitor centers and chambers of commerce.

For a complimentary copy, write to Madden Publishing, P.O. Box 42915, Tucson 85733, or go to the Web at www.azzoomers.com.

Mature Living Choices focuses on retirement communities for active adults (age 55-plus) and offers comprehensive, reader-friendly guides in full color, with easy-to-read descriptions, maps, and directions. You can request a free copy at www.maturelivingchoices.com, or call (800) 222-5771.

services, and housing in Sun City, Sun City West, and Sun City Grand, and to make referrals when more information is needed.

Sun City's seven recreation centers are conveniently dispersed around town. A look around will tell you in an instant that residents in these parts don't like sitting still. The centers encompass seven swimming pools (six outdoor and one indoor); two libraries; a variety of classes in crafts, hobbies, and fine arts; square dancing and ballroom dancing; fitness rooms; and bowling alleys. Add to that therapy pools, lawn bowling, tennis courts, miniature golf, and shuffleboard. Eight golf courses belong to the recreation centers and three country clubs. The recreation centers are: Bell Recreation Center, 16828 North 99th Avenue, (623) 876-3040; Fairway, 10620 West Peoria Avenue, (623) 876-3044; Marinette, 9860 West Union Hills Drive, (623) 876-3054; Mountain View, 9749 North 107th Avenue, (623) 876-3042; Oakmont, 10725 West Oakmont, (623) 876-3046; Sundial, 14801 North 103rd Avenue, (623) 876-3048; and Lakeview, 10626 West Thunderbird Boulevard, (623) 876-3000.

The motto "Keeping Sun City Beautiful" rings true thanks to the Sun City residents who volunteer for the Sun City Prides. They spend untold hours picking up litter, raking the landscaped medians, trimming bushes, painting the trunks of the community's 1,800 orange trees, caring for the automatic watering systems, and reporting needed street repairs. County government officials once estimated the Prides' services to be worth more than $500,000 a year. The Sun City Sheriff's Posse, volunteers coordinated by the Maricopa County Sheriff's Office, helps Sun City maintain one of the lowest crime rates for a U.S. city of its size. Posse members help with neighborhood watches, search and rescue, and home-security surveys.

Sun City West
13950 Meeker Boulevard, Sun City West
(623) 546-5000
www.delwebb.com/activeadult/arizona
Buoyed by the success of Sun City, Del Webb Corp. moved 2 miles west in 1978 to begin building a second active-adult community. The first homes were completed in 1978, and the final home was delivered in 1998, for a total of 17,000 homes and 31,000 residents. Like its neighbor, Sun City West is self-contained, with dozens of

shops, banks, restaurants, several golf courses, four recreation centers, and a hospital. In the same vein, it mandates that at least one member of a household be age 55 or older. The median home price is $151,000.

Sun City West also has a Sheriff's Posse to keep crime down and a Prides volunteer organization to keep neighborhoods tidy. It calls itself "Flag City U.S.A." owing to the hundreds of American flags lining the major thoroughfare, R. H. Johnson Boulevard, under the guidance of the local American Legion post.

The residents' get-up-and-go attitude is reflected in the diversity of clubs and social groups at their disposal. A club list from the visitor center, for instance, lists over 100 organizations, from the Agriculture Club to the Yoga Club. Folks regularly get together for jazz dancing, water therapy, bicycling, and other sports.

And don't forget the ubiquitous golfing. The community has nine golf courses, seven of which are owned by the residents. One is a public course, and another is part of a private country club.

The Property Owners and Residents Association, 13815 Camino del Sol, (623) 584-4288, is Sun City West's watchdog over legislative and governmental matters affecting retirees and their pocketbooks. It also runs town halls with community leaders, provides consumer information, raises funds for charity, and answers gardening questions.

Sun City West's four recreation centers are R. H. Johnson Recreation Center, 19803 R. H. Johnson Boulevard, (623) 584-2050; Beardsley Park, 12755 Beardsley Drive, (623) 584-6078; Fred P. Kuentz Recreation Center, 14401 R. H. Johnson Boulevard, (623) 546-0737; and Palm Ridge, 13800 West Deer Valley Road, (623) 214-1398. Amenities include an Olympic-size swimming pool at each of the centers as well as tennis, bowling, billiards, racquetball, miniature golf, fitness rooms, slow-pitch softball, and horseshoes. Social halls host various kinds of dancing, bingo, and other weekly activities. Arts and crafts rooms let rec center members try their hands at ceramics, stained glass, painting, woodworking, and many other endeavors.

The Sun City West Visitor Center, 13823 West Camino del Sol, (623) 214-8629, (800) 482-3798, is a good first stop. Members of the Sun City West Ambassadors are ready and waiting to answer questions, show you an informational video, and direct you to the walls lined with fliers, pamphlets, maps, and other take-home information. The center will also arrange tours of the community. It's open from 9:00 A.M. to 4:00 P.M. Monday through Saturday and from noon to 3:00 P.M. Sunday. Although Sun City West is sold out, resale homes are available through brokers or owners.

Sun City Grand
19726 North Remington Drive, Surprise
(623) 546-5149, (800) 528-2604
www.delwebb.com/activeadult/arizona
Sun City Grand opened October 1, 1996, in Surprise, Arizona, just west of Sun City. Still in development, the 400-acre community will have 9,800 homes and around 17,500 residents upon completion. The community was the first in the Del Webb family to target the newly retiring baby boomer and has been the best-selling master-planned community in Arizona since its opening and is one of the top-selling active-adult communities in the country. There are 20 on-site models with all floor plans ranging from 1,100 to 2,900 square feet, priced from the low $100s to the $290s.

Designed to reflect a Southwestern desert resort with all the related resort amenities, Sun City Grand features state-of-the-art recreational facilities, championship golf courses, and Del Webb's trademark amenities. The Village Center is located at the community's hub. With its inviting, pleasant courtyard design, cascading water features, and lush landscaping, the Village Center provides an ideal environment for socializing and meeting neighbors. The centerpiece for that mingling is the Sonoran Plaza, a beautiful 21,000-square-foot structure that offers a 9,100-square-foot ballroom, a performing-arts stage, several smaller meeting rooms, a reading room/lounge, an outdoor patio area with fireplace, and the offices of the Community Association Management. It also provides the setting for the Adobe Spa and Fitness Center, a sophisticated facility with the latest exercise and weight training equipment, indoor and outdoor pools, an indoor walking track, and aerobics classrooms.

The center also includes bocce and tennis courts, lawn-bowling greens, and a fishing pier, as well as an outdoor amphitheater for festivals and special events and activity rooms for interests ranging from billiards to computers. The four golf courses include Desert Springs Golf Course, a public course designed by Billy Casper and Greg Nash, featuring playability for players of all levels, 17 lakes, and panoramic views. Granite Falls South, a second course designed by Casper and Nash, opened in December 1997. Designed more like Midwestern U.S. courses with rolling fairways and large greens, Granite Falls South offers a picturesque 18th hole that features two lakes linked by a cascading waterfall and a fountain as a backdrop. Granite Falls North, the third Casper and Nash–designed 18-hole golf course, opened in January 2000 and features more that 20,000 native shrubs and trees, including burrage, brittlebush, mesquites, palo verdes, and a variety of cacti.

Sun Lakes Resort Community
25025 South E. J. Robson Boulevard, Sun Lakes
(480) 895-9600, (800) 223-7317
www.robson.com
On the opposite end of the Valley from the Sun Cities lies the community of Sun Lakes, which has grown to more than 16,200 people, is about 20 miles from downtown Phoenix, but is still considered part of the Valley because of its proximity to Interstate 10. As you're heading south-

Potential home buyers should know: Many retirement communities have either wholly or partially de-annexed themselves from school districts so that they don't have to pay the districts' property taxes. It's a controversial subject with many Valley residents of all ages.

east to Tucson, Sun Lakes springs out of agricultural fields like an oasis of towering trees and ample golf courses. Here, too, active adults find plenty of ways to have fun and stay busy with social clubs, recreation opportunities, places of worship, and performing arts.

You'll find travel groups, social groups, 45 holes of golf, aerobics, dancing, card groups, and computer clubs—to name just a few of the hundreds of activities listed at clubhouses and in community newspapers. Every major holiday brings some kind of get-together at the luxurious clubhouses.

Sun Lakes was conceived about 30 years ago when developer Ed Robson envisioned an active-adult community with a "youthful spirit." The community was built in three phases, beginning in 1972, and is 94 percent sold out.

Its 3,500 acres are organized around the five country clubs, called Sun Lakes, Cottonwood, Palo Verde, Ironwood, and Oakwood. Many of the streets are circular, with the golf courses and lakes as the focal points. The homes range in price from $178,000 to $300,000 and range in size from 1,444 to 3,497 square feet. Sun Lakes also offers condo living at the Renaissance. Beautiful one- and two-bedroom luxury condos are available for sale or lease.

Although the growing city of Chandler and regional shopping malls are fairly close to home, Sun Lakes residents can get much of their shopping done within the community. Supermarkets, banks, professional offices, a health center, and specialty shops are at the major intersections.

OTHER COMMUNITIES

Arizona Traditions
17212 White Tank Vista, Surprise
(623) 546-5613, (800) 226-9214
www.drhorton.com
Built by D. R. Horton, Arizona Traditions is an active-adult 55-plus community in Surprise on Bell Road, about 5 miles west of Grand Avenue. Nine models are offered, with prices starting at $129,800. It's a gated community with an 18-hole golf course, a sports complex, pickle ball courts, and community centers offering not only swimming and tennis, but also a computer room, woodworking shop, crafts classes, and a fitness center.

Leisure World
908 South Power Road, Mesa
(480) 832-7451
www.leisureworldarizona.com
One of the more established active-adult communities, Leisure World, located 30 miles from metropolitan Phoenix, consists of 2,664 homes and over 4,000 residents. It has two large recreation centers, two 18-hole golf courses, security gates, a 24-hour mobile patrol, and minibuses that shuttle to nearby shopping centers. Resale homes are one-, two-, or three-bedroom. You can also choose from one-, two-, or three-bedroom condominiums, garden homes, and duplexes, with prices starting in the $100,000s.

Pebble Creek Resort Community
3639 Clubhouse Drive, Goodyear
(602) 935-6700, (800) 795-4663
www.robson.com
Voted one of the best master-planned communities in the country by *Where to Retire* magazine, Pebble Creek is located in Goodyear, 17 miles west of downtown Phoenix. With 6,500 units, this community is for age 40-plus. Priced from the $140s to the $300s, Pebble Creek showcases professionally decorated model homes as well as an abundance of recreational and social activities to enjoy, including two championship golf courses (Eagle's Nest and Tuscany Falls), exceptional clubhouses, tennis, swimming, dining, arts and crafts, a state-of-the-art fitness center, classes, and more.

Rio Verde
18815 Four Peaks Boulevard, Rio Verde
(480) 471-1962, (800) 233-7103
www.rioverdeaz.com
An adult golf community (age 55-plus) in the Northeast Valley (Scottsdale area), Rio Verde began development in 1973 and today is close to completion. There are approximately 1,080 residential homesites (single family and townhomes) priced from $200,000 to $1 million, 6 commercial buildings, 3 recreation buildings, and a church. Rio Verde's population is over 1,600 and is expected to grow to approximately 1800. The country club offers two 18-hole championship golf courses, a driving range, and several putting and chipping greens interspersed within the community. An 18,000 square foot clubhouse contains two dining rooms. Amenities include six lighted tennis courts, a large swimming pool with four 75-foot lap lanes, Jacuzzi, fitness center, and hiking trails. The community center also has a library, arts-and-crafts room, pool table, table tennis, multipurpose room, and two large card rooms. Ice-cream socials, Gammage Theatre events, potluck dinners, Western dance classes, art classes, and other special-interest group activities are all available to residents.

Solera by Del Webb
6360 South Mountain Boulevard, Chandler
(480) 802-6999, (888) 303-4353
www.delwebb.com
Solera, in Chandler, a short drive from metropolitan Phoenix, is an active-adult community for folks age 55-plus. This 600-acre community will have approximately 1,150 single-family homes. It offers 10 floor plans for homes from $140,000 to $220,000 ranging from 1,151 to 2,400 square feet. You'll find the usual great amenities here; an 18-hole championship golf course features breathtaking fairways and bunkers as

Frequently Called Numbers

The Phoenix area has an ever growing number of community services that, if not directly related to seniors, can still be of help. Here are the telephone numbers for some important resources:

AARP—(602) 256-2277
Alzheimer's Association Helpline—(602) 528-0550
Area Agency on Aging Help Line—(602) 264-4357, (888) 264-2258
Catholic Social Services Phoenix Area—(602) 997-6105
City of Phoenix Human Services Department—(602) 262-4520
Community Information & Referral—(602) 263-8856
Foundation for Senior Living—(602) 285-1800
Sun City Visitor Center—(623) 977-5000
Sun City West Visitor Center—(623) 214-1340

well as undulating greens and six lakes. Facilities also include a state-of-the-art fitness center, two outdoor pools and spa, tennis courts, and a billiards room.

Sunland Springs Village
2233 South Springwood Boulevard
(480) 984-4999, (800) 777-7358
www.sunlandsprings.com
Located in Mesa, close to the Superstition Mountains, the slightly more affordable active-adult community (age 55-plus) of Sunland Springs Village offers 3,000 units of two- to three-bedroom homes and condominiums with prices ranging from the $130s to the $190s. You'll find pools, tennis, shuffleboard, and an 18-hole golf course with driving range and chipping and putting greens.

Westbrook Village
19281 North Westbrook Parkway, Peoria
(623) 561-0099
www.westbrookvillage.org
Westbrook Village includes about 4,000 single-family homes. It's an active-adult community open to those age 40 and older. No children are allowed as permanent residents. Amenities include two championship golf courses, a golf club, and two recreation centers with swimming, tennis, and arts-and-crafts classes.

MOBILE-HOME COMMUNITIES

With its alluring climate and long-standing reputation as a haven for seniors, the Valley of the Sun has developed a variety of lifestyle options for those ready to settle into retirement. Age-restricted (55-plus) mobile-home communities are an option to consider. Like the Sun Cities and Sun Lakes, many of these parks are happy to assist you in your pursuit of an active retirement full of recreation and socializing. If quiet and solitude are more to your liking, they can accommodate that, too. Plus, mobile-home parks are usually the more economical route.

Mobile-home parks in the Valley number literally in the hundreds and can accommodate as few as two dozen homes or as many as 600. An alternate term for mobile homes is manufactured homes, referring to the large, prefabricated homes trucked into a community

There are tons of terrific places to take courses from ballet to drawing. Here are some places to check out if you're looking for something to do!

Arizona Ballet School
(602) 965-0188
www.azballet.org

The Drawing Board
Family Art Studio
(602) 992-5678

Scottsdale Artists School
(480) 990-1422
www.scottsdaleartschool.org

from a factory. Once a site is chosen, the homes pretty much stay put for decades until they're replaced by newer models.

Manufactured homes are a growing trend in the U.S. housing market. The Valley of the Sun is keeping up with the trend, judging from the number of manufactured-home communities developing on its fringes. Their architectural amenities rival those of custom homes, yet manufactured homes can save buyers 25 to 50 percent per square foot. At Crescent Run in Mesa, there are seven styles of model homes available; they range in size from 970 to 1,706 square feet and are priced from $60,000 to $90,000. When comparing costs, be sure to factor in the cost of leasing space for the manufactured home.

Mobile and manufactured homes are a favorite roost of snowbirds. And each mobile-home community varies in its ratio of permanent residents (those who brave the summer) to winter residents, who tend to stay from three to eight months each year and either leave their homes vacant during the summer or rent them out.

Following are several of the larger age-55-plus mobile- and manufactured-home parks scattered around the Valley. Being larger, they are more likely to offer their residents a potpourri of leisure activities and social groups. Amenities typically include heated pools, billiards, shuffleboard, tennis courts, card groups, bingo games, holiday-themed parties, and small golf courses.

Phoenix

Friendly Village of Orangewood
2650 West Union Hills Drive, Phoenix
(623) 869-7498
www.neighborhoodhomes.com
This gated community likes the fact that it has 75 percent permanent residents—a fairly high number among mobile-home communities. In addition to planned activities, residents enjoy the village's 5-hole golf course, pool, hot tub, shuffleboard, and other recreational opportunities.

Paradise Peak West
3901 East Pinnacle Peak Road, Phoenix
(480) 515-2043
Boasting a view of the McDowell Mountains, this community has 415 spaces for manufactured homes. It's known for its nine-hole golf course.

Southeast Valley

Crescent Run
8500 East Southern Avenue, Mesa
(480) 373-8500, (800) 437-9910
www.hometownamerica.com
An 11,000-square-foot recreation center is the centerpiece of this community of 300 manufactured homes with over 330 lots available. It's also a gated community, with amenities that run the gamut from pools, putting green, and tennis to craft rooms, exercise classes, and a library. On the grounds is an eight-acre park with a natural grass amphitheater.

Hacienda de Valencia
201 South Greenfield Road, Mesa
(480) 832-6081
www.mhchomes.com
The Hacienda has room for 365 mobile homes. Amenities include two pools, a hot

tub, a horseshoe pit, a gazebo area for barbecues, a social hall, a card room, a billiards room, an exercise room, and wellness center.

La Casa Blanca
2208 West Baseline Road, Apache Junction
(480) 983-1344

This gated, 198-space community has pools and other recreation amenities and hosts hiking and golfing trips, potlucks, and lectures. About 70 percent of the residents call it home all year. A sister community, Desert Harbor, is nearby, with 207 spaces.

Las Palmas
215 North Power Road, Mesa
(480) 396-2172
www.laspalmasmesa.com

Las Palmas is huge—539 spaces to be exact. Recreation facilities include swimming and therapy pools, with a continuous roster of planned activities within the community. There's also tennis, shuffleboard, bocce ball, horseshoes, and a large clubhouse with meeting and game rooms.

The Meadows
2401 West Southern Avenue, Tempe
(602) 438-1865
www.mhchomes.com

This manufactured-home community boasts lush landscaping and room for 391 houses. A guard stands at the front entrance. For recreation, there are a clubhouse, pool, sauna, exercise room, shuffleboard, and areas for cards and billiards. Many planned activities are available.

Palmas del Sol Country Club
6209 East McKellips Road, Mesa
(480) 641-3385
www.palmasdelsolmesa.com

Tennis, anyone? There are courts aplenty here, along with pools, hot tubs, and shuffleboard. The manufactured-home sites number 467.

Northeast Valley

Roadrunner Lake Resort
1149 North 92nd Street, Scottsdale
(480) 945-0787

This 627-space community promotes resort living with a miniature-golf course, a pool, a hot tub, and shuffleboard as well as many activities in its large clubhouse.

Shadow Mountain Village
8780 East McKellips Road, Scottsdale
(480) 947-8393

Conveniently located near the new Pima and Red Mountain Freeways, this 55-plus community has 586 spaces and a number of recreation amenities, including a tennis court, a horseshoe pit, shuffleboard, pools, exercise equipment, and billiards, all located in and around two clubhouses and a dance hall. Planned activities include holiday parties, pancake breakfasts, and dances.

Northwest Valley

Apollo Village
10701 North 99th Avenue, Peoria
(623) 933-0166
www.mhchomes.com

Apollo Village is relatively compact at 236 spaces, but it's large enough to offer a clubhouse, pool, hot tub, picnic area, car wash bay, RV storage, library, and beauty shop.

Blue Sky Mobile Home Estates
4800 West Ocotillo Road, Glendale
(623) 939-5425

Blue Sky, a 55-plus community, has only 160 spaces but plenty of amenities—a clubhouse, pool, hot tub, exercise room, billiards area, and library. Add to that lots of bunco and bingo games, potlucks, and breakfasts.

Grand Missouri Mobile Home Park
4400 West Missouri Avenue, Glendale
(623) 937-7721
www.grandmissouri.com

Retirees 55-plus with an interest in ceramics will find company here in the various classes offered. Planned activities include bingo games and potlucks; exercise options include swimming and therapy pools, tennis, shuffleboard, and aerobics. The park has 303 spaces.

Palm Shadows Mobile Home Park
7300 North 51st Avenue, Glendale
(623) 934-1308
www.mhchomes.com
Bingo every night? You'll find it here, along with horseshoes, shuffleboard, billiards, pools, and spas. Palm Shadows also has an auditorium. A mix of winter and permanent residents occupy the 294 spaces.

INFORMATION AND ASSISTANCE FOR SENIORS

Valleywide

American Association of Retired Persons
302 North First Avenue, Suite 410,
Phoenix
(602) 256-2277
AARP is a nonprofit, nonpartisan service organization for people age 50 and older. By design and mission AARP helps members achieve goals of independence, dignity, and purpose. There are several active AARP chapters in the Valley. The number above is for the statewide office, which can put you in touch with local groups.

Area Agency on Aging
1366 East Thomas Road, Suite 108,
Phoenix
(602) 264-2255
www.aaaphx.org
The Area Agency on Aging's Region One office serves the elderly and disabled adults in all of Maricopa County. It administers contracts with various services and agencies for benefits assistance, transportation, counseling, home repair, assisting the homebound, recreation, socialization, and respite services. It also

runs specialized programs, for instance, dealing with elder abuse prevention or assisting someone in making the transition from hospital to home. In addition, the Area Agency on Aging advocates on behalf of the elderly, provides information and referral services, and runs a Senior Help Line, (602) 264-HELP, and an Elder Resource and Referral line (ERRL), (800) 686-1431, which provides 24-hour statewide assistance for the elderly, their families, and caregivers throughout Arizona. The agency is also home to the Dr. R. Alice Drought Gerontological Resource Center (GRC), a comprehensive full-service library with books, journals, newsletters, videos, magazines, and national and international databases related to the topics of aging and public policy, death and dying, elder abuse, legal concerns, and intergenerational issues. A professional librarian is available to assist. The library is open to the public 8:00 A.M. to 5:00 P.M. Monday through Friday.

The AAA publishes a list and provides information on the Valley's more than three dozen senior centers. The centers are bustling with activities, including recreation, arts and crafts, hobby clubs, health screenings, and educational and intergenerational programs. Plus, they regularly provide nutritious meals and opportunities for socializing. The directory is available by calling (602) 264-4357.

The senior centers reach out to all areas of the Valley and to all income levels. Some are freestanding, and some are housed in churches or YMCAs. A few are affiliated with ethnic communities such as the Chinese Senior Center, Chicanos Por La Causa Senior Center, the Jewish Community Center, and the Phoenix Indian Center. A few are run by city parks and recreation divisions. And a handful have their own support organizations to raise funds to provide even better services. At Los Olivos Senior Center in east Phoenix, seniors enjoy regularly scheduled bingo, dancing, singing groups, walking groups, and coffeehouses.

Arizona Senior Citizens Law Project
1818 South 16th Street, Phoenix
(602) 252-6710

This service helps age-60-plus Maricopa County residents who have problems concerning government benefits, housing, consumer affairs, wills, probates, guardianship, and other legal matters. Financial accommodations are made for those in hospitals or nursing homes and for those seeking the reduced-fee services of a private attorney.

Beatitudes Center DOAR (Developing Older Adult Resources)
555 West Glendale Avenue, Phoenix
(602) 274-5022
www.centerdoar.org

This organization lends a hand in a variety of ways, including a parish nursing/ministry network, a library with books and videos related to aging, care-giver support groups, a volunteer base that makes home visits and phone calls to seniors living on their own, and an interfaith volunteer network that runs errands and does small home repairs for those in need.

Foundation for Senior Living
1201 East Thomas Road, Phoenix
(602) 285-1800

The foundation's aim is to protect seniors as well as adults with disabilities from institutional placement that may be both costly and inappropriate. Its many flexible, individualized, personal care programs are the means to do that, through counseling, adult day care, home health care, low-cost remodeling, apartments and supervised private homes geared to their needs, and senior centers. Another important program is OASIS (Older Adult Services and Information System), which offers seniors many cultural and educational activities such as outings to museums and discussion roundtables.

Phoenix Advocacy and Counseling for the Elderly
200 West Washington Street, Phoenix
(602) 262-6631
www.phoenix.gov

PACE is open to Phoenix residents ages 60 and older who need help with or referrals for food, clothing, counseling, assistive devices, insurance bills, housing, transportation, and legal aid. It is a City of Phoenix program.

Interfaith Community Care
17749 North El Mirage Road, Surprise
(623) 584-4999
www.interfaithcommunitycare.org

This agency provides a number of services, including adult day care, in-home respite care, grocery shopping and transportation help, and counseling on options in assisted living and long-term care.

Meals on Wheels
Scottsdale
(480) 675-4140

Sun City
(623) 974-9430

Sun City West
(623) 214-4233

Surprise
(623) 937-0500

Residents who are unable to prepare their own meals are eligible for this service. Hot and cold meals are prepared, then delivered by volunteer drivers for a nominal fee.

Sun Health
10401 Thunderbird Boulevard, Sun City
(623) 977-7211
www.sunhealth.org

Many of the health care services in the Sun Cities come under the aegis of Sun Health, including Boswell Memorial Hospital in Sun City and Del E Webb Memorial Hospital in Sun City West. Sun Health also runs a physician referral service, a community education program, and hospice and home health care services.

EDUCATIONAL OPPORTUNITIES

Southeast Valley

Mesa Community College
1833 West Southern Avenue, Mesa
(480) 461-7000
www.mc.maricopa.edu
Mesa Community College reaches out to retirees with a program called New Frontiers for Learning in Retirement. Of interest to seniors are classes in computers, history, Spanish, and more.

Sun Lakes Education Center
25105 South Alma School Road,
Sun Lakes
(480) 857-5500
www.cgc.maricopa.edu/slec
An arm of Chandler-Gilbert Community College, this center offers a special program for seniors called New Adventures in Learning. Classes include Spanish, creative writing, financial planning, Southwest history, art, fitness, and nutrition.

Northeast Valley

Scottsdale Community College
9000 East Chaparral Road, Scottsdale
(480) 423-6000
www.sc.maricopa.edu
The college's Senior Adult Program offers courses of interest to seniors, along with lecture series and special events. Choose from courses on history, the environment, religion, English literature, contemporary cinema, computers, yoga, and "cerebral aerobics." The program also sponsors 55-Alive driving classes and a Silver Striders walking club. Call the program directly at (480) 423-6559.

Northwest Valley

Lifelong Learning Academy
Sun City Grand
19726 North Remington Drive, Surprise
(623) 546-7429
An innovative continuing education program that partners Del Webb's Sun City Grand retirement community and Arizona State University. Courses and programs of all types are offered at Sun City's Academy, a 22,000-square-foot facility that serves as the on-site campus. Lectures and special events will also take place here.

Rio Salado College
12535 West Smokey Drive, Surprise
(623) 583-0548
www.rio.maricopa.edu
With support from Rio Salado College, seniors can take a number of noncredit classes by enrolling in R.I.S.E. (Rio Institute for Senior Education). The program asks for a nominal annual membership fee and lets you take a variety of classes. A few for-credit computer classes are also available.

VOLUNTEER OPPORTUNITIES

Arizona CASA Program
1501 West Washington Street, Suite 119,
Phoenix
(602) 542-9683
www.supremecourt.az.gov/casa
Donate your time to help protect abandoned, abused, and neglected children through the Court Appointed Special Advocate (CASA) program. Volunteers are trained to help the court system determine what is best for children who have come under the court's care.

Retired Senior Volunteer Program
1366 East Thomas Road, Phoenix
(602) 264-2255

450 West Fourth Place, Mesa
(480) 775-1466

RSVP assists people age 55 and older in discovering uses for their creativity, energy, and expertise. Volunteers are placed with nonprofit organizations and public agencies.

Sun Cities Volunteer Placement Services
13815 West Camino del Sol
Sun City West
(623) 584-4288
The Property Owners and Residents Association (PORA) handles volunteer opportunities for Sun City West. Among the many organizations served by volunteers are AARP, Habitat for Humanity, the Arizona Humane Society, and Northwest Valley schools.

Volunteer Center of Maricopa County
1515 East Osborn Road, Phoenix
(602) 263-9736, (800) VOLUNTEER
www.volunteerphoenix.org
The center works with more than 750 nonprofit and public agencies, such as the Salvation Army, the Association of Arizona Food Banks, and local hospitals.

JOB OPPORTUNITIES

Age Works & C-POW+ER
1366 East Thomas Road, Phoenix
(602) 264-4357
www.aaaphx.org
These two programs, affiliated with the Area Agency on Aging, work together to help persons age 50 and older find work.

Extra time on your hands? Many worthwhile organizations in Arizona are looking for mature, experienced volunteers. You can contribute and learn new skills at the same time. Become a volunteer for the state park system as a host or guide. Call Nicole Armstrong-Best at (602) 542-7152 or sign up on the Web at www.asstateparks.com. Want to learn more about Arizona history? Become a docent at the Arizona Historical Society or work in the fascinating archives. There are lots of opportunities; check www.ahs.state.az.us. Not sure what you want to do? Contact the Maricopa County Volunteer Center at (800) VOLUNTEER, or visit www.volunteer phoenix.org where they will match you with the right organization looking for help.

Experience Plus Placement Center
5119 North 19th Avenue, Phoenix
(602) 246-0260
Operating on funds from the United Way, grants, and contributions, this nonprofit job placement and counseling service is geared to those age 50 and older. There is no charge for placement on the part of the employer or employee. Experience Plus has offices in Sun City, Mesa, Scottsdale, Sunnyslope, and Tempe.

HEALTH CARE (H)

I f you have adequate health-care coverage, you'll be glad to know that Phoenix and the Valley of the Sun are home to a number of nationally prominent health-care facilities such as Barrow Neurological Institute, the Arizona Heart Institute, and the Mayo Clinic, among others. This reflects a forward-looking attitude toward health-care innovations that the Valley has maintained since the earliest days of Maricopa Medical Center, the oldest health-care institution in the Valley, which was established in 1883.

Phoenix's early hospitals emerged from a need to combat various epidemics—small pox for Maricopa Medical Center and tuberculosis for St. Joseph's Hospital and Medical Center, John C. Lincoln Hospital, and Banner Good Samaritan Medical Center.

The Valley embraced chiropractic, osteopathic, and holistic medicine before more traditional parts of the country did, and it has become home to Midwestern University's College of Osteopathic Medicine in Glendale.

The Valley also had the first freestanding, outpatient surgical center in the nation. Innovative techniques such as radial keratotomy and other eye procedures quickly became popular here.

Sports medicine as a separate discipline had its roots here in the work that Dr. Paul Steingard did as the first team physician of the Phoenix Suns. Steingard developed ways to help his athletes recover faster from injuries and helped them learn how to prevent injuries. (Of course, it helped that his patients were highly motivated to stay in the games.) By the early 1970s Steingard's own clinic had become the first sports medicine practice in Arizona. Today, the Steingard Medical Group, 5830 North 19th Avenue in Phoenix, (602) 336-1966, does both sports medicine and general practice and is leading the way in making high school sports safe for teens

by offering free annual physicals and doing research on teens at risk for sudden cardiac death.

Today, all of the hospitals feature state-of-the-art equipment and the latest ideas in patient care—such as single rooms where mothers can go through labor, delivery, and recovery in relative comfort, instead of being wheeled around from the labor area to the delivery room and then to the recovery room. Most of them also offer preventive medicine, either in the form of classes or wellness programs. In this chapter we give you a selection of Valley hospitals, as well as some walk-in clinics, emergency numbers, and mental-health resources. We also touch briefly on alternative medicine in the Valley.

HOSPITALS

Phoenix

Arizona Heart Hospital
1930 East Thomas Road, Phoenix
(602) 532-1000, (800) 345-4278
www.azhearthospital.com
The 59-bed Arizona Heart Hospital, dedicated to the diagnosis and treatment of heart disease, opened in early 1998 and has received international recognition for its work. It has close ties to the Arizona Heart Institute (see next listing), and its medical director and founder is Dr. Edward B. Diethrich. The facility was built to function as an advanced coronary-care unit and has a staff of more than 300 physicians, including the world's leading cardiologists and cardiovascular surgeons. The hospital has 4 operating rooms; 4 cardiac catheterization and electrophysiology suites; 59 private inpatient rooms, including 14 cardiac intensive-care rooms; a special peripheral vascular suite, and a

24-hour emergency center. It also encompasses the Wound Healing and Hyperbaric Oxygen Center, which treats nonhealing wounds such as diabetic ulcers, and a congestive heart failure clinic, which offers individualized intensive programs to congestive heart failure patients.

Arizona Heart Institute
2632 North 20th Street, Phoenix
(602) 266-2200, (800) 345-4278
www.azheart.com
In 1971 Dr. Edward B. Diethrich founded the Arizona Heart Institute, the nation's first freestanding outpatient clinic devoted to cardiovascular diseases.

Affiliated with the Arizona Heart Hospital, where the institute's patients are referred if necessary, its multispecialty outpatient facility is dedicated to the prevention, detection, and treatment of cardiovascular, pulmonary, and neurological disorders. The Heart Institute has an open-door policy and offers same-day service for testing and exams. It specializes in advanced nonsurgical interventional therapies that replace traditional scalpel-and-suture treatment for heart and blood vessel disease and is currently conducting research on myoblastic and gene-cell therapies.

The Arizona Heart Institute's hours are 7:00 A.M. to 4:00 P.M. Monday through Friday. Treatments offered include advanced alternatives to surgery, angioplasty, cardiac rehabilitation, general medical care, cardiovascular and thoracic surgery, pulmonology, check-ups, and preventive medicine, among others. The institute's Vein Center provides treatment for varicose veins, with most taking place in the doctor's office.

Banner Estrella Medical Center
9201 West Thomas Road, Phoenix
(623) 327-4000
www.bannerhealth.com
Banner Estrella Medical Center opened in 2004 with a 50-acre campus that includes a 172-bed hospital, a surgery center, and a medical office building. It serves the rap-

idly growing West Valley communities of Avondale, Glendale, Goodyear, Litchfield Park, Peoria, and Tolleson. The hospital was designed with an eye toward the future and incorporates the latest in health care technology and health care delivery processes. Services include inpatient and outpatient surgery, cancer care, cardiac services, ambulatory care, emergency services, and a comprehensive women and infants services center. An electronic physician information system eliminates handwritten flip charts to reduce or eliminate medical errors. Banner Estrella was designed with soothing colors and comfortable furnishings, and all the hospital's rooms are private and look like bedrooms. The hospital also offers room-service meals to all patients and their families.

Banner Good Samaritan Medical Center
1111 East McDowell Road, Phoenix
(602) 239-2000
www.bannerhealth.com
Banner Good Samaritan began its days as a tuberculosis sanitarium, the Deaconess Hospital and Home, which was founded by a Methodist group in 1911. In 1928 it was renamed Good Samaritan Hospital and began to offer a wider range of services to the local community. Today, Banner Good Samaritan Medical Center is run by Banner Health and is one of the largest hospitals in Arizona, with 625 licensed beds. Banner Good Sam has 1,650 physicians representing 54 specialties. It features 16 inpatient operating suites and 8 outpatient operating suites. The hospital leads the state in heart procedures and is a prominent research center for Alzheimer's and spinal-cord injuries. The hospital specializes in heart and cancer care and is a leader in kidney and liver

Many hospitals offer community education classes on all aspects of staying healthy, from child care tips to maintaining a healthy heart. Call a hospital nearest you for more information.

transplants, high-risk obstetrics, and multiple births. It also offers general maternity services, a sleep-disorders program, a Level I trauma center, rehabilitation, and outpatient services. The institute's Vein Center provides treatment for varicose veins, mostly in the doctor's office.

The hospital has 92 beds dedicated to intensive-care and intermediate-care services. Banner Good Sam's emergency room trauma center treats patients from around the Southwest and Mexico. Banner Good Sam has the state's first positron emission tomography (PET) scanner, which is used to monitor the chemical activity of living cells within tissue. The hospital's oncology services include a bone-marrow transplantation program run in conjunction with the City of Hope National Medical Center in Los Angeles. The campus also houses the 60-bed Banner Good Samaritan Rehabilitation Institute, one of the top rehab centers in the state, and Banner Good Samaritan Behavioral Health Center, which offers both inpatient and outpatient mental health services. Banner Poison Control Center is also on campus. Its phone number is (800) 222-1222.

Barrow Neurological Institute
St. Joseph's Hospital and Medical
Center, 350 West Thomas Road, Phoenix
(602) 406-3000
www.thebarrow.com
Named in 2003 as the 10th-best hospital for neurology and neurosurgery by *U.S. News & World Report*, Barrow Neurological Institute opened at St. Joseph's Hospital in 1962 as advances in brain surgery and neurology made such a center feasible. The institute treats aneurysms, vascular tumors, malformations, occlusions, ischemia, epilepsy, chronic pain, and trauma. Barrow is one of the largest neuroscience centers in the Southwest, with 8 dedicated surgical suites, a postanesthesia care area, 24 intensive-care beds, 15 intermediate-care beds, 24 acute-care beds, a 38-bed neurorehabilitation inpatient unit, a stroke unit, a spine unit, an epilepsy monitoring unit, a subacute rehabilitation

unit, and outpatient neurology specialty clinics. A pediatric neurosurgery section helps children with complex conditions such as spina bifida, cerebral palsy, craniofacial abnormalities, brain tumors, and head injuries. The institute is part of a Level I trauma center for brain and spinal-cord injury victims in central Arizona. It is also a teaching hospital and a research facility. Treatments pioneered at Barrow are now being used around the world.

Carl T. Hayden Veterans Affairs
Medical Center
650 East Indian School Road, Phoenix
(602) 277-5551
www.phoenix.med.va.gov
In 1947, Senator Carl T. Hayden was approached by a group of Maricopa County residents who felt that Phoenix needed a hospital to serve veterans recently returned from World War II. A land deal was arranged with the Phoenix Indian School for a 27-acre parcel on the northwestern corner of Seventh Street and Indian School Road. Approximately 290,000 veterans live in Maricopa County, and the facility serves about 60,000 of them annually through its programs. The hospital has 132 medical and surgical beds, 102 nursing-home beds, and 48 mental-health beds. It is also a teaching and research hospital. Its services include an emergency life-support unit, services for homeless veterans, a substance-abuse disorders program, and a post-traumatic stress disorder program. General medical and surgical services are offered, as are mental health and behavioral science services, physical medicine, rehabilitation, and neurology. In addition, the hospital has its own pharmacy and complete laboratory services and a 60,000-square-foot ambulatory-care center.

Hacienda de Los Angeles
1402 East South Mountain Avenue,
Phoenix
(602) 243-4231
www.haciendainc.org
Hacienda de Los Angeles is a long-term residential care and hospital-to-home tran-

Emily Center

If you have a sick child, you might want to check out the Emily Center, a pediatric health library at Phoenix Children's Hospital. Founded in 1990 by the family of Emily Anderson—who lost her life to leukemia at age seven—the Emily Center is the most comprehensive pediatric health library in the Southwest. It is free, open to the general public, and provides accurate and up-to-date information on children's health and diseases. A large collection of resources in Spanish is available. The center is located on the main corridor of the Phoenix Children's Hospital at 1919 East Thomas Road, at 20th Street. Hours vary, so call ahead. You can find them on the Web at www.phxchildrens.com/illnesses/emily center. You can also ask the staff questions by calling them directly at (602) 546-1400, or through e-mail at emilyc@phxchildrens.com.

sition center serving infants, children, and young adults. It was founded in 1967 by Eileen Butler, who shared her mobile home on South Mountain to care for these patients. In 1970 a group of supporters called the Madrinas secured funding for a proper facility, and in 1976 Hacienda de Los Angeles moved to its current location. The hospital serves patients who have genetic disorders or have suffered from birth trauma, physical abuse, or accidents such as near-drowning and car accidents. The hospital-to-home transition program is meant to speed recovery and the patient's return home. A respite-care program provides short-term care (including medical services and recreation) to allow the families of the patients to take a respite from caregiving. The long-term care program is a home away from home for chronically ill patients. Services include medical and therapeutic care, on-campus and public-school education, social and recreational activities, respiratory therapy, and physical, occupational, and speech therapy.

John C. Lincoln Hospital–Deer Valley
19829 North 27th Avenue, Phoenix
(623) 879-6100
www.jcl.com
The Deer Valley location of John C. Lincoln Hospital began its days as Phoenix General Hospital, and for most of its existence it has been known as Phoenix General Hospital and Medical Center. It was purchased by John C. Lincoln Health Network in 1997. The hospital's 127-bed facility, with all private rooms, offers inpatient and outpatient medical and surgical care. The hospital also offers a 24-hour emergency department, an intensive-care unit, cardiac care, and diagnostic imaging, among other services. Its pediatric center, called Mendy's Place, is the only after-hours pediatric-care center in the North Valley.

John C. Lincoln Hospital–North Mountain
250 East Dunlap Avenue, Phoenix
(602) 943-2381
www.jcl.com
John C. Lincoln Hospital has its roots in the Desert Mission Sanitarium, which was opened by the Presbyterian Church in then-remote Sunnyslope to serve poor people who were ailing from tuberculosis. It grew through the years and became John C. Lincoln Hospital. Today, it's a 262-bed facility that provides 24-hour Level I trauma and emergency services, intensive-care and cardio intensive-care units, inpatient and outpatient surgery, an orthopedic unit, a breast care center, a sleep disorders center, diagnostic imaging, oncology services, and outpatient rehabili-

tation services. Part of its legacy as a one-time tuberculosis sanitarium are the respiratory wellness and pulmonary rehabilitation programs, which combine exercise and education to make daily life easier for people with chronic conditions such as emphysema. The birthing center at the hospital was designed by women, and it features private rooms with whirlpool tubs and a quiet, calming atmosphere.

Los Niños Hospital
2303 East Thomas Road, Phoenix
(602) 954-7311
www.losninoshospital.com
This 15-bed facility opened in 1994 and is the acute-care facility for Hacienda de Los Angeles. The children's hospital offers medical care for children suffering from a variety of ailments. It specializes in acute care for infants, children, and teens, including medical monitoring, urgent care, and transitional care. The hospital also offers physical, occupational, and speech therapy and training to prepare family members and others for patients' post-hospital care. Los Niños Hospital allows 24-hour visitation by parents and encourages them to spend the night. The hospital is locally owned and features a cheerful, homelike setting.

Maricopa Medical Center
2601 East Roosevelt Street, Phoenix
(602) 344-5011
www.maricopa.gov/mdcenter/ourfacility/
mmc.html.
Maricopa Medical Center was honored in 1999 as one of the best hospitals in the country by *U.S. News & World Report*. The original Maricopa County Hospital was built at Seventh Avenue and Roosevelt Street in 1883 to handle smallpox victims. The site was very close to downtown Phoenix even then, so the county was pressured to move the contagious patients farther out. The county bought a site at 35th Avenue and Durango Street in 1885, where the hospital was built. By the early 1960s the Valley had outgrown its

existing hospitals, and a $10.8-million bond issue was approved to fund a new 425-bed county hospital. Site selection dragged into the late 1960s, when a document was uncovered showing the county owned a site at Roosevelt and 24th Streets. The new hospital opened in 1971. The Arizona Burn Center was established at Maricopa County Hospital in 1965 and is the state's only regional burn center. Maricopa Medical Center was the first Arizona hospital to establish a Level I trauma unit to handle all types of life-threatening injuries and emergencies.

The 541-bed hospital also features one of the few emergency centers in Phoenix dedicated to the special needs of children, a pediatric intensive-care unit, a neonatal intensive-care unit, three adult intensive-care units, and a family birthing center, among other services. Maricopa Medical Center (MMC) is part of the Maricopa Integrated Health systems, a network that includes not only the MMC but also 12 family-health centers throughout the Valley, a behavioral-health care center in Mesa and 3 health plans. Maricopa Medical Center is a teaching hospital affiliated with the University of Arizona College of Medicine, Arizona State University, and the Mayo Graduate School of Medicine.

Maryvale Hospital
5102 West Campbell Avenue, Phoenix
(623) 848-5000
www.maryvalehospital.com
Maryvale Community Hospital opened with 60 beds in 1961 to serve the needs brought on by the first wave of explosive growth in the Maryvale area. Samaritan Health System bought the hospital in 1968, renaming it Maryvale Samaritan Hospital, and built the current, 239-bed hospital in 1978. In 1998 the hospital was acquired by Vanguard Health Systems and renamed Maryvale Hospital Medical Center. The hospital is now managed by Vanguard's Abrazo Health Care and serves west Phoenix and the Southwest Valley. The Center for Mother and Child offers each patient a private room for labor,

delivery, recovery, and postpartum care. The hospital has a special-care unit for oncology, cardiology, medical, and surgical patients needing intensive services. It has operating rooms where both inpatient and outpatient surgeries are performed. The hospital also has a skilled nursing facility and oncology and rehabilitation services. Its outpatient therapeutic aquatics program is nationally recognized.

Mayo Clinic Hospital
5777 East Mayo Boulevard, Phoenix
(480) 342-2000
www.mayoclinic.org/mchospital-sct

The Mayo Clinic Hospital opened in 1998. It is the first hospital planned, designed, and built by the Mayo Clinic. A 205-bed facility, its focus is to provide inpatient care to support the 66 medical and surgical specialties practiced at the Mayo Clinic Scottsdale. The hospital has 148 medical-surgical beds, 20 intensive/critical-care beds, 10 beds in a short-stay unit, 9 skilled-nursing beds, and 7 rehabilitation beds. It also has an emergency room and a full-service clinical laboratory, urgent-care services, an intensive-care unit, a bone-marrow transplant facility, and a sleep studies lab for the diagnosis and treatment of sleep disorders. The hospital also offers a liver, kidney, and pancreas transplant program, with success rates higher than the national average.

Paradise Valley Hospital
3929 East Bell Road, Phoenix
(602) 923-5000
www.paradisevalleyhospital.com

As the Northeast Valley grew in the early 1980s, the need for a hospital became apparent. This 163-bed facility was built in 1983 to serve an area within a 10-mile radius of 40th Street and Bell Road. Today, Paradise Valley Hospital is owned by Vanguard Health Systems and is run by their Abrazo Health Care, with a staff of 700 physicians. The hospital has eight surgical suites available for outpatient procedures and general surgeries. The diagnostic imaging department features

an open scan MRI unit. Paradise Valley Hospital also has a Women's Center that provides women's health care services and includes a labor and delivery center. In addition to recovery units for orthopedic, oncology, and pediatric patients, the hospital also has a 14-bed intensive-care and coronary-care unit. The hospital offers outpatient surgery, rehabilitation services, spinal treatment, and hyperbaric wound treatment, and is currently undergoing a $5.8-million expansion of its emergency room facilities.

Phoenix Baptist Hospital
2000 West Bethany Home Road, Phoenix
(602) 249-0212
www.baptisthealth.com

Phoenix Baptist Hospital began as a small children's hospital in 1963. As the Valley grew, the hospital expanded its focus to all-purpose care for patients of all ages. Since 2000 Phoenix Baptist has been owned by Vanguard Health Systems and is part of their Abrazo Healthy Care network of hospitals.

Phoenix Baptist is a 216-bed facility that offers general medical and surgical services, an emergency room, an intensive-care and coronary-care unit, oncology services, a cardiology center, the Center for Arthritis and Joint Replacement, a mammography center, maternity services with labor-delivery-recovery-postpartum suites, and a perinatal department that can handle premature infants. Phoenix Baptist also houses a six-bed hospice unit and provides home health care.

Phoenix Children's Hospital
1919 East Thomas Road, Phoenix
(602) 546-1000
www.phxchildrens.com

The concept of a children's hospital had languished for about a decade when, in 1978, the Maricopa County Pediatric Society began considering ways to make the concept a reality. In 1980 a group of community leaders joined the pediatric doctors to form the nonprofit Phoenix Children's Hospital Inc. The founders

i

911 is for life-threatening emergencies only. This may seem like a no-brainer, but 911 operators are often called by people who don't understand this. Please, don't get in the way of someone else's rescue. If something is non-life threatening, seek help at a walk-in clinic or emergency room.

decided that Phoenix Children's Hospital would best accomplish its mission in conjunction with an existing hospital, and hospitals throughout the Valley were invited to submit proposals. A blue ribbon committee accepted a proposal from Good Samaritan Regional Medical Center (now called Banner Good Samaritan Medical Center). Phoenix Children's Hospital opened in 1983 in space leased from Good Samaritan. There were no construction or equipment costs incurred. Instead, Good Samaritan transferred its pediatric services and beds to Phoenix Children's Hospital through the lease arrangement.

Recently, the hospital outgrew its facility at Banner Good Samaritan, and in 2002 Phoenix Children's Hospital moved into its current 20-acre campus. The hospital is now the largest freestanding children's hospital in the United States and the only licensed pediatric hospital in Arizona. It also runs three outpatient specialty care centers, in Glendale, Mesa, and Scottsdale. The hospital has 308 beds, playrooms, school rooms, and family sleep areas in patient rooms and throughout the hospital. Services include pediatric critical care; the state's only 24-hour, 7-day-a-week pediatric emergency department; neonatal intensive care; a blood and marrow transplant unit; a kids' kidney center; a children's cancer center; a cystic fibrosis center; a neurosciences center for neurology and neurosurgery; a children's heart center; a hemophilia center; and endocrinology, gastroenterology, pulmonology, and rehabilitation services.

Phoenix Indian Medical Center, United States Department of Health and Human Services
4212 North 16th Street, Phoenix
(602) 263-1200
www.ihs.gov
The Phoenix Indian Medical Center started its days as a tuberculosis sanitarium for Native American children. The sanitarium opened in 1909 on land owned by the Phoenix Indian School, and it was administered by the school until 1931. After a few years as an independent facility, the sanitarium administration changed its mission, deciding to serve adults as well as children, and Phoenix Indian Hospital was born. Today, it serves the medical needs of six Native American communities under the aegis of the Phoenix Area Indian Health Services. The hospital has more than 100 acute-care beds and a complete array of health services. Because diabetes is a serious health issue for tribal members, the National Institutes of Health maintains a National Institute of Diabetes, Digestive, and Kidney Diseases at the hospital. The hospital's Auxiliary Association provides scholarships for Native American students who are pursuing education in the health field. The auxiliary also purchases equipment for various departments and donates time and money to hospital-sponsored community events.

Phoenix Memorial Hospital
1201 South Seventh Avenue, Phoenix
(602) 258-5111
www.phxmemorialhospital.com
Phoenix Memorial Hospital has been honored as one of the most innovative hospitals in the country. It began as St. Monica's Mission, Arizona's first maternity-care clinic, in 1934. In 1944 the hospital began the first interracial nurses training program west of the Mississippi. In 1951 the hospital opened the region's only polio treatment center, a unit with 40 iron-lung machines. The hospital opened the Southwest Cancer Institute in 1961, which still serves all of Arizona and parts of Nevada and New Mexico. The hospital has been owned by Vanguard Health

Systems since 2001 and is now managed by their Abrazo Health Care. It has 109 beds and, because of its joint venture with MedPro, a multispecialty physicians group, now offers full-service medical care. Services include cardiac catheterization, open-heart surgery, and cardiac rehabilitation; critical-care and intensive-care units; orthopedics and joint replacement; women's services including maternity, well-woman care, and mammography; a nurse-midwifery program; pediatrics; physical, occupational, and speech therapy; a rehabilitation center; a comprehensive cancer services center; and skilled-nursing and hospice units. The hospital also runs health clinics at nearby schools, where a traveling nurse practitioner provides medical check-ups to students.

St. Joseph's Hospital and Medical Center
350 West Thomas Road, Phoenix
(602) 406-3000
www.ichosestjoes.com
The Sisters of Mercy came to Phoenix in 1892 to teach. When they got here, they were moved by the suffering of tuberculosis victims. By 1895 the sisters had raised enough money to rent a six-room cottage at Fourth and Polk Streets, where the original St. Joseph's Sanitarium was established. A year later, the sisters were forced to find larger quarters and changed the name to St. Joseph's Hospital. As the city grew, so did the hospital. The sisters opened a school of nursing in 1910. They moved the hospital to its current location in 1953, and it continued to grow, adding a kidney dialysis unit in 1956, the Barrow Neurological Institute in 1962 (see listing), a coronary-care unit in 1965, a neonatal intensive-care unit in 1967, a respiratory intensive-care unit in 1968, and pediatric intensive-care unit in 1972. The hospital also changed its name to add the words "medical center" to reflect its expanded role. On his trip to Phoenix in 1987, Pope John Paul II visited the hospital.

The Sisters of Mercy continue to guide the institution in partnership with secular hospital professionals. Its services include more than 500 patient beds, a Level I

trauma center, general surgery, hyberbaric medicine, maternity services, the Muhammad Ali Parkinson's Research Center, outpatient surgery, an adult–day hospital, an audiology center, behavioral and developmental pediatrics, a blood bank, a cardiac catheterization lab, cardiac rehabilitation, a child-abuse assessment center, dialysis, general medical education, and much more. The hospital is part of Catholic Healthcare West, one of the largest health care systems in the United States.

St. Luke's Medical Center
1800 East Van Buren Street, Phoenix
(602) 251-8100
www.stlukesmedcenter.com
St. Luke's Medical Center opened in 1907 as the St. Luke's Home serving tuberculosis patients. Tuberculosis was pretty well under control in 1949, when St. Luke's expanded its mission. As St. Luke's Hospital, the facility specialized in respiratory and cardiovascular diseases as well as general medicine and surgery. Today, St. Luke's Medical Center is a 225-bed facility that provides services and programs in cardiology, pulmonology, orthopedics, general medicine and surgery, neuroscience, emergency medicine, gastroenterology, oncology, and ophthalmology. Facilities include the Charles A. Barrow Heart Lung Center, the Jane Eslick Johnson Physical Rehabilitation Center, and the Bridges Center for Surgical Weight Management, which opened in 1996 and is the oldest center of its kind in the Valley. The hospital also offers robotic surgery for heart, prostate, and other ailments, and a wound care center that treats nonhealing wounds such as diabetic ulcers.

Southeast Valley

Banner Baywood Heart Hospital
6750 East Baywood Avenue, Mesa
(480) 854-5000
www.bannerhealth.com
Banner Baywood Heart Hospital is the second-largest freestanding heart hospital

in the United States. It opened in 2000 with 60 beds. After recently completing a $13.2-million expansion, the hospital is now a 111-bed facility. The hospital offers a wide variety of cardiac services, including advanced capabilities in cardiac catheterization, electrophysiology, noninvasive cardiology, heart surgery, and vascular care.

Banner Baywood Medical Center
6644 East Baywood Avenue, Mesa
(480) 981-2000
www.bannerhealth.com

Banner Baywood Medical Center, formerly known as Valley Lutheran Hospital and now owned by Banner Health Systems, opened in 1984 with 120 beds. It has grown into a 241-bed, full-service hospital providing general surgery and medical care, critical care, and maternity care. The hospital has an emergency room, a women's health center, a joint-replacement program, and an outpatient services center.

Banner Desert Medical Center
1400 South Dobson Road, Mesa
(480) 835-3000
www.bannerhealth.com

Banner Desert Medical Center, formerly known as Desert Samaritan Hospital, opened in 1973, but its roots go back to 1921 when Genevieve LeSueur donated her two-story, 12-room house to become Mesa Southside District Hospital. As Mesa grew, so did the hospital. By 1958 it had moved to Main Street and Country Club Drive and expanded to become a complete hospital facility with operating rooms, a recovery room, and emergency room. In 1968 Southside merged with Good Samaritan Hospital (now known as Banner Good Samaritan Medical Center), and Samaritan Health Service was born. The corporation built Desert Samaritan to replace Southside Hospital, and in 2003 the hospital was purchased by Banner Health Systems and renamed Banner Desert Medical Center. Banner Desert primarily serves Mesa, Tempe, Chandler, Gilbert, and Apache Junction. A full-service community hospital, Banner Desert has 600 licensed beds, including private rooms with patios. It features a Level II emergency room with 53 beds. Banner Desert also provides 26 private labor-delivery-recovery rooms. Banner Desert Children's Center is a Level III neonatal intensive-care unit and also offers pediatric intensive-care facilities. Thousands of inpatient and outpatient surgeries are performed each year at Desert Banner, including more than 500 open-heart surgeries. The hospital also has a radiation oncology department, 88 critical-care and intermediate-care beds, a 32-bed orthopedic and neurology unit, and a sleep disorders center. Banner Desert also offers various therapy programs, such as aquatic therapy, community health education classes, and an orthopedic and sports-rehabilitation program.

Banner Mesa Medical Center
1010 North Country Club Drive, Mesa
(480) 834-1211
www.bannerhealth.com

Banner Mesa Medical Center, formerly known as Mesa Lutheran Hospital, opened in 1963 with 165 beds. Today, Banner Mesa, owned by Banner Health Systems, is a 258-bed hospital, with a 60-bed skilled-nursing facility. Its services include an emergency room, obstetrical services, a joint-replacement program, a woman's health center, and general medical and surgical services. The John J. Rhodes Rehabilitation Institute, the Center for Women's Health, and the Generations Behavioral Health unit, which offers inpatient and outpatient psychological services for seniors, are also on campus. The hospital recently underwent a $2-million renovation project, which added MRI capabilities, additional beds, and a new bariatric surgery department and provided for the renovation of its obstetrics suites.

Chandler Regional Hospital
475 South Dobson Road, Chandler
(480) 963-4561
www.crhaz.com

A citizens group established Maricopa County Hospital District #1 in 1961 and, through it, built Chandler Regional Hospital. The 210-bed facility provides all private rooms. Its major services include an emergency center featuring Level II trauma care, an intensive-care unit, inpatient and outpatient surgery, physical rehabilitation services, a pediatrics unit, and cardiopulmonary services. The Family Birth Center offers full-service care and features labor-delivery-recovery rooms. In addition, the East Valley Regional Cancer Center, which offers comprehensive oncology services, is on the campus. The recently completed construction of a $20-million Ambulatory Surgery and Imaging Center to expand the hospital's emergency, surgery, and diagnostic imaging services and added a heart vascular center, which offers a full range of cardiovascular services.

Mesa General Hospital
515 North Mesa Drive, Mesa
(480) 969-9111
www.mesageneralhospital.com

Mesa General Hospital opened in 1965 as a physician-owned community hospital. Today, it is a 130-bed facility that offers a full range of services, including an emergency room, an intensive-care unit, maternity services, outpatient surgery and rehabilitation, a women's care center, and a robotic surgery program for heart, prostate, and other diseases. It is home to the Arizona Diagnostic and Surgical Center as well as a wound center for the treatment of chronic wounds.

Tempe St. Luke's Hospital
1500 South Mill Avenue, Tempe
(480) 784-5500
www. tempestlukeshospital.com

Tempe St. Luke's Hospital opened in 1944 as a small, 10-bed community hospital in the home of Dr. Ernest Pohle. It remains the only acute-care hospital in Tempe. A 109-bed facility, Tempe St. Luke's has an emergency room, general surgery, a radiology lab, a sleep disorders center, a wound care center, and outpatient surgery. The hospital's labor and delivery department

offers full-service care, including certified nurse midwives on staff. Also on the hospital campus is a 63,000-square-foot medical office complex housing more than 50 specialized medical practices.

Northeast Valley

Mayo Clinic Scottsdale
13400 East Shea Boulevard, Scottsdale
(480) 301-8000
www.mayoclinic.org/scottsdale

Mayo Clinic Scottsdale opened in 1987 and, owing to the Mayo Clinic reputation, it serves a varied clientele. More than 280 physicians are available to patients at the Mayo Clinic Scottsdale. It is also part of an integrated, multicampus system that includes the 205-bed Mayo Clinic Hospital, located in northeast Phoenix, several primary care centers throughout the Valley, and the Mayo Center for Women's Health. It is a multispecialty outpatient clinic with more than 240 exam rooms, an outpatient surgery center, a full-service laboratory, a pharmacy, a patient-education library, and an endoscopy suite. The Mayo Clinic's Samuel C. Johnson Medical Research Building is a basic science research lab and is currently conducting research in such areas as molecular genetics and cellular and molecular biology. Clinical research trials give patients access to the latest medical treatments. It is also a teaching institution. More than 65 medical and surgical specialties are practiced at the clinic, which includes an NCI-designated comprehensive cancer center, organ transplantation, a breast clinic, a gastrointestinal endoscopy program, a sleep disorders center, and state-of-the-art radiation oncology treatment. The Mayo Clinic Scottsdale also offers a patient-education library and a 188-seat auditorium for patient- and physician-education programs. Also on the clinic's campus is Courtyard by Marriot, a 124-room hotel that is available for overnight stays for patients and their families.

Scottsdale Healthcare Osborn
7400 East Osborn Road, Scottsdale
(480) 675–4000
www.shc.org

City Hospital of Scottsdale was founded in 1962 as a 120-bed facility. As the Northeast Valley grew, so did the hospital and its mission. For most of its existence, it has been known as Scottsdale Memorial Hospital, but in 1998 changed its name to Scottsdale Healthcare Osborn. It is a 305-bed, full-service hospital, known for its cardiovascular medicine, obstetrics, orthopedics, and oncology services. Its emergency department is a Level I trauma center that serves the East Valley and much of south central Arizona. The hospital also provides an urgent-care center; outpatient surgery and recovery care; inpatient and outpatient facilities for physical, occupational, and speech therapy; a cardiac center; 15 operating suites, including 2 specifically equipped for open-heart surgery; a critical-care unit; a freestanding birth center with 12 couplet care rooms and 9 labor and delivery rooms; and a Level II nursery. The hospital also houses hyperbaric oxygen treatment, adult day care, an outpatient cardiopulmonary rehabilitation and fitness center, an outpatient surgery center with a dedicated recovery care nursing unit, and primary care through the Family Practice Center.

Scottsdale Healthcare Shea
9003 East Shea Boulevard, Scottsdale
(480) 860–3000
www.shc.org

Scottsdale Healthcare Shea, consistently ranked among top hospitals in the nation, is a 343-bed hospital that features all private rooms and is known for its cardiology, oncology, and women's and children's services. The hospital's Kenneth M. Piper Outpatient Surgery Center offers surgical specialties, such as reconstructive, orthopedic, urology, and gynecology, and houses the Scottsdale Healthcare Reproductive Medicine program. The Piper Center contains eight operating rooms and a nine-room overnight-services pavilion to serve patients requiring postsurgery observation, pain control, or IV therapy. The hospital also has an emergency room, cardiology services that include open-heart surgery, cardiac catheterization, and inpatient and outpatient cardiac rehabilitation facilities. The hospital also has an intensive-care unit, medical and surgical services, obstetric services, a bone-marrow transplant unit, a 24-bed oncology unit, a sleep disorders center, and an epilepsy monitoring center. Also available through the hospital are pediatric services; outpatient physical, occupational and speech therapy; laboratory services; and lithotripsy, a special treatment for kidney stones.

Also on campus is the Virginia G. Piper Cancer Center, an outpatient center that provides a myriad of programs and services including hematology, bone-marrow transplants, a genetic risk program, occupational therapy, diet and nutrition advice, and a team of medical oncologists. There is also a boutique featuring makeup and prosthetics. The center is also affiliated with the Arizona Cancer Center of Tucson and will participate in various clinical trials and special research programs.

Northwest Valley

Arrowhead Community Hospital
18701 North 67th Avenue, Glendale
(623) 561–1000
www.arrowheadhospital.com

This 115-bed facility has served the Northwest Valley since 1988. Part of the Vanguard Hospital group since 2000, and now managed by their Abrazo Health Care, the hospital offers state-of-the-art equipment and technology. Services available include angioplasty, a cancer resource center, cardiac catherizaton lab, cardiac rehab, a Level II obstetrics unit, oncology and mammography services, labor and delivery suites, orthopedic and outpatient surgery, and a variety of wellness programs such as exercise classes or a diabetic education course through the Wellness Connection, just north of the main hospital building at 6670 West Sack Drive.

Banner Thunderbird Medical Center
5555 West Thunderbird Road, Glendale
(602) 865-5555
www.bannerhealth.com
Northwest Hospital—Glendale's first hospital—opened in 1960. In 1983, when it had outgrown its original site, the hospital moved to its current location and was renamed Thunderbird Samaritan Medical Center. Today, the hospital is called Banner Thunderbird Medical Center and is owned by Banner Health Systems. The hospital has 335 licensed beds, plus 62 licensed behavioral-health and rehabilitation beds, and primarily serves residents of the Northwest Valley. Its emergency department features 45 fully equipped treatment rooms. The hospital also offers a complete range of gynecological and obstetrical services, including a labor, delivery, and recovery unit, and a nursery that provides expert care for premature infants. The hospital has 12 operating rooms, including several suites for open-heart surgery. Banner Thunderbird offers general surgery, orthopedics, pediatrics, pulmonary care, a critical-care and intensive-care unit, an oncology and urology unit, occupational therapy and rehabilitation services, cardiac care, and renal care. There is also a sleep-disorders program, an outpatient center, and a hospice program. In addition, Banner Thunderbird Behavioral Health offers psychiatric, behavioral-health, and substance-abuse treatment for adults and adolescents on an inpatient basis. In recent years the hospital has undergone a $50-million expansion and continues to grow to meet the needs of the community.

Del E Webb Memorial Hospital
14502 West Meeker Boulevard,
Sun City West
(623) 214-4000
www.sunhealth.org/delwebb
The 254-bed Del E Webb hospital, built in 1988, serves the communities of the

Northwest Valley. Focused on medicine for adults, the hospital offers an emergency center, general medical and surgical services, a cardiac-catheterization laboratory, outpatient surgery and services, rehabilitation services, medical-psychiatric services, mobile MRI and lithotripsy services, and extended-care facilities. It is a leading center for hip and knee replacement, as well as other follow-up rehabilitation programs. It is the site for the Sun Health Pain Management Center and the Sun Health Center for Adult Behavioral Health, the Valley's only nursing home unit for med-psych care. The Louisa Kellam Center for Women's Health offers extensive services for women, including obstetrics and gynecology.

Sun Health Boswell Memorial Hospital
10401 Thunderbird Boulevard, Sun City
(623) 977-7211
www.sunhealth.org/boswell
When Boswell Memorial Hospital was built in 1970, Sun City was a long way from Glendale, Peoria, and the mainstream of the Valley. Reflecting the nature of the retirement community, Boswell focused on adult care and medicine. As the Northwest Valley has grown, Boswell has maintained that focus. This 357-bed community hospital provides inpatient and outpatient medical and surgical services as well as a skilled-nursing facility. Boswell offers an emergency center, an outpatient center, a cancer program, cardiovascular surgery, an intensive-care unit, and extended-care and rehabilitation services. The Heart Center in the hospital includes catheterization labs and office space on-site for cardiologists and surgeons.

Southwest Valley

West Valley Hospital
13677 West McDowell Road, Goodyear
(623) 882-1500
www.wvhospital.com
West Valley Hospital opened in 2003 and is part of the Vanguard Health Systems/

Abrazo Health Care network. The acute-care hospital currently has 74 beds, but will grow to approximately 140 beds by 2004. The hospital provides general medical care to Phoenix's West Valley communities and also offers obstetrics services, a cardiovascular operating room, an emergency room, and radiology services.

Don't underestimate the power of the Arizona sun. Skin cancer danger is very real in Arizona, so you should always apply a heavy-duty sunblock when you go out—and this goes double for the small tykes. Wearing a light, long-sleeved shirt will help, and donning a hat will also combat heat stroke. Succumbing to dehydration is also easy here, even in the winter. Try to drink at least eight cups of water a day—even more during periods of heavy activity. Heat stroke can kill, so if you or someone you know succumbs to the heat, seek medical attention immediately.

WALK-IN CLINICS

Walk-in clinics come in a number of flavors. If the clinic doesn't have the word "urgent" in its name somewhere, then the clinic generally will turn out to be a general practice that accepts walk-in patients. Most of these general-practice clinics work the Monday through Friday, 9:00 A.M. to 5:00 P.M. shift. The urgent-care clinics tend to work the odd hours (some offer 24-hour services), and they're geared to handle accidents and conditions that need immediate care but are not life threatening. They're not the place to go if you think you're having a heart attack, but a good place to go if you think you've broken a limb. Next Care Urgent Care clinics are sprinkled throughout the Valley and are open seven days a week (www.nextcare.com). Call beforehand to ascertain hours and what insurance carriers are covered. In addition, many of the

hospitals such as Mayo Clinic, Chandler Regional Hospital, the Banner Samaritan group, and others have affiliated walk-in, general-practice clinics, and a call to the hospital can help you find a good clinic. (Most of the hospitals also have lines for doctor referrals.) The following list of additional clinics is not complete, but representative.

Phoenix

Ahwatukee Foothills Urgent Care
4545 East Chandler Boulevard, Phoenix
(480) 961-2300

Jesse Owens Urgent Care Center
325 East Baseline Road, Phoenix
(602) 824-4350

STAT Clinix
4530 East Ray Road, Phoenix
(480) 598-7500

U.S. Healthworks
2010 North 75th Avenue, Phoenix
(623) 245-6695
www.ushealthworks.com

Southeast Valley

Gilbert Health Center Urgent Care
1501 North Gilbert Road, Gilbert
(480) 503-5400

Minor Medical Care Center
4427 South Rural Road, Suite 1
Tempe
(480) 838-2289

Northeast Valley

Primary Care Walk-In Center
8102 East McDowell Road, Scottsdale
(480) 946-3800

U.S. Healthworks
10335 North Scottsdale Road, Scottsdale
(480) 991-9358
www.ushealthworks.com

Northwest Valley

Surprise Health Center
14800 West Mountain View Boulevard,
Suite 230, Surprise
(623) 815-2900

MENTAL HEALTH

Mental-health services are available at a
number of the hospitals listed in this
chapter and through the services and hospitals listed below.

Arizona State Hospital
2500 East Van Buren Street, Phoenix
(602) 244-1331, (800) 242-7837
www.hs.state.az.us/azsh

**Banner Behavioral Health
Hospital-Scottsdale**
7575 East Earl Drive, Scottsdale
(602) 254-4357, (800) 254-HELP
www.bannerhealth.com

Banner Desert Behavioral Health Center
2225 West Southern Avenue, Mesa
(602) 254-4357, (800) 254-HELP
www.bannerhealth.com

St. Luke's Behavioral Health Center
1800 East Van Buren Street, Phoenix
(602) 251-8535

ALTERNATIVE HEALTH CARE

Ever since settlers started coming to the
Valley of the Sun in the 1800s, interest in
alternative health care has been high.
Back then, it was difficult to find practitioners well-versed in medical science

anyway, so home cures, folk cures—and
even out-and-out quackery—often filled
health-care needs that included bullet
wounds, rattlesnake bites, and tuberculosis. By 1870 Arizona's settlers numbered
10,000, with 22 doctors to serve them.
The few doctors out here had to live life
on the road, traveling from settlement to
settlement to treat people.

The first doctors in Arizona were
undoubtedly Native American medicine
men. A number of frontier doctors incorporated the many herbal and botanical
cures that the medicine men used
because they worked. Science has only
recently begun to verify what these frontier doctors knew by experience. Today,
herbal and botanical cures from many different cultures, including that of Native
Americans, are considered part of the vast
umbrella known as "alternative"—and even
mainstream—health care.

The Valley offers a full range of alternative medical services that complement
or step outside the bounds of traditional
Western medical practices. For example,
chiropractors are virtually mainstream
practitioners in Arizona and the Yellow
Pages listings for chiropractors fill numerous pages. You'll also find homeopaths,
naturopaths, acupuncturists, aromathera-
pists, massage therapists, bioelectric therapists, and just about any other
practitioner of alternative medicine you
can think of.

Unfortunately, alternative medicine is a
vast and decentralized realm, and there
are no authoritative referral sources in the
Valley. So the best sources for finding an
alternative-medicine practitioner are the
phone book and word of mouth. You can
also often stop by a local health food
store to get recommendations on practitioners in the region.

The best advice we can offer is similar
to what we would give when seeking a
conventional medical practitioner. Find
out where the physician studied, how long
the physician has been practicing, and
whether the physician is licensed with the

state. Then, check with the licensing boards for any complaints. Arizona licensing boards include the Board of Chiropractic Examiners, 5060 North 19th Avenue, Suite 416, Phoenix, (602) 864-5088, www.azchiroboard.com; the Board of Homeopathic Medical Examiners, 1400 West Washington Street, Suite 230, Phoenix, (602) 542-3095, http://home .mindspring.com/~bhme; and the Naturopathic Physicians Board of Medical Examiners, 1400 West Washington Street, Suite 230, Phoenix, (602) 542-8242, www.np bomex.az.gov.

EDUCATION AND CHILD CARE

There's much to praise about the education scene in the Phoenix area: the ever improving Arizona State University, one of the largest community college systems in the nation, and private schools whose fame reaches beyond Arizona's borders. In comparison, though, the Valley's public school system is not as dynamic as it could or should be for such a large metropolitan area. There are many bright spots—progressive, high-minded elementary and secondary schools in the urban core as well as in suburban areas. But those who rank livable cities say Phoenix's public schools are part of the reason the city doesn't make it to the top echelon.

Looking at Arizona public schools as a whole, the state has made vast strides during the past few years. In the national rankings for state and local revenues for public schools, Arizona places 18th and 19th, respectively, out of 50 states. Arizona's high-school dropout rate is half the national average, and the state ranks near the middle nationally in high-school graduation rates. Arizona also ranks 28th nationally in public-school teacher salaries, a big improvement from a few years ago. However, Arizona still sits near the bottom nationally—48th out of 50 states—in per-pupil spending and also ranks 49th out of 50 states for having one of the highest student-teacher ratios in the United States. In addition, because of the state's exponential population growth, Arizona is plagued by teacher shortages and a building crunch.

If you talk to Phoenix area residents with young children, you'll find that many of them shop school districts as much as they do real estate when they are ready to move into new homes. (Homebuyers should consult the Relocation chapter.) Certain districts have excellent reputations, while others limp along because of inequities in Arizona's system for school funding. Some schools have enough money to build swimming pools and top-notch computer labs, while others get by with bare-bones classrooms and the simplest of gymnasiums. Since statehood in 1912, Arizona schools have relied on bonds, repaid through property taxes, to build and improve schools. In 1994 the Arizona Supreme Court ruled that funding school construction through local property taxes was unconstitutional because of the disparities it created among classrooms. The Arizona Legislature has been struggling with the school-financing issue ever since.

In this chapter we start our list of educational facilities with public and private universities, including Arizona State University, which for many years played second banana to the University of Arizona in Tucson. Some would argue that the two schools are now about equal.

Those looking for a community college will find an impressive selection in the Phoenix area. The Maricopa Community College District of 10 colleges is the largest such district in the country. It draws more than a quarter of a million students, some of whom like the cost savings versus a four-year university and some of whom seek the specialized skills and training that community colleges can offer. Community colleges are also a great way to gather prerequisite classes before launching into a bachelor degree at another institution. The colleges represent a wide range of ages and ethnic groups, and students include retirees, homemakers, and those seeking a career change.

Education opportunities trickle down to the youngest of Arizonans too. The Valley of the Sun has a number of good preschool programs, including ones endorsed by the National Association for the Education of Young Children, Montessori programs, and parent-cooperative programs. See the Child Care section of this chapter for important phone numbers as well as information on finding babysitters, nannies, and child care centers.

EDUCATION

Arizona State University

From a humble teachers college more than a century ago, Arizona State University has grown to a multipurpose institution of 57,000 students on three campuses. It has undergone several name changes over the decades. It started out as Tempe Normal School in the 1890s, later became Arizona State Teachers College, then Arizona State College, until becoming Arizona State University in 1958. The university is one of the top-five largest universities in the nation. ASU is very much a part of the Valley community based on its contributions toward education, research, business, and the arts. The campuses are a source of pride for local residents, because ASU has been able to continually ascend in the ratings of universities nationwide. In addition, ASU continues to improve in reputation as a research university. For instance, it has been highly involved in the Mars Pathfinder project and the fields of bioengineering and biomedicine.

In athletics ASU is known for having an excellent overall program, one that has risen to the national rankings in several of its more than 22 varsity programs. The football team went to the Rose Bowl in 1987 and 1997. The teams' mascot, Sparky, is the maroon-and-gold Sun Devil, an impish-looking devil complete with pitchfork. Top-notch athletic amenities include Sun Devil Stadium, the Karsten golf course, and the Plummer Aquatic Center.

ASU has more than 400 student organizations, including those that have religious or ethnic affiliations and certain political or environmental interests.

The ASU library system boasts 3.2 million volumes, making it the 37th-largest research library in the United States and Canada, according to the Association of Research Libraries. Hayden Library on the main campus houses the Arizona Collection and research sites in Chicano and Native American studies. A two-level underground addition to Hayden opened in 1989. Also on campus are the Noble Science & Engineering Library, housing a vast map collection and data on U.S. patents, and law, music, and video research libraries.

ASU's newspaper, *The State Press,* is published Monday through Friday. A literary magazine called *Hayden's Ferry Review* comes out twice a year and highlights local and national writers and artists. It is considered one of the best literary magazines in the country.

The Arizona Board of Regents is the governing board for the state's public university system, which also includes the University of Arizona in Tucson and Northern Arizona University in Flagstaff.

Here we give overviews of the campuses of ASU.

ASU, Main Campus
University Drive and Mill Avenue, Tempe
(480) 965-9011
www.asu.edu
With 47,000 students taking day and evening classes, the main campus is by far the focal point of the ASU system. The 700-acre campus takes up several city blocks in downtown Tempe, and it regulates the pulse of the city. When the students leave for the summer, the usually bustling Mill Avenue falls quiet. There's little open space and landscaping between

campus buildings and Tempe businesses, so there's an overall feeling that this is an urban, commuter campus. On the other hand, the interior of the campus has several malls—wide, tree-lined pedestrian walkways—that give that feeling of seclusion and seriousness associated with institutions of higher learning. Plus, there are 14 residence halls and ASU-run apartment complexes, proving that the campus is a good mix of commuters and those who hang out close to campus.

Architecture buffs should have a look at Grady Gammage Memorial Auditorium on Mill Avenue, a grandly executed circular building with lighted ramps leading out from it. It was the last public building designed by Frank Lloyd Wright. Nearby, you will see the round and tiered Music Building and the futuristic Nelson Fine Arts Center.

ASU Main students pursue a choice of 87 undergraduate degrees, 95 master's degrees, 48 doctoral or terminal degree programs, and 1 law degree program. The colleges ASU is best known for are in liberal arts and sciences, engineering, fine arts, architecture and environmental design, business, nursing, and education. To keep up with technology, the campus has several computing sites for use by students, faculty, and staff. The huge Computing Commons is near the center of campus.

ASU West
4701 West Thunderbird Road, Phoenix
(602) 543-5500
www.west.asu.edu

Established in 1984 to serve the West Valley, ASU West continues to grow, serving more than 6,000 students. Undergraduate and graduate level courses lead to 38 degree programs, plus professional certificates offered through the Colleges of Arts & Sciences, Education, and Human Services as well as the School of Management and Division of Collaborative Programs.

ASU East
7001 East Williams Road, Mesa
(480) 727-3278
www.east.asu.edu

ASU's newest campus is the home campus for ASU's College of Technology and Applied Sciences, the Morrison School of Agribusiness and Resource Management, and East College, serving more than 3,000 students.

The Arizona State University Visitor Center, located at 826 East Apache Boulevard, (480) 965-0100, in Tempe can provide you with maps of campus and brochures about ASU programs. The visitor center also houses the alumni office. Hours are 8:15 A.M. to 4:45 P.M. Monday through Friday. Diagonally across the intersection is the Tempe Chamber of Commerce, with other information to help you find your way around.

ASU Extended Campus
502 East Monroe Avenue, Phoenix
(480) 965-9696
www.asu.edu/xed

ASU Extended Campus is now considered the university's fourth campus and is located downtown in the ASU Downtown Center. The campus offers degree programs, noncredit classes, and certificate programs for professional development. All classes are held in the evening and on weekends to accommodate both full- and part-time students wanting to continue their education. A great number of classes, however, are held through distance learning via the Internet—either on campus or off. ASU Extended Campus also offers a number of community programs, such as workforce development, outreach programs, and noontime lectures on a variety of topics.

Other Universities

Grand Canyon University
3300 West Camelback Road, Phoenix
(602) 249-3300, (800) 800-9776
www.grand-canyon.edu
The 3,011-student Grand Canyon University is Arizona's only private, traditional, Christian liberal arts institution. It has 60 programs of study, all with a Christian perspective. The six colleges are nursing, liberal arts, science, business and professional studies, Christian studies, and education. The university is continually ranked among the best private liberal arts programs in the nation in surveys by *U.S. News & World Report*. The 90-acre campus, lined with palm trees and featuring fairly modern red-brick buildings, is easily accessible from busy Camelback Road in west Phoenix and also houses the Canyon Institute for Advanced Studies, a Christian interdisciplinary research center. The student population is a mix of commuting students, those transferring from other colleges, and first-time college students living on campus. There is one residence hall, and the university can arrange for apartment housing. The university says it has a broad religious and ethnic representation, with students from all over the country and all over the world. In athletics Grand Canyon won the 1996 Men's Soccer NCAA Division II Championship, and has also competed for national collegiate titles in baseball and basketball.

If you want to learn a new skill but aren't interested in earning college credit, consider auditing a course at a regular college or signing up for a community education class. Whether you want to paint or learn how to write your family history, your local city library or parks and recreation department should have information on community classes. If you look in the Yellow Pages, you can also find schools for everything from ballroom dancing to horseshoeing.

University of Phoenix
4635 East Elwood Street, Phoenix
(480) 804-7600, (800) 697-8223
www.phoenix.edu

Ahwatukee Foothills Campus
14647 South 50th Street, Phoenix
(480) 557-2700

Chandler Campus
2975 West Linda Lane, Chandler
(480) 557-2800

Gilbert Campus
2160 South Power Road, Chandler
(480) 557-2600

Mesa Campus
1620 South Stapley Road, Mesa
(480) 557-2550

Northwest Campus
15601 North 28th Avenue, Phoenix
(602) 863-2600

Scottsdale Campus
8801 East Raintree Drive, Suite 100
Scottsdale
(480) 557-2650

Tempe Campus
1150 West Grove Parkway, Tempe
(480) 557-2130
The Arizona-based University of Phoenix is the nation's largest for-profit, accredited university. University of Phoenix classes are offered at more than 139 campuses and learning centers in 29 states, Puerto Rico, Canada, and around the world via the Internet and currently enrolls 186,169 students. The University of Phoenix bills itself as the nation's leading university for working adults, with degree programs in areas such as business, information systems, counseling, nursing, and education. An important note, though: The university accepts only gainfully employed students age 21 and older. A recent study indicated that nearly half of all higher-education students are in this age group. Flexible scheduling of classes allows working professionals to earn degrees or certifications without interrupting their careers. This means week-

Important Phone Numbers

Here are several addresses and phone numbers you might find helpful as you research the education scene in the Valley.

Arizona Department of Education, 1535 West Jefferson Street, Phoenix, (602) 542-5393, www.ade.az.gov

Arizona Congress of Parents and Teachers/PTA, 2721 North Seventh Avenue, Phoenix, (602) 279-1811, www.azpta.org

Arizona Private School Association, 202 East McDowell Road, Suite 273, Phoenix, (602) 254-5199, www.azpsa.org

Arizona State Board for Charter Schools, 1700 West Washington, Suite 164, Phoenix, (602) 364-3080, www.asbcs.state.az.us

Maricopa County Superintendent of Schools, 301 West Jefferson Street, Suite 660, Phoenix, (602) 506-3866, www.maricopa.gov/schools/contact_home_school.asp

end and evening classes, usually lasting for compressed amounts of time compared with similar classes at traditional universities.

Community Colleges

Maricopa Community Colleges
2411 West 14th Street, Tempe
(480) 731-8000
www.maricopa.edu

Ten colleges, two skill centers, and several satellite campuses in Maricopa County are organized into the Maricopa Community College District, which is the largest provider of postsecondary education in Arizona and one of the largest in the country. The district formed in 1962 with a single college and has since grown to serve more than 250,000 students annually in credit and noncredit programs. Students have their choice of professional, occupational, special interest, and continuing education programs. In other words, you can study just about anything somewhere within the Maricopa Community College system. Many students attending Arizona State University have taken pre-

requisites in the liberal arts and other subjects at a community college, either before starting at ASU or while at ASU. Dramatic growth, innovative partnerships, and outstanding faculty and staff have created a community college district known for contemporary programming, technological advances, and an imaginative environment for learning. The Maricopa Community Colleges offer 9,057 credit courses and 607 occupational programs as well as 7 degrees, including Associate in Arts (AA), Associate in Science (AS), Associate in Applied Science (AAS), Associate in Business (ABus), Associate in Transfer Partnership (ATP), Associate in Elementary Education (AEE), and Associate in General Studies (AGS).

The colleges serve many diverse communities, with students ranging in age from 15 to 91. Women comprise 53 percent of the student population and more than 47 percent of all students plan to work full- or part-time. The student body includes more than 15,000 students aged 50 plus, 25,000 Internet students, as well as more than 57,000 students who are culturally and ethnically diverse and more than 18,000 international students.

Currently, about 40 percent of all adults residing in Maricopa County have received educational services at one of the Maricopa Community Colleges. More than half of all Arizona State University baccalaureate degree recipients transfer credits from the Maricopa Community Colleges, and articulation agreements exist with numerous public and private colleges and universities in Arizona and nationally.

Campuses, for the most part, have a few thousand students, but some are smaller. District growth has enabled campuses to build not only classroom buildings, but also such things as fitness centers, child care centers, and computer labs.

Flexible scheduling and evening classes help accommodate working adults. Rio Salado Community College is known as the college without walls, because most of the classes take place at various satellite learning centers. Some of its campuses also offer distance learning via the Internet. These programs help make the community college experience accessible to everyone.

The community colleges pride themselves on being able to serve every corner of the Valley. For addresses and phone numbers, call the district's 24-hour hotline at (480) 731-8333.

Other Higher Education Institutions

East Valley Institute of Technology
1601 West Main Street, Mesa
(480) 461-4000
www.evit.com
EVIT is Arizona's first regional, technological public school district, open to students in 10th through 12th grade from throughout the East Valley. It's free for those students, although adults out of high school pay a small tuition. Financial assistance is available. The idea is to prepare students for immediate employment in such areas as health occupations, commercial art, computer programming, electronics, draft-

ing, construction, culinary arts, and many other areas of business and industry. Students typically spend half the school day at their regular school and half at EVIT.

Scottsdale Culinary Institute
8100 East Camelback Road, Suite 1001
Scottsdale
(480) 990-3773, (800) 848-2433
www.scichefs.com
We mention this school because Scottsdale—with its many resorts, hotels, and fine restaurants—is a natural location for training chefs. The institute, in operation since 1986, offers an Associate of Occupational Studies degree in Le Cordon Bleu Culinary Arts, a 15-month program, and the Le Cordon Bleu Patisserie and Baking Certificate Program, which lasts 9 months. Both programs provide intensive, hands-on learning, and the school's graduates have gone on to great jobs, locally and elsewhere, as sous chefs, pastry chefs, and banquet managers. The Institute's L'Ecole Restaurant, rated three stars by Mobil, is a classroom, laboratory, and public restaurant. The restaurant is open for lunch and dinner Monday through Friday. The institute opened a second campus, Sky Bridge, in downtown Scottsdale in 2001, with additional classrooms, kitchens, and a new student-run bistro-style cafe, L'Academie Cafe, which is open for lunch and dinner Monday through Friday.

Thunderbird, The American Graduate School of International Management
15249 North 59th Avenue, Glendale
(602) 978-7000
www.t-bird.edu
This private graduate school enjoys a global reputation as one of the top schools of international business. It was established in 1946 on the principle that to do business on a global scale, one must be able to combine functional business skills—such as finance and marketing—with the ability to understand the culture, language, and business climate of one's customers and business associates. To that end, Thunderbird offers a three-part

curriculum: the study of one or more languages, international studies, and international business. Students have their choice of studying Arabic, Chinese, French, German, Japanese, Portuguese, Russian, or Spanish. International students may opt for thorough training in English as a Second Language. Many international students are sent here by their home country's graduate schools or corporations for further polishing in the ways of international business. All students earn an MBA in international management. Thunderbird, with 933 full-time students in 2003, bills itself as the oldest graduate management school in the United States devoted exclusively to the education of college graduates for international careers. It also boasts a large multimedia library called the International Business Information Centre. Tracking of graduates shows that most go into marketing/sales, finance/ accounting, or consulting and work in the manufacturing and financial services sectors. The school says it has 33,000 alumni working in 12,000 companies, represented in 135 countries, making for an impressive global network of contacts for graduates. About 5,000 students go through the school's nondegreed executive programs annually, which offer short-term training, certification, and continuing education. The average age of Thunderbird students is 29, while the average for the executive programs is 37. Thunderbird has centers in Tokyo, Japan; Moscow, Russia; Sâo Paulo, Brazil; and Archamps, France.

Valley School Districts

The Valley is a crazy quilt of 58 school districts serving nearly half a million students. Some districts—especially in central Phoenix—are at a disadvantage in regard to academic programs, staffing, facilities, and amenities. Certain schools have been found to be substandard. On the other hand, districts in the suburbs with high growth typically enjoy excellent facilities and amenities,

along with all kinds of extra programs to expand students' knowledge. Homebuyers flock to these newer areas, which leads to one drawback—overcrowding when supply can't keep up with demand.

The Arizona Legislature has been struggling to address this issue of inequality for years, not only in the Phoenix area, but also around the state.

In 1997 Arizona schools started giving the Stanford 9 Achievement test to selected grades and found that overall scores were less than glowing when compared to national scores on the standardized test, which looks at reading, math, and vocabulary. Some individual schools scored well, though, especially sites in Scottsdale, Paradise Valley, and areas of the southeast Valley.

Arizona's open-enrollment law means that you can send your child to a public school outside of your home district, provided that school has room. Deadlines for open enrollment are usually early in the calendar year. Call the school district you are interested in for more information. The only state requirements for enrolling your children in public school are birth certificates and immunization records. Some individual districts, however, require a proof of residency. State law requires children to be 5 years old before September 1 to start kindergarten.

Paradise Valley Unified School District
15002 North 32nd Street, Phoenix
(602) 867-5100
www.pvusd.k12.az.us
This district—the state's fourth largest—encompasses all kinds of neighborhoods, from low-income housing to multimillion-dollar hillside homes. Some parts of the district are seeing high growth, and most of the schools were built in the last 16 years. Organized in 1919, the district became a unified elementary and high school district in 1976 and currently boasts 30 elementary schools, 7 middle schools, and 5 high schools. It also runs 2 alternative schools. There are more than 35,000 students in all.

Peoria Unified School District
6330 West Thunderbird Road, Glendale
(623) 486-6000
www.peoriaud.k12.az.us
The Peoria Unified School District is nestled in the midst of two of the fastest-growing cities in the Phoenix metropolitan area—Glendale and Peoria. The school district has grown to encompass nearly 150 square miles due to a voter-approved annexation in November 2000. The Peoria Unified School District now stretches south from Glendale Avenue all the way north to the Maricopa–Yavapai County borders. As Arizona's third-largest district in terms of enrollment, the Peoria Unified School District boasts 29 K–8 schools and 5 high schools, serving over 36,000 students. Interestingly, 32 of the 34 schools have been built since 1972, indicating what a high growth area this has been. Many of the original campuses have received improvements and renovations thanks to a voter-approved bond election in 1996.

In 1999 the Peoria district completed the state's first Challenger Learning Center, one of about 30 around the world dedicated to space-themed programs in remembrance of the space shuttle *Challenger*. The center is located next to the campus of Sunrise Mountain High School in Peoria. For more information, call (623) 322-2001 or visit www.azchallenger.org.

Phoenix Union High School District
4502 North Central Avenue, Phoenix
(602) 764-1100
www.phxhs.k12.az.us
Phoenix Union is one of the largest high school districts in the nation, serving more than 23,000 students. But what sets this district apart from other high school districts in the Valley is its 11 magnet programs and 1 magnet high school, which currently educates more than 3,000 students. The magnet concept is how the district complies with a federal court order to desegregate its schools. Students often choose schools outside their neighborhoods because they're interested in a certain program at another school. What-

ever their choice, they receive free transportation to that school. A magnet school, as described by the district, provides both specialized and advanced preparation to students with special needs or ambitions. In addition to specialized courses, the schools offer a full slate of basic curriculum, athletics, clubs, and student government. Here are a few examples of magnet programs: medical and health studies at Alhambra High School in west Phoenix; computer and marine/environmental studies at Carl Hayden High School in west Phoenix; agribusiness, equine science, and natural resources management at César Chávez High School in west Phoenix; an international baccalaureate program for college-bound students at North High School in central Phoenix; and performing/visual arts, aviation/aerospace, and law-related studies at South Mountain High School in south Phoenix. For 25 years the district's students' SAT score averages have remained above the national average.

Metro Tech High School, formerly a vocational-technical school, has now become a comprehensive four-year high school and offers both regular academic classes and more than 25 career-vocational programs. It's at 1900 West Thomas Road; the phone number is (602) 764-8000.

Scottsdale Unified School District
3811 North 44th Street, Phoenix
(408) 484-6100
www.susd.org
This district of 27,000 students celebrated its centennial in 1996. It enjoys a good reputation, although you may find newer schools in the growth areas of north Scottsdale are at an advantage in facilities and programs over older schools in south Scottsdale. The district incorporates Scottsdale as well as portions of east Phoenix and has 20 elementary schools, 7 middle schools, 5 high schools, and 1 alternative school. One of the elementary schools is a "learning center," where the emphases are on hands-on learning, whole-language reading, and cross-grade

classrooms in a multicultural environment. Another elementary school focuses on back-to-basics instruction.

Charter Schools

Arizona is a leader in the concept of charter schools—state-funded K through 12 schools that market their specialized programs and offer Arizonans a choice besides traditional public schools for free education.

Arizona law defines a charter school as "a public school established by contract with a district governing board, the State Board of Education or the State Board for Charter Schools to provide learning that will improve pupil achievement." In addition, charter schools "provide additional academic choices for parents and pupils." Charter school statutes support flexibility and innovation in operations and structure, including governance, scheduling, curriculum, and instructional methodologies. Arizona's charter school laws are said to be among the most liberal in the nation.

Thus charter schools are owned and operated by private individuals or companies, but funded by taxpayers, to the tune of about $5,000 per student. There are close to 500 charter schools in the state (at least half of them in Maricopa County), with enrollment of 75,000-plus students and the number continues to rise.

In the past few years, many charter schools have sprung up in new buildings or have taken the place of existing schools. They are an eclectic bunch, and they receive state funding as long as they comply with the laws set up for them.

Charter schools advertise various focuses; examples are science/technology, back-to-basics, workplace skills, Montessori, college-preparatory, the arts, and integrated approaches. Most charter schools stick to either kindergarten through 8th grade enrollment or high school students. They are in a variety of neighborhoods; some take hundreds of students and others are as small as 50 students.

If you are looking for information on how schools stack up, call the Arizona School Report Card Program at (602) 542-5022 or visit www.ade.az.gov and click on "School Report Card."

For a list of charter schools, call the Arizona Department of Education Charter School Info Line at (602) 542-5094, or visit www.ade.az.gov/charterschools/info.

Private and Parochial Schools

You will be awash in choices if private schools are your preferred route. The Valley is home to several dozen. In addition, there are good Catholic, Protestant, Jewish, and Islamic schools whose focus is also on religion.

There's an enormous tuition range, with some of the parochial schools asking for a $1,000 to $3,000 annual tuition, midrange private schools asking about $5,000 annually, and the more exclusive private schools asking for as much as $11,000 annually. Some schools test students prior to admitting them and may ask for interviews as well. You'll also find that siblings of current students have the edge in admissions. Ask about financial assistance; some schools offer scholarships or can set up flexible payment plans.

All Saints' Episcopal Day School
**6300 North Central Avenue, Phoenix
(602) 274-4866
www.allsaints.org**
All Saints' philosophy is to identify academically talented youth and develop their abilities through a curriculum that balances academic excellence, physical education, and spiritual awareness. There are many enriching programs, such as computers and drama, as well as extracurricular activities, such as chorus, sports, and community service. The school has

been around since 1963 and now serves kindergartners through 8th graders. The student–teacher ratio is 8 to 1, with a maximum class size of 15 (grades K to 3) and 22 (grades 4 to 8).

The Arizona Commission for Post-Secondary Education publishes a directory of the state's private and public colleges and universities. **The Arizona College and Career Guide** *costs $5.00 and may be obtained by writing the commission at 2020 North Central Avenue, Suite 550, Phoenix 85004, or by calling (602) 258-2435. The directory is also available in the state's public libraries and online at www.rbbalch.com/accg.*

Brophy College Preparatory
4701 North Central Avenue, Phoenix
(602) 264-5291
www.brophyprep.org
Brophy Prep sits on a lovely 17-acre campus at Central Avenue and Camelback Road and encompasses a historically significant private chapel built when the school opened in 1928. The all-male Catholic Jesuit high school serves 9th- through 12th-grade students. The school's curriculum is college prep, and 99 percent of its graduates go on to four-year colleges and universities. The ratio of students to teachers is 25 to 1.

Phoenix Country Day School
3901 East Stanford Drive, Paradise Valley
(602) 955-8200
www.pcds.org
This is a popular option for Northeast Valley parents who want and can afford the private-school experience. The school opened in 1961 and has expanded over the years to a sprawling campus near Camelback Mountain. It's open to preschoolers through 12th graders. It calls itself a student-centered school and has many electives and extracurricular activities. The student–teacher ratio is 10 to 1, with a maximum class size of 15. Current enrollment is 700.

Rancho Solano Private Schools
5656 East Greenway, Scottsdale
(602) 996-7002
www.ranchosolano.com
Founded in 1954, Rancho Solano has five campuses in the Valley, including one in Scottsdale. It's open to preschoolers through 8th graders, and adheres to the philosophy that basic skills and appropriate study habits—mixed in with lots of activities, a positive attitude, and fun—are necessary to accomplish optimum personal, educational, and career goals. Rancho Solano has a college-preparatory focus, with arts, athletics, and bilingual education as pluses. The student–teacher ratio is 20 to 1 in grades K to 8, 10 to 1 in the preschool. The schools are popular, so expect a waiting list to get in.

Scottsdale Christian Academy
14400 North Tatum Boulevard, Phoenix
(602) 992-5100
www.scottsdalechristian.org
The Scottsdale Christian Academy is quite large, with top-notch facilities on a sprawling campus in north Phoenix. Current enrollment is nearly 1,100 students, ages preschool through high school. All students must sign a statement of faith in Christianity before admission. Older students receive a college-preparatory curriculum, and athletic programs are popular here.

Tesseract
4800 East Doubletree Ranch Road
Paradise Valley
(480) 991-1770
www.tesseractpv.org
The word *tesseract* comes from Madeleine L'Engle's book *A Wrinkle in Time* and refers to a fifth-dimensional learning experience. The school opened in Paradise Valley in 1988 and features an "inquiry-based way of learning" that emphasizes self-esteem and communication skills for preschoolers through 8th-graders. The student–teacher ratio is 12 to 1, (10 to 1 in the preschool).

CHILD CARE

You are sure to find the type of child care you're looking for in an enterprising area like the Valley of the Sun. There are hundreds of options in day-care centers, in-home care, and preschools.

One of the best ways to start your search is by talking to your neighbors who have children. Usually, you will want something close to home for a day-care center or preschool, and neighbors will be able to recommend nearby places. When seeking out child care, be sure to ask the provider about hours of operation, full-time versus part-time care, and cleanliness and safety standards. Look for a variety of toys and playground equipment and colorful surroundings. Beyond that, of course, you'll want to know whether it's a place where your child will have ample opportunities to learn, develop socially, and generally have fun. Find out if a preschool program tends to be open-ended and child-oriented or more academically oriented with a structured curriculum. The Valley has a number of parent-cooperative programs in which parents volunteer a few hours a week in the center. Many of these are affiliated with churches and temples.

To find a state-licensed day-care program, contact the following offices. For centers and family child-care homes serving more than five children, call the Department of Health Services Office of Childcare Licensing at (602) 364–2536, www.hs.state.az.us/als/childcare/index.htm. For family child-care homes serving one to four children, call the Department of Economic Security's Childcare Administration at (602) 542–4248, www.de.state.az.us/childcare. You can search the files of preschools that interest you and find out if there have been any complaints or violations listed against them, but remember, not all child-care facilities are required to have state licenses.

You might also want to contact Arizona Childcare Resources and Referral, which runs a resource and referral service and other programs in support of child care for all income levels. Call (800) 308–9000, or visit www.arizonachildcare.org.

Montessori programs are well represented in the Phoenix area, with about 75 schools listing themselves as having a Montessori philosophy. That philosophy embraces learning activities that are related to real-life experiences and that are highly interactive and hands-on. The various schools cater to toddlers, preschoolers, and elementary school-age children. For more information on Montessori schools in the Valley, contact the Foundation for Montessori Education, 9215 North 14th Street, Phoenix, at (602) 395–0292.

Among the child-care chains operating in the Valley are Children's World Learning Centers, www.childrensworld.com; Childtime Learning Centers, www.childtime.com; KinderCare Learning Centers, www.kindercare.com; La Petite Academy, www.lapetite.com; and Tutor Time Child Care/Learning Centers, www.tutortime.com.

If you're looking for in-home care provided by a babysitter or nanny, try calling one of the Valley's many nanny referral agencies. One longtime company is Peace of Mind Referral Service, (480) 732–1234. Agencies will help you find a live-in nanny or someone who works in your home full-time or part-time. The agencies will have done various background checks on potential babysitters before setting up interviews with you.

If you're a visitor in town seeking babysitting services, your hotel or resort can put you in touch with a number of caregivers. One Valley company that specializes in serving the tourist market is the Granny Company, (602) 956–4040.

MEDIA 📺

As the sixth-largest city in the United States, Phoenix has a wide variety of media options. It's a real eclectic mix, with more than 40 radio stations offering everything from Christian to Talk to Spanish; scores of newspapers, daily and weekly, conservative and liberal; special-interest magazines from gay to women's business to gourmet, and all manner of highly specialized local and ethnic publications like the bilingual Asian American Times and the monthly Arizona Muslim Voice.

The local television news is dominated by happy talk. You would be hard-pressed to figure out what is Arizonan about these broadcasts, except when the anchors gloat about the sunny winter weather after the East and Midwest are snowed in. Local news is a rare commodity on all but a few radio stations.

But the media isn't just the news, it's entertainment as well. On TV, local non-news broadcasts are rare, but radio is driven by its local personalities. It's probably on radio that we get the truest media reflection of this community and its diverse interests and concerns.

NEWSPAPERS

There are scores of newspapers across the Valley covering the minutiae of the neighborhoods—the potlucks and the PTA meetings, the open houses and the class reunions. It would be impossible for us to

---

ℹ️ *What's happening around town this weekend? You've three reliable sources for information on concerts, special events, and the bar scene in the weekly* New Times, *the* Arizona Republic's "The Rep," *and the* Tribune's "Get Out." *These tabloids are distributed free.*

---

list and describe all the neighborhood papers, many of them freebies that show up on people's driveways. The following list covers English-language newspapers that have circulations of more than a few thousand. Subscription plans are available for most newspapers.

Dailies

The Arizona Republic
200 East Van Buren Street, Phoenix
(602) 444-8000
www.arizonarepublic.com
The *Arizona Republic* is the big gun in town and has been the largest paper in Arizona since 1915 and ranks 15th among U.S. dailies. With a circulation that tops 400,000 daily and 500,000 on Sunday, it penetrates the Phoenix market like no other newspaper, magazine, television or radio station. Politically conservative, the paper was founded in May 1890 as the *Arizona Republican* by territorial Governor Lewis Wolfley and Attorney General Clark Churchill. The paper was as partisan as its name. The name changed to the *Arizona Republic* in 1930. Since its growth rested on the Valley's growth, the paper has consistently acted as a booster for business interests. On the plus side, that meant championing statehood. Yet oddly enough for a pro-growth cheerleader, the paper stood against freeways until the metropolitan area almost choked on its size. The *Republic* was influential enough to get its way on such issues for many years.

The paper was owned by Central Newspapers Inc., an Indianapolis-based corporation founded in 1934 by Eugene C. Pulliam, Dan Quayle's grandfather. The Gannett newspaper chain purchased it in 2000. The *Republic* has a Pulitzer Prize winner on staff: political cartoonist Steve Benson. The paper's only other Pulitzer was also won by a cartoonist, the late Reg Manning.

In 1997 the paper began publishing "The Rep," a tabloid-size entertainment guide to compete with *Phoenix New Times* and the *Tribune*'s "Get Out." It appears in The *Republic* on Thursday.

The *Sunday Republic* features *Parade* magazine as a mark of distinction. The *Republic* also publishes an annual best-of-the-Valley section called "AZ Best."

The Tribune
120 West First Avenue, Mesa
(480) 898-6500
www.aztrib.com

The *Tribune* has a long and complicated history. Suffice it to say that the paper was founded in 1891 as Mesa's first newspaper. After changing hands numerous times since its founding, the paper has been owned by Freedom Communications, Inc., of Irvine, California, since August 2000.

The current *Tribune* consists of eight different papers, four dailies (the *East Valley Tribune, Scottsdale Tribune, Ahwatukee Foothills,* and the *Daily News Sun*) and four weekly papers (the *Chandler Connection, Gilbert Guardian, South Tempe Voice,* and *Scottsdale Views*). The entertainment and recreation guide, "Get Out," appears as a special section of the *East Valley Tribune* on Thursday and is available free at newsstands around town.

Weeklies

Arizona Business Gazette
200 East Van Buren Street, Phoenix
(602) 444-7300
www.abgnews.com

The *Business Gazette,* published each Thursday by the same parent company as The *Arizona Republic,* downsized during 1997, becoming essentially a vehicle for legal advertising. The news copy it contains focuses on the always-burgeoning Arizona business and real-estate scene.

The first issue of the **Arizona Republican,** *a partisan paper, was published May 19, 1890. In the opposing Democrat camp was the* **Arizona Gazette,** *which later became the* **Phoenix Gazette.** *In 1930, within a week of shortening* **Republican** *to* **Republic,** *the paper's owners bought the* **Phoenix Gazette.** *The purchase left the* **Arizona Republic** *as Phoenix's major player, with the* **Phoenix Gazette** *chugging along as a small afternoon daily until its closure in January 1997.*

Arizona Capitol Times
1835 West Adams, Phoenix
(602) 258-7026
www.azcapitoltimes.com

Arizona Capitol Times focuses on the goings-on at the State Capitol. The news coverage is straightforward with few graphic geegaws filling the pages. Among its features is a listing of bills being considered and passed. Some stories focus on issues, but all have the state government at their center. It is published weekly, with an extra year-end wrap-up issue. Subscribers also receive a magazine-style *Government Resources Directory* as an extra issue in December.

Arizona Informant
1746 East Madison Street, Phoenix
(602) 257-9300

The *Arizona Informant* is the major African-American newspaper in the Valley, with a circulation of about 15,000. A booster of the African-American community, the paper keeps an eye on race and social issues. Besides a general news section, it breaks down its coverage into sections on business, women, youth, sports, entertainment, health, and religion.

The Business Journal of Phoenix
3030 North Central Avenue, Phoenix
(602) 230-8400
http://phoenix.bcentral.com

One of a chain of *Business Journals* across the United States, the Phoenix edition focuses on the Valley's business scene, trends, and local business figures.

ℹ️ **Many area publications, especially smaller community newspapers, offer discounted subscriptions to new residents. When ordering a subscription, make sure to mention that you are a newcomer.**

Independent Newspapers
23043 North 16th Lane, Phoenix
(623) 445-2800
www.newszap.com
Independent Newspapers is a chain that publishes 11 community weeklies across the Valley. The primary concern of the papers is the very local news and human-interest stories that the big papers tend to miss.

The papers are: *Apache Junction Independent* and the *East Mesa Independent,* 201 West Apache Trail, Apache Junction, (480) 982-7799; the *Gilbert Independent* and *Chandler/Sun Lakes Independent,* 375 East Elliott Road, Chandler, (480) 497-0048; the *Paradise Valley Independent, North Phoenix Independent,* and *Northeast Scottsdale Independent,* 11000 North Scottsdale Road, (480) 483-0977; *Peoria Independent* and *Surprise Independent,* 10202 West Bell Road, Suite 116, (623) 972-6101; and *Sun Cities Independent* and *Arrowhead Ranch Independent,* 10327 West Coggins Drive, Sun City, (623) 972-6101.

Jewish News of Greater Phoenix
1625 East Northern Avenue, Phoenix
(602) 870-9470
www.jewishaz.com
An independent journal of the Jewish community in Arizona, the *Jewish News* focuses on covering the diverse segments of the local community. It augments its local coverage with Jewish newswire stories to provide news on national and international events important to the community. The paper publishes many special sections in the course of the year on such themes as fashion, back to school, and finance. It publishes an annual *Community Directory* that is especially helpful to Jewish newcomers to Phoenix.

Phoenix New Times
1201 East Jefferson Street, Phoenix
(602) 271-0040
www.phoenixnewtimes.com
New Times started out as an underground newspaper, but today is part of Phoenix's mainstream. Still, a booster it is not. The feature writers at *New Times* work on extended investigative stories on topics that often are not covered in the mainstream papers. People routinely turn to its "Flashes" column for the current juice on local public figures and to read the latest installment in the paper's running feud with the *Arizona Republic.* The meat and potatoes of the paper are magazine-length stories featuring in-depth reporting on government malfeasance and public affairs (often the same thing) and social issues as well as the occasional major profile of local artists and performers and quirky attractions and people in the Valley. The dessert course is its comprehensive guide to Valley dining, events, arts, and nightlife. The "Best of Phoenix" issue, which appears in the fall, is an excellent reference guide and worth keeping around on a shelf to look at throughout the year when you're thinking about what to do and where to eat. You'll find awards for the best fish tacos, best used-book stores, and best public art work in town.

Phoenix New Times, which is distributed free, is the flagship paper of a chain of weeklies that includes *WestWord* in Denver, *Los Angeles New Times,* and the *Houston Press.*

MAGAZINES

With the rapid population growth in the area, Phoenix recently has become a growing magazine market. As a result, you'll find lots and lots of magazines available in the Valley from specialty publications to monthlies, covering everything from sports to lifestyle to dining, gay lifestyle, and women's business. Here's a sampling.

Arizona Business Magazine
3111 North Central Avenue, Phoenix
(602) 277-6045
This bimonthly magazine offers profiles of businesses across the state, but its primary focus is those in the Valley. The magazine also covers many issues that affect business, such as the impact of water policy on growth.

Arizona Food & Lifestyles
8655 East Via de Ventura, Suite E160, Scottsdale
(480) 998-5810
www.foodandlifestyles.com
Do you live for food? Rush to the very newest restaurant in town as soon as it's open? Search high and low for that special ingredient? If so, don't be without your copy of Arizona Food & Lifestyles, which covers cooking, dining out, and entertainment both in the Valley and beyond. You'll find celebrity chef profiles, party tips, recipes from four-star restaurants, and a food-only events calendar that will make you drool.

Arizona Foothills Magazine
8132 North 87th Place, Scottsdale
(480) 460-5203
www.azfoothillsmag.com
See how the rich live with this sophisticated monthly lifestyle publication that covers the affluent in the Valley and the state. Some of the most expensive houses you've ever seen, fashion, shopping, events, architecture, local upscale happenings—it's all between these shiny pages.

Arizona Highways
2039 West Lewis Avenue, Phoenix
(602) 712-2200, (800) 543-5432
www.arizhwys.com
Published by the Arizona Department of Transportation for the last 75 years, Arizona Highways is the state magazine with the highest profile nationally and even internationally. Essentially a travel magazine about our fair state, it features photography that is among the best anywhere. The prose attempts to match the vistas for color and excitement. Once you move here, it is fun to give your distant relatives a subscription so they can learn about your new home (and turn green with envy).

bizAZ
5151 North 16th Street, Suite E128, Phoenix
(602) 667-3008
www.bizaz.com
Published bimonthly, this pub makes doing business look cool with great graphics and elegant writing. Magazine sections cover marketing strategies, people, technology, and even dining, with insightful looks at businesses and trends statewide.

Desert Living Magazine
342 East Thomas Road, Phoenix
(602) 667-9798
www.desertlivingmag.com
Formerly CityAZ, this slick bimonthly focuses on fashion, design, dining, architecture, and interior decorating. While not as edgy as its predecessor, the clean design and good writing make this a pleasing magazine to flip through. The frequent articles on top places to eat or visit are useful for newcomers.

Echo Magazine
P.O. Box 16630, Phoenix 85011
(602) 266-0550, (888) 324-6624
www.echomag.com
News and features, arts and entertainment, restaurants, classifieds, and

no-holds-barred editorial make this a top choice for the gay community in town. It's free and available at bookstores, cafes, and some specialty shops.

Native Peoples
5333 North Seventh Avenue, Suite C224, Phoenix
(602) 265–4855
www.nativepeoples.com
Affiliated with the Heard and several other nationally prominent museums and art institutes, this bimonthly is the largest magazine devoted solely to Native American art and culture in the world. Dedicated to sensitively portraying the arts and lifeways of Native Americans, it features gorgeous photography, fascinating features, and an extensive calendar of events nationwide.

Phoenix Downtown Magazine
P.O. Box 34798, Phoenix 85067
(602) 279-9070
www.phoenixdowntown.com
This free monthly is part of an effort to revitalize the Phoenix downtown area. Once the heart of the city, it was left to decay as people and investment fled to the suburbs. Now the city is trying to breathe new life and money into the area. *Phoenix Downtown* is the effort's main booster and helps out with extensive listings of downtown art and cultural events. Each issue also includes a handful of articles on local artists and entrepreneurs. The magazine can be found in many cafes and restaurants around Phoenix.

PHOENIX Magazine
4041 North Central Avenue, Phoenix
(602) 234-0840
www.phoenixmag.com
PHOENIX Magazine aims for the sass and excitement of other big-city magazines, but the monthly magazine actually achieves something better—conversations with its readers. The subjects of those conversations are all over the map—quiet

hiking trails and a trip down Indian School Road on the one hand, and a discussion of grandparents who kidnap their grandchildren on the other. In addition, you'll find plenty on Valley dining, a good events calendar, and a column that blends bright and hip short items called "The PHXFiles."

Raising Arizona Kids
4545 East Shea Boulevard, Suite 201, Phoenix
(602) 953-5437
www.raisingarizonakids.com
Do you have kids? Are you always searching for things to keep them busy? Here's the answer. This subscription-based monthly magazine is chock-full of local resources, articles, and a comprehensive calendar of family events for kids 15 and younger. Problem solved.

Shade
P.O. Box 790, Phoenix 85001
(602) 288-3974
www.shademag.com
A relative newcomer to the Valley magazine scene, *Shade* has distinguished itself with its award-winning design and in-depth articles on art, both local and international. There are no listings here; many other publications take care of those. Instead, the reader will find thoughtful articles on the place of art in Phoenix life, current trends, and lengthy interviews with leading artists. Its recent award for design was well deserved; *Shade* is perhaps the best-looking magazine coming out of Phoenix.

Today's Arizona Woman
4425 North Saddlebag Trail, Scottsdale
(480) 945-5000
www.taw.com
Are you a woman? Do you live and work in Arizona? If you answered yes to either of these questions, pick up a copy of this magazine, a serious look at women doing business in the Grand Canyon State.

RADIO

Phoenix radio is volatile, and the landscape is littered with new formats that failed. Although the primary motivation for format changes is usually the sale of a station, some longtime owners have changed formats on their stations repeatedly, searching for the key to winning in a very competitive market. Even as this is being written, local stations are changing formats and searching for the highest ratings.

Listening to the radio is a popular hobby for Valley locals. Stuck in their cars for commutes that range from 20 minutes to more than an hour, people tend to find their favorite stations and stay with them. The five top stations in the Valley are country station KNIX-FM (102.5), talk station KTAR-AM (620), urban/top-40 station KKFR-FM (92.3), smooth jazz station KYOT-FM (95.5), and oldies station KOOL-FM (94.5), which demonstrates the diversity of Phoenix's listening audience.

Longtime market leaders are talk-news station KTAR, which carries the ever popular Phoenix Suns basketball games all season; blue-collar rocker KUPD, propelled by morning jock Dave Pratt's decades of success; urban-contemporary KKFR, better known as Power 92; adult rocker KDKB; easy-listening KOY; and adult-contemporary KESZ, better known as KEZ and noted for morning personalities Beth McDonald and Bill Austin. Public radio station KJZZ has served its niche for many years and for the past few has been primarily an NPR talk-radio station, with acoustic jazz music filling in the off-hours. A second public radio station, KBAQ, programs classical music and features opera broadcasts on Saturday afternoons. Unfortunately, its weak signal does not reach all parts of the Valley.

Because the Valley is so large, a number of stations simulcast on two frequencies to cover the entire Valley.

FM STATIONS

KNAI 88.3 (Spanish regional)
KBAQ 89.5 (Classical)
KFLR 90.3 (Christian)
KGCB 90.9 (Christian)
KJZZ 91.5 (NPR news/talk/jazz)
KKFR 92.3 (Urban Top 40)
KDKB 93.3 (Album rock)
KOOL 94.5 (Oldies)
KYOT 95.5 (Contemporary jazz)
KSWG 96.3 (Country)
KMXP 96.9 (80s, 90s, current)
KRXS 97.3/103.1 (Country/Oldies)
KUPD 97.9 (Modern rock)
KKLT 98.7 (Adult contemporary)
KAJM 99.3/104.3 (R&B oldies)
KESZ 99.9 (Adult contemporary)
KMRR 100.3 (Spanish love songs)
KSLX 100.7 (Classic rock)
KNRJ 101.1/92.7 (Dance)
KZON 101.5 (Rock alternative)
KNIX 102.5 (Country)
KLNZ 103.5 (Spanish regional)
KZZP 104.7 (Contemporary hits)
KSSL 105.3 (Spanish regional)
KLVA 105.5 (Christian, Contemporary)
KHOT 105.9 (Spanish regional)
KDVA 106.9/92.7 (Contemporary Spanish)
KVVA 107.1 (Spanish contemporary)
KMLE 107.9 (Country)

AM STATIONS

KFYI 550 (News/talk)
KSAZ 580 (Adult standards)
KTAR 620 (News/talk)
KUET 710 (Oldies)
KIDR 740 (Spanish news/talk)
KMVP 860 (Sports, ESPN radio)
KGME 910 (Sports/talk)
KKNT 960 (News/talk)
KXEM 1010 (News/talk)
KDUS 1060 (Sports)
KFNX 1100 (Talk)
KCKY 1150 (Spanish)
KMYL 1190 (Talk)
KOY 1230 (Adult standards)
KXEG 1280 (Christian)

It's only natural that radio station KTAR is the Valley's full-time news station. It was launched by the Arizona Republican *on February 4, 1930.*

KXAM 1310 (Talk)
KPXQ 1360 (Christian talk)
KSUN 1400 (Spanish)
KSLX 1440 (Gold oldies)
KPHX 1480 (Spanish)
KFNN 1510 (Business)
KASA 1540 (Christian/Spanish)
KMIK 1580 (Children/Radio Disney)

Don't expect to hear the phrase "Film at 11" in Phoenix. The late-evening news comes on at 10:00 P.M. (This town goes to bed early.)

TELEVISION

Phoenix television includes affiliates of all four major networks as well as PBS, UPN, and the WB network. Channels 45 and 61, the stations that offer the limited platter of WB and UPN network offerings, are otherwise independent stations. Channel 45 has retained the rights to air Phoenix Suns basketball, Channel 61 airs Phoenix Coyotes hockey, and Channel 3 airs Arizona Diamondbacks baseball.

Cable television is available in most areas of the Valley, with more than 50 percent of TV households wired in. All local broadcast outlets are carried on cable, unless otherwise noted in the listings below.

LOCAL STATIONS

KTVK Channel 3 (Independent)
KPHO Channel 5 (CBS)
KAET Channel 8 (PBS)
KSAZ Channel 10 (Fox)
KPNX Channel 12 (NBC)
KNXV Channel 15 (ABC)

KPAZ Channel 21 (TBN—Religious)
KDMA Channel 25 (CAN—shopping)
KAZ Channel 27 (Independent)
KTVW Channel 33 (Univision—Spanish language)
KFPH Channel 35 (Independent/Spanish language)
LDTP Channel 39 (Daystar)
KUTP Channel 45 (UPN)
KDRK Channel 48 and 56 (Telemundo—Spanish language)
KPPX Channel 51 (PAX Family)
KASW Channel 61 (WB Fox Children's Network)
KFE Channel 67 (Spanish Independent Broadcasting)

LOW-POWER UHF STATIONS

The FCC approved low-power outlets to increase the availability of alternative television programming in markets like the Valley. KBI Channel 39 has family network and religious programming, while BOX Channel 58 Video Jukebox, or The Box, is an interactive station. Viewers call up and order (for a price) the video they want played. It is not carried on cable.

CABLE TV COMPANIES

Cox Communications, 20401 North 29th Avenue, (623) 594-9390, serves most of Phoenix and the Valley.

Cable America Corp., 4120 East Valley Auto Drive, Mesa, (480) 558-7260, serves portions of Mesa and eastern Maricopa County.

Fox Sports Net Arizona, 2 North Central, Suite 1700, Phoenix, (602) 257-9500, holds the exclusive nonbroadcast rights to the Arizona Diamondbacks, Phoenix Coyotes, Arizona State University, and the University of Arizona sports events.

WORSHIP

n a typical suburban development on the far west side of Phoenix, everything is as it should be. Palm trees shade the rows of tract houses, kids race bicycles along the low-traffic streets, soccer moms rush children to their games, and a pair of orange-clad Buddhist monks tend a little garden plot beside a home.

Whoa! Hold on there! Buddhist monks in the 'burbs?

If Valley boosters really wanted to demonstrate how cosmopolitan the Valley of the Sun is, they would boast about its religious scene. In this arena, the Valley is as diverse as the United Nations. Whatever your religion, or lack thereof, there is a place for you in the Valley.

The simple fact is that when you attract people from around the world, most of them bring their religions along with them. Our fair Valley holds more than 1,700 houses of worship—churches, synagogues, mosques, shrines, reading rooms, halls, and temples.

There is no centralized source of religious information that's adequate for everybody. To find out what's going on, you can check the following sources. The *Arizona Republic* carries "Religion Roundup" in the Religion section of its Saturday editions, listing special worship services, concerts, and meetings occurring Valleywide, but not regular worship schedules. In the East Valley the *Tribune* offers a similar listing in its Saturday Spiritual Life section.

The best bet for people seeking a place to worship, whether as a visitor or as a resident, may be the Yellow Pages, where you'll find pages of church listings, covering more than 125 denominations— and that's not to mention the separate listings for synagogues and mosques.

All of this means that the subsequent overviews are necessarily incomplete. The diverse histories of each mainline Protestant and Baptist subgroup in the Valley

could fill a tome twice the size of our humble guide. We have instead opted to mention a few representative churches that we hope will offer our readers an introduction into the diversity of worship in the Valley.

ROMAN CATHOLIC INFLUENCE

Roman Catholics represent the largest identifiable religious group in the Valley. Within that group, there is quite a bit of diversity. There are parishes of Maronite (Lebanese) and other Eastern Rite Catholic Churches, among other ethnic churches.

Before Phoenix began to develop, Catholic missionaries had nearly 300 years of history in the Southwest, seeking to convert Native Americans and ministering to the needs of the Hispanic Catholic community. As more people settled in the Valley, Hispanics and Mexican Americans were the first big block of Catholics, although other groups of ethnic Catholics moved in quickly. Disadvantaged and, due to prejudice, essentially shut out of the Anglo power structure, the Hispanic community forged its own subculture, and much of its communal life revolved around the first St. Mary's Church, built in 1881.

In 1915 a new St. Mary's Church was built. The church's style was like an exalted version of the mission churches found in isolated outposts throughout the Southwest. Spanish-influenced, the church's stained-glass windows, artwork, high ceilings, and wooden pews hark back to the pre–Vatican II world of Catholic worship.

In the mid-1980s Pope John Paul II elevated St. Mary's Church to the rank of a minor basilica, a special status within the church. John Paul II made it a point to speak from the front balcony of the basilica when he visited Phoenix in 1987. And well he might, since the basilica sits across Monroe Street from the Phoenix Civic Plaza. In fact, St. Mary's Basilica stands out in Phoenix's redeveloping downtown and is renowned for its stained-glass windows imported from Germany. Its address is 231 North Third Street in Phoenix, but the church's front entrance sits on Monroe Street. The basilica is open Monday through Friday, from 10:00 A.M. to 2:00 P.M. Daily masses are at 12:05 P.M. Monday through Friday, 5:00 P.M. on Saturday, and 9:00 and 11:00 A.M. on Sunday. Admission is free. For more information, call (602) 354-2100. It's best to sign up for tours ahead of time.

There are about 89 Catholic parishes and 28 missions in the Valley as well as support services and charitable efforts. For more information, contact The Catholic Diocese of Phoenix, 400 East Monroe Street, Phoenix, (602) 257-0030, www.diocesephoenix.org.

MORMONS' SECOND HOME

The true home of the Mormons is Utah, but Mesa—and to a lesser extent, the rest of the Valley—is a sort of second home to the Church of Jesus Christ of Latter-day Saints. The Latter-day Saints' Arizona Temple was the most impressive structure in Mesa when it was built in 1927.

At that time, prejudice against Mormons was high elsewhere in the Valley, but Mesa, which Mormon farmers settled in February 1878, was the city of their own making. They were influenced by the plan of Salt Lake City and plotted out wide streets, squares, and big lots. Prejudice in Mexico also forced an exodus of Mormon settlers from south of the border into the Valley in 1912.

Today, Mormons are dispersed throughout the Valley, but the East Valley— including Mesa, Gilbert, and Chandler—still is the major bastion of the LDS church in Arizona.

The temple, a large, bright cube atop a rectangle, is located in Mesa at 525 East Main Street, right behind the visitor center. Old photos show that when it was built the structure was out in the middle of nowhere, but downtown Mesa has grown around it. That's not to say that the city has swallowed the building—Mesa's well-planned spaciousness has left it impressive. Its Christmas lighting display draws 100,000 visitors, and since 1938 church members have presented an annual Easter pageant, Jesus the Christ, that attracts more than 225,000 visitors.

In addition to worship, the Mormons have support services and missionary programs and charitable programs. The visitor center general information number is (480) 964-7164, or check www.lds.org.

CHRISTIAN CHURCHES IN GENERAL

When you add the percentages of Catholics, Mormons, Baptists, and mainline Protestants, it's clear that Christian churches dominate the religious landscape of Phoenix. Beyond the Catholics and the Mormons, who may be the most readily identifiable groups, the variety of adherents to Jesus and the Gospels is great.

From the independent gospel churches that dot the disadvantaged neighborhoods, to the cluster of African Methodist Episcopal congregations in South Phoenix, to scores of Baptist, Lutheran, Methodist, Presbyterian, and Episcopal congregations throughout the Valley, Christian worship is huge. What follows is the barest tip of what's out there.

According to those in the know, the Community Church of Joy in Glendale, located at 21000 North 75th Avenue, is admired nationwide for its successful growth into a megacongregation. The sanctuary, built in 1998, holds 2,200 people, so the church holds multiple services to accommodate its growing membership, which has hit 11,000 people. The Lutheran congregation bills itself as "a friendly place that really believes in you." The church, affiliated with the Evangelical Lutheran Church in America (ELCA), uses a contemporary worship style, including music, dance, drama, and multimedia, to reach beyond the traditional church-going public. For more information, call (623) 561-0500, or visit www.joyonline.org.

A similarly huge congregation is North Phoenix Baptist Church, 5757 North Central Avenue, a Southern Baptist congregation. With more than 7,000 members, this church prides itself on the theatrical production values of its services. Its worship services are aired on local TV. The church melds drama, video montages, and live music into services that have received great word of mouth and always pack the church's ample parking lot. For more

information, call the church at (602) 707-5757 or visit www.npbc.org.

Episcopalians who want to learn more about their worship options in the Valley should contact the local diocese. The headquarters of the Episcopal Diocese of Arizona is at 114 West Roosevelt Street in Phoenix, (602) 254-0976, www.episcopal az.org.

Many churches have gay and lesbian ministries, but a very few have principally gay and lesbian membership. The largest such congregation in Phoenix is the independent, nondenominational Community Church of Hope, 4121 North Seventh Avenue in Phoenix, (602) 234-2180, www .communitychurchofhope.com.

If you are looking to explore your individual path spirituality in an open, rational, and liberal environment, check out the Unitarian Univeralist Church at 17540 North Avenue of the Arts, Surprise, (623) 875-2550, or one of the three other Unitarian Universalist churches in the Valley.

You will probably see kachina (kah-CHEE-nah) dolls for sale in the Phoenix area. These colorful Hopi wood carvings are representatives of spirits essential to Hopi religion. Sculpted from cottonwood and painted bright colors, they may represent the corn maiden, a ceremonial dancer, a singer, an ogre, the buffalo, the badger, the crow, the hawk, clouds, the sun, or the rainbow.

THE JEWISH COMMUNITY

By 1870 Jews were a visible minority in Phoenix. Unlike the case in many other cities, overt discrimination against them was rarely seen. Barry Goldwater's ancestors were among the prominent Jewish families in the Valley.

By the 1880s worship services were being held in private homes around the city. In 1922 Temple Beth Israel, built at Second and Culver Streets, became the first synagogue in Phoenix. A Reform synagogue, Temple Beth Israel is now at 10460 North 56th Street in Scottsdale, (480) 951-0323, http://templebethisrael.com. Its facilities include the Sylvia Plotkin Judaica Museum, http://spjm.org, which features a permanent collection of historical and contemporary ceremonial objects used to observe basic holidays and life cycle events, including Shabbat candlesticks, Seder plates, and Kiddush cups. The museum also has a reconstructed Tunisian synagogue, and features two to three temporary exhibits per year. The museum is open Tuesday through Thursday, 10:00 A.M. to 3:00 P.M.; by appointment on Friday and after Friday-night services; and Sunday on special occasions.

Phoenix's Jewish community numbers approximately 100,000, and it is diverse in spirit. There are Orthodox, Conservative, Reform, Jewish Renewal, and Humanistic congregations in the Valley of the Sun.

The Jewish Federation of Greater Phoenix conducts the annual UJC/Federation Campaign to benefit the United Jewish Appeal and local social services. Its constituent agencies include two Jewish community centers, the Jewish Family and Children's Service, and the Bureau of Jewish Education of Greater Phoenix, among others. The federation's offices are at 12701 North Scottsdale Road, Suite 201, Scottsdale, (480) 634-4900 or visit www.jewishphoenix.org.

Jewish News of Greater Phoenix publishes an annual directory of Jewish congregations, agencies, services, and schools in the Valley. The cost is $6.00. It's available at the *Jewish News* office, 1625 East Northern Avenue, Suite 106, Phoenix, (602) 870-9470, www.jewishaz.com.

MUSLIMS

With increased immigration from the Middle East, Africa, and Asia, the Islamic community in the Valley of the Sun is also growing. Adherents also include many African-American converts to Islam.

The Islamic Cultural Center, 131 East Sixth Street, Tempe, (480) 894-6070, www.tempemasjid.com, with its minaret, stands out in downtown Tempe. The cultural center and mosque work hard to fight stereotypes while raising Valley awareness of Muslim beliefs. The congregation includes immigrants and first-generation members as well as American converts. Located as it is near Arizona State University, the center's air of scholarly prayerfulness is a welcome relief from the hustle and bustle.

There are a handful of other mosques in the Valley, and the Islamic Cultural Center can provide information on those.

BUDDHISTS

Buddhism first found its way to Phoenix via an influx of Chinese railroad workers and the community that formed around them as they settled here. Many of their descendants remained, and Chinatown flourished in Phoenix until the early 1930s.

Successive waves of Asian immigration to the Valley helped broaden Buddhism's reach here. In the early 1980s the Thai community began a growth spurt that prompted establishment of Wat Promkunaram, a temple in west Phoenix.

The oldest Buddhist congregation in the state is the Arizona Buddhist Temple, established out of the concerns of a smaller Asian immigrant group—the Japanese. Only a few hundred Japanese resided in the Valley when the Arizona Buddhist Temple was established in 1932. The temple became central to the small group's community life. Today, the temple, at 4142 West Clarendon Avenue in Phoenix, (602) 278-0036, www.azbuddhisttemple.org, serves not only an immigrant community, but also Western followers.

Possibly the saddest day in the state of Arizona's religious history, however, involved Wat Promkunaram Temple. Six Thai monks, plus three others, were slaughtered there in 1991. The mass murder raised questions, particularly among the Thai community here and in Thailand, of whether modern-day Arizonans were religiously tolerant. Locally, though, most people were shocked at the bloody crime in the temple. Wat Promkunaram had been established three years earlier to meet the needs of Thai immigrants, and it continues to serve them. To contact Wat Promkunaram call (623) 935-2276 or visit www.watprom. iirt.net. The temple is located at 17212 West Maryland Avenue in Waddell, a small town on the far west side of the Valley. Services are open to everyone on Sunday at 10:00 A.M.

OTHER DISCIPLINES

There are many other religious and spiritual disciplines practiced in the Valley of the Sun. Most of them have arrived in the past few decades. Phoenix is the site of Yogi Paramahansa Yogananda's only U.S. temple outside California. The Self-Realization Fellowship Temple and Ashram Center offers services on Sunday through Thursday that mix Hindu mysticism with discussions on Western scriptures at 6111 North Central Avenue in Phoenix, (602) 279-6140, www.yoga nanda-srf.org/temples/phoenix.

Phoenix also has a Sikh community with a number of American adherents. Many of them can be found at congrega-

The Franciscan Renewal Center, 5802 East Lincoln Drive, Scottsdale, (480) 948-7460, www.thecasa.org, offers retreats and classes. Although it's a Catholic institution, it's open to anyone. Classes have included studies of Islam, taught by a representative of the Islamic Cultural Center, and even tai chi. Its 25 acres of desert space between Camelback and Mummy Mountains offers a spiritually refreshing place for a retreat, and it has conference rooms for groups as large as 120 people.

tional services at the Kundalini Yoga Center, 2302 North Ninth Street, Phoenix, (602) 271-4480. Classes are seven days a week in the evening. Call ahead to register.

Another aspect of life in the Southwest is the rise of New Age religious and spiritual groups. Because of the blend of sources for their beliefs and practices, it is sometimes difficult to distinguish New Age believers from practitioners of Eastern mysticism, Native American religions, pagan, and Wiccan ideas, but it is precisely the blending of these ancient beliefs into new forms that marks New Age. Because of this diversity of practices, it's difficult to find a characteristic group or church to profile here. Suffice it to say that there are numerous groups of this type listed in the phone book. Other sources of information on these groups are the various New Age stores, where meeting places and times are often posted.

INDEX

ABOUT THE AUTHORS

SEAN MCLACHLAN

Sean McLachlan first came to Arizona to study archaeology at the University of Arizona in Tucson. Originally from the Great White North, he fell in love with the rugged terrain, clear skies, and mix of cultures that make up the Southwest. After excavating sites in Arizona, Israel, Cyprus, and Bulgaria, he turned to writing. His work has appeared in various newspapers and magazines, including *Yoga Journal, The World and I, Global Journalist,* and *Ancient Egypt.* He is also the author of *Byzantium: An Illustrated History,* published by Hippocrene Books. Besides writing, his greatest passion is travel. He has spent several years on the road, exploring everything from the snow-capped mountains of Peru to the ancient cities of Iran. His two careers have taken him to more than 25 countries, but he always ends up back in the Sonoran Desert.

When not on assignment, Sean spends his time traveling, hiking, hunting for petroglyphs, watching obscure films, reading even more obscure books, and practicing Spanish. He divides his time between Madrid and Arizona, living with his wife and best friend, Almudena.

MARY PAGANELLI

A graduate of Vassar College and the New School Culinary Arts Program, Mary Paganelli is a food and travel writer, editor, and chef. She developed and wrote an international dining guide for VISA and CondeNet and worked with *New York Magazine,* the Food Network, and Fodor's. She contributes to cooking, lifestyle, and travel publications, and she is working with Tohono O'odham Community Action on a book about traditional foods. Originally from New York City, Mary, husband Ernest, and son Eric now call southern Arizona home.

ERNEST VOTTO

ALMUDENA ALONSO-HERRERO

HELP US KEEP THIS GUIDE UP TO DATE

Every effort has been made by the authors and editors to make this guide as accurate and useful as possible. However, many things can change after a guide is published—phone numbers change, facilities come under new management, etc.

We would love to hear from you concerning your experiences with this guide and how you feel it could be improved and be kept up to date. While we may not be able to respond to all comments and suggestions, we'll take them to heart and we'll also make certain to share them with the authors. Please send your comments and suggestions to the following address:

The Globe Pequot Press
Reader Response/Editorial Department
P. O. Box 480
Guilford, CT 06437

Or you may e-mail us at:

editorial@GlobePequot.com

Thanks for your input, and happy travels!

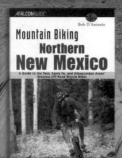
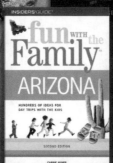